AMERICAN CULTURAL HERITAGE SERIES 5
Jack Salzman, *General Editor*

America
as Utopia

Edited by

KENNETH M. ROEMER

BURT FRANKLIN & COMPANY

DEDICATED TO

my family,

Hennig Cohen, and Clayton Eichelberger

for their encouragement and guidance

Published by Burt Franklin & Co.
235 East Forty-fourth Street
New York, New York 10017

Library of Congress Cataloging in Publication Data
Main entry under title:
America as Utopia.
(American cultural heritage series; 5)
Includes bibliographical references and index.
1. American fiction—History and criticism.
2. Utopias in literature. I. Roemer, Kenneth M.,
1945–ㅤ II. Series: American cultural
heritage; 5.
PS374.U8A47ㅤ813'.009'372ㅤ79-24626
ISBN 0-89102-169-8

Designed by Bernard Schleifer
Manufactured in the United States of America

Contents

Contents

Acknowledgments

MY FIRST ACKNOWLEDGMENT of gratitude goes to the contributers to this collection. I thank them for their willingness to put up with the inconveniences of finding obscure utopian works, for their analyses of obscure and well-known works, and for their patience with my requests for revisions. I would also like to thank my wife, Micki, for suggestions about the structure of the book and for her patience; H. Bruce Franklin of Rutgers University and Khaching Tololyan of Wesleyan University for reading an earlier version of the manuscript and making valuable suggestions for revision; the editors at Burt Franklin & Co. for their copy-editing; Sarah Crouch, for helping me prepare the index; the English Department at the University of Texas at Arlington, which supported Ms. Crouch's work with me; Hannah Goolsby, for checking bibliographic entries; the Graduate School Office at the University of Texas at Arlington, which gave Ms. Goolsby a research grant and awarded me a summer stipend (1978); Arthur K. Roemer, Leslie Branyan, and Wyndell Speers, for proofreading help; and Yvonne and Michael, who—while perched on my lap—typed several words in my historical essay.

The following authors and publishers kindly granted me permission to reprint the following essays, which in several cases were revised for this collection: B. F. Skinner and Prentice-Hall, Inc., "Utopia as an Experimental Culture"; Ursula K. Le Guin and Harper & Row, Publishers, Inc., Chapter 11 of *The Dispossessed*; Thomas M. Disch and Harper & Row Publishers, Inc., "Buck Rogers in the New Jerusalem"; and Darko Suvin and Yale University Press, "Anticipating the Sunburst—Dream and Vision." The appropriate permission credit appears with each essay.

vi

Social Contract, idealistic city plans, and even the advertising layouts included in Ian Tod and Michael Wheeler's *Utopia*. Though a decade old, Frank Manuel's collection *Utopias and Utopian Thought* is still a good introduction to this type of utopianism. A more recent and more comprehensive survey can be found in Frank and Fritzie Manuel's *Utopian Thought in the Western World*, published in the fall of 1979. (Because the Manuels' book appeared while *America as Utopia* was in press, it was not available to the contributors to this volume.)

Utopian communities are a bit easier to pin down. They are often the offspring of utopian thought—witness the communities inspired by the writings of Cabet, Fourier, Owen, and Skinner. For all the diversity of utopian communities, they are linked by their "attempts to create ideal, or at least significantly better, societies."[6] In America mid–nineteenth century communities such as Brook Farm, New Harmony, and Oneida have received much attention. But the existence of utopian communities can be traced back to our colonial origins and up through and beyond the tragedy of Jonestown, Guyana, in 1978. For example, Robert S. Fogarty estimates that between 1862 and 1919, 120 utopian communities were established in America, and "in 1971 a spokesman for the National Institutes of Health estimated that there were 3,000 communes across the country."[7] A good introduction to this utopian phenomenon is Fogarty's collection *American Utopianism*.

Several of the essays in the present collection—especially Joel Nydahl's surveys of early utopian thought and writing, Jean Pfaelzer's analysis of relationships between political theory and literary form, Robert Plank's interpretation of the modern shrunken utopia, and B. F. Skinner's "Utopia as an Experimental Culture"—use the concepts of utopian thought and utopian communities. But the main focus of *America as Utopia* is on the third category, utopian literature. This literature, which to some degree is a subcategory of utopian thought, is almost as difficult to define as utopian urges and quests. But the following definition of a literary utopia should be a useful guide to this collection: *A literary utopia is a fairly detailed description of an imaginary community, society, or world—a "fiction" that encourages readers to experience vicariously a culture that represents a prescriptive, normative alternative to their own culture.* This alternative, according to the author, is much better than his own culture. It is a "eutopia," or to use the more familiar term, a "utopia": the depiction of a good time and place, for example, the alternative described in *Looking Backward* or *Walden Two*. When the author creates an imaginary alternative that is much worse than the present, we have the negative image of utopia—"dystopia": the depiction of a bad time and place, for instance, *1984*, *Brave New World*, or *Player Piano*. In other words, utopian literature suggests a family of literatures. The traditional head of the clan is the utopia, and the best-known relative—especially during the twentieth century—is the dystopia. (Other relations are discussed below.)[8]

I realize that using "utopia" and "eutopia" almost interchangeably may seem confusing or even downright sloppy. It would be much neater simply to use the more "correct" term "eutopia" to represent the depiction of the good place and time. Unfortunately, it is often quite difficult to find purely eutopian works, as I argue below. Furthermore, since the birth of More's pun the term "utopia" has become almost entirely associated with the good place and time. Hence it is dubious as to whether the self-righteous, exclusive use of "eutopia" would lead to clarity, to misleading implications, or to the popularization of another bit of jargon in a world already saturated with that form of verbal blight. Therefore, in the following essays and bibliographies, when an author wants to stress—to make it very clear—that he means the good place in contrast to the bad place of dystopia, he will use the term "eutopia," sometimes even "eutopian." Otherwise, when the context makes the meaning of the words clear, the more familiar "utopia" and "utopian" will be used to suggest the imaginary culture that represents the good place and time.

Before noting any other loopholes in this terminology, some explication of the general definition is necessary. "Fairly detailed" is important because, as Sargent argues, "too many works that are sometimes thought of as [u]topias actually fail to provide sufficient material for analysis."[9] Brief, vague glimpses of alternative worlds also often fail to encourage readers to experience utopia—there simply isn't enough to hold on to—and they certainly do not create the illusion of a total culture. Contrast, for example, the detailed (too detailed for some readers) descriptions of utopia in *Looking Backward* and *Walden Two* to the delightful vagueness of *The Wonderful Wizard of Oz* or the lyrics of "The Big Rock Candy Mountain." Oz and the song certainly express a utopian desire for a spectacular fairyland and a tempting free-lunch land. But, really, all we get are fantasy visions occasionally tied down by sparkling images of emeralds or streams, lakes, and fountains of lemonade, whiskey, and soda.

"Imaginary" is another important characteristic, because it helps us to distinguish between utopian literature and utopian communities. It also implies freedom. A utopist, the author of a literary utopia, is free to imagine any setting that will adequately express his concepts of goodness or, in a dystopia, badness. The founders of utopian communities, on the other hand, are severely constrained by nagging realities: "The pigs ate up all the potatoes on the flat today; also the squash. Oh, Hell!" reads a diary entry by a founder of a utopian community in California.[10] But one occupational hazard of the utopist's freedom is exposure. The founders of communes can blame their failures on uncontrollable forces—hungry pigs, for instance. Utopists cannot hide; they set the ground rules for their utopias. Therefore, they consciously or unconsciously reveal their deepest desires and fears as they describe the worlds they have created with their imaginations.

Encouraging readers to "experience vicariously" utopia is closely linked to the imaginary or fictional nature of literary utopias, because one of the primary goals of most writers of fiction is to create an identifiable illusion of reality; Coleridge's "willing suspension of disbelief" applies to romantics, realists, and utopists. Ayn Rand, the author of *Atlas Shrugged* and other influential works, stresses the importance of this fictional quality especially for idealistic art forms: "The *primary* value is that it gives [humanity] the experience of living in a world where things are *as they ought to be.*"[11] Although this "experience" is central to many of the arts, it is an especially crucial ingredient in a literary utopia, and thus it is surprising that the experiencing of utopia has rarely, if ever, been stressed in definitions of utopia. This quality is important in part because the shaping of the reader's experience in a literary utopia achieved through the author's use of narratives, narrators, dialogue, characterization and character conflicts, evocative descriptions, and other literary devices helps us to distinguish between utopian literature and utopian thought—between, say, Skinner's *Walden Two* and his essay in this volume, "Utopia as an Experimental Culture." Furthermore, encouraging the reader to experience utopia facilitates the dual psychological (actually perceptual) function of utopian literature: to disengage him from present reality so that he can see and feel better alternatives to the present and see and feel the present in new ways. Utopia is a seeing experience.

An inclusive seeing experience: That is why "culture" is a more appropriate frame than "sociopolitical institutions" or even "society." Here, "culture" is used in the anthropological sense of "an evolving system of beliefs, attitudes, and techniques, transmitted from generation to generation, and finding expression in innumerable activities people learn: religion, politics, child-rearing customs, the arts, professions, *inter alia.*"[12]

Of course, every example of utopian literature does not survey all eighty-eight major cultural areas presented in George P. Murdock's *Outline of Cultural Materials*. Most utopists have pet reforms and gripes, which are often related to the whims of personality or to more general trends in their countries or their eras. Nevertheless, the desire to create an "experience" for the reader and the fictional conventions of literary utopias force utopists to transcend limited reforms and criticisms. Even if an author confines his narrator to long dialogues with one utopian guide, for example, the West-Leete dialogues in *Looking Backward*, or limits his visit to one community, as in *The Blithedale Romance* and *Walden Two*, the reader will begin to sense a network of "beliefs, attitudes, and techniques" that characterize the utopian experience. This is primarily because the visitor, who is frequently the narrator, is naturally inquisitive, and his guide is usually eager to explain and justify his utopia. We, the readers, often identify with the visitors because we are also strangers to each new utopian experience; hence we too are curious and expect the utopians to provide explanations of what we see. All this curiosity and explaining can lead to tiresome acculturation sessions, but they ensure that the author will suggest how one area of his imaginary culture relates to other areas in response to the visitor's sequences of questions and the reader's curiosity.

Another assurance of cultural inclusiveness is that even the most inarticulate utopists realize that readers lose interest in nonstop intellectual discussions. So, as Jean Pfaelzer points out in her essay in this collection, utopists break up their initiation and indoctrination talks with narrative episodes. Sometimes this takes the form of tours, such as Burris's visits to nurseries, schools, and living quarters in *Walden Two* or Shevek's carefully monitored shopping trips and unauthorized escape to the slums of Urras in Ursula K. Le Guin's *The Dispossessed*. Romantic interludes also counterpoint lectures, for instance, Mr. Homos's interest in Eve in William Dean Howells's *A Traveler from Altruria* and Julian West's infatuation with Edith Leete in *Looking Backward*. Another type of narrative break is the narrator's or protagonist's crisis episode: Shevek's fits of depression, West's physical and psychological collapses, and Frazier's impassioned confession, for example. Then too, there are the introductory and concluding shenanigans that explain how the visitor reached utopia, how he returned, or why he didn't. Readers who ignore these breaks as mere sugar-coating for, or diversions from, the author's "message" are missing much of the inclusive experience of utopian culture. As they strip away and forget these episodes in their search for "raw" ideas, such readers miss not only the flesh but a good deal of the marrow of utopia. After all, West's agonizing passage to A.D. 2000 and Edith's role as catalyst, mother, adviser, sister, and lover may reveal more about Bellamy's utopia than all of Dr. Leete's elaborate discourses on distribution and production.

The final element of the definition of a literary utopia—the depiction of a prescriptive, normative alternative to the present—is related to the cultural approach of the utopists, as both elements help us to distinguish between utopian and science fiction. Such distinctions are extremely difficult to make; as Sargent suggests in his historical survey of 1950 to 1975, utopian literature has practically become a subcategory of science fiction. And yet some boundary lines are useful. First, as the term *"science* fiction" implies, science-fiction writers often emphasize the scientific and technological aspects of their alternate worlds or "thought experiments," whereas utopists usually offer their readers information on "a variety of aspects" of a utopian culture.[13] Second, the author's intentions behind the creation of his alternative world often separate utopian from science fiction. Science fiction writers, especially those interested in mass markets, create alternatives primarily as frameworks for ingenious speculation or for entertaining adventures: *What-could-be* settings provide all sorts of opportunities for thought-provoking and exciting episodes, as the titles listed in Lyman Tower Sargent's bibliography and even the "Star Trek" books and television series demonstrate. Utopists create alternative cultures as didactic frameworks: *What-ought-to-be* (eutopia) and *what-ought-not-to-be* (dystopia) become "norms by which to judge existing societies."[14] Of course, such distinctions are arbitrary. Not all science fictions are just scientific-technological adventure stories, and utopian fictions are not all purely didactic tales set in imaginary cultures. But the cultural approach of the utopists and their prescriptive, normative intents to encourage readers to experience good (or bad) alternatives do suggest ways to discriminate between the two merging genres.

Now for the loopholes: The foregoing definition of a literary utopia raises at least two important questions. If we focus on imaginary settings that encourage a vicarious experience, does that mean a ban on expository writing? Can utopia be captured only in fiction, poetry, and drama? This is a very difficult question. If the item at hand is the Declaration of Independence, then it is fairly easy to place it in the realm of utopian thought as opposed to utopian literature. But if an expository work conforms to all the specifications of a literary utopia—for example, Sargent points to Edgar Chambless's *Roadtown* in an article defining utopia,[15] and I mention King Camp Gillette's *The Human Drift* in my historical survey of 1888 to 1899—should it be excluded? Such an exclusion seems overly arbitrary. Therefore, expository works are occasionally discussed in this collection.

The other large loophole undermines the neat symmetry of the utopian family of literatures: the mapping of the family tree in white and black—utopia (or eutopia) and dystopia. This division assumes that it is always possible to discover an author's intent and that the intent is consistently optimistic or pessimistic. Even a cursory knowledge of utopian literature betrays these assumptions. When *Walden Two* appeared, there was disagreement as to whether it reflected a behaviorist's dream or his nightmare. It has even been suggested that the granddaddy of them all, More's *Utopia*, might be a satiric dystopia.[16]

This problem becomes particularly acute with the study of American utopian literature. As Ernest Lee Tuveson, Michael Kammen, and others have observed, strange combinations of catastrophism and ebullience have always stalked the American landscape, and these mixtures permeate our utopian literature. Furthermore, American literary utopias often express mixed desires for reform and refuge—pleas for multiple change that lead to a changeless culture. These combinations of dynamism and static resistance to change often make it difficult to determine the author's intent. Therefore, it is quite difficult to find "pure" American eutopias and dystopias. To illustrate, in this collection both Robert Plank and Sargent comment on the tendency to tack happy endings onto American dystopias. Even during

the Golden Era of American eutopian literature during the late nineteenth
and early twentieth centuries there were dire warnings. Julian West expected Boston to be a "heap of moss grown ruins" by the year 2000;[17] John
Ames Mitchell's Persians do indeed find the ruins of America in the satiric
The Last American; Ignatius Donnelly mixed bloodbaths with visions of a
pastoral, Populist eutopia in *Caesar's Column*; Jack London wrote of eutopian dystopias and dystopian eutopias, as Gorman Beauchamp reminds
us in his essay in this collection; and even the utopists less prone to catastrophe than Donnelly and London gave warnings about the possibility of
future upheavals in explicit jeremiads or in bursts of volcanic imagery. But
it is not only the American "penchant for paradox" that muddies the precise
labeling of eutopias and dystopias. When perceptive novelists—novelists
who avoid one-dimensional re-creations of reality—turn toward utopia, the
usual contradictions are compounded by their awareness of the complexities
of the experience into which they draw their readers. Sometimes the result
is an almost uncontrolled ambivalence, such as Mark Twain's vacillations
between a democratic technocracy as eutopia and dystopia in *A Connecticut
Yankee in King Arthur's Court*. Other times the utopia is shaped by a
calculated ambiguity, as in Hawthorne's narrative voice in *The Blithedale
Romance* and the alternations between Urras and Anarres in Le Guin's *The
Dispossessed*, which is even subtitled *An Ambiguous Utopia*.

One solution to these categorical dilemmas is to suggest that utopian
terminology must be flexible. Utopias (or eutopias) and dystopias are the
most notable branches. But most eutopias must be supple enough to admit
the seeds of their dystopias, and vice versa. Therefore, when the contributors
to this collection label a book a "utopia," they do not necessarily imply that
the work is purely eutopian; and when a book contains healthy portions of
both eutopianism and dystopianism, then the general term, utopian, is often
used. (To simplify the terminology, the authors of utopian works are called
utopists or utopian authors rather than eutopists and dystopists, and the
citizens of their imaginary worlds are called utopians.)

One further elaboration: When specific works are discussed, labels besides utopia, eutopia, and dystopia are often very useful. Hence the contributors occasionally use terms such as "satiric utopia" (a work presenting
a "negative vision which indirectly presents an improved or ideal society
by portraying an imaginary society as an absurd reflection of the author's
own [society]," for example, *Gulliver's Travels*);[18] "antiutopia" (a work that
is a direct, negative response to a specific concept of utopia but often implies
an alternative utopia, for example, Richard C. Michaelis's *Looking Further
Forward: An Answer to Looking Backward by Edward Bellamy*); "partial
utopia" (a work that fulfills part but not all of the definition of a literary
utopia, for example, Garden of Eden and Golden Age mythology or a novel
such as Charles M. Sheldon's *In His Steps*); or an "ambiguous utopia," for

example, Le Guin's *The Dispossessed*. The selective bibliographies of literary utopias that follow each historical survey often include such labels. Of course, too many subcategories could lead to acute cases of multiple hyphenation. After all, isn't *The Blithedale Romance* a satiric-ambiguous antiutopia? And *A Connecticut Yankee* is most likely a partial-ambiguous-ambivalent-satiric-antieutopian-dystopian utopia. But at least the combination of the general definition offered in this introduction and the discreet use of more specialized terms in the following essays should point readers in the right direction and make them aware of the gentle dunes, jagged rocks, and combinations thereof that form the utopian landscape.

III

In this collection the emphasis will be on the American portion of that utopian landscape viewed from several different angles.

Admittedly this is but one continent of the utopian world. Diligent bibliographers, especially Glenn Negley and Lyman Tower Sargent, have discovered hundreds of non-American utopias; Darko Suvin has demonstrated the importance of Russian utopian and science fiction; and at the first Conference on Utopian Studies held in 1976 there were separate sessions on Spanish, Austrian, and Oriental utopias. But American utopian literature certainly deserves separate attention. The utopian urge has permeated our history. This impulse has been translated into hundreds of literary utopias, more than in any other country, and several of them—*Looking Backward, Walden Two, Atlas Shrugged, The Harrad Experiment*, and the partial utopia, *In His Steps*, for instance—have attracted millions of readers and thousands of active supporters.

But *America as Utopia* is not an isolationist collection; the many non-American authors and titles listed in the indexes should attest to that. Too frequently Americanists stare at their navels, and from this rather confined perspective they utter grand pronouncements about the uniqueness of certain "American" traits. The contributors to this collection realize that in order to understand American utopian literature fully, it is sometimes necessary to place it within the context of non-American literature and history. This awareness is especially evident in Joel Nydahl's examinations of the roots of the earliest American utopias. But it is also obvious in numerous cross-cultural comparisons throughout the collection—notably in my historical survey of 1888–99, which incorporates certain elements of Anglo-American Victorianism as a backdrop for the discussion of literary utopias; in Sargent's comments about the important British science fiction produced from 1950 to 1975; in Teitler's introduction to his Ten Lost Tribes checklist; in Plank's interpretations of *1984* and *Brave New World* and his generalizations about modern European history; in Suvin's comparisons between *Looking Backward* and William Morris's *News from Nowhere*; and in Hughes's comparisons of the historical perspectives of Huxley, Orwell, Zamiatin, and Vonnegut.

These international contexts add depth and variety to the collection. Another source of diversity comes from the division of *America as Utopia* into four different types of essays. One of the weaknesses of many studies of utopian literature is that their authors often approach utopia from only one angle. The results often seem logical and coherent, but they can be very misleading. Therefore, one of the chief goals of this collection is to present a wide variety of ways to study American utopian literature. Such a collection will not, of course, be as "unified" or as "definitive" as a comprehensive study undertaken by one competent scholar; nor will each approach included appeal to every reader. But this collection should introduce both the novice and the expert to a spectrum of provocative approaches that will help him or her to understand American utopian literature and to elaborate upon the methods offered here or to develop new approaches.

In the brief introductions to the four parts and to the Epilogue I attempt to define the general and specific characteristics of each section. But I should at least offer a few words about the overall organization and the variety of essays here. The four parts offer a tour of American utopian literature that begins with essays by utopists expressing their particular views of utopia and utopian literature; continues with discussions of specific utopists, comparisons between utopists, and broad thematic studies by students of utopia; and concludes with general bibliographic and historical surveys. Thus the collection moves from the specific to the general, allowing the reader first to become acquainted with individual utopias, which—along with other utopias—are gradually placed into larger and larger contexts. (Within each section the order of the essays is chronological, with the initial essays relating to earlier utopian literature. All the essays and bibliographies are original except for three of the contributions to Part I and one of the contributions to Part II, which are reprints that have been revised slightly for this collection.)

Although each of the four parts represents one general approach, there is diversity within each section. In Part I the essays express the views of four authors who have written important utopian works from different historical and philosophic perspectives. In *Looking Backward* (1888) Edward Bellamy blended Christian and Victorian attitudes with his enthusiasm for socialism and modern technology; in *Walden Two* (1948) B. F. Skinner used the conventional setting of a utopian commune to dramatize the effectiveness and morality of twentieth-century behavioral engineering; in *The Harrad Experiment* (1966) Robert Rimmer focused on the college students of the 1960s and on alternative ways of developing personal relationships; and in short stories, novels, and *The New Improved Sun: An Anthology of Utopian SF* (1975), Thomas Disch has explored the literary and philosophic implications of mixing utopian and science fiction.

In Part II the "case studies" range from a close reading of the evolutionary process in Kurt Vonnegut's *Player Piano*; through comparisons between two works by one author, Jack London, and comparisons between the alternatives posed by several works by William Dean Howells and Mark Twain; to a broad literary and socioeconomic examination of Bellamy and William Morris.

In Part III there is still some emphasis on several well-known utopias, for example, Arthur O. Lewis's discussion of James Fenimore Cooper's *The Crater* and Ayn Rand's *Atlas Shrugged*, and Robert Plank's examination of *Walden Two* and *The Harrad Experiment*. But in this section the focus has changed. The emphasis is upon important themes, types of characters, and theoretical problems. Therefore, the contributors investigate a wide variety of well-known and obscure literary utopias. In this section the approaches range from Stuart Teitler's annotated bibliography of the Lost Tribes in utopia; through Lyman Tower Sargent's survey of one type of utopia, which clearly demonstrates that all American utopias were not socialistic or even cooperative; the topical essays by Donald C. Burt and Barbara Quissell on ecology and women; and the character study that spans two centuries by Arthur O. Lewis; to the broad theoretical and historical essays by Jean Pfaelzer and Robert Plank. (Readers with little background in utopian literature might want to read Pfaelzer's essay before any other in the collection, for it provides an excellent introduction to several salient characteristics of utopian literature.)

The essays in Part IV constitute a more cohesive unit than the essays in the other sections, because these bibliographic and historical surveys offer a chronological order and completeness lacking in the previous parts. Nevertheless, Part IV still reflects a variety of ways to approach utopian literature. Two of the contributors—Joel Nydahl in his second essay and Charles Rooney—take the book-by-book approach, which is appropriate for such periods as 1798 to 1887, when relatively few utopias appeared. In their surveys of the twentieth century Howard P. Segal and Lyman Tower Sargent were confronted with hundreds of works; therefore their surveys emphasized broad trends rather than book-by-book descriptions. Sargent also chose to concentrate on the eutopias and dystopias within science fiction. In his first essay, Nydahl emphasizes the tremendous impact of English and European concepts upon the American view of utopia, which is an appropriate treatment for the earliest phases of American utopianism. In my examination of late-nineteenth-century utopias I was, in one way, more fortunate than the other contributors to Part IV. Much of the bibliographic and historical spadework has been done for this period. Therefore, I was freer to attempt a speculative survey that placed the utopias within the context of Victorian "culture" in America. Part IV concludes with a selective checklist of secondary sources that focuses on general historical studies.

No matter which type of historical or bibliographic essay in Part IV appeals most or least to readers, this section should make it perfectly clear that the late nineteenth century is not the only period worthy of study. The utopias of the earlier and later periods, which are often ignored, deserve close attention.

Considering the diversity of the essays in all four parts and the fact that more than seven hundred literary utopias are either examined or listed, it would be rather difficult—and more than arbitrary—to attempt to tie everything together in a neat concluding essay. But one alternative to such a strained finale is an example of what this collection is all about—American utopian literature. The particular example I selected for the Epilogue is from Ursula K. Le Guin's *The Dispossessed: An Ambiguous Utopia*. Ms. Le Guin is one of several contemporary novelists, including Thomas Disch, who have experimented with new types of utopian fiction. *The Dispossessed*, the winner of the 1975 Nebula Award, is respected as one of the most interesting of these experiments. Ms. Le Guin felt that Chapter 11 would make an appropriate Epilogue to this collection, because the episode incorporates echoes of many of the visions of perfection and nightmarish prophecies that intrigued the contributors to this collection and have inspired American utopian literature from the European discovery of the New World through the appearance of modern utopian science fiction.

IV

"Until we have a clear idea of what we want and are sure we want it . . . it would be a waste of time to discuss how we get it." So wrote the most famous American utopist, Edward Bellamy.[19] So far this introduction has responded to two of his three requirements: The definition of utopian literature is an attempt to offer "a clear idea of what we want," and the descriptions of the collection's organization and the variety of types of essays included define one way to "get it." But are we "sure we want it"? Is there really a need for a collection of diversified essays on American utopian literature?

Two quick, easy answers: yes, because utopian studies are "in" and because there are no books that cover American utopian literature in its entirety. It took twenty-four pages to list addenda to recent checklists and the 1978 utopian-studies scholarship, conferences, and papers in the spring 1979 "News Center" section of *Alternative Futures: The Journal of Utopian Studies*. These projects included two book-length bibliographies of utopian literature by Glenn Negley and Lyman Tower Sargent and two national conferences. But as the selective secondary source listing at the end of the collection indicates, there are no books or even dissertations that attempt comprehensive surveys of American utopian literature. Vernon Louis Parrington, Jr.'s, pioneering work, *American Dreams* (1947; reprint 1964), pays very little attention to pre-Bellamy utopias and even less to the twentieth century; Ivan Doig's *Utopian America* (1976) is an interesting reprint anthology, but it offers only a few examples of American utopian fiction; and my book, *The Obsolete Necessity; America in Utopian Writing, 1888–1900* (1976), like the dissertations on American utopian literature, covers only one important period. Thus, *America as Utopia* does seem to respond to a "popular" demand and a "real" need.

But even if there were other books that covered American utopian literature and even if utopian studies were not currently fashionable, there would be a need for *America as Utopia*. Such a collection draws attention to many unanswered literary questions about all utopian literature and encourages speculation about the social and personal value of utopian speculation. Literary questions are especially obvious: How do the best utopists make readers see how to extrapolate the present into new alternatives and simultaneously see the present in new ways? How can contemporary utopists give coherence, value, and meaning to utopia and still be honest about the pluralism, relativity, and doubts of the present and the future?

In spite of the obsolescence of much utopian literature, its study also offers many social and personal rewards. Because many of the recurring issues in the literature are still with us, utopias can be read as hypothetical case studies in the application of specific reforms. On a more abstract plane, past and present utopias are checks on the present. It is impossible to read Julian West's nightmarish return to the slums of Boston or Shevek's bizarre encounters with the shopping malls of Urras without feeling the shortcomings of American culture. On the other hand, by creating the illusion of a better America as a *fait accompli*, American utopists challenge readers with the need for and hopes of improvement.

As for personal rewards, every time readers allow themselves to experience a literary utopia, they know themselves a bit better. Once seduced by a utopia, we naturally begin to speculate about why it is attractive to us or about what we would modify to suit our needs. To quote Doig, "Utopia is not a tent city of oddballs; it's a site where any of us can mull our values."[20] Another personal reward is that reading good utopias can be an antidote for future shock. They prepare us for rapid change by thrusting us into new worlds. But to encourage our entry, utopists must provide enough of the familiar—enough confusion, awe, and doubt to identify with, for instance—and enough of a moral and ethical judgment about the goodness or badness of the new world to enable us to understand and judge what is going on while we shudder at the strangeness of it all. This simultaneous pushing and comforting can help to dull the bite of the future.

Finally, studies of American utopian literature are essential for anyone who wants to understand America. The inclusiveness of the utopias and their revelations about basic hopes and fears make them fascinating indices to American attitudes. This is especially so because American history is in part a history of potential dystopias and eutopias: the dystopian aura of the "howling wilderness," the genocide in the name of Manifest Destiny, the horrors of slavery, the nightmares of rampant commercialism, technology, urban squalor, Vietnam, Watergate and energy shortages; and the eutopian impulse of Winthrop's "Citty upon a Hill," Jefferson's Declaration of Independence, the possibilities for rebirth in the "virgin" West, the idealism of youth and civil rights movements, New Deals, New Frontiers, and Great Societies, and the technology and spirit that sent Americans to the moon and a bicentennial Viking to Utopia. To know America, we must have knowledge of America as utopia.

NOTES

1. "Mars Pictorial," *Astronomy*, November 1976, p. 18.

2. See Darko Suvin, "SF Theory: Internal and External Delimitation and Utopia," *Extrapolation*, 19 (December 1977), 14, and "Youtopia" illustration in Tony Jones, "The Utopian Urge: You Make the Future Today," *Harper's Magazine*, March 1973, p. 11.

3. See especially Darko Suvin, "Defining the Literary Genre of Utopia: Some Historical Semantics, Some Geneology, A Proposal and a Plea," *Studies in the Literary Imagination*, 2 (Fall 1973), 121–45; Lyman Tower Sargent, "Utopia: The Problem of Definition," *Extrapolation*, 16 (May 1975), 137–48; Ivan Doig, "This Is the Way the World Mends," in *Utopian America; Dreams and Reality*, ed. Ivan Doig (Rochelle Park, N.J.: Hayden, 1976), pp. 1–6; Oscar A. Haac, "Toward a Definition of Utopia," *Studies in Eighteenth-Century Culture*, 6 (December 1976), 405–14; Glenn Negley, "Introduction" to *Utopian Literature: A Bibliography* (Lawrence: The Regents Press of Kansas, 1977), pp. xi–xiv; Robert Plank, "Remarks on the Nomenclature We Use," *Alternative Futures*, 1 (Spring 1978), 95–96; Raymond Williams, "Utopia and Science Fiction," *Science-Fiction Studies*, 5 (November 1978), 203–14; and Tom Kitwood, " 'Science' and 'Utopia' in the Anticipation of Social Change," *Alternative Futures*, 1 (Summer 1978), 24–46. Later in my introduction I use Haac's concept of utopia as a combination of "reform and refuge."

4. Raymond Trousson, "Utopie et roman utopique," *Revue des sciences humaines*, 155 (September 1974), 372–73, as quoted in Haac, "Toward a Definition," p. 409.

5. Sargent, "Problem of Definition," p. 139; see also Sargent's "The Three Faces of Utopianism, *Minnesota Review*, 7, No. 3 (1967), 222–30.

6. Sargent, "Problem of Definition," p. 139.

7. Robert S. Fogarty, "Community Organization After Mid-19th Century," paper delivered at the First Annual Conference on Utopian Studies, Troy, N.Y., October 2, 1976, and Jones, "Utopian Urge," p. 11.

8. For a slightly different approach to this family of literatures see Joel Nydahl, "Introduction" to Timothy Savage, *The Amazonian Republic* (Delmar, N.Y.: Scholars' Facsimiles & Reprints, 1976), p. vii.

9. Sargent, "Problem of Definition," p. 141.

10. As quoted in Ivan Doig, "The United States of Utopia" in *Utopian America*, p. 8.

11. Ayn Rand, "The Goal of My Writing," *The Objectivist Newsletter*, November 1963, pp. 40–41.

12. Daniel Walker Howe, "American Victorianism as a Culture," *American Quarterly*, 27 (December 1975), 509.

13. J. Max Patrick, "Introduction" to R. W. Gibson and J. Max Patrick, "Utopias and Dystopias, 1500–1750" in R. W. Gibson, *St. Thomas More: A Preliminary Bibliography of His Works and of Moreana to the Year 1750* (New Haven: Yale University Press, 1961), p. 293.

14. Ibid.

15. Sargent, "Problem of Definition," p. 142.

16. Merritt Abrash, "Missing the Point in More's *Utopia*," *Extrapolation*, 19 (December 1977), 27–38.

17. Edward Bellamy, *Looking Backward, 2000–1887* (Cambridge, Mass.: Belknap Press of Harvard University Press, 1967), p. 123.

18. Nydahl, "Introduction," p. vii.

19. As quoted in John Thomas, "Introduction" to Bellamy, *Looking Backward*, p. 66.

20. Doig, "Way the World Mends," (note 3 above), p. 3.

THE AUTHORS' VIEWS

PART I IS AN important counterbalance to Parts II–IV. Most collections of essays on a particular subject are written by either scholars or "practitioners." The scholars can usually be more objective than the practitioners, because often they are not in the "thick of things": They are political scientists, not politicians; historians, not history makers; critics, not novelists. But this lack of direct involvement can also limit the scholars' views. Probably the contributors to Part I have not read as much utopian literature as many of the scholars who contributed to Parts II–IV. But they have confronted head on the complexities and frustrations of creating utopia. They certainly deserve our attention; they deserve to speak first.

It seems appropriate to begin a collection of essays about American utopian literature with two contributions by the most famous American utopian author, Edward Bellamy (1850–98). A sketch of his life story is readily available in the *Dictionary of American Biography*: The Bellamy entry emphasizes his tendency to stay close to his home in Chicopee Falls, Massachusetts; the influence of his father, a Baptist minister; the impact of his visit to Germany, where as a boy of eighteen he was shocked by the poverty he saw; his brief encounter with the legal profession; his journalism; his early fiction, which included several stories with utopian content; and, of course, how the tremendous popularity of *Looking Backward* (1888) changed Bellamy's life. (For a list of more thorough biographies than the DAB entry, see notes 3 and 5 to Darko Suvin's essay in Part II.)

The way *Looking Backward* affected Bellamy's life is, in part, reflected in the two short essays included in Part I as "How and Why I Wrote *Looking Backward*." The original titles for the essays—"How I Came to Write 'Looking Backward,'" and "How I wrote 'Looking Backward'"—suggest duplicate pieces; and yet the first essay, published in 1889 shortly after *Looking Backward* became a best seller, offers quite a different version of the origins of the novel from the one in the second essay, which was published in 1894

17

after Bellamy had become actively involved in reform journalism and political battles.

The first essay expresses a tone of modesty and innocence—traits that
evidently were quite characteristic of Bellamy's pre–*Looking Backward* days
as an obscure journalist and novelist. He maintains that he had only intended
to write a "literary fantasy," "a cloud-palace for an ideal humanity," "a mere
fairy tale of social perfection." But suddenly he was captivated by the concept
of the Industrial Army; he realized that his fantasies might have important
practical applications as solutions to social and economic ills in America.
After this revelation, he stripped away many of the episodes and details he
had intended for his tale of Asheville, North Carolina, in A.D. 3000 and
focused on his reform ideas. He even claims that he only kept the fictional
form in hopes of "inducing" more Americans to "at least" read the book—in
other words, the old sugar-coating-the-pill argument.

The second essay almost seems as if it were written by a different author
about another book. There is no mention of cloud-palaces or fairy tales. Now
the impression offered is that Bellamy "sat down at [his] desk with the
definite purpose of trying to reason out a method of economic organization."
Bellamy hints at the fiction-as-sugar-coating pose when he mentions the
"popular attention" paid to stories. But now fiction has become much more
than a pleasant lure; it is a form of expression that offers a rigorous testing
ground for the logic, consistency, and practicality of his reform proposals.
The rhetoric of the second essay is also much more businesslike or, one
might argue, propagandistic.

All these changes suggest Bellamy's transformation from a retiring novelist known for provocative psychic speculations to an embattled public
figure who wanted to emphasize the practical as opposed to the fanciful
aspects of his writing. Thus Bellamy's re-creations of the origins of *Looking
Backward* dramatize basic opportunities and problems confronting utopian
authors: the exciting cross-fertilization of ideas and imagination, and the
tensions of the dual role of storyteller and practical ideologist. (Darko Suvin's
essay in Part II, Jean Pfaelzer's in Part III, and mine in Part IV directly or
indirectly examine how Bellamy approached these opportunities and problems. See also R. Jackson Wilson's provocative essay "Experience and Utopia," which appeared in the April 1977 issue of the *Journal of American
Studies*.)

Next to *Looking Backward*, B. F. Skinner's *Walden Two* (1948) has
probably been the most influential American literary utopia. (A close runner-
up would be Ayn Rand's *Atlas Shrugged* [1957]. But, unfortunately, Miss
Rand would not grant me permission to reprint her interesting essay "The
Goal of My Writing.") Skinner (1904–   ) has had a distinguished academic
career, including positions at the University of Minnesota, Indiana University, and Harvard and the publication of thirteen influential books. He has

received numerous honorary degrees and is recognized as the leading ex-
ponent of behavioral psychology. Skinner has also gained notoriety for inventions such as the "Skinner Box," the "Air-Crib," and teaching machines.
But it is as the author of *Walden Two* that he is best known.

There are several similarities between Bellamy's essays and Skinner's
"Utopia as an Experimental Culture" (which was originally prepared as BBC
talks and then revised for publication in Skinner's *Contingencies of Reinforcement.)* Both authors present their literary utopias as "serious proposals"; both admit to being criticized; both perceive a crucial role for
America in their utopias; and both their essays are designed as defenses of
their utopias.

But Skinner's defense has a much broader scope than Bellamy's. In order
to define his concept of a behavioral utopia, he provides a thumbnail sketch
of utopian literature that surveys the writings of, among others, Plato, Saint
Augustine, More, Bacon, Cabet, Marx, Morris, and Bellamy. Some readers
may argue that Skinner manipulates this survey for his own purposes. But
his overview is a marvelously concise attempt to delineate the fundamental
differences between the "classic" utopists' dependency on religious and
economic appeals and his emphasis on behavioral conditioning. The survey
will also help to acquaint readers having little or no background in utopian
literature with several of the most important non-American utopists mentioned throughout this collection.

One other notable quality of Skinner's essay is that he confronts one of
the principal criticisms voiced by his detractors: People don't like to be
"designed." In part, as Skinner explains, this aversion is related to a fear
of being controlled, for control has so many negative connotations. But
repugnance toward a designed utopia based upon behavioral engineering
also springs from our deep-seated beliefs about personal worth and individuality. Skinner is fully aware that we tend to give a person "credit" if he or
she struggles against adversity and accident. But how can we "credit" individuals who live in an "ideal" environment and are conditioned from birth
to behave in appropriate ways? Skinner's answer—that our concepts of personal worth and individuality are obsolete and must be replaced by concepts
of people and culture that encourage creative and humane control over
accidental development—will not appeal to all the readers of this collection.
His analysis of one of the main criticisms of *Walden Two*, however, certainly
demonstrates his awareness of the complexity of writing modern literary
utopias and also indicates his willingness to confront questions that many
utopian authors tend to ignore and evade. (For further discussions of Skinner, see Robert Plank's essay in Part III and Lyman Tower Sargent's bibliographic survey in Part IV.)

The third contributor to Part I, Robert Rimmer (1917–   ), has much
in common with Bellamy and Skinner. Like his predecessors, Rimmer never

intended to be a "utopian author." He was and still is a businessman who for many years headed the Relief Printing Corporation, which he finally sold in 1977. Although his novels, especially *The Harrad Experiment* (1966), have sold millions of copies, he still lists writing as a "major hobby" on his vita. But it is clear that Rimmer, like Bellamy and Skinner, considers his writing serious business. His afterword to the new (1978) Bantam edition of *The Harrad Experiment* is entitled "Who Is Going to Start Harrad," and like Bellamy's postscript to the second edition of *Looking Backward* and Skinner's introduction to the new (1976) Macmillan edition of *Walden Two*, the afterword stresses that the ideas in his utopian works are intended as practical reform measures.

It is also evident that Rimmer has been influenced by Bellamy and Skinner. The "Human Values" course taught at Harrad draws heavily upon behavioral psychology as well as other types of psychologies. Rimmer is very concerned about equality, an issue that pervaded Bellamy's utopianism as evidenced by the title of his second book-length utopia, *Equality* (1897). Titles also reaffirm the links between Rimmer and Bellamy. Rimmer's newest novel, *Love Me Tomorrow*, was originally entitled *Looking Backward II*. (The title was changed because the publisher felt that the original title no longer had mass appeal.)

In his essay in Part I Rimmer offers provocative biographical insights about the origins of *The Harrad Experiment* and his other "entopian" novels, about his decision to express his views in fiction instead of nonfiction, and about his proposals for improved educational systems and family structures—the two aspects of his novels that have made them popular and controversial. Rimmer also articulates some of the occupational hazards of being a "utopian author." He has discovered that "laymen," especially businessmen, are suspicious of a president of a printing corporation who writes novels; one prestigious Boston bank even kept a copy of *The Harrad Experiment* tucked away in Rimmer's personal file! (This episode in Rimmer's life sounds like a twentieth-century version of the suspicions heaped upon the "scribbling farmer" by wife and neighbors in Crèvecoeur's *Letters from an American Farmer*.) On the other hand, "experts" and "academics" are often leery of the utopist, especially when he treads upon their areas of specialization without having the proper "credentials," which, of course, is almost inevitable considering the broad scope of most utopian narratives. But despite the suspicions of laymen and experts, it is obvious that Rimmer has found many sympathetic readers, notably high school and college students. As Robert Plank argues in Part III, this popular appeal of Rimmer's works indicates that they deserve serious consideration as influential developments in the evolution of the modern utopia.

Thomas M. Disch (1940–   ), the youngest and final contributor to Part I, speaks out of a different literary tradition from the explicit, practical literary utopianism defended by Bellamy, Skinner, and Rimmer. His achievements as a writer of science fiction have lead to critical praise; visiting lectureships at the University of Minnesota, Michigan State, and Wesleyan; and the 1975 O. Henry Prize. As his essay reveals, his experience as a science fiction writer has also made him aware of some of the important literary reasons for a decline in the number of the type of positive, explicit eutopias created by Bellamy, Skinner, and Rimmer. (The statistics of this decline are presented in bibliographic essays by Howard P. Segal and Lyman Tower Sargent in Part IV and analyzed by Robert Plank in Part III. For a different approach to this decline, see James R. Simmons's "The American Historical Novel in Historical Perspective," a paper presented on October 14, 1979, at the Fourth Annual Conference on Utopian Studies in Denver.)

Specifically, Disch points to the dullness, silliness, impracticality, and downright repugnance of many utopian works. And yet he, along with several other talented contemporary writers of science fiction (see introduction to the Epilogue of this collection), has attempted such literature; his essay is a slightly revised version of the introduction to his anthology, *The New Improved Sun: An Anthology of Utopian S-F* (1975); and he, like the other contributors to Part I, believes that our ability to maintain hope for the future of an ever changing America depends in part upon our ability to produce a fresh crop of utopian speculation "each season."

E D W A R D   B E L L A M Y

How and Why I Wrote Looking Backward

I ACCEPT more readily the invitation to tell . . . how I came to write *Looking Backward* for the reason that it will afford an opportunity to clear up certain points on which inquiries have been frequently addressed to me. I never had, previous to the publication of the work, any affiliations with any class or sect of industrial or social reformers nor, to make my confession complete, any particular sympathy with undertakings of the sort. It is only just to myself to say, however, that this should not be taken to indicate any indifference to the miserable condition of the mass of humanity, seeing that it resulted rather from a perception all too clear of the depth and breadth of the social problem and a consequent skepticism as to the effectiveness of the proposed solutions which had come to my notice.

In undertaking to write *Looking Backward* I had, at the outset, no idea of attempting a serious contribution to the movement of social reform. The idea was of a mere literary fantasy, a fairy tale of social felicity. There was no thought of contriving a house which practical men might live in, but merely of hanging in mid-air, far out of reach of the sordid and material world of the present, a cloud-palace for an ideal humanity.

In order to secure plenty of elbow room for the fancy and prevent awkward collisions between the ideal structure and the hard facts of the real world, I fixed the date of the story in the year A.D. 3000. As to what might be in A.D. 3000 one man's opinion was as good as another's, and my fantasy of the social system of that day only required to be consistent with itself to defy criticism. Emboldened by the impunity my isolated position secured me, I was satisfied with nothing less than the whole earth for my social palace. In its present form the story is a romance of the ideal nation, but

This essay combines two short essays: "How I Came to Write 'Looking Backward,' " *The Nationalist*, May 1889, pp. 1–4, and "How I Wrote 'Looking Backward,' " *The Ladies Home Journal*, April 1894, p. 2. The introduction to the latter has been omitted.

in its first form it was a romance of an ideal world. In the first draft of *Looking Backward*, though the immediate scene was laid in America (in Asheville, North Carolina, instead of Boston, by the way), the United States was supposed to be merely an administrative province of the great World Nation, whose affairs were directed from the World Capital which was declared to be the city of Berne, in Switzerland. The action of the story was made to begin in the thirtieth century.

The opening scene was a grand parade of a departmental division of the industrial army on the occasion of the annual muster day when the young men coming of age that year were mustered into the national service and those who that year had reached the age of exemption were mustered out. That chapter always pleased me and it was with some regrets that I left it out of the final draft. The solemn pageantry of the great festival of the year, the impressive ceremonial of the oath of duty taken by the new recruits in presence of the world-standard, the formal return of the thanks of humanity to the veterans who received their honorable dismissal from service, the review and march past of the entire body of the local industrial forces, each battalion with its appropriate insignia, the triumphal arches, the garlanded streets, the banquets, the music, the open theatres and pleasure gardens, with all the features of a gala day sacred to the civic virtues and the enthusiasm of humanity, furnished materials for a picture exhilarating at least to the painter.

The idea of committing the duty of maintaining the community to an industrial army, precisely as the duty of protecting it is entrusted to a military army, was directly suggested to me by the grand object lesson of the organization of an entire people for national purposes presented by the military system of universal service for fixed and equal terms, which has been practically adopted by the nations of Europe and theoretically adopted everywhere else as the only just and only effectual plan of public defense on a great scale. What inference could possibly be more obvious and more unquestionable than the advisability of trying to see if a plan which was found to work so well for purposes of destruction might not be profitably applied to the business of production now in such shocking confusion. But while this idea had for some time been vaguely floating in my mind, for a year or two I think at least, I had been far from realizing all that was in it, and only thought then of utilizing it as an analogy to lend an effect of feasibility to the fancy sketch I had in hand. It was not till I began to work out the details of the scheme by way of explaining how the people of the thirtieth century disposed of the awkward problems of labor and avoided the evils of a classifed society that I perceived the full potency of the instrument I was using and recognized in the modern military system not merely a rhetorical analogy for a national industrial service, but its prototype, furnishing at once a complete working model for its organization, an arsenal of patriotic and national motives and arguments for its animation, and the unanswerable demonstration of its feasibility drawn from the actual experience of whole nations organized and manoeuvred as armies.

Something in this way it was that, no thanks to myself, I stumbled over the destined corner-stone of the new social order. It scarcely needs to be said that having once apprehended it for what it was, it became a matter of pressing importance to me to show it in the same light to other people. This led to a complete recasting, both in form and purpose, of the book I was engaged upon. Instead of a mere fairy tale of social perfection, it became the vehicle of a definite scheme of industrial reorganization. The form of a romance was retained, although with some impatience, in the hope of inducing the more to give it at least a reading. Barely enough story was left to decently drape the skeleton of the argument and not enough, I fear, in spots, for even that purpose. A great deal of merely fanciful matter concerning the manners, customs, social and political institutions, mechanical contrivances, and so forth of the people of the thirtieth century, which had been intended for the book, was cut out for fear of diverting the attention of readers from the main theme. Instead of the year A.D. 3000, that of A.D. 2000 was fixed upon as the date of the story. Ten centuries had at first seemed to me none too much to allow for the evolution of anything like an ideal society, but with my new belief as to the part which the National organization of industry is to play in bringing in the good time coming, it appeared to me reasonable to suppose that by the year 2000 the order of things which we look forward to will already have become an exceedingly old story. This conviction as to the shortness of the time in which the hope of Nationalization is to be realized by the birth of the new, and the first true, nation, I wish to say, is one which every day's reflection and observation, since the publication of *Looking Backward*, has tended to confirm.

The same clearer conviction as to the method by which this great change is to come about, which caused me to shorten so greatly my estimate of the time in which it was to be accomplished, necessitated the substitution of the conception of a separate national evolution for the original idea of a homogeneous world-wide social system. The year 3000 may, indeed, see something of that sort, but not the year 2000. It would be preposterous to assume parity of progress between America and Turkey. The more advanced nations, ours surely first of all, will reach the summit earliest and, reaching strong brotherly hands downward, help up the laggards.   (1889)

II

According to my best recollection it was in the fall or winter of 1886 that

I sat down to my desk with the definite purpose of trying to reason out a method of economic organization by which the republic might guarantee the livelihood and material welfare of its citizens on a basis of equality corresponding to and supplementing their political equality. There was no doubt in my mind that the proposed study should be in the form of a story. This was not merely because that was a treatment which would command greater popular attention than others. In adventuring in any new and difficult field of speculation I believe that the student often cannot do better than to use the literary form of fiction. Nothing outside of the exact sciences has to be so logical as the thread of a story, if it is to be acceptable. There is no such test of a false and absurd idea as trying to fit it into a story. You may make a sermon or an essay or a philosophical treatise as illogical as you please, and no one know the difference, but all the world is a good critic of a story, for it has to conform to the laws of ordinary probability and commonly observed sequence, of which we are all judges.

The stories that I had written before *Looking Backward* were largely of one sort, namely, the working out of problems, that is to say, attempts to trace the logical consequences of certain assumed conditions. It was natural, therefore, that in this form the plan of *Looking Backward* should present itself to my mind. Given the United States, a republic based upon the equality of all men and conducted by their equal voice, what would the natural and logical way be by which to go about the work of guaranteeing an economic equality to its citizens corresponding with their political equality, but without the present unjust discrimination on account of sex? From the moment the problem first clearly presented itself to my mind in this way, the writing of the book was the simplest thing in the world.

Looking Backward has been frequently called a "fanciful" production. Of course, the notion of a man's being resuscitated after a century's sleep is fanciful, and so, of course, are the various other whimsies about life in the year 2000 necessarily inserted to give color to the picture. The argument of the book is, however, about as little fanciful as possible. It is, as I have said, an attempt to work out logically the results of regulating the national system of production and distribution by the democratic principle of the equal rights of all, determined by the equal voice of all. I defend as material no feature of the plan which cannot be shown to be in accord with that method.

Many excellent persons, not without sympathy with the idea of a somewhat more equal distribution of this world's wealth, have objected to the principle of absolute and invariable economic equality underlying the plan developed in *Looking Backward*. Many have seemed to think that here was an arbitrary detail that might just as well have been modified by admitting economic inequality in proportion to unequal values of industrial service. So it might have been if the plan had been the fanciful theory they supposed it, but regarding it as the result of a rigid application of the democratic idea to the economic system, no feature of the whole plan is more absolutely a matter of course, a more logical necessity than just that. Political equality, which gives all citizens an equal voice in government, without regard to the great differences between men as to intelligence, public service, personal worth and wealth, is the recognition that the essential dignity of human nature is of an importance transcending all personal attributes and accidents and is, therefore, not to be limited by them. In applying the democratic idea to the economic organization, economic equality, without regard to differences of industrial ability, is necessitated by precisely the same logic which justifies political equality. The two ideas are one and stand or fall together.

Nor is economic equality any more an ethical than a necessary physical consequence of democratic rule extended to the productive and distributive system. Political equals will never legislate economic inequality. Nor should they do so. Self-preservation forbids it, for economic inequality presently undermines and nullifies political equality and every other form of equality as well.

Moreover, under any system proportioning wealth distribution to industrial performance, how could women be assured an indefeasible equality with men, and their yoke of economic dependence upon the other sex, with all its related and implied subserviences, be finally broken? Surely no social solution not securely guaranteeing that result could claim to be adequate.

I have stopped by the way to say these few words about the plan of *Looking Backward* as the result of the rigid application of the democratic formula to the social problem, and concerning the feature of absolute economic equality as a necessary effect of that method, because it is in these points and their implications that Nationalism, as suggested by *Looking Backward*, is, perhaps, most strongly differentiated from some other socialistic solutions.

As to the form of the story, my first notion was, while keeping the resuscitated man as a link between the two centuries, not to make him the narrator, or to write chiefly from his point of view, but rather from that of the twentieth century. This would have admitted of some very interesting effects and about half the story was at first written on that line. But as I became convinced of the practical availability of the social solution I was studying, it became my aim to sacrifice all other effects to the method which would enable me to explain its features most fully, which was manifestly that of presenting everything from the point of view of the representative of the nineteenth century.

I have been very frequently asked if I anticipated any considerable effect from the publication of *Looking Backward*, and whether I was not very much surprised at the sensation it produced. I cannot say that I was surprised. If it be asked what was the basis of my expectations, I answer the effect of the writing of the book upon myself. When I first undertook to work out the results of a democratic organization of production and distribution based on the recognition of an equal duty of individual service by all citizens and an equal share by all in the result, according to the analogies of military service and taxation and all other relations between the State and the citizen, I believed, indeed, it might be possible on this line to make some valuable suggestions upon the social problem, but it was only as I proceeded with the inquiry that I became fully convinced of the entire adequacy of the principle as a social solution, and, moreover, that the achievement of this solution was to be the next great step in human evolution. It would, indeed, be a most impassive person in whose mind so mighty a hope could grow without producing strong emotions.

Knowing that "as face answereth to face in water, so the heart of man to man," I could not doubt that the hope that moved me must needs, in like manner, move all who should come even in part to share it.

As well as I can remember *Looking Backward* began in earnest to be written in the fall or winter of 1886, and was substantially finished in the following six or eight months, although rewriting and revising took up the following spring and summer. It went to the publishers in August or September, 1887, and although promptly accepted did not appear till January, 1888. Although it made a stir among the critics, up to the close of 1888 the sales had not exceeded ten thousand, after which they leaped into the hundred thousands.   (1894)

B. F. SKINNER

Utopia as an Experimental Culture

Walden Two DESCRIBES an imaginary community of about a thousand people who are living a Good Life. They enjoy a pleasant rural setting and work only a few hours a day, without being compelled to do so. Their children are cared for and educated by specialists with due regard for the lives they are going to lead. Food is good and sanitation and medical care excellent. There is plenty of leisure and many ways of enjoying it. Art, music, and literature flourish, and scientific research is encouraged. Life in Walden Two is not only good, it seems feasible. It is within the reach of intelligent men of goodwill who will apply the principles which are now emerging from the scientific study of human behavior to the design of culture. Some readers may take the book as written with tongue in cheek, but it was actually a quite serious proposal.

The book was violently attacked as soon as it appeared. *Life* magazine called it a "slander on some old notions of the 'good life' . . . Such a triumph of mortmain, or the 'dead hand,' [as] has not been envisaged since the days of Sparta . . . a slur upon a name, a corruption of an impulse."[1] In *The Quest for Utopia* Negley and Patrick, while agreeing that sooner or later "the principle of psychological conditioning would be made the basis of the serious construction of utopia . . . ," found they were quite unprepared for "the shocking horror of the idea when positively presented. Of all the dictatorships espoused by utopists," they continued, "this is the most profound, and incipient dictators might well find in this utopia a guide book of political practice."[2] And Joseph Wood Krutch soon devoted a substantial part of *The Measure of Man* to an attack on what he called an "ignoble utopia."[3] The controversy grows more violent and puzzling as the years pass.

There is clearly a renewal of interest in utopian speculation. A pattern is probably not set when, as two psychoanalysts have suggested, "in need of and in despair for the absent breast, the infant hallucinates the fulfillment

B. F. Skinner, *Contingencies of Reinforcement: A Theoretical Analysis,* © 1969, pp. 29-49. Reprinted by permission of Prentice-Hall, Inc., Englewood Cliffs, New Jersey.

and thus postpones momentarily the overwhelming panic of prolonged frustration,"[4] but there are other possibilities. For many people a utopia serves as an alternative to a kind of political dream which is still suppressed by vestiges of political witch-hunting. For some it may show dissatisfaction with our international stance; an experimental community is a sort of domestic Peace Corps. Whatever the explanation, there is no doubt that many people are now inclined to scrutinize the way of life in which they find themselves, to question its justification, and to consider alternatives.

But this is also an anti-utopian age. The modern classics—Aldous Huxley's *Brave New World* and George Orwell's *Nineteen Eighty Four*— describe ways of life we must be sure to avoid. George Kateb has analyzed the issue in *Utopia and Its Enemies*, a title obviously based on Karl Popper's *The Open Society and Its Enemies* which was itself an early skirmish in the war against utopia. The strange thing in all this is the violence. One of Plato's characters calls his *Republic* "a city of pigs," but never before have dreams of a better world raised such a storm. Possibly one explanation is that now, for the first time, the dream must be taken seriously. Utopias are science fiction, and we have learned that science fiction has a way of coming true.

UTOPIAN TECHNIQUES

We can take a step toward explaining why Utopia only now seems within reach by looking at some classical examples. In his *Republic* and in parts of other dialogues, Plato portrayed a well-managed society patterned on the Greek city-state. He suggested features which would presumably contribute to its success, but he put his faith in a wise ruler—a philosopher-king who, as philosopher, would know what to do and, as king, would be able to do it. It is an old and not very honorable strategy: when you do not know what should be done, assume that there is someone who does. The philosopher-king was to patch up a defective governmental design as the need arose, but it was not clear how he was to do so.

There are those—among them theologians—who argue that the next great utopian vision was the Christian heaven. St. Augustine developed the theme in his *City of God*. It was certainly a good life based on the highest authority, but important details were missing. Everyone who went to heaven was to be happy, but it was not clear just why. No one, in fact, has ever portrayed a very interesting heaven. St. Augustine's mundane version set the pattern for the monastic communities of early Christianity, but it would be hard to defend it as a good life. The monastery was a transitory state to which men turned with assurance that it was to be followed by a better life in a world to come.

Plato hoped to find the good life *sub homine*, and St. Augustine sought it *sub deo*. It remained for Thomas More to propose that it might be found *sub lege*. More was a lawyer, and history had begun to show the importance of charters, constitutions, and other agreements which men might make among themselves in order to live peacefully together. The title of his book, *Utopia*, which gave the name to this kind of speculation, has an ambiguous etymology. The Greek root of Utopia denotes a place, but the prefix means either good or nonexistent—or possibly, and cynically, both. Within a century another lawyer, Francis Bacon, had extended More's appeal to reason in his fragmentary utopia, *The New Atlantis*, in which he also looked to government and law for a solution—although he suggested that scientists might be called on as advisers. (The scientific institution he described—Solomon's House—was in fact the model on which the Royal Society was soon founded.)

But was law and order the answer? Erasmus thought not. He supported More's utopian vision, but with reservations. Reason might contribute to the good life, but it was a mistake to overlook other things. Erasmus was amused by the fact that More's name was the Latin root for "fool," and he whimsically defended his friend by writing *The Praise of Folly*. Government, he said, is all very well, but were it not for the folly of sex, no one would be born, and were it not for the folly of appetite, no one would survive, to be governed.

It was not long before further doubt was cast on the necessity or sufficiency of law and order. Round-the-world voyagers returning from the South Seas brought back stories of a good life which flourished without benefit of civilization on the European pattern. Men were peaceful and happy although completely ignorant of western morals and with little or no visible government. Diderot developed the theme in his *Supplement to the Voyage of Bougainville*—for example, in the amusing scene in which a Catholic priest and a Tahitian chief discuss sexual morality. Jean-Jacques Rousseau took a stronger line: government was not only unnecessary, it was inimical to the good life. Natural man—the noble savage—was wise and good; government corrupted him. Here were the beginnings of a philosophy of anarchy which still finds a place in utopian speculation.

(The South Seas proved that natural man was not only good but self-sufficient. Governments made men dependent upon other men, but the shipwrecked sailor, aided by the abundant resources of a tropical isle, could be master of all he surveyed. A special kind of utopian writing began to take shape when Robinson Crusoe put the solitary good life to the test. Frontier America offered many opportunities to the individual *coureur de bois*, and the theme was still strong in the middle of the nineteenth century when Henry David Thoreau built his own tropical island on the shores of Walden Pond.)

Exaggerated reports of life in the South Seas led to a rash of idyllic utopias, many of them set in the tropics. And now, for the first time, such a world seemed feasible. It is true that the Greeks dreamed of Arcadia, which was a real place, and proposals to found a utopia were occasionally made (according to Gibbon the Emperor Gallienus was on the point of offering the philosopher Plotinus a captured city so that he might try Plato's experiment when, perhaps fortunately for Plotinus, he was called away on emergencies of state), but More and Bacon were not drawing blueprints; they were simply describing societies with which contemporary life might be compared. The South Seas were real, and life on that pattern could therefore be taken seriously. Etienne Cabet's *Voyage en Icarie* was one of the most popular of the idyllic utopias, and Cabet actually came to America in the 1850's planning to set up Icaria on the Red River in Texas. He died in St. Louis, Missouri, but a community on the Icarian principle survived for some time in the Middle West.

It was the idyllic utopia which Karl Marx attacked. To portray a good life was one thing, to bring it about quite another. In this sense Marx was anti-utopian, but he had his own vision, and it was not entirely unrelated to the South Sea idyll. It was possible that human happiness might be traced not so much to the absence of government as to an abundance of goods. Nature could not always be counted on to supply what man needed to be happy in the style of the South Seas, but man would provide for himself if he were able. A Utopia hinged on economic principles.

The notion had been developing for a long time. Goods were essential to the good life, but where were they to be found? Bacon had argued that science was power, and the technology which he advocated and which began to emerge in the seventeenth century seemed a possible answer. If men were not producing the wealth they needed to be happy, it was because they did not know how. Science must come to the rescue. The great encyclopedia of Diderot and d'Alembert was to have this effect. Many recipes, formulae, and systems for the production of wealth which had been trade, guild, or family secrets had only to be made public and men would go busily to work.

Marx thought he saw another reason why men were not producing the wealth they needed for happiness: the means of production were being sequestered by selfish people. The good life would follow when the necessary tools were made available to everyone. This was the solution emphasized in nineteenth-century utopias, exemplified in England by William Morris's *News From Nowhere* and in the United States by Edward Bellamy's *Looking Backward*. The doctrine that the good life will follow when each has been supplied "according to his need" is scriptural: it is St. Augustine, not St. Karl. It has remained, of course, a strong utopian theme: technology is to solve our problems by making everyone affluent. A few years ago Mr. Khrushchev announced that before long all food, clothing, and housing in Russia would be free. The good life was just round the corner.

An irritating problem survived. Given both the skills and the means, men may still not produce wealth. Nineteenth-century theorists found it necessary to appeal to a natural compulsion to work. William Morris describes a man looking for work, not to earn money but simply to express a need. A Russian economist when asked why men will work when all food, clothing, and housing are free, replied with a confident smile, "For the common good," but that is by no means certain. "To each according to his need" must be balanced by "from each according to his ability," and that is an assignment which has so far proved to be beyond the reach of economics. And there are other kinds of goods which physical technology has not yet been able to supply. A more comprehensive behavioral science is needed.

BEHAVIORAL UTOPIAS

Rousseau knew that natural man would not solve all his problems, and Marx knew that economic principles would not suffice, and both took other characteristics of human behavior into account. A thoroughgoing behavioral utopia, however, was to wait for the twentieth century. The two leading figures of behavioral science in that century are Freud and Pavlov. Curiously enough, no utopian novel seems to have been written on Freudian principles. Pavlov was drawn into utopian speculation by accident. In 1917 the Russians needed the principle of the conditioned reflex to support their ideology, and they made Pavlov a national hero. If men were neither productive nor happy, it was the fault of their environments, and with the help of Pavlovian principles the Russian government would change the world and thus change men. But by the early nineteen-thirties the position had become embarrassing, as Bauer has noted.[5] The government had had its chance, and Russians were not yet conspicuously productive or happy. Pavlov went out of favor, and for twenty years Russian research on conditioned reflexes was confined to physiological processes not closely related to behavior. When the Second World War restored Russia's confidence, Pavlov returned as an intellectual hero, and the conditioned reflex was given another chance to build the good life.

Meanwhile, Aldous Huxley had explored the utopian implications of Pavlov's work in Brave New World. The book is, of course, a satire, heralding the threat rather than the promise of the conditioned reflex. There is nothing really new about conditioning, and Huxley seems to have known it. When Miranda in The Tempest exclaims, "Oh, brave new world that has such creatures in it," she is talking about creatures washed up on the shores of her utopian island who have come from the contemporary world.[6] For Huxley the conditoned reflex was a means of determining what the citizens of his brave new world would call good. It was important, for example, that certain kinds of workers should not be distracted by literature or nature, and babies who were destined to be workers of that sort were therefore appropriately conditioned. They were put on the floor of a laboratory near a few attractive books and bouquets. As they moved toward them and touched them, they were electrically shocked or frightened by loud noises. When they tried again, the treatment was repeated. Soon they were safe: they would never again take an interest in literature or nature. Pavlov had something to say about changing what is good about the good life because he had studied responses which have to do with what one feels. The good life which Huxley portrayed (with contempt, of course) *felt* good. It is no accident that it included an art form called the "feelies" and drugs which produced or changed feelings.

The good things in life have other effects, however. One is the satisfaction of needs in the simple sense of the relief of distress. We sometimes eat to escape from the pangs of hunger and take pills to allay pain, and out of compassion we feed the hungry and heal the sick. For such purposes we design a culture which provides for each "according to his need." But satisfaction is a limited objective; we are not necessarily happy because we have everything we want. The word *sated* is related to the word *sad*. Simple abundance, whether in an affluent society, a benevolent climate, or a welfare state, is not enough. When people are supplied according to their needs, *regardless of what they are doing*, they remain inactive. The abundant life is a candy-mountain land or Cockaigne. It is the *Schlaraffenland*—the idler's land—of Hans Sachs, and idleness is the goal only of those who have been compulsively or anxiously busy.

Heavens are usually described by listing the good things to be found in them, but no one has ever designed a really interesting heaven on that principle. The important thing about the good things in life is what people are doing when they get them. "Goods" are reinforcers, and a way of life is a set of contingencies of reinforcement. In utopian literature, the arrangements of contingencies have seldom been explicit. As we have seen, contingencies of reinforcement are not the most conspicuous aspects of life, and the experimental analysis which has revealed their nature and their effects is of recent origin. There is probably a better reason, however, why they have been overlooked. The very reinforcers which figure in utopian writing exert too powerful an effect upon the writer. If we ask someone to describe the kind of world in which he would like to live, he will probably begin to list the reinforcers he would want to find in it. He will go straight to the things which make life good, and probably simply because he will be reinforced for doing so. Food, sex, security, the approval of one's fellow men, works of art, music, and literature—these are the things men want and act to get and therefore the things they mention when they are asked to describe a world in which they would like to live. The significant fact is that *they seldom mention what they are to do to get them.* They specify a better world simply as they wish for it, dream of it, or pray for it, giving no thought to the manner of their getting it.

A much more interesting possibility arises when we recognize the role of contingencies of reinforcement, for we can then apply something like the "behavioral engineering" of *Walden Two* to cultural design. A utopian community is a pilot experiment, like the pilot plant in industry or the pilot experiment in science, where principles are tested on a small scale to avoid the risks and inconvenience of size. Utopias have usually been isolated geographically because border problems can then be neglected, and they have usually implied a break with tradition (symbolized in religious communities, for example, by a ritual of rebirth) because problems raised by conflicting cultures are then minimized. A new practice can be put into effect more easily in a small community than in the world at large, and the results more easily seen. Given these helpful simplifications and the demonstrated power of a behavioral technology, a successful utopia is not too hard to imagine. The necessary physical environment is being analyzed in the field of urban design. The micro-rayons in Russia, the Newtownes of Great Britain, and many urban experiments in the United States, while still largely concerned with physical aspects, have also been designed with some attention to the basic principle that a city or a building is meaningful only as an environment in which people live and must rest upon an understanding of the interaction between behavior and the environment. It is true that the special communities represented by hospitals for psychotics, homes for retardates, training schools for delinquents, camps, and standard classrooms are not typical communities because the population at large is not properly represented, but the problems which arise in designing communities of that sort are not far from those in communities in the utopian sense. As solutions to those problems grow more successful, the plausibility of a utopian design increases. To most people "utopian" still means "impossible," but that usage may have to be changed.

LIKING A WAY OF LIFE

A common objection to *Walden Two* (and no doubt to other utopias) goes like this: "I shouldn't like to live there. I don't mind doing the things the author is at pains to save me from doing, I don't like to do some of the things I should be expected to do, and I like to do things I could not do. Granted that life there meets many traditional specifications of the Good Life and compares favorably with existing cultures, it is still a world designed to please the author, and he is bound by his own culture, not mine. *He* would like to live there, of course, but he must not expect me to join him."

We "like" a way of life to the extent that we are reinforced by it. We like a world in which both natural and social reinforcers are abundant and easily achieved and in which aversive stimuli are either rare or easily avoided. Unfortunately, however, it is a fact about man's genetic endowment and the world in which he lives that immediate rewards are often offset by deferred punishments, and that punishments must often be taken for the sake of deferred rewards. To maximize net gains we must do things we do not like to do and forgo things we like. A culture cannot change these facts, but it can induce us to deal with them effectively. Indeed, this is its most important function.

It is not too often successful. A common practice, for example, is to extract rules from the prevailing contingencies, natural or social, and to make positive and negative reinforcers contingent upon the behavior of following them. The rule-following contingencies are often unskillfully designed, and members of a culture seldom take net consequences into account. On the contrary, they resist control of this sort. They object to what they are asked to do and either drop out of the culture—as hermits, hobos, or hippies—or remain in it while challenging its principles.

Contingencies of reinforcement which maximize net gains need to be much more effective. Conditioned reinforcers can be used to bridge the gap between behavior and its remoter consequences, and supplementary reinforcers can be arranged to serve until remote reinforcers can be brought into play. An important point is that effective contingencies need to be programmed—that is, they are effective only when a person has passed through a series of intermediate contingencies. Those who have reached the terminal contingencies will be productive, creative, and happy—in a word, maximally effective. The outsider confronted with the terminal contingencies for the first time may not like them or be able to imagine liking them.

The designer must take something else into account which is still more difficult to bring to bear on the individual member. Will the culture *work*? It is a question which is clarified by the concept of a community as an experiment. A community is a thing, having a life of its own. It will survive or perish, and the designer must keep that fact in mind. The problem is that survival is often furthered by behavior which is not only not reinforced but may have punishing (even lethal) consequences. Phylogenic contingencies of survival supply examples. When a member of a herd of grazing animals spots the approach of a predator and utters a warning cry, the group is more likely to escape and survive, but the member who emits the cry calls attention to himself and may perish. Ontogenic contingencies of reinforcement work in the same way: a culture induces a hero to die for his country or a martyr for his religion.

Contingencies which promote survival are also usually badly designed. Something seems to be gained if the culture can be identified with a race, nation, or religious group, but this leads to jingoistic excesses. Contrived sanctions, positive and negative, are often spurious. The result is a different kind of dropout, who objects to taking the survival of a culture as a "value." The protest sometimes takes this form: "Why should I care whether my way of life survives or contributes to the way of life of the future?" An honest answer would seem to be, "There is no good reason, but if your culture has not convinced you that there is, so much the worse for your culture." The thoughtful person may inquire further. Why should the *culture* care whether it survives? Survival for what? How do we know that a culture is evolving in the right direction? Questions of this sort show a misunderstanding of the nature of evolution, biological and cultural. The processes of mutation and selection do not require, and may not provide, any advance plan of the state toward which they lead.

A well-designed culture is a set of contingencies of reinforcement under which members behave in ways which maintain the culture, enable it to meet emergencies, and change it in such a way that it will do these things even more effectively in the future. Personal sacrifice may be a dramatic example of the conflict of interests between the group and its members, but it is the product of a bad design. Under better contingencies behavior which strengthens the culture may be highly reinforcing. A jingoistic nationalism may be an easy way of underlining the good of a group, but the survival of a culture regarded simply as a set of practices, quite apart from those who practice them, can also be made the basis for a design. (It is significant that current discussions of survival are likely to speak of competition between ways of life rather than between nations or religions.) Here again effective contingencies must be programmed, and the terminal contingencies will not necessarily be "liked" by those who confront them for the first time.

The problem, in short, is not to design a way of life which will be liked by men *as they now are*, but a way of life which will be liked by those who live it. Whether those who are not part of a culture like it may have a bearing on whether they join and therefore on the promotion of a new culture and possibly on the design of early features intended to attract outsiders or prevent the defection of new members. It has no bearing on the ultimate goodness of the design. It is nevertheless in its effects on human nature—on the genetic endowment of the species—that any environment, physical or social, is to be evaluated.

The man who insists upon judging a culture in terms of whether or not he likes it is the true immoralist. Just as he refuses to follow rules designed to maximize his own net gain because they conflict with immediate gratification, so he rejects contingencies designed to strengthen the group because they conflict with his "rights as an individual." He sets himself up as a standard of human nature, implying or insisting that the culture which produced him is the only good or natural culture. He wants the world he wants and is unwilling to ask why he wants it. He is so completely the product of his own culture that he fears the influence of any other. He is like the child who said: "I'm glad I don't like broccoli because if I liked it, I'd eat a lot of it, and I hate it."

OBJECTIONS TO A DESIGNED CULTURE

Many of those who like a given way of life may still object to it if it has been deliberately designed. Suppose one of the critics of *Walden Two* were to happen upon a small isolated community where—to repeat the first paragraph of this essay—people were working only a few hours a day and without compulsion, children were being cared for and educated by specialists with due regard for the lives they were going to lead, food was good and sanitation and medical care excellent, and art, music, literature, and science flourished. Would he not exclaim, "Here is the good life!" But then let him discover that the community was explicitly designed, and the spectre of the designer would spoil it all. Why?

Design implies control, and there are many reasons why we fear it. The very techniques are often objectionable, for control passes first to those who have the power to treat others aversively. The state is still identified with the power to punish, some religious agencies still claim to mediate supernatural punishments, and schoolboys are still caned. This is "control through fear," and we naturally fear it. There is historical evidence that men have slowly turned to nonaversive methods. They have thereby escaped from some aversive stimuli, but they have not necessarily made other kinds of control acceptable. Even when a wealthy government can reinforce the behavior it wants instead of punishing the behavior it does not want—the result may still be exploitation.

The archetype of a nonexploiting controller is the benevolent dictator. We suspect him because we cannot imagine why he should control benevolently. Yet in some of the special communities we have noted the contingencies which control the designer do not conflict with those he uses in his design. When contingencies are well arranged in a hospital for psychotics, for example, the fact that patients make fewer demands on the staff and yet display as much dignity and happiness as their pathology permits is enough to explain the behavior of the designer. In a home for retarded children, if aversive control is minimal and happiness and dignity therefore maximal, and if some of the children learn enough to be able to move into the world at large, these effects will be among the important reinforcers of those who have designed the community. If juvenile delinquents behave well in a training school and at the same time acquire skills which permit them to lead nondelinquent lives after they leave it, the design can be explained. In each of these communities a way of life is designed both for the good of those who live it and for the good of the designer, and the two goods do not conflict. Nevertheless, technologies of this sort are often opposed just because control is exerted.

Democracy is an effort to solve the problem by letting the people design the contingencies under which they are to live or—to put it another way—by insisting that the designer himself live under the contingencies he designs. It is reasonable to suppose that he will not use aversive techniques if he himself will be affected by them or positive techniques which lead to exploitation if he himself will be exploited. But specialization is almost inevitable (minorities readily understand how difficult it is to keep the controller and the controllee in the same skin), and specialization implies special contingencies which are still open to suspicion.

One safeguard against exploitation is to make sure that the designer never controls; he refuses to put his design into effect himself or is forbidden to do so or—better still—dies. In *Walden Two* the protagonist, Frazier, has simply abdicated. (As an additional assurance that he exerts no current control, he was given what might be called negative charisma.) But he may still be feared because a particularly subtle kind of exploitation survives. No matter how benevolent he may be, or how far from the exercise of power, the designer gets credit for the achievements of the community, and the credit is taken from those who live in it. A ruler who discovers a better way of inducing people to behave well gets credit for an orderly society but at the expense of those who live in it, who would be more admired if they behaved well in a disorderly society. A man who designs a better way of teaching gets credit for the benefits of improved education but at the expense of the students, who would be more admired if they learned when badly taught or not taught at all. The industrialist who designs a better way of producing goods gets credit for increased production but at the expense of the workers, who would get more credit for being efficient and enterprising under another system. A utopia as a completely managed culture seems to work a wholesale despoliation of this sort. Its citizens are *automatically* good, wise, and productive, and we have no reason to admire them or give them credit. Some critics have gone so far as to say that they have been robbed of their very humanity. Mr. Krutch has accused me of dehumanizing men, and C. S. Lewis entitled a book on this theme *The Abolition of Man*.[7]

We admire people and give them credit for what they do in order to induce them to behave in admirable ways.[8] We are particularly likely to do so when no other kind of control is available, as I have shown elsewhere. When alternative practices are invented, or when the world changes so that the behavior at issue is no longer necessary, the practice of admiration is dropped. (It is a temporary measure, the weakness of which is suggested by the fact that we do not admire those who are obviously behaving well simply because they have been admired for doing so.) Admiration often supplements aversive control (we admire those who meet their responsibilities and hence need not be punished), and it may indeed represent an early form of an alternative practice, but it must eventually yield to other alternatives. As we come to understand human behavior and its role in the evolution of cultures, and particularly the contingencies which induce men to design cultures, we must dispense with the practice of giving personal credit. But that step is disturbing for other reasons.

MAN AND HIS DESTINY

The notion of personal credit is incompatible with the hypothesis that human behavior is wholly determined by genetic and environmental forces. The hypothesis is sometimes said to imply that man is a helpless victim, but we must not overlook the extent to which he controls the things which control him. Man is largely responsible for the environment in which he lives. He has changed the physical world to minimize aversive properties and maximize positive reinforcements, and he has constructed governmental, religious, educational, economic, and psychotherapeutic systems which promote satisfying personal contacts and make him more skillful, informed, productive, and happy. He is engaged in a gigantic exercise in self-control, as the result of which he has come to realize more and more of his genetic potential.

He has reached a very special point in that story. He is the product of an evolutionary process in which essentially accidental changes in genetic endowment have been differentially selected by accidental features of the environment, but he has now reached the point at which he can examine that process and do something about it. He can change the course of his own evolution through selective breeding, and in the not too distant future he will quite possibly change it by changing his chromosomes. The "value judgments" which will then be demanded are beginning to attract attention. The point is that *we have long since reached a comparable stage in the evolution of cultures.* We produce cultural "mutations" when we invent new social practices, and we change the conditions under which they are selected when we change the environments in which men live.

To refuse to do either of these things is to leave further changes in our culture to accident, and accident is the tyrant really to be feared. Adventitious arrangements of both genetic and environmental variables have brought man to his present position and are responsible for its faults as well as its virtues. The very misuse of personal control to which we object so violently is the product of accidents which have made the weak subject to the strong, the dull to the sharp, the well-intentioned to the selfish. We can do better than that. By accepting the fact that human behavior is controlled—by things if not by men—we take a big step forward, for we can then stop trying to avoid control and begin to look for the most effective kinds.

Whether we like it or not, survival is the value by which we shall be judged. The culture which takes its survival into account is most likely to survive. To recognize the fact is not, unfortunately, to resolve all our difficulties. It is hard to say what kinds of human behavior will prove most valuable in a future which cannot be clearly foreseen. Nor is it easy to identify the practices which will generate the kinds of behavior needed, but here at least we have made some progress. The design of behavior to specification is the very essence of a technology derived from an experimental analysis.

The authors of the classical utopian literature proposed to achieve the good life they described in ways which are now seen to be inadequate, but the value of utopian thinking must not, therefore, be underestimated. In a curious way it has always taken cultural evolution into account. It has scrutinized the sources of social practices, examined their consequences, and proposed alternatives which should have more desirable consequences—and all in the experimental spirit characteristic of science.

In the long run, of course, we must dispense with utopian simplifications, for the real test of a culture is the world at large. (The anti-utopians, of course, are talking about that world too; they would scarcely be so violent about a community of a few hundred people.) And the persistent question about that test is this: Is it to be *our* culture which survives and contributes most to the culture of the future? We can point to certain reassuring features. We enjoy the advantages which flow from the very practice of changing practice; until recently we have been perhaps unique in our disposition to try new ways of doing things. We give thought to consequences. Our practice of asking whether something works or whether something else would work better is often criticized as a crude pragmatism, but it may prove to have been an important cultural mutation. We readily change practices because we are not greatly restrained by revelation or immutable decrees, and for similar reasons we are free to pursue a science of behavior. Above all, we have recognized the need for the explicit design of a way of life.

But not all signs are propitious. The contingencies of reinforcement which shape and maintain the behavior of the cultural designer are not yet very clear. Obvious economic contingencies bring yearly improvements in automobiles, for example, but there are no comparable forces at work to improve governmental and ethical practices, education, housing, or psychotherapy. The survival of the culture has not yet been brought to bear in a very effective way on those who are engaged in government in the broadest sense.

Another danger signal is anti-utopianism itself (the clarification of which may be one of the most important contributions of utopian thinking). Anti-utopian arguments are the utopian arguments of an earlier era; that is why we call them reactionary. At one stage in the evolution of a culture, for example, aversive control may be effectively centralized in a despotic government. The appropriate philosophy or literature which supports it may outlive its usefulness without losing its power and will continue to support those who oppose any change—say, to democratic practices. Something of the same sort is now happening with respect to the doctrine of individual freedom. In undermining despotic control it is important to convince the individual that he is the source of the power to govern, that he can free himself of restraining forces, that he can make unique contributions, and so on. This is done by calling him free and responsible, admiring him for meeting his responsibilities, and punishing him for failing to do so. The supporting philosophy and literature have remained effective and are responsible for much of current anti-utopianism.

A scientific analysis of human behavior and of genetic and cultural evolution cannot make individual freedom the goal of cultural design. The individual is not an origin or source. He does not initiate anything. Nor is it he who survives. (The doctrine of survival after death is a source of personal reinforcers appropriate only to an earlier design.) What survives are the species and the culture. They lie "beyond the individual" in the sense that they are responsible for him and outlive him. Nevertheless, a species has no existence apart from its members or a culture apart from the people who practice it. It is only through effects on individuals that practices are selected or designed. If by "man" we mean a member of the human species with its unique genetic endowment, its human nature, then man is still the measure of all things. But it is a measure we can use effectively only if we accept it for what it is, as this is revealed in a scientific analysis rather than in some earlier conception, no matter how convincing that conception may have seemed or how effective it may have proved to be in another culture.[9]

It has been argued that it was the well-governed city-state which suggested to the Greeks that the universe itself might show law and order and that in their search for the laws which governed it, they laid the foundations of modern science. The problems of government have grown more difficult, and no modern state is likely to be taken as the model of a lawful system. It is possible that science may now repay its debt and restore order to human affairs.

NOTES

1. *Life*, June 28, 1948, p. 38.
2. Glenn Negley and J. Max Patrick, *The Quest for Utopia* (New York: Schuman, 1952), p. 580.

3. Joseph Wood Krutch, *The Measure of Man* (Indianapolis: Bobbs-Merrill, 1953).

4. Rudolph Ekstein and Elaine Caruth, "From Eden to Utopia," *American Imago*, 22 (1965), 128–41.

5. Raymond Bauer, *The New Man in Soviet Psychology* (Cambridge, Mass.: Harvard University Press, 1952).

6. The title of the French translation—*Le meilleur des mondes*—makes the same point. Pangloss assures Candide that it is *this* world, in spite of its diseases, earthquakes, and famines, which is the best of all possible worlds. Nor were Huxley's economics part of any world of the future; they were early Keynesian or Rooseveltian. His psychedelic drug "soma," though it anticipated LSD, was used like mescaline or alcohol.

7. C. S. Lewis, *The Abolition of Man* (New York: Macmillan, 1957).

8. See B. F. Skinner, "Man," *American Philosophical Society Proceedings*, 108 (December 1964), 482–85.

9. For a more detailed analysis of the concept of freedom and dignity from this point of view, see B. F. Skinner, *Beyond Freedom and Dignity* (New York: Alfred A. Knopf, 1971).

ROBERT H. RIMMER

I Write Entopian Novels

IN HIS 1966 LECTURES, published under the title *Between Dystopia and Utopia*, Constantinos Doxiadis, the famous city planner, introduced the concept of entopia: "The present city—without reason, without dream—leads to dystopia and disaster. Utopia—without reason, with dream—cannot get us out of the impasse. There is only one road left—*with reason and dream*—which should take us out of the bad place into a good place, which is not out of place, but in place—an entopia" (pp. 49–50).

I am an enthusiastic utopian, and believe, with more than one writer, that at this time in world history we can't afford to think in any less concepts than utopian ones. And I believe the well-known pronouncements of Marie Louise Berneri, who said, "Out of dreams come the beneficial realities. Utopia is the principle of all progress and the essay into a better future," and of Oscar Wilde, who contended, "A map of the world that does not include Utopia is not worth glancing at, for it leaves out the country at which Humanity is always landing." Yet the plain truth is that I am both shocked and amused when my alternate–life-style novels are labeled "utopian" or "shrunken" utopias, as Robert Plank has characterized *The Harrad Experiment* in one of the essays in Part III of this book. Not that I object to the word "shrunken." If my novels are shrunken utopias, then they are also achievable utopias.

But before I extract the main proposals in my alternate–life-style novels, of which there are now eight, let me briefly explain why I have used the novel form to present sociological, humanist, and psychological ideas rather than attempted to reach an audience through magazines or relevant journals. One reason is obvious: If you want a mass audience, you must cater to a mass audience. So my readers get the Rimmer theses, with a nice sugar-coating of plot and sex. But sex in my novels is warm, loving, and wondrous. The lack of it in a complete sense of caring and involvement, in much of life and fiction, which I am arguing against, is one reason the fictional form is more appropriate than a scholarly article in some abstruse journal read by a few specialists. But fiction has a very big disadvantage. No one at the level of academia believes me! Or believes that even Bob Rimmer cares whether the wheat is separated from the chaff.

Actually, the real reason that I write entopian novels is that I am a strange (by present-day standards) product of a liberal-arts education that ranged through all areas of human knowledge, took root in my brain, and produced an inextinguishable interest in learning and knowing just about anything my mind could encompass. Now that I am sixty-two, my Faustian quest, which I believe is transmittable and joyous, continues unabated. Although I realize that in many areas I am inevitably a dilettante, I have had the lifelong satisfaction of slowly discovering that all knowledge is interrelated. I have also discovered that the quest for the philosopher's stone is the only truly joyous and happy way to live—especially when it is a shared quest with a female collaborator.

Unfortunately, for my potential prestige, I'm unable to reach the top areas of academia and communicate fully with those who hold the reins. Why? Because I didn't pursue any specific liberal-arts interests within the walls of academia. In essence, I never made any attempt to obtain a doctorate in sociology, philosophy, or psychology. I didn't even venture into the world of marital therapy or family planning and counseling. Instead, after graduation from Bates College with a Bachelor's Degree in a dual major of psychology and English literature (which shocked one of my good professor friends and college mentor, Peter Bertocci, who has written many books in the areas of philosophy and psychology), I applied to the Harvard Graduate School of Business Administration, was accepted, received my M.B.A. in 1941, and became a first lieutenant in the Finance Department of the Air Transport Command. Fortunately, I was eventually assigned to the China–India–Burma theater and spent nearly two years in China and what is now known as Bangladesh. My never ending curiosity led me to Indian bookstores, where I discovered Swami Vivekananda (a much neglected nineteenth-century guru who exerted a great influence on Emerson and Whitman) and, guided by him, I was led into the complete areas of Vendanta and Eastern philosophy, including Tantra—many years before Tantra was "discovered" by the Human Potential Movement.

Keep in mind that the only purpose of this biographical excursion is to orient you to my reality. The only avenue I could use to express any ideas, utopian or entopian, which didn't specifically deal with the business world was via the novel. There really was no other choice. In the Western world today, businessmen for the most part are extremely one-dimensional, and, unfortunately, so are most educators. A man who could manage millions of dollars of Army base payrolls and read Indian philosophy at the same time or, later, who ran a printing business for thirty years, as I did, after World War II (unfortunately it had no capacity to print books) and had a personal library of more than twenty thousand books was and is considered very suspect by his peers. Businessmen rarely read novels. And educators want to know, as Robert Plank does in his article: Who the hell is Bob Rimmer? What are his academiic credentials?

If I labor this point, it's because it is one of the theses in my novels. Sadly, it's both a utopian and an entopian act to assume that most people can discuss any subject that isn't within their vocational specialty, be it academic, business, or scientific, for more than ten minutes with another person. I am a cultural lag: the educated man who knows that the more he knows, the more he doesn't know, and who accepts the idea with a blissful determination to keep learning despite the odds.

In today's society, this is a dangerous kind of pursuit. During the past thirty years, while I built a national mail order printing business doing a sale in excess of $6 million annually, I continued to write novels on weekends and gradually discovered that I could run with neither the lambs nor the wolves. Two amusing cases in point (I mention them because I'm utopian enough to believe that the kind of society they illustrate is not the kind that can create an environment of self-realization for most people): When the printing business I ran needed to do some heavy borrowing in the area close to a million dollars, I discovered that my personal file in one of Boston's most prestigious banks contained a folded-in-half copy of *The Harrad Experiment*. If you were a bank loan officer would you trust an entrepreneur who wrote books such as *Harrad* and *Proposition 31* with a million-dollar loan? On the other side of the fence, when I appeared in a lengthy *Psychology Today* interview a few years ago, the editors were avalanched with letters from both general readers and academia wanting to know what my credentials were. Even a recent article I wrote for *Forum*, the sex digest published by *Penthouse*, titled "Open Marriage Doesn't Work," brought the same kind of complaints. How could a mass-market novelist know anything about sexually open marriages? The bitter frosting—really rather chuckly—on the cake occurred in 1977, when I sold the family printing business and offered myself *free* to any college or university in the Boston area that would provide me with an office (no secretary) and would like to have an interesting gadfly around to relate to both students and faculty and to teach a course in Human Values along the lines proposed in *The Harrad Experiment*. So far, there have been no takers. Not even Harvard Business School would accept me.

So much for autobiography. My experiences are interesting commentaries on the so-called controversy over educational specialization versus liberal-arts training, which, once again, is in the news with Harvard College's new approaches. Eliminating this dichotomy, which is touched upon in all utopian literature since Plato, is at the heart of many of my proposals. But perhaps if I had been more realistic, if instead of using the novel as a vehicle to push particular philosophies or programs (an approach that incidentally is an anathema to literary critics), I had flowed with the tide and, like Harold Robbins, Sidney Shelton, Irving Wallace, or Mario Puzo, written sick, sadistic sex coupled with violence, then I might have sold many more millions of books than I have. But I can't complain. Any person who incorporates the words rebellion, challenge, and experiment into his life-style threatens more people than he intrigues.

Against this personal background, I began writing novels at the age of thirty-nine. My first novel, *The Rebellion of Yale Marratt*, which is still in print (and has reappeared with a new and sexier cover in 1979), not only proposes a new religion based on Ten Humanistic Commandments but, in the course of a long story, advocates the legalization of bigamy. Yale marries Anne, a Red Cross girl in India during World War II, in an Indian wedding ceremony. He loses track of her in the shifting war scene and after the war marries a college sweetheart, Cynthia. Then he discovers that Anne is alive and has his child. Cynthia is pregnant by a close friend of Yale's and Cynthia's who was killed in an automobile accident. Yale brings the women together, and they decide that a ménage à trois is preferable to a divorce, which would restore Yale to a socially approved monogamous relationship—but with which wife? The novel concludes with Yale Marratt and his wives challenging the monogamous laws of the United States and trying to legalize bigamy in Connecticut.

Is Yale Marratt's Challenge Foundation utopian? It is finally funded by several hundred million dollars to underwrite a new kind of world where millions of men and women could realize much more of their potential. The novel concludes on a note of hope that the Foundation's proselytizing book *Spoken in My Manner* (titled after Socrates) is being read by millions of people, and that Yale will probably win his case, which may be precedent-making.

We live in a society where the only legal form of marriage is monogamy. Of course, most utopian proposals offer some new approaches to marriage and the family. But in suggesting that a marriage of two men and one woman, or two women and one man, be legalized, all I am saying is that we no longer live in a world where a one-to-one monogamous marriage, and a family with two children, is the sure road to Mecca. Is it a shrunken utopia when one man challenges the status quo and believes that many of us in the Western world are capable of what Lawrence Kohlberg would call a Stage 5 and 6 morality—the kind of morality that places the highest value on human life, equality and dignity, and individual principles of conscience? A kind of society where there is no place for a Great White Father or Big Brother in Washington or any other seat of government? Is that utopian or quite realistic?

The fact is that there are thousands of households in the United States that are already based on a one man and two women, or two men and one woman, interpersonal and sexual relationships. Legalization of bigamy on an a priori basis would allow many of these families to surface and function in a different but fully responsible marital pattern. The Ten Commandments of Challenge, beginning with Number One, that Man is God, are not utopian. They are "dreams which are not out of place." They are entopian!

Basically, the underlying theme of all my proposals revolves around the beliefs, to paraphrase Lester Kirkendall's words, that all men and women have a greater capacity to trust others; the potential for a greater integrity in relationships; the potential for a dissolution of barriers that separate people; a greater potential for cooperative attitudes; a belief that all people prize brotherhood and a sense of living; and a need for a fulfillment of individual potentialities.

Because most of my characters react vis-à-vis each other, as if this were a possible way of life, some readers label me not only as a utopian but also as a Polyanna. But the sad truth is that if we prefer the belief that man is dominated by a territorial imperative that today is mass-marketed in the form of looking out for number one, or how to be your own best friend, or "I gotta be me," or "I'll do it my way," then we deserve the whirlwind that we are sowing.

Sequentially, after Yale Marratt, in *The Harrad Experiment*, I proposed a new kind of postsecondary education where, at the age of seventeen, young men and women could study for their college degrees at colleges and universities in the area of a particular Harrad dormitory. They would live together, unmarried, in Harrad-style dormitories—a male with a female—*not of their own choosing*, through their entire four undergraduate years. Each year they would have a different roommate, of the other sex, not of their own choosing. The unifying aspect of this living-together environment would be not only that each of the roommates of the other sex was studying for his or her undergraduate degrees, but a concomitant requirement, which was that they would all take a continuing seminar in Human Values, which would run continuously over the four-year period and would be built around a specific reading program. Not only would the Human Value Seminar expand the boundaries of their physical and interpersonal sexual knowledge, it would also be designed to provide a wider perspective on the shuck values of our civilization; in one sense it would be a deconditioning process, an exploration of many false values being inculcated by the corporate, educational, and religious establishment.

While there is a Skinnerian overtone in all of my proposals—a firm belief that we won't get better human beings until we create better human environments—it is obvious that critics, such as Robert Plank, and many academicians (not the younger generation) haven't read *The Harrad Experiment* or *The Premar Experiments* (a ten-year further elaboration of the Harrad idea) very carefully. The Tenhausens *are not* typical utopian authoritarian figures. The Harrad students, and later the Premar students, live in a total environment of thought-provoking, stimulating ideas. The Human Values course is essentially a liberal arts training that releases the creative mind by making a wide variety of input possible. The Tenhausens are continuously surprised at the response from the Harrad students. In *Harrad* and in all my novels, I have even gone a step further. I have attempted to involve at least some of the readers, not with utopian ideas, but with the reality of changing patterns of marriage and the family. I have stressed that the nuclear family, for example, is not the typical historical family; families, as well as premarital and postmarital relationships, are continuously evolving. Reader involvement is often the result of my annotated bibliographies (which include many authors who don't believe in what I am saying or consider it utopian) and my attempts to create a sense of reality in the novels (which leads hundreds of readers to write letters to Harrad or Premar or to Father Lereve—in *Thursday, My Love*—seeking a synergamous marriage, or to Future Families of America in search of the Hershe corporate family and the hope that *Proposition 31* can be made legal).

I am not yet, however, in the line of Robert Owen or John Humphrey Noyes, whose communal ideas were tried and eventually failed, because time is proving me out. I have reinforced the almost universal trend to coeducation that has eliminated most of the all-male or all-female colleges, which were so prevalent ten to fifteen years ago. Eventually, a new breed of educators will realize that the highest priority in education is to educate young men and women for each other and to eliminate completely the adversary relationship that, in Western societies, is built into the male-female relationship from childhood. A twelfth-anniversary edition of *The Harrad Experiment* was published in 1978; it contains an afterword by me entitled "Who Is Going to Start Harrad?" and a new chronological bibliography. The answer to "who is going to start Harrad," is *you*—the younger readers of this book—because there is no alternative. A society without some common human perspective besides the accumulation of wealth and material goods, a society geared to bottom-line profits at the expense of human loving and the sheer joy of eternal curiosity about all aspects of life, is deep on the road to decadence and ultimate disappearance.

I am emphasizing the Harrad/Premar–style education, which is not compulsory and, most certainly, doesn't envision some beneficent dictator or leader to make it universal, because I believe that Kohlberg's Stage 5 or 6 kind of moral development, which a Harrad education anticipates, is crucial to the kind of interpersonal relationships and caring sexuality, and alternate marriage styles that I have proposed in my later novels—such as *Proposition 31; Thursday, My Love; Come Live My Life; Love Me Tomorrow;* and a new one that was published in late 1980 called *Soufriere, the Volcano*. If you are interested in a comparison sheet between entopian proposals in most of of these novels and the realities of the United States in the 1970s, I shall be happy to send it to you. Many teachers of courses in marriage and the family have found these "utopian ideas"—I'm grinning—very provocative to general discussion of current realities.

Let me give you a swift summary of a few of these concepts, to show you that if they seem to be utopian, they really are achievable utopias. All that some one or group has to do is to try them out. No one will ever know whether Harrad/Premar is utopian until some daring college administration creates a Harrad/Premar. Premar pushes the Harrad idea to its logical conclusions. Premar is available to all high school graduates. Premar students earn their own education on a thirteen-week alternating work-study cycle. The work cycle is subsidized by the government, working with private industry and local government, to an amount of $100 a week (increasing with inflation), of which the students, living in Premar Communes (in groups of forty-eight, with leaders who are married graduate students), pay all but $15 a week to the Commune. The balance is used to pay for the individual student's food and housing and tuition to undergraduate and vocational colleges in the vicinity. Not all Premar students are working for undergraduate degrees, but all their education is unified by the Human Values Seminar comprising one book a week, fifty-two a year, for four years. Roommates are of the opposite sex, not of one's choosing, unmarried, and for the first two years a roommate shift occurs every six months. After that, for the final two years, the choice of roommates, still unmarried, is up to the individual students. If you'd like to read a detailed economic analysis of the effect of this total approach to education, which could be developed without the roommate exchange and without making Premar compulsory, read "The Premar Solution" in my book of essays, *The Love Adventurers*, published in 1979.

Graduates of Harrad/Premar would, in many cases, enter a monogamous phase of their lives that would persist into their early thirties and possibly for a lifetime. But for those who weren't content with the narrow boundaries of monogamy and two-people relationships, there would be legalized bigamous marriage and also corporate marriages, synergamous marriages, LovXchanges, Love Groups and succedaneum marriage.

In my novel *Proposition 31*, I have proposed corporate marriage. Up to three couples, past thirty, and their children would establish a government-recognized corporation in which all were equal shareholders. The Proposition, which is described in detail in the novel, tells how such marriages could function financially and how such marriage corporations could be dissolved. The value of this kind of marital relationship for many Americans, obviously not all, is covered in great detail in the novel. In *Love Me Tomorrow* I have proposed a different type of federally approved family incorporation of four couples, which has a ten-year age spread between the couples and becomes a self-sustaining group of people who eliminate the need for nursing homes, welfare, and child care, and provide easy sexual variety and cross-generational companionship throughout one's life. The time of *Love Me Tomorrow* is 1996. Is the idea utopian? Is Proposition 31 utopian? My prediction as a futurist is that economics will prevail and people will be forced to function together in environments that still give them privacy but make possible the material possessions and wealth we now take for granted.

In *Thursday, My Love* I have proposed synergamous marriages, which are not legal but are church-approved. A monogamous couple could make a caring commitment to another person in addition to one's spouse and, to expand one's life, he and she could enjoy another family and a sexual variety with another person once or twice a week. This and LovXchange, as developed in my novel *Come Live My Life*, are not sexually open marriages but expanded human relationships with varying degrees of structure and commitment.

Because I am convinced that the kind of marriages, families, and sex lives we have now, and will have in the future, are closely related to our government and our economic environment, in my novel *Love Me Tomorrow* I have proposed a totally new kind of economic system based on the United States's becoming a People's Corporation and paying dividends to you and me, the stockholders, and taxing all of us with only one tax, a Floating Instant Skim Tax (FIST). I'm sure that if you read this proposal in detail—it occupies some fifty pages of the novel—you will agree that the only thing utopian about it is whether the people of this country would elect Newton Morrow (the charismatic leader who is proposing the idea) President of the United States, which eventually will include Canada and become the United People of America. Whether you think my economics are utopian, entopian, or even, in some aspects, self-fulfilling prophecies, it may amuse you to know that before my publisher would accept this novel (which he complained "wasn't vintage Rimmer"), I was forced to write three additional sex scenes for a novel that I already considered pretty sexy. That's the penalty and the reward(?) for reaching a mass audience.

But it's not only the problem of being either a utopianist or an entopianist. The sad truth is that if I am really writing utopian novels and if the basis of my utopias is a belief that the human kind are slowly moving upward and not in a circle, then I am one of the few people who is writing utopian novels. Today, as Lyman Tower Sargent's bibliographic essay in Part IV demonstrates, the popular genre is science fiction, which occasionally presents eutopian worlds. But more often the authors revel in dystopias and expend most of their storytelling on scientific devices and not on how people in the future will live as full human beings. Science fiction writers have their own writing associations and conclaves. By contrast, utopianists have societies of futurists, many of whom are writing science fiction and calling it nonfiction. But where are the entopians?

REFERENCES

Doxiadis, Constantinos. *Between Dystopia and Utopia*. Hartford, Conn.: Trinity College Press, 1966.

Kirkendall, Lester. *Premarital Intercourse and Interpersonal Relationships*. New York: Gramercy Publishing, 1961.

Rimmer, Robert H. *The Love Adventurers*, New York: Dell, 1980. All Rimmer novels are published by New American Library except *The Harrad Experiment*, which is published by Bantam. The 40th printing of *Harrad* has a long afterword and a new bibliography. All the novels are available in paperback.

Scharf, Peter. *Readings in Moral Education*. Oak Grove, Ill.: Winston Press, 1977. A good survey of Lawrence Kohlberg's theories.

THOMAS M. DISCH

Buck Rogers in the New Jerusalem

IN ONE SENSE, all science fiction is utopian. In the sense that u-topia is not only the good place but no-place-at-all. To describe in patient, plausible detail a world that doesn't exist—what else is that but to write science fiction?

The fact is, however, that with the looming exception of Wells there has been very little overlap between science fiction and utopian fiction. Anti-utopias there have been by the droves: *Brave New World*, *1984*, *The Space Merchants*, *Player Piano*, and all their vast progeny. But the genuine ameliorative article is rarely encountered. Except, sometimes, inadvertently. For it may be that good old hard-core sci fi of triple-A vintage (Amazing-Astounding-Analog) represents an implicit program for reforming society along technocratic lines: the world *as* a better mousetrap. Surely the most delectable diorama of such a utopia has been the monolithically bland, sublimely monotonous *mise en scène* of *2001*, a movie unanimously loathed by the surviving Gernsbackian contingent of the science fiction fraternity, who saw more clearly than those who had never shared their dream that Clarke and Kubrick had decisively betrayed the utopia between the billion lines of all their stories.

In that respect, *2001* epitomizes the relations between science fiction and utopian speculation. No sooner does a bright hope glimmer on the page than it is shown to be delusive, specious, or downright sinister. Even in a solid, progressive, triple-A story, the nice inventions have decided kinks in them, so the good scientists have something to cope with (if aliens are lacking).

There are several reasons why there has been so little utopian science fiction, and the best of these is that utopias are notoriously dull. How can

In a slightly different form this essay first appeared as the introduction to *The New Improved Sun; An Anthology of Utopian S-F*, pp. 1–4, published by Harper & Row Publishers, Inc., New York, New York. Reprinted by permission of the author; copyright © 1975 by Thomas Disch.

there be conflicts when everyone is nice? And without a conflict, what story is possible?

Basically, only one. The story of the Visitor from Here-and-Now who goes to utopia, misunderstands and misjudges its citizens, and finally comes round to seeing that it is, verily, utopia. At which point narrative ceases and the Virtues take over. This scheme can accommodate any number of worthy books (such as the *ur-Utopia* of Thomas More, Bellamy's *Looking Backward*, even the longest of them all, Austin Wright's *Islandia*). . . . In the story of the Visitor, what is required is that the utopist's bare ideas be so good, so ingenious, so just, that all by themselves they can arouse and sustain the reader's interest.

This, however, should not be an insuperable requirement for science fiction writers. Isn't it the commonest complaint against us that we're all too willing to offer mere ideas in place of fully fleshed-out fiction? And why not, after all? A good idea doesn't *need* to be dressed up as a narrative. Accordingly, some utopian science fiction—for example, long passages in both Russ's *The Female Man* and Heinlein's *Stranger in a Strange Land*—aren't fictions so much as manifestoes, recipes, calls to arms, more or less barefaced as the case may be.

A much more serious impediment to the creation of utopias than their inherent dullness is that they're silly—in real life as much as in literature. The same dolts who expect Babylon to go sliding into the Pacific tomorrow morning are also expecting their messiah, what's-his-name, to lead them to the Promised Land by tomorrow night. Utopia is the reciprocal of Armageddon, and neither locality can survive long in the cruel world of reality. After the ninth or tenth trip to the mountains to escape a certain doom, anyone may legitimately conclude that the world isn't coming to an end. And as for the bright new day a-dawning, that hope is surrendered along with one's dreams of becoming a movie star, a great ballerina, or a saint. Even the truest believers seem to run out of good intentions before they've paved the road all the way to hell. Shakers end up selling homemade jam, Flower Children wilt and die, Mormons become advisers to Nixon, and life goes on, a mixed bag at best.

And isn't it just this, the grand equivocalness of everything, that's always been the subject of good fiction, science fiction included? Utopias require a deliberate singleness of vision, a decision to accentuate the positive, that can be death to a limber intelligence. If science fiction writers characteristically have portrayed antiutopias, it isn't due to their inherent pessimism or contrariness, but simply because there is a natural tendency for logical minds to pick nits and look for loopholes. I remember that Gordon Dickson, surely the least black-hearted of men, once described the process by which, knowing the background of a story, he finds the ideal protagonist to place against it: He considers who will be most seriously harmed or threatened by the world of his invention. This, while a quite workable principle for storytellers, would never do for a sincere utopist, whose only interest in loopholes is in plugging them. The better the utopia one devises, the freer it should be from all that we post-lapsarians regard as drama, and what cannot be achieved by ingenuity is accomplished by fiat. In Campanella's *City of the Sun*, for instance, there are only beautiful women, since "ugliness is unknown among them. Because the women exercise, they acquire good complexions, become strong of limb, tall and agile; and beauty among them consists of tallness, liveliness, and strength." Well, certainly we all benefit from exercise, and a good complexion doesn't need make-up. But still. I think of all the strong, tall, agile women (and men) I've known who were, nonetheless, rather uglier than not. Even Campanella wasn't wholly persuaded by his own prescription, it seems, for he added: "Therefore, if any woman were to paint her face in order to make herself beautiful, or use high-heeled shoes so as to look tall, or wear lengthened garments to cover her thick legs, she would be subjected to capital punishment."

Which takes us to the final consideration that can be urged against utopias as a class: They are repugnant. Once one has eliminated all that is dull, silly, and unworkable, there usually remains a great unredeemable mass of black bile. Often, as with Campanella, it is that touchiest of all utopian problems, Sex, that brings out the city planner's worst, but it can be anything. Plato had it in for the arts, as did Francis Bacon, who forbade the inhabitants of his New Atlantis—"under pain of ignominy and fines, that they do not show any natural work or thing adorned or swelling, but only pure as it is, and without all affectation of strangeness." Shades of Mies van der Rohe! But, in all fairness to Plato and Bacon, utopias bring out the totalitarian in all of us, for the simple and sufficient reason that whatever a utopia's ostensible mode of government, it is always ruled by an absolute tyrant, the author.

Nevertheless.

Nevertheless we need utopias, and we need them, like other necessaries, fresh each season. Our hopes must be a function of our possibilities, and these keep changing at an ever increasing rate, as both our environment alters (no full-scale utopia of our time, for instance, can ignore ecological problems) and our own image in the age's mirror changes—and changes again.

PART II

CASE STUDIES

THEMATIC INTERPRETATIONS, historical surveys, and bibliographies can delineate general trends in America utopian literature. But they can also obscure the complexities of individual works and blur important distinctions between utopias. In Part II the contributors attempt to avoid the shortcomings of general studies by concentrating upon comparisons between two utopists (Bellamy and Morris, Howells and Twain), by analyzing two works by one author (London), or by focusing on one book (*Player Piano*).

In the first essay Darko Suvin uses his wide-ranging knowledge of American, English, and European literature and history to produce a balanced comparison of Edward Bellamy's and William Morris's concepts of utopia. Suvin's ability to trace the roots of the utopias is especially noteworthy. He demonstrates how Bellamy combined the Bible, sermon oratory, Victorianism, Christianity, middle-class attitudes, sentimental romance, and socialism in *Looking Backward* and how Morris combined socialism with the medieval dream genre and pre-Raphaelite perspectives to create the crowning example of the utopian legend of the Earthly Paradise in *News from Nowhere*. (Suvin's comments about Bellamy's and Morris's contributions to science fiction and his analysis of Bellamy's Victorianism illuminate important aspects of the surveys by Sargent and me in Part IV.)

Frederick Pratter also uses a comparative approach in his examination of William Dean Howells and Mark Twain; furthermore, he discusses the importance of the dream motif, which Suvin links to *News from Nowhere*. But Pratter's primary concern is how the concept of formula speculative fiction and the mysterious traveler figure can be used to understand the psychological and cultural tensions of Howells's Altrurian Romances and Twain's *Connecticut Yankee* and *The Mysterious Stranger*.

In his treatment of Jack London's *The Iron Heel* and "Goliah," Gorman Beauchamp picks up on a tendency noted by Pratter in Twain's *Connecticut Yankee*: the mixing of eutopia and dystopia that often accompanies the act of writing a literary utopia. Beauchamp's essay also reinforces Suvin's view of Bellamy by constrasting London's awareness of the importance of class conflicts to Bellamy's (and Howells's) hopes for a radical yet totally peaceful transition period.

In the final case study David Y. Hughes examines a vision that may be even darker than the darkest passages in *Connecticut Yankee* and *The Iron Heel*. Hughes argues that Kurt Vonnegut's *Player Piano* is more terrifying than most modern dystopias, including *We*, *Brave New World*, and *1984*, because the citizens of Vonnegut's Ilium have chosen to be slaves to modern technology, commercialism, and bureaucracy.

DARKO SUVIN

Anticipating the Sunburst—Dream and Vision: The Exemplary Case of Bellamy and Morris

> The great cry that rises from all our manufacturing cities,
> louder than the furnace blast, is all in very deed for
> this,—that we manufacture there everything except men;
> we blanch cotton, and strengthen steel, and refine sugar,
> and shape pottery; but to brighten, to strengthen, to re-
> fine, or to form a single living spirit, never enters into our
> estimate of advantages.
>
> JOHN RUSKIN

> Is the Earth so?
> Let her change then.
> Let the Earth quicken.
> Search until you know.
>
> BERTOLT BRECHT

> Was it a vision, or a waking dream?
> Fled is that music:—do I wake or sleep?
>
> JOHN KEATS

I HAVE ARGUED ELSEWHERE that the gloom and recantation of science fiction (including utopian or social-science fiction) writers from Mary Shelley and Herman Melville to Jules Verne and Villiers de l'Isle Adam reflected the increasing closure of bourgeois horizons.[1] Yet simultaneously, during the nineteenth century the thirst for *anticipations*—fictional pictures of an ex-citingly different future—rose sharply (one statistic puts their frequency in 1871–1916 at about thirty-five times the pre-1870 rate of publication).[2] In science fiction, a literary genre concerned with humanity's farthest horizons, the radical alternative of a socialist dawn erupted even more strongly than in the contemporary political surge in Germany, Britain, the United States, and elsewhere. In addition to its thematic and ideational appeal, this alter-native had the merit of solving the racking dilemmas opened by the time of the radical Romantics such as Blake—movement forward versus the closed circle, wish versus realization, freedom versus brotherhood, skepticism ver-sus belief, individual versus society. A whole century had dealt with these dilemmas by ingenious or feeble evasions within a spatial symbolism and had in the plot endings washed its hands of the cognitive reason for the

This essay is a revised version of Darko Suvin's *Metamorphoses of Science Fiction: On the Poetics and History of a Literary Genre*, © 1979, pp. 170–93. Reprinted by permission of Yale University Press, New Haven, Connecticut.

57

story's existence. Therefore, the science fiction narrations of Mary Shelley, Herman Melville, Jules Verne, or Villiers de l'Isle Adam culminated in destructions and murders as the logical end and outcome of the quantitative, individually anguished Faustian quest, as opposed to the qualitative, collectively subversive Promethean quest of earlier utopian and science fiction writers, from More and Cyrano to Percy Shelley. Even Goethe felt he could avoid such an outcome only by tacking on to his *Faust* a religious happy ending incompatible with the wager that had set the whole story off. The socialist vision of a classless Paradise on Earth was thus a solution both to the ideational and to the formal problems of nineteenth-century science fiction. It flourished for a brief time in Bellamy and Morris, the absence of its open horizon explains Mark Twain's impatience and despairing failure in *A Connecticut Yankee*, and at the end of the century it provided one of the basic ingredients for Wells's ambiguous synthesis. This essay will deal only with Bellamy and Morris, though Twain's disenchanted retraction of such a sunburst would be necessary for a full account of the horizons in late Victorian social-science fiction.

In *Looking Backward 2000–1887* (1888) Edward Bellamy[3] started not only from the widespread Victorian observation that, as Disraeli put it, the rich and the poor were two nations, but also from the observation that "the working classes had quite suddenly and very generally become infected with a profound discontent with their condition, and an idea that it could be greatly bettered if they only knew how to go about it."[4] Bellamy was willing to show them how, for it was not "only the toilers of the world who are engaged in something like a world-wide insurrection, but true and humane men and women, of every degree, are in a mood of exasperation, verging on absolute revolt, against social conditions that reduce life to a brutal struggle for existence" (LB, 285). In *Equality* (1897), a sequel that set out to plug the gaps left by the first novel, he added to these sources of discontent the ruin of prairie farmers by capitalist mortgages, the degradation of women fostered by economic exploitation, the recurrent economic crises of the last third of the nineteenth century, the concentration of three-quarters of all national wealth in the hands of 10 percent of the population. Bellamy's utopianism was the point at which all these deep discontents—which in the decade of the Chicago Haymarket trial ran the whole gamut between bankrupt smaller businessmen and striking industrial workers (almost 6,000 strikes per year)—met with the earlier utopian-socialist tradition of American religious and lay associationism and with the experiences of the nineteenth-century socialist movement in Europe. As a spokesman of the American "immense average of villagers, of smalltown-dwellers," Bellamy believed in "modern inventions, modern conveniences, modern facilities"[5]—in Yankee gadgetry as a white magic for overcoming drudgery. This perspective differed from the Populist revolt, which inveighed in the name of the smallholder against the financial trusts of Wall Street that were enslaving the countryside by means of railways. Bellamy accepted the trusts as more efficient and—following their own logic—condemned only their private character as economically too wasteful and politically too dangerous to tolerate. Instead of the corporate tyranny, his practical and democratic streak of "Yankee communism, or, to be more precise, 'Associationism' "[6] led him to envisage "the nation . . . organized as the one great corporation . . . , the sole employer, the final monopoly . . . in the profits and economies of which all citizens shared" (LB, 48).

Bellamy's new frontier, replacing the West traversed by the irreversible rails, is the future. It offers not only better railways, motor carriages, aircars, telephones, and television, but also a classless social brotherhood of affluence that will make these means of communication generally accessible and socialize all other upper-class privileges, including culture. Comfort and security are the ends of Bellamy's utopia, and economic reorganization the means. In this pragmatic socialism, unhappiness is ethical waste: *Looking Backward* shows forth "the economy of happiness."[7] This is brought about by universal high education, universal industrial service from the twenty-first to the forty-fifth year, equal and guaranteed income (in nontransferable yearly credits—there is no money) for every citizen including the old, children, and the sick, a flexible planning adjusting workloads and production according to demand, and a highly developed system of public bestowal of honors. Government is reduced to the operations of the Great Trust or—because the economy is run on the lines of universal civic service analogous to the military service—the Industrial Army. In it, every citizen rises through the ranks as far as his capacity will carry him. The generals of each guild or industrial branch are, however, not appointed from above but chosen by all the retired members or alumni of the guild, and so on up to the head of the army, who is president of the United States. Doctors and teachers have their own guilds and regents outside this army, and a writer, artist, journal editor, or inventor can be exempted from it if a sufficient number of buyers sign over a part of their credit to support him. In *Equality* Bellamy adds that economic equality gives free play to the greatest possible expansion of individuality, that there is a reservation for Thoreau-like objectors to "work out a better solution of the problem of existence than our society offers"[8] (a recurring escape hatch of later utopias), that the population of the cities has drastically shrunk, and that all tools are electrically powered and garments made from disposable paper.

Bellamy's economic blueprint is integrated into the story of Julian West, who wakes from a mesmeric sleep begun in 1887 into the year 2000, is given information about the new order by Dr. Leete, and falls in love with Leete's daughter Edith. Further, all this is a "romantic narrative" (LB, 6) by an anonymous historian writing in the festive year 2000 to instruct his readers in the contrasts of past and present by "looking backward." This system of mirrors and receding vistas in time is memorably reactualized in the nightmarish ending, when Julian dreams of awakening back in the capitalist society of 1887. He encounters its folly and moral repulsiveness with an anguished eye, which goes the Romantics such as Shelley or Baudelaire one better by supplying to each spectral place and person a counter-possibility. This utopian estrangement culminates in the hallucination about "the possible face that would have been actual if mind and soul had lived" (LB, 275), which he sees superimposed upon the living dead of the poor quarter. The lesson is that living in this nightmare and "pleading for crucified humanity" (LB, 281) might yet be better than reawakening into the golden twenty-first century—as, in a final twist, Julian does.

Thus, *Looking Backward*—intimately informed by Bellamy's constant preoccupation with human plasticity, with memory and identity (concerns of his tales *Dr. Heidenhoff's Process*, 1880, and *Miss Ludington's Sister*, 1884, as well as a number of his short stories), with brute reality and ideal possibility—reposes on a symbolic balance of time horizons. Its plot is, in fact, Julian's change of identity. In two of Bellamy's later science-fiction stories, the improvident and "imprevident" Earthmen, sundered from their neighbors and self-knowledge, are contrasted to worlds of brotherhood and transparency where men are "lords of themselves" ("The Blindman's World" and "To Whom This May Come," 1898). Julian West, the idealistic and insomniac rich idler with a revealing name, becomes an apostate from such a life in the West of 1887 through his education into a citizen of 2000 by a healer's reasonable lectures and his daughter's healing sympathy and intercession. *The construction of a social system for the reader is also the reconstruction of the hero*. This innovation in the utopian tradition responds to the epoch-making—if implicit—challenge of *Gulliver's Travels* that a different kind of Man is indispensable if one wants a different World, and is therefore a pointer to all future science fiction. It is an insight that came up precisely with the American Revolution and its radical-democratic paradigm of dynamic changeability, of new Adamic figures (for example, Blake). It can thus be considered a specifically American contribution to utopian and science fiction.

However, Bellamy immediately retreated from this discovery. Just as Julian is the mediator between two social systems for the reader, so Edith Leete—the descendant, projection, and as it were reincarnation of Julian's fiancée from 1887—is the steadying emotional mediator in his passage to a new world, a personal female Christ of earthly love and brotherhood. Bellamy's is an ethical socialism, abhorring violence and hatred. The "sunburst" of the new order, "when heroes burst the barred gate of the future" (LB, 240–41), is validated equally by economics, ethical evolution, and Christian love; unethical economics was for him unworkable. Such a millenary future brings a different, purified space as well as man. The sheltering house of Dr. Leete stands on the burned-down remnants of Julian's house and on top of his underground shelter, which has to be excavated as a feat of archeology for the twenty-first century. For Julian, the Leete household is the hearth of the spacious, reasonable, clean, classless Boston of the year 2000, and Edith is not too far from an image from his favorite writer Dickens, the cricket on the hearth. The hard-headed civic pragmatism is only the obverse of a soft-hearted petty-bourgeois romance or "fairy tale of social felicity."[9]

This fairy-tale character is most evident in Bellamy's sanguine expectation of a nonviolent, imminent, and almost instantaneous abandonment of private capitalism through universal recognition of its folly. With telling effect he extrapolated bourgeois rationality, ethics, and institutions to a logical end-product of universal public ownership. But this consistent pedagogic starting from the known signifies a sanitizing of capitalism to ensure the freedom, equality, brotherhood, and abundance of the Rationalist or Jeffersonian dreams. Bellamy remained limited by such ideals, which form an important part but by no means the final horizon of a socialist future. It is perhaps unfair to judge his fascination with the army as a model of rational organization by the normative ethical reaction toward armies today, for he acquired it in Lincoln's days and translated it into peaceful and constructive terms, just as Fourier did. Further, any self-respecting utopia before automation had to ensure its working by a certain harshness for recalcitrants, and Bellamy—possibly learning from Morris—clearly evolved toward greater openness and participatory democracy in *Equality*, where all officials are subject to recall. Nonetheless, his stress on a blend of state mobilization and "public capitalism,"[10] his patronizing dismissal of "the more backward races" (LB, 119) and of political efforts by narrow-minded "workingmen," and above all his faith in technocratic regimentation within economic production as the obverse of liberal classless relations outside them strike an alienating note, in the tradition of Saint-Simon and Cabet rather than Fourier and Marx. That note is out of harmony with his basic libertarian preoccupations and introduces into his romance a cold and static element.

But if Bellamy is a pragmatist who is not comfortable when depicting sweeping processes of change, he is at his strongest in the shrewd treatment of the economics of everyday life—of the dressing and marriage, the distribution of goods, the cultural activities—and in the brilliant passages on making democratic supply-and-demand work outside a capitalist framework, for example, in organizing a journal or in solving brain drain between countries. On such occasions, Bellamy is quite free from a state socialism regulating everything from above. When contrasting such warm possibilities with the irrationality and dead-end character of private competition, his clear and attractive, though not infrequently pedestrian, style rises to little

parabolic inserts of great force, as the initial allegory of the Coach, the
parables of the Collective Umbrella and of the Rosebush, or (in *Equality*)
the parables of the Water Tank and of the Masters of the Bread. All such
apologues, exempla, and parables come from a laicized and radical pulpit
style, openly displayed in the sermon on the sunburst from *Looking Backward*. It is within this New England oral and public tradition, from the
Bible and the Platonic dialogues and not from the genteel literature of Gilded
Age mandarins, that Bellamy's rhetorics arise as a respectable and sometimes
splendid accomplishment of its kind. Such addresses were at the time primarily meant for middle-class women, and Julian's sentimental plot as well
as the whole ethical tone of *Looking Backward* addressed itself to them—and
generally to that part of the educated classes that felt insecure and unfree
in bourgeois society. Thus, Bellamy's homely lucidity made his romance,
with all its middle-class limitations, the first authentically American socialist
anticipation tale.

Bellamy's success can—as always in significant science fiction and, indeed, in all significant fiction—be expressed in terms of a creative fusion
of various strands and traditions. These were not only literary but reached
back to the hundreds of religious or lay utopian communities in the young
United States. Though all of them finally collapsed *qua* utopian communities
under the violent pressures of an inimical environment, their legacy to
American thought from the Puritans through Hawthorne and Melville to
our days is larger than commonly assumed. An attenuated lay vision of the
glorious City had now and then crossed from the oral and tractarian into the
written fictional tradition, in works such as Mary Griffith's feminist, abolitionist, and technological anticipation "Three Hundred Years Hence" (1836),
Edward Kent's and Jane S. Appleton's future Bangor in *Voices from the
Kenduskeag* (1848), and several descriptions by Edward E. Hale culminating
in "My Visit to Sybaris" (1869) and *How They Lived in Hampton* (1888).[11]
Although Howells exaggerated when he claimed for Bellamy "a romantic
imagination surpassed only by that of Hawthorne,"[12] Bellamy did interfuse
these narratively helpless precursors—to whom one should add some French
and British utopian writers—with an effective Romantic system of corre-
spondences. In particular, the conclusion seems inescapable that he drew
on a number of important elements from John Macnie's *The Diothas* (1883),
such as a utopia with an industrial army, love with a descendant of the
nineteenth-century sweetheart named Edith like her ancestress, or the use
of radio.[13] But, most important, Bellamy was the first to go all the way with
such a lay millenarianism. Therefore, his ending—which refuses the easy
alibi of it all being a dream, a norm from Mercier's *L'An 2440* (1770; translated in the United States in 1795) and Griffith to Macnie—marks the historical moment when this tradition came of age and changed from defensive
to self-confident. The new vision achieves, within the text, a reality equal

to that of the author's empirical actuality. This ontological claim translates into historical cognition Hawthorne's psychological fantasy and especially the long sleep of Irving's Rip van Winkle, itself cognate to folk tales such as the Sleeping Beauty or the Seven Sleepers (Hawthorne and Irving are the only American authors in Dr. Leete's library). Bellamy thus links two strong American traditions: the fantastic one of unknown worlds and potentialities and the practical one of organizing a new world, both of which avail themselves of powerful biblical parallels while translating them from religion to economics. His materialist view of history as a coherent succession of changing human relationships and social structures was continued by Morris and Wells, and thence lay into the fundaments of subsequent science fiction. The same holds for the plot, which educates the reader into acceptance of the strange locus and its values by following the puzzled education of a representative protagonist. Modern science fiction, although it has forgotten its ancestor, builds on *Looking Backward* much as Dr. Leete's house was built on Julian's burned-down ruins and on top of the hermetically sealed sleeping chamber under its foundations.

Particular traits from Bellamy's other works also found their way into science fiction, such as the cosmically exceptional blindness of Earthmen into C. S. Lewis or the transferral by spirit to Mars into Edgar Rice Burroughs (from "The Blindman's World"), and the despotic oligarchy as alternative to revolution into Wells and London (from *Equality*). Most immediately, the immense political echo of *Looking Backward* reverberated through Howells, Twain, and numerous writers of sequels and rebuttals. Bellamy had hit exactly the right note at a time of widespread search for alternatives to ruthless plutocracy, and between 100 and 200 fictional utopias expounding or satirizing social democracy, state regulation of economy, a Populist capitalism, or various uncouth combinations thereof were published in the United States from 1888 to World War I. Though none of them approached Bellamy's coherence, the most notable were Ignatius Donnelly's melodramatic *Caesar's Column* (1890) and Howells's politely satirical discussions in *A Traveler from Altruria* (1894). Bellamy's fame spread to Germany, where Hertzka had just published *Freeland* (1889), and inspired at least three dozen works there too. But the perfect complement and answer to *Looking Backward* was written by William Morris.

Like so many other utopian works, Morris's *News from Nowhere* (1890)[14] was, among other things, a direct reply to *Looking Backward*. Reviewing it, he had denounced Bellamy's "unhistoric and unartistic" temperament, which "makes its owner (if a socialist) perfectly satisfied with modern civilization, if only the injustice, misery and waste of class society could be got rid of " and whose ideal of life "is that of the industrious *professional* middle-class man of today, purified from [the] crime of complicity with the monopolist class"; whence it follows "that he conceives of the change to Socialism as taking place without any breakdown of that life, or indeed disturbance of it." Morris especially objected to Bellamy's stress on both technological and social machinery, leaving the impression "of a huge standing army, tightly drilled," to the corresponding "State Communism" as opposed to direct participatory democracy, and to the reduction of labor instead of its change to work as pleasure, work blended with an art that "is not a mere adjunct of life . . . but the necessary and indispensable instrument of human happiness."[15]

Accordingly, it is direct, sensual relationships of people to each other and to nature—a different civilization where useful work is pleasure—that provide the fundament of *News from Nowhere*. It adopts the frame of *Looking Backward*, beginning with the narrator's falling asleep and waking up in the future house built on the site of his own home, and ending with his terrible return to his own time. But from the very beginning, Morris's story is a counterproject to Bellamy's. It is presented neither as a safe retrospective from the year 2000 nor as the voice of a lone member of the upper class, but as one privileged voice and vision of the future among several others possible and indeed held within the socialist party of which Morris was a member and in whose periodical *News from Nowhere* was published. The whole story is informed by the tone of a man displaying his personal vision for consent to potential comrades in bringing it about and yet very aware of its distance in the future. This approach blends collective validity and personal heartbreak. It is much richer than the easy Christian Socialist resolution of Julian West's private anguish by means of a resurrected bride, for it takes into full consideration both the collective difficulty of arriving at and the personal impossibility of setting up an abode in the promised classless land: The narrator William Guest—Morris's *persona*—is in the position of Moses walking through a vision of Canaan. Therefore, the narration adds to the obligatory Mercier-to-Bellamy tradition of outlining the future (the ride from Hammersmith to the British Museum, that repository of collective memory) two further and historically new elements. First, it introduces an account of the revolution that led to the future. Today this account may seem still too naive and optimistic, but it is of a different order of credibility than the sudden wholesale social conversions depicted by previous writers in this tradition up to and including Bellamy. Second, the bittersweet rowing up the Thames shows what the future might have meant to the author-narrator in terms of a personally more satisfying, nonalienated life. Together with the ubiquitous guide Dick, the average Nowherean, Guest's main partner and interlocutor in the first part of the story is Old Hammond, the custodian of history, and in the second Ellen, the incarnation of the "pleasure of life" of the future present.

The narrator's vision is also a dream. Not only can it naturalistically be considered a dream in his nineteenth-century Hammersmith bed, it is also a wish-dream. Reacting against the capitalist use of machinery that polluted the life of man and the earth and created ugliness and misery, Morris began with the pre-Raphaelite tradition of art as daydreaming. In its refusal to look deeper into the basic problems of reality, however, such an art became its complement, as green complements red, and thus directly dependent upon it—pretty where actuality is ugly, sweet where it is bitter, brightly shaped where it is amorphous and sooty, a pastoral where it is an ulcer of slums:

> Forget six counties overhung with smoke,
> Forget the snorting steam and piston stroke,
> Forget the spreading of the hideous town;
> Think rather of the pack-horse on the down,
> And dream of London, small, and white, and clean,
> The clear Thames bordered by its gardens green. . . .
> Morris, *The Earthly Paradise*

Steam-age capitalism's totalizing development of the war of each against each into global imperialisms was accompanied and indeed prepared by its ruthless transformation of towns into "an extension of the coal mine"[16] and of the countryside into spoils for the railway that Thoreau had already fulminated against. In a technique similar to More's, *News from Nowhere* is primarily a counterproject to that bourgeois life:

> The hope of the past times was gone. . . . Was it all to end in a counting-house on the top of a cinder-heap, with Podsnap's drawing-room in the offing, and a Whig committee dealing champagne to the rich and margarine to the poor in such convenient proportions as would make all men contented together, though the pleasure of the eyes was gone from the world . . .?[17]

At this high point of the paleotechnic world, any sensitive artist might have wished, with Guest, "for days of peace and rest, and cleanness and smiling goodwill."[18] For its "realities were money, price, capital, shares: The environment itself, like most of human existence, was treated as an abstraction. Air and sunlight, because of their deplorable lack of value in exchange, had no reality at all."[19] On the contrary, *News from Nowhere* is an airy and sunny environment, where only direct interhuman relations are clearly envisaged. As opposed to the capitalist gospel of toil, its moral and creative center is work as playful human necessity. As opposed to the Victorian starvation of the mind and the senses, its figures are perhaps the fullest and least embarrassed Epicureans in modern English literature. As opposed to the terrible anxieties of blood-and-iron progress, its subtitle is *An Epoch of Rest*.

Thus there is a strong element of mere escape in *News from Nowhere*. Most disturbing for a utopian tale, Morris overreacted to the extent of a total refusal to envisage any machinery, technological or societal. This amounts to leaving his future society without any economic or organizational basis. In economy a "force-barge" (NFN, 140) with an undisclosed new energy is the only exception to a turning away from and indeed dismantling of technology in Nowhere. "Power" (that is, energy) is available everywhere, and people who are so minded can collect together in workshops to draw on it, but this is used only for handicrafts (NFN, 38); for the rest, "England . . . is now a garden" (NFN, 61). Morris makes some telling points about the "never-ending series [of] sham or artificial necessaries" (NFN, 79) imposed by the capitalist world market, which necessarily enslaves colonial countries as a counterpart to the corruption of consumer taste. But to reject resolutely not only useless forms of technology and industrial organization but technical productivity and inventiveness in general while keeping the population stable and affluent, as *News from Nowhere* does, is to leave the future society without an economic basis. Any utopist has the right to fashion his Land of Heart's Desire; but he has a corresponding obligation to make it at least an arguable alternative possibility.

It could be argued that the gap left by Morris's disgust with modern economics might today be filled in by an imaginative reader supplying his own economics, based on the possibilities of automation and other ways of "postindustrial" productivity that Morris could not know about—though his vision did assume humanity would somehow evolve "immensely improved machinery" (NFN, 82) for irksome tasks if only basic problems of social organization were solved. Unfortunately, the absence of *sociopolitical* organization in Nowhere is a gap that cannot be argued away and makes it impossible to treat it as a full-fledged utopian tale. True, there is a classical Marxist glimpse of "communes and colleges" (NFN, 24) run by participatory democracy. However, overcompensating for Bellamy's state apparatus and clear lines of power, *News from Nowhere* omits all machinery for determining priorities between communes or any other basic units. Yet all production, including very much the automated kind, requires—as long as it is not simply magical—coordination and a (however truly participatory) system of vertical decision-making. As Bellamy astutely countered in his review of Morris, "[no] degree of moral improvement [will] lessen the necessity of a strictly economic administration for the directing of the productive and distributive machinery."[20] *News from Nowhere* throws the baby of human productivity out with the dirty water of Statism and technocracy.

But if it is not a utopia, much less prophetic anticipation, *News from Nowhere* is the finest specimen of Earthly Paradise story in modern literature. As I have argued elsewhere,[21] the Terrestrial Paradise—a place of thisworldly fleshly contentment, magical fertility, happiness, health, and youth—is a wish-dream that does not have to work out an alternative economical and sociopolitical organization; it is a magical parallel world akin to folk tale and pastoral, yet of collective import as an alternative community to be striven for. Morris's story has almost all of these elements. The weather and the people are (perhaps a shade monotonously) perpetually summery, the salmon are back in the Thames, and Shelleyan consentaneous love inspires all breasts, with just enough exceptions to avoid making it too saccharine. Liberated from grim capitalism, the world has entered upon its "second childhood" (NFN, 87, 116) very similar to an idealized version of the fourteenth century and characterized by a childishly unspoiled enjoyment in artful work not sundered from play; all of its people look younger than they would in our civilization. Above all, the dryness of the usual utopian panoramic sweep is avoided by fashioning most of the narration as a personal working out of the new country, as a glimpse of the narrator's alternative—happy and wholesome—life. His journey up the magical waters of the fertile Thames, signposted with references to a range of legends from the Grimm tales "from the childhood of the world" (NFN, 85) to Tennyson's Lotus Eaters, shows a rich and contrapuntal use of the Romantic fairy tale. The newly fertile land and happy relationships in the future England are the result of a metamorphosis from the ugly Victorian past—a past still inscribed in Guest's clothes, looks, and memories—to the clear and colorful beauty of the Nowherean present, a metamorphosis analogous to Andersen's Ugly Duckling reborn as a beautiful swan. Under the spell of his rejuvenating journey toward the sources, the narrator also moves toward the happiness felt in his childhood.

Nonetheless, "shades of the prison-house" are inescapably upon the narrator-protagonist: He personally can only testify to, not accomplish for himself, the happiness-bringing metamorphosis. The tension between the report about collective happiness and the personal melancholy of the guest-reporter in that Earthly Paradise—for him truly a Nowhere—refuses a Bellamy-type sentimental happy ending. The radically more mature resolution is not one of ethical salvation, as in *Looking Backward*, but one of political strife. We are back at Blake's great oath not to let "the sword sleep in my hand" until Jerusalem is built "in England's green and pleasant land." But here, such a strife is translated from Blake's arena of a single mind to public political struggle, as personal compensation for and collective justification of Guest's visit and departure:

> Ellen's last mournful look seemed to say, "No, it will not do; you cannot be of us; you belong so entirely to the unhappiness of the past that our happiness even would weary you. . . . Go back and be the happier for having seen us, for having added a little hope to your struggle. Go on living while you may, striving, with whatsoever pain

and labour needs must be, to build up little by little the new day of fellowship, and rest, and happiness."

Yes, surely! and if others can see it as I have seen it, then it may be called a vision rather than a dream. [NFN, 182]

For this "dream" is, finally, to be understood in the tradition of the medieval genre of the same name whose convention, for example, in Chaucer, is that the author relates the dream as a nonnaturalistic analogy—often using the fable or other allegorical means—to public problems of great personal import. Morris had already used this convention in his story about the peasant revolt in the Middle Ages *A Dream of John Ball* (1888). Its narrator, double horizon of defeat and victory, historical assumptions, and time scheme combined with color imagery (night and moon opposed to "the east crimson with sunrise"), prefigure the fuller use in *News from Nowhere*. But just as *A Dream of John Ball* was not an individualistic historical novel, so the later work is not to be taken for positivistic prophecy but for the figure or type of a fulfillment that could or should come. In that roundabout, dialectical way, *News from Nowhere* and its "ideal of the old pastoral poets" (NFN, 131) can, through its nucleus of frank and beautiful human relationships to other humans and to nature, be reintegrated into anticipatory utopianism. Its Earthly Paradise is an analogy to the classless socialist day. Its collective dream, "if others can see it," will finally also be a vision reinserted into history.

Dawn or sunburst, a favorite image of the socialist movement, is here particularly appropriate because of the close correspondence among people, vegetation, and the seasons of day and year. Morris's narrator went to sleep in a wintry night, whose young moon portended renewal; he wakes up, "by witness of the river-side trees" (NFN, 3), in a bright morning of spring or summer. The sunlight denotes happiness, as the moonlight's colorless pallidity throughout the story reminds the narrator of the dark past. Colors too are connected with the opposed tempers and historical epochs, "the sombre greyness, or rather brownness, of the nineteenth century" versus "the gaiety and brightness" (NFN, 118) of the twenty-first. Mankind has again become a part of nature, "men and women [are] worthy of the sweet abundance of mid-summer" (NFN, 123), and the riverside trees are emblems as much as witnesses to it. The representative denizen of the future, Ellen, sums it up in her cry: "O me! O me! How I love the earth, and the seasons, and weather, and all things that deal with it, and all that grows out of it" (NFN, 174). She is the ideal partner or *anima* of Morris, who characterized himself as a man "careless of metaphysics and religion, as well as of scientific analysis, but with a deep love of the earth and the life on it, and a passion for the history of the past of mankind."[22]

The arrested moment of Earthly Paradise is conveyed by a series of descriptive *pictures*—perhaps Morris's basic stylistic device. The vision in *News from Nowhere* etches sharply in colors and shades, time and place—especially the topography of London and the Thames valley—but it is most attentive to the sensual nuances of behavior and movement of humans amid a nature produced by their hands' work, literally a nature as handiwork or handicrafts. The beautiful bridges, the garden-like banks of the Thames, the haysels, the old house that grows out of the earth are of the same stuff as the nut-brown maids "born out of the summer day itself" (NFN, 122), flowers amid the green countryside. Yet this pictorial, at times somewhat picturesque, vision is ever and again clouded by the dreamlike melancholy and alienation of the beholder. The bemused and never quite sunny narrator does not fully fit into the bright day of the pictorial narration. He comes from the wrong, moony or night side of the dawn, and he finally has to step outside the picture frame and fade from the Earthly Paradise. Yet, in their turn, the translucent characters, scenery, and style all harmonize with the yearning of the narrator in an "identity of situation and feeling."[23] Nowhere and William Guest are two polar aspects of Morris the author—the healing, achieved hope and the wounded, hoping subject. Both the subject and his hope are in some ways akin to a narcissistic pre-Raphaelitism very much at odds with modern taste. But the sensual immediacy and clarity of their interaction render with great fidelity and economy a genuine poetry of human beauty and transience. The characters take up a graduated spectrum ranging from the clouded narrator to Ellen, the personification of sunshine loveliness. Nearest to Guest are Old Hammond with his knowledge of, and the "grumbler" with his eccentric penchant for, the old-time unhappiness, while the fulcrum of the narration is taken up by Dick with Clara. Because this is "a land of fellowship rather than authority, there are no fathers: a generation is always skipped."[24] But all characters are mirror-images of the narrator (Old Hammond) or of the landscape, and all elements of the story a system of stylistic mirrors, which would easily become tedious were it not for the fundamental existential estrangement and opposition between Nowhere and England, the twenty-first and the nineteenth century, light and soot, summer and winter, sunlight and moonlight. The narration glides in a leisurely way among these clarifying mirrors, progressing from Guest's first immersions into the Thames of the future and the deurbanized London to the historical explanation, the beauty of the river journey, and—as he cannot be in at the fruition—his final expulsion from the harvest celebration.

The horizons of *News from Nowhere* are a variant of Marxism, with a bias toward Fourier's passionate attraction toward work and pleasure but without his maniacal systematization. Human history is seen as a dialectical development from tribal communism, or from Morris's beloved Middle Ages, through capitalism to classless society, "from the older imperfect communal period, through the time of the confused struggle and tyranny of the rights of property, into the present rest and happiness of complete Communism" (NFN, 160). The chapter "How the Change Came" extrapolates from the experience of French revolutions and English working-class agitation, such as the Bloody Sunday demonstration of 1887, a first approximation to realistic revolution in utopias and science fiction. There are also shrewd hints about the transitional period after the revolution. True, the resulting life, where mathematics is an eccentric foible on a par with antiquarian novels and education is left to haphazard communion with the society of people and things, is in many important aspects a multiplication *ad infinitum* of ideals from Morris's arts-and-crafts circle. However, if life is envisaged somewhat too exclusively as a pre-Raphaelite work of art, at least Morris went to the logical end of his whole generation's demand that life should become a work of art. He took it seriously—literally and collectively—and tried to depict its realization. If the attempt was not wholly successful because of Morris's well-founded but one-sided distrust of science, the further horizons of such life are open-ended. As with any Golden Age or Eden from Morris's favorites Homer, Hesiod, and the Bible onward, this is a static society. But in Morris's scheme of history it is explicitly an epoch of cleansing rest, which might well evolve further.

News from Nowhere is an alternative not only to what Morris felt as mawkish bourgeois novels and as the technocracy of *Looking Backward*. In the spectrum of science fiction, it is also an alternative to W. H. Hudson's wholly escapist and idiosyncratic pastoral in *A Crystal Age* (1887) and to Richard Jefferies's embracing of "hard" barbarism and primitivism in *After London* (1885). Both of these works have some elements similar to Morris's, insofar as they totally reject the present and the city. Morris read *After London* before he wrote his book and was stimulated to "absurd hopes" by its picture of deurbanization.[25] But his romance is a third way, transcending the opposition between Bellamy's ethicoreligious pacification and Jefferies's politicogeological devolution, as well as between escapism of the Hudson type and naturalistic sentimentality. Guest and his hosts are obscurely conscious of meeting "as if I were a being from another planet" (NFN, 46). But he is also the link between the universes of darkness and sunlight, and Morris overcomes the one-sidedness of his various traditions by a blend of verisimilitude and pastoral, by a future sunlight constantly contrasting with our darkness—as befits a dawn.

Finally, the underlying view of world and man is simply and beautifully but inexorably materialistic. Logically, there is no immortality in Nowhere (the only feature of the traditional Earthly Paradise not picked up), yet death and sorrow, as in the episode of the jealousy killing, do not destroy but confirm the paradise. For in this view the individual is bound up with his fellows and nature in an existence that has wholly eradicated the social and cosmic alienation of man. Morris "seems to retire far from the real world and to build a world out of his wishes; but when he has finished, the result stands out as a picture of experience ineluctably true."[26] In Bellamy's romance, the new vision evolved systematically out of facets of the old. In Morris's, the new vision as a whole is incompatible with the old. As noted, Bellamy's vision achieved within his book a reality *equal* to that of the author's empirical environment; but Morris's achieved an "ineluctable" reality *superior* to that of the class civilization. That is why the narrator tragically marked by the old has to end up extruded from the vision.

Accordingly, unlike Bellamy, it is not discrete scenes of estrangement and parables that stand out in *News from Nowhere*. Learning from Bellamy, Morris has a few jolting examples of them too, such as the phantasmagoric vision of Bloody Sunday superimposed upon the sight of the orchard leading to "the Parliament House, or Dung Market" (NFN, 34), or the shocking final reacquaintance with the black cloud and the servile men of the nineteenth century. But it is the tone of the whole vision-dream—the book-length parable of new human relations in a society of "wealthy freemen" (NFN, 74), beauty and "free exercise of the senses and passions of a healthy human animal, so far as this [does] not injure the other individuals of the community"[27]—that remains with the reader. It is the historical horizon, the spectacle of people who "pass [their] lives in reasonable strife with nature, exercising not one side of [themselves] only, but all sides, taking the keenest pleasure in all the life of the world" (NFN, 48–49) in counterpoint with a Marxist "optimistic tragedy" borne by the narrator bereft of such a life, that gives *News from Nowhere* its bittersweet, tensile strength. Within a well-defined, deep but narrow sensibility, its dialectics of consciousness and unconsciousness establishes an Earthly Paradise more real and more human than the reader's tawdry actuality. If Morris's romance harks back to almost animistic elements, it does so as the crown of a plebeian tradition of legends and folk tales. As Fourier had said, unlike the best political economists who wanted to throw light on the chaos, he wanted to lead out of it. Although *News from Nowhere* only partly avoids the weakness of utopias, their abstractness, it fully shares their strength, which lies in "*the ineluctable and the absolute.*"[28] And the abstractness too is overcome in Morris's late essays, his crowning and truly utopian works such as "How We Live and How We Might Live," "The Society of the Future," "How I Became a Socialist," and "Communism." In them he even accepted the cognitive necessity of "time [teaching] us that new machinery may be necessary to the new life."[29] This is Morris's final marriage of art with history.

Thus, Morris bequeathed to science fiction several key elements. He endowed Bellamy's suffering narrator in the new country with philosophical and poetic value. He transferred a believable revolution from political tracts into fiction, fathering a line that stretches from Wells's *When the Sleeper Wakes* through Jack London, Alexei Tolstoi, Shaw, and Heinlein to the flood of science-fiction revolts in the last thirty-five years. His utopian pastoral or Earthly Paradise had had less success than Jefferies's neobarbarism or Hudson's titillating escapism, though it can be felt as the endangered alternative from Wells's Eloi to C. S. Lewis's Venus or Le Guin's *The Word for World Is Forest*. But his dialectic, tragic, and victorious socialism remains the mature horizon of all science fiction that draws on hopes for an open future of men and of the earth. Nobody has yet surpassed Morris in his intimate understanding that "times of change, disruption, and revolution are naturally times of hope also."[30] Nobody in nineteenth-century utopian or science fiction, and few outside it, have embodied this understanding in such lucid and warm prose.

In conclusion, there is no doubt that the political surface or indeed backbone of a utopian tale is of a high and possibly central significance to it. That level is, however, isolatable from the whole of the narration only at the expense of not treating it as what it primarily and irreducibly is—a *narration*. In fact, other structural levels—such as the fictional treatment of characters, time, and space—and the degree of their congruence with the ideologicopolitical level largely account for the success or failure of the tale, including its message. Thus, Bellamy's "colder" political stance is accompanied by a closed and often oppressive narrative structure, whereas an open and airier structure is fully homologous to Morris's warmer, less regimenting politics. A striking and symbolical example is that of the dining room. Dr. Leete's private room in the communal dining house stands for Bellamy's general treatment of the public whole as a sum of rationalized and sanitized private elements, no doubt spatially transposed and regrouped but qualitatively unchanged. It is a dining room for a monogamous family and its private guests, just as the speech, furniture, dress, maidenly blushes, and so forth—in short the whole life-style of the future Bostonians—is for all practical purposes simply extrapolated from the style of "their cultured ancestors of the nineteenth [century]" (LB, 38). Furthermore, the whole narration of *Looking Backward* progresses as a retrospective series of West's topographical and ideological sallies into the new Boston from the individual, monogamous hearth of the Leetes and under their reassuring guidance. Any unaccompanied personal venture from this safe cocoon immediately provokes in West a "horror of strangeness" (LB, 40), an existential or indeed existentialist nausea that is—most revealingly—quite as violent in the supposedly safe new Boston of the future as in the nightmare of returning to the competitive old Boston of the past. There is a strong agoraphobic air about Bellamy's millennium, a panic fear for which only the closure of space, of ideas (that is, state socialism), and of the narration itself can provide a remedy. The underlying metaphoric cluster of his book is one of static healing, whereas in Morris's book it is one of dynamic gazing during a journey. That is why, though Bellamy came within an ace of returning his narrator to the nineteenth century in order to work there for his new vision, and furthermore made it clear that this would have been the ethically proper course to follow, it was left for the more open Morris, with his less hidebound readership, actually to effect this large step. The supreme sacrament of acceptance into Bellamy's society is a mystically subromantic marriage into which the narrator once and for all escapes in a sentimental happy ending of ethical, rather than political, salvation. Quite homologously, Bellamy's fear of existential openness unshielded by a personal savior or vertical hierarchy is also the motivation for his ideological stance, for example, toward industrial organization and a forcible political revolution: In utopian writings, politics is based on the author's simultaneously deeply personal and deeply class-bound psychology.

On the contrary, Morris's dining rooms, such as the Hammersmith one, harbor truly communal feasts, open to the garden and river glimpsed beyond, and with a large nonmonogamous cast of erotically sympathetic and obviously erotically open "neighbors" who transmit information to the narrator and to us by asking him curious questions rather than by simply lecturing him, and us, as affable but omniscient teachers. Morris's narration as a whole is thus not only open-ended, requiring an inner-directed rather than other-directed reader; its whole texture is also much richer. In space/time it has a double movement through "town" (past memory) and "country" (truly changed future existence at least marginally experienced by the narrator). Correspondingly, it not only more than doubles the number of characters (two main women and two main guides instead of one each in Bellamy—plus a great number of subsidiary characters instead of the lone Mrs. Leete and some disembodied voices and faces), it also deepens the overall complexity of their relationships. In brief, Morris transcends Bellamy's model of fraternity under the "fatherhood of God" (LB, 240) and of lay elders (the alumni, the father figure of Dr. Leete) in favor of the youthful, self-governing, and as it were parthenogenetic model of potential lovers. Where Bellamy goes in for a psychological repression of self-determination, equally of the workers at their working place and of the sexual relationships (demurely identical to those in the current sentimental novel), Morris goes in for an extension of sympathy or libido to the whole of gardenlike nature, a sinless Earthly Paradise. The supreme sacrament of acceptance into his society is therefore, dialectically, not sentimentality but the actual journeying and working together, as far as that is realistically feasible for a *guest* to a radically different civilization.

This is not to belittle the achievements of Bellamy or to ignore the gaps in Morris, as discussed earlier. It is simply to point out that, in some ways, *News from Nowhere* is a sublation or fulfillment of Bellamy's inconsistent attempts or ambiguities. Both writers are deeply committed to an anguished distancing from nineteenth-century capitalism and to a different life. Nevertheless, Bellamy's transfer results mainly in a sentimental dream and a tight and earnest embracing of *security*, where anguish is discharged upon a series of personal mediators, whereas Morris's journeying results mainly in a painterly vision and an attempt at direct *creativity*, which being open-ended is inseparable from a possible anguish to be resolved only in self-determined practice or praxis. Yet, in other ways, the dreams or visions of Bellamy and Morris can also be treated as complementary: There is, finally, no need to make an exclusive choice between them. The paradox of *Looking Backward* being both more limited than and complementary to *News from Nowhere* is finally the paradox of Christian Socialism itself, simultaneously committed to the patriarchal vertical of the "fatherhood of God" and to the libertarian horizontal of the "brotherhood of Man." Such conflicting Protestant and middle-class abstractions are resolved by Morris: Radically careless of the fatherhood, he explores the meaning and price of brotherhood in terms of an intimate neighborliness. Staying within the bourgeois—or indeed WASP—existential horizons, Bellamy pursued the everyday need for security to its logical end and ended up with the socialist dawn as a safe order of *things*, a *societas rerum*. Reneging on the bourgeois existential horizons but opposing to them unrealistically idealized preindustrial—or indeed bohemian—horizons, Morris pursued the arrested timeless moment, the visionary dream (in all the mentioned senses) of Earthly Paradise to its logical end, and ended up with another aspect of that same dawn, the creative and therefore beautiful *human relations*, a *societas hominum*. Between them, Bellamy and Morris covered the technical premises and sensual horizons of the dawn: In a way each has what the other lacks. For a brief but still exemplary historical moment—which extended to Wells, London, and Zamiatin—the significant literary discussion about darkness and dawn became one inside the international socialist movement.

It might, of course, be fairly easy to fault Bellamy's and Morris's texts in comparison to the norms of nineteenth-century fiction, as a number of critics have already done. But perhaps such fault-finding is not only too easy, and therefore banal, but also wrong-headed. After all—despite both the aesthetic and the political ideologies one suspects are responsible for the negative stance dominant in twentieth-century literary criticism toward utopian and allied fiction in general, and toward nineteenth-century texts in particular—after all, the norms of individualistic fiction from, say, Defoe to James, as well as the critical instruments elaborated therefrom, are themselves historically fleeting and already unsatisfactory. Perhaps the time has come to re-evaluate much hitherto scorned utopian or social-science fiction as being not (or not so much) a series of bad attempts at the individualistic norm but a series of more or less successful attempts at a different, oppositional or submerged, norm. For such a reevaluation it is, to begin with, necessary to tease out of such ideologically and aesthetically heretical texts their own norm.

NOTES

1. See Darko Suvin, *Metamorphoses of Science Fiction: On the Poetics and History of a Literary Genre* (New Haven: Yale University Press, 1979), Ch. 6 and 7; this essay is part of that book's historical survey of main science fiction models from More to the twentieth century. The case for including utopian fiction in science fiction has been argued in Chapter 3 (earlier in *Studies in the Literary Imagination*, 6 [Fall 1973], 121–45) and in Darko Suvin, "The River-side Trees, of SF & Utopia," *The Minnesota Review*, N.S. 2–3 (Spring–Fall 1974), pp. 108–15. The first of these two arguments is also an attempt at a summarizing discussion of the utopian genre; it cites a number of works relevant to a general approach to it. I am grateful to McGill University for the sabbatical leave of 1973–74, during which the present text was written, to the Canada Council for a Leave Fellowship, and to the services of Cambridge University Library.

2. Calculated by me from Ian Clarke, *The Tale of the Future*, 2d ed. (London: Library Association, 1972).

3. For the general context of Bellamy's writings see (besides some Ph.D. dissertations) Daniel Aaron, *Men of Good Hope* (New York: Oxford University Press, 1961); Sylvia E. Bowman, *The Year 2000* (New York: Bookman Associates, 1958); Van Wyck Brooks, *New England: Indian Summer* (New York: Dutton, 1950); Jay Martin, *Harvests of Change* (Englewood Cliffs, N.J.: Prentice-Hall, 1967); Arthur E. Morgan, *Edward Bellamy* (New York: Columbia University Press, 1944); idem, *The Philosophy of Edward Bellamy* (New York: King's Crown Press, 1945); Vernon L. Parrington, *Main Currents in American Thought*, Vol. 3 (New York: Harcourt, Brace, 1930); Joseph Schiffman, "Edward Bellamy's Altruistic Man," *American Quarterly*, 6 (Fall 1954), 195–209; "Introduction" to *Looking Backward* (New York: Harper's, 1959); and "Edward Bellamy and the Social Gospel," in *Intellectual History in America*, ed. Cushing Strout, 2 vols. (New York: Harper & Row, 1968); Walter F. Taylor, *The Economic Novel in America* (Chapel Hill: University of North Carolina Press, 1942); and John L. Thomas, "Introduction" to *Looking Backward* (Cambridge, Mass.: Belknap Press of Harvard University Press, 1967). On Bellamy's connections with science fiction, see H. Bruce Franklin, *Future Perfect* (New York: Oxford University Press, 1968); J. O. Bailey, *Pilgrims Through Space and Time* (Westport, Conn.: Greenwood Press, 1972); and Martin, *Harvests*. On his connections with utopian fiction, see note 11 below.

4. Edward Bellamy, *Looking Backward 2000–1887* (Leipzig: Bernhard Tauchnitz, 1890), p. 15. Hereafter this edition will be cited in the essay parenthetically by the page number, preceded by "LB."

5. W. D. Howells, "Edward Bellamy," in Edward Bellamy, *The Blindman's World and Other Stories* (London: A.P. Watt & Son [1898]), pp. vii, ix. On Bellamy's audience and the rhetorical structuring of *Looking Backward*, see David Bleich, "Eros and Bellamy," *American Quarterly*, 16 (Fall 1964), 445–59; Robert J. Cornet, "Rhetorical Strategies in *Looking Backward*," *Markham Review*, 4 (October 1974), 53–58; Virgil Lokke, "The American Utopian Anti-Novel," in *Frontiers of American Culture*, Ray Browne et al., eds. (West Lafayette, Ind.: Purdue University Studies, 1968); Martin, *Harvests*; Bernard Poli, *Le Roman américain 1865-1917* (Paris: Colin, 1972), Ch. 12; Barbara Carolyn Quissell, "The Sentimental and Utopian Novels of Nineteenth Century America," Ph.D. dissertation, University of Utah, 1973; Ken-

neth M. Roemer, *The Obsolete Necessity* (Kent, Ohio: Kent State University Press, 1976); and Tom H. Towers, "The Insomnia of Julian West," *American Literature*, 47 (March 1975), 52–63.

6. Aaron, *Men of Good Hope*, p. 95.
7. Unlocated quote, apparently from Bellamy's diary, in ibid., p. 97.
8. Edward Bellamy, *Equality* (New York: Appleton 1897), p. 41.
9. Edward Bellamy, "How I Came to Write 'Looking Backward.' " *The Nationalist*, May 1889; see the first page of this essay reprinted in Part I of this collection.
10. Bellamy, *Equality*, p. 176.
11. For the tradition of utopian fiction in the United States and Bellamy's position within it, see Lokke, "Anti-Novel"; Martin, *Harvests*; Quissell, "Sentimental and Utopian Novels"; and Roemer, *Obsolete Necessity*. Roemer supersedes earlier writing on nineteenth-century American utopias except where the previous studies deal with writings earlier than his *terminus a quo* of 1888, such as Allyn B. Forbes, "The Literary Quest for Utopia, 1880–1900," *Social Forces*, 6 (December 1927), 179–89, and Vernon L. Parrington, Jr., *American Dreams* (Providence: Brown University Press, 1947). For other studies of American utopian literature, see the secondary sources checklist in Part IV of this collection.
12. Howells, "Bellamy," p. xiii.
13. Arthur E. Morgan devotes most of his booklet *Plagiarism in Utopia* (Yellow Springs, Ohio: Arthur E. Morgan, 1944) to a refutation of Bellamy's supposed plagiarism from *The Diothas* (see Robert L. Shurter, "The Utopian Novel in America, 1865–1900," Ph.D. dissertation, Case Western Reserve University, 1936, and Taylor, *Economic Novel*). While Morgan examines a number of interesting but rather tangled trails possibly pointing to a personal acquaintance and exchange of opinions, including some tenuous hints at an exchange of manuscripts between Bellamy and Macnie, he does not solve the question. The only hard fact we are left with up to now is that Macnie's book was published five years before Bellamy's, and that there are some major structural similarities, as well as major differences in value and message between the two books. Perhaps literary critics should stop using the bourgeois legal terminology of "plagiarism" when talking about fiction in general and utopian fiction in particular.
14. For Morris's ideational context see Granville Hicks, *Figures of Transition* (New York: Macmillan, 1939); Lewis Mumford, *Technics and Civilization* (New York: Harcourt, 1963); and Raymond Williams, *Culture and Society, 1780-1950* (London: Penguin, 1961). For a general overview of his work see E. P. Thompson, *William Morris, Romantic to Revolutionary* (London: Lawrence & Wishart, 1955); for his writing, G. D. H. Cole, "Introduction" to the selection *William Morris* (London: Nonesuch Press, 1948); C. S. Lewis, "William Morris," *Rehabilitations* (London: Oxford University Press, 1939); and Jack Lindsay, *William Morris, Writer* (London: William Morris Society, 1961). On his use of dream and imagery, mainly in *A Dream of John Ball*, see John Goode, "William Morris and the Dream of Revolution," in *Literature and Politics in the Nineteenth Century*, ed. John Lucas (London: Methuen, 1971); and Jessie Kocmanová, "Two Uses of the Dream-Form as a Means of Confronting the Present with the Past: William Morris and Svatopluk Čech," *Brno Studies in English*, 2 (1960), 113–48. Specifically on *News from Nowhere*, see also Blue Calhoun, *The Pastoral Vision of William Morris* (Athens: University of Georgia

Press, 1975); V. Dupont, *L'Utopie et le roman utopique dans la Littérature Anglaise* (Toulouse and Paris: Librairie M. Didier, 1941), whose section IV collocated *News from Nowhere* into the context of nineteenth- and twentieth-century English utopias; Tom Middlebro', "Brief Thoughts on *News from Nowhere*," *Journal of the William Morris Society*, 2 (Summer 1970), 8–12; A. L. Morton, *The English Utopia* (London: Lawrence & Wishart, 1969); and James Redmond, "Introduction" to the Routledge & Kegan Paul ed. (London, 1972). Parallels between Morris's and Bellamy's utopias are briefly drawn by a number of critics, for example, Morton, but rarely sustained. A somewhat rambling parallel biased toward Bellamy is Peter Marshall's "A British Sensation" in Sylvia E. Bowman et al., *Edward Bellamy Abroad* (New York: Twayne, 1962). The first and so far the most voluminous parallel, Graham Stanhope Rawson's dissertation printed as *William Morris's Political Romance "News from Nowhere": Its Sources and Its Relationship to "John Ball" and Bellamy's Political Romance "Looking Backward"* (Borna and Leipzig: Noske, 1914), is not very helpful, nor is T. M. Parssinen's article "Bellamy, Morris and the Image of the Industrial City in Victorian Social Criticism," *Midwest Quarterly*, 14 (Spring 1973), 257–66—despite the grandiose titles.

15. William Morris, "*Looking Backward*," *The Commonweal*, 22 June 1889, reprinted in *Science-Fiction Studies*, 3 (November 1976), 287–90, together with Morris's introduction to his Kelmscott Press edition of More's *Utopia*.

16. Mumford, *Technics*, p. 159; see also all of Ch. 4.

17. "How I Became a Socialist" (1894), in *Political Writings of William Morris*, ed. A. L. Morton (New York: International, 1973), p. 244. This book is an indispensable companion to *News from Nowhere*. See also note 27 below.

18. William Morris, *News from Nowhere* (London and Boston: Routledge & Kegan Paul, 1972), p. 2. Hereafter this edition will be cited in the essay parenthetically by page number preceded by "NFN."

19. Mumford, *Technics*, p. 168.

20. [Edward Bellamy], "News from Nowhere," *New Nation*, 14 February 1891, p. 47, quoted in Bowman et al., *Edward Bellamy Abroad*, p. 94.

21. See my Chapters 3 and 5 in *Metamorphoses of Science Fiction* (note 1 above); an ample bibliography is included. See also Calhoun, *Pastoral Vision*.

22. "How I Became a Socialist," in *Political Writings*, p. 244.

23. Williams, *Culture*, p. 234.

24. Middlebro', "Thoughts" (note 14 above), p. 10.

25. Quoted from an unidentified letter of Morris's in Morton, *English Utopia*, p. 204.

26. Lewis, "William Morris" (note 14 above), p. 54.

27. "The Society of the Future" (1887), in *Political Writings*, p. 202. This essay is the nearest thing to an ideological nucleus of *News from Nowhere*.

28. Ernst Bloch, *Das Prinzip Hoffnug*, 2 vols. (Frankfurt: Suhrkamp, 1959), 1: 679; from here, 1: 677, is also the paraphrase of Fourier's dictum.

29. "Communism" (1893), in *Political Writings*, p. 239.

30. "The Hopes of Civilization" (1885), ibid., p. 159.

FREDERICK E. PRATTER

The Mysterious Traveler in the Speculative Fiction of Howells and Twain

ONE IMPORTANT but frequently overlooked function of utopian literature is its value as a way of working out social anxieties in imaginary, hence harmless, forms. The term "utopian" applied to fictive writing need not be synonymous with "ideal." Instead, the central feature of this kind of literature is the displacement from the here-and-now to some alternative (but not necessarily perfect) setting. Much of the derogatory connotation associated with the term "utopian" arises as a result of this misunderstanding, that the literature of alternative worlds is somehow by its very nature escapist.

In order to avoid this kind of value judgement, several students of utopian literature have introduced the use of the term "speculative fiction." Usually used in connection with science fiction (in order to get away from the connotations of *that* label), "speculative" refers to the displacement of the setting to some alternative world, whether in the past, on some remote island, or into the future.[1] The uses of this device for the author are obvious; the alternative world can be held up as a model of perfection (a eutopia), as a nightmare (the "dystopian" vision), or simply as somewhere different, a different way of looking at familiar values and habits.

If one is concerned with literature as a cultural artifact, it is important not to overlook the unconscious dimension of speculative writing. The creation of imaginary societies seems to provide a way to ease psychological conflicts in a way analogous to the function of dreaming. Dreams act within the individual consciousness, perhaps connecting the dreamer in some fashion to an inbuilt collective imagination. Speculative fiction similarly provides an outlet for individual and societal uneasiness within a culturally approved pattern and without alienating the author from the supportive effect of the shared culture. If a particular kind of fantasy literature becomes extremely widespread at a particular historical moment, the analysis of the structure of that fantasy ought to provide insights into the popular culture of the period.

The spate of utopianizing surveyed in Kenneth Roemer's historical essay covering 1888 to 1899 can be approached as the working out of social problems resulting from expansion and industrialization, in terms of traditional cultural and psychological norms. These utopian novels all share a common structure, the speculative fiction formula. Just as the analysis of the formula Western led John Cawelti and Henry Nash Smith to an understanding of the mythic nature of nineteenth-century American culture, so recently several students of utopian fiction have attempted to describe the formulaic nature of speculative writing.[2]

The typical pattern of American speculative fiction in the nineteenth century was the dream or dreamlike voyage—a technique also used by William Morris, as Darko Suvin points out in his essay. By the 1880s and 1890s the question of dream or reality had become somewhat muddled, even in the literature of American sentimental idealism. The dreaming narrator was transformed into the hero as dreamer, or visionary. A kind of American "power vision," the dream was the democratic ideal, the Whitmanic vision of comradeship and progress.[3] The reality was increasing class oppression and industrial strife, the poverty and misery that were the daily life of the working-class majority. Thus the voyage of escape was to dream of ante-bellum rural America.[4]

The geography of utopia is always significant; it provides a place of safety and isolation. Speculative regression to the "lost island" or "happy valley" is clearly a rejection of reality for the fantasy warmth of the womb. Both the island and the valley, protected from their surroundings by expanses of ocean or impenetrable mountains, are strong images of remoteness and security.[5] An important functional component of utopian speculation is this element of retreat, of turning backward to a past of imagined safety and simplicity. For the *fin de siècle* American author this meant a psychological return to the "lost Agrarian Eden."[6] Paradoxically, the American utopists of the period based their projections of an ideal future on this longing dream of an imagined past, which can be viewed as interchangeable with the voyage through space to the island.

This lost world of the Agrarian myth—a world examined in Donald Burt's thematic essay—is central to the utopian writings of Mark Twain and William Dean Howells, in the imaginatively reconstructed boyhood life, which provides a sense of values for their speculative works as well as the ostensibly realistic ones. Their novels, which are most clearly in the speculative tradition, are Howells's Altrurian Romances, *A Traveler from Altruria* and *Through the Eye of the Needle*, and Twain's medieval pastorals, *A Connecticut Yankee in King Arthur's Court* and *The Mysterious Stranger*.[7] By analyzing these novels as formula speculative fiction, it is possible to gain a better understanding both of their place in the authors' canons and of their function as cultural artifacts.

The formula hero of the speculative fiction of this period is the Mysterious Traveler who observes and comments on the alternative society from the perspective of an outsider. At the same time the traveler is a romantic idealist who has set forth, often in a dream, in quest of some better place. (The case of the observer who visits America from a utopian world, as in the first of Howells's Altrurian Romances, is a special subtype, considered in detail below.) This dual role, as dreamer-hero and as observer, is a symbolic representation of the novelist's role. At once longing for a better world and very much aware of the defects of this one, the utopist dreams of an alternative world in order to confront and come to terms with the social stresses of his own time.

In most of the utopian novels of the 1880–1900 period the hero, after a period of disorientation and confusion, comes to terms with the imaginary society and wins happiness and riches. Thus Julian West, in Bellamy's *Looking Backward,* is not so much removed from his milieu as alienated from it. Frustrated and dissatisfied in Brahmin Boston, he is more at home in the future, where there are others of his moral quality. The future dream voyage is a metaphorical extension of his alienation. The helplessness and insignificance he feels in the face of the moral perfection of the year 2000 can be considered as a trial to be undergone before, purified, he may take his place in the utopian social order.

In its simplest form, the speculative novel is an optimistic plan for a better world. In contrast, the utopian vision of Samuel Clemens was considerably more complex. In his time-travel adventure story *A Connecticut Yankee in King Arthur's Court* (1889), the journey into an imaginary medieval past serves the same function as Julian West's utopian future voyage. The hero, Hank Morgan, is unhappy in nineteenth-century Hartford, as his chances for advancement are slim. As he says:

> After that, I was just as much at home in that century as I could have been in any other; and as for preference, I wouldn't have traded it for the twentieth. Look at the opportunities here for a man of knowledge, brains, pluck, and enterprise to sail in and grow up with the country. The grandest field that ever was; and all my own; not a competitor; not a man who wasn't a baby to me in acquirements and capacities; whereas, what would I amount to in the twentieth century? I should be foreman of a factory, that is about all; and could drag a seine downstreet any day and catch a hundred better men than myself.[8]

It is no accident that Twain uses the phrase "sail in and grow up with the country," an idea that was basic to the settlement of the frontier. Twain had himself gone west in an attempt to make his fortune in the new country, turning his back on the exhausted South. As he well knew, there was little room in the America of 1889 to get in on the ground floor. As Henry Nash Smith points out, Hank contains in himself the conflict of his era: Is he an American Adam or the new Promethus?[9] There is clearly an association in Twain's mind between industrial progress and republican virtue, which gradually dissolves as the story progresses.

Hank's ambitions in Camelot are not just for himself; he wants to drag the whole century along with him; to remake it according to his own utopian view of society. The Mysterious Traveler becomes the Boss. At home in Hartford, there was little he (or Twain, for that matter) could do to ameliorate the injustices of the established order, but in Camelot there seems at first to be a real chance for social progress. That, finally, the dream goes awry is a clear demonstration of the author's growing fatalism about "that damned human race."

The formula plot line prescribes that the discoverer of a lost world make good by his discovery. Sometimes the lost world will yield gold or a beautiful princess, sometimes only a vision of idealized human happiness. Hank is at times deficient in sensibility (as when he fails to reckon with the power of the established church), but the real ironic power of his situation is that he, the hero, lacks the ability to affect his surroundings. One man acting alone against the forces of his time cannot hope to redirect them, whether that time be nineteenth-century Hartford or sixth-century Camelot. Even though Hank thinks himself the most powerful man in the kingdom ("I was no shadow of a king; I was the substance; the king himself was the shadow"), finally he is powerless. Twain's awareness of this condition of powerlessness and absurdity is a foretelling of the twentieth-century preoccupation with existential despair. In going back to Camelot and trying to grow up with the new country, Hank is attempting to assert the Promethean ideal, the capacity of an individual to effect a change in his world. That the attempt is a failure indicates how for Twain the disintegration of safety and stability, the two props of the ideal sensibility in post-Civil War America, had become a major concern. By the end of his life, this concern was to amount almost to an obsession.

In *The Obsolete Necessity*, Roemer's perceptive analysis of *Connecticut Yankee* in the context of the speculative novels of the period emphasizes the schizoid nature of much late-nineteenth-century utopian literature.[10] This novel is both utopian and dystopian; Hank's new chance in the "virgin land" of Arthurian Britain seems a bright utopian promise at first, only to degenerate into the dystopian last chapters and "The Battle of the Sand Belt":

In most instances the utopian heroic figure harnesses the turbulent forces of his age and directs them into constructive and peaceful channels. But here Hank ultimately becomes the explosive, blind Samson who destroys his enemies and in the process wrecks his own civilization and falls prey to the champion of Old-World superstition, Merlin. Instead of achieving a rejection of the past, this hero of Progress only succeeds in engineering a massacre that rivals any "senseless" Old-World war for its barbaric carnage.[11]

If we accept the elemental equation between the speculative hero, trying to understand this strange new world into which he has been thrown, and Clemens the utopian author, it becomes clear that the artistic failure of this novel embodies the "clash between fears and hopes" so characteristic of the utopian works of the period.

Like his friend Sam Clemens, William Dean Howells took many of the values of his later life and work from his recollection of boyhood life on the river. In Howells's case, the river was the Miami, which flowed through the small Ohio town subsequently elegized in A Boy's Town (1890). Significantly, the river has an island—"the boys called it The Island; and it must have been about the size of Australia."[12] It is certainly no coincidence that Altruria, the imagined ideal society, should be located on just such an island. One of Howells's straw figures in A Traveler from Altruria (1894) comments that "it is perfectly astonishing that an island so large as Altruria should have been lost to the knowledge of the world ever since the beginning of our era," and this is precisely the point.[13] The true location of the Christian Commonwealth is in "the human heart," and it is indeed singular, as Howells suggests, that it has been so long ignored while all have gone about their business.

Howells's ventures into utopian romance use many of the characteristic devices of formula speculative fiction. Altruria is an idealized future America; thus in A Traveler from Altruria, as Aristides Homos (the best man) makes the mythic journey from Altruria to rural New England, he goes back into a cruel and competitive past. Life in Altruria, the hoped-for utopian future, has certain clear links with the remembered world of the author's boyhood. The Altrurian past is much like Howells's American present; it was filled with industrial greed and strife. Altruria has transcended the Age of Accumulation, however. The moral and economic order of the new world (and it is significant that these are linked in this way) is a kind of Swedenborgian Christian Socialism. It is an idealized pastoral society based not on a new social and economic order, as in Bellamy's utopia, but on a vision of human brotherhood and trust, clearly derived from Howells's internalization of the agrarian myth.[14]

Altruria is an extremely genteel vision of utopia; it is perfectly possible to read this work as a call for a return to the principles of an earlier America.[15] In the author's vision, the eighteenth-century notion of society in harmony with the natural order of the universe is coupled with the nineteenth-century image of Christ the meek and gentle lover. Christianity in Altruria is not sectarian or even particularly theological; the guiding principles of this society are simplicity and trust. The Altrurian Romances embody the paradox of a retreat from the highly complex and competitive society of Howells's era, without the concomittant loss of an industrial standard of living.

The isolation of Altruria, Howells's misunderstanding of the implications of industrialism, and his sympathy for the oppressed farmer are all ideologically consonant with other utopian works from this period. But, also like other utopian novels of the period, *A Traveler from Altruria* is not a very good piece of social engineering. Howells disagrees with Bellamy about the influence of the social order on the individual; *A Traveler from Altruria* is intended to illustrate that no utopian society can come about without a change in the moral basis of human society. Twain would probably agree. Twain disagreed violently, however, with Howells's conclusion that the humane reordering of American culture could be accomplished by political activity. The history of Altruria climaxes with the victory of Christian Socialism at the ballot box. Howells's regard for the traditional apparatus of political change can only be regarded as the literary expression of a wistful hope.

The value of the Altrurian Romances is not as prediction, nor even as social philosophy; the important issue is the conflict between Christian conscience and social decorum. In *A Traveler from Altruria*, Aristides Homos and Mr. Twelvemough, the narrator, are the two sides of the authorial persona. As Howells concludes ironically, "As for the more cultivated people who had met him, they continued of two minds upon both points."[16] This is it precisely—Howells is himself of two minds. One is Christian and humane, his conscience as represented by Homos; the other is petty and middle class, the author of "women's novels," concerned only that he may be embarrassed by this outlandish (literally) stranger. This is of course the liberal dilemma—how to provide social justice without giving up the personal comforts that proceed, ultimately, from the inequalities of the present system.

This specific issue, the confrontation of conscience and comfort, is treated in a slightly different but parallel fashion in Howells's continuation of the story, published in *Cosmopolitan* as "Letters of An Altrurian Traveller," and later as part of *Through the Eye of the Needle.*[17] In this talky series of sermons on the life of rich and poor in New York, Howells comes closer to realism than in those idyllic sections of the novel set in Altruria. The contrast between Homos, the wholly good man, and Eve, the well-bred bourgeoise, is a metaphor for the seductions of idealism. Roemer has outlined the author's dilemma:

[Howells's] desire to convey realistically the reactions of an upper-class woman led him dangerously close to denying that a sudden awareness of the horrors of the present and a vision of a better world could transform the heart. [Eve] is too much of a lady to call Homos a madman, but she does call him a silly "goose" and refuses to go. Homos reacts by first depicting her as a victim of "false conditions" that have "warped" her. Then he realizes that the real reason for her decision is that if she did accept Altruria, she would be "in a manner ceasing to be." She had invested so much of her intellectual and emotional self in an upper-class way of seeing America that to deny this would be an act of self destruction.[18]

The first part of *Through the Eye of the Needle* ends with Eve rejecting Homos and Altruria. The "jump cut" to Altruria at the start of the second part is false to the sense of the work. Just as Twelvemough in *Traveler from Altruria* is a foil for the Stranger, Eve is an idealist who is reluctant to make the commitment to action. She does finally go to Altruria, as Howells never can; one cannot imagine the portly dean of American novelists cavorting in flowing utopian robes in the Christian commonwealth.

Howells's utopian romances are one response of the nineteenth-century bourgeois conscience to the real problems of American life. Their escapist aspects enabled the author to circumscribe his anxieties without really confronting them. In contrast, Howells's friend Twain was unable to create a synthesis that could resolve his moral dilemma. The structural flaws of several of his later works, such as *A Connecticut Yankee* and *Huckleberry Finn*, come largely from this inability, and it may be said that his disturbing speculations prevented the publication of his last major work during his lifetime.

The Mysterious Stranger was published by Harper's in 1916, after the author's death; it is a collection of bits and pieces assembled by Paine and Duneka, the author's literary executors. It was long thought to be the resolution of the Twain canon, the coming together of the raveled strands of his psychological development. Bernard De Voto, for example, felt that in his work Twain was escaping from his personal anguish—the death of his wife and daughter Jean, the bitterness of old age—by assuming the mask of philosophic detachment.[19] The omniscient narrator of the concluding section (published as Chapter XI) sees the world as a shadow play, the symbolic dream of human experience. In fact, the work was never finished. The textual scholarship of John Tuckey,[20] William Gibson,[21] and Sholom J. Kahn[22] has demonstrated that the position of extreme solipsism that marks this chapter was not intended to conclude the version of the tale to be published. The author himself seems to have repudiated this section, in which he denies the phenomenological world; it was probably written in a period of intense despair at the time of his wife's death in Florence in 1904. Certainly, he felt dissatisfied with the version of the story to which this ending properly belongs, for he set it aside not once but twice for alternative attempts. Thus all of the critical analysis of this novel published prior to Tuckey was working with a text that did not represent the author's true intentions. Nevertheless, it is evident that this device (the Mysterious Stranger) was important to the author, because he tried without success to use it in three separate plots. An analysis of this work in terms of the speculative formula suggests some of the functions of the novel. It is here that one must look for a final statement of the great ironist's literary career.

The dominant strain in Twain's fiction in the last decades of his life is ironic; the progressive bitterness that infected *Connecticut Yankee* during the course of its composition is present throughout the Mysterious Stranger manuscripts.[23] This sense of futility and disgust is integral to the author's use of the Mysterious Stranger theme. Only as an outsider, commenting on the human race from a position of detachment, could he come to terms with the real suffering and unhappiness of the last decades of his life. By this time he himself had become something of a stranger in the world.

The "Schoolhouse Hill" version of the tale is the shortest and weakest of the attempts, and the only one set in the remembered past. His clear failure with that portion of the manuscript set in Hannibal illustrates the distance Twain had traveled from his literary beginnings. The agrarian myth, for him the myth of the river and his Missouri boyhood, had provided him the emotional resonance for his best writing. Eseldorf, the Austrian village of the other two versions, was another attempted return to Hannibal, but after fifty years the author could not go home again. He had been too long the traveler and citizen of the world to play the country bumpkin; *Connecticut Yankee* represents his last endeavor in the pastoral mode, and it too is deeply flawed and ambiguous in intent. As the big houses of his later years, Nook Farm and finally Stormfield, became progressively emptier of life, he lost that essential sense of a place to stand that every American novelist seems to need.

Deprived of an American past, Twain turned to Europe. The largest portion of the Mysterious Stranger manuscripts is set in Austria, and as he reworked the story he put it farther and farther back into the Middle Ages. It is as though the author were re-creating the dream-voyage that brought Hank Morgan, the hero of *Connecticut Yankee*, back to an earlier pastoral epoch. Twain was led inescapably back to the device of the Mysterious Stranger who passes through life but is not *of* it.

Like Aristides Homos, Satan (the spirit guide of the manuscripts) is a mysterious visitor from a better world, but in many ways the Twain character is the reverse of Howells's. For Satan (a nephew of the Infernal One) sneers at that "moral sense" that Howells valued as the Christian path. One would like to know what Howells thought of his friend's new novel. There is some indication in *My Mark Twain* that he had heard part of the fragment set in Saint Petersburg (the location of *Tom Sawyer* and *Huckleberry Finn* and the setting of the "Schoolhouse Hill" attempt), but there is nothing in their published correspondence to suggest that Twain ever showed him any more than that. Perhaps his friend realized how horrified Howells would have been by the utter blackness of the tale. Twain's other moral censor, his wife Livy, thought it was "perfectly horrible—and perfectly beautiful!"[24]

In *A Traveler from Altruria* Howells uses Homos and Twelvemough as the two aspects of his dual hero, the author as dreamer. Twain's manuscripts all have this same device. The story is told by an adolescent boy very much like Huck or Tom (or young Sam Clemens, for that matter), while his spirit guide is variously denominated Philip Traum, Little Satan, or #44. It is characteristic of the speculative fiction formula to use a dichotomous hero in this way.

The sources for this convention are diverse. As Arthur O. Lewis suggests in his essay on the utopian hero, in the model for the genre, *Utopia* by Thomas More, the mysterious stranger is Raphael Hythloday, who tells of his voyage to the utopian island. In Bellamy's *Looking Backward*, the guide is Dr. Leete, who explains many of the mysteries of the year 2000 to Julian West. In many of the American utopian works of the period there are spirit guides who tell of the World Beyond to the longing hero, usually in a dream vision.[25] It is important to recognize that *both* the narrator *and* the guide function as the hero of a speculative novel; the tension between the characters reveals the two sides of the author's dilemma. On the one hand he is a man, bound by his culture and by other people's expectations; on the other he is free to travel to the outermost bounds of his imagination in the setting and description of his work.

The dual hero is a literary representation of the author's relationship to his creation; the writer of a work of speculative fiction bears the same relation to his invention as the individual to the culture that nourishes him.[26] There is a significant difference, however. Culture is not created by individuals but by social groups; we are all subject to the patterns and assumptions of our society, but the universe of the dream-voyage is literally created by the dreamer-author. To be thus omnipotent—to control totally the structure of the world—is the emotional power and the reward of the artist's role.

Of course, it is one of the conventions of culture criticism that literary artifacts bear the traces of the culture out of which they come. No one would deny, for example, that all the utopian works of this period reflect the hopes and fears of American society at the end of the nineteenth century. One must also bear in mind, however, that art has a "superorganic" aspect that lifts it above the everyday world into the realm of the universal. (That modern day utopian, Kurt Vonnegut, who is examined in David Hughes's essay, plays with the authorial role by teasing the reader; in his novel *Breakfast of Champions*, characters are introduced and disposed of with a studied disregard for the laws of storytelling.)[27]

In most speculative fiction, though, the author conceals his megalomania behind the cloak of his dream-self, his "doppleganger." Interestingly, there is evidence in the final "Print Shop" version of the "Mysterious Stranger" manuscripts that Sam Clemens had become aware of how much he needed the mask of "Mark Twain." When the human "devils" go out on strike in the print shop, Satan calls up a labor force of "shades" to perform the tasks of their counterparts. The boy hero, Theodor, has a hard time trying to determine which he really is, boy or shade. All traces of this identity crisis are absent from the published version of the tale, where Theodor is the son of a church organist!

The reasons for Twain's executors' choices are sometimes obscure, but it is likely that they were trying to obscure the emotional crisis the author is working through in this story:

> This prophecy [about the Boxer rebellion] was delivered by a fantastic stranger in a romance which, since Mark Twain may in 1900 still have intended to publish it, insulated its author from direct criticism. Probably the most important fact in Mark Twain's life in 1900 was his tentative exploratory removal of his fictional disguise, which he was unable to make in his case. [28]

The evidence is perfectly clear; in this first version of the manuscript the "fantastic stranger's" name is Philip Traum (*dream*, in German). Hamlin Hill is suggesting, in the quote above, that the author used the utopian dream vision form because he was afraid of direct criticism of his political opinions. The real nature of Clemens's personal struggle, of this attempt to throw off the mask of the dreamer, was that conflict between the authorial perspective—the mysterious stranger—and the man himself.

Sam Clemens could not write without Mark Twain, his "mysterious stranger." His attempts to do so motivate his obsession with this device in the last years of his life. The dream vision can be an attempt at escape, a longing for "power," or a metaphor for the authorial condition. For Clemens, in the years after 1900, it was all three.

The dream function of speculative fiction is the attempted transformation of the present; the escape into the past, for Twain and Howells, was a way of dealing with their alienation and frustration resulting from the changes in American society taking place during their lifetimes. These utopian romances are a lament for the lost agrarian myth. The main functional element of speculative fiction is the sense of retreat to an imagined past of safety and simplicity. But Clemens, at least in his final years, had become aware of the shallowness of the hope for America and the whole damned human race. In *A Connecticut Yankee* he satirically contrasted ante-bellum rural America with the new Industrial Age. As he became more distant from his native roots, he became troubled with the problems of dream and reality; of the pious hypocrisy of idealism and progress. His dream had turned to nightmare as he came to confront the inescapable fact that America *had* changed, from an agrarian pastoral society to an urban industrial one.

In their utopian romances of the 1880s and 1890s, the pioneer realists Twain and Howells tried to deal with this transformation metaphorically, to understand it in terms of traditional cultural and psychological values. They cannot be blamed for failing, for they and their contemporaries had set themselves an impossible problem; we are still dealing with the consequences of that failure.

NOTES

1. Kate Wilhelm, *The Infinity Box: A Collection of Speculative Fiction* (New York: Harper & Row, 1975), p. 12:

> Speculative fiction as I define and use it involves the exploration of worlds that probably will never exist, that I don't believe in as real, that I don't expect the reader to accept as real, but that are realistically handled in order to investigate them, because for one reason or another they are the worlds we most dread or yearn for.

2. Henry Nash Smith, *Virgin Land: The American West as Symbol and Myth* (New York: Vintage, 1950), pp. 99–125, and John Cawelti, *The Six-Gun Mystique* (Bowling Green, Ohio: Bowling Green University Popular Press, 1971). See also the dissertations listed in the "Secondary Sources" bibliography in this collection.

3. For a discussion of the "power vision" as a central theme in Native American mysticism, see Weston La Barre, *The Ghost Dance: Origins of Religion* (Garden City, N.Y.: Doubleday, 1970), pp. 43–44. A body of utopian writings such as those by Howells and Twain discussed in this essay can be seen as a kind of national dream vision, a "power quest" for the most deeply rooted cultural myths.

4. In his dissertation and his essay in this collection, Donald C. Burt points out how the utopian novels of the post–Civil War years effected a compromise between "the virtues of the agrarian past and the practical advantages of the industrial present."

5. Robert Plank, "The Geography of Utopia: Psychological Factors Shaping the 'Ideal' Location," *Extrapolation*, 6 (May 1965), 39.

6. Richard Hofstadter, *The Age of Reform: From Bryan to F.D.R.* (New York: Knopf, 1955), pp. 23–36.

7. William Dean Howells, *The Altrurian Romances*, ed. Clara Kirk and Rudolf Kirk, text est. Scott Bennett (Bloomington and London: Indiana University Press,

1968). For most of Twain's novels there are no correct editions; I have used the facsimile edition of the 1889 text, *A Connecticut Yankee in King Arthur's Court*, ed. Hamlin Hill (San Francisco, 1963) and *Mark Twain's Mysterious Stranger Manuscripts*, ed. William Gibson (Berkeley: University of California Press, 1969). Unfortunately, the new CEAA-approved edition (Berkeley: University of California Press) of *Connecticut Yankee* was not available to me before this collection was in press.

8. *Connecticut Yankee*, pp. 56–57.

9. Henry Nash Smith, *Mark Twain's Fable of Progress: Political and Economic Ideas in "A Connecticut Yankee"* (New Brunswick: Rutgers University Press, 1964), pp. 69, 106 ff.

10. Kenneth M. Roemer, *The Obsolete Necessity: America in Utopian Writings, 1888-1900* (Kent, Ohio: Kent State University Press, 1976), p. 6.

11. *Ibid.*, p. 31.

12. William Dean Howells, *A Boy's Town* (New York: Harpers, 1890), p. 2.

13. *Altrurian Romances*, p. 32.

14. Barbara C. Quissell, "The Sentimental and Utopian Novels of Nineteenth Century America: Romance and Social Issues," Ph.D. dissertation, University of Iowa, 1973, points out the links of this form to earlier sentimental romances; see also Donald C. Burt, "Utopia and the Agrarian Tradition in America, 1865–1900," Ph.D. dissertation, University of New Mexico, 1973.

15. See Burt, "Utopia and Agrarian Tradition," for the principles on the agrarian democratic faith.

16. *Altrurian Romances*, p. 179.

17. For an account of the publishing history of this work, see Clara M. Kirk, *W. D. Howells, Traveler from Altruria, 1889-1894* (New Brunswick, N.J.: Rutgers University Press, 1962).

18. Roemer, *Obsolete Necessity*, p. 62.

19. Bernard De Voto, *Mark Twain at Work*, quoted in Hamlin Hill, *Mark Twain: God's Fool* (New York: Harper & Row, 1973), p. 91: "Mark Twain 'saved himself in the end, and came back from the edge of insanity, and found as much peace as any man may find in his last years, and brought his talent into fruition and made it whole again.' "

20. John S. Tuckey, *Mark Twain and Little Satan: The Writing of "The Mysterious Stranger"* (West Lafayette, Ind.: Purdue University Studies, 1963), p. 9.

21. William Gibson, "Introduction," *Mark Twain's Mysterious Stranger Manuscripts* (Berkeley and Los Angeles: University of California Press, 1969), pp. 1–34.

22. Sholom J. Kahn, *Mark Twain's Mysterious Stranger; A Study of the Manuscript Texts* (Columbia: University of Missouri Press, 1978).

23. Howard Baetzhold, "The Course of Composition of *A Connecticut Yankee*: A Reinterpretation," *American Literature*, 33 (May 1961), 195–214.

24. Henry Nash Smith, William D. Gibson, and Frederick Anderson, eds., *Mark Twain–Howells Letters*, Vol. 2 (Cambridge, Mass.: Belknap Press, Harvard University Press, 1960), p. 699.

25. See the discussion of spiritualism in the literature of the period in Howard Kerr, *Mediums, and Spirit-Rappers, and Roaring Radicals* (Urbana: University of Illinois Press, 1972), pp. 108–20.

26. This suggestion is made in Thomas Blues, *Mark Twain and the Community* (Lexington: University of Kentucky Press, 1970), pp. 37–50.

27. Kurt Vonnegut, Jr., *Breakfast of Champions, or, Goodbye Blue Monday* (New York: Delacorte Press, 1973), pp. 292–93:

> I laughed there in the dark, tried to turn on the light again, activated the windshield washer again. "I don't need a gun to control you, Mr. Trout. All I have to do is write down something about you and that's it. . . . I am approaching my fiftieth birthday, Mr. Trout," I said. "I am cleansing and renewing myself for the very different sorts of years to come. Under similar spiritual conditions, Count Tolstoi freed his serfs. Thomas Jefferson freed his slaves. I am going to set at liberty all the literary characters who have served me so loyally during my writing career."

28. Hill, *Mark Twain: God's Fool*, p. 16.

GORMAN BEAUCHAMP

Jack London's Utopian Dystopia and Dystopian Utopia

JACK LONDON, as both man and artist, was an anomaly: a subproletarian autodidact who gained wealth and fame through intellectual pursuits, an enormously popular writer who boldly espoused a most unpopular political philosophy, a revolutionary who owned a vast ranch and a magnificent yacht, a believer in the brotherhood of man who was a racist, a proponent of egalitarianism who admired the powerful individual standing above and dominating the crowd, a preacher of universal peace who was irresistibly drawn to destruction and violence. While he assimilated elements from a variety of intellectual systems—Herbert Spencer's sociology, for instance, and Darwin's evolutionary biology and Freudian psychology—he was hardly a systematic thinker, possessing no single, all-embracing formula for explaining either individual or historical experience. In this respect, as in a great many others, he resembled H. G. Wells, who once professed: "I make up my beliefs as I want them. I do not attempt to distil them out of facts as physicists distil their laws. I make them thus and not thus exactly as an artist makes a picture so and not so."[1]

This epistemological license accounts for the varied array of alternative, even conflicting futures in Wells's fiction: Not bound to extrapolating *one* plausible future out of existing fact, in accord with some "scientific" methodology, he could devise as many futuristic scenarios as his imagination would allow. "A story teller, of course, has the privilege of dreaming up any kind of a universe that fits the exigencies of his tale, nor does he have to believe in the reality of what his imagination has created"[2]—so writes one critic of London, who shared with Wells a fascination with the future. Freed in this sense from fact, London's imagination had free reign to destroy the old world and create new ones on a grand, apocalyptic scale. He neither destroys nor creates, however, in consistent support of any dogma or system—not even the revolutionary Marxism he professed—but only in accord with the conflicting antinomies of his own protean mind and character.

I

London's most noteworthy and sustained fictive future is *The Iron Heel*, published in 1908.[3] In *H. G. Wells: Critic of Progress* Jack Williamson claims that every work depicting the future must take a stand on progress, pro or con; must, that is, show the future as having ameliorated man's condition or worsened it. In this work, however, London has it both ways, for *The Iron Heel* is a dystopian novel set within a utopian frame. This dual perspective on the future is achieved by an unusual narrative device. The memoir of Avis Everhard recounts the events of the early twentieth century (from 1912 to 1932) that led to the triumph in America of a brutal, oligarchic dictatorship, the proto-fascist Iron Heel, and reads much like a prologue to *1984*; but appended to her manuscript are the comments of an editor, writing from the vantage of the twenty-seventh century, after "three centuries of the Iron Heel and four centuries of the Brotherhood of Man" (p. 273).[4] As these comments make clear, the oligarchy's initial triumph could not be sustained, despite the most repressive totalitarian measures, against the inexorable evolution of socialism. The immediate pessimism of the novel is thus superseded by an ultimate optimism, dystopia gives way to utopia—the only utopia, surely, ever to be couched entirely in footnotes.[5]

London's utopia, the shape of which the reader must assemble for himself from the fragments of information scattered through the editorial apparatus and from the vaticinations of the novel's hero, Ernest Everhard, accords with the quotidian nineteenth-century socialist formula for the ideal state. It is, of course, a society without classes and thus without class conflict and, because all nations are united in socialism, without national wars as well; the citizens of this era know of violent bloodshed only by reading the history of the presocialist dark ages (p. 248). A whole array of evils—rent, strikes, thieves, lawyers, lap dogs, Wall Street—must be explicated by the editor, because they no longer exist in the twenty-seventh century. Freed of their taint, London's utopians live lives of sensible simplicity, in magnificent Wellsian mega-cities, consuming synthetic foods and celebrating their cooperative superiority to the criminally competitive past.

But the artist in London, as opposed to the ideologue, was clearly more drawn to the heroic struggle to achieve utopia than to the calm delineation of utopia already achieved. In this regard he resembles the Reverend Barton of Bellamy's *Looking Backward*, who "would fain exchange my share in this serene and golden day for a place in that stormy epoch of transition."[6] Given his penchant for the violent and the cataclysmic, London reverses the usual balance found in utopian fictions, in which the new social order is lengthily detailed, while its birth pangs (if any) are but briefly related. But this reversal of emphasis—from contemplation to action—has its own ideological significance, for it underlines London's dissent from the prevailing opinion of other radicals and reformers concerning the sort of action necessary to bring about the "revolution" in America that they all agreed in desiring.

The critical consensus once held that the vast bulk of American eutopian writing predicated a peaceful change from the bad old world to the brave new one, an enlightened evolution of the sort found in *Looking Backward* or in the Altruria novels of Howells. Recently, however, Kenneth Roemer has shown that this notion of the painless transition is too simplistic: that violent action, or at least the threat of it, accompanied the establishment of a number of utopias, and that the image of a volcano building toward eruption was a commonplace metaphor for the preutopian society.[7] Even so, London's position among his fellow utopists must be unique, not only for the intensity and internecine ferocity of the struggle he depicts in *The Iron Heel*, but even more for his conviction of its absolute historical inevitability. (Unlike London, Ignatius Donnelly, in *Caesar's Column* [1890], protested that it pained him to depict violent class conflicts.) London's is an uncompromising Marxist analysis of American capitalist society, acknowledging and welcoming class struggle as the worker's weapon against his oppressors. Like Marx, London believed that power is never relinquished from above, but must always be wrested from below: Significant systemic reform was thus impossible, peaceful evolution a delusion, the ballot box revolution a hoax. The capitalist class would surrender its power and status only at gunpoint.

The distinction that the Marxists draw between the "utopian" socialism of bourgeois reformers and their own "scientific" sort hinges on just the matter of transition: The steps necessary to effect the socialist society, rather than the structure or content of that society, are the crux that divides them. While the utopian socialists had once played a historically significant role in exposing the evils of capitalism, they had become retrograde, Engels wrote, in persisting in the belief that "socialism is the expression of absolute truth, reason and justice, and had only to be discovered to conquer the world by virtue of its own power."[8] The scientific socialism of Marx had exposed this error by demonstrating the inevitability of class conflict as the dynamic of all historical change—conflict not willed by individual men, and therefore not amenable to conscious choice, but ordained by the materialist dialectic of history. "Since the historical appearance of the capitalist mode of production," Engels continues, "the appropriation by society of all the means of production has been dreamed of . . . by individuals, as well as by sects, as the ideal of the future." But this condition will be brought about "not by men *understanding* that the existence of classes is in contradiction to justice, equality, etc., not by the *mere willingness* to abolish these classes"—not, that is, by the enlightened voluntarism envisioned by bourgeois utopists—"but by virtue of certain new economic forces," namely, the industrial proletariat, whose triumph over its creator-exploiters is decreed by the laws of history.[9]

When Julian West awakes in Bellamy's twenty-first century, he conjectures that the "stupendous changes" that he sees "did not, of course, take place without bloodshed and terrible convulsions." But his host assures him that, "On the contrary, there was absolutely no violence."[10] The Mellons, the Morgans, and, we must assume, the Rockefellers and Harrimans had simply seen the light, dismissed their Pinkertons and congressmen, and enlisted in the Industrial Army along with everyone else. Indeed, such is precisely what happened, *mutatis mutandis*, among Howells's Altrurians. Mr. Homos, the traveler from Altruria, explains that the Accumulation—the clique of monopolists in his mirror-image America—was "simply snowed under" in a great national election:

> The Accumulation had no voters, except the few men at its head, and the creatures devoted to it by interest or ignorance. It seemed, at one moment, as if it would offer an armed resistance to the popular will, but, happily, that moment of madness passed. Our evolution was accomplished without a drop of bloodshed, and the first great political brotherhood, the commonwealth of Altruria was founded.

Were this recitation not heartwarming enough, Howells adds a coda: "But perhaps I shall give a sufficiently clear notion of the triumph of the change among us, when I say that within half a decade after the fall of the old plutocratic oligarchy one of the chief directors of the Accumulation publicly expressed his gratitude to God that the Accumulation had passed away forever."[11]

In *The Iron Heel* London sets out to demolish this myth of the obliging oligarch. Not moral suasion, he wants to show, nor lessons in comparative economics, but superior force would alone suffice to overthrow the capitalist system and institute the era of socialist brotherhood. This is the challenge that Ernest casts down to the Philomaths, the elite assembly of San Francisco's ruling class. The electoral strength of the socialists, he proclaims, is growing year by year, so that soon they will command a majority. But, one of the Philomaths demands, "What if you get a majority, a sweeping majority, on election day? Suppose we refuse to turn the government over to you after you have captured it at the ballot box?" The question proves prophetic—London's are no paper plutocrats—but so does Ernest's answer, a Marxist scenario for the second American revolution:

> . . . we shall give you an answer in terms of lead. Power, you have proclaimed the king of words. Very good. Power it shall be. And in the day that we sweep to victory at the ballot-box and you refuse to turn over the government that we have constitutionally and peacefully captured, and you demand what we are going to do about it—in that day, I say, we shall answer you; in the roar of shell and shrapnel and in the whine of machine-guns our answer shall be couched.

You cannot escape us. It is true that you have read history aright. . . . Power will be the arbiter, as it has always been the arbiter. It is a struggle of classes. Just as your class dragged down the old feudal nobility, so shall it be dragged down by my class, the working class. . . . It does not matter whether it be one year, ten, or a thousand—your class shall be dragged down. And it shall be done by power. [pp. 98–99]

While the capitalists of London's novel accept the inevitability of the class struggle, the truth escapes Ernest's fellow socialists, who, in typical menshevik fashion, "still insisted that victory could be gained through elections. . . . Ernest could not get them seriously to fear the coming of the Oligarchy. . . . There was no room in their theoretical revolution for an oligarchy, therefore the Oligarchy could not be" (p. 175). London's point, of course, formed in part from reading W. J. Ghent's *Our Benevolent Feudalism*, was that the Oligarchy *could* be and the latter half of his novel chronicles how it came to be: how, under the pressure of challenge to its continued dominance, the capitalist class forged itself into a para-military, rigidly disciplined party, the Iron Heel.

In his prediction of the resiliency of capitalism, of its ability to adopt the counterrevolutionary measures necessary to forestall its fall from power, London contributed a novel stage to the class struggle that had not been anticipated, and was greeted derisively by his fellow socialists of all stripes. He imagined, that is, fascism. In 1937, having just read *The Iron Heel* for the first time as the fascist tide was flowing in Europe, Trotsky expressed his admiration for "the audacity and independence of its historical foresight" and found the novel's " 'romantic' hyperboles . . . much more realistic than the bookkeeperlike calculations of the so-called sober politicians" who had dismissed London's efforts "to force them to open their eyes and see . . . what approaches."

It is easy to imagine [Trotsky continues] with what a condescending perplexity the official socialist thinking of the time met with Jack London's menacing prophecies. [Yet he] saw incomparably more clearly and farther than all the social democratic leaders of the time taken together. But Jack London bears comparison in this domain not only with the reformists. One can say with assurance that in 1907 not one of the revolutionary Marxists, not excluding Lenin and Rosa Luxemburg, imagined so fully the ominous perspective of the alliance between finance capitalism and labor aristocracy. . . . In reading it one does not believe his own eyes: it is precisely the picture of fascism, of its economy, of its governmental technique, its political psychology![12]

History was following, all too faithfully, London's art.

What London envisioned was the multitude of coercive and co-optive strategies that a determined ruling class could employ to retain its power, even in the face of overwhelming popular opposition. At the outset of the struggle in *The Iron Heel* not only are the army and police the private instruments of the capitalists, but this class also exercises control over the churches, the universities, and the press, systematically eliminating any elements that oppose their oppression. Furthermore, as all means of communication are in capitalist hands, the only news the people receive is the news their exploiters want them to receive. And as the loose association of plutocrats develops into a tightly unified oligarchy, their controls become even more totalitarian. The property-owning middle class is obliterated. More important, the laboring class is divided against itself, with the "aristocracy" of skilled workers in the central industries segregated in special cities and well provided for: "They had better food to eat, less hours of labor, more holidays, and a greater amount and variety of interests and pleasures. And for their less fortunate brothers and sisters, the unfavored labor, the driven people of the abyss, they cared nothing" (p. 298). The regular citizen army is dissolved, replaced by the Mercenaries, "a race apart," with "their own class morality and consciousness" (p. 298), who feel no compunction at leveling whole cities or slaughtering whole populations, as their Guernica-like destruction of Chicago demonstrates.[13]

Indeed, it is in this climactic, cataclysmic episode, awhirl with chaos and carnage, that London's writing becomes most vividly energized; and herein lies the paradox that disturbs many readers of *The Iron Heel*: Its destructive, dystopian impact is rendered with such dramatic force that its ultimate utopian promise seems compromised. True, even the brutal, devastating repression of the proletarian uprising appears to Avis Everhard as only a temporary check in the inevitable progress toward socialism: "The Cause for this one time was lost, but the Cause would be there to-morrow, the same Cause, ever fresh and ever burning" (p. 327). But London's programmatic pronouncements discord disturbingly with his dramatic realities. Though he claims that the capitalists are "doomed to perish as all atavisms perish," still, within the novel, as David Ketterer remarks, "the socialists do most of the perishing." In fact, Ketterer continues, the "critical reader . . . being unable to accept the reality of London's socialist utopia, can only conceive of a reality in which the dystopian situation continues indefinitely."[14]

In other words, London's imaginative commitment to the dystopian destructiveness in *The Iron Heel* is greater and carries more conviction than does his ideological commitment to the distant utopian resolution of this suffering: The artist is at odds with the ideologue. His creative imagination, as Walter Rideout has noted, "always functioned increasingly well the more it was able to disintegrate the fabric of social life or the civilized responses of the individual personality, reducing that life, that personality to its simplest level, a condition of complete violence."[15] Thus, for instance, the detailed, almost psychopathic, power with which he projects the apocalypse in such tales as *The Scarlet Plague* or "The Unparalleled Invasion." London himself seems to have realized as much, at least obliquely, when he confessed "gleefully" to a friend about the scenes of mass destruction in "Goliah": "Oh, I haven't a bit of conscience when my imagination gets to working."[16] In *The Iron Heel* this conscienceless imagination triumphs *dramatically* over his conscious socialist schema, unsettling the dialectical balance between utopia and dystopia that the novel's dualistic structure seeks to establish. Even London's prescience here in adumbrating fascism, with its unparalleled will to destruction, seems to have stemmed not so much from any profound analysis on his part as from a similar impulse within himself, an imaginative penchant for the cataclysmic that fascism reified historically. Indeed, he seems to have been attracted to Marxism more for its celebration of conflict as the essence of history, for its promised destruction of a hated social order, than for its esoteric economics or abstruse sociology.[17]

And yet, when all this is said, to set London down as an unwitting partisan of the devil's party will, finally, not do. While his artistic proclivity for violent, destructive action undercuts to some degree his projection of a world at last serene in its socialism, calm of mind and all its passion spent, it does not negate that ideal. His professed intent—which even in the aftermath of the New Criticism must still count for something—is manifest: to offer a glimmering vision of the distant millennium, discernible through even the darkest, most degraded epoch of human experience. The verses he affixes as an epigraph to *The Iron Heel* indicate, in brief, both the message of his novel and his strategy for conveying it:

> At first, this Earth, a stage so gloomed with woe
> You almost sicken at the shifting scene.
> And yet be patient. Our Playwright may show
> In some fifth act what this Wild Drama means.

London offers us his "four acts" of sickening violence and woe, but his fifth act—those footnotes—redeems his wild drama from hopeless dystopianism; his Marxist teleology posits a utopian denouement for history's anfractuous drama, thus making his sociomachy an apocalypse in the fullest sense: "the fulfillment of the apocalyptic imagination demands that the destructive chaos give way finally to a new order."[18]

In this sense, then, *The Iron Heel* is an optimistic book, free of the unrelieved pessimism that permeates, for instance, that quintessential dystopia, Orwell's *1984*, a pessimism epitomized in O'Brien's claim, "If you want a picture of the future, imagine a boot stamping on a human face—forever."[19] London's oligarchs make a similar claim for their own omnipotence: "We will grind you revolutionists down under our heel, and we shall walk upon your faces" (p. 97). But the historical perspective in which London frames the action of his novel is meant to convert this boast into irony, a resolution utterly different from Orwell's nightmare of endless evil. If, then, *The Iron Heel* is a dystopia, it is the most utopian of dystopias.

II

In the same year that London was writing *The Iron Heel*, he published a tale of utopian science fiction, "Goliah."[20] Goliah is the pseudonym taken by a secretive scientific genius, one Percival Stultz, who, through the discovery and ruthless application of a mysterious power source called Energon, topples kings and capitalists to bring universal socialism to a stunned but grateful world. As literature the tale is nugatory; philosophically it is jejune; but juxtaposed to *The Iron Heel*, it casts a revealing light on the heterodox nature of London's utopian speculation—and, indeed, on utopianism generally.

If all the works in a writer's canon can be assigned equal ideational weight, then "Goliah" in Jack London's demands that we rethink the sort of seriousness accorded *The Iron Heel* as social prophecy, in that the pseudo-historical dialectic of that novel, however much affirmed or denied by actual historical events, becomes but one more *imaginative* entree into utopia, with no more contextual cogency as an explanation for the arrival of the millennium than Energon. In other words, the artist, as I noted at the outset, imagines the future rather than extrapolating it; and thus all his futures have equal validity *as fictions*, whatever their incidental vatic merits. With the artist's epistemological license, then, London provides alternative paths into the fictively ideal world of the future: here by Marxist dialectic, there by Wellsian fantasy. To claim this sort of parity for a fantastic work like "Goliah" need not imply that London was frivolous in his stance as a socialist, but rather to insist that his was the socialism of a fabulist and not that of a "scientist."

The crux for utopists, as we have seen, is the question of transition from the bad old world to the brave new one. For those like Bellamy and Howells, utopia evolves, peacefully, out of the unsustainable contradictions of the capitalist order; for London in *The Iron Heel*, as for William Morris in *News from Nowhere*, it results from violent revolution against that order by its own creation—the proletariat. In "Goliah," however, utopia is simply imposed from outside the existing order, by one mastermind and a miracle. The single-founder device is, in fact, the most venerable imaginative technique for establishing utopia; Plato's king-who-has-become-a-philosopher (or vice versa) and Plutarch's Lycurgus, More's Utopus, and Bacon's Solamona exemplify this tradition. To such utopists, according to J. B. Bury, it never occurred "that a perfect order might be attained by a long series of changes and adaptations. Such an order, being the embodiment of reason, could be created only by a deliberate and immediate act of a planning mind. . . . Hence the salvation of a community must lie in preserving intact . . . the institutions imposed by the enlightened lawgiver."[21] Goliah functions as such an "enlightened lawgiver," despite some spurious concessions to participatory democracy, and "Goliah," in this respect, represents a throwback to an earlier stage of utopian thinking, one seemingly outmoded by the nineteenth century's passionate faith in Progress.

That very faith in Progress, however, would seem to be embodied in London's reliance on a scientific innovation as Goliah's means of realizing utopia; but like most of the "science" of science fiction, Energon is really magic-*manqué*, a miracle posing as technology. And once miracles are allowed, the problem of transition, of course, disappears. The miraculous conversion has always been the easiest—even, at times, the only possible—explanation for the genesis of utopia. More's Utopia, A. L. Morton claims, "*had to be* a miracle. . . . [H]e would have been more than human to see at that time the historical process by which socialism could be realized."[22] The disjunction Morton makes here between history and miracle—a reflection of his own Marxist faith in the former's ability to achieve the latter—separates those utopists who seek to ground their fictions in some evolutionary development out of the actual conditions obtaining at the time from those who simply obviate existing conditions by fiat: the essential demarcation, perhaps, between social-science fiction and science fiction. *Looking Backward, News from Nowhere*, and *The Iron Heel*, for all their other differences, claim an evolutionary-historical justification for the futures they envision;[23] "Goliah," however, can claim only Energon. Like *Vril* in Bulwer-Lytton's *The Coming Race* or *Rial* in Martin Atlas's *Die Befreiung*, those analogous mystery sources of energy, or the green gas in Wells's *In The Days of the Comet*, Energon does all the work of the dialectic, quickly and efficiently.

The new order that Goliah creates wielding Energon differs little, if at all, from the socialist millennium forecast in *The Iron Heel*, except that it is more specifically detailed. The means of production and distribution are "nationalized"—even though the nation-states give way to an international government; the labor of women and children is abolished; and "all the splendid force of the men who had previously worked for themselves was now put to work for the good of society."

With this rational organization of society amazing results were brought about. The national day's work was eight hours, and yet production increased. In spite of the great permanent improvements and of the immense amount of energy consumed in systematizing the competitive chaos of society, production doubled and tripled upon itself. The standard of living increased, and still consumption could not keep up with production. [p. 100]

Crime, primarily economic in origin, virtually ceases. "The courts became shadows, attenuated ghosts, rudimentary vestiges of the anarchistic times that had preceded the coming of Goliah" (p. 107). "Kings and emperors, with fear in their hearts . . . abdicate[d] thrones and crowns," and all nations, threatened with Energonian annihilation if they resisted, beat their swords into plowshares and studied war no more. Yet, for all the orthodoxy of the content of London's brave new world, socialists would have to pronounce it heretical, for the new order arises not out of the class action of the proletariat but through the agency of a philanthropic superman: a gift rather than a victory.

London's attraction to the superman has, of course, proved a source of embarassment for those who want to make of his maverick socialism something consistent and theoretically sound. Ernest Everhard—huge, dauntless, *echt* Nordic—is struck from London's supermanly mold, but he at least acts as a proletarian among proletarians: *primus inter pares*, to be sure, but not *sui generis*. Goliah, by contrast, is simply the greatest man the world has ever known, "a superman, a scientific superman," alongside whose achievements "the deeds of Alexander, Caesar, Genghis Khan and Napoleon were as the play of babes" (p. 113). Physically unprepossessing—indeed on his first appearance before an awed world, he proves to be short, fat, balding, and afraid of cats—Goliah is the purely intellectual hero, the egghead as *Ubermensch*. Whether by brain or by brawn, however, the man marked off from his fellows as clearly superior, as one of nature's elite, ill accords with the ideal of egalitarian brotherhood preached in the socialist gospels. Imaginatively, London could never distribute the dynamic power and force of will he so admired among a whole class of people, as his political faith ought to have dictated, but had to delegate them to a single, exceptional individual. In *The Iron Heel* the exceptional man and the mass movement are balanced, albeit precariously, but in "Goliah" that balance has collapsed completely, replaced by a cult of personality.

More disturbing to more readers, however, than London's recourse to the superman motif will be this particular superman's reliance on death and destruction as means for guaranteeing the good life. As an apocalyptic tale, "Goliah," like *The Iron Heel*, generates the new order out of the death throes of the old; but unlike the sociomachy of that novel, in which the role of destroyer is assigned to evil capitalists and that of creator to good socialists, the drama of Goliah casts him in both roles, destroyer and creator. In the abstract, such a schema may be plausible enough, but London's specific realization of it is more than a little grotesque, chilling in its implications, as frightening, in its way, as any dystopia. Indeed, as I want now to argue, "Goliah" presents for our approbation the very philosophy, with its attendant *modus operandi*, that dystopians have attacked with savage irony or horrific warnings.

In brief, this philosophy holds that one man or group of men has exclusive access to final Truth; thus they, and they alone, can determine the ends of life and the proper means for achieving them. Because Truth is a priori, questioning of ends and means is precluded: Whatever is done to reify Truth is right. Perhaps one sentence from H. G. Wells's *Men like Gods* sums up this position: "The age of economic disputes and experiments had come to an end; the right way to do things had been found."[24] From Plato's philosopher kings to B. F. Skinner's behavioral engineers, the guardian class justifies its measures, however extreme, on the basis of its apodictic knowledge, whether that knowledge be the gift of the philosophic dialectic or "the scientific method."

Goliah is London's guardian, a self-appointed majority of one, blithely certain that he alone can determine the destiny of all men for all time. This he declares quite candidly: "I have decided to step in and become captain of this world-ship for a while. I have the intelligence and wide vision of the skilled expert. Also, I have the power. I shall be obeyed. The men of all the world shall perform my bidding and make governments so that they shall become laughter-producers" (p. 75). Goliah is big on laughter, which he appoints the true end of social life, and will kill as many people as it takes to keep the survivors laughing. Consider his telegram to the political leaders of the United States:

> It is my wish and my will that you confer with me . . . in the matter of reconstructing society upon some rational basis. Do not misunderstand me when I tell you that I am one with a theory. I want to see that theory work, and I therefore call upon your cooperation. In this theory of mine, lives are but pawns; I deal with quantities of lives. I am after laughter, and those that stand in the way of laughter must perish. The game is big. There are fifteen hundred million human lives today on the planet. What is your single life against them? It is naught, in my theory. And remember that mine is the power. Remember that I am a scientist, and that one life, or one million of lives, means nothing to me as arrayed against the countless billions of billions of lives of the generations to come. It is for their laughter that I seek to reconstruct society now; and against them your own meager little life is a paltry thing indeed. [p. 80]

The politicians—sensibly enough—treat the summons as the raving of a crackpot and so are killed: the first of many. "When Goliah spoke to politicians (so-called 'statesmen'), they obeyed . . . or died" (p. 108).

Now, one need hold no particular brief for the world's politicians or for the social orders they uphold, to be appalled at Goliah's draconic means of dealing with them. But London reveals thereby, though admittedly to an unusually sanguine degree, the utopist's usual phobia of politics—of the necessity, that is, to accommodate, compromise, and persuade rather than to command *ex cathedra*. Politics involve, of course, conflict, and the utopist seeks to rid the world of conflict once and for all, to decide finally the ultimate questions that divide men, and then to maintain inviolable the social order that embodies Truth. The ideal, as Howells's Altrurian puts it, is "an order so just that it cannot be disturbed."[25] But such an ideal begs the very question of justice, establishing by dictum what must be determined by discussion. By exalting the conflict-free society, utopists tend, imaginatively at least, toward totalitarianism. "A free and open society is an ongoing conflict," argues Saul Alinsky, "interrupted periodically by compromises—which then become the start for the continuation of conflict, compromise, and on ad infinitum. . . . A society devoid of compromise is totalitarian."[26] But compare this affirmation with the claim made by Bellamy's Dr. Leete to Julian West: "The fundamental principles on which our society is founded settle *for all time* the strife and misunderstandings which in your day called for legislation."[27] Because the ultimate questions have all been answered, no politics is possible, and politicians are, of course, superfluous: All Bellamy's trappings of democracy really serve only to select the ablest technicians to oversee the smooth running of the social mechanism, never to alter the mechanism itself.[28] The laws of Bensalem, Bacon tells us in the *New Atlantis*, were established by King Solamona 1,900 years ago and not one has been changed since, an arrangement every utopist seems to want to emulate.

London differs from his fellow utopists, however, in the candor with which he sanctions coercive measures—murder when necessary—as a means to utopia, making explicit the covert threat of force that underlies the insistence on total harmony. His politicians do not see the light so much as they are shown the sword poised over their heads. Nor are they Goliah's only victims in his campaign for joy: "Here and there, it is true, there were atavisms, men who yearned for the fleshpots and cannibal feasts of the old alleged 'individualism' . . . ; but they were looked upon as diseased, and were treated in hospitals. A small remnant, however, proved incurable, and were confined to asylums and denied marriage" (p. 111). From these ranks, no doubt, would emerge the protagonists of the dystopias—the D-503's, the Helmholtz Watsons and the Winston Smiths; for the dystopian hero is always an atavism in eutopia, seeking to escape its enforced perfection.[29] And Goliah, too, is prototypical of the know-it-all dictators of the dystopias—the Well Doer, the World Controller, Big Brother—who crush the protests of proponents of "the old alleged 'individualism.' "

For the dystopist, the lessons of history preclude accepting Goliah's intentions at his own valuation; rather, they contend, unquestioning "virtue" fused with unrestrained power tends inevitably toward inquisitorial despotism. "Robespierre believed in virtue," Anatole France reminds us, "he produced the Reign of Terror; Marat believed in justice, he demanded two hundred thousand heads."[30] And, of a later millenarian experiment, Andrei Siniavski sadly concludes: "So that not one drop of blood be shed any more, we killed and killed and killed."[31] The evidence of the last two centuries, dominated by what Shaw once called "the new Catholicisms"—political movements certain that they alone are possessed of ultimate Truth and willing to sacrifice countless lives to manifest it on earth—renders London's faith in his scientist on horseback historically suspect, politically pernicious. The road to hell, we have learned, can be paved with utopian intentions.

London does attempt to mitigate Goliah's absolutism by presenting it as merely a ground-clearing, a dictatorial prelude to greater self-government than the world has ever known. Thus:

> With the exception to putting a stop to war, and of indicating the broad general plan, Goliah did nothing. By putting the fear of death into the hearts of those who sat in the high places and obstructed progress, Goliah made the opportunity for the unshackled intelligence of the best social thinkers of the world to exert itself. Goliah left all the multitudinous details of reconstruction to these social thinkers. He wanted them to prove that they were able to do it, and they proved it. [p. 108]

This strategy offers a sop, of sorts, to the modern faith in the right of people to determine their own social destiny; but that faith is highly attenuated and the strategy clearly a sleight of hand. To understand that, one has only to ask what Goliah's response would have been had all that assembled "unshackled intelligence"—selected, of course, by him—come up with some policy that contravened his "broad general plan." Knowing in advance what conclusions he would allow, Goliah tolerantly encourages the world to play out its charade of deciding—rather like those spurious Socratic dialogues endemic in American classrooms in which the instructor allows students to discover for themselves his answers to the questions. The reality of Goliah's relationship to the new order he permits others to establish is, in any case, best summed up in a single sentence: " 'Goliah has spoken' . . . was another way of saying, 'He must be obeyed' " (p. 98).

Utopian fictions are usually most effective as critiques of the irrational, unjust social order extant at the time; they usually falter, however, when they offer, in any great detail, an ideal new order to replace the condemned old one. In fact, the more concrete and complete the detail, the more the reader is inclined to cavil, to question, to dissent. An inverse ratio seems to exist between the concreteness of a utopia and the assent it can command. The distant eutopian vision that frames *The Iron Heel* commands the reader's assent partly because the dramatic action depicting the preutopian society is so horrifying, so morally outrageous, but partly also because the vision *is* distant and remains vague enough in its outline to be untroubling. When the vision becomes immediate and detailed, as in "Goliah," the reader becomes conscious of some sinister implications.

It is no new discovery that one man's utopia will be another's dystopia: Perhaps the only really significant difference between *Walden Two*, for example, and *Brave New World* is each author's attitude toward his creation. Readers, however, "if forced to make a choice," as one critic remarks, might "find some aspects of Huxley's model preferable to Skinner's."[32] In fact, *Walden Two* was originally widely mistaken for a parody of utopia rather than an affirmation of it. Similarly, readers would, I think, despite London's intent to provide a utopian future in "Goliah," an image of the socialist millennium, find his tale more frightening than promising. Perhaps, to some degree, this affect holds true for all such projections of "perfection": Even of Sir Thomas More's *Utopia*, utterly benevolent in its intent, a sympathetic commentator is forced to ask, "Has any State, at any time, carried terrorism quite so far?"[33] Indeed, Lewis Mumford concludes: "In the end, utopia merges with dystopia . . . and one suddenly realizes that the distance between the positive ideal and the negative one was never so great as the advocates or admirers of utopia had professed."[34] If this is so—and I think it is—still the realization comes more slowly and with greater regret about some works than about others: about *Utopia* and *Looking Backward*, for instance, which embody so many of man's noblest feelings and highest aspirations. "Goliah," by contrast, forces this realization quickly and almost painlessly, so heavy-handed is its exposure of the darker side of paradise. Few dystopias can have managed to cast as much doubt on the wisdom of utopianizing as London has in this dreary little fable. Reading it, one wants to echo (allowing for some exaggeration) Max Beerbohm's wry refrain:

> So this is Utopia,
> Is it? Well—
> I beg your pardon;
> I thought it was Hell.

NOTES

1. H. G. Wells, *First and Last Things*, rev. ed. (London: Cassell, 1917), pp. 38–39.

2. Conway Zirkle, *Evolution, Marxian Biology and the Social Scene* (Philadelphia: University of Pennsylvania Press, 1959), p. 321.

3. Much of my commentary on *The Iron Heel* is drawn from my earlier essay, "*The Iron Heel* and *Looking Backward*: Two Paths to Utopia," *American Literary Realism*, 9 (Fall 1976), 307–14.

4. Jack London, *The Iron Heel* (New York: Macmillan, 1908). Page references are included parenthetically in the text.

A recent study by Nathaniel Teich, "Marxist Dialectics in Content, Form, Point of View: Structures in Jack London's *The Iron Heel*," *Modern Fiction Studies*, 22 (Spring 1976), 85–99, elaborates, sometimes overingeniously, on the ideological significance of this structure: "Avis' uncompleted 20th-century MS is the body of the text to which the footnotes are added by the annotator 700 years later. These two technical points of view are juxtaposed in our reading. The way they inform each other produces the cumulative effects and meaning of the novel" (p. 91). Nadia Khouri, in another recent study—"Utopia and Epic: Ideological Confrontation in Jack London's *The Iron Heel*," *Science-Fiction Studies*, 3 (July 1976), 174–81—stresses the effect London achieves with his mixing of two genres, the dynamic heroic epic as tempered by the static descriptive utopia: "by yoking ideological and generic tensions together and by conducting them towards a dialectic resolution, *The Iron Heel* significantly expresses the tensions of its own historical reality, and also ushers in . . . utopias that (both conceptually and narratively) do not in fact have to be static" (p. 175).

5. *The Iron Heel* is not treated in standard studies of utopian fiction: There is no reference to it, for instance, in Vernon L. Parrington's encyclopedic *American Dreams: A Study of American Utopias* (New York: Russell & Russell, 1964). The exception is a brief mention by the Marxist critic A. L. Morton in *The English Utopia* (London: Lawrence & Wishart, 1952). The most perceptive comment on *The Iron Heel*'s place among American utopian fiction is that of Jay Martin, *Harvests of Change: American Literature 1865-1914* (Englewood Cliffs, N.J.: Prentice-Hall, 1967), pp. 234–39.

6. *Looking Backward, 2000-1887*, ed. John L. Thomas (Cambridge, Mass.: Belknap Press of Harvard University Press, 1967), p. 281.

7. Kenneth Roemer, *The Obsolete Necessity: America in Utopian Writings, 1888-1900* (Kent, Ohio: Kent State University Press, 1976), pp. 20–24.

8. Friedrich Engels, *Socialism: Utopian and Scientific*, trans. Edward Aveling (New York: International Publishers, 1968), p. 43. While for Marx and Engels "utopian" was a term of opprobrium when applied to other brands of socialism, their own was certainly utopian in the sense of positing a new Golden Age at the end of dialectical history. See, for example, Martin Buber, *Paths in Utopia*, trans. R. F. C. Hull (Boston: Beacon Press, 1958), pp. 7–15; Fred Polak, *The Image of the Future*, trans. Elise Boulding (Amsterdam: Elsevier, 1973), pp. 117–24; Jerome M. Gilison, *The Soviet Image of Utopia* (Baltimore: Johns Hopkins University Press, 1975), pp. 23–52; and Martin G. Kalin, *The Utopian Flight from Unhappiness: Freud Against Marx on Social Progress* (Chicago: Nelson-Hall, 1974), pp. 13–108. For two recent studies of the utopian component in Marxism, see Pavel Kovaly, "Marxism and Utopia," in Peyton E. Richter, ed., *Utopia/Dystopia* (Cambridge, Mass.: Schenkman, 1975), pp. 75–92, and Gorman Beauchamp, "Alienation and Utopia: Marx, Morris and the Machine," *Science/Technology and the Humanities*, 1 (Spring 1978), 145–58.

9. Engels, *Socialism, Utopian and Scientific*, p. 70 (emphasis added).

10. Edward Bellamy, *Looking Backward*, p. 127.

11. William Dean Howells, *A Traveler from Altruria* (New York: Hill & Wang, 1957), p. 181.

12. *Leon Trotsky on Literature and Art*, ed. Paul Siegel (New York: Pathfinder Press, 1970), pp. 221–24. For critical reaction to *The Iron Heel*, see Philip Foner, *Jack London: American Rebel* (New York: Citadel Press, 1947), pp. 95–97; Richard O'Connor, *Jack London: A Biography* (Boston: Little, Brown, 1964), pp. 249–50; and Francis Lacassin, "A Classic of Revolt," *Jack London Newsletter*, 6 (May–August 1973), 76–77.

13. London's Battle of Chicago is clearly indebted to similar scenes in H. G. Wells's *When the Sleeper Wakes* (1899). Indeed, it seems likely that London's idea for the rise of the Iron Heel may owe something to the argument of Wells's own oligarch, Ostrog, that an elite minority has the right to exploit the rest of mankind for its benefit.

14. David Ketterer, *New Worlds for Old: The Apocalyptic Imagination, Science Fiction and American Literature* (Garden City, N.Y.: Anchor, 1974), pp. 130, 132. Or again: "Clearly, whatever hopes London may have entertained of a utopia, he could only describe the preceding dystopia" (p. 127).

15. Walter Rideout, *The Radical Novel in the United States, 1900–1954* (Cambridge, Mass.: Harvard University Press, 1956), p. 45.

16. Martin Johnson, *Through the South Seas with Jack London* (1913), quoted in Dale L. Walker, ed., *Curious Fragments: Jack London's Tales of Fantasy Fiction* (Port Washington, N.Y.: Kennikat Press, 1975), p. 87.

17. It seems to be generally conceded that London was poorly read in the primary literature of Marxism. Joan London, in *Jack London and His Times* (New York: Doubleday, 1939), p. 209, states that "Marx, save for *The Communist Manifesto*, went by the board," there being no evidence "to indicate that Jack studied even the one volume" of *Capital* available in English in 1906. Thus his Marxist ideas were mostly acquired from journalistic, and presumably somewhat simplified, redactions. See Sam S. Baskett, "A Source for *The Iron Heel*," *American Literature*, 27 (May 1955), 268–70.

18. Ketterer, *New Worlds for Old*, p. 14.

19. George Orwell, *1984* (New York: Signet Classics, 1961), p. 220.

20. Jack London, *Revolution and Other Essays* (New York: Macmillan, 1910). Page references are included parenthetically in the text.

21. J. B. Bury, *The Idea of Progress* (1922; reprint, New York: Dover Books, 1955), p. 11. Bury is referring specifically to the Greeks, but his conclusion holds for most utopists before the late eighteenth century. The distinction between the "classical" and the modern utopia has been examined in the greatest detail by Elisabeth Hansot, *Perfection and Progress: Two Modes of Utopian Thought* (Cambridge, Mass.: MIT Press, 1974). I cannot, however, subscribe to a great many of her conclusions.

22. Morton, *The English Utopia*, (note 5 above), p. 68.

23. Cf. Bellamy's comment: "*Looking Backward*, although in form a fanciful romance, is intended, in all seriousness, as a forecast, in accordance with the principles of evolution, of the next stage in the industrial and social development of

humanity." From a letter to the Boston *Transcript* (1888), printed as a postscript to the Signet Classics edition of *Looking Backward* (New York, 1960), p. 222.

24. H. G. Wells, *Men Like Gods* (New York: Macmillan, 1923), p. 170. See Gorman Beauchamp, "Utopia and Its Discontents," *Midwest Quarterly*, 16 (Winter 1975), 163–66.

25. Howells, *Traveler from Altruria* (note 11 above), p. 151.

26. Saul Alinsky, *Rules for Radicals* (New York: Random House, 1971), p. 59. For this view as it is related to utopias, see Karl Popper, "Utopia and Violence," *Hibbert Journal*, 46 (1948), 109–16, and Ralf Dahrendorf, "In Praise of Thrasymachus," in *Essays in the Theory of Society* (Stanford, Calif.: Stanford University Press, 1968), pp. 129–50. London's disgust with politics is evident in a passage such as this one from "These Bones Shall Rise Again," in *Revolution*, p. 220, where he speaks of "the unstable, mob-minded mass, which sits on the fence, ever ready to fall this side or that and indecorously clamber back again; which puts a Democratic administration into office one election, and a Republican the next; which discovers and lifts up a prophet to-day that it may stone him tomorrow."

27. Bellamy, *Looking Backward*, p. 230. Italics added.

28. Cf. Sir Isaiah Berlin, *Four Essays on Liberty* (New York: Oxford University Press, 1969), p. 118: "Where ends are agreed, the only questions left are those of means, and these are not political but technical, that is to say, capable of being settled by experts or machines like arguments between engineers or doctors. That is why those who put their faith in some immense, world-transforming phenomenon, like the final triumph of reason or the proletarian revolution, must believe that all political and moral problems can thereby be turned into technological ones."

29. I have dealt with these dystopian rebels in "Of Man's Last Disobedience: Zamiatin's *We* and Orwell's *1984*," *Comparative Literature Studies*, 10 (December 1973), 285–301, and in "Cultural Primitivism as Norm in the Dystopian Novel," *Extrapolation*, 19 (December 1977), 88–96.

30. Anatole France, *Les Dieux ont soif* (1912), quoted in Liam Brophy, "Grave New Worlds," *Catholic World*, 17 (April 1954), 41.

31. Abram Tertz (pseud.), *On Socialist Realism* (New York: Vintage Books, 1965), p. 162. Though he exaggerates somewhat, Joseph Wood Krutch is probably right when he claims that "the determination to settle for nothing less than perfection has been at least as much a curse as a blessing. Without utopian thinking neither Nazi Germany nor Communism could ever have come into existence." Joseph Wood Krutch, "Danger: Utopia Ahead," *Saturday Review*, August 20, 1966, p. 18.

32. Gilison, *The Soviet Image of Utopia* (note 8 above), p. 33.

33. R. W. Chambers, *Thomas More* (1935; reprint, Ann Arbor: University of Michigan Press, 1958), p. 137.

34. Lewis Mumford, "Utopia, the City and the Machine," in Frank E. Manuel, ed., *Utopias and Utopian Thought* (Boston: Beacon Press, 1967), p. 9.

DAVID Y. HUGHES

The Ghost in the Machine: The Theme of Player Piano

KURT VONNEGUT'S ILIUM, U.S.A., exhibits the familiar topography of a twentieth-century dystopia. "As usual," writes Mark Hillegas, summarizing the situation,

> [*Player Piano*] society is a pyramid topped by an elite, with the great mass of people faceless and nameless—the line of descent runs direct from the blue-clad workers [of Wells's *When the Sleeper Wakes*] through Huxley's Gammas, Deltas, and Epsilons to Orwell's Proles. As usual the elite rules with the help of a strong police force, who employ the latest, most efficient means of surveillance. . . . And as usual [it is] a machine civilization, one in which machines are replacing men. The only difference between Vonnegut's nightmare and its ancestors is that Vonnegut's seems closer to coming reality as we may come to know it.[1]

This is a useful inventory of basic dystopian features. The reason Hillegas put it together was to establish a dystopian pedigree from Wells to all later practitioners, including Vonnegut. While I welcome the inventory, I disagree that Vonnegut belongs in this line of descent. For one thing, at mid-twentieth century Vonnegut was both young and an American; furthermore, and more important, the bondage of Ilium is not dictated by Big Brother: The reason Iliumites are servile is that they would have it no other way. *Player Piano*'s enslavement is terrifying because it is inner-directed, unlike that of *Brave New World* and *1984*.

How did Ilium come about? It evolved. It evolved from present urban America sometime in the latter part of the twentieth century without a break with the past. The discontinuity of the customary leap into a planned fu-

I wish to thank Miss Julia F. Hewitt, reference librarian of the General Electric Company in Schenectady, for her kind and indispensable assistance.

ture—as in Zamiatin's, Huxley's, and Orwell's dystopias—has no place in *Player Piano*. The topography of Ilium relates to no rational social model—Platonic, Skinnerian, or other. It simply grew, naturally and irrationally, conforming to three ongoing historical determinants: first, the accident of a third world war; second, the war's legacy of a new cybernetic technology serving the nation in time of peace; and third, and most important in my opinion, the continuing vitality of that unexamined hunger after the good life—the so-called American dream—which historically has driven us to the conquest of land and the conquest of toil.[2]

Seventy years ago Henry Adams linked this dream to the material force and attraction of the machine in America, which he associated with a degradation of the spiritual force and attraction of the Virgin Mary in the Middle Ages.[3] In 1950 Marshall McLuhan termed the machine *The Mechanical Bride* loved by America as Narcissus loved his image. Norbert Wiener, in the same year, added that technology would soon enable us to leave our decisions to machines, that is, to put our heads where our hearts already are. The day approaches, claimed Wiener (Vonnegut's chief technical source),[4] when complex commands transmitted at indefinitely low orders of power will govern machine responses of any magnitude, for any number of reduplications, at any remove from the transmitter (itself perhaps machine-directed). As we become more and more what Freud calls "prosthetic gods"[5] remote from the arena of action, the risk, warned Wiener, is that we "transfer to the machine made in [our] own image the responsibility for [our] choice of good and evil."[6] If so—if we the responsible rational and ethical agents fail to review machine decisions—we will sooner or later fall victim to the powers we have brought into play. We will in real life enact the story of the monkey's paw, and, ironically, the fatal wishes will be granted us by our creations, the machines.

True to the terms of Wiener's prophecy, the machine civilization of Ilium arose in default of conscious guidance, not as a result of it. For this reason, *Player Piano* diverges radically in its view of man's instinctual life from dystopias it otherwise resembles. In works such as *We* or *1984*, a D-503 or a Winston Smith faces an array of probes and controls, which—insofar as he can get in touch with his instincts—he may successfully resist, at least until the state manages to root out his instincts or turn them against him. Only then is he irreversibly a robot. But in *Player Piano*, getting in touch with his instincts by no means secures Paul Proteus against the beguilements of regimentation. True to the dictates of the American dream, Paul acquires a farm, and true to the historical course of the dream, he soon rejects the reality of farming, "coarse and sluggish, hot and wet and smelly," and returns to his beloved paperbacks of the hairy-chested bargemen, cattlemen, and pioneers of old. Moved by the same instincts, his wife, Anita, runs a real colonial kitchen with electronic innards.[7]

In fact, what distinguishes the behavior of Iliumites of all walks of life when left to their own devices, is their spontaneous standardized regressive role-playing. On the one hand, each summer the busy executive plunges into the emotional "homogenized pudding" of the mass games and rituals at The Meadows.[8] On the other, the unemployed, the so-called Reeks and Wrecks of Ilium's Homestead area, engage in perpetual dress-ups and costume parades, partaking of a form of mass regression. These are unconstrained demonstrations, outbursts of the joiner's instinct. The Meadows is stage-managed by members of management, who are also among the participants; the Homestead parades are quite unprompted happenings.

The originals of these doings in America are not difficult to find. Relative to its date of publication in 1952, *Player Piano* is remarkable for assimilating institutions both past and present into the future. The marriage of Paul and Anita is a 1950s-modern, company marriage.[9] The Reeks and Wrecks—officially known as the Reconstruction and Reclamation Corps—are descended from the WPA and CCC of the 1930s (the men leaning on their implements call to mind the standard jokes about the corps of the unemployed under Roosevelt). The events at The Meadows reflect an earlier period still. For a time after World War II Vonnegut worked for General Electric. The thinly disguised historical source for The Meadows is General Electric's Association Island, a retreat that had had its heydey between 1910 and 1930; by the 1950s it was in disuse.[10]

But these ruling-class retreats are a continuing fixture of American life. As at The Meadows men stand before the Sacred Oak with hands "clasped before their genitals," so, writes John van der Zee of a visitor to San Francisco's famous Bohemian Grove, "I knew that I was in Bohemia . . . when I saw Eisenhower and Nixon pissing on the same tree."[11] Of GE's Association Island Vonnegut elsewhere recounts that in early days the representatives of a number of electric light companies would meet there in friendly competition and "what the competitors did not know for quite a while was that they were all owned by General Electric" and that, no matter what, "General Electric won."[12] Paul Keating's admiring history of GE bears witness to Vonnegut's accuracy on this point. Also, Keating describes the Island camps—the games, the in-house skits, the fraternal societies, the hazing of the neophytes by the graybeards—all as Vonnegut has it at The Meadows.[13] Two years after the publication of *Player Piano*, former GE President Charles Wilson addressed his erstwhile co-workers at a reunion specially held on the Island, as of old. He spoke in part as follows:

> I know it would be trite to tell you how much the invitation to be with you at the Island, and to be here tonight, means to me. It was a great joy and a great inspiration just to come back and step on this beloved Island. I have read stories of men who went overseas for a year or two and came back to their native heath, got off the ship and kissed the

ground. I'll admit to you that as I stepped on the Island night before last, I knew why they did it.[14]

As Vonnegut would say, "Yesterday's snow job becomes today's sermon."

In *Player Piano*, as on Association Island, life is both regimented and rigged. Most of the players would have it no other way. But to what extent is it rigged? Well, ubiquitously; and it hurts its victims. An old joke in Ilium has it that the machines hold all the cards. Into each person's card are punched the holes that determine his life absolutely. Life is a flow chart. Below a certain IQ cutoff, one is punched out into the Reeks and Wrecks or the army. Above that cutoff, one is punched into college, where in due course one's Achievement and Aptitude Profile perforations punch one into whichever branch of industry or the civil service is appropriate.[15] Private Elmo C. Hacketts's flow chart, for example, sent him into the Stateside army, where the troops are never issued guns but stand inspections and engage in exercises and close-order drill. Hacketts, shoulders back, eyes front, legs marching, daydreams profanely what his superiors will hear from him when in just twenty-three more years his discharge will come through.[16]

Sometimes the worm turns. Consider the story of Edgar Rice Burroughs Hagstrom—Reeks and Wrecks #131313, Undercoater First Class, 22nd Surface Preserving Battalion, 58th Maintenance Regiment, 110th Reclamation Corps—who "liked Tarzan as much as his father had, and hated being a little man . . . in Chicago." The story is that Paul Proteus observed the features of Edgar R. B. Hagstrom being fashioned by a police radiophoto machine because Hagstrom went berserk, cut up his M-17 home with a blowtorch, stripped naked, and, though rebuffed by the Jane of his choice, escaped Tarzanlike into a bird sanctuary.[17]

Similarly, near the beginning of the novel, a cat dies in the act of gaining its freedom, fried on an electric fence. This cat against the symbol of totalitarianism resembles the animals electrocuted by the fence surrounding the Reservation in *Brave New World*, the animals and birds beyond the green glass wall of the city in *We*, and the singing birds in the open countryside so near the hidden microphones of the secret police in *1984*.[18] The spontaneity of these creatures is testimony that the will to freedom is aboriginal and owes nothing to civilized life. But what is splendid in animals is absurd and pathetic in people, as in the case, say, of Edgar R. B. Hagstrom.

Some Iliumites go mad, but most collaborate with the system, as suggested by one of the central images in the novel, the ghost in the machine. To define this image, I have selected two instances: first a player piano in a bar in Homestead, and second the television set in the same bar.[19] A player piano is not a new invention.[20] Thinking of it, one thinks of some tinkly ragtime tune. The keys move, and a ghost seems to play. There is a nostalgia to a player piano, an echo of a younger and less disillusioned age. Vonnegut's player piano stands in the bar where the unemployed gather in Homestead. Paul Proteus—sometimes drawn to such haunts away from his proper world as manager of the Ilium Works—encounters in the bar an old man, Rudy Hertz, formerly a master machinist, the movements of whose wonderful hands Paul had taped years earlier, with youthful exuberance, programing the essence of Rudy into a bank of machines in Building 58 of the Ilium Works. Rudy, maudlinly delighted to see the man who immortalized his hands, drops a nickel into the slot of the piano in honor of Paul.[21]

Another prominent fixture of the bar is the television, which is generally on video only. Habitués of the bar contend with each other in a game to see if by watching the movements of the orchestra on the silent screen they can guess the tune it is playing.[22] This game constitutes both an analogue of the condition of the society as a whole and a sort of voiceless protest of it. The society has chosen to "turn the sound off," that is to tape the functions and tune out the performers, who, wraithlike, live on in the machinery, spooking the player piano, the radiophoto machine, the television, the Building 58 ensemble, and the giant corporate mechanism itself. The tune-guessing game play-acts fulfillment of a wish for a performance "live," by and for people.

The television and player piano images illustrate the degree to which Iliumites have identified the emotional substratum of life with machines. As McLuhan says, the medium is the message; and in these images, the machine-medium speaks poignantly of the dream once dreamed by its creator, the people.

This relationship between people and technology suggests one of the novel's themes: the ambivalent response to machinery that ensures its supremacy. I take as prototypical a single example, namely, Paul Proteus's ambivalent feelings toward Building 58.[23] On the one hand, as Paul looks down the length of the shed, he sees machines which to him are beautiful in their harmonious and concerted activity. He calls the ensemble of the machines and their sounds and motions the Building 58 Suite. Moreover, the shed runs back into time (the far end dates from the days of Edison) and with various additions it runs forward to his own day. Edison would know and delight in the scene, Paul realizes, for the individual machines would be well known to him in principle, automation being the one great innovation. Thus Paul loves both the machines and the feeling of human drive and aspiration that he has in looking back into the time of this shed. On the other hand, looking at a favorite photograph on his desk of crew chiefs and men of Edison's time, Paul sees in their eyes the light of the dream he has lost. What he has, rather than the dream, is the dream's legacy, the machines: The shed hasn't a single human operator in it. Nonetheless, he, Paul, once taped the hands of Rudy Hertz, in obedience to the dream—and thereby ensured automation.

At the end of the book, after the people have risen in a fit of rage and demolished the machines, they cannibalize the remains in order to begin again to fashion new machines—specifically, the absurd orange-O machine. As always, they labor at the instruments of their own demise (like Bud Calhoun, who earlier invented himself out of a job category).[24] Yet their fury against the machines, so recently at peak, is an equally authentic emotion. The very ambivalence itself is a pure emotion in its own right. The cycle of destruction and construction has repeated itself often in the past and will repeat itself, perhaps, forever; it is the human cycle. Vonnegut, therefore, is not saying that science and technology are the enemy of people and that the fight against science and technology is the hope of salvation; nor is he saying that totalitarianism is the enemy of people and that the preservation of freedom and dignity is the hope of salvation. What he is saying is that human beings are fallen and that, being fallen, whatever they conceive or create will carry within it the seeds of destruction. To the extent that *Player Piano* conveys these convictions, it is a more disturbing book than *We, Brave New World,* or *1984.*

NOTES

1. Mark Hillegas, *The Future as Nightmare* (New York: Oxford University Press, 1967), p. 161.

2. Of the three determinants, the first two might suggest the operation of an impersonal process—the sort of "inevitable" historical dialectic underlying the monopoly socialism of *Looking Backward* or the monopoly capitalism of *When the Sleeper Wakes*—but the third determinant, the main one, resides in the promptings of the dream. The imperatives are psychological rather than economic.

3. See *The Education of Henry Adams*, Ch. 25. Though Vonnegut's bases are mostly American, mention should also be made of Samuel Butler's seminal "Book of the Machines" (in *Erewhon*, 1872), wherein the Erewhonians have halted machine-evolution as a threat to man's hegemony.

4. For mention of Wiener, see *Player Piano* (hereafter *PP*), Ch. 1. Vonnegut appears indebted not to Wiener's 1948 monograph *Cybernetics*, but to its popularization, *The Human Use of Human Beings* (Cambridge, Mass.: Riverside Press, 1950). The latter was revised and toned down in the second edition (1954), after *PP* was published. No mere catalog of borrowings can reveal Vonnegut's assimilation of the 1950 edition, but some of the salient references follow: Wiener on "economic slavery" and its relation to upcoming automation, pp. 168, 180, 187–89; on chess-playing machines, pp. 204–06; on a "machine à gouverner" (Epicac-like), pp. 207–10; on player pianos, p. 210; on "The Monkey's Paw" and the Bottled Djinnee, pp. 211–13; and on the typically American nucleation of the ideas of pioneering-progress-primitivism, pp. 30–31, 56–57.

5. Sigmund Freud, *Civilization and Its Discontents*, trans. James Strachey (New York: Norton, 1962), p. 39.

6. Wiener, *Human Use*, p. 211.

7. *PP*, Chs. 27 and 10.

8. Ibid., Ch. 19.

9. See William H. Whyte, Jr., *The Organization Man* (New York: Simon & Schuster, 1956), pp. 258–63. Other companion materials for *PP*: Whyte's section on General Electric's Management Training Program, pp. 119–28; on scientism, aptitude testing, and personality testing, pp. 8–9, 26–27, 175–201; and on "togetherness," *passim*.

10. See note 13 below.

11. John van der Zee, *The Greatest Men's Party on Earth: Inside the Bohemian Grove* (New York: Harcourt Brace Jovanovich, 1974), p. 82. Van der Zee's waiter's-eye view of Bohemia parallels Vonnegut's view of The Meadows at many points. Ch. 12, "The Scenery's the Thing," is a fascinating account of the dwarfing of the redwoods by the scenery set up for the Grove plays.

12. Robert Scholes, "A Talk with Kurt Vonnegut, Jr.," in *The Vonnegut Statement*, ed. Jerome Klinkowitz and John Somer (New York: Dell, 1973), p. 93.

13. Paul Keating, *Lamps for a Brighter America* (New York: McGraw-Hill, 1954), pp. 83–86.

14. Charles Wilson, "The Ethics of Business Leadership," in *Responsibilities of Business Leadership: Talks Presented at the Leadership Conferences, Association Island* (General Electric, 1954), p. 61. On the title page appears the silhouette of the Island's Sacred Elm (Vonnegut's Sacred Oak). Wilson's rise from seventh-grade dropout to office boy to president of the corporation to a power in the nation's defense councils has similarities to Gelhorne's (*PP*, Ch. 22). Another famous GE figure, known as GE's first pure theoretician, was Charles *Proteus* Steinmetz.

15. *PP*, Ch. 8.

16. Ibid., Ch. 7.

17. Ibid., Chs. 17, 27.

18. Ibid., Ch. 1; *Brave New World*, Ch. 6, No. 3; *We*, Record 17; *1984*, Part 2, No. 2.

19. A few other instances of the metaphor I have mentioned in the text: the cat spewed out of the sweeper and fried on the fence; Anita's "pioneer" kitchen; Hagstrom telegraphed by the radiophoto machine; and Paul's museum-piece farm deeded to be kept "as is" in perpetuity. A few other samples: the dirtiest word in the language is "saboteur," or machine-killer (Ch. 23); Epicac XIV is "baku" to the Shah of Bratpuhr—"figure of straw and mud" worshiped ignorantly—since he alone perceives it as a piece of dead metal (Ch. 11); and the name of the rebels against the machines is the Ghost Shirts, named after the Indians who, in the year that Edison set up shop in Schenectady, stood firm in the faith they were invulnerable to the bullets that mowed them down. Examples might be multiplied.

20. The heart of a player piano, the perforated music sheet, was invented in 1842 (*Encyclopaedia Brittanica*, 11th ed.) and by about 1890 it was brought to perfection in the United States. It affords Vonnegut the blend he wants of nostalgia, technical proficiency, and corporealization of the spiritual world.

21. *PP*, Ch. 3.

22. Ibid., Ch. 9.

23. Ibid., Ch. 1.

24. Ibid., Ch. 3.

THEMES, TYPES, AND FORMS

THE ESSAYS IN PART III are arranged in a less rigid chronological order than the essays in the other parts of the collection. True, the section begins with three essays that focus on the nineteenth century, continues with two that bridge the gap between the nineteenth and twentieth centuries, and concludes with an analysis of one type of modern utopia. But the contributors to Part III are attempting thematic approaches to American utopian literature, and the pursuit of themes often calls for a more flexible historical scope than the time frames of the case studies in Part II or the historical and bibliographic essays in Part IV. For example, in spite of Arthur O. Lewis's emphasis on nineteenth-century authors, his study of utopian heroes includes Ayn Rand's John Galt, and Robert Plank uses Shakespeare and Montaigne to illuminate modern utopias.

Several of the contributors to Part III discuss utopias written earlier than the late-nineteenth-century works examined by Jean Pfaelzer. But I decided to place Pfaelzer's essay first because it goes beyond a perceptive interpretation of the relationships between a specific era and a particular group of books to define many of the general characteristics of utopian literature—for instance, the episodic balance between manifesto and fable, the dependence upon guides and visitors, the monotonous characterization, and the ahistorical quality of the narratives. Thus Pfaelzer's essay serves as an excellent introduction to the thematic approaches in Part III. (For a complementary treatment of the late nineteenth century, see my essay in Part IV.)

Arthur O. Lewis's "The Utopian Hero" continues two interests of Pfaelzer's essay: the concentration on the late nineteenth century and a concern with literary problems. Specifically, he analyzes the two most common types of protagonists in utopian fiction, the agent and the observer. To support his views, he selects examples from well-known works such as *Utopia*, *Looking Backward*, and *Atlas Shrugged*; less familiar works such as James Fenimore Cooper's *The Crater*; and obscure works such as *The Milltillionaire*, *Perfecting the Earth*, *A.D. 2000*, and *The Legal Revolution of 1902*.

The next three essays deal with themes that should interest readers involved with women studies, ecological studies, and ethnic studies. There

115

have been several surveys of women in utopian literature, but to my knowledge, Barbara Quissell's "The New World That Eve Made" is the first thorough study of feminist utopian works that have been written by women. She divides her nineteenth-century utopias into two categories: those dealing primarily with the status of women, and those depicting a two-stage transformation beginning with a change in the role of women and culminating in broad social and economic changes. Quissell notes that many of the arguments offered by these forgotten women writers are similar to recently proposed reforms that are often considered new and revolutionary. Donald C. Burt analyzes the agrarian longings in American utopian literature—a theme that is mentioned by Suvin and Pratter in Part II and by Nydahl, Rooney, and me in Part IV. Burt's essay is an interesting complement to wilderness and landscape studies by such scholars as Roderick Nash and Leo Marx, because he discovers a dominant longing for a "middle state"—a controlled and domesticated Nature. But Burt goes beyond this typical attitude to survey attitudes that range from extreme conservation stances (in D. L. Stump's utopia the use of lumber for homes is forbidden) to reckless ventures in terraforming, such as flooding the Sahara, altering ocean currents, and decreasing the orbital speed of our planet so as to lengthen the year! Stuart Teitler's introduction and annotated bibliography examine one aspect of Lost Race literature—the tale of the Lost Tribes of Israel in utopia. The novels described offer images of Judaism that include caricatures of materialistic Jews as well as idealistic visions of societies characterized by physical health and beauty, equality, and religious devotion. The flavor of this type of utopian adventure story is captured in Teitler's lively annotations.

Lyman Tower Sargent's "Capitalist Eutopias in America" represents an important criticism of the common assumption that all American utopias depict socialistic or cooperative economies. He surveys more than fifty capitalistic eutopias, including works by such well-known figures as Ayn Rand and H. L. Hunt, written between 1836 and 1973. Sargent concentrates on four types of utopian visions: pure free-enterprise economy; reformed capitalism; antiutopian critiques of socialism; and socialistic dystopias.

In the concluding essay in Part III, Robert Plank examines a fascinating twentieth-century phenomenon, the shrunken utopia. His study combines the case study method of Part II and the thematic, and to some degree the historical, approaches of Parts III and IV. First Plank establishes the literary context of European and American utopian literature after the decline in popularity of the nineteenth-century eutopia. Then he presents Skinner's *Walden Two* as the paradigm of the shrunken utopia and traces the continuity of the paradigm in Rimmer's *The Harrad Experiment*. Finally, he relates his topic to the psychology of writing utopias and to crucial historical forces that created the appropriate climate for the shrinking of utopia.

JEAN PFAELZER

The Impact of Political Theory on Narrative Structures

THE NARRATIVE STRUCTURES OF late-nineteenth-century utopian fiction demonstrate the contradictory historical function of this form of fantasy literature. In response to America's first prolonged postindustrial depression, liberal authors offered utopias that functioned as both satire and revelation, criticizing the age while positing an improved future. These popular utopian novels, which flooded America in the late nineteenth century, were a cultural reaction to militant struggles of labor, farmers, and women. From 1886, the year of the Haymarket Riots, until 1896, the year of the restoration of conservative hegemony (emblemized in the Bryan-McKinley elections), more than one hundred works of utopian fiction appeared, written by middle-class authors, politicians, clergymen, businessmen, and reformers who were reacting to demands by masses of people for economic and political equality.[1] Despite their egalitarian and, at times, socialist solutions, these utopias were alternatives to real equality because they lacked formalized reform strategies.

The 1880s and 1890s were among the most active periods of class, race, and sex struggles in American history. In 1886, 340,000 people demonstrated, for example, in May Day demands for the eight-hour day. During those years railroad expansion, the growth of heavy industries, and government support of monopolies and trusts institutionalized and consolidated the Industrial Revolution—already stimulated by the military's needs for arms, uniforms, canned foods, and transportation during the Civil War. Women, children, and immigrants provided the new industries with a pool of cheap labor. Cities and slums developed, permanently altering the patterns and appearance of American life.

The period that coincides with the popularity of utopian fiction can be characterized as one long depression. The panic of 1893, a crisis caused by

Several paragraphs of this essay appeared in "American Utopian Fiction 1888–1896: The Political Origins of Form," *Minnesota Review*, NS 6 (Spring 1976), 114–17.

the completion of the nation's basic steel and transportation requirements, signified the end of an era of easy domestic investment and massive profit. Entire agricultural districts were impoverished, while one-fourth of the urban unskilled labor force was out of work. Six hundred banks closed before the autumn of 1893. Meanwhile capitalists demanded that government suppress radicals, women, unions, and Populists and provide business with channels for foreign commerce. Industry did not yet recognize the industrial and marketing potential of the cities. The production of utopian fiction waned after McKinley's election, as America adopted imperialist solutions to the crises of production gluts and unemployment. By 1898 America was at war with Spain over hegemony in Cuba and the Philippines.

Basically there were two categories of response to the conditions of inequality, poverty, and alienation in the Gilded Age. One view held that Property accepted the responsibility for the general welfare of the state. It assumed that the community would be served best by satisfying the needs of business. Industrial prosperity would guarantee that benefits would "trickle down" to the community through employment and goods. Therefore, business should control politics. Continued expansion in the West and overseas would underwrite the source of all national prosperity: private property. Such conservative utopian authors as Alvarado Fuller in *A. D. 2000* (1890), described in detail in Arthur O. Lewis's essay, projected mock histories culminating in capitalistic societies run, with full employment, by the military. Walter H. McDougall's *The Hidden City* appeared in 1891, the year of the Wounded Knee Massacre. He projected a utopia in which the Native American is absorbed in an appropriately isolated stratum of an industrialized urban society.

The second solution to the depression replaced private property with social property, and competition with various forms of cooperation and communalism. The most famous progressive utopia was, of course, *Looking Backward* (1888) by Edward Bellamy. However, despite *Looking Backward*'s expression of economic equality, Bellamy's utopia preserved the existing political, social, and sexual relationships, because Bellamy accepted as "givens" contemporary ideas often used to justify capitalism: Social Darwinism, the rights of private property, and the inferiority of women and working-class people. Progressive utopian fiction prematurely resolved social contradictions. Although contemporary reformers were proposing a variety of methods for social change, ranging from electoral politics to militant actions against the corporations, utopists chose instead from the range of ahistorical devices of time travel such as long sleep, drugs, and mesmerism, which had been introduced in sentimental and gothic fiction. The absence of historical change in much of the utopian fiction limits the possibility for extended narrative activity, while the characters become irrelevant because they cannot affect the process of social and material progress.

CONTENT AND FORM

Although, as both Joel Nydahl and Charles Rooney point out in this collection, the genre of utopian fiction had been tried by many prominent American authors earlier in the century, the wide popularity of late-nineteenth-century utopian fiction reflects the genre's successful representation of the reform currents of the time. Strikes, meetings, rallies, and petitions were political manifestations of the recognition that industrialization had not fulfilled its promises. Evangelical religion, industrial novels, science fiction, labor songs, and utopian fiction represent the cultural extension of those political articulations. Utopian fiction was not, as Joyce Hertzler suggests, "the audible expression of murmurings so faint that few could notice them."[2] Authors of that generation of utopian fiction sought to maximize the contrast between the real world and the utopian world for political purposes. In these utopias the authors' political goals determine the structure of the fiction, including genre, characterization, plot, setting, and literary organization, as well as the proposed economic reforms.

Utopian fiction is a category of prose fiction in which the author's political statement controls the narrative structures. If the author succeeds, the reader can formulate a statement of the author's political belief; all the narrative elements serve this end. I will apply the term *apologue*[3] to this form. Because of the satiric as well as programmatic function of utopianism, as readers we expect to refer to our experience *outside* the fictional world. The goals of psychological realism and consistency of character, which empower the novel, would, in utopian fiction, destroy the continuity of the comparison between the reader's society and the utopian society. If we become concerned with characters in the novelistic sense, it would undermine our recognition that in utopia the individual is usually less important than the society as a whole. Writers of utopian fiction must keep our interest in the hero's fate below the point where his destiny becomes more important than our acceptance of the proposed social program.

The necessity of establishing a controlling "statement" determines the principle of selection in utopian fiction. In the genre of utopian fiction, the content affects the form in specific ways. Unlike *The Dispossessed* by Ursula Le Guin, which argues for permanent revolution, in the late nineteenth century "utopia" implied a historical situation of perfection, with the explicit denial of future growth or development. In the 1880s and 1890s realistic fiction vividly portrayed the antagonistic character of social contradictions. Technological and progressive utopian fiction prematurely resolved the era's political contradictions in a static industrial future. This denial of change, which philosophically became a denial of history, past as well as future, was politically related to a fear of change that informed the literary structures of utopian fiction. Without a concept of change, it was impossible to use the novel form as it existed in the 1880s. The Victorian novel was predicated on development and growth of character as the individual interacted with his or her society. But because of their need to reveal a whole rather than show development, utopian authors turned to such literary genres as diaries and travelogues. To replace novelistic development, the action in utopian fiction centers on revelation. The guide reveals the utopian society to the hero. There is no extended conflict, because utopia marks the end of history; without history there can be no fictional activity.

This fictional consequence of political conservatism in turn produces an emotional disengagement in the readers of utopian fiction. The construction of the narrative is episodic; our involvement in situations is momentary. Characters are quickly introduced and quickly disappear. They generally exhibit only those traits relevant to the doctrinal statement. Utopian fiction establishes a pattern in which commentary and analysis alternate with fictional portrayal. As in a Brecht play or a Godard film, we soon interpret events and relationships as examples and demonstrations. The utopian author describes characters, rather than shows them in action. They emerge through their typicality rather than their individuality; they become one of many. Finally, because everything in utopia is controlled for the general good, we know we do not have to worry about the fates of the characters.

Technological and progressive utopias such as *Looking Backward* project no dialectic between character and environment. We recognize instead the deterministic situation of the characters. They cannot make choices that indicate their development. Utopias achieve their political effect by piling up enough details to convince the reader of the perfection of the new system. We do not await the stabilization of relationships, the recognition of social truth, or the attainment of self-knowledge. The hero changes only to the extent that he becomes informed of the institutions of the new society and convinced of its benefits.

In American utopian fiction of the late nineteenth century the apologue involves two interacting forms, which I shall term *manifesto* and *fable*. The *fable* contains the action and its implicit morality. In the *manifesto*, the action stops while the guide and his marriageable daughter interpret the experiences and institutions to the visitor. The *manifesto* sections adopt the realists' style and often include detailed descriptions of the exploitation of labor, the impact of technology on civilization, and the effects of industrial capitalism on agrarian society.

The action, description, and characterization in the *fable* sections show the influence of the sentimental romance, a popular contemporary form known to utopian authors through such domestic novels as Maria Cummins's *The Lamplighter* (1854) or Susan B. Warner's *The Wide Wide World* (1850) and through the current popularity of Shakespeare and Scott. Utopian authors adopted traditional devices to weld social commentary to the romance form. In utopian fiction, as in romance, the physical appearance of the state and the citizens measures the society's virtues. The beauty of the people reflects the beauty of the social architecture, although these parallels did not impel utopian romancers to investigate supernatural correlations between society and soul. Utopian fiction also inherited plot structures from the romance tradition. As in *The Tempest*, the stranger enters the new society through a fortunate accident. A potentially serious misfortune, such as a shipwreck, drug overdose, or accident in space thrusts the visitor into utopia. Utopian fiction also borrows such romance devices as lost family ties, characters near death restored to life, periods of wandering and exile, recognitions through a physical trait or a piece of jewelry, and a beautiful woman (princess surrogate), who is usually the daughter of the wise old guide (benevolent father king surrogate) and who assists the visitor in his initiation.

In addition to progressive technological utopias, the late nineteenth century produced pastoral utopias, such as *A Traveler from Altruria* (1894) by William Dean Howells, or procapitalist utopias, such as *A Journey in Other Worlds* (1894) by John Jacob Astor. (See the essays by Frederick E. Pratter and Lyman Tower Sargent in this collection.) Fundamentally escapist, pastoral or retrogressive utopias borrowed from romance the optimistic tone of human life renewing itself. The purity of the country is contrasted to the unhealthy industrialized city (the plague-ridden city of romance). History is a lost period of innocence; nature alone can re-establish the order that industrialization destroyed. Nevertheless, although the literary forms come from the romance tradition, the particular construction of the scenes, situations, and characters in nineteenth-century retrogressive utopias also show the influences of populist ideology and agrarian nativism.

Ernst Bloch suggests two political functions of utopian romances. They can be: "distracting, gilded con-dreams . . . daytime dreams of pulp literature in which an impossible stroke of good fortune befalls some poor devil, and in which the happy ending is unhappy deceit."[4] Thus utopia can divert the reader, permitting us to be happy in experiencing utopia by proxy. Bloch also cites old tales in which there is "no mere distraction and voyeuristic palliation, but a vital stimulus and direct relevance. The brave little tailor conquers the ogres with cunning, that Chaplinesque weapon of the poor, and wins the beautiful princess."[5] A utopian romance can thus be a "vital stimulus." According to Bloch, the difference depends on whether the hero arrives in utopia by "an impossible stroke of good fortune" or whether he enters on his own strength. As a socialist, Bloch criticizes those visions which describe "plenty without labor." He believes that utopias can stimulate action if they "evoke longing" and if they contain demonstrations of change relevant to their historic context. The aesthetic and political tension of utopian fiction arises, then, from the contrast between "what is and what might be," between reality and potential. Thus utopists' ideas are not direct "reversals" of the ethics and institutions of their own time. The nineteenth-century utopia instead is a society in which social tendencies are developed, tested, experienced, yet delayed. Utopian authors escaped the social contradictions by adding the dimension of the remote future or, as Ernst Bloch puts it, by relying on "the utopian interpolation, the adverbial 'not yet.' "6

Because utopian fiction was written by intellectuals and bourgeois reformers, it was colored more by the American belief in democracy than by the developing ideas of European socialism. Unable to come to grips with a new methodology for change, utopian authors were stuck with the contemporary notion of laissez-faire progress and evolutionary growth. Utopian fiction was one of the few literary movements up to that time that did not have a contemporary source in England. It was provincial and chauvinistic, concerned only with the fate of America. Nineteenth-century American utopian authors rarely showed international or world-state consciousness. They were influenced by Owen, St. Simon, and Fourier only insofar as their thought was translated through such American social theoreticians as Charlotte Perkins Gilman, Henry George, and Laurence Gronlund. In America there was also the memory of the experimental utopian communities.

More immediate ideological influences on American utopian authors were the post–Civil War erosion of the doctrine of original sin and its replacement by a participatory form of evangelical religion, which promised that heaven was available to all believers. Similarly optimistic, Henry George, Francis Walker, and David Wells promised that financial problems could be scientifically solved, while in the realm of "social biology" Francis Galton announced that most medical and social problems could be cured genetically. In Arthur Bird's *Looking Forward* (1899), the inhabitants of China turn white under the "civilizing" influence of American dominion.

American utopian authors attempted to reconcile the new industrialism to well-established American myths. They advocated a democratic form of possessive materialism in which acquisition of property would become a general rather than an individual phenomenon. Characters in utopian fiction, despite the socialistic nature of their societies, demonstrate the virtues of competition, acquisitiveness, and individual effort. During a period of a developing reading public and the growing popularity of fiction, utopian literature thus became an instrument in the reform movement. It was particularly suited to those thinkers who believed that social change should come slowly and peacefully and be led by intellectuals.

CHARACTER IN UTOPIA

The creation of a character in a work of utopian fiction presented peculiar stylistic problems arising from the effect of equality on individuality. For some authors social and economic equality led to uniformity, implying the necessity of conflict for the development of idiosyncrasy and individuality. Tragedy, accident, and competition, the traditional sources for character development, are supposed to be absent in utopia. Consequently, either the characters are dull and homogenized or nonutopian factors are artificially maintained by introducing tensions from the pre-utopian world. The goal of regulated behavior also destroys character differences. Efficiency, shared scarcity, indeed uniformity as a goal in itself also contribute to monotonous characterization.

The *apologue* narrative form also affected characterization. Because the form does not permit the author to proceed through dramatic interaction of characters, the burden of exposition falls on one or two main characters, traditionally a guide and a visitor. Completely identified with the society, the guide is usually powerful, smug, male, and older than the visitor. The visitor is typically liberal, naive, male, and often critical of his own society. As he becomes initiated and indoctrinated, we see through his eyes. Occasionally, as in *The Man from Mars* (1891) by William Simpson or *A Traveler from Altruria* by William Dean Howells, the pattern reverses and the visitor comes to America. It is significant that many heroes enter utopia with an injury or sickness, suggesting a painful loss at leaving the old society.

During periods of high unemployment, domesticity is often promoted through fiction. While many utopias provided for political equality for women, they did not translate this status into portrayals of strong, competent, independent female characters. Utopian authors did not understand that social and economic equality would imply new forms of female characterization. Because women share the roles of economic producers in utopia, utopian authors introduced new technology for household labor. Although the authors saw housework as lonely and degrading work and replaced it with hotels or central kitchens, no nineteenth-century utopian author understood that childrearing and housework provide the reproduction, maintenance, and socialization of the laboring class.

Women citizens in utopia were, like their sister characters in the sentimental and gothic novel, promoted as domestic, pious, modest, and maternal creatures. The family is still the metaphor for social order. Despite their economic function, on the level of fictional activity, utopian women exist to inspire utopian men. In 1880 there were more than 4 million American women employed, 17.2 percent of the total working force. In 1886 women workers averaged ten hours per day at an average pay of $10 per week. Nonetheless, with the exception of a few works, such as *The Garden of Eden, U.S.A.* (1894) by W. H. Bishop, we never see women characters at work in utopia, indeed rarely outside the home or dormitory. Despite the fact that women's assemblies in the Knights of Labor included textile and other factory workers, teachers, waitresses, even servants, laundresses, and cooks (people traditionally difficult to organize, as they work in separate places and live in their employers' houses), women rarely participate in the political indoctrination of the visitor to utopia. Women in utopia promoted the new spiritual and cultural institutions without taking direct responsibility for the institutions themselves. The older women were hostesses, and the younger women were generally the passive romantic prey of the visitor.

Finally, faith in utopia as a solution rests on faith in the perfectibility of the individual. Because society determines the individual's capacity for good or evil, the outer limit of each utopia is the point at which the author thinks the individual is wicked or selfish. This faith in human perfectibility further distinguishes utopias from satire on the one hand and pastoralism on the other. Satire conventionally ridicules humanity. Pastoralism responds to the influences of urbanization and competition on character by insisting on a nonindustrial setting. Characters who inhabit progressive utopias, however, are not the rustics George Kateb calls "untouched natural growths fresh from their maker's hands."[7] In progressive utopias the individual realizes his or her capacity for perfection through the influence of highly developed educational and economic institutions. Utopia is not a land of pastoral repose and sensuality, but rather a society with a highly circumscribed moral code. Virtue in utopia comes from the interaction of human potential and benevolent social institutions. A person's capacity for evil is not ignored.

This wave of utopianism predated the sense of powerlessness expressed by the Freudian and naturalist views. Late-nineteenth-century utopists did not believe that aggression is instinctual in all humans. If the individual is inherently perfect, fictional representatives of the forces of good or evil need not do battle for the soul or social conscience. Society causes evil; evil exists external to character. Therefore the citizens of utopia do not need to change. Although the possibility of human perfection would soon be repudiated by the notion that there is an innate depravity not curable by social change, utopianism was still linked to the eighteenth-century view of man as a rational being. Antiutopianism or "dystopia" became popular genres in the twentieth century.

IDEOLOGY AND UTOPIAN FICTION

American utopian authors assumed the bourgeois ideologies of the nineteenth century: laissez-faire, social evolution, and the progressive tendency of industrialism and democracy. During a long period of falling prices, capitalism managed to sustain the momentum of economic and industrial development through a coalition with a strong national government, while attacking the unions for attempting to interfere with the "free market place." Nonetheless, utopian authors frequently accepted capital's rationalization for its attack on unions: There is a strong link between the precepts of utopianism and noninterventionism. In late-nineteenth-century American utopias, the forces of good enter the competitive arena and beat the capitalists at their own game.

Writing in an era of militant protest against the social injustices resulting from monopoly capitalism, utopian authors tried to show that change would come eventually and automatically. Reform certainly could be won without violence. The dates they assigned to their new societies, such as 2050, 2894, and 2000, demonstrate their belief that change must take place slowly. Several utopian authors, like E. E. Hale in *How They Lived in Hampton* (1888), advocate co-ops for production and distribution. Co-ops would make better and cheaper products and defeat capital in the market place. William Dean Howells in his Altrurian utopias supported nationalization of industries, a form of change that would also win in the traditional open market. No one seizes the industry for the people or state. Bellamy and many of his followers vote themselves into utopia, often ignoring their own critique of capital's manipulation of the electoral process. Frequently the adoption of one contemporary demand, such as abolition of the gold standard or inheritance, readjusts the financial environment so that a social economy simply emerges.

These views encouraged the ahistorical belief that one new invention would manufacture socialism. Friedrich Engels described this phenomenon in *Socialism, Utopian and Scientific*. For utopian reformers, "socialism is the expression of absolute truth, reason and justice, and has only to be discovered to conquer all the world by virtue of its own power. And as absolute truth is independent of time, space, and of the historical development of man, it is mere accident when and where it is discovered."[8] As Gorman Beauchamp notes in his essay on Jack London, many utopian authors avoided the issue of change altogether, presenting ongoing societies without describing their origins, or creating the utopian societies through magic.

Marxist critics writing in the 1920s and 1930s, like Allyn Forbes and Christopher Caudwell, showed that this ahistorical attitude can be linked to the class background of utopian authors. In *Studies in a Dying Culture* Caudwell describes the utopianism of H. G. Wells. Because Wells experienced the life of an intellectual, it was easy for him to believe that analysis ruled the world. Caudwell argued that because the proletariat did not exist in Wells's vision, he assumed that change would come only from the middle class. Wells made it the responsibility of utopian authors to enlighten bourgeois reform leaders.[9]

The major critique of utopian thought has come from Marxists, who believe that socialism will come only through class struggle when capitalist culture breaks down. Nineteenth-century utopian authors failed to under-

stand that because of its components of industrialism and technology, capitalism is a necessary precondition of socialism. It cannot be wished away
by space travel, a long sleep, or drugs. Because utopists do not have a causal analysis of history, they are indeterminate about what must specifically
happen before utopia will occur. Thus in *Socialism, Utopian and Scientific*,
Engels defines the function of socialism in opposition to that of utopianism.
Socialism is not

> . . . an accidental discovery of this or that ingenious brain, but the
> necessary outcome of the struggle between two historically developed
> classes—the proletariat and the bourgeoisie. Its task was no longer to
> manufacture a system of society as perfect as possible but to examine
> the historico-economic succession of events from which these classes
> and their antagonisms had of necessity sprung, and to discover in the
> economic conditions thus created the means of ending the conflict.[10]

Karl Mannheim, in his seminal work *Ideology and Utopia* likewise shows
that utopian authors believe that ideas rather than class struggle influence
the trend of history. For a utopian reformer, according to Mannheim, the
idea is the "driving force" of history.[11]

That the intellectuals, clerics, and businessmen who wrote utopias *on
behalf* of workers were unable to imagine what work, workers, and social
change were like is almost inevitable. Their attempts led, for example, to
Chauncey Thomas's romanticizing of working people in *The Crystal Button*
(1891) or Ignatius Donnelly's portrayal of workers as unthinking brutes in
Caesar's Column (1890). Working people rarely enter the utopian panorama
as leaders. Utopian authors make a distinction between working or poor
people's lives and beliefs, which they assert are formed by environment,
and their own existence, which they assume is socially untainted and free.
Utopian authors, including Bellamy, Howells, Donnelly, and Bradford Peck,
describe working people with either fear, pity, or contempt. This paternalism creeps into their utopian structures in various forms: an aristocracy
of experts, a fear of social or economic equality, and the maintenance of an
intellectual elite.

In addition to the class background of the utopian authors, George Kateb,
a passionate defender of utopian thought, gives other explanations as to why
utopian writers avoided portrayals of class struggle and revolution. Kateb
suggests that they feared violence because they sensed that if violence were
introduced, it would become a permanent phenomenon of the new society.
According to Kateb, utopian reformers were patriots who defined revolution
as "destruction" of America. "Common sense" also told them that revolution
was impractical. Furthermore, they shared a "Lutheran sense" that the
powers-that-be are ordained by God and should not be rearranged. Finally,

utopian authors had a "moral absolutism" expressed in love for all human beings, rather than in love of one class.[12]

Nevertheless, a few authors, including Ignatius Donnelly, Frank Rosewater in *'96, A Romance of Chicago* (1894), Mrs. C. H. Stone in *One of "Berrian's" Novels* (1890), and Henry Salisbury in *The Birth of Freedom* (1894), introduce fictional revolutions that define the limits and potential of social change. However, through the paired images of creation and catastrophe, destruction and millennium, Jerusalem and retribution, revolutions in their utopias become two-edged swords: destroying the ruling class with delicious violence on the one side, but destroying faith in human and technological potential on the other. Revolutions in nineteenth-century utopian fiction precede world destruction and gothic annihilation.

Change is a deterministic rather than historical process in nineteenth-century utopian fiction. Utopia, according to Northrop Frye, "presents an imaginative vision of the *telos* or end at which social life aims."[13] The *telos* orders the events in the fiction. As Karl Mannheim suggests, in utopia "events which at first glance present themselves as mere chronological cumulation take on the character of destiny."[14]

Utopian fiction emerged in an era that was fascinated with time itself.[15] This was the century in which geological time confronted biblical time. Geology, biology, and anthropology had totally revised man's notions of the past, and introduced new concepts of a primeval past and prehistoric life forms that permanently changed ideas about history, change, and progress. During the late Renaissance More, Bacon, and Campanella set their utopias on remote islands in uncharted seas, which coexisted with nonutopian societies. In the late eighteenth century, when Sébastien Mercier projected the first utopia into the future in *L'an 2440*, he provided important indications of the emerging idea of progress. In the nineteenth-century utopia time was not synonymous with the millenarian concept of time. The nineteenth-century utopian *telos* is secular, while the millenarian end is eternal salvation. Utopia, by the late nineteenth century, was not a manifestation of a supernatural truth or system.

Another category of utopias, the "retrogressive" utopias, solved these contradictions by being placed in a glorified and romanticized past. The authors did not explain their method of reversion from the present to the past; they merely defined the present as evil and the future as dangerous and uncertain. Retrogressive utopists sought a return to a lost age of a simple agrarian arcadia, which they claimed existed in preindustrial America. Somewhere in the past, real or fictional, was the real life. Because it was preindustrial, it was stable. The sources of authority were traditional and therefore natural. These authors refused to accept science as a necessary condition of material security and equality. They returned to the classical model in which the farm and family are the ultimate units of social life. Typified by Howells in *A Traveler from Altruria* (and familiar today in Richard Brautigan's *In Watermelon Sugar*), retrogressive utopias show peasant societies at a handicraft stage of production. Their ethic is leisure as much as it is equality. Domesticity, artisanship, and natural piety order these self-sufficient societies. In both Howells's and Brautigan's works, technology exists primarily in museums. History is reversed.

The attitude toward history in retrogressive utopias requires different literary devices. Because utopia is not progressive, it can be reached by a journey through space, rather than time. Because utopia is nonscientific, it does not, by implication, have to be worldwide. Retrogressive utopias coexist with nonutopian lands and only await discovery. Thus, newcomers reach this type of utopia through voyage rather than sleep. The setting can be an isolated island, as in Howells's *A Traveler from Altruria*, a lost valley, as in Joaquin Miller's *The Building of the City Beautiful* (1894), or a distant mountaintop, as in the pastoral finale of Ignatius Donnelly's *Caesar's Column*. Retrogressive utopias often retain an apocalyptic version of history. The civilized world explodes, destroys itself, and is born anew in a virgin Eden state. By contrast, in "progressive" or industrial utopias, typified by *Looking Backward*, we move through time rather than space. Either we observe the hero's movement in consciousness back and forth in time or we become the time-traveler, projected into the future through a first-person narrator.

Neither retrogressive nor progressive utopias prescribe tactics for social change. In the tradition of the communitarian movement, utopian societies in literature exist as models to be contemplated and imitated. Judith Shklar terms this the "classical" function of utopia. The ahistorical nature of utopias was "in keeping with the Platonic metaphysics, which inspired More and his imitators as late as Fenelon. For them, utopia was a model, an ideal pattern that invited contemplation and judgement but did not entail any other activity. It is a perfection that the mind's eye recognizes as true, and which is described as such, and so serves as a standard of moral judgement."[16] Shklar makes a distinction between Renaissance or classical utopias, which were created to be contemplated, and nineteenth-century utopias, which she contends were "calls to action." However, the classical function also applies to nineteenth-century utopias and was an expression of nineteenth-century utopian authors' attitude toward change and "activity."

Technology rather than political activity delineated the possibilities of the utopian age. Progressive authors optimistically predicted how the new technology could benefit masses of people. The new industrialism in America required scientific explanations for the physical properties and processes of nature. After the Civil War, a scientific revolution paralleled the Industrial Revolution. The age became fascinated with the new technology. By the 1870s science fiction was an established genre. Crowds attended scientific lectures, large audiences supported popularized scientific journals, and literary journals began to include science fiction stories.

In utopian fiction, however, technology is not included just because it is new and fascinating. Through science, progressive utopias show people's need and ability to control their environment. Science, nonetheless, produces an important contradiction in the technologically advanced utopias. Science is temporal and impermanent in a supposedly changeless, permanent world. As modern readers, we are in a superior position to look back on and evaluate the authors' scientific predictions. H. Bruce Franklin suggests that because of our own experiences with science, no matter how much we admire utopian societies, we also look down on them.[17]

Utopian fiction borrowed many scientific devices from contemporary popular fiction. American time-travel fiction, dating back to Rip Van Winkle, had already introduced mesmerism, drugs, long sleeps, freezings, immortality, and injuries as literary devices. Psychic phenomena, wondrous inventions, lost worlds, telepathy, and voyages in time and space were familiar in American literature. Many prominent American authors who wrote at least one utopian novel also tried their hands at science fiction: Charles Brockden Brown, James Fenimore Cooper, Herman Melville, Mark Twain, Howells, and Bellamy all tried both.

Antiutopias and dystopias were other species of conservative utopian literature in the late nineteenth century. While one part of the antiutopian movement was stimulated by the political popularity of *Looking Backward,* another part was written in response to the technological age per se. By the 1890s people were disillusioned with technology's promises of infinite improvement. Like retrogressive utopists, antiutopians seek the Golden Age in a romanticized past. They fear the consequences of industrial technology: Machines develop volitions of their own, technology turns people into machine-tenders, and scientists become dictators.

In addition to technology, antiutopias parody collectivism, which they portray as the destruction of the individual. The anti-utopian writers feared the socialists' demands for economic equality and the abolition of private property. Anna Bowman Dodd wrote the antiutopia *The Republic of the Future* (1887), described in Charles Rooney's essay. In her futuristic view of New York, socialism has erased ambition, imagination, and the dominant white Protestant community. Socialism has even produced physical uniformity in the human race.

The antiutopian views required different literary techniques from progressive and pastoral utopias. Some antiutopias are parodies, relying for their effect on the readers recognizing the exaggeration of typical elements of utopian literature. Other antiutopias are satires, mocking social conditions in the real world. Antiutopias generally were more novelistic than utopias in that they describe an individual confronting his or her society. In a society that annihilates individualism, one character emerges who attempts to eradicate the suffocating sameness of the socialist utopia. The heroes are anachronisms, throwbacks to the presocialist world. They are criminals to the degree that they express their individuality.

The cultural phenomenon of social Darwinism contributed to the production of antiutopian literature. Although social Darwinism distorted Charles Darwin's evolutionary theories, phrases such as "struggle for existence" and "survival of the fittest" took on popularized meaning in the 1880s and 1890s. They undid the utopian axiom of human perfectibility by implying that conflict and competition are part of our biological makeup. Time and evolution are no longer progressive forces. Instead, Social Darwinists justified the ossification of the class structure as genetically and racially inevitable.

Thus, utopianism served contradictory political goals in the late nineteenth century. On one hand, utopianism judged society as it existed in the 1880s and 1890s and then provided the dimension of an egalitarian future. It aesthetically realized the economic if not the social potential of socialism for a technological society. Utopian fiction showed that the dimensions of both the present and the future are necessary for social change to occur. In this way utopian literature could promote action. As Ernst Bloch suggests, "all the worse if the revolutionary capacity is not there to execute ideals which have been represented abstractly . . . nonetheless action will release available transitional tendencies into active freedom only if the utopian goal is clearly visible, unadulterated, and unrenounced."[18] Or, as Lewis Mumford puts it, "one of the main factors that conditions the future is the attitude people have toward it."[19] Nineteenth-century utopian literature was consistent with the era's faith in progress.

Frederick Polak characterizes this contradictory attitude toward the future as a passive-versus-active paradox. Utopianism has "a passive essence—optimism, which rests its case on the laws of social dynamics, and an active influence—optimism, which strives toward the goal of hidden utopia."[20] In other words, when utopian authors suggest that the laws of progress will automatically lead to happiness, the individual becomes passive. At the same time, when they describe social goals as already realized and instituted, the reader is encouraged to imitate and reconstruct the model actively. Thus, utopian literature conditioned an attitude toward the future in the mind of the reading public. Because utopianism presented its heroes as capable, perfectible, and sinless, it stimulated the belief that progress would come through people, not God. This in turn facilitated a new conception of the individual's relationship to society. Utopianism helped break down nineteenth-century individualism by encouraging a focus on the development of society as a whole. The notion that prosperity is a collective process is an important contribution to American thought.

Utopian literature written in the last decades of the nineteenth century was also an important instrument of opposition and social criticism. The ideal state became a criterion by which readers compared and judged the conditions of industrial America. Furthermore, utopian literature popularized significant progressive ideas, in particular the basic socialist concept that the land and the economy should belong to the community as a whole. Nineteenth-century utopias realized many contemporary reformist demands. Although the radical aspect of these ideas has been diluted as they have been adopted and institutionalized in modified forms, in their *fictional* assumption of social security, universal suffrage, universal education, trade unionism, and limited emancipation for women, nineteenth-century utopists anticipated today's welfare state.

Thus utopian literature played an important role in the development of fiction. Utopian literature, along with the industrial novel, was part of a new use of fiction in America as a device for popularizing social and political ideas and for bringing about social change. Utopianism insisted that economic and scientific progress is a valid realm for art. This body of literature demonstrates the dialectical possibilities of the relationship between culture and politics.

Nonetheless, utopian literature may have contributed to the period of political reaction that followed McKinley's election in 1896. Utopian literature perpetuated the American myth of political freedom by asserting that individuals could be free before they created the conditions through which their freedom could be realized. Utopia was still predicated on the individualist assumption that the dreams of a single person ought to be realized in society as a whole. Utopia exists on the author's terms alone.

Utopianism, like other reform movements of the 1880s and 1890s, was unsuccessful in bringing about any general social change. It failed in part because it was neither addressed to nor written by the people who were the victims of the economic and social injustices of the era. American utopian literature expressed the authors' fear of working-class and unemployed people who were demanding economic relief and social equality. Intellectuals could institute utopias simply through an alliance of technology and democracy. Like the union leaders and Populist politicians, utopian authors ultimately failed to reject the national rationalizations—inevitable progress, laissez-faire, and social determinism—which permitted the social and economic contradictions to develop so rapidly and painfully in the decades following the Civil War.

NOTES

1. See Kenneth M. Roemer, *The Obsolete Necessity* (Kent, Ohio: Kent State University Press, 1976), pp. 186–208, for an excellent bibliography of late-nineteenth-century utopian literature.

2. Joyce O. Hertzler, *The History of Utopian Thought* (New York: Cooper Square, 1965), p. 265.

3. I am indebted to Sheldon Sachs, *Fiction and the Shape of Belief* (Berkeley: University of California Press, 1966) for the concept of *apologue*.

4. Ernst Bloch, *A Philosophy of the Future* (New York: Herder & Herder, 1970), p. 87.

5. Ibid.

6. Ibid., p. 41.

7. George Kateb, *Utopia and Its Enemies* (New York: Schocken, 1972), p. 140.

8. Friedrich Engels, *Socialism, Utopian and Scientific,* ed. Lewis Feuer, in *Basic Writings on Politics and Philosophy* (Garden City, N.Y.: Doubleday, 1959), p. 81.

9. Christopher Caudwell, *Studies and Further Studies in a Dying Culture* (New York: Monthly Review Press, 1971), pp. 74–95. See also Allyn B. Forbes, "Literary Quest for Utopia, 1880–1900," *Social Forces* 6 (December 1927), 179–89.

10. Engels, *Socialism,* p. 89.

11. Karl Mannheim, *Ideology and Utopia* (New York: Harcourt, Brace, 1952), p. 219.

12. Kateb, *Utopia and Its Enemies,* pp. 113–25.

13. Northrop Frye, "Varieties of Literary Utopias," in *Utopias and Utopian Thought,* ed. Frank Manuel (Boston: Beacon Press, 1966), p. 25.

14. Mannheim, *Ideology and Utopia,* p. 188.

15. For example, see Roemer, *Obsolete Necessity* (note 1 above), pp. 15–40.

16. Judith Shklar, "The Political Theory of Utopia," in Manuel, *Utopias and Utopian Thought,* p. 109.

17. H. Bruce Franklin, *Future Perfect: American Science Fiction of the Nineteenth Century* (New York: Oxford University Press, 1966), p. ix.

18. Bloch, *Philosophy of the Future* (note 4 above), p. 92.

19. Lewis Mumford, *The Story of Utopias* (New York: Boni & Liveright, 1922), p. 298.

20. Frederick Polak, *The Image of the Future,* Vol. I (New York: Oceana Publications, 1961), p. 287.

ARTHUR O. LEWIS

The Utopian Hero

UTOPIAN STUDIES have recently become a focus of scholarly interest. Most studies have emphasized the nonliterary aspects of utopian writings. But most of the significant utopian proposals are presented in a form that purports to be fiction. This study is a brief examination of several such works, with the view of assessing the impact of the chief character on the success or failure of the work as literature.

The heroes of utopian novels may be divided into two general classes: agents, that is, those who bring about utopia, and observers, those who describe utopia after its creation. In the work from which the genre has drawn its name, Utopus, the legendary king who founded Utopia, is the prototype of the agent hero, and Hythloday, the philosopher-traveler who visited and later described Utopia, is the prototype of the observer hero. The present study is concerned with a few examples of each type of hero with a view to seeing what purposes they may serve and what effect those purposes may have upon the success of the utopian work. The works considered are, for the most part, American utopian novels of the last few years of the nineteenth century, with minor glimpses of both earlier and later examples. A more thorough examination of a larger number of works, spread over a longer period of time, makes possible the generalization that in the last century or so more careful characterization of utopian heroes has been attempted than previously. The earlier agent heroes for the most part appear only briefly, but the later ones have often been genuine flesh-and-blood protagonists with significant roles in forwarding the action. Similarly, the earlier observer heroes are little more than cardboard figures who stumble around utopia describing their experiences in stilted phrases, whereas in the later works the observer hero is a character in his own right, whose feelings and beliefs become an important part of understanding the utopia.

This essay was first presented at a session on Utopia and the Novel at the Sixth Annual Comparative Literature Symposium, University of Tennessee, March 30, 1974, and on two later occasions, locally and slightly modified, at the Pennsylvania State University.

It should also be noted that in the dystopian and antiutopian novels the observer hero frequently is more fully developed than in the utopian novels.

A brief look at Thomas More's *Utopia* (1516),[1] a work that is obviously not a novel though cast in fictional form, demonstrates an immediate and important distinction between the agent hero Utopus and the observer hero Hythloday. Utopus appears by name only four times in the entire work. He is described first as the "Conqueror [who] gave the Island its name . . . and who brought the rude and rustic people to such a perfection of culture and humanity as makes them superior to all other mortals" (p. 113). This introductory statement is followed by a description of the manner in which he created the island and set up the new state: "that the whole plan of the city had been sketched at the very beginning by Utopus himself" (p. 121). Two other references mention his decision to lay down regulations in regard to religious freedom (pp. 219, 221).

On the other hand, although Hythloday is not a part of Utopia itself, he is of course a major character in Book One, and it is he who gives the details of the new land he has discovered. During the discussion with Thomas More and Peter Giles, which leads to his story about Utopia, a great deal is learned about Hythloday's character. He is, as Edward Surtz has pointed out, "one of the neglected great figures of European literature" (p. cxl), and although he is not mentioned by name in the description of the island, there are several indications of his activity while visiting Utopia. It is worthy of note that, although this observer hero is given both character and actions leading to a deeper understanding of the society he is describing, such thoroughness is seldom the case in so early a work. More typical of the kind of characterization of both agent hero and observer hero is that found in two American works, written almost four hundred years later, which may be used to demonstrate the superficiality with which the characters of utopian works were generally portrayed.

Like Utopus in *Utopia*, the Milltillionaire of Albert Waldo Howard's *The Milltillionaire*, a short but eclectic utopian pamphlet of the mid-1890s, appears only at the beginning of the work.[2] Very little is known of him except that "his personal history" would be "more like a romance than real life" (p. 4). He achieves utopia by the very simple means of "having with his unlimited wealth possessed himself of all landed property of all civil countries"; then, "virtually owning the earth" (p. 5), he proceeds to transform earth into "the true millennium" (p. 6). What the Milltillionaire has in common with the King Utopus is that each has achieved utopia through personal conquest, in the one case through war and in the other case with money, after which the leader is able to produce a society to suit his personal taste. In neither case does the author attempt motivation or characterization of the agent hero.

For General Theodore Goodwill, the agent hero of C. W. Wooldridge's

Perfecting The Earth (1902),[3] the existence of a large, unneeded army in a society weary of war and plagued by unemployment provides the means to bring about utopia through technological advances and huge public works. But after the initial introduction of General Goodwill as having "recently come into command" (p. 25) and a brief description of the manner in which he places his proposition before Congress—in both cases he is reported, not actually seen—there is little specific reference to him throughout the rest of the book. Typical of these references are the appearance early in the book of an order signed by Goodwill, explaining what the soldiers will do (p. 27), and a statement some seven years later signed by Goodwill and others in regard to funeral arrangements for citizens (pp. 202–4). He appears in person in 1915 at a widely reported press interview (pp. 91–93) and again to deliver an address to "fellow citizens and soldiers of the army of industry" (p. 212). The occasion is July 4, 1929, when, as had been promised earlier, the order is issued to disband the army. General Goodwill seizes this occasion to tell his people of their accomplishments and to point the way to even greater and more civilized possibilities in the future. His final appearance is in 1947, the last pages of the book being devoted to the funeral services for this leader who brought about a better world. As in the case of King Utopus and the Milltillionaire, one knows little about General Goodwill other than that he lives up to his name. The documents quoted and the 1929 valedictory address tell us something of his ideals but little of his character or, for that matter, of his motivation in leading the nation to utopia.

There is certainly nothing complex about the portrayal, or much interest in the character, of the agent hero in any of the three works considered so far. Such development as there might be is that from the simple naming of a king as conqueror, through a brief mention of the Milltillionaire as one whose life might be interesting if it were examined, to a twentieth-century military man who, without being well described, is perhaps a little better understood because of the words put in his mouth or shown to flow from his pen.

Even the most superficial comparison of the observer heroes in the three works demonstrates that Hythloday is far more carefully developed than are the observers of the other two. The observer of *The Milltillionaire* is an unidentified narrator who devotes all his energies simply to describing the wonders of the world and who departs, almost in midsentence, with no particular reason for doing so; thus, the work itself simply stops on an unfinished note. In *Perfecting the Earth*, the unidentified observer is, again, only a narrator who does, however, visit the new world on various occasions and talks with persons such as "the Conductor," "a Guide," and a number of teachers and students, as well as a few unidentified companions who join him on one of his trips through the communities of New Utopia, Mount Ceres, and Fort Goodwill. He also listens to a long sermon by a minister, who may very well be quoting from one of Wooldridge's other works, but nothing is really known about this observer other than that he is much impressed by what he sees and hears.

Perfecting the Earth differs from *Utopia* and *The Milltillionaire* in that, despite the superficiality of the characterization of General Goodwill, the focus of the book is basically on the *creation* of the new society. *Utopia*, on the other hand, with its "annals, embracing the history of 1760 years" (p. 121), has existed for some time, and although *The Milltillionaire* describes "The Earth in the Inaugural Century of the Millennium" (p. 6), some length of time has obviously passed in order to permit completion of the huge constructions that are described. *Perfecting the Earth* is thus an example of a kind of utopian work popular in the late nineteenth century and even more so in our own time, where the interest is not in describing an existing utopia but in the way in which it is brought about. Only at the end of the work do the agent hero and his followers enjoy the fruits of their labors. Because the agent hero is thus an integral part of the story, it is essential that he be invested with a complete character and a life of some interest to the reader other than simply as creator of a new society. General Goodwill does not fill these requirements as a character and never comes alive.

The late nineteenth century in America was a period when the conflict between the ideals of the previous century and the reality of the present was most conspicuous. Reformers of all kinds arose, each with his scheme for making the promise of the past become the reality of the future. It was to such a time that Bellamy referred, "when heroes burst the barred gate of the future and revealed . . . a vista of progress whose end . . . still dazzles us" (p. 281).[4] Although Bellamy himself never wrote of such heroes, many others did, most of them with little attempt to create anything but cardboard characters.[5]

Some writers, however, have been somewhat more concerned with characterization than others. Three novels, separated by intervals of half a century, can be used as examples: James Fenimore Cooper's *The Crater* (1847), Bert J. Wellman's *The Legal Revolution of 1902* (1898), and Ayn Rand's *Atlas Shrugged* (1957).[6] The three writers begin from very different premises: Cooper suggests that some of his readers may see "grounds for a timely warning in the events here recorded" (p. 6); Wellman wishes "to show the people their power, wherein it lies, and the methods of exercising it to right their grievances" (p. 3); and Rand urges that "only a *philosophy of reason* can lead to an intellectual renaissance."[7] But all three works are part of the utopian realm, and all three were written, at least in part, to propagandize the author's view of what is wrong with existing society, what a better society might be, and how such a society might be brought about. Their common solution is a strong leader who sees what is wrong and sets about correcting it.

It may be argued that *The Crater* is not really a utopia, that indeed it is simply a more complicated *Robinson Crusoe*, in which a castaway, at first alone and later in company with others, builds what only happens to be a reasonably ideal society. The utopian novel, it might be maintained, implies a *deliberate* attempt to create a perfect world; but one might argue equally well that any utopian work is merely illustrative of the author's ideas of what a perfect society might be; if he chooses, as has Cooper, to bring about that society through a fortuitous accident or, as have many twentieth-century utopian writers, following a catastrophic event that wipes out much of the present society, surely this approach is not much removed from that of the utopian writer who chooses to show the overthrow of the old society necessary to creation of the new.

Cooper's strong man, Mark Woolston,[8] is a young ship's officer who, with one companion, is cast ashore on an uncharted reef where only a very small crater rises much above sea level. The book deals with the way in which Mark and his companion, Bob Betts, begin to build a fertile land from seaweed, guano, and the ship's cargo and to establish a livable world for themselves. The loss of Betts in a storm does not appreciably slow Mark down. He continues his activities, and when a year later Betts miraculously returns together with Mark's wife and other friends and relatives, the new society develops rapidly. It is a typical Cooper device that an earthquake has raised even more land above the water just in time to accommodate the new arrivals. The society they create comes about chiefly through a combination of Mark's drive and energy and a common acceptance of his leadership ability, an acceptance stemming only in part from the fact that he was, in a sense, the discoverer and sole owner of the land, but more from a kind of respect for one of his position, as well as for his perceptivity and intelligence. A successful, capitalistic, reasonably democratic, though class-conscious society is developed but—from Cooper's point of view—falls upon perilous ways following the introduction of too many ministers, journalists, and demogogic lawyers. Mark, who has been governor by acclamation and an occasional perfunctory vote, loses an election, having refused to lower himself to any kind of political infighting, and leaves with his family and closest friends for a visit to America. There is a certain poetic justice in the fact that upon Mark's return nothing is left of the ingrates, for another earthquake has put all but a small reef beneath the waves again. Cooper seems to be saying that the perfect society cannot survive without enlightened but powerful leadership, but he is also saying much more.

The Crater has been much underrated, and yet, as Thomas Philbrick has written, "perhaps no single novel better demonstrates the full array of Cooper's mind and art than *The Crater*" (p. viii). When considered as representative of his mature work, viewing life as both rich and uncomplicated and supporting the belief that man's sole hope for perfection is an increased knowledge of God, Cooper's choice of a utopian vehicle makes a great deal of sense. The development of an ideal community from a small reef on which two castaways have somehow managed to flourish and the downfall of that community in what has become almost an antiutopian work are embodiments of several salient aspects of Cooper's own political theory: his belief in paternalistic government, democratic but grounded in the rule of those best qualified by education, wealth, and experience, and his view that popular sovereignty with its unceasing blowing with the winds of change can lead only to destruction.

Parallel with the development of the society from simple community to the complicated society that falls is the development of the agent hero. In Mark Woolston, Cooper has created a character who, though often stereotyped and molded in his own image, is a strong leader who has brought about an ideal society through the force of his own personality. But Mark changes from a likable, eager man of taste and few needs to a proud, arrogant, complex being surrounded by all the perquisites of rank and authority, even perhaps sharing "in the corruption of his subjects" (Philbrick, p. xxvi). Thus when Mark's reef disappears beneath the ocean, what might from the point of view of the character be a kind of poetic justice is from the standpoint of Cooper's deeper intention a reminder that man does not yet control his destiny; that whatever attempts, successful or unsuccessful, he may make to establish a just society, in the end a Being greater than man makes the final decision.

The Legal Revolution of 1902, first published in 1898, has both an agent hero whose life is the heart of the book and an observer hero who creeps into the action through the author's oversight. The agent hero, Mark Mishler, is less real than Mark Woolston, but what happens to him sometimes overshadows what happens to society. Although he does not appear in person until the beginning of the second chapter, Mishler's name is mentioned in the very first paragraph of the book. As leading characer, he achieves a great deal of political success, including election to two terms as President of the United States following a successful legal revolution that transformed the nation into a cooperative commonwealth. But more important from a literary point of view, he has also achieved a great deal of personal success. At the beginning of the book he is a widower mourning the death years earlier of his wife and children in a train wreck, but at the end of the book he has found his wife's grave and has his son, his daughter, and a grandson by his side. In this highly romantic tale the personal and political stories run side by side, but the political story is far more important and frequently submerges the personal story for several chapters. Such interest as there may be today in the personality of Mark Mishler is developed almost completely from the effect of his political story rather than his personal story. However, the events of this fantastic tale—the kidnapping of his wife as a little girl by gypsies, her "death" in a train wreck, her brother's unknowing adoption of her son Glen, Mark's support of Glen simply because he is a promising young man, the friendship of Glen and his sister Ethel as students in college not knowing of their relationship, the false leads that at each point in the discovery of the real facts of Mishler's loss, seem to indicate that only a part of the mystery will be solved, the accidental discoveries which lead to the real solution—all may well have seemed much more possible in 1898 than they do today, and they do help to move the political story along. In some ways Glen is a kind of junior agent hero, because his father—both before and after they learn of their relationship—accepts and carries out some of his political suggestions. There is no observer hero as such except that the author of the book occasionally forgets that he is writing in the third person and introduces a passage in which "I" intrudes. Such lapses, evidence that the book is not especially well written, point up the polemic intent of the author and explain why the political events are more carefully treated than the personal.

Ayn Rand is even more polemic than Cooper and Wellman, and she needs more space to deliver her message, for *Atlas Shrugged* runs to almost 1,200 pages. Commensurate with its length is the number of major characters on whom the agent hero, John Galt, works his persuasion. Of these, Dagny Taggart is perhaps the most important from the point of view of what happens, and much of the book deals with her conversion to John Galt's view of society. Thus part of the appeal of *Atlas Shrugged* springs from the general appeal of conversion narratives. Dagny and the other converts are strong people, leaders in their chosen fields of activity, and it is only through the efforts of a superleader that they can be brought to help in developing the new society—especially one which on the surface appears to be completely hostile to their own beliefs. Although John Galt does not appear in person until the book is more than half finished, the opening words, "Who is John Galt?," set the tone, and it is the force of his personality and the strength of his accomplishments that will bring about his utopia.

John Galt brings about the beginnings of his utopia through a "strike of men of the mind" (p. 738). A brilliant engineer, he had stood up at a meeting of the workers who were to share in the company under a new "one big family" plan and refused to join: "I will put an end to this, once and for all" (p. 671), he said. And this he did in the next twelve years by gathering together "those great departed whom you had not seen on earth . . . from all the past centuries, the great men you would like to meet" (p. 735). These are leaders and potential leaders in each of their fields: the great composer, the great judge, the great financier, Galt's own professor and the other two of that professor's three greatest pupils, the great scientists, the great engineers, the great production men, and eventually the great female transportation expert for whom they all have been waiting. As each joins the cause, he makes his home in a valley cut off from the rest of the world, venturing forth only to carry out his assignments, always living by the oath that is at the heart of Galt's and Rand's philosophy: "I swear by my life and my love of it that I will never live for the sake of another man, nor ask another man to live for mine" (p. 732). A seventy-page speech, heard on all radio stations at the same time, describes Galt's motivations and his views of the necessity of this movement toward a new world, the best kind of government, and the responsibilities of the individual. But throughout the speech, as throughout the book, it is not the rightness of his beliefs but the force of his personality that brings to Galt's side those whom he needs in his conquest of society. And it is in the moment when all the motors of the world are actually stopped, the rather melodramatic attempt to force Galt to change the course of his revolution, the torture that follows on his refusal, and his rescue by his followers that the love and concern of his associates become most evident. On the purely personal level so great is this near-worship of their leader that two of the party who have themselves been lovers of Dagny find it only right and proper that she now be John Galt's. One almost has the feeling that in fact not until she was ready to join Galt could the world finally be set right.

The last few pages of the book show this band of devoted and brilliant leaders in their peaceful valley making final plans to move out into the world and restore mankind to what they regard as its rightful heritage. Within the book one is ready to believe that the symbol of this new world will be the dollar sign and that the most important new clause of the Constitution will be: "Congress shall make no law abridging the freedom of production and trade" (p. 1168). John Galt is in many ways the strongest of the agent heroes. Utopia has not yet been achieved, but on the last page of the book he stands looking beyond his mountain retreat, Dagny, once his most powerful opponent, at his side, and says: "The road is cleared. We are going back to the world" (p. 1168). At this point the reader is near the conviction that it might work. Such near conviction is the result of the care with which the character of this hero has been portrayed, somehow credible in spite of his unusual beliefs and actions. Fictionally, at least, Rand succeeds as well as almost any proponent of the utopian dream.

Cooper, Wooldridge, Wellman, and Rand all agree to some extent that American society needs reformation because it has strayed from the principles of the Declaration of Independence and the Constitution. But there are vast differences in their manner of achieving the new society.

Cooper offers no specific program—perhaps because of the accidental nature of so much that happens, but he seems to say that the mission can be accomplished through acceptance of leadership by one qualified to exert it, because "education and practice gave a man certain claims to control" (p. 222). If society were permitted to grow in accord with the belief that "certain great moral principles existed as the law of the human family" (p. 301), all would be well. It is the failure of some to remember these principles that causes the downfall of the Crater society and provides Cooper's "timely warning." Wooldridge proposes to change those national energies devoted to war to "constructive work for the public benefit" (p. 25), and through wise employment of manpower and machinery his leader turns society around so that great economic and political reforms are brought about simply by the will of the people. Wellman uses Article V of the Constitution as the key to reform. By means of a convention called for the purpose of amending the Constitution, great political changes are wrought, and from these follow the economic and social changes which make up the legal revolution leading to the new society. John Galt's weapon is to "stop the motor of the world" (p. 671), that is, to destroy the present industrial society and start over again. Only a complete overthrow of perverted society can cleanse and make possible the truly moral society, and twelve years of preparation are required before the industrial complex is brought to a complete standstill so that Galt can begin to build his utopia.

As characters these leaders are quite different. Mark Woolston is patient, intelligent, and resourceful, but his actions are often purely reactive to events around him. General Goodwill, as indicated earlier, is too vaguely portrayed to be more than a kind of shadowy incarnation of what his name implies. Mark Mishler does what needs to be done, but despite the romantic aspects of his personal life is still little more than a mouthpiece for the author. John Galt, on the other hand, is more interesting as a man and thus more effective as a leader. He feels anger, rage, and pain, falls in love, is injured, reacts violently to injustice, engages in physical battle—in short, he lives. He comes through as a human being, a superman perhaps, but human.

The four leaders have in common the fact that they are completely benevolent: Their chief goal is to permit men to attain the greatest fulfillment in life. Other writers who have agreed that only a strong leader can bring about reform have recognized that unfortunately not all strong men are benevolent and, perhaps fearing the consequences of change brought about by evil strong men, have produced the dystopian works so characteristic of the last five decades. In recent years both utopian and dystopian writers have generally preferred the active, rebellious John Galt kind of character to the more passive, legal-minded Mark Mishler model.

In quantitative terms alone utopias in which the observer hero is important are far more numerous than those in which the agent hero dominates, and the completeness of the observer's character has an important bearing on the credibility of what he describes. Thus, Bellamy's *Looking Backward* (1888), possibly the best-known and most popular of all utopias, has a carefully developed observer hero in Julian West. On the other hand, Lieutenant

Alvarado M. Fuller's *A.D. 2000* (1890) is not very well known.[9] First published complete with a disclaimer that it had been written before publication
of *Looking Backward*, this often naive but frequently entertaining picture
of society still a quarter-century in our own future reflects some of the
utopian interests of the period. It has considerable merit, and despite its
obvious faults the young hero, Junius Cobb, is eminently likable. Like
Bellamy's hero, he sleeps for a number of years to awaken in a new world.
Unlike Bellamy's hero, he *intended* to sleep, and some of the things that
have happened to bring about the new world were the result of his own
earlier work, though he had no such idea in mind at the time. I have
elsewhere noted that Junius Cobb's story is a kind of Tom Swift–Horatio
Alger artifact,[10] and I would add now, a few years later, with perhaps a dash
of Richard Harding Davis as well. Junius is an interesting and often charming
hero, and he and his friends, although frequently just as wooden and stereotyped as some of the worst of Cooper's or Alger's or Appleton's orDavis's
characters, go through adventures sufficiently interesting to lead the reader
to learn of the marvels of twenty-first–century America. The book is a useful
example of the kind of sugar-coating—a reasonably interesting plot and
attractive characters—that ensnares the reader even at the expense of his
being brainwashed into accepting the possibility that the author's is an
accurate view of the future.

   A.D. 2000 is an excellent example of the way in which the character of
the observer serves as a literary filter. Junius Cobb reflects his creator's
views and is, as are many other such heroes, frequently little more than the
author's mouthpiece, a fact made explicit in this case by the coincidence of
his rank as lieutenant with the emphasis on the title page of the author's
lieutenancy. The hero's point of view is that of an army officer, one who
takes pride in his career and regards his comrades as the best of men,
obviously qualified to assume positions of civilian leadership. Thus, while
part of Junius's motivation for undertaking his experiment is that he would
"have to serve for fifty years to become a colonel" (p. 33), he carefully
assures himself of a place in the army upon awakening from sleep by obtaining an indefinite leave of absence. That a descendant of one of his old
army friends should be President, that a descendant of another should be
in command of his old cavalry troop, and that he himself should become the
ranking major of cavalry with immediate promotion to lieutenant colonel are
no surprise: Things are just as they should be. He learns with approbation
of the successful war with England and the ensuing unification of North
America, about the volunteer army with its supplemental system of the
draft, and about the excellent career development within the army. Prior
to his experiments, in addition to his military activities, Junius had "given
many of his days and nights to hard study in science, in political economy,
and, in fact, had taken a deep interest in almost all of the progressive

undertakings of his day" (p. 12). Further he "had employed every spare moment of his time in experimenting in chemistry and electricity" (p. 12). Thus upon his revival it is reasonable to find him devoting much of his time to the discussion of new matters of technological, political, and scientific interest and, indeed, to helping in further development of several inventions. He is eager to understand the mysteries of submarine, pneumatic train, malleable glass, and other technological developments. His previous study of progressive ideas makes equally reasonable his questions about the new systems of legislative, executive, judicial, economic, and social operation—always necessary in a utopian observer but seldom so well explained. Even the wealth, fame, and high rank bestowed upon Junius Cobb at the end of the book follow logically from the kind of society he has joined, and these perquisites and honors come to him because he is a person who *belongs* and because—unlike most observers—he actually takes an active role. From a literary standpoint his personal characteristics make him an excellent observer hero. Fuller has, in other words, tried to make utopia more believable by portraying it through the eyes of one who is not only sympathetic with but also prepared for the new experience.

But, as noted earlier, Fuller's work is almost unknown and Bellamy's is an all-time bestseller. The difference is not in the kind of utopia they describe, for there is more agreement than disagreement between them. It is not in Bellamy's having a more exciting plot, for Fuller's is much more adventuresome and far less prone to stop for long-winded explanations of why things were as they were or are as they are. Nor is there much to choose between Bellamy and Fuller as stylists of the English language. The most plausible explanation is the simple fact that Bellamy's hero is a more complex, more carefully created human being than Fuller's. Despite the more immediately attractive nature of Junius Cobb, Julian West is a more thoughtful, more perceptive, and more credible witness to the wonderful new world he has been privileged to join. Where Junius Cobb more or less expects what he finds, for Julian New Boston is a revelation of something he had never really thought about. The discussions with Dr. Leete and others are really rather dull, but what happens to Julian's own thinking is what counts. Unlike many observer heroes, he does not passively accept everything. His new surroundings actually change him.

Much of Julian's credibility derives from the growth of his personality during the course of the book. In 1887 he is, as John L. Thomas has pointed out, "a prisoner of his own selfishness" (p. 51). His awakening in the new world becomes not only a physical but a mental process, in which the freedom from physical want of the new world is reflected in the new freedom of thought, which replaces Julian's own spiritual dullness. He becomes literally a new man, in a process culminated by the dream of his return to old Boston. As I have pointed out elsewhere, this dramatic confrontation of the nineteenth with the "golden century" is one of the most convincing episodes in all of utopian literature.[11] Its power derives in large part from the interest the reader has in the fate of a character who has been portrayed realistically enough to deserve the reader's concern. And it is typical of the way in which good characterization contributes to the utopian writer's success as polemicist.

Of the two heroes Junius Cobb is much better prepared for what he observes than Julian West. As a consequence, in reading *A.D. 2000* one's sense of wonder is muted while his sense of the fitness of the new society is enhanced. But Julian West's struggle for "redemption," as Thomas has named it, is so genuine and so closely paralleled by the needed social change that the reader of *Looking Backward* is caught up and convinced of the rightness of New Boston. Both heroes have performed their function well, but Bellamy's art is, in the end, greater than Fuller's, and it is Bellamy's book that has lasted as the most impressive of American contributions to utopian fiction.[12]

Such examples of characterization as those here discussed could be multiplied many times, but the conclusions to be drawn following a more exhaustive investigation would not be much different. In so short an essay as this, it is necessary to draw conclusions from a very small sample of the works that might possibly have been considered. There have been hundreds of utopian novels in America alone, and the numbers are especially impressive in the period with which most of this essay has been concerned. For example between 1888 and 1920 there were more than two hundred such works, and in the year *A.D. 2000* appeared, at least nineteen utopian works of various types were published.[13] Nevertheless, the seven works here considered provide opportunity for some conclusions.[14]

The comparison of Bellamy and Fuller demonstrates the literary superiority of Bellamy's work. A different comparison of Wooldridge and Bellamy would note that although their proposed utopias are somewhat similar, Bellamy has been more successful in promulgating his views. Wooldridge uses an unneeded army to achieve utopia but disbands it as soon as the cooperative commonwealth has been established; Bellamy shows a world in which the Industrial Army is the central organization of society. Appealing as Wooldridge's utopia might be, it never had any measurable impact on American society, but Bellamy's provided impetus for several periodicals and the beginnings of a political party. At least some of the reason for Bellamy's greater practical success must be the superiority of the characterization of Julian West over that of General Goodwill.

Similarly, the impact of Cooper was almost zero, but Rand has attracted responsive and energetic followers and a regularly published periodical to spread her message. Yet Cooper's view of the best government was not far removed from that of Ayn Rand, as comparison of a few passages will indicate. Cooper writes: "So long as a man toiled for himself and those nearest and dearest to him, society had a security for his doing much, that would be wanting where the proceeds of the entire community were to be shared in common; and, on the knowledge of this simple and obvious truth, did our young legislator found his theory of government. Protect all and their right equally, but, that done, let every man pursue his road to happiness in his own way; conceding no more of his natural rights than were necessary to the great ends of peace, security, and law" (pp. 324–25). John Galt tells his radio audience: "The only proper purpose of a government is to protect man's rights, which means: to protect him from physical violence. A proper government is only a policeman, acting as an agent of man's self defense, and, as such, may resort to force only against those who start the use of force" (p. 1062). And, again: "Every man is free to rise as far as he is able or willing, but it's only the degree to which he thinks that determines the degree to which he'll rise" (p. 1064). Presumably, the long neglect of *The Crater* and the instant bestseller status of *Atlas Shrugged* have less to do with differences of political view than with creation of greater interest in the characters.

Although none of these authors is a "great" writer, Cooper, Bellamy, and Rand might be called "competent" writers. Howard, Wellman, Wooldridge, and Fuller must be placed much lower on the scale, with Fuller perhaps a little higher than the others. Of the seven, Bellamy and Rand have had the most impact, Bellamy through the Nationalist movement, which helped to bring about major reforms in American society, and Rand whose Objectivist system continues to attract large numbers of followers in our own society. All seven are polemicists with goals to be sought, but only Bellamy and Rand have presented proposals by means of a story that interests the reader largely through identification with the hero. One conclusion must be that polemicists who expect to have any real impact on society need to be good writers, and if they choose the utopian mode, they would do well to devote at least as much of their efforts to careful characterization of their heroes as to describing their ideal societies.

In any utopian work there must be someone who serves as mouthpiece for the author. The agent hero is generally one who carries out the plan of action the author would use to achieve utopia if he had the power. The observer hero is the author's means for showing the superiority of the pro-. posed utopia over his own contemporary society, or—in the antiutopian or dystopian novel—for showing why the proposed society would be less satisfactory than his own.

In the seven novels considered here, the better the characterization of either agent hero or observer hero, the less obviously is he the author's mouthpiece, and the more credible the utopia becomes. It is thus not surprising that Bellamy, who created a character with whom the reader can develop genuine empathy, and Rand, who created a hero (and for that matter several other characters) who are most appealing to substantial numbers of present-day society, should have had the most significant influence of the seven writers considered. Only the specialists read *The Milltillionaire, The Legal Revolution of 1902, Perfecting the Earth, A.D. 2000*, or *The Crater*, but *Looking Backward* and *Atlas Shrugged* have never been out of print and continue to be read for pleasure. From a literary standpoint these are the true marks of success.

NOTES

1. Thomas More, *Utopia*, ed. Edward Surtz, S.J., and J. H. Herter, the Yale Edition of the Complete Works of St. Thomas More, Vol. 4 (New Haven and London: Yale University Press, 1964). All references to *Utopia* are to this edition and are inserted parenthetically in the text.
2. Waldo Howard, *The Milltillionaire* (1895?; reprinted in Arthur O. Lewis, ed., *American Utopias: Selected Short Fiction* (New York: Arno Press, 1971). References are inserted parenthetically in the text.
3. Charles William Wooldridge, *Perfecting the Earth, A Piece of Possible History* (Cleveland: Utopia Publishing, 1902; reprint, New York: Arno Press, 1971). References are inserted parenthetically in the text.
4. Edward Bellamy, *Looking Backward 2000–1887*, ed. John L. Thomas (Cambridge, Mass.: The Belknap Press of Harvard University Press, 1967). References are inserted parenthetically in the text.
5. Excellent studies of such works in this period are Kenneth M. Roemer, *The Obsolete Necessity: America in Utopian Writings, 1888-1900*, (Kent, Ohio: Kent State University Press, 1976), a revision of "America as Utopia, 1888–1900: New Visions, Old Dreams," Ph.D. dissertation, University of Pennsylvania, 1971, and Frederick Earl Pratter, "The Uses of Utopia: An Analysis of American Speculative Fiction, 1880–1960," Ph.D. dissertation, University of Iowa, 1973. See especially pp. 63–70 in Roemer and pp. 31–52 in Pratter for two investigations of the utopian hero differing somewhat from this essay. (It should also be noted that there are a few works in which the hero becomes a kind of Moses who leads his people to a promised land he will never himself enjoy. For example, Marc Bradley of John Hawkinson's *We, the Few* [1952] leads his people from catastrophe to a reborn world but lives only long enough to see it firmly started before his death.)
6. James Fenimore Cooper, *The Crater, or, Vulcan's Peak*, ed. Thomas Philbrick (Cambridge, Mass.: The Belknap Press of Harvard University Press, 1962); Bert J. Wellman, *The Legal Revolution of 1902* (Chicago: Charles H. Kerr, 1898; reprint, New York: Arno Press, 1971); and Ayn Rand, *Atlas Shrugged* (New York: Random House, 1957). References to these works are inserted parenthetically in the text.
7. "A Message from the Author," *Atlas Shrugged* (New York: Signet, 1959) p. 1086.
8. Cooper is careful to point out that this name is pronounced *Wooster*.
9. Alvarado M. Fuller, *A.D. 2000* (Chicago: Laird & Lee, 1890?; reprint, with

introduction by Arthur O. Lewis, New York: Arno Press, 1971). Page references to this work are inserted parenthetically in the text.

10. "Introduction," *A.D. 2000*, p. vi.

11. Arthur O. Lewis, "The Utopian Dream," *Directions in Literary Criticism*, Stanley Weintraub and Philip Young, eds. (University Park and London: Pennsylvania State University Press, 1973), pp. 192–200. See also Roemer, pp. 59–63.

12. Possibly also the circumstances of publication were partly responsible: Fuller was published by the relatively unknown Chicago firm of Laird & Lee two years after Bellamy had been published by the well known Boston firm of Ticknor & Company, and later by the even better-known firm of Houghton, Mifflin. Thousands of copies of *Looking Backward* had been sold before *A.D. 2000* appeared.

13. See Roemer's bibliographies in Part IV of this collection.

14. It is tempting to continue with an examination of some of the antiutopian or dystopian works of the last few decades, for in these the character of the observer hero appears to be more important in conveying the writer's message than in the utopian novels. Aldous Huxley's *Brave New World* (1932), for example, derives much of its meaning from the reaction of John the Savage to a world he cannot really understand. (One could also make a strong case for the similar mission of Lemuel Gulliver.) Of equal interest might be an examination of the specific role of those heroes of antiutopian or dystopian works who, while not agent heroes (because they are not responsible for the world in which they find themselves), are not observers in the sense in which those considered in this paper have been. For example, Bernard Marx in *Brave New World*, D-503 in Eugene Zamiatin's *We* (1924), Kuno in E. M. Forster's "The Machine Shops" (1909), Equality 7-2521 in Ayn Rand's *Anthem* (1939), and the heroes of other twentieth-century works are born into the presumed utopian society but rebel against it.

BARBARA C. QUISSELL

The New World That Eve Made: Feminist Utopias Written by Nineteenth-Century Women

I

IN HER ANALYSIS of the "sphere, condition and duties of woman" published as *Women in the Nineteenth Century*, Margaret Fuller asserted that "as the principle of liberty is better understood, and more nobly interpreted, a broader protest is made on behalf of woman."[1] But as women's rights advocates of the century discovered, the extension of fundamental liberties to women, even with limited objectives such as the vote, was a lengthy and discouraging process. The protest became a battle fought by organized women using lobbying tactics, speeches, marches, newspaper and magazine articles. The nineteenth-century women's views that have been studied generally are those expressed in the highly visible public forums by such leaders as Susan B. Anthony, Elizabeth Cady Stanton, and Carrie Chapman Catt and women's rights advocates or personalities such as Frances Wright, Antoinette Brown Blackwell, Victoria Woodhull, and Charlotte Perkins Gilman (who was a well-known figure and the author of three early twentieth-century utopias serialized in *The Forerunner: Moving the Mountain*, 1911; *Herland*, 1915; and *With Her in Ourland*, 1916). But another group of women chose a different approach to what the century called the "woman question": They ignored the public platform and national press and instead recorded their visions of women's lives in utopian works. The views of these women, published in obscure novels, never reached a large contemporary audience, and although mentioned in studies of American utopianism, their contribution to the debate on woman's place has not been fully delineated.

The advantage of the utopian genre was that women could pursue in its ideal form the same analysis as Margaret Fuller's, unhindered by gradual methods or the amelioration of individual opinions in organized protests. To a woman dissatisfied with or outraged by the treatment of her sex, the

148

utopia provided a stage for rehearsing the stifling mores and laws of American society and for presenting the effects of a feminist reordering of society. In their works the women utopists revealed an impatience with narrow objectives such as those of the suffragists—women's right to vote and to control their own income and property were minor details. These authors sought the complete transformation characteristic of the genre; their views were at once more fundamentally radical and more idiosyncratic than the issues debated by other nineteenth-century feminists.

The number of feminist utopias is small. My study includes ten that were published between 1836 and 1902, approximately one-third of the utopias written by women during the century.[2] None of the writers achieved the success of Lydia Maria Child or Harriet Beecher Stowe with her reform writings or the influence of Edward Bellamy in *Looking Backward* (1888), which precipitated the golden age of American utopian writing. Nevertheless, the feminist utopias are notable for the counterpoint they provide to moderate views on women's issues during the century. Many of their solutions are the same as those advanced within the last ten years and treated as revolutionary. Their utopian focus is appropriate, too, considering that the first utopia written by a professional American author was Charles Brockden Brown's *Alcuin* (1798), which described the legal and social bondage of women, especially as imposed by marriage.

As fiction, the feminist utopias are very readable; the soporific prose too often found in the genre has been replaced by wit, indignation, and delight in reversing sex roles. The utopian dialectic always features contrast between the imperfect present and the ideal world, but because of the emotional, personal nature of their subject, the women writers could startle a reader by exchanging the male and female stereotypes or by contrasting the norm with the unusual. One must admit another advantage that the writers realized—sex is much closer to comedy than economics will ever be.

The feminist utopias can be divided into two groups on the basis of the writers' approach to the genre. Half of the women redefined the utopian perspective. Instead of accepting the comprehensive view of society and all its institutions, present and future, they limited their discussion to the status of women. Unlike most nineteenth-century utopian writers in America who were concerned with the economic conditions of industrialization and its political manifestations, these women focused on the laws, cultural attitudes, and social conditioning that confined their sex. The details of government, politics, wages, and jobs, when included, complemented women's new roles and influence. In this group utopia was not a matter of the "good place" for everyone; rather it was defined as the best of all possible worlds for women.

The second group of writers proposed a two-phase utopian progression. First, the condition of women had to be changed, and then once they were free to exercise their abilities, they would take part in or take charge of the transformation from the imperfect contemporary society to the ideal world. The writers maintained that no effective reconstruction of America was possible without first eliminating the restraints on women's actions and power. Liberating women, not a new economic or political system, was the key to utopia. All the feminist utopian writers insisted that contemporary assumptions about woman's nature and her role in society must be thoroughly examined. A design for a new world was not possible without confronting the question of what women could and should achieve.

II

In the first group—utopia as a protest for women's rights—the authors portray their contemporary situation with sharp detail. As the women react to how their sex is treated, whether with disgust or rage, the tone of their work becomes strongly dystopian. They attack the notion that women already occupy a favored position because as wives and mothers they receive the flattery and homage of the entire culture. The following six authors regard a further institutionalization of the nineteenth-century image of ideal womanhood as catastrophic for all women.

The genesis of Jane Sophia Appleton's utopia can be pieced together from details within the collection *Voices from the Kenduskeag* (1848) where her "Sequel to the 'Vision of Bangor in the Twentieth Century' " was published.[3] Appleton had begun with a fund-raising idea, a collection of prose and poetry by local writers that would help solicit money for the Female Orphan Asylum in her community of Bangor, Maine. Appleton's methods as a coeditor are revealed in Governor Kent's sketch, "A Vision of Bangor in the Twentieth Century": The reluctant contributor pleads that the editor think of the reviewers, and she insists that he think of the orphans and remember the printer is waiting. Kent's brief sketch describes a prosperous, industrialized Bangor of 1978 in a United States freed from slavery and extending its empire throughout South America. An important feature of his utopian projection is the news that all women's rights agitation had disappeared; after a brief trial period in which women proved too frivolous and impressionable to be politicians and legislators, the society was peaceably divided between the sexes, women ruling in the home and men in the outer world. Obviously, when Appleton collected this essay, she could not let its chauvinism go unchallenged. Her own utopian vision begins after reading Kent's manuscript and continues with the same narrator and the 1978 setting.[4]

Before presenting the new rights for women in her "Sequel," Appleton surveyed other improvements—a peaceful community, beautiful city buildings, ecumenical church leaders, and a monument to the end of all wars.

Then she subjected the nineteenth-century male narrator to a session of consciousness-raising. The young man tries to flatter the first pretty girl he meets in utopia by asserting that after seeing her no one could doubt that "woman was to man the 'morning star' that shone through his youthful dreams, the 'day-star' that gilded his manly pride, the 'evening-star' that shed a halo over his declining years—and—"(p. 251). But the twentieth-century woman is no coquette or demure maid, and she interrupts his paean with "You might add the 'dog-star.' " Appleton's guide to the 1978 America admits the change in attitudes toward women came only after a long period of reform—a battle between the sexes in which "Still woman cried 'Onward,' and still man groaned 'Darn stockings!' " (p. 259). The outcome, however, was a complete freedom of personal development and career choices for women and absolute equality between the sexes that Appleton made clear did not obliterate individual or constitutional differences. The genial mockery of the young narrator is a prelude to Appleton's statement of belief: "*Your* age [nineteenth century] fondled women. *Ours* [the twentieth century] honors her. You gave her *compliments*. We give her *rights*. . . . With you, all things in woman had a reference to *man*. We think not so, but regard her as *complete in herself*" (pp. 251–52).

The ideas of Charles Fourier are given credit for the changes that have assisted in women's liberation: the communal dining halls, the mechanized and large-scale handling of domestic chores such as laundry and cleaning, and, most important, the cooperative economy and the necessity of some work for every citizen. Yet Appleton's utopia is not radically constructed, for the nuclear family and its childrearing functions still exist. Women still marry, but their financial independence has removed the economic and social compulsions for them to marry in order to survive.[5]

The only surprising feature is that even though women freely work at all kinds of "head and hand labor," they do not vote or legislate. In the past the love of money had become an epidemic disease afflicting the male population; it was a "money-leprosy," which induced dollar-sized copper spots on the skin. Women temporarily took charge of the government, gave it a thorough moral housecleaning, and when "beauty and order" were restored, returned the political affairs of the country to the rehabilitated men.[6] Apparently this better world is so justly and equitably regulated that women need not participate directly in the government.

There is an appropriateness in Appleton's utopia—the care given to the health and education of women would make the notion of a Female Orphan Asylum obsolete. No longer would girls be pitiable victims who required an "asylum" until they found another protector. Although 1978 did not fulfill many of Appleton's utopian details, the charitable institution that she raised money for still exists. Its change in names indicates a practical transition as women have responded to the needs of children in their community—from the Bangor Female Orphan Asylum & Society to the Bangor Children's Home to the present Bangor Day-Care Center.[7]

Appleton's utopia dealt with ways in which cultural attitudes shaped women's lives and the legal and social means by which women might become free to exercise their abilities. Elizabeth T. Corbett in "My Visit to Utopia" (1868) presents a narrowed definition of the ideal world: Utopia is a place where "one finds husbands quite perfect and wives quite satisfied."[8] In her brief magazine sketch Corbett investigates marriage as a psychological environment and traces its effects on women. The laws and political structure of the American society are mentioned only as they impinge upon the interpersonal relationships. The fact that women vote, for example, testifies to the respect accorded to them by the men in the society.

Corbett's utopia illustrates what ought to be in the best of all possible marriages. The woman narrator visits an old friend at home in Utopia and observes that men have been trained to share child care, to consider their wives' opinions, and to treat all women thoughtfully. The husband who fails to uphold this ideal relationship is sent to the House of Correction, where he is forced to wait on others who make the same inordinate demands as he made on his wife. Men have no recourse to the male prerogatives in their marriage vows, because the "obsolete and useless sentence" requiring the wife to honor and obey as well as the notion that a wife submit her will to her husband's have been dropped. The Utopians emphasize "mutual effort and forbearance" and "reciprocal tenderness and courtesy" in an equal partnership (pp. 202–3).

The Utopian home as pictured is economically very conventional in that the husband provides the support for his wife and child and a comfortable living standard that includes a cook and nanny. Corbett, accepting the stereotype of women's weaker physical nature, demonstrates its advantage in Utopia, where men are assigned the laborious tasks such as scrubbing and housecleaning, which require "the application of mere muscular force without mind" (p. 203). The visit to Utopia affects the narrator's marriage (her husband says she is very unreasonable and exacting) and her feelings toward the feminist critics of American society: "I have become very tolerant of all those reformers, as they are too often derisively called, who are fighting with too much violence and too little grace, perhaps, in the cause of progress, on the side of liberality" (p. 204).

However trivial some of Corbett's discussion may seem—a wife can automatically divorce a chronic grumbler—this utopia reveals the agony for women in a relationship that does not drift off into "happy ever after." In the popular nineteenth-century formulation, the man may have thought of his home as an emotional sanctuary he ruled,[9] but the underlying thought of Corbett's vision is that marriage can be dangerous to a woman's mental health, especially when her emotional needs are not recognized and her sense of worth degraded by a husband's intolerance.[10]

Corbett focused on the social institution of marriage; in Annie Denton Cridge's *Man's Rights; or, How Would You Like It?* (1870) the entire social context of laws, traditions, and attitudes is under attack.[11] Cridge intended that her readers feel the indignities women suffer, and she fixed the blame—one of her prefatory quotations plainly stated, "It is *my* cow that was gored by *your* ox." In a series of five dreams the narrator visits a strange society on Mars where she finds the familiar nineteenth-century sex role stereotypes, but the genders are reversed. The narrator is startled by her discovery that all the women are beautiful, noble, dignified, and strong and that politically and socially they oppress the "vain, silly, half-educated" men.

With simply a change of "he" for "she" and "men" for "women," Cridge catalogs the same abuses reiterated by the century's women's rights reformers. In the Martian households the narrator finds the men "pale, nervous, over-worked as house-keepers," in fact, close to hysteria: "I saw anxiety and unrest, a constant feeling of unpleasant expectancy" (pp. 3–4). Only in the homes of a few rich women do men have leisure time, but they and their sons spend it chatting about fashions, gossiping, and speculating on how a young man can catch a wealthy wife to provide for his future. Shocked by the fact that women control all professions, the narrator reluctantly notes that the men themselves and their dress seem to encourage the picture of masculine helplessness: The men wear cumbersome, frilled calico suits and have submitted to the latest fashion, the Grecian Bend, which forces them into a stooped position.

Cridge takes current events as her script, the common platitudes as dialogue, and with Swiftian delight pictures a men's rights meeting. The speakers protest that men are paid one-third the wages of women, that the suffrage and inheritance laws are formulated by women for their benefit only, and the speakers demand that "men be educated as liberally as women" (pp. 27, 29). The women in the audience (who dislike the "womanish man") cheer a notable member of their community as she refutes the speakers' claims. She voices the culture's prejudices: "The sphere of man is *home!*" and "how well Nature knows the superiority of woman and the inferiority of man, inasmuch as she has chosen woman for maternity" (pp. 30–31).

In this mirror-image world Cridge demonstrates the theme of many women reformers that depriving one sex of an adequate education and confining these individuals to a limited domestic sphere guarantee that the cultural prejudices will be self-fulfilling. The narrator on Mars admits, "I was almost tempted to believe Nature intended—in this part of the world at least—that woman and only woman, should legislate and govern" (p. 17). As a final touch in her "Modest Proposal," Cridge includes glimpses of the narrator's husband in between the dreams of a Martian world. He complains about the new servant girl, yells for his breakfast, and grumbles about the narrator's burning a lamp to write by late at night. He is a reminder of the individual, typical man.

Evidence within *Man's Rights* suggests that Cridge's motivation for writing came from a discouraged sense of how long the women's suffrage movement had been active and how little change had been made in American society. When the narrator in her dreams sees the men's rights leaders twenty years later, the plainly dressed "Susan Anthony" figure is grayhaired, and although the movement has more supporters (some, unfortunately, sympathetic because it is a touch of social adventure), the issues are still the same. Writing in 1870 Cridge was measuring the distance from the 1848 Seneca Convention's proclamation of women's rights and wondering if she, now in her sixties, would see a feminist awakening and an equitable new world.

Although most of *Man's Rights* is dystopian in that the Martian world illustrates the abusive and imprisoning treatment of one sex by the other, to a certain extent Cridge does outline how a change in attitudes toward the "weaker sex" would affect the details of living. First, machines and organized communal kitchens would remove the physical drudgery of housekeeping, "emancipation from the kitchen." Then, the child-spouses would be free to develop their minds and to participate in all aspects of economic and political life. Because the authoritarian rule of one sex oppresses children, an interest in children's rights would develop. Finally, Cridge believed that men and women could be free and could develop a joyful family unit only after the degraded state of one sex was eliminated from the culture.

Cridge hoped to shock her readers into recognizing the pervasiveness of sex discrimination. She chose the novel for its affective powers, like Harriet Beecher Stowe in *Uncle Tom's Cabin*, encouraging a sense of moral outrage. But instead of using pathos to make the issue personal and immediate, in *Man's Rights* Cridge's weapon is ridicule aimed at complacent American men who laugh at the idea of change and ignore rational argument. Her utopian view omits economics and the Industrial Revolution to focus on sexual politics.

In Eveleen Laura Mason's *Hiero-Salem: The Vision of Peace* (1889) eutopia is not found on another planet or in another century but instead in a single, prototypical family.[12] Mason contends that the essential first step toward a higher civilization is a transformation in the character of men and women, as indicated by her prefatory quotation, "The truth is, a great *mind* must be androgynous."[13] The lengthy novel follows the lives of an independent Althea Eloi and a wandering social theorist, Daniel Heem, who join last names to form the Eloiheems and become godlike pioneers of a new race.

Althea as the "father-mother" earns the family income with shrewd land and money speculations on the Wisconsin frontier; she refuses to be the "self-sacrificing, wrapper-wearing, pork-cooking" kind of mother. Daniel as "mother-father" decorates and furnishes the houses they live in, cares for the garden, and educates their son and daughter at home in a Froebel-influenced, free school. Mason visualizes these characters as representative figures, and indeed they move like gods and goddesses on the shores of Lake Michigan. For example, during an all-night vision of the history of women's exploitation, the daughter's hair turns white and she becomes known as the Lady of Life, a prophetess of the new order.[14]

The main conflict in the novel is psychological, as the son refuses to accept the family's androgynous ideal. After struggling with his authoritarian desires and his hatred of women,[15] at the close of the novel the son experiences what can only be described as an ecstatic conversion experience in which he acknowledges the feminine element: "Self-unioned beings are the generators of a force which creates a new centre of gravity on Alpine Heights, a force which will draw men to upflow those heights for love of the Eternal Womanly there" (pp. 507–8). Mason's emphasis on the feminine does not exclude the masculine but would correct an imbalance in the contemporary definition of male and female characteristics that draws up a list of opposites, strength and weakness, for instance, to divide between the sexes.

Stylistically, *Hiero-Salem* is the worst of decadent romanticism visited upon the utopian genre. Mason disregards plausibility of events and the simple declarative sentence for characterization of larger-than-life figures and dialogue punctuated with exclamations. Mythological references, occult designs, and abstractions flourish in this expansive novel. For the reader trying to find a design for utopia in spite of Mason's prose, there is another difficulty. Mason does not construct a program-oriented eutopia with its answers to political and economic questions but rather defines a psychological new world and assumes other details are of secondary importance once the polarization of sexes is banished from American society.

Mason suggests that the state will follow the example of the smallest group, the family, and thus will be a democratic association among equals and will practice an altruism exemplifying the androgynous harmony within an individual—"of-all-in-each-and-each-in-all" (p. 210). Mason foresees little difficulty in moving from the family unit to the entire nation as she explains that if men treated the law of liberty within their own homes, "society would reconstruct itself in less than another forty years" (p. 409). Although Mason does not provide the steps by which the new society can be achieved, she does state that women will have to have a greater share of the leadership: "[We] have yet to learn what *Woman's* ideal of liberty would do for woman and the race" (p. 247). Mason requested that instead of "The End" to label the conclusion of her novel a picture of a Valkyrie be printed—spear in hand and riding heavenward, this militant woman figure signals the new age.

The satiric method of Cridge and the denunciation of contemporary practices appears again in the next feminist utopian work. *Unveiling a Parallel* (1893), co-authored by Alice Ilgenfritz Jones and Ella Merchant, is a thoroughgoing exposé of the double standard and its institutionalization in American life.[16] Following the pattern of utopian romance as established by Edward Bellamy's *Looking Backward* (1888), Jones and Merchant satirized the comfortable acceptance of sexist attitudes and the glorified terms with which they were justified.

One of Bellamy's important gifts to the utopian genre was the adaptation of the popular sentimental romance to utopian description, replacing the classical dialogue format. His synthesis of love story and economic theory quickly established a set of literary conventions for the late-nineteenth-century American utopists: A young man journeys in time or space to utopia; there he meets a citizen who takes him into a family group, which serves as an illustration and guide to the ideal world. Almost immediately the young adventurer also meets a beautiful young woman (often within the family), and so to his indoctrination is added the love of a perfect woman. Alexander Craig's title *Ionia; Land of Wise Men and Beautiful Women* (1898) summarizes the neatly divided commitment between the head and the heart, the rational and the emotional attractions of utopia. Jones and Merchant used this predictable format to demonstrate that the accepted cultural definitions of woman's character were erroneous, inappropriate, and silly.

When the young American in *Unveiling a Parallel* arrives on Mars, he finds the sister of his guide a beautiful, attractive woman, and like Julian West he becomes enamored with the possibilities of a new life. But the young man soon discovers that his adventure has become an unsettling examination of how he treats women; his gallant and therefore condescending approach does not fit in a society where women have the same rights, privileges, and vices as an upper-class American man.

In order to demonstrate the absurdities in American society, Jones and Merchant created the most unusual heroine in all of nineteenth-century utopian fiction. The earthling is understandably shocked by a woman who is a dynamic financier-philanthropist, who nurses a hangover instead of a baby, who discusses her illegitimate child, and who dismisses marriage as a luxury too costly in demands and burdens for her. The young man had visions of marrying this fascinating woman and establishing a blissful home with a devoted wife, but he is left disillusioned and fighting to maintain his notion that women are "the preservers of our ideals, the interpreters of our faith, the keepers of our consciences" (p. 80).

In the Martian society with no double standard for behavior, women form secret clubs for speech-making, parading, and banqueting lavishly; they "vaporize" the valerian root just as men smoke cigars; they marry respectable husbands and keep lovers; they visit Cupid's gardens with male prostitutes. Jones's and Merchant's theme is as familiar as the comedy of manners tradition; the dazed adventurer asks his host, "Do you in your inmost soul believe that men and women have one common nature,—that women are no better at all than men, and that men may, if they will, be as pure as—well, as women ought to be?" (p. 185).

For Jones and Merchant prevailing attitudes must be desentimentalized and then human rights extended to women before elevation to an ideal world is possible. They note the discrepancy between the "loyalty and tender devotion to individual women" and the "antagonistic attitude toward women in general" (p. 187), which in economic and political terms justifies a protective tyranny. Their rewriting of the Christian creation myth opposes the Pauline view of God-ordained sex roles as well as Milton's version, which prescribed guilt and male dominance: "A pair of creatures, male and female sprang simultaneously from an enchanted lake in the mountain region of a country. . . . They were only animals, but they were beautiful and innocent. God breathed a Soul into them and they were Man and Woman, equals in all things" (pp. 57–58). Because Jones and Merchant desire equality in practical terms, they ridicule a society that flatters and idealizes women and yet will not grant voting rights, just wages, and equal education; they condemn a society that in withholding political and social rights damages a woman's strength, dignity, and self-respect.

Toward the end of the novel Jones and Merchant briefly describe an ideal community high in the mountains where men and women have formed a spiritualized, egalitarian society in which those with great skills and education receive the highest honors. A cook, for example, does not feel degraded by her position; she writes scholarly articles in chemistry and botany, complementary interests for her profession. In this purified society the natural good in human nature predominates, so that the "Rise of Man" rather than the control of his vices occupies the citizens.[17] The representative young American, however, retains his pedestal-mania to the end of the novel: "I have reverenced womanhood all my life as the highest and purest thing under heaven, and I will, I must, hold fast to that faith" (p. 182). In his visit to the model society he thinks he has at last found the ideal woman, and looking into her eyes he marvels, "I saw a new heaven and a new earth" (p. 269). But considering the ridicule Jones and Merchant have subjected him to throughout the novel, this concluding scene is merely the last laugh.

The most striking feature of the first five utopias examined is the vehemence with which the women refute the image of what they are supposed to be and supposed to do for society. In her essay "The Cult of True Womanhood: 1820–1860" Barbara Welter outlined the various demands placed on women by their nineteenth-century culture.[18] She listed piety, purity, submissiveness, and domesticity as the cardinal virtues of an ideal woman's character. Such virtues put into action meant woman's job was to inspire and to nurture those around her, usually in an individual home, and by her example to assure the stability of the society.

The women utopists could not accept the century's popular definition of their nature; their works proclaim different views of the relationship between woman and American society. These women not only condemned the nonactivist roles and the restrictions of domestic life but also showed that radical changes in women's activities would not bring chaos, death, and destruction.

The six utopian feminists in this group demanded the substance, not the sentiments—in Appleton's words, rights, not compliments. In any scene where women are being flattered or idolized, the attitude of the author is satiric. As Jones and Merchant pointed out, flattery only disguised the unequal treatment within a society and did not compensate for direct influence. Instead of beginning the Mother's Day sort of observances, the women sought changes in all concerns that touched their daily lives—social mores, education, political representation, personal property, and economic independence.

None of the writers was tolerant of the image of woman as guardian angel who hovered over men and children, gently murmuring the dos and don'ts of behavior. Most of the utopists described woman as a moral agent with the freedom to act within her society, to participate equally with men, and to be a leader—effective action, not inspiration, was most important. Mason's androgynous ideal, for example, countered the identification of feminine character with passive virtues only. The sharpest attack on piety and purity as woman's duty can be found in Jones's and Merchant's utopia; their theme is that any good traits of human behavior should be encouraged for both sexes. Appleton and Cridge demonstrated that women did not have a special mission in life or a special realm but rather belonged in the midst of society.

All these utopists saw domesticity as in one way or another a curse on women. Cridge and Corbett attacked the notion that the individual household protected women by pointing out that the isolation stifled abilities and that the lifetime effects were damaging to a woman's psyche. For Mason's and Jones/Merchant's heroines, being the center of a domestic circle was dull and potentially claustrophobic. Appleton would break the restrictions on a housewife's duties and her dependency by having more services available in the public sector and by encouraging women in their self-determination.

The fact that each writer focused on different topics (the double standard, marriage, or political and economic equality) illustrates the unifying assumption of all that as women they wanted to define their own ideals and be able to work them out in a sympathetic society. Because women utopists were consciously refuting accepted social patterns and codified injustices, they often directed their message to the men who perpetuated erroneous notions of woman's place. The writers' approaches varied: Appleton's correction of Kent's utopia, Corbett's delineation of happy wives, Cridge's blunt question "How would you like it?," Mason's discussion of misogyny, and Cridge's and Jones/Merchant's treatment of the typical American male as a comic figure. In each instance the women use the utopian genre to question the comfortable supposition that men speak for all humanity.

III

In the following five utopian works the awakening of women to their powers for changing society marks the beginning of utopia. The authors portray this phase in different ways: The process may have begun offstage in the early history of the narrative or it may be part of the immediate development of a new order; the women shaping a better society have come to the realization individually or gradually as part of a woman's group or organization. Many of the good things in the utopias are directly attributed to women's leadership, and in all instances the shape of the ideal society reflects the active participation of women.

Mary Griffith, author of one of the early-American utopias, "Three Hundred Years Hence" (1836), discussed by Nydahl, constructed her vision of the nation's future on the basis of values in her own life experience.[19] Widowed early, Griffith assumed control of the family's farm in Charles Hope, New Jersey, and managed it while developing her interest in horticulture.[20] She dedicated her first published work, *Our Neighbourhood* (1831), to the horticultural societies of Pennsylvania and Massachusetts.[21] Written to excite "a love of horticulture and of rural pursuits," *Our Neighbourhood* anticipates the emphasis on agrarianism and women's rights that characterizes Griffith's utopian sketch.

In general outlines *Our Neighbourhood* resembles the utopian romance pattern of Bellamy's *Looking Backward*: In letters to his English relatives a young man praises the classless American community in which each man is valued for his industry; he learns how the economy flourishes (the details on grafting fruit trees, rotating crops, and so forth); and he searches for a suitable wife in the new land. The prosperous and contented society that Griffith describes is a testimonial to Jeffersonian democracy; however, not all conditions are ideal. Griffith includes a lengthy public lecture on woman's condition that details her narrow existence. Through the voice of a respected doctor, Griffith insists that women must be given a broad education, trained in financial affairs (especially those of their own families), exposed to all cultural and intellectual trends, and encouraged in their self-development.[22] Speaking from her own disgruntled experience, Griffith remarks, "God did not intend that the female mind should never aspire to higher things than to dress chicken salad, and to compound whiskey punch" (p. 267). Griffith's main concern is with the effects of woman's condition on an entire civili-

zation: "We are persuaded that all the misery in this world, which is dependent on vice, arises from the limited sphere of action in which woman
is compelled to move" (p. 283). In her utopia woman-power determines the
course of American history.

The frame story in "Three Hundred Years Hence" pictures a young man,
comfortably settled on a Pennsylvania farm, who is buried by a snow avalanche and found by his descendants three hundred years later. He discovers
that women have purified the American society during the intervening centuries by eliminating the mistreatment of children, banning capital punishment, and exterminating the "war seed." Women have made possible the
tranquil, nonviolent way of life because they were so sensitive to cruelty
and injustice. Griffith traces the beginnings of this transformation to the
volunteer charity organizations of the nineteenth century that were formed
by women to aid the poor and the orphaned. Once women were fully
educated and had entered the business world, they curbed all aspects of
bloodthirstiness in society, including economic rapaciousness: "In every
benevolent scheme, in every plan for meliorating the condition of the poor,
and improving their morals, it was woman's influence that promoted and
fostered it" (p. 87).

Repeatedly Griffith deals with women's need to understand business
methods and their ability to control their own finances.[23] One can assume
Griffith speaks from her own experience as a widow when she insists women
must have economic independence and should learn how to use that power.
Sometime before the twenty-second century, women had assumed control
of money matters and had also received the necessary education and experience: "As soon as [women] themselves were considered as of equal
importance with their husbands—as soon as they were on an equality in
money matters, for after all, people are respected in proportion to their
wealth, that moment all the barbarisms of the age disappeared" (p. 68).
Women's influence extended to such details as removing "coarse and in-
delicate allusions" from Shakespeare's plays, limiting alcoholic beverages to
wine and cider, and prohibiting smoking. Individual women are mentioned
for their success in protecting America's cultural heritage and improving the
daily conditions of life with their inventions.

Along with equality Griffith maintains that women must be given recognition for all their contributions to society, illustrating with the praise
given to Dr. Jenner but denied to Lady Mary Montagu for equal contributions to the eradication of smallpox.[24] In America as utopia the "degraded
state" of women has been changed so that they can participate fully in the
economic as well as cultural affairs of the nation.

The better America provides services for all citizens ranging from nationalized, inexpensive railroads and post offices to consumer-protective
regulation of weights and sanitation standards. No one can obtain a monopoly

on goods, and everyone is subject to an equitable single tax. Griffith assumes a predominantly agricultural economy even though she predicts "internal machinery" vehicles for transportation and for farmwork and long-distance balloon travel. Farmers occupy a respected place in the society. In "Three Hundred Years Hence" Griffith combined the best of Jefferson's agrarianism with an insistence, like Mary Wollstonecraft's, on the importance of women's rights.

Griffith as a farmer and horticulturalist was living the imperfect version of her utopian society. For another writer, Marie Howland, the demonstration of the utopian ideal was equally important, although Howland's economic model, communalism, presented a radical alternative to the American system. In her pursuit of an ideal society Howland explored the theoretical and the experimental. As a student in France she became interested in the theories of the Socialist Godin and the Fourieristic colony he founded at Guise—the *Familistère* or Social Palace, as it is often translated. Howland utilized this colony as a model for the community in *Papa's Own Girl* (1874).[25] The novel drew the attention of Albert K. Owen, who enlisted both Marie and her husband, Edward, in the establishment of a communal society at Topolobampo, Mexico.[26] For the rest of her life Marie Howland was a participant in and advocate of the intentional community as a model for American development. She edited the newspaper *The Credit Foncier of Sinaloa* from its beginning, when it solicited members, and after its move to the colony at Topolobampo. After seven years in Mexico, she returned to the United States and spent her last years in the single-tax colony at Fairhope, Alabama, furnishing the books for its first library and serving as librarian and as associate editor of the Fairhope *Courier*.[27] It should be noted that before Bellamy published his famous *Looking Backward* and the popular Nationalist Clubs were organized to promote his eutopia, Marie Howland was helping to direct an experimental utopian community.

Both the title and the first half of *Papa's Own Girl* may strike readers as unrelated to utopian discussion, because Howland focuses on the domestic life of her heroine. However, if viewed as a special trial by experience, the events in the heroine's personal life are essential to preparing her for her role in founding a new communal society. Howland subjects her heroine to the ideal woman's life as defined by the nineteenth-century culture, and only after the young woman learns that the "perfect image" stifles her talents and indeed separates her from participation in the larger society outside an individual home is she ready to pursue her work as a reformer.

The heroine of *Papa's Own Girl* is reared in a home where her physician father actively encourages her education and preaches the importance of woman's liberation from prejudice and custom;[28] nevertheless, the young woman chooses a conventional marriage to a wealthy, arrogant young man.

She soon discovers that the popular, sentimental view, which glorified woman's mission as household angel, obscured the possibility that the bride may make a mistake or that marriage can become a socially acceptable form of misery. After a divorce, which sets her apart from polite society, the heroine joins a childless widow and a former servant girl with her illegitimate daughter in building a florist and nursery business. The women support themselves and gradually develop a feeling of sisterhood with other single working women. The heroine, at last, is fulfilling her father's belief that women must work out their own political and social salvation and that an age of strong women is necessary to break the male-defined inequalities in society.

Howland includes as part of a conversation her brief description of sex role reversal, designed as was Cridge's and Jones/Merchant's with satiric intent. The heroine conjectures:

> [We women would] be fearful tyrants, having so old a precedent before us, or rather behind us. We'd get all the wealth into our own hands, and when our sometime lords wanted money, we'd ask him how much, and what for, and quibble about the amount, and recommend home-made cigars instead of Havanas. We'd give them donkeys and a side-saddle to ride on, lest immodesty and ambition sould be fostered by riding astride fine horses. We'd have them do hard work all the time, and yet we'd kiss only the hands that were soft and white. Then we'd set up our ideal for male chastity, which would be unattainable, through our system of tempting them; and then we'd laugh at the presumption of any who presumed to demand the same standard for us. If they wished to vote, we'd howl at and persecute them for getting out of their sphere, and show them they had no need of the ballot because we their heaven-appointed protectors, represented them at the polls. [pp. 341–42]

The heroine can ridicule the status quo definition because she has painfully liberated herself from the cultural model for a woman's life, and she has helped develop a separate small community. Having achieved self-determination within the American society, she is free to welcome the ideas of a European reformer and join him in building a socialistic colony that closely follows the *familistère* pattern.

In the latter part of the novel the love story of the heroine and Count Frauenstein takes second place to the building of a communal group. The Count finances and supervises the construction of a self-contained village and factory system where all workers have comfortable housing and access to group dining rooms, shops, libraries, a museum, and a concert hall. The primary emphasis in the Social Palace they build is on the equality of all laborers and the dignity of labor: Every able-bodied member works and receives payment; even the older children have two- and three-hour jobs. Goods purchased at the colony's stores as well as services such as the communal meals (including a choice of French wines) are priced at cost and paid for in the colony's scrip. Education is stressed, beginning with Froebel exercises for the preschoolers, and everyone is encouraged to attend the cultural events held at the community. All women and teenagers sixteen and older have a vote in the governing of the Social Palace.

The Count champions women's rights, insisting that only when women are freed from culturally enforced injustices will men be free. In the establishment of the colony he urges all women to exercise their political power and to ignore the remarks they might receive about being "out-of-her-sphere," "strong-minded," and "losing respectability." Within the new community each woman receives her own salary for her work. A centralized laundry, large kitchens, and twenty-four-hour free nursery care are available for every woman so that no one need be confined to a life of laundry, cooking, and babies. The florist business and its all-woman management are incorporated into the community, which includes brickmaking and silk-weaving factories.

Beginning with two thousand workers, Howland envisions a well-organized city-state sustained by its manufacturing. (Centralized planning has, however, preserved the rural beauty of its surroundings.) The communal life is especially important for women, because it removes them from the isolation of an individual house or farm, offers them a choice of jobs, and assures them economic and political equality.

The heroine of *Papa's Own Girl* marries the Count (they write their own marriage contract), assists him in the formative stages of the colony, and at the end of the novel gives birth to the first child in the new community. Howland concludes on a festival day in this village eutopia—everyone is happy. She leaves unanswered any problems regarding the Count's paternalistic leadership or the heroine's adjustments to motherhood and the nuclear family.

In the next utopia the heroine rejects the traditional woman's role, first by subterfuge and disguise and then, after her voyage to the utopian realm, by her creation of a new role. The adventurer in Alcanoan O. Grigsby's *Nequa; or, The Problem of the Ages* (1900) is "Jack Adams," a woman who has disguised herself as a sailor in order to receive the kind of training and salary she wanted.[29] Akin to the lady buccaneers of nineteenth-century popular fiction, this woman hires on to a ship going to the South Pole and along with the crew is swept into the center of the earth, where an ideal state, Altruria, has mastered the problems of an industrialized America.[30]

Inspired by the highly organized, egalitarian civilization, the heroine decides her mission is to study every detail of the utopian world and then bring its reforms to earth's topside. When the woman guide, a respected teacher and leader, recognizes the heroine's disguise, "Jack Adams" gratefully takes the utopian name of Nequa, or teacher, and responds to the sympathetic friendship. Grigsby has used the Amazonian figure of popular adventure tales in the making of a woman reformer—her adventuresomeness, her independence, her leadership ability—and with the emotional support from a wise, older woman prepares Nequa for her role as social prophet.[31] At the conclusion of the novel Nequa rejects an offer from her long-lost lover to be a fireside wife, insisting that she be "free to think and act" for herself, and she turns from marriage to "labor for the upbuilding of all humanity" (p. 386).

In the characterization of the heroine and in the description of women's contributions to utopia, Grigsby accepts the typical nineteenth-century definition of woman as by nature humanitarian:

> . . . the women of the outer world take the lead in all humanitarian work, because they are naturally more sensitive and sympathetic than men. The women of this inner world are even more inclined to extend a helping hand to the distressed, and they are not handicapped by usages which restrict the influence of the woman of the outer world. Here, both sexes are placed upon terms of absolute equality, and every individual has an opportunity to find the place that is best suited to his or her inclinations. Men are also engaged in this work, but the women here, as in the outer world, are more sympathetic, and as there is nothing to prevent it, they have carried their humanitarian work to such perfection, that all the oppressive conditions which afflict humanity have been well nigh removed. To this, more than to all other causes combined, do we attribute the existence of the ideal conditions which you will find throughout this inner world. [pp. 128–29]

In the history of Altruria the sensitivities of women brought an end to war and removed "the vicious commercial, financial and governmental systems that enable one class of people to oppress another" (p. 129). Grigsby explains that the documented examples of cruel women in the past do not illustrate another side of woman's nature but rather were the result of "domination of man-made laws and prerogatives." Once all women secured their personal freedom, "Mother-love completed the work of human redemption" (p. 130).

Grigsby's optimism is bolstered by her definition of human nature as essentially good: "I believe that nature has planted the germs of all that is good and noble in every human soul, and if this is true, all that is good and noble can be developed in them by the proper influences" (p. 46). For this reason, too, women must be freed from all social and legal restraints so that their special abilities can be utilized for the benefit of the entire civilization. In the ideal world at the center of the earth, special provisions are made for prenatal care and the health of mothers as well as for education, beginning with the very young. The potential of each influence for accomplishing good animates Grigsby's utopian vision. Thus it is not surprising that the heroine chooses to "trace the progressive evolution of these people and discover the fundamental principles and practical business methods that had enabled them to reach their present ideal civilization" (p. 174) and with such powerful knowledge to return to the outer world and convert American society. As a sea captain's wife the heroine could never fulfill her mission, and so she rejects the one-family direction of her sympathies in marriage for the in dependent role of reformer.

Many other aspects of Grigsby's utopia are recognizable features of the post-Bellamy technological visions. The gadgetry, for example, a combined TV and telephone form of communication and electrically powered "chairs" for intracity travel, attest to Grigsby's acceptance of an industrial society and the importance of machines in a better world. Life in the center of the earth is wholesome with less drudgery (two hours of work a day), a vegetarian diet, and better housing (clean cities and communal houses with two thousand private rooms in each). Because the state owns all land and industries, wealth can be equitably distributed. Only the brief touches of Populist rhetoric such as the "Thirteen Usuries on One Hog" parable distinguish Grigsby's discussion of cooperative economics from that in the majority of late-nineteenth-century utopian works.

In naming her inner world Altruria, Grigsby relied on the typical formula of many late-nineteenth-century utopian writers who avoided the adverse connotations of communism or even socialism with a publicly acceptable label.[32] In works such as Titus Smith's *Altruria* (1895), John Brisben Walker's *A Brief History of Altruria* (1895–96), and William Dean Howells's Altrurian Romances, the social and political theories are discussed in the context of government as a Christian brotherhood. Grigsby also pictures the inner world as following the lessons of a Krystus and implementing the Golden Rule as the basis of all laws: She dedicated her book to "all lovers of humanity, wherever found, who believe that the application of the Golden Rule in human affairs would remove all the burdens that ignorance and greed have imposed upon the masses of mankind." In Grigsby's utopia the best interpreters of the Golden Rule or Social Gospel approach to governing are women; for example, the narrator at the beginning of the adventure reminds all the ship's crew, locked in Arctic ice, that "common sense and our common interests dictate that we should be a unit and realize that 'an injury to one is the concern of all' " (p. 84). Woman as humanitarian and as mother is most sensitive to what needs to be changed, and once she is given the utopian world's freedom of action, she selflessly leads the "elevation of the human race." In Grigsby's vision the woman, Nequa—predisposed to follow her altruistic nature—has the answer to the problem of the ages.

In general the nineteenth-century women wrote larger roles for their sex in the utopian scripts. Often, as in *Nequa*, both central characters of the novel, the narrator-adventurer and the guide or representative utopian citizen, are women. In Winnifred Harper Cooley's utopian sketch, "A Dream of the Twenty-first Century" (1902), an old woman in her dream greets another generation, the "radiant young maiden of the new reign of freedom," who explains the ideal century.[33] It should be noted that Cooley is the closest of any of the utopian writers to the nineteenth century's national suffragist leaders. Her mother, Ida Hustad Harper, served as publicist for the National American Woman Suffrage Association, and as the association's historian she wrote Volumes IV, V, and VI of the *History of Women's Suffrage* and the official Susan B. Anthony biography. Unfortunately Cooley's utopia is too brief to do more than hint at her own feminism and her intimate knowledge of several generations of women fighting for their rights. A volume of essays, *The New Womanhood*, which Cooley published two years later, does contain substantial discussion of woman's past contributions to society and her future roles.[34]

In Cooley's utopian dream women are credited with beginning the reform of American society by abolishing the slums, at first using an "insidious, left-handed influence" that was their only power. Later, when the vote was granted them, women's vigorous activities transformed the "unclean bodies and tainted morals of the nation" (p. 513). In *The New Womanhood* Cooley expanded her discussion of "woman's place in the world's work" with chapters on women's role in civic reform, woman as citizen, and women in the trades, professions, and civil offices.

Monogamous marriage in the twenty-first century has become more successful because men and women marry later (usually after the four years of compulsory college education) and because marriage is no longer an economic refuge for women.[35] Cooley notes that public opinion approves families of only two children, the entire society benefiting by the greater care given each child and the improved health of all mothers. In *The New Womanhood* Cooley justified zero population growth with Malthusian arguments and with her belief that a higher civilization brought a concomitant decrease in children per family.

The main features of Cooley's utopia are nationalized industries, the abolition of trusts and monopolies, and nominal fees for services to those with lower incomes. A universal "Religion of Humanity," which replaced the old dogmatic, ritualistic, and conservative forms, now suffuses America with a spirit of rational, simplified Christian religion; like the Social Gospel movement of the age, this religion concentrates on practical ethics and philanthropy. Cooley's utopia ends dramatically with the old woman awakening to the cries of ragged newspaperboys calling out the daily financial crashes, murders, suicides, and scandals. The dream of the ideal inspires the narrator to dedicate herself to the cause of reform and to work toward the vision that the next century's woman had pictured.

Although Mary Bradley Lane's *Mizora: A Prophecy* (1889)[36] was published shortly before Grigsby's, I have placed it at the conclusion of my discussion because it presents the most extreme rejection of male leadership and the most thorough condemnation of patriarchal government. In Lane's *Mizora* the journey to a utopian country at the center of the earth follows the same adventure-novel pattern found in *Nequa*. An upper-class Russian woman, Princess Vera Garovitch, is exiled to Siberia after protesting the killing of her Polish friend, but her family bribes her escape on a whaling ship bound for the North Sea. After desertion, shipwreck, and a brief stay with the "Esquimaux," she drifts to a tropical land of enchantment in the center of the earth.

The conventional frame story does not prepare the reader for the utopian society that Lane describes. The narrator Vera exclaims, "In my world man was regarded, or he had himself regarded, as a superior being" (p. 41); however, in Mizora she sees no men, only a race of blond, agile, strong, and beautiful women who resemble the Aphrodite of Praxitiles. These women live a happy, edenic existence in their scientifically advanced society. Lane's utopian world is an absolute matriarchy—men have been extinct for three thousand years.

By means of the narrator's puzzled inquiries, Lane contrasts the patriarchal governments of nineteenth-century civilizations with the utopian realm where all references, natural and supernatural, are exclusively female. The citizens who live for the good they can do during their lifetimes do not attend churches, for there are no elaborate creeds or religions. In the Mizorian pantheism, "Nature is God and God is Nature. She is the Great Mother who gathers the centuries in her arms, and rocks their children into eternal sleep upon her bosom" (p. 255). A sophisticated technology is responsible for the idyllic comfort of Mizorian life: "Science . . . is the goddess who has led *us* out of ignorance and superstition; out of degradation and disease and every other wretchedness . . . humanity has known" (p. 256). Women, of course, occupy all professions and run the country with a self-sufficiency that amazes the narrator, whose cultural background had taught her "to regard man as a vital necessity" (p. 39).

In the history Lane writes for Mizora, it is clear that men were responsible for all the disruptive evils in society. Women first organized for their own protection, and then with their experience in governing and the discovery of the chemical secret of propagation, they allowed men to simply "die out," although as the Director of the College of Experimental Science tells the narrator, it took centuries before the coarser nature of men was eliminated from the race. A combination of eugenics, special care for mothers, and permissive, loving treatment of children has brought the women to a highly evolved state.

As if proving the amazing civilization women can create, Lane details a complex, marvel-filled world. Many conveniences make life comfortable:

an "elastic glass," mechanical housecleaning, electrically powered carriages, hot air heating, airships, a public broadcasting system. Beautiful and quiet cities built of marble and granite offer their citizens libraries, museums, theaters, and galleries. At its minimum, the Mizorian standard of living provides healthful food (fruits, vegetables, and synthesized meats), ample housing, and universal free education. Each woman works, but no one is a servant in this society, because science has been the magic that eliminated all "menial, degrading, and harassing" toil (p. 39). Everyone has time for cultural refinement and perpetual education.

A striking feature of Lane's utopia is that no change has been made in family structure or in the raising of children; each woman maintains her own home, and although there are infant schools, each woman supervises her young daughters' lives. Lane does not advocate communal housing or a kibbutz grouping that would seem to complement the sisterhood nation. Her praise for the single-family home is extravagant: "Human nature finds its sweetest pleasure, its happiest content, within its own home circle; and in Mizora I found no exception to the rule. . . . In Mizora the home is the heart of all joy, and wherever a Mizora woman goes, she endeavors to surround herself with its comforts and pleasures" (pp. 79, 153). The most serious punishment in the land, exile, is reserved for mothers who mistreat their daughters. A harmonious mother-daughter relationship provides the emotional security and love that is reflected throughout the society in the tranquil and kindly tone of everyday life.

Mizorians are governed by a meritocracy. Personal ambition is recognized, but the educational system and the noble character of all Mizorian women determine the proper direction: "Ambition of the most intense earnestness was a natural characteristic but was guided by a stern and inflexible justice" (p. 53). The narrator learns that all candidates for office in this democracy must first be certified as competent, and then their campaigns are conducted on the basis of their commitment to the public good; no vote-buying or dirty politicking occurs. In Mizora there are no hereditary or social class divisions, for all the citizens are well-educated and refined. Although differences in intellect as well as wealth are recognized, they cannot become the means of gaining unrestrained power.

The narrator marvels at the freedom from sorrows in Mizora—personal and public life is serene with no harassments, and furthermore the usual curses of civilization such as disease, early deaths, poverty, and wars have long since been eliminated: "The very atmosphere seemed to feed one's brain with grander and nobler ideas of life and humanity" (p. 183). The narrator convinces one of the Mizorian young women to go to America with her and explain the ideal system. But the young woman's "lofty ideal of humanity" is laughed at or ignored by the nineteenth-century Americans, and during her return to Mizora she dies.

Lane concludes her novel with no hopeful predictions or optimistic future. The Russian narrator lives in America. Her husband and child have died, and she daily contrasts her life with that in Mizora. Although hoping for the "issue of universal liberty," the woman who has lived in utopia concludes: "Life is a tragedy even under the most favorable conditions" (p. 312).

Griffith, Howland, Grigsby, and Cooley contended that freeing women to use their sensitivities and talents was essential to utopian change. For Lane woman's character and abilities were all-sufficient in establishing the ideal world. The first four writers proposed replacing patriarchal rule with a sexually egalitarian approach to developing and governing a civilization; however, in Lane's view sharing leadership with men inevitably tainted the social order, and the only solution was complete banishment of men. The five writers did agree that the primary ills of their contemporary America such as poverty, economic oppression, monopolies, child abuse, immorality, and the scourge of mankind, war, should be blamed on patriarchal rule.

IV

The greatest advantage of the utopian genre for the eleven feminists was its scope. Cultural models of women effecting social change were inadequate or nonexistent in nineteenth-century America; in utopia the full impact of women's participation could be demonstrated. In each feminist utopia the recitation of evils in the "old world" always featured discrimination against women, and then the false notions and injustices were contrasted with the women's successes in the "new, good" world.

When applying utopian solutions to the problem of woman's status, the writers also benefited from the fact that in utopia the solutions generally are to be found in social, political, and economic systems. For the feminists it meant that with the utopian form came the assumption that woman was not doomed by Nature or God to her present role. The blame for women's exclusion from education, the professions, and politics could not be found in woman's hereditary nature or in her individual weaknesses and inabilities—the fault was in the social order. Furthermore, if the problem was not genetic or teleological, then women did not have to endure their situation because there was no hope. By fashioning their own utopias, the women writers illustrated the concept of planned social change and the extraordinary possibilities of human design for a better life. Eve could create her own garden and organize its management, even to such details as a curfew or "No Trespassing" regulations.

Although these utopists did not join other women reformers on the speaker's platform or in the rallies and marches or at kitchen tables writing position papers, they adamantly believed that their contemporary American society did not meet the needs of women. The eleven writers in this study were activists, too, but they chose as their form of expression the utopia and its personal, yet cosmic, statement.

NOTES

1. Margaret Fuller, *Woman in the Nineteenth Century* (New York: W. W. Norton, 1971), p. 24.

2. Many of the women who wrote or co-authored utopias during the century supported the status quo definition of women's roles. For example, Mary Agnes Tincker in *San Salvador* (1892) succinctly explained, "Now we [women] are going to make a race of noble men. We will rule the state through the cradle." I have extended my survey slightly beyond 1900 in order to include the utopian enthusiasm that followed Edward Bellamy's *Looking Backward* (1888) during the first years of the twentieth century. Twentieth-century feminist utopias—beginning with Charlotte Perkins Gilmans's and extending through the science fiction of Ursula K. Le Guin and Joanna Russ—have continued the nineteenth-century tradition of the feminist literary utopia.

3. Jane Sophia Appleton, ed., *Voices from the Kenduskeag* (Bangor, Me.: David Bugbee, 1848). Mrs. Cornelia Crosby Barrett is listed as coeditor with Appleton. All contributions were anonymous in the original printing. Both Kent's and Appleton's utopias are reprinted in Arthur O. Lewis, Jr., ed. *American Utopias* (New York: Arno Press, 1971). Parenthetical text references are to this edition.

4. In the collection the feminist note mingles with sentimental love poetry and short stories. One poet criticized women for giving their approval to the Mexican War when love, peace, and mercy should be woman's work. Another poet responded to women being called the "poetry of life" with unsentimental lines such as:

> "Life is real, life is earnest," says some ninny;
> *He'd* keep us in a charming flutter!
> But we, being proved life's "Poetry,"
> No longer mean to mind life's clutter. [p. 114]

5. The obituary and eulogy in the *Bangor Daily Whig & Curier*, April 10, 1884, and March 31, 1884, described Appleton as a writer on reform issues, both temperance and the "cause of Women's Progress." Unfortunately, I have not been able to locate a copy of her essay "End and Aim of the Present System of Female Education."

6. Appleton explains that the first guide the narrator met in utopia (in Kent's sketch) was a misogynist whose deceased wife had been servile and obedient. Even though he was very rich, he could not find another woman to marry him, and so he was bitter. The extravagant conduct by women as legislators had been part of a practical joke to ridicule men for their stated fears of feminine power.

7. The Asylum and adjunct supporting member Society illustrate the nineteenth century's independent charitable organizations controlled solely by women, which

historians have begun to study. In this instance all the trustees, directors, and yearly member contributors were women. They managed the education of the early residents, controlled the finances in addition to raising money, and had legal authority to supervise adoptions. See Mary L. Patten, *Historical Sketch of the Bangor Female Orphan Asylum* (Bangor, Me.: Smith & Hill, 1868).

8. Elizabeth T. Corbett, "My Visit to Utopia," *Harper's* 38 (1868–69), 200–204; quotation, p. 201. Further references to this and other works are inserted parenthetically in the text.

9. See William E. Bridges, "Family Patterns and Special Values in America, 1825–1875," *American Quarterly*, 17 (Spring 1965), 3–11, and idem, "Warm Hearth, Cold World: Social Perspectives on the Household Poets," *American Quarterly*, 21 (Winter 1969), 764–79.

10. I have adapted the phrase "marriage can be dangerous for a woman's mental health" from the studies by sociologist Jessie Bernard. For her discussions of the past, future, and ideal conditions for women in marriage see *The Future of Marriage* (New York: World, Bantam, 1973) and *Women, Wives, Mothers: Values and Options* (Chicago: Aldine, 1975).

11. Annie Denton Cridge, *Man's Rights; or, How Would You Like it?* (Boston: William Denton, 1870). Alfred Denton Cridge, in an advertisement following his *Utopia: or, The History of an Extinct Planet* (1884), identified himself as the son of the late Mrs. Annie Denton Cridge and nephew of Prof. William Denton. The son's utopia seems to have been written as proof of his prophetic ability, because he advertises himself as a psychometrist who can delineate character by a letter or a lock of hair (and since he is in California, can examine minerals to locate mines). His utopia describes a catastrophic history on another planet; the individual civilizations evolve to higher states while the planet goes through a disintegrating evolution. Alfred Cridge's utopia shows the influence of his mother's feminism: In each society that reaches a higher civilization, women are given equality in the government and in all the arts and sciences. Writing before Bellamy's popular success, Alfred Cridge had his mother's example of eutopia as a vehicle for social commentary.

12. Eveleen Laura Mason, *Hiero-Salem: The Vision of Peace* (Boston: J. G. Cupples, 1889).

13. Interestingly, Carolyn G. Heilbrun in *Toward a Recognition of Androgyny* (1973) quotes the same statement by Coleridge in her introduction. Heilbrun's purpose is consciously utopian, too, as she urges, "that the ideal of androgyny must be realized for our very survival" (p. xx).

14. The mother tells a suitor that her daughter has another mission in life and that he should "join the army of honorable men who are working for women's enfranchisement before the law; and when the amendment is added to the National Constitution, then, with other suitors, you can plead your case before Miss Eloiheem yourself. Till then, I doubt if our daughter will marry" (p. 247). The mother supports her views with a quotation from John Stuart Mill: "the legal subjection of one sex to another is a wrong in itself, and is now one of the chief hindrances to improvements" (p. 247).

15. Mason identifies the source of the son's hatred of women as an archetypal fear of the female's mysterious connection with the source of life. The son cries that women's "self-knowledge and endurance, yes, their endurance of loneliness and the

pangs of child-birth—and of sights and sense of the unseen worlds—what *don't* they endure? What *do* they enjoy? What do they get or ask for—I mean—what am I saying? I am saying that they are devils! . . . devils and tricky fools, and they outwit us every time! Would there had never been a woman made!" (p. 400).

16. Alice Ilgenfritz Jones and Ella Merchant, *Unveiling a Parallel* (Boston: Arena, 1893), originally published anonymously by "Two Women of the West." Jones had published a novel earlier, *Highwater Mark* (1879), under the pseudonym Ferris Jerome. She also wrote a historical romance, *The Chevalier de St. Denis* (1900), and a novel using the tragic quadroon figure, *Beatrice of Bayou Teche* (1895). Her solution to the quadroon's tragic dilemma is unusual in that instead of choosing self-sacrifice (not marrying the white lover) or death, the quadroon finds a sisterly companionship with an exiled Italian patriot and lives with her on an untroubled Batavian island. I have found no references to other publications by Merchant.

17. In the ideal community all individuals live in their own rooms; sexual relations are only for the divine purpose of propagation. And contrary to what one might expect because of the women's rights positions in most of the novel, in the ideal society women exercise primarily a mothering, nurturing function. The leadership of the group is that of a single man, called the Master.

18. Barbara Welter, "The Cult of True Womanhood," *American Quarterly*, 18 (Summer 1966), 151–74.

19. Mary Griffith, "Three Hundred Years Hence," published in *Camperdown; or, News from Our Neighborhood* (Philadelphia: Carey, Lea & Blanchard, 1836). Griffith dedicated the volume to Mrs. William Minot, "a lady distinguished as a writer and artist; and esteemed by her friends for her domestic virtues" and who had the good fortune to live in Boston, "where woman receives high respect and the consideration" she is entitled to.

20. See Vernon Louis Parrington, Jr., *American Dreams* (Providence: Brown University Press, 1947), pp. 17–18, for biographical information.

21. Mary Griffith, *Our Neighborhood, or Letters on Horticulture and Natural Phenomena: Interspersed with Opinions on Domestic and Moral Economy* (New York: E. Bliss, 1831).

22. Griffith's life illustrates the importance of widows' careers that often cannot be widely documented. See Elisabeth Anthony Dexter's discussion in "When Eve Delved," *Career Women of America: 1776–1840*. Griffith in *Our Neighbourhood* confirmed the historical analysis of Dexter and others, which traces the gradual loss of women's professions during the increased mechanization of early-nineteenth-century America. Griffith contended that men had "usurped" every former industry—teaching, keeping of boarding houses, retail shopkeeping, silkworm raising, tailoring (except for needlework)—and she advocated legal measures to restrict certain employments for women only and to guarantee them just salaries (pp. 270–73).

23. Two other sketches in the collection *Camperdown* are noteworthy for the portraits of women actively managing family incomes. In "The Seven Shanties" a rich benefactor helps a small group of poor families set up a gardening community and develop a cooperative, self-supporting existence. Most of the seven families consist of women and their children, barely eking out a living; even in these adverse conditions women are credited with powers of endurance because they "have a

higher spirit than a man" (pp. 188–89). The successful gardens (agrarianism in an Irish setting) improve both the living standard and the habits of the poor—another example of Griffith's faith in horticulture as social improvement. In "The Baker's Dozen" a shrewd woman manages all property and her household of thirteen daughters (the husband absenting himself most of the time after having failed to father a son). One of the woman's favorite projects is building neat, well-kept cottages to rent to widows, providing housing no one else thought necessary.

24. Griffith, "Three Hundred Years Hence," pp. 48–49. In *Our Neighbourhood* Griffith deplored the centuries of prejudice and abuse women had suffered and mentioned the witchcraft trials as an extreme instance of the generally accepted treatment. She also noted that while John Rogers, who was accused and burned, had been declared a martyr and recorded in children's history books, the many women who had been burned were not mentioned. She implied that the writers of history were reluctant to give women any credit.

25. Marie Howland, *Papa's Own Girl* (New York: John P. Jewett; Boston: Lee & Shepard, 1874). Subsequent editions were printed in 1885 and 1890 by John Lovell, New York. In 1918 a final edition was published under the title *The Familistère* (Boston: Christopher, 1918). A French translation of Howland's novel appeared in 1880 as *La Fille de Son Père*. Howland translated the writings of Jean Baptiste André Godin, *Social Solutions* (New York: J. W. Lovell, 1887).

26. For details on the Topolobampo experiment see Thomas A. Robertson, *A Southwestern Utopia* (Los Angeles: Ward Ritchie, 1964). The interest in communal living was shared by Marie and her husband. Edward Howland published "The Social Palace at Guise," *Harper's*, 44 (April 1872), 701–16, in which he described the facilities and the organized life at Guise. Edward was a joint editor of the newspaper for the Topolobampo colony. The Howlands were among the first colonists, arriving in 1886. Edward died in 1890, and Marie remained in the colony until 1893.

27. Paul E. Alyea and Blanche R. Alyea, *Fairhope, 1844–1954* (University: University of Alabama Press, 1956), pp. 76–77.

28. It is in the father's statements that Howland most vehemently condemns male dominance: "Brute force and ignorance have oppressed women in all history making her a slave to petty cares, denying her the political and social equality that belongs by right to human beings, and making her dependent like a slave" (p. 93). When discussing the sexual double standard, he states that the "inhumanity of men to women is enough to make fiends hide their heads in shame. If the whole sex should go mad with vengeance and murder us all in our sleep, it would scarcely be an injustice to us" (p. 332).

29. Alcanoan O. Grigsby, *Nequa; or The Problem of the Ages* (Topeka, Kans.: Equity, 1900). The heroine explains: "Protected by this disguise, I had filled almost every position on shipboard and had succeeded in earning a competency, something I never could have accomplished as a woman. It was not an experiment. I had tried it successfully for years and would try it again" (p. 18). She later notes the penalties for wearing her disguise but justifies it as the only means she had for being free from the inequitable legal restrictions on women's activities.

30. The notion of the earth's hollow center sheltering a race of people was advanced by John Cleves Symmes, who in 1822–23 urged Congress to appropriate

funds for an expedition to the center of the earth. Grigsby discusses Symmes's theories in her novel, pp. 100–104. Mary Bradley Lane uses the same concept in *Mizora*.

31. The friendship with an understanding woman is crucial for the heroine as she works out her own destiny: "A chord of sympathy and affection had been touched, that enraptured while it bound me in bonds of friendship to this grand woman, a relationship of the most enjoyable character, as well as of incalculable value, in opening up for me a life work" (p. 179).

32. See Louis J. Budd, "Altruism Arrives in America," *American Quarterly*, 8 (Spring 1956), 40–52.

33. Winnifred Harper Cooley, "A Dream of the Twenty-First Century," *Arena*, 28 (November 1902), 511–16.

34. Winnifred Harper Cooley, *The New Womanhood* (New York: Broadway Publishers, 1904). Cooley dedicated the volume to her mother, "not only a great writer, but the most maternal of women," and to her husband, the Reverend George Eliot Cooley, "who is my great inspiration,—the sympathizer with my successes, the comforter of my failures,—one who believes in the highest opportunities for women being the only salvation of the race." For Cooley's views on suffrage see "Suffragists and Suffragettes," *World Today*, 15 (October 1908), 1066–71, and "The Younger Suffragists," *Harper's Weekly* 58, (September 27, 1913), 7–8.

35. In *The New Womanhood* Cooley emphasized the ideal marriage of equals that did not force women to sacrifice their own ambitions. See also her discussion "The First Cause of Divorce," *Arena*, 32 (September 1904), 291–93, for the importance of social structures accommodating women's rising expectations and independence.

36. Mary Bradley Lane, *Mizora: A Prophecy* (New York: G. W. Dillingham, 1889). Subtitled "The Narrative of Vera Zarovitch. Being a true and faithful account of her journey to the interior of the earth, with a careful description of the country and its inhabitants, their customs, manners and government. Written by herself," the novel was first published serially in the Cincinnati *Commercial* from November 6, 1880, to February 5, 1881. In the novel's preface Murat Halstead states that at the time of the newspaper publication the story created a great deal of interest and that not even the author's husband knew who wrote it (pp. v–vi). Lane stated that she had written the narrative "for the sole purpose of benefitting Science and giving encouragement to those progressive minds who have already added their mite of knowledge to the coming future of the race" (p. 9).

DONALD C. BURT

The Well-manicured Landscape:
Nature in Utopia

INTELLECTUAL HISTORIANS HAVE often defined the peculiar attitude of European Americans toward nature by contrasting it to the attitude of Indian
Americans. Merle Curti, for one, writes, "By and large the whites understood little of Indian nature worship, of the poetical Indian love of the land
as it was rather than as it might become under cultivation."[1] The European
American, with his agrarian orientation, accepted paradoxically what Henry
Nash Smith calls "the paired but contradictory ideas of nature and civilization."[2] Jefferson, the chief prophet of American agrarian democracy,
felt—according to David W. Noble—that "the task of Americans . . . was
to develop a way of life in harmony with nature";[3] but in that harmony man
was always to carry the melody and nature the accompaniment. In other
words, the American agrarian believed that a life lived close to nature was
a wholesome life, but he insisted that the nature one lived with be well-
mannered and civilized: Howling wilderness as a neighbor deflated the
moral value of the neighborhood. To the agrarian, farming was the noblest
of occupations. Farming, of course, required that nature be subdued to
man's needs for sustenance and regularity. The American agrarian thus
rejected not only the city but the savage wilderness as well. One cannot
find in American agrarian philosophy the roots of the twentieth-century
concern for preserving nature in the raw.

The attitude toward nature typical of the American utopist of the last
third of the nineteenth century was a compromise between American agrarian principles and the demands of urbanism. The citizens of utopia typically
lived in park-cities—clean, pollution-free, and gardenlike. But they seemed
to have little awareness of or concern for the ecological consequences of
free-wheeling exploitation of the earth and the living things upon it. They
blithely engineered mammoth projects for changing climate, altering topography, and exterminating troublesome and "useless" species. And they
possessed an assurance that natural resources were limitless and would never
run out. In other words, these utopians—and their creators—had an exploitative optimism typical of the American frontier mentality.

But having said as much, one must keep in mind that it was not until the last third of the nineteenth century that Americans, and then only a few, became aware of the importance of preserving wilderness. In 1872 the federal government established Yellowstone National Park, and in 1885 New York established the Adirondacks Forest Preserve—the first such large-scale attempts.[4] The concern that prompted these early and somewhat grudging attempts to preserve wilderness is reflected in the concern of a few utopists for saving and restoring wilderness areas, particularly forest lands. Among this small group of preservationists, some of the most interesting proposals are offered by Albert Chavannes, Edward Bellamy, Bert J. Wellman, Alexander Craig, D. L. Stump, and Milan C. Edson.

Albert Chavannes's Sociolanders establish, near their cities, parks in which nature is left in a wild state except in the areas near the entrances to the cities. Roads and rough picnic facilities are the only concessions to civilization allowed in the parks. Edward Bellamy, a staunchly urban utopist, foresees under Nationalism a parklike United States in which wilderness areas and forests ravaged by capitalism are restored and reforested. In these restored areas the only marks of civilization are the roadways that allow access to them. Bert J. Wellman's "law-abiding revolutionists" make the unagrarian move of allowing large tracts of agricultural land to revert back to wilderness filled with game animals. Great portions of the country thus become a sportsman's paradise. Alexander Craig's Ionia also has an extensive and widely diverse system of national parks, but his utopian parks are not actually wilderness preserves: In them the government has provided elaborate facilities for tourists and visitors. In D. L. Stump's parallel-Earth utopia, conservation of forests and trees is paramount. In fact, lumber is never used for houses, and trees must be planted around farms.[5]

A particularly interesting preservationist is the agrarian utopist Milan C. Edson. Among active conservationists of the late nineteenth century, two not always compatible arguments for preservation were presented. One argument stressed the material benefits of preservation, for example, the assurance through preservation of an adequate water supply. The other argument, of course, was the aesthetic argument—that exposure to the wild beauties of nature was good for the soul.[6] In *Solaris Farm* (1900) Edson proposes a grand national scheme for planting trees. In addition he, through his utopian hero, calls for setting aside as a public park the entire Rocky Mountain range—to be called the "Pride-of-the-World-Park." Not only that, but he wants "all of the most available portions of the mountains of the Pacific Coast Range, the Sierra Nevadas, the Alleghenies, the Adirondacks and the White Mountains . . . reserved by the government, and set apart." His arguments are that such projects will increase the water supply and will provide "such beauty of scenic grandeur and magnitude of picturesque proportions, as the world never saw before."[7] Material and aesthetic—the arguments are those of the conservationists of the late nineteenth century.

It should be made clear, though, that the few utopists who stressed the need for conservation and wilderness preservation were in no way calling for a return to nature. Practically all American utopists of the post–Civil War nineteenth century equated civilization with utopia.[8] They seemed to agree with Thomas Paine's contention in "Agrarian Justice" that "the natural state is without those advantages which flow from agriculture, arts, science and manufactures."[9] Typical of the late-nineteenth-century utopian attitude toward nature and civilization is the utopian socialist Laurence Gronlund's remark that "Civil society is man's natural state." Indeed, he continues, the state struggles against nature.[10] A historian of the American idea of nature and the wilderness, Roderick Nash, has written that "for most of their history, Americans regarded wilderness as a moral and physical wasteland fit only for conquest and fructification in the name of progress, civilization, and Christianity." To the pioneer, "the rural, controlled state of nature . . . the pastoral condition," was the ideal.[11] With all the optimism of the American frontier ethic of exploitation, with all the faith of the American agrarian belief in the limitless abundance of nature, the citizens of utopia polluted their lakes, engineered changes in geography and climate, destroyed entire animal species, and plowed under the wilderness. They were as quintessentially American as the mountain men, pioneers, and empire builders.

Water pollution is the least of the ecological problems American utopian practices would cause. King C. Gillette, the safety-razor king, envisions a mighty metropolis run with machine-like efficiency in the vicinity of Niagara Falls. This monolithic "Central City" complacently uses Lake Ontario as an open sewer into which waste materials are discharged. And Albert Adams Merrill is assured that by forcing the exhaust particles of electric-powered boats into the water, his twenty-second-century utopians are eliminating, not causing, pollution.[12]

Far more outrageous from an ecological point of view are the schemes to alter massively the face of the earth and to change the climate. Again, the American utopists, like nineteenth-century Americans generally, were dedicated to the agrarian proposition that man was duty-bound to adjust nature to his comfort rather than to conform man to the delicate balance of nature. The citizens of America's fictional utopias, oblivious to the possibilities for catastrophe, eagerly exerted their control over nature to alter the natural world in the most highhanded ways. A favorite scheme of the late-nineteenth-century citizens of utopia is the flooding of the Sahara Desert, turning it into a huge lake and altering the climate of the region.[13] Another, proposed by a group of Merrill's twenty-second-century engineers, is to lengthen the year by slowing down the earth.[14] Other fantastic schemes for altering climate include quelling storms and volcanic action and equalizing the earth's temperature from the poles to the equator;[15] altering ocean currents to bring temperate conditions to the Arctic regions;[16] and using high-powered electric lights, which not only turn night into day but also emit enough heat to make the temperate zones semitropical and condense water, which falls as rain when needed.[17] Even William Dean Howells, with his antimachine and pro-rural instincts, is fascinated by the possibilities of climate modification. The southwestern peninsula of Altruria has been cut off to allow the equatorial current to warm the polar regions to an Italian-like moderation in climate. The Altrurians also entertain a recommendation that the western shore of Alaska be cut off to let in the Japanese current.[18]

Not only do the utopists seem oblivious to the possibly dire consequences of altering the earth's climate, they also seem blissfully ignorant of the consequences of shattering links in the biological chain. By the forty-ninth century, according to Chauncey Thomas's utopian prediction, "more than fifty well-known species of mammalia, and more than double that number of oviparious animals, have become extinct [owing to] direct and systematic warfare in the interests of humanity." These include the great dogs and cats, hippos, rhinos, crocodiles, and all serpents. Alexander Craig's utopians also reveal the worst instincts of the American frontier tradition. During their hunting expedition the narrator and his Ionian friends proceed to shoot at every wild creature in sight. "In the course of the day we passed over at least a hundred square miles of territory, and cleared that district of some very formidable pests." Albert Merrill's twenty-second–century utopians have similar murderous frontier inclinations, combined with the tools of an advanced technology; one of their greatest "sports" is hunting eagles on the wing from flying machines. (Merrill's illustrator draws attention to this sport in a full-page frontispiece.) Even the gentle Altrurians of the gentle Howells have cleared all wild beasts from their "sylvan" countryside.[19]

Indeed, for a great many of the utopists wildness has no place at all in utopia. The agrarian impulse to subdue nature, to bring it under full cultivation, is a dominant motive in the American utopia of the late nineteenth century. Typical is John Macnie's utopia of the far future, in which land is cultivated to the hilt and no wildness remains. There are no longer any forests or waste places of any kind, because land is much too valuable—"the very hills were cultivated to their summits." In Amos K. Fiske's utopian world, "no parts of the planet were given up to wilderness or desert, but labor had brought the wilderness into subjection and made the desert like a garden, to minister to the wants of the people." Chauncey Thomas and James Cowan foresaw population pressures necessitating full cultivation of all available land. (Large populations are typical of late-nineteenth-century American utopias.) In Thomas's forty-ninth-century utopia, because of its tremendous population, "there are now few if any waste places." In fact, soil is manufactured on barren places, such as rocky hillsides, and these places are used for agriculture. Cowan's Martian host informs his earthly visitors that the pressures of population demand that all land surface be cultivated: "All the surface of our planet is brought into use; the waste places are reclaimed, and there is abundant room for all."[20]

Were there, then, no utopian voices prophesying ecological doom in the last third of the nineteenth century? Yes, but very, very few. Two utopists clearly warn against the dangers of thoughtless tampering with nature—Edward Everett Hale and Alfred Denton Cridge. Hale's Sybarites oppose changing the face of nature by draining swamps, building dams, and other earth-altering projects. "If one of them tries to mend, he is apt to mar." Cridge illustrates, with his Utopia, "an extinct planet," the dangers of tampering with nature. His utopians' project of draining water from the ocean into an inland area only aggravates the condition of barrenness, which steadily becomes a serious problem on their planet.[21]

But more typically, the utopist rarely felt a pang of regret for the loss of irreplaceable nature and wilderness. Indeed, such a sense of loss is portrayed as frivolous and romantic by the Bellamyite Mrs. C. H. Stone. The heroine of her novel (with the outlandish name of "Fleur-De-Lys Standish") indulges in what is treated as a momentary lapse into romantic regret by an ordinarily level-headed and patriotic Nationalist, when she writes in a letter that in the "rustic" past "mother earth had time and room to be wasteful and idle, and held in her rugged bosom miles and miles of just trees and grass and flowers; the homes of countless wild, free creatures, that our inhospitable days have crowded out of existence."[22]

Like all would-be Edens, then, the landscape of the American utopia was that of a garden, the pastoral landscape of cultivated land. This, as Leo Marx has pointed out, was the ideal landscape of the agrarian, the "middle state" between the primitive and the urban.[23] The American utopia was set in a garden, its roads ran through parks, its farms were parks, and even its cities flourished with cultivated nature. The words "park" and "garden," indeed, were an insistent refrain in the descriptions of the utopian landscape.

One manifestation of the utopian impulse to make America over into a garden is the magnificent parklike highways and country roads that run through the American utopia of the late nineteenth century. The drab and dusty country roads of the rural Midwest, typical of the late nineteenth century as they are typical today, were not allowed in the new Garden of Eden. Cultivated nature was employed to grace even the most utilitarian of man's marks on the landscape. Typical in the magnificence of their scope are the highway systems of Daniel Bond's and Albert Merrill's utopians. Bond foresees a system of highways ("magnificent boulevards") crisscrossing the entire country. These will be multilane highways: A beautiful park 100 feet wide, filled with fountains and flowers, will be laid out between 200-foot-wide roads running on each side. Merrill describes a similar stretch of road: "This boulevard, like all the other streets, was two hundred feet wide. In the centre there were walks, with flower beds and beautiful trees. It was an earthly paradise."[24] In such projects the American passion for bigness is as apparent as the agrarian love of cultivated, gardenlike nature.

Not only have roads in utopia become like parks, so have farms. Under socialism, Bert J. Wellman predicts, the farm will become a "lovely park, with fountains and blooming flowers." On Milan Edson's cooperative farm, "all industrial buildings, are surrounded by well-kept lawns," and the farm cottages are surrounded "by gardens and lawns." The setting of the cooperative farm village is a "pastoral picture." The agricultural district of Alcanoan O. Grigsby's *Nequa* is an even more elaborate and artificial park: It has "much of the surface . . . given up to parks, shaded driveways, miniature rivers, artificial lakes, fountains, ornamental gardens and orchards." And in Bradford Peck's countryside there are "beautiful fields and orchards, which were laid out like one vast and continuous park." Indeed, Peck's nineteenth-century protagonist learns from a utopian of the future that "the entire farming section of our country [is] made into a vast park like those in our greatest cities."[25] The utopian farm, thus, was to be pastoral and parklike, unlike the drab, unkempt farmsteads on which farmers labored away their dreary lives—according to the Midwestern regional literature contemporary with the utopian fiction under discussion. Hamlin Garland's Middle Border farms were the antithesis of the Jeffersonian agrarian image. America's utopian thinkers of the last decades of the nineteenth century suggested changes in the natural setting of the American farm that would bring some beauty to farm life and thus bring it closer to the agrarian ideal.

But the garden of the utopian countryside paled before the garden of the utopian city. The citizen of the American utopia tended to be a city dweller, but he was also fond of country greenery. What these utopians achieved, thus, was a compromise between urban togetherness and efficiency, and agrarian rural love of cultivated nature. American utopian literature of the last decades of the nineteeenth century is filled with descriptions of tree-lined city streets, rooftop gardens, public parks, and lush lawns and gardens surrounding marvels of city architecture.

Tree-lined streets and buildings surrounded with well-kept lawns and gardens are a nearly universal feature of the city in the utopian cosmos. Cridge, for example, offers a rather typical urban-pastoral description of a utopian city: "Where were once the narrow roughly-paved streets and alleys of the lower portion of the city, now are broad smoothly laid avenues with shaded sidewalks, a row of handsome trees in the center and statues or drinklng [sic] fountains at every corner." In Ignatius Donnelly's Populist utopia in the African mountains, each town is required by law to line its streets with *fruit* trees, no less, and each house is expected to be surrounded with a garden. In Howells's Altrurian towns the dwellings "are built round courts, with gardens and flowers in the courts, and wide grassy spaces round them." The utopian city was a garden, a well-manicured landscape in which the citizen was always in sight of trees and flowers and shrubbery. Fiske's and Stump's "flowery" descriptions of city garden-scapes echo descriptions to be found in dozens of utopian novels of the late nineteenth century. In Fiske's otherworldly city, "spread for miles around along the diverging avenues were the habitations of the people, each occupying ample space, with fruitful gardens and shaded walks and a profusion of rich herbage and trees and flowers." And in the city of Stump's extraterrestrial utopia, "the wide and smooth-mown lawns with their carpets of velvety green, the profusion of beautiful flowers, the elegant shrubbery and stately trees combined to make a scene most wonderfully enchanting." No adman writing copy for suburban townhouses could have said it more appealingly.[26]

Indeed, one might get the impression from these limited examples that the utopian city is an idealization of the twentieth-century suburban community of the real estate developers, with its moderate-sized one-family dwellings and well-kept lawns—the quintessential compromise between urban and rural values. Such, however, is not often the case. The dwelling places in many utopian cities consist of vast apartment buildings in which the citizen lives like a bee in a hive or an ant in an anthill. So concerned were most utopists with the isolation and loneliness of life in rural America—an experience many of them had endured as youths[27]—that they often suggested an urban plan for social togetherness with a vengeance. Two extreme but representative examples are found in the utopias of Chauncey Thomas and Albert Waldo Howard. Thomas offers one of the more original designs for his multiunit and multiuse apartment buildings; they each cover a city block and are tapered like pyramids, so that all floors have access to light and ventilation. Each of these apartment pyramids has more than 4,000 units; one pyramid has a population of 22,000. The professor who conducts Thomas's nineteenth-century protagonist through the wonders of the forty-ninth century proudly calls the pyramids anthills. In Howard's tall-tale utopia the smallest residence buildings of 10,000 to 15,000 feet in height hold 1 million citizens. The "grand Salon" of one of these buildings seats 1 million people. Nevertheless, some country greenery is incorporated with these mountainous urban nightmares. In order to enjoy a vestige of rural nature in their anthill apartment-pyramids, Thomas's urban citizens of the forty-ninth century are allowed a "little strip of soil" at the entrance of each apartment unit in which to plant trees and shrubs. And Howard's gargantuan residence buildings all have roof gardens.[28]

It is chiefly, though, the public park that gives the utopian city-dweller his taste of nature. Like their contemporary, Frederick Law Olmsted, landscape architect and designer of Central Park in New York City, practically all the American utopists insisted that an ideal city must have large areas of land set aside for satisfying the pastoral longings. Cridge's utopia, for example, sets aside one city block in sixteen as a public park or garden. The government of Donnelly's pastoral utopia requires all towns to set aside space for parks, and Craig's Ionian city of Iolkos has a great deal of space taken up by parks, one of which consists of four blocks. Even the gigantic apartment complexes of Howard are surrounded by luxurious parks.[29]

Clearly, thus, the prevailing attitude toward nature of the American utopists of the last third of the nineteenth century was a reflection of the agrarian desire for a well-manicured landscape. In that landscape uncontrolled nature did not belong. The American utopist was no Natty Bumppo, disdainfully wishing the settlements would clear out and let the forests grow wild again. He was no Thoreau, seeking spiritual solitude, away from civilization, in the woods. Even the handful of utopists who stressed preservation allowed easy access to their utopian wilderness areas. Wild nature, it was always understood, was for man's use and enjoyment. Civilization and civilized men were always to make their presence felt.

Nature domesticated and controlled—that is the keynote. And the generation following the Civil War was a generation becoming increasingly aware of the possibilities of controlling the physical world through the forces of science and technology. The continent had been spanned by railroad and telegraph; men controlled massive machinery with steam and electricity.[30] It is to be expected that utopian thinkers of that generation would speculate about ways in which the new forces at mankind's command could be used to shape and alter the earth to make it a more comfortable home for mankind. Both the new science and the old agrarian tradition called for control of nature. And both the new science and the old agrarian tradition insisted on the never failing abundance of nature. Thus the utopian speculators of the generation after the Civil War could propose ecologically questionable schemes such as altering the rotation of the earth, drastically altering its climate, radically changing its surface, and blithely exterminating its wildlife. The last third of the nineteenth century was a period of exploitative optimism almost without equal in American history, and agrarianism and science certainly supported that optimism.

But the agrarian landscape was a garden, not bare pavement, stone, and steel like the typical American city. And though the citizens of American utopias typically lived in cities, agrarian love of cultivated nature was reflected in the gardenlike landscape that dominated both city and country. The utopian city was a city of parks, of tree-lined avenues, of apartment houses surrounded by large, well-kept lawns and flowers, and of buildings topped with roof gardens.[31] The move to the suburbs, which began in earnest after the Civil War, was one compromise between the convenience of city living and the agrarian wholesomeness of country living. The garden-city of the American utopia of the period was another. The American utopists of the last third of the nineteenth century, for all their affection for urbanization and technology, did not see the city and the machine as irreconcilable with the pleasures of nature. They had a healthy awareness of man's need for contact with growing things—even if that growth was rigidly controlled by man. What these authors were eager to see created was a pastoral garden landscape over the entire countryside, and parks and gardens in—and of—every city.

NOTES

1. Merle Curti, *The Growth of American Thought* (New York and London: Harper & Brothers, 1943), p. 18.

2. Henry Nash Smith, *Virgin Land* (New York: Vintage, 1950), p. 305.

3. David W. Noble, *Historians Against History* (Minneapolis: University of Minnesota Press, 1965), p. 14.

4. See Roderick Nash, *Wilderness and the American Mind* (New Haven and London: Yale University Press, 1967), pp. 108–21, for a discussion of the progress of the preservationists during the period.

5. Albert Chavannes, *The Future Commonwealth; or, What Samuel Balcom Saw in Socioland* (New York: Nationalist Publishing Company, 1892; reprint, New York: Arno Press, 1971), p. 87; Edward Bellamy, *Equality* (New York: D. Appleton, 1897; reprint, Upper Saddle River, N.J.: Gregg Press, 1968), pp. 296–97; [Bert J. Wellman], *The Legal Revolution of 1902*, by a Law-Abiding Revolutionist (Chicago: Charles H. Kerr, 1898; reprint, New York: Arno Press, 1971), pp. 307–9; Alexander Craig, *Ionia; Land of Wise Men and Fair Women* (Chicago: E. A. Weeks, 1898; reprint, New York: Arno Press, 1971), pp. 189–91; D. L. Stump, *From World to World* (Asbury, Mo.: World to World, 1896), pp. 40–41.

6. Again, see Nash, *Wilderness*, pp. 108–21. This conservationist debate between the pragmatic and the esthetic can be found in American literature as early as James Fenimore Cooper's *The Pioneers* (1823). Judge Temple argues for conservation of resources for future use. Natty Bumppo asserts the spiritual good of unsullied wilderness.

7. Milan C. Edson, *Solaris Farm; A Story of the Twentieth Century* (Washington, D.C.: published by the author, 1900; reprint, New York: Arno Press, 1971), pp. 187–214. Quoted passages are from p. 211.

8. One exception is Mrs. M. A. (Weeks) Pittock, the thesis of whose romance, *The God of Civilization* (Chicago: Eureka, 1890), is that natural man is purer, nobler, and more moral than the "dissipated and vicious creatures" of civilization (p. 84).

9. Thomas Paine, "Agrarian Justice," in *The Life and Works of Thomas Paine*, ed. William M. Van der Weyde, Vol. 10 (New Rochelle, N.Y.: Thomas Paine National Historical Association, 1925), 10.

10. Laurence Gronlund, *The Coöperative Commonwealth* (1884) (Cambridge, Mass.: The Belknap Press of Harvard University Press, 1965), pp. 72–73.

11. Nash, *Wilderness*, pp. vii, 30.

12. King C. Gillette, *The Human Drift* (Boston: New Era, 1894), pp. 87–88, and Albert Adams Merrill, *The Great Awakening: The Story of the Twenty-second Century* (Boston: George, 1899), p. 189.

13. Byron A. Brooks, *Earth Revisited* (Boston: Arena, 1893), p. 240, and Solomon Schindler, *Young West, A Sequel to Edward Bellamy's Celebrated Novel "Looking Backward"* (Boston: Arena, 1894; reprint, New York: Arno Press, 1971), pp. 254–55.

14. Merrill, *Great Awakening*, p. 52.

15. Calvin Blanchard, *The Art of Real Pleasure* (New York: published by Calvin Blanchard, 1864; reprint, New York: Arno Press, 1971), p. 18.

16. Alvarado M. Fuller, *A.D. 2000* (Chicago: Laird & Lee, 1890; reprint, New York: Arno Press, 1971), pp. 249–51, and Chauncey Thomas, *The Crystal Button; or, Adventures of Paul Prognosis in the Forty-Ninth Century* (Boston and New York: Houghton, Mifflin, 1891), pp. 103–4.

17. [John McCoy], *A Prophetic Romance: Mars to Earth*, by the Lord Commissioner (Boston: Arena, 1896), p. 37.

18. William Dean Howells, *Through the Eye of the Needle* (1907), in *The Altrurian Romances*, eds. Clara and Rudolf Kirk (Bloomington: Indiana University Press, 1968), pp. 389–90.

19. Thomas, *Crystal Button*, pp. 100–102; Craig, *Ionia* (note 5 above), pp. 261–64; Merrill, *Great Awakening*, p. 230; Howells, *Eye of the Needle*, p. 390.

20. [John Macnie], *The Diothas; or, A Far Look Ahead*, by Ismar Thiusen (pseud.) (New York: Putnam's 1883; reprint, New York: Arno Press, 1971), pp. 83–85, 303; Amos K. Fiske, *Beyond the Bourn: Reports of a Traveller Returned from "The Undiscovered Country"* (New York: Fords, Howard & Hulbert, 1891), p. 88; Thomas, *Crystal Button*, pp. 114, 117–18; and James Cowan, *Daybreak: A Romance of an Old World* (New York: George H. Richmond, 1896; reprint, New York: Arno Press, 1971), p. 97.

21. Edward Everett Hale, *Sybaris and Other Homes* (Boston: Fields, Osgood, 1869; reprint, New York: Arno Press, 1971), p. 54, and Alfred Denton Cridge, *Utopia; or, The History of an Extinct Planet* (Oakland, Cal.: Winchester & Pew, 1884), p. 27 *et passim*.

22. Mrs. C. H. Stone, *One of "Berrian's" Novels* (New York: Welch, Fracker, 1890), p. 15.

23. Leo Marx, *The Machine in the Garden* (New York: Oxford University Press, 1964), pp. 100–116.

24. Daniel Bond, *Uncle Sam in Business* (Chicago: C. H. Kerr, 1899), pp. 38–39, and Merrill, *Great Awakening*, p. 39.

25. Wellman, *Legal Revolution* (note 5 above), p.293; Edson, *Solaris Farm* (note 7 above), pp. 314–15; Alcanoan O. Grigsby, *Nequa; or, The Problem of the Ages* (Topeka, Kans.: Equity Publishing, 1900), p. 147; and Bradford Peck, *The World a Department Store: A Story of Life under a Coöperative System* (Lewiston, Me.: Bradford Peck, 1900; reprint, New York: Arno Press, 1971), pp. 194–95, 205.

26. Cridge, *Utopia*, p. 16; Ignatius Donnelly, *Caesar's Column: A Story of the Twentieth Century* (1890) (Cambridge, Mass.: The Belknap Press of Harvard University Press, 1960), pp. 308–12; Howells, *Eye of the Needle*, p. 401; Fiske, *Beyond the Bourn*, p. 97; and Stump, from *World to World* (note 5 above), p. 46.

27. See Kenneth M. Roemer, *The Obsolete Necessity: America in Utopian Writings, 1888–1900* (Kent, Ohio: Kent State University Press, 1976), p. 9.

28. Thomas, *Crystal Button*, pp. 51–52, 77–78, and [Albert Waldo Howard], "The Milltillionaire," by M. Auburré Hovorrè (pseud.) (1895?), reprinted in Arthur O. Lewis, Jr., ed., *American Utopias: Selected Short Fiction* (New York: Arno Press, 1971), pp. 9, 19, 22.

29. Cridge, *Utopia*, p. 6; Donnelly, *Caesar's Column*, p. 308; Craig, *Ionia*, pp. 148–49; and Howard, "Milltillionaire," p. 5.

30. In the pre–Civil War utopia, typically, science and technology were satirized as the work of "projectors," to use the eighteenth-century Swiftian word. Almost without exception the post–Civil War utopia was machine-based, and electricity was a utopian obsession of almost mystical quality.

31. Besides the foregoing examples see also Roemer's survey in *The Obsolete Necessity*, pp. 153–70.

STUART TEITLER

In Search of Zion: An Annotated Bibliography of the Ten Lost Tribes of Israel in Utopia

BIBLICAL LORE HAS it that at first there were twelve tribes of Israel. Ten of them scattered hither and yon in search of a land of milk and honey—Zion—and the other two are more or less accounted for. With so venerable a source as the Good Book, it is no wonder that the whereabouts of the mysterious Lost Tribes has fascinated writers for centuries and thus created a substantial body of speculative fiction and nonfiction. The annotated checklist below attempts to trace through American fiction the exodus of the wayward Lost Tribes and how they found utopia in its differing aspects and climes.

Stories dealing with the discovery of the Ten Lost Tribes form only a tiny part of a vast body of popular fiction that has become known as Lost Race fiction—a type of literature that has been examined recently by Thomas D. Clareson in "Lost Lands, Lost Races: A Pagan Princess of Their Very Own," one of the essays in Clareson's collection, *Many Futures, Many Worlds: Theme and Form in Science Fiction* (1977). The formula for this type of adventure tale emerged fully developed with all its trappings in the late nineteenth century. Its popularity was largely due to the influence of the novels of the British author H. Rider Haggard, especially *She* (ca. 1886), *Allan Quatermain* (1887), and *Queen Sheba's Ring* (1910). A stream of imitations and adaptions of Haggard's basic formula appeared in pulp science fiction magazines into the 1940s, and it was probably at that time that fans coined the term Lost Race. Voyages to previously unknown civilizations are, however, about as old as stories themselves, with some foundations in Eastern romances and, of course, in utopian writings. To the science fiction and fantasy reader Lost Race means escape fiction, the wonders of archaeology, barbaric kingdoms with lusty heroes and heroines, and ample touches of super-science or the supernatural. But Lost Race really refers not to a theme so much as to a plot device, a skeletal framework to which an author might

186

attach his or her concepts of social satire, romantic escape, or utopian philosophy.

The Lost Race framework was employed in most of the earliest classic utopias. The dialogues of Timias and Kritias in *The Republic* of Plato formed the basis of the Atlantis legend, one of the standard Lost Race settings. Campanella's *City of the Sun* and Bacon's *New Atlantis* are seventeenth-century utopias that are also Lost Race narratives. Andreae's *Christianapolis* (1619) is not only utopian Lost Race but possibly the first book in a long cycle to be set at the North Pole, a favored location among nineteenth-century American authors, as suggested by the following checklist. The lesser-known but superb *Memoirs of Sigr. Gaudentio di Lucca* (1737) describes the advanced and socially enlightened "Mezzoranians," found in untrodden parts of Africa. *Di Lucca* was an early story to depart from the strictly travelogue utopian formula. It offers readers some character development, love interest, and personal rivalry. It also appears to be the first English-language utopia to feature the Ten Lost Tribes.

There have been more than two thousand adult Lost Race books published in English, and a generous portion of these qualify as utopian. By the late nineteenth century, the Lost Race story with varying degrees of utopian content had emerged as one of the most popular types of adventure fiction in the United States. Hundreds of such novels were published in both England and America from around 1870 to 1905. As suggested already, much of this popularity can be attributed to the success of Haggard's African epics, although the nineteenth-century interest in Lost Race utopias was also fostered by such British works as *The Coming Race* (1871) by Edward Bulwer-Lytton and the satirical utopia *Erewhon* (1872) by Samuel Butler. As Kenneth Roemer notes in his historical survey, in America the popularity of Bellamy's *Looking Backward* (1888) inspired numerous utopists, and many of these, unlike Bellamy, employed a Lost Race framework—for example, William Dean Howells in the Altrurian Romances, Walt McDougall in *The Hidden City* (1891), William R. Bradshaw in *The Goddess of Atvatabar* (1892), and Alexander Craig in *Ionia; Land of Wise Men and Fair Women* (1898).

The following chronological checklist focuses on the utopian Lost Tribes of Israel version of the Lost Race tale. The list begins with 1888, the year after the publication of Haggard's *Allan Quatermain* and the year *Looking Backward* appeared. It continues by surveying the Lost Tribes utopias published in America during the late nineteenth and early twentieth centuries. This survey makes no claims to "completeness." There are undoubtedly other utopian Lost Race books that contain allusions to the Ten Lost Tribes buried within their narratives. But the following list is the most complete of its kind, and it does suggest the importance of the search for Zion in

American utopian literature and the variety of plots and themes inspired by the Biblical account of the Ten Lost Tribes of Israel.

1888   [De Mille, James]. *A Strange Manuscript Found in a Copper Cylinder*. New York: Harper & Brothers.
Spurred by the popularity of *Looking Backward*, this novel appears to be the first utopian story by a North American writer (De Mille was a native Canadian) to feature the Lost Tribes. (De Mille's popularity antedated publication of this book as a result of many boys' adventure novels and a few good mysteries.) This beautifully produced novel tells of a manuscript, plucked from the bosom of the sea, that records the experiences of Antarctic voyagers on a warm subcontinent inhabited by the "Kosekin." Through long centuries of isolation these people have evolved an elaborate but topsy-turvy economy that holds poverty and suffering as the highest honors achievable. Scenes portray the Kosekin engaged in suicidal forays with the monstrous saurians of this lost land. The life mission of these people is the attainment of poverty. As entertainment, this story is quite successful. It is only partially dystopian, as there are areas of social equality—womens rights, for instance—that are superior to any on earth. *A Strange Manuscript* is also clearly a satiric utopia that criticizes materialism and, one suspects, the Jews, who De Mille feels are its most devout disciples. The book includes terrific illustrations.

1889   Fleming, Andrew Magnus. *Captain Kiddle; A Fantastic Romance*. New York: John B. Alden.
Kiddle and his variegated crew of racial stereotypes, including a Jew and a black, cruise for unknown waters in the Arctic Circle. The original Eden and the Fountain of Youth are soon discovered among a degenerate race of giants living under a mildly communistic system. Later the grandeur of their past achievements is uncovered—a stupendous modern city with mummies of the rulers. It is suggested that they are descendants of the Tribes. This novel is predominantly an adventure yarn, filled with ethnic barbs and Fleming's feeble attempts at humor.

1891   Makeever, John L. *The Wandering Jew; A Tale of the Ten Lost Tribes of Israel*. Osceola, Neb.: E. A. Walrath.
This brief novel tells of the "New Jerusalem," sequestered among the cliffs of Colorado. The Tribes have lived in peace and prosperity here for countless centuries. They have a simple religious utopia, but there is some conflict between the "True-Believers," the "Pagans," and the "Baal-Worshippers." The perfectly preserved bodies of all the great Jewish patriarchs rest in this community. Later the Wandering Jew himself arrives and tells of his immemorial wanderings. A natural upheaval destroys the country. Only the narrator and the Wandering Jew escape.

1893   Warren, Benjamin C. *Arsareth; A Tale of the Luray Caverns*. New York: A. Lovell.
A Virginian theosophist proves his theory that the Tribes migrated to America and found their Zion in the fabulous Luray Caverns. He accomplishes this

by mesmerizing his daughter, who, while entranced, tells of her pre-existence (before reincarnation) among the Tribes. *Arsareth* is marginally Lost Race and only slightly utopian.

1896 [Burg, Swan]. *The Light of Eden; or, A Historical Narrative of the Barbarian Age. A Scientific Discovery* . . . Seattle: S. Burg.

Light of Eden begins as a pure adventure story: The heroes are rescued in the nick of time from savages in Borneo and flown by airplane to a lovely country, called "Eden," that lies across the North Pole. The classically beautiful inhabitants had sometime ago sought and found solutions to the questions of politics, economy, and religion. Burg emphasizes land rent and single tax. The hero returns with an Edenic bride and billions in gold that upset the American economy and pave the way toward a new order.

1896 Chipman, De Witt C. *Beyond the Verge; Home of the Ten Lost Tribes of Israel.* Boston: J. H. Earle.

This is a fantastic pseudo-history that alternates between fictional narrative and treatise, the latter supporting Symmes's hollow-world theory. The story deals with a great Hebrew patriarch and scientist who leads his people in ancient times to the paradise that lies at the earth's core. En route to the Pole, the Tribes mingle with the Mound-builders, and some remain among these Indians. The book can be characterized as religious utopian and science fiction.

1897 Kerr, Artemus P. *The Lost Tribes and the Land of Nod. An Original Natural Gas Story.* Indianapolis: Indiana Newspaper Union.

This tall, thin volume relates the adventures of a trapper who is supposed to have accompanied the Lewis and Clark expedition and never returned. In a place suggestive of Northern California, the hero finds the Tribes in a severely static and tradition-bound but peaceful and prosperous community. As in Twain's *Connecticut Yankee*, the outsider attempts to implement social and technological improvements. In doing so, he only makes things worse and incurs the ire of the elders of the Tribes. He is finally forced to leave the country. As in many Lost Race stories, the country is destroyed shortly thereafter. Again like Twain's work, *The Lost Tribes* is satiric.

1897 Mentor, Lillian F. *The Day of Resis.* New York: G. W. Dillingham.

This novel is not listed in Wright and is listed by the Library of Congress as being authored by a writer of unknown nationality. The style, American characters, and New York publisher argue American origin. A rare map brings travelers across remote parts of Africa to an unknown country called "On." The Onians are of Egyptian-Hebrew heritage, having fled their homeland during the Biblical plague set upon them by the God of the Jews; they now follow a bastardized form of Judaism. On is clearly a utopia, governed by a form of communism under a hereditary king. There is complete equality; all types of employment are shared; a form of eugenic marriage is practiced; and population control and physical culture have become obsessions. The people are giants and magnificent human specimens, even in advanced years. They believe in much leisure time. "The Day of Resis" is an annual human-sacrifice ritual that serves to purge the populace, who are otherwise peaceful folk.

1899   Jackson, Ambrose Lester. *When Shiloh Came*. New York: J. S. Ogilvie.
       This is a fantastic allegory of pre- and postflood events. It attacks the worship
       of false gods and values.

1900   Harney, Gilbert Lane. *Philoland*. New York: F. T. Neely.
       In the author's note he claims that *Philoland* was conceived and written
       before many books of similar theme and long before the principal one,
       presumably *Looking Backward*. The narrative recounts a balloon flight to
       the all-too-familiar world inside the earth. This interior world supports a vast
       and sophisticated civilization that outstrips the known world in the natural,
       paranatural, and social sciences: The people's accomplishments include lon-
       gevity without disease and other ravages of old age, airplanes, phonographs,
       telephones, and moving roadways (which anticipate a famous story by Robert
       A. Heinlein). The novel is a readable and inventive piece of science fiction
       as well as a "hard-core" utopia, which offers a detailed account of a coop-
       erative socialist system under a benevolent monarch. The population is of
       ancient Hebrew stock; they were the earliest converts to Christianity. They
       found their new country shortly after the resurrection.

1901   McGrady, Thomas. *Beyond the Black Ocean: A Story of Social Revolution*.
       Terre Haute, Ind.: Standard.
       A paperback edition published by Charles H. Kerr of Chicago exists.
       McGrady constructs a parallel, pseudo-history of America and England with
       the countries of "Todia" (America) and "Dan" (England). In the late eigh-
       teenth century two hundred Irish flee their homes to enter a mysterious
       polar channel that brings them beyond the Arctic ice to an entirely new
       planet, earth's twin, connected at the polar cap by an umbilical channel that
       opens only periodically. (The same idea had been used as early as the sev-
       enteeth century.) The new world was populated by the descendants of the
       Tribes. With the help of the fighting Irish, the Todians defeat the Dans and
       establish a socialistic cooperative commonwealth. By the nineteenth century,
       war, disease, and suffering have been abolished, and there has been much
       technological progress, including the development of airplanes and com-
       munication with Mars.

1903   Lindelof, Otto Julius Swenson. *A Trip to the North Pole; or, The Discovery
       of the Ten Tribes, as Found in the Arctic Ocean*. Salt Lake City: Tribune
       Printing.
       Here the great cities of "Vau" and "Thebboth" support a flourishing civili-
       zation that mingles the ancient with the ultramodern. The lovely people
       follow the old faith, customs, and dress of the ancient Jews. There are chariot
       races and gladiatorial matches along with airplanes, shaped like beautiful
       birds, and other machines. The wealth of the land is shared in a socialistic
       fashion; peace and prosperity reign.

1908   Hatfield, Frank (pseud.). *The Realm of Light*. Boston: Reid.
       A people called the "Zoeians," of ancient Biblical origins suggesting the
       Tribes, dwell in unknown parts of Africa. They have tapped the secrets of
       solar energy and increased longevity. The Zoeians have begun evolving into
       a higher human form. Under the guidance of a lifetime elected ruler, the
       three distinct classes of the populus thrive in a form of cooperative com-
       monwealth.

1915 Gratacap, Louis P. *The New Northland; Krocker Land, A Romance of Discovery.* New York: T. Benton.
The stunted and macrocephalic descendents of the Tribes are found in an abyss near the North Pole. Their huge skulls and dwarfish bodies are the results of mutations caused by a neighboring radium pool that is also the source of their wonderful technology. The people are deeply religious and are ruled by a hierarchy of priest-scientists in a moneyless, communal society. They have learned the transmutation of baser metals into gold. Though marred by awkward and pretentious writing, the ideas in this eventful tale are utterly fantastic and often interesting. Gratacap wrote five other science fiction novels, two of which were utopian.

1920 Winslow, Belle Hagen. *The White Dawn.* Minneapolis, Minn.: Augsburg.
The narrative is set around the eleventh century. A Viking discovers the remnants of the Tribes in an extinct volcano in the Arctic Circle. The visit is brief, and much of the novel is taken up with Christian proselytizing.

1927 Barker, Arthur W. *The Light from Sealonia.* Boston: Four Seas.
An old rivalry, war, and invention are the major ingredients of this science fiction thriller, which includes an aerial voyage to the North Pole to the domains of the "Sealonians" and the "Nodolians." Both stem from the Tribes, or at least from the Biblical Israeli, but are fierce enemies.

1934 Aronin, Benjamin. *The Lost Tribe; Being the Strange Adventures of Raphael Drale in Search of the Lost Tribes of Israel.* Chicago: Simons Press.
The Lost Tribe depicts the descendants of the Tribe of Dan in a simple-life and deeply religious agrarian utopia of vegetarians. The goods and services of this small country are shared by all. This is an adventure story intended for rather sober-minded and unimaginative boys. A loose sequel entitled *Cavern of Destiny* was published in 1943.

1937 Aronstam, Noah E. *The Lost Nation.* Detroit: Duo-Art Press.
This novella tells of an edenic volcanic valley in Africa that for a millennium has concealed a remnant of the "Chazars." They speak a mixed Arabian dialect but use the Hebrew alphabet and live in accordance with old Jewish laws. The Chazars are not the Lost Tribes; they are converts to the faith who had a prosperous empire in Southern Russia in the eighth and ninth centuries.

[no date] Argo, Madeline. *My Trip to the Ten Lost Tribes Inside the Earth.* n.p.: n.p.
Probably an occult pamphlet presented as nonfiction. It is not listed in the Library of Congress Printed Cards.

LYMAN TOWER SARGENT

Capitalist Eutopias in America

UTOPIAS, defined as a species of prose fiction that describes in some detail a nonexistent society located in time and space,[1] have recently been receiving considerable attention. Unfortunately this attention has rarely been informed by any very serious study of the utopian genre. Usually there has simply been a continuation of the tradition of focusing on a few of the "best" or best-known examples. In the process many errors have been made. Here I want to explore and attempt to correct partially one of those errors.

It appears to be generally assumed that utopias describe socialist societies. In fact, some studies have gone so far as to define the utopia as a genre that describes such societies.[2] While it is true that most utopias do so, it certainly must be unusually reckless scholarship to define out of existence works that are in every sense the same as those one includes except for one factor.

In order to explore this error, I have examined "all" of the utopias written in English between 1516 and 1975. In spite of this broad sampling, it would be incorrect to assume that all the capitalist eutopias and important criticisms of socialist eutopias have appeared in English. Non-English utopias and science fiction also provide important examples of capitalist eutopias and antisocialist dystopias. Nevertheless, because most utopias have been of American origin and the capitalist-socialist debate has been particularly significant in American thought, I have chosen to analyze the American capitalist eutopia.

There have been a significant number of capitalist utopias throughout the history of the utopian novel in America, from the earliest works at the beginning of the nineteenth century to the present. Here I want to look at four categories of such utopias in order to rescue the works from oblivion and, more important, to explore what the writers thought to be the key elements of a good capitalist society. The four categories are (1) works that

Research for this essay was supported by grants from the Office of Research Administration, University of Missouri–St. Louis.

192

picture a completely or nearly completely free-enterprise economy; (2) works that suggest that although capitalism is the best economic system, it needs reform; (3) antisocialist works, usually picturing the problems of a socialist utopia; and (4) a subcategory of the above, socialist dystopias. The last category cannot be dealt with in the same way as the other three, for there are hundreds of twentieth-century examples. Also, it is more interesting and important to examine the capitalist eutopias, because the socialist or communist dystopia has a deadly sameness about it.

The first problem in undertaking such an analysis is the problem of definition. I have ignored a large number of works that simply assume that whatever economic system existed at the time of the book was unchanged in the utopia.[3] I have also ignored the very large number of cooperative utopias, which exist somewhere on the borderline between capitalism and socialism. But there are still problems.

For example, in *Caesar's Column* (1890) Ignatius Donnelly proposes the following changes: "I should grant one or two years time, in which the great owners of land should sell their estates, in small tracts, to actual occupants, to be paid for in installments, on long-time, without interest."[4] He does not reject differential wealth, although he would limit land ownership to 100 to 500 acres.[5] These limitations are restrictive enough to make it misleading to include Donnelly in this survey, even though his point is to make competition fairer. A similar problem exists with some advocates of the single tax.

Another problem is posed by those works depicting one giant corporation that takes over the world's economy. In some of these works, such as Lebbeus Harding Rogers's *The Kite Trust* (1900), there is little reason for considering them to be capitalist. But in others, such as Felix and Elizabeth Pedroso's *The World the World Wants* (1947), the society is specifically called "a free stateless universal capitalist society."[6] And somewhere in between there are King Camp Gillette's *The Human Drift* (1894), "*World Corporation*" (1910), and *The People's Corporation* (1924).

In order to make the point that capitalist utopias do exist and are important, I have used a fairly simple and restrictive criterion of capitalism. If the work emphasizes the element of private property as opposed to public ownership, I have included it. If there is a large portion of property held privately, but the focus is on public ownership, I have excluded it.

Turning now to a consideration of the several types of works involved, I shall note the ways in which these utopias support and criticize capitalism.

LAISSEZ-FAIRE CAPITALISM

Very few of the works argue for a completely unregulated capitalist system. In fact, the most striking characteristic of these utopias is that most of them readily admit that capitalism, as it had functioned so far, had serious problems. But they believe that reform, a bit of tinkering with the system, can change a bad situation into a good one. The authors of two antisocialist works express the feeling of many of the authors. In *Looking Further Forward* (1890) Richard Michaelis writes:

> I do not deny that our society stands in need of many desirable reforms; but I am not prepared to follow blindly Mr. Bellamy, John Most, or anybody else who pretends that he is ready to deliver humanity from all evils on short notice, and I do not intend to jump head over heels into the dark. [p. vi]

Similarly in *Looking Further Backward* (1890) Arthur Dudley Vinton argues: "The benefit which these books [Bellamy's *Looking Backward* (1888) and Laurence Gronlund's *The Coöperative Commonwealth* (1884)] have done is very great; but the utopian schemes which they recommend as remedies for the evils which exist to-day are fraught with danger" (p. 6).

A few in the nineteenth century and others in the twentieth century do contend that the economy should be completely unregulated. Among the nineteenth-century works, for example, Wheeler (1895) argues that utopia already exists in 1895. (For the titles of works designated by the author's last name and a publication date, consult the biblography that follows this essay.) Giles (1894) and Welcome (1894) believed that all our problems were the result of restraints on competition. As Welcome (1894) said:

> With our people . . . it is a maxim that individuals or corporations, being directly interested in the results of skill, industry and labor-saving appliances, are more alert and efficient concerning such matters than are public officials. For that reason, such enterprises as railroads, telegraph lines, the express and postal service, public schools, and industries of a public nature generally, have within the last forty years, passed from governmental control into private hands. It may seem incredible to you . . . but it is true, nevertheless, that governmental operation of any public service ever tried here has proved inefficient, and been superseded by private enterprises. Not that we have arbitrarily displaced the one with the other, but by the natural law of competition, private individuals have taken the place of public officials. [p. 89]

Or, as Michaelis (1890) put it, "For the purpose of reaching the state of mock-equality, Mr. Bellamy would have as a matter of course had to *sacrifice competition*, the gigantic power that has elevated us all, and Mr. Bellamy with us, to the present state of evolution!" (p. iii; italics in the original).

Twentieth-century works that stress greater competition and less governmental concern include, in chronological order, Griesser (1923), Rand's *Anthem* (1938) and *Atlas Shrugged* (1957), Morley (1956), H. L. Hunt's *Alpaca* (1960) and *Alpaca Revisited* (1967), Palmer (1968), Judson (1973), and various science fiction works by Poul Anderson and Robert A. Heinlein. For example, Griesser expresses a common approach when he states:

> No combinations of Capital, no Combinations of Labor, no Combi-
> nations of Dealers, Producers or Manufacturing Interests are permit-
> ted on the Welcome Island. It shall always be a genuinely free country;
> free to work for the best wages obtainable, giving first class service,
> free to sell and manufacture anything not otherwise protected or pro-
> hibited. [p. 136]

Ayn Rand makes the point even more strongly, arguing for little or no government of any sort and the central role of the capitalist entrepreneur.

REGULATED CAPITALISM

But, for most, some regulation is necessary, and in some cases very extensive regulation is felt to be desirable. In the nineteenth century for example, Bachelder (1890) would limit wealth:

> While everything to aid and encourage the accumulation of property
> and ownership of homes is done, inordinate accumulation is restricted
> by limiting the wealth of any individual to $100,000. The effect of this
> restriction has had a marked influence upon our institutions. This class
> of persons is now quite numerous, and the restriction of further ac-
> cumulations has resulted in the aiding and founding of many public
> institutions and charities; also, in aiding and encouraging the poorer
> classes to rise, and it produces a more general equalization of social
> fabric. [pp. 21–22]

Others, such as Phelps (1895), would directly limit profit or establish estate taxes so that no one would begin life with an inordinate advantage over another. For example, in Craig's (1898) utopia, "no person shall become possessed by inheritance of more than a certain limited amount of wealth" (p. 200).

Other suggestions in the nineteenth century include public control of utilities (Schellhous, 1893; Craig, 1898), public ownership or control of land (Schellhous, 1893; Welcome, 1894; Fuller, 1890), free coinage (Everett, 1892), and graduated land and income taxes (Norton, 1895; Moore, 1856). According to Moore,

. . . all taxes whatsoever, for any and every purpose, under the law or Government, shall be levied and collected from such estates, belonging to individuals and corporations, as shall exceed in value the sum of Twenty Thousand Dollars. Such estates as shall exceed in value that amount by Ten Thousand Dollars or over, shall pay double the proportion of taxes paid by the smaller estates. And for each additional Ten Thousand Dollars the ratio of taxation shall be thus increased, geometrically! [p. 254; in the original this is all in italics]

Clearly he wishes to limit wealth severely, but property is still held privately and great fortunes can still be accumulated.

The twentieth-century works tend simply to repeat the basic criticisms and propose similar answers, such as all transport on a nonprofit basis (Posnack, 1946), more political power to the wealthy (Hunt, 1960, 1967), and the representation of occupational groups in the legislature (Palmer, 1968). But it should be noted that at least some of the twentieth-century works stress political solutions to the problems brought about by capitalism, whereas the nineteenth-century works tended more to economic solutions. There are, of course, other twentieth-century works that completely reject political solutions and argue for a libertarian or anarchocapitalist position (Griesser, 1923; Rand, 1938, 1957).

So far the reforms mentioned have been directed at controlling aspects of capitalism that, according to the authors, have a pernicious effect on society. On the more positive side, there are a number of suggestions about how to improve the lives of the people, particularly the workers. For example, in *The Beginning* (1893) the anonymous author favors vocational education, as did Griffith (1836), whose utopia was largely brought about by training the daughters of the poor so that they could earn a living. The daughters of those who had seen better days were taught accounts and bookkeeping. The daughters of the long-term poor were taught to cut out and sew.

Bunce (1889) and Hale (1867, 1871, 1888) believed that great changes could be brought about simply by providing better physical surroundings. As Bunce put it, "It is better, we think, to be cleanly than to be splendid; to have assurance of health and comfort, than to be entertained by great shows; to have about us in our daily life the things that are pure and worthy, than to be dazzled with occasional magnificence" ("The City Beautiful," p. 100). Roberts (1893) challenges Bunce's view by arguing that although it is possible to provide excellent buildings with fine exteriors, these changes will not produce any reformation in the people. Thus the interiors will be a continuation of the slums the buildings were meant to replace. This is, of course, a point commonly made today.

Other positive reforms in the nineteenth century include an insurance system in which "all workmen must insure against accidents and for old age" through private companies (Giles, 1894, p. 137). And there is also some suggestion for a property qualification for voting. In John Bachelder's Atlantis, "when admitted to citizenship they were not made electors or voters until they were possessed of property of the value of $500 or more, it being deemed proper that only persons interested in taxable property should have a voice in taxing it" (p. 21).

Twentieth-century positive reforms develop along similar lines. One early example makes a utopia out of a company town. In Frederick Fairfield's *City of Works* the good worker is taken care of and leads a decent life if he conforms, but the process of oversight is thorough to say the least:

> Little kids from seven to ten watch out and tell him [the Recreation Doctor, in charge of amusements and general overseer of neighborhoods] if anybody throws paper on the street or marks on the houses and fences or swears, or uses bad language, or are impolite or rude. [Fairfield (1919), p. 27]

This is supposed to keep the people in line and teach the children to be more aware of their own behavior. The title of the book denies that there are capitalists in the society, but the content presents a managerial class that controls all property.

The twentieth-century works appear to be more concerned with the need to enforce virtue than the nineteenth-century utopias.[7] For example, Griesser (1923) spends considerable time instructing parents in the appropriate raising of their children so that they will remain virtuous. He is particularly concerned with women, whom he treats as virtually a separate species:

> Womanhood stands out and compares favorably with Manhood. It is the feminine in Nature, in spirit and culture. Under Womanhood you cannot combine the new woman who wants to be all but a woman. There cannot be equality with man. One standard of morality for both sexes is impossible to adopt, and would mean the destruction of womanhood. [p. 256]

Although this attitude is fairly common among utopists,[8] it is illustrative of an attitude found particularly among the twentieth-century capitalist works.

The twentieth-century authors imply that America has lost the virtue it once had. The reasons for the loss are usually ascribed to "liberal" social reforms such as welfare programs. But it should be noted that in most cases a high degree of control is advocated, at least in the interim, when the welfare system is replaced and while everyone returns to work and regains a recognition of his appropriate place in life. For example, Bacas (1954) lays out a set of principles for his America the Substantial movement that neatly illustrate these points:

Life should be enjoyed
A philosophy of life should be developed
Real patriotism should be developed
Orderly habits should be developed
Illegal speeding should be curbed
Extreme individualism should be curbed
Persons should not follow the mob
Human nature should be controlled
Persons should not glorify themselves
The worker's principal intent should be his product
Persons should earn their fame
Home conditions should be improved
Morale of the employed should be improved
Class legislation should be discouraged
The public should not be irritated unnecessarily
Enjoyment of motor transportation should be improved
Enjoyment of recreation should be improved
Lawyers should work for the good of the public
Clergymen should emulate the Lord
Physicians should observe professional standards
Financial advisors should be responsible
Labor leaders should be business statesmen
Personal savings should be encouraged
Education should be developed sanely
New buildings should be limited in height
Business men should observe a code of ethics
Individuals should be protected against financial emergencies
Candidates for office should be qualified
Legislative bodies should be smaller
Former Presidents should be Senate members
The Judiciary should have life tenure
Government should regulate, not control
Government should forgo business activity
Government employees should observe a code of ethics
Price increases should be halted
High living standards should be maintained
Government expenditures should be reduced [pp. 107–22]

This incredible miscellany of points is important for two reasons. First, it illustrates the shotgun approach of most utopian authors. Second, the dominant concern is demonstrated in the constant references to a code of ethics, controlling human nature, and the like. Bacas is fairly typical of the twentieth-century capitalist utopian writers.

One other reform, proposed by Dalton (1931) and Van Petten (1959), albeit in very different forms, deserves mention. Dalton says that workers should receive a bare pay sufficient to support a family and provide a college education for his children. Van Petten goes a step farther and argues that everyone over a specified age, twelve at the beginning, should receive a set amount of money ($10.00 per week at the beginning). This would ensure prosperity; the payments are called the Prosperity Fund. In both cases the approach was designed to protect private property by ensuring that everyone was sufficiently well off and to stimulate the economy by ensuring that money was constantly available.

PRIVATE PROPERTY

This leads to one of the important points found in virtually all these novels, the importance of private property. For Phelps (1895) it is "sacred" (p. 175); many of the other authors agree. In *The Crater* (1847) James Fenimore Cooper proclaims that "civilization could not exist without property, or property without a direct personal interest in both its accumulation and its preservation" (Vol. 2, p. 283). Dalton (1931) echoes this view: "Private property and self-interest is the basis of all that is best in man" (p. 171). Craig's *Ionia* (1898) is typical of a more moderate approach to private property:

> Nearly all our large business houses are joint stock companies, but the shareholders are generally those who are engaged in carrying on the business. Not only the managers but the bookkeepers, clerks and salesmen, and in manufacturing business the foremen and mechanics very commonly own more or less of the stock. The privilege of purchasing it is one of the rewards of zeal and ability. [p. 140]

It should also be noted that at least some of the writers believe that the establishment of unions is an unfair limitation on the use of property (Athey and Bowers, 1898; Fuller, 1890; Giles, 1894; and all the twentieth-century works).

THE REJECTION OF EQUALITY

This relates to another area of agreement, the rejection of equality. Athey and Bowers (1898) write that

. . . discontent is the natural corollary of that pernicious doctrine of
equality which is the perpetual burden of harangues and writings
launched by ignorant demagogues. We *should*, of course, be equal
before God and before the law, and would be, were this last but
rightfully administered; but nature never intended that we should be
otherwise equal, and, therefore, as long as the world lasts, *we never
shall* be. [p. 80]

Similarly Cooper (1847) remarks that "Mark Woolston was much too sensible
a man to fall into any of the modern absurdities on the subject of equality"
(Vol. 2, p. 283), and Griffith (1836) notes approvingly: "People . . . are
respected in proportion to their wealth" (p. 68). Perhaps Dodd (1887) puts
it most strongly in her antisocialist novel, *The Republic of the Future; or,
Socialism a Reality*:

A superior class, a class composed of scholars, students, artists and
authors, arose, whose views and whose political ideas threatened the
very life and liberties of the community. The aristocracy of intellect,
it was found, was as dangerous to the State as an aristocracy founded
on pride of descent or on the possession of ancestral acres. It became
necessary, therefore, to make a law against learning and the sciences.
All scholars, authors, artists and scientists who were found on examination to be more gifted than the average, were exiled. [p. 66]

The most vehement antiegalitarians, however, are found in the twentieth
century. The best known among them are, of course, Rand (1938, 1957) and
H. L. Hunt (1960, 1967). As Rand declares, "the word 'We' must never be
spoken, save by one's choice and as a second thought. This word must never
be placed first within man's soul, else it becomes a monster, the root of all
the evils on earth, the root of man's torture by men, and of an unspeakable
lie" (*Anthem*, p. 111).

PRESENT-DAY SCIENCE FICTION

Any serious study of capitalism in the utopian literature found in contemporary science fiction would extend this essay to an intolerable length,
for at least half of the dystopias in the twentieth century are attacks on
socialism or communism.[9] (For further examinations of modern American
dystopian works, consult the essays by Sargent and Hughes in Parts II and
IV of this collection—Ed.) Even listing the hundreds of titles involved would
be pointless. Suffice it to say that they all portray a society gone wrong by
stressing equality and abolishing private property, and the result is a total-

itarian system with most of the population docile or degenerate. There is, of course, usually a lone rebel who wins in the end.

Still, there are two science fiction writers who deserve brief mention here, Poul Anderson and Robert A. Heinlein. Heinlein's recent work has attracted considerable attention from the youth culture because of the communal eutopia built into his best-known work, *Stranger in a Strange Land* (1961). Many readers of Heinlein simply did not believe that he could present such a utopia because it seemed so opposed to the ideas presented in his other works. To some extent the seeming contradiction has been explained in his novel *Time Enough for Love* (1973), in which a similar eutopia is presented but with the clear statement that this is simply an extended family to be treated as an individual fighting against a hostile world. In this work he makes clear his basic belief in private property and his rejection of equality.

While Heinlein briefly confused his interpreters, there has never been any question about Anderson. His main character has usually been a robber baron type, and he explicitly states his position. Still, that position is an interesting one: "private action, where everybody concerned is needful to everybody else's income, that's stable. Politics, they come and go, but greed goes on forever."[10] Or, again:

> You wanted to re-establish the centralized state, didn't you? Did you ever stop to think that maybe feudalism is what suits man? Some one place to call our own, and belong to, and be part of; a community with traditions and honor; a chance for the individual to make decisions that count; a bulwark for liberty against the central overlords, who'll always want more and more power; a thousand different ways to live. We've always built supercountries here on Earth, and we've always knocked them apart again. I think maybe the whole idea is wrong. And maybe this time we'll try something better. Why not a world of little states, too well rooted to dissolve in a nation, too small to do much harm—slowly rising above petty jealousies and spite, but keeping their identities—thousands of separate approaches to our problems. Maybe then we can solve a few of them . . . for ourselves![11]

An earlier twentieth-century capitalist utopia, Austin Tappen Wright's *Islandia* (1942), an influential and significant work, also re-created a feudal system, this one agrarian, as the basis for the ideal society.

Although the form of the capitalist utopia changes, the foregoing survey reveals that the concern remains fairly constant, and while the capitalist utopia may be rare, its existence should not be ignored. The belief that a good society can be built on the basis of inequality and private property is certainly not uncommon, and descriptions of the economic base of such societies deserve notice. Also, it is particularly interesting to see how believers in capitalism thought it needed to be reformed at the time of its most unfettered development in America.

In conclusion, it may be worthwhile to speculate briefly about the reasons for the neglect of the capitalist utopia. First, it must be admitted that most utopian literature, and virtually all of the best-known works, do in fact depict socialist societies. Second, we have tended to adopt Engels's pejorative phrase "utopian socialist" even though none of his examples could be very accurately labeled either utopian or socialist.[12] Third, much of the scholarship on utopias has been very poor. Among other problems, there is no generally agreed upon definition of the genre, and most analyses simply ignore the problem. In addition, there was no adequate bibliography until recently. Without definition or a bibliography, poor scholarship seems almost inevitable.[13] Therefore, perhaps it is not surprising that a significant subgenre has been ignored.

But there is one final question that should be considered. Having, I hope, demonstrated the significance of the capitalist eutopia in America, there is still the problem of why, in comparison to socialist eutopias, they are so rare. There is no way of convincingly demonstrating why a particular genre of literature tends to be used for one purpose rather than another, but there is one characteristic of the utopian genre that may provide at least a partial answer in this case. Utopias are primarily vehicles for criticism. A picture of the good society is something like a distorting (rectifying is a better word) mirror held up to a society to show the population how their society should look. In the United States the defender of capitalism has generally believed, with Wheeler (1895), that the best possible world already exists. Thus the main criticism implied in the construction of an alternative society would be inappropriate. The prevalence of the antisocialist dystopia in the twentieth century makes the same point; it is designed to show that we are falling away from the good society. Also, it is likely that the more common use of the utopia to present socialist societies did not endear the genre to the advocates of capitalism. But the genre was used, and it was used to criticize the failings of the capitalist system and to show that improvements were possible.

Thus the capitalist eutopias have been similar in form and purpose to the other inhabitants of this odd genre. From the perspective of a significantly better life, the utopists have pointed out the strengths and, more often, weaknesses of the life we lead. The solutions proposed—economic, social, political, or, increasingly, psychological—vary depending on the times and place and the predilections of the authors, but they hold out hope where so many social critics only point to problems.

NOTES

1. For my definition of utopia, see Lyman Tower Sargent, "Utopia: The Problem of Definition," *Extrapolation*, 16 (May 1975), 137–48.

2. There are many examples of this approach. For two, see Jerome Davis, *Contemporary Social Movements* (New York: Century, 1930), pp. 50–51, and Allyn B. Forbes, "The Literary Quest for Utopia, 1880–1900," *Social Forces*, 6 (September 1927), 179–82. There are exceptions to this rule, but they have other problems. Two works, both originally doctoral dissertations, that treat capitalist eutopias, Vernon Louis Parrington, Jr., *American Dreams: A Study of American Utopias*, 2d ed. (New York: Russell & Russell, 1964), and Robert L. Shurter, *The Utopian Novel in America, 1865–1900* (New York: AMS Press, 1973), have such a severely limited bibliography and cavalier treatment of definitional problems as to be useless. A third, Charles J. Rooney, "Utopian Literature as a Reflection of Social Forces in America, 1865–1917," unpublished doctoral dissertation, George Washington University, 1968, is significantly better, but the time and bibliographical limits are too restricted.

3. See, for one example, Robert Grimshaw, *Fifty Years Hence: or What May Be in 1943: A Prophecy Supposed to be Based on Scientific Deductions by an Improved Graphical Method* (New York: Practical Publishing Company, 1892).

4. Ignatius Donnelly, *Caesar's Column: A Story of the Twentieth Century*, ed. Walter B. Rideout (Cambridge, Mass.: Belknap Press, 1960), p. 105 (c. 1890).

5. *Ibid.*

6. Felix Pedroso and Elizabeth Pedroso, *The World the World Wants (A Sociocratic Order)*, (Sao Paulo, Brazil: n.p., 1947), p. 99.

7. For more on this point, see Lyman Tower Sargent, "A Note on the Other Side of Human Nature in the Utopian Novel," *Political Theory*, 3 (February 1975), 88–97.

8. For more on this point, see Lyman Tower Sargent, "Women in Utopia," *Comparative Literature Studies*, 10 (December 1973), 302–16.

9. For partial essays on this literature, see Lyman Tower Sargent, "Utopia and Dystopia in Contemporary Science Fiction," *The Futurist*, 6 (June 1972), 93–98.

10. Poul Anderson, "Territory," in his *Trader to the Stars* (London: Panther Science Fiction, 1967), pp. 102–103.

11. Poul Anderson, "No Truce with Kings," in his *Time and Stars* (London: Panther Science Fiction, 1966), p. 64.

12. See the discussion of this phrase in John Wahlke, "Charles Fourier and Henri Saint-Simon: Two Theorists of the Reaction," unpublished doctoral dissertation, Harvard University, 1952, pp. 1–14.

13. Significant improvements in all areas of utopian scholarship have begun to appear or are promised for the near future, and one can expect that the standards of such scholarship will continue to rise dramatically based on the new bibliographies and more careful definition. See the recent titles in the secondary sources checklist in Part IV and note 3 to the introductory essay, "Defining America as Utopia."

SHORT-TITLE BIBLIOGRAPHY

1836   [Griffith, Mary]. "Three Hundred Years Hence," in *Camperdown; or, News from Our Neighborhood*.

1845   [Judd, Sylvester]. *Margaret*.

1847   [Cooper, James Fenimore]. *The Crater; or, Vulcan's Peak. A Tale of the Pacific*.

1856   Moore, David A. *The Age of Progress; or, A Panorama of Time*.

1867   Hale, Edward Everett. "My Visit to Sybaris." *Atlantic Monthly*, 20 (July 1867), 63–81.

1871   [Hale, Edward Everett]. *Ten Times One Is Ten; the Possible Reformation*, by Colonel Frederic Ingham (pseud.).

1887   Dodd, Anna Bowman. *The Republic of the Future; or, Socialism a Reality*.

1888   Hale, Edward Everett. *How They Lived in Hampton: A Study in Practical Christianity*.

1889   Bunce, Oliver Bell. "The City Beautiful," in *The Story of Happinolande, and Other Legends*.

1889   Bunce, Oliver Bell. "The Story of Happinolande," in *The Story of Happinolande, and Other Legends*.

1890   [Bachelder, John]. *A.D. 2050. Electrical Development at Atlantis*.

1890   Fuller, Lieut. Alvarado M. *A.D. 2000*.

1890   Michaelis, Richard C. *A Sequel to Looking Backward or Looking Further Forward*. Also entitled *Looking Forward* and *Looking Further Forward*.

1890   Satterlee, W. W. *Looking Backward; and What I Saw*.

1890   Vinton, Arthur Dudley. *Looking Further Backward*.

1891   Fitch, Thomas, and Anna M. Fitch. *Better Days; or, A Millionaire of To-morrow*.

1891   Leland, Samuel Phelps. *Peculiar People*.

1891   Norton, Seymour F. *Ten Men of Money Island*.

1891   Simpson, William. *The Man from Mars. His Morals, Politics and Religon*. 3d ed., Rev. and enl. by an Extended Preface and a Chapter on Woman Suffrage, 1900.

1892   Everett, Henry L[exington]. *The People's Program; The Twentieth Century Is Theirs. A Romance of the Expectations of the Present Generation*.

1893   *The Beginning. A Romance of Chicago As it Might Be*.

1893   Roberts, J. W. *Looking Within: The Misleading Tendencies of "Looking Backward" Made Manifest*.

1893   Russell, A[ddison] P[eale]. *Sub-Coelum: A Sky-Built Human World*.

1893   Schellhous, E. J. *The New Republic. Founded on the Inalienable Rights of Man, and Containing the Outlines of Such a Government as the Patriot Fathers Contemplated and Formulated in the Declaration of Independence, When Struggling for Liberty*.

1893   [Jones, Alice Ilgenfritz, and Ella Merchant]. *Unveiling a Parallel. A Romance*, by Two Women of the West.

1894   Giles, Fayette Stratton. *Shadows Before; or, A Century Onward*.

1894   Welcome, S. Byron. *From Earth's Centre, A Polar Gateway Message*.

1895   [Fitzpatrick, Ernest Hugh]. *The Marshall Duke of Denver; or, The Labor Revolution of 1920*, by Hugo Barnaby (pseud.).

1895   Phelps, Corwin. *An Ideal Republic; or, Way Out of the Fog*.

1895   Wheeler, David Hilton. *Our Industrial Utopia and Its Unhappy Citizens*.

1897   [Caryl, Charles W.]. *New Era*.

1898   Athey, Henry, and A. Herbert Bowers. *With Gyves of Gold.*
1898   Craig, Alexander. *Ionia; Land of Wise Men and Fair Women.*
1898   [Wellman, Bert J.]. *The Legal Revolution of 1902,* by A Law-Abiding Revolutionist.
1909   Dixon, Thomas. *Comrades; A Story of Social Adventure in California.*
1919   Fairfield, Frederick Pease. *Story of the City of Works; A Community of Peace and Plenty Where Every Man is His Own Policeman. A New Order of Government. Anti-Socialistic. Free Street Cars and Telephones. No Middleman. No Capitalist Class. All Profit Accrues to Labor. Farm and City Life Conjoined.*
1923   Griesser, Wilhelm. *The Welcome Island, Story and Laws.*
1931   Dalton, [Charles] Test. *The Richest Man on Earth.*
1938   Rand, Ayn. *Anthem.*
1940   Gieske, Herman Everett. *Utopia, Inc.*
1942   Wright, Austin Tappen. *Islandia.*
1946   Posnack, Emanuel R[obert]. *The 21st Century Looks Back.*
1954   Bacas, Paul E[dmond]. *Thirty Years to Win.*
1956   Morley, Felix. *Gumption Island; A Fantasy of Coexistence.*
1957   Rand, Ayn. *Atlas Shrugged.*
1959   Van Petten, Albert Archer. *The Great Man's Life 1925–2000 A.D.*
1960   Hunt, H. L. *Alpaca.*
1967   Hunt, H. L. *Alpaca Revisited.*
1968   Palmer, William J. *The Curious Culture of the Planet Loretta.*
1969   Saxton, Mark. *The Islar; A Narrative of Lang III.*
1973   Judson, [Lyman Spicer] Vincent. *Solution PNC and PNCland.*

ROBERT PLANK

The Modern Shrunken Utopia

I

TWO YOUNG VETERANS, Rogers and Jamnik, just back from World War II, find civilian life disappointing. Jamnik, while browsing in the PX, had seen an article by a man named Frazier about a commune, and it intrigued him. They visit Rogers's old professor, Burris, who had occasionally mentioned utopias in his lectures, thinking he might find Frazier for them. (Frazier had been Burris's fellow student in graduate school, and he remembers him, a bit vaguely, as brilliant and not fitting into a groove.) Eventually Rogers, Jamnik, and the professor visit Walden Two, accompanied by Jamnik's and Rogers's girl friends and by a philosopher, Castle, whom Burris takes along and who serves as Frazier's outspoken antagonist in the debates that follow and that make up the bulk of the book. The visitors are given the grand tour of the place, a large and thriving commune. Frazier has founded it and runs it, unobtrusively, using the most modern psychological methods, notably positive reinforcement. All arguments for and against the new system are thoroughly discussed. Some of the guests join up. Some, unconverted, leave. Burris finds upon reentering the outside world that his eyes have been opened to its defects; he returns.

Stripped to its bare bones, this is the plot of *Walden Two*,[1] unique among American utopias, indeed among all twentieth-century utopias. Hence, a bewildering work. It is the task of this essay to beat through the thicket of bewilderment an approach to a better understanding of Skinner's remarkable book. This approach does not offer explanations of why it was written as it was written; every individual work contains, although Skinner would deny this, too much of the mysterious—or, if you prefer, of the aleatory—to be totally accessible to explanation. Rather it is the purpose of this essay to analyze the category of which *Walden Two* is the paradigm, the twentieth century's shrunken utopia.

This focus does not, of course, suggest that there weren't any small-scale utopias before *Walden Two* or that the only type of utopias being written today are shrunken utopias. The bibliographic essays in the last section of this collection demonstrate the presence of earlier shrunken utopias and the continuity of large-scale utopias.

To achieve my examination of the modern shrunken utopia, this essay has been divided into three parts. I shall first establish a literary context by examining several types of American and European utopian works that filled the vacuum left by the decline of the nineteenth-century eutopia. Then I shall concentrate upon *Walden Two* and a contemporary offspring, *The Harrad Experiment*, published in 1966. The final section relates the shrunken utopia to the psychology of writing utopias and to the crucial historical and cultural forces that created the appropriate climate for the shrinking of utopia.

II

For a long time utopias presented to the inquiring historian merely one simple, almost monotonous aspect. A graph of their development could be plotted as a straight rising line. Like so much else, utopias were getting "bigger" and "better." But then, some seventy years ago, something happened: The straight rising line suddenly broke. The luscious and seemingly so healthy growth of eutopias withered. A new growth sprang up on the vacant lot and soon proliferated.

Specimens of the new were collected by the Linnaeuses of this branch of descriptive science. They variously named it negative utopia, dystopia, kakotopia, and antiutopia. On a more popular level it was classified as a weed.

This would not do; the weed grew too lustily. The almost total reversal of the centuries-old trend was more conspicuous in the Old World than in the New, but it was marked in the United States as well. In Europe there were some of the most successful works of H. G. Wells; there was the last chapter of *Penguin Island* by Anatole France; later, Huxley; much later, Orwell. In America, the paradigm of the old eutopia was Bellamy; of the new dystopia, Jack London's *The Iron Heel*. (See Gorman Beauchamp's essay in Part II of this collection.) A later example was furnished by Sinclair Lewis's *It Can't Happen Here*. Then, as Sargent observes in his bibliographic essay, the floodgates opened; the cataract of modern science fiction stories poured out. Many of them are really utopias disguised as science fiction; many others contain casual snippets of utopias. *Gravy Planet* (better known by its later title, *The Space Merchants*) by Kornbluth and Pohl may serve as the paradigm of this stream, including its flotsam and jetsam.

The sharp break in the development of utopias has of course long been observed. It has much puzzled observers. An attempt must be made to explain it. At the present stage of our art and science, though, we do not have precise standards of either quality or quantity. If we are willing to risk being smug, we can say that the importance of raising questions is still greater in our field than the possibility of answering them. Furthermore, lots of spadework would have to be done to isolate pure types of utopias. This situation imposes several caveats.

First, because we cannot consider any specific work of utopian literature unique in the sense that it would represent an attribute of utopism not found elsewhere, and because we do not have representative samples or averages, we had best make use of paradigms—works that show the characteristics of a type in high profile without necessarily exhibiting all the characteristics or exhibiting them all to an average degree.

Second, America is part of the Western World. American utopias, especially twentieth-century utopias, are part of a broader development. To grasp their history it is essential not to ignore their foreign antecedents and their effects abroad.

Third, terminology. It had little chance to raise its ugly head in the nineteenth century. "Eutopia" was practically all there was, so the term "utopia" sufficed for everything. More had coined both words, but only to denote different aspects of his imaginary commonwealth, not different societies. The England of his day was bad enough for him; there was nothing worse in his imagination. Now we need different terms for different types of utopias. "Kakotopia" is an ugly word for an ugly thing, so it would not be inappropriate. Of the various terms that have been proposed for the opposite of eutopia, both "kakotopia" and "dystopia" are clear, and both have an irreproachable linguistic pedigree. Dystopia is the one that Doxiades, who did not write the best book on utopias[2] but has the estimable advantage of being Greek, prefers. So "eutopia" and "dystopia" it will be. Later I shall use "antiutopianism," but in a different context.

The development of the genre in the twentieth century has made it increasingly clear, though, that there has not been a simple polarization. Once the line was broken, the tree toppled, a variety of new branches sprang from the crippled stem. To speak merely of eutopia and dystopia no longer does justice to the complexity of the literature. We shall now turn to the increasing differentiation of utopias.

III

Though ascribed in particular to the residents of Missouri, healthy skepticism, sometimes shading into less healthy cynicism, is a generally established American trait. Pessimism and defeatism are not. So there is no

American *Brave New World*, no American *1984*. Here the vacuum left by the demise of eutopia was not filled by straight dystopia. Not that there aren't American dystopias; there are. But the predominant types, though close enough to the classical dystopias to be usually confused with them, differ from them on a rather important point: American utopists have been loath to leave the field completely to the enemy.

It is a common feature of utopias, particularly of those displaced into the future, that the author gives an account of how the system prevailing in his utopic society came into being. That fictitious historical process not unnaturally often involves violent conflict. The oppressive total state of *1984* has emerged from a revolution. The revolution is shadowy—not because Orwell would not have been able to describe it in detail if he had wanted to, but because the obliteration of the past is a point he greatly stresses. It is more usual for authors of dystopias not to devote much attention to the origins of the regimes they depict. In *Brave New World*, the other paradigmatic European dystopia, the regime has also been established through revolutionary upheavals and counterrevolutionary atrocities. The last of these were the massacres of Golders Green, where 800 "Simple Lifers" were mowed down by machine guns, and the "famous British Museum Massacre" where "two thousand culture fans" were killed by poison gas. The very flippancy of the tone shows that the author's main interest was elsewhere—in depicting the victors and their system. Once the opponents of the new order are vanquished, as it has been clear from the beginning they must be, the dystopian regime is supposed to last: in *Brave New World*, for the foreseeable future; in *1984*, emphatically forever.

This would not do for Americans. Neither the cavalier treatment of the process that leads to dystopia (pragmatists that they are, Americans always want to know what makes it tick) nor the despair of its ever being overthrown is acceptable to American utopists. The crucial fight is not the one at the beginning, before the hated regime is established, but the one at the end, when it is destined to fall. The dystopian tyranny is not accepted as fate. It is, however horrid, a mere episode. Even Sinclair Lewis, writing at a time when international politics had reached a nadir[3] (more perceptible to Americans, though most of them couldn't have cared less, than to Europeans unable to see the forest for all the poisonous trees), ends with a vision of liberation. It is only a vision, not a fact. But the struggle goes on, whereas in *Brave New World* and *1984* it distinctly does not. Both European paradigms end with the destruction of the only opponent of the regime that we have been allowed to glimpse. Both American paradigms—*It Can't Happen Here* and *The Iron Heel*—show massive resistance remaining very much alive. As Gorman Beauchamp points out, Jack London ends his utopian history with the actual overthrow of the oligarchy and the triumphant reversal of the historical trend, with the establishment of a new eutopia.[4]

While Jack London's fame has reverberated through the world (not everybody makes it to the pantheon of Soviet saints while serving as one of the few tourist attractions of Oakland, California) and while *The Iron Heel* is a true paradigm of American utopia, Ira Levin's concept of the historic process is closer to that of the TV addict and the reader (if that is the word) of comic strips. The struggle between world-shaking forces becomes in his utopia, *This Perfect Day* (1970), a duel of the glorious boy hero with the wily old Oriental.[5] Still, the duel does take place, with its unsurprising outcome, and the dystopic regime is overthrown. All these are what we might call *reversal utopias*.

They represent America's answer to the obsolescence of eutopia. The reversal utopia is not exactly dystopia, but close to it: It is dystopia with an added twist. *The Iron Heel* has quite justly been said to have a "Janus-headed form of discourse."[6] The impression becomes inescapable, though, in reading reversal utopias, that the author's real interest is in the dystopic part, just as with authors of pure dystopias. His overriding purpose is to hold before our eyes a warning. We are insistently told of the horrors awaiting us if we do not act in time to avert them. That in the end they turn out to have been only passing plagues is but a sop to the reader. (See Gorman Beauchamp's treatment of the novel in Part II.)

Though there have been segments of our nation, notably the slaves and Indians, who have suffered from intolerable oppression, Americans as a nation have been lucky enough not to have personal experience with a tyrannical regime, at least not for the last two hundred years. And what was George III, after all, compared to Hitler and Stalin and all the rest! Europeans, less favored by history, may be deemed more inured to political suffering. Authors such as Orwell and Huxley did not feel they needed the sop.

Next to the reversal utopia, there is another type available to take the place left vacant by the disappearance of eutopia: the *ambiguous utopia*. The term has obtained an admission ticket to our discussion through its use by Ursula Le Guin as the subtitle to *The Dispossessed*.[7] And ambiguous it is, with a vengeance. There is the planet Urras, which has all the natural advantages; people make an unholy capitalistic mess of it. Some who don't fit there take sail (rocket, rather; the *Mayflower* has long been replaced by a spaceship) to a neighboring moon, Anarres, which has chiefly disadvantages and is beautiful only for pilgrim feet whose stern, relentless stress beats a thoroughfare for solidarity and community. All of life there gets pretty stern and relentless, while Urras, the home planet, rots in opulent iniquity. Which of the two—? Loyal and brave, the hero goes back to his bleak utopian land. The reader, no doubt, gets much enjoyment out of empathizing with such a Chinaman's choice, especially as he doesn't have to make it himself.

Some more intrepid if perhaps less sophisticated authors have been unwilling to put up with ambiguity. Choosing neither the ambiguous nor the reversal utopia—as to the true dystopia, there is no reason why it should have entered their minds—they resolutely stuck to writing eutopias, just as the great nineteenth-century utopists had. But we do not have the nineteenth century's certitudes. Like other lovable human virtues, naiveté, once lost, can never be regained. We are not going to erect another Statue of Liberty either, or build another Pennsylvania Station. In the hands of twentieth-century re-creators, the old clay wouldn't form a new colossus. Eutopia lost the eloquent pathos, the missionary righteousness, the promise beyond doubt, the exclusive scope. In one word, it shrunk.

IV

It would be a grave mistake to think of American utopias as an outgrowth of European ones and to neglect the obverse side of the coin. In some aspects American utopism has been leading. Bellamy's *Looking Backward*, as American as apple pie, was by far the most successful and influential of the classical utopias. It made an impact in Europe as no other utopia had made before or was to make since.

It was not a wholly positive impact. The second most sincere form of flattery, parody, was perhaps more frequent than the sincerest, imitation. Eugen Richter, leader of the Liberals in Imperial Germany, a then powerful party equally set against Bismarck's authoritarian and militaristic regime as against the Socialist aspirations of the working class (and eventually ground to dust between these two millstones), wrote an anti-Bellamy utopia, a charming if intellectually lightweight pamphlet that became quite popular. And this was but one of a large number of critical and satirical responses to the American "Nationalist." The negative utopia established itself as a new category by way of reacting to Bellamy's success.

These were modest beginnings. Against the sweeping claim of eutopia to be able to save a country, to redeem a continent, dystopia could only offer a response of small scope. It had as yet no independent existence. In a history of utopism, Bellamy would have a chapter; Richter a footnote.[5]

Eventually history was to reverse the proportion. Dystopias sprang up spontaneously, out of their authors' primary initiative, and became wider and wider in scope. Eutopias were gradually reduced to limited responses. Two paradigms demonstrate the gradual shrinking of eutopia in Europe.

Theodor Herzl's career was meteoric. In a few years he had founded the modern Zionist movement, established himself firmly as its leader, found access to the chambers of the mighty, and got the foreign offices and great banking houses of Europe busy on his plan for a Jewish homestead in Palestine. Yet success eluded him—the only success, that is, that would have mattered: No real steps were taken toward his goal. By 1902 he realized this. And he knew that he had little time left; he was suffering from a then untreatable heart disease, from which he was to die only two years later. He decided to try a new tack. Seven years before, he had written down, more playfully than in earnest, some notes that might become a novel. Now he took them seriously and wrote *Altneuland* (*Old-New-Land*).[9]

Propaganda was its purpose. As he was a writer at heart, it became a true novel. Social conditions are not merely described but embodied in events. The characters are not mere stock characters as usual in utopias, but men and women of flesh and blood, bound to each other by the web of emotions. As he was not a first-class writer, though, it became a sentimental novel.

In some respects *Old-New-Land* follows the classical pattern of eutopia; in others it does not. The book is sharply divided in two parts, just as is More's: The first part is a grim description of what is, and the second shows what the author hopes and wishes will be. Cardinal Morton's banqueting hall has become a Viennese coffeehouse, where the hero broods at an engagement party of Jewish bourgeois who do not have the slightest inkling what is lurking around the corner. The burden of the critique in both *Utopia* and *Old-New-Land* is carried mainly by discussion, though Herzl also uses genuine narrative. The two works castigate the existing with the same brilliance and charm.

In the second part, however, the difference is sharp. In Herzl's work the imaginary country is imaginary only insofar as it is described as it would be in the future—Palestine in 1923, two decades after he wrote. For various reasons, especially Herzl's failure to foresee World War I and the British mandate, much less Nazism and World War II, his vision is in some respects quite off the mark; in others it is uncannily accurate. Eutopias in general have stood up rather less well; but of course, only the "man in the street" thinks that prediction is their concern. Where Herzl really belongs to a new era in utopism is in his goals. When classical eutopia describes only one imaginary country, they present it as a model. Their transparent intention is to have the world remodeled—a public extension of Omar Khayyam's intimate wish:

> Ah love! Could thou and I with Fate conspire
> To grasp this sorry Scheme of Things entire,
> Would not we shatter it to bits—and then
> Re-mould it nearer to the Heart's Desire! [LXXIII]

Such aims are entirely alien to Herzl. He desires a Jewish state established, a state rather like any other. He does not envisage any change in the world at large or any radical innovation to take place in what since has become

Israel. This is undoubtedly the main reason why the work is largely forgotten in the country it helped create. Yet *Old-New-Land* is one of the few instances in history, if not indeed the only one, of a literary utopia having played a role in shaping events, having become triumphantly realized. (Harrington's utopia—which is often mentioned as a source for the U.S. Constitution—was limited, and so was its influence. His target had been England. Although his work was consulted by the Founding Fathers, one would not call the United States a realization of *Oceana*.)

Lost Horizon seems at first glance hardly even a utopia, shrunken or otherwise, but a lighthearted fantasy. The term "escapist" fits it to a T. Characteristically, few people have bothered to remember the title or the author, while the name of his imaginary garden of delights, Shangri-La, has long been a household word. Yet is is also a serious political utopia. Shangri-La serves not only the rejuvenation and delectation of the elite gathered there, but also as a repository for the cultural values threatened with destruction through the wars and disasters looming on the "lost" horizon. It is a eutopia, but one shrunken almost beyond recognition.

The classical eutopias had aimed at nothing less than to remake the world "nearer to the heart's desire." Herzl, writing at the time of their collapse, eschewed shattering the sorry scheme of things entire and limited himself to one country; Hilton, contemporary with the great dystopias, working under the shadow of World Warr II, limited himself to one small refuge. There was only one more step to take to complete the process, and Skinner took it.

V

No utopia has in recent years been talked and written about nearly as much as *Walden Two*. As Skinner indicates in his essay in Part I of this collection, critique has quickly turned into attack. Skinner has defended himself vigorously and has untiringly expounded and expanded his views. Few have come to his aid, and he would probably disdain it if they did. The role of the noble stag warding off the howling pack of hounds seems much to his liking. Because neither he nor his hounds are afflicted with either lack of intelligence and knowledge or the habit of hiding their light behind a bushel, discussions, both spoken and in print, have ranged far and wide. They have covered most of the problems that the human mind can comprehend and perhaps some it cannot. It would be foolish to try to sum up the raging debate, and foolhardy to enter into it. I shall limit myself to comments on a few points of psychological or literary interest that can be useful as starting points for various considerations later in this essay.

Walden Two is here considered as the paradigm of the American shrunken utopia. I believe that it is indeed very American and different from its European counterparts but not in respect to its being shrunken. We have seen that there are European shrunken utopias, though such an authoritative writer as Irving Howe seems inclined to deny it: "Our literature is incorrigibly romantic. . . . It is a romanticism somewhat different from its European sources, for it proposes what no European imagination ever could—an end-run past history, into the freedom of unconditioned selfhood, or in its more moderate versions, into a mini-utopia of friends."[10]

Walden Two, which would be a "more moderate version" (it surely doesn't aim at unconditioned selfhood), can hardly be called a utopia of *friends*. Skinner himself only claims that his utopians would "treat each other with friendship and affection,"[11] which is something different; and the term "mini-utopia" is not as telling as "shrunken utopia," because it fails to indicate that in being "mini" it deviates from the previously prevailing type. This, however, is the case. Classical utopia was traditionally thought of as having far greater scope. To cite but two examples for many, Gerber speaks of utopias as "clearly defined imaginary *countries* with strange institutions" (my italics)[12] and a German scholar notes that "utopias habitually claim general validity."[13]

Walden Two is clearly not a country, and the story leaves doubt whether it claims general validity. Writing as a theoretician rather than as a novelist, Skinner, in his new preface (1976), leans heavily on E. F. Schumacher's book *Small Is Beautiful* and ventures that "Frazier might call" Walden Two a pilot project. The underlying idea is that eventually our entire nation, or perhaps the entire world, might consist of a vast number of communes on the pattern and of the size of Walden Two.

But this is begging the question. A successful pilot project shows that an operation can be performed and, by implication, repeated; but it does not show that it can be performed on a larger scale unless we can be assured that the larger operation would offer no other difficulties than the smaller one. We cannot be sure of this. In fact, we can rather be sure of the opposite. To prick a patient's finger and draw a drop of blood is not a pilot project for draining him of a gallon of blood.

Undaunted, Skinner advances claims for his utopia that nobody will call unduly modest. In a celebrated debate held at the convention of the APA in 1956 between Skinner and Carl R. Rogers[14]—a psychologist whose theoretical orientation is relatively close to Skinner's; one wonders what the debate would have been like if Skinner's antagonist had been chosen from the opposite side of the spectrum—Skinner said that *Walden Two* "was essentially a proposal to apply a behavioral technology to the construction of a workable, effective, and productive pattern of government . . . where—in short—people are truly happy and secure, productive, active, and forward-looking." When Rogers compared *Walden Two* to *1984*, Skinner rose sharply to the defense:

It saddens me to hear Rogers say that "at a deeper philosophical level" *Walden Two* and George Orwell's *1984* "seem indistinguishable." They could scarcely be more unlike—at any level. The book *1984* is a picture of mediate aversive control for vicious selfish purposes. The founder of Walden Two, on the other hand, has built a community in which neither he nor any other person exerts any *current* control. His achievement lay in his original *plan*.

Skinner wrote *Walden Two* in "the early summer of 1945." It "was not a bad time for Western Civilization. Hitler was dead, one of the most barbaric regimes in history was coming to an end."[15] Ten years earlier—Hitler had taken Germany; much of Europe was in the power of fascism; World War II was glowering on the horizon—R. Brunngraber, a writer rooted in a different tradition, had the hero of his novel spend a date with his girl speculating on the future of mankind. (Yes, that's what some people did in those days.) They agree that utopia is the future. Yet he cannot silence misgivings: Things may not turn out as expected.

It may also turn out that mankind is altogether but a more complicated species of ape; that in that very farthest future, when we imagine the Earth a checker board of gardens and architecture, the violent will abuse the weak with a cynical brutality that we cannot even imagine. . . . It is also possible that the madness will not be limited to one stratum of the population. It is not unthinkable that the general leisure and affluence will bring an upsurge of the very lowest in man: that then with drug-infested bodies, gorged to nausea and pitiably full of appetite—that then in utter despair everybody will massacre everybody.[16]

Which of the two is right, Skinner or Brunngraber? Or does it *entirely* depend on the place in history where one happens to stand? Is objective prediction out of reach?

Decades have passed since those two novels were written. Has very much happened to give us confidence that the horrors foreseen by Brunngraber will not come to pass? Ironically, about the only passage that sounds really dated is the one about the "checker board of gardens and architecture." We would scarcely place the elimination of nature and spontaneity by the spread of civilization and its regularity into the "very farthest future." It is coming closer and closer.

So Skinner thinks that the people in his utopia will be, among other things, happy. It is not easy to see how that could be proved. Personally I have encountered only one product of authentic Skinnerian conditioning. It was on one of those dismal November days full of rain and fog, as they will be in Seattle (where we were house guests of friends), and infinitely more depressing because on the day before President Kennedy had been assassinated. But we had promised the children of our hosts to take them to the World's Fair on Saturday, and so we did. The Fair had officially closed some time before. Only a few buildings were still open, and some activities of interest to children were still going on. The immense Hall of Science was empty—except, attached to one pillar was a cage, with various tubing leading to it, and corn came rustling through one tube in a steady stream. In the cage was Skinner's pigeon.

The bird pecked at the grains as they fell down, and he did so with such speed and energy that we thought the poor creature would soon get exhausted. But he didn't. He pecked selectively. I do not recall exactly what he did—I believe he picked up grains of a certain color, eschewing all others. In any event, he did what Skinner had trained him to do. The hammering of the beak was the only sound in the vast building. It kept going on—indefatigable as well as "secure, productive, active" and, for all I know, forward-looking. Was the pigeon happy?

The scene reminded me forcefully of one I had seen many years earlier, at a time just shortly before Skinner wrote *Walden Two*. I was riding in a truck convoy through the city of Aachen in Western Germany; or rather, through what was left of the city. Houses lined the streets we traveled, but on closer look they were only façades of former houses. Everything behind the front had been bombed into rubble. There were no people. For miles there was no sign of life. But on one tower that was still standing (there was no more church behind it) there was a clock, and the clock showed the time. It evidently had its own power source (hygroscopy, I presume), and nobody had made it stop. So it went on. It was secure, productive (we set our watches by it), active, and forward-looking (it would go on showing the correct time). Was the clock happy?

Skinner's answer to Brunngraber's somber pronouncement and to my carping would logically be that the future conjured up by Brunngraber will not be allowed to happen; that people will be happy because they will be conditioned not to get what they want, but to want what they get. But why stop there?

It is written that the meek shall inherit the earth, but it is not written that they shall be meek humans. If we are to be so conditioned that our responses to the world will be different from what they are now, if we are to be made over into what we are not, why not give up on this refractory species altogether and plan for some other entities to be the lords of the earth? Ants have often been suggested for the assignment (small is beautiful!). If that is too corny by now, we might go farther: Why not concentrate on making pigeons, or clocks, happy and secure, productive, active, and forward-looking?

If this seems absurd, it is well to remember that utopias have long toyed with this very idea—that is, science fiction has; but utopia has gone under the guise of science fiction for so long that the garment has become thread-bare: Utopia shines through.

In its fully developed form the idea goes back at least half a century, when Karel Capek gave to the non-Slavic world the word robot in his play *R.U.R.*[17] The initials stand for "Rossum's Universal Robots." The word *rossum* is derived from the Czech word for intellect. In the play he is the elder scientist, not unlike the mad scientists of so much science fiction, who has started the world of robots. And the play ends with mankind eliminated and a robot Adam with a robot Eve starting a new epoch in the history of earth, one where robots will be masters and will, no doubt, be happy and secure.

Capek has had both forerunners and successors.[18] Samuel Butler had pondered the same problem and arrived at similar solutions more than a hundred years ago, first in a newspaper article and later (1873) in *Erewhon*, particularly in that section of it called "The Book of the Machines." A writer of our time, Arthur C. Clarke, of "2001" fame, is fairly explicit:

> To Bruno, as to many of his colleagues, the machines with which he was working were a new species, free from the limitations, taints, and stresses of organic evolution. They were still primitive, but they would learn. Already they could handle problems of a complexity far beyond the scope of the human brain. Soon they would be designing their own successors, striving for goals which *homo sapiens* might never comprehend.
>
> Yes, it was true that—for a while—men would be able to outbreed robots; but far more important was the fact that one day robots would outthink men.
>
> When that day came, Bruno hoped that they would still be on good terms with their creators.[19]

Or else the creators—*homo sapiens*—would be unhappy and insecure, unproductive, inactive, and backward-looking. But who would care?

VI

When in the Greek theater the audience had achieved catharsis by watching several tragedies, a farce was performed for a chaser. Among shrunken utopias, the *Harrad Experiment*[20] follows *Walden Two* as the Attic farce followed the tragedy.

Proudly hailed on the paperback cover as "the sex manifesto of the free love generation," *The Harrad Experiment* has sold more than three million copies and appeared in a new paperback edition in 1978. The novel presents an imaginary college where students are rather less free than they are in more conventional institutions of learning and indulge in feelings that only select people will call love. The plot is beguilingly simple: An experimental college is established, called Harrad (*Har*vard—*Rad*cliffe; get it? nothing in the book is very subtle). The college is coeducational, to put it mildly. One boy and one girl each are assigned to a suite in the dormitory, and the college authorities fondly hope that eventually they will "have normal sexual relations" (p. 15) with each other. Behold, this comes to pass. Applicants for admission are "preselected on the basis of careful psychological tests" (p. 1), as they well nigh must, to eliminate those who would say, thanks, I'll pick my own, you go jump in the lake.

Intellectual standards are high: "During the four year seminar in Human Values, Harrad students cover more than a thousand books in the general area of psychology, history, sociology and sexology as well as selected novels and autobiographies" (p. 307). That comes to about a book a day, not counting vacation days, and this is only one class. Students are evidently also preselected for their skill in using their brains as sponges.

The account above is, of course, a highly condensed synopsis. Much must happen to fill three hundred pages before the end—marital bliss—is attained, and much does happen. There are many experiments within the experiment, chiefly with group sex and with promiscuity. There is no homosexuality, and the more florid perversions are equally conspicuous by their absence.

Anthony Burgess, who as the author of such renowned dystopias as *The Wanting Seed* and *A Clockwork Orange* must know something about sex in utopia, writes: "Pornography depersonalizes, creating an abstract paradise Steven Marcus called Pornotopia, in which the only emotion is lust and the only event orgasm and the only inhabitants animated phalluses and vulvae."[21] I do not know whether either Professor Marcus or Burgess was thinking of Harrad, but they well might have been.

Nevertheless, and whatever one may think of the literary qualities of *Harrad*, the book is not to be ignored, not only because of its success as a campus craze but also because it is another paradigm of the American shrunken utopia. It is a shrunken utopia not only in the sense that it presents but a small unit (one college) as the arena of its fictitious realization, it is also limited to one aspect of life (sex). The classical utopists who advocated free love (some of the French, naturally, and to some extent William Morris in *News from Nowhere*) did so by showing free love prevailing in a much broader setting. For an author to restrict his scope to one aspect of life instead of revamping the entire life-style and society, as both the eutopias and the dystopias do, is another way of shrinking and has been done for various reasons. Szilard, for instance, who was a leading nuclear scientist and an activist concerned with control of atomic energy, limited himself in the title story of his collection of utopic tales to that one area of his expertise.[22] This also is a response, by shrinking, to the demise of the classical eutopia, though it might seem that *New Atlantis* could serve as a much older paradigm; but *New Atlantis* is, of course, a fragment, and we can not know what else Bacon would have put in had he lived to complete the work.

Though the ideologies that inform *Walden Two* and *Harrad* respectively (in the latter case, the word "ideology" may be too strong) are quite different, the structure of the two works is the same. A charismatic leader (in the case of *Harrad*, a married couple, the Tenhausens) with a clear and supposedly original idea of how people should be made happy establishes a commune of moderate size to translate a plan into practice. Young people who feel stymied in the outside world are attracted and chosen. They are not subjected to orders—their leader's yoke is gentle—but the environment is systematically and cleverly manipulated so as to nudge them toward certain choices of behavior. The system works, just as its constructor thought it would and as the rest of the world, sitting on the bench of the scoffers, had been sure it would not.

At the end all are happy. Everything is fine, even finer than it had been all along, and nothing is left to be done but to spread the glad tidings to the rest of the world. One might expect the successful graduates of the experiment to go out and preach the new gospel. Curiously, this is not emphasized in either novel. There is, instead, interest in infiltrating units of the indifferent or even hostile outside world: Frazier concedes the possibility, not without embarrassment, in Chapter 27 of *Walden Two*, and in *Harrad* bold strategies are laid down (pp. 272–75).

Both authors evidently expect that the unenlightened outsiders will never see through the stratagem and will take the inroads from utopia lying down. No doubt, many people indulge in daydreams wherein they win glorious victories with great ease because their opponents never fight back. Daydreams, however, are not generally known for mature wisdom and great realism. To underestimate one's potential adversary is inviting disaster. One can't help wondering how Skinner, a scientist renowned for his keen intellect, could fall into the trap. As to Rimmer, we don't know much about his intellect. Is this how immersion in utopian thinking affects a man? So I shall now attempt to take a crack at the puzzling psychology of writing utopias.

VII

It has long been held that poets may be more reliable guides through the labyrinth of the human mind than scientists. Freud, though the most eminent, was neither the first nor the last of the psychologists who readily conceded this. We can do no better than turn to Shakespeare to enlighten us as to why people write utopias.

Montaigne's essay "Of the Caniballes" purports to describe the American Indians and their country. Florio's translation was published in 1603. *The Tempest* was first performed in 1611. Montaigne says:

> It is a nation . . . that has no kind of traffike, no knowledge of Letters, no intelligence of numbers, no name of magistrate, nor of politike superioritie; no use of service, of riches or of povertie; no contracts, no successions, no partitions, no occupation but idle; no respect of kindred, but common, no apparell but naturall, no manuring of lands, no use of wine, corne, or mettle. The very words that import lying, falshood, treason, dissimulations, covetousness, envie, detraction and pardon, were never heard of amongst them. . . . They have great abundance of fish and flesh . . . and eat them without any sawces, or skill of Cookerie, but plaine boiled or broiled.[23]

Shakespeare transformed Montaigne's prose into these verses (*The Tempest*, Act II, Scene 1):

> Had I plantation of this isle, my lord, . . .
> And were the king on 't, what would I do? . . .
> I' the commonwealth I would by contraries
> Execute all things; for no kind of traffic
> Would I admit; no name of magistrate;
> Letters should not be known; riches, poverty,
> And use of service, none; contracts, succession,
> Bourne, bound of land, tilth, vineyard, none;
> No use of metal, corn, or wine, or oil;
> No occupation; all men idle, all;
> And women too, but innocent and pure:
> No sovereignty— . . .
> All things in common nature should produce
> Without sweat or endeavor: treason, felony,
> Sword, pike, knife, gun, or need of any engine
> Would I not have; but nature should bring forth
> Of its own kind, all foizon, all abundance
> To feed my innocent people. . . .
> I would with such perfections govern, sir,
> To excel the golden age.

Shakespeare has adorned Montaigne's story with some details and skipped others: For example, he was not as impressed as the Frenchman was with the Indians' habit of eating meat without sauces, but he made one radical change: Montaigne reports what allegedly is, Shakespeare a project of what might be. The anthropological study has been transformed into a utopia.

The lines are spoken by Gonzalo, "an honest old counsellor of Naples." Shakespeare is keenly aware of the vulnerable spot in Gonzalo's utopia. So are Sebastian and Antonio, the two wicked lords. They keep taunting and interrupting Gonzalo. As he says, "No sovereignty," they quickly hook in: *Sebastian*: "Yet he would be king on 't. / *Antonio*: The latter end of his commonwealth forgets the beginning."

Gonzalo ignores them, as he must, for their argument is unanswerable. They have uncovered the trap into which shapers of utopias can fall—are likely to fall, because it is so well baited. It is hard to see how any writer can avoid projecting himself in some role in the imaginary world he is creating, and it is most apt to be a role that flatters him, that could as easily be an element out of his daydreams. When it comes to utopia, no role is more suitable than that of the founder and ruler, the savior of the people. If it is an authoritarian utopia, no contradiction results. But Gonzalo is a good man, a nonauthoritarian—Prospero will later address him as "Holy Gonzalo, honorable man." He delights in the imagined welfare, freedom, and innocence of the people who are to inhabit his island. Yet he cannot renounce the more basic satisfaction of fantasizing himself as king, even while he sees things as so perfect that little remains for a king to do, and so the end of his utopia forgets its beginning, just as will happen in daydreams.

Not all writers of utopias succumb to the lure. Shakespeare didn't, but then he was not advocating Gonzalo's utopia, he was mocking it. Sir Thomas More was another writer—and, in contrast to Shakespeare, a true utopist—who proved immune to the lure. It is no wonder that he became a saint.

With the obsolescence of eutopia, the problem of the trap lost its sting. In dystopias, reversal utopias, and to some extent ambiguous utopias, the identification of the author with a character in the story is even more manifest and more important than in eutopias, but it is clearly identification with the leading rebel.

If Gonzalo's candid disclosure of his identification drew derision even in Shakespeare, then in our psychologically more sophisticated age a writer could hardly even admit that much to himself. It would be like revealing a daydream, which most people are restrained by a feeling of shame from doing—unless it is softened by some device that blunts its point, essentially by indicating that it is not to be taken as seriously as it appears. The shrinking of the utopia is such a device, and so is shifting it into the realm of fantasy literature. The explosiveness of the disclosure is defused by making its object less grand or less credible.

The Gonzalo type of identification therefore still thrives in such works of fantasy or allegory as C. S. Lewis's trilogy, where Elwin Ransom, the hero who shows clear marks of the author's person projected onto him, is raised to almost divine honors. A somewhat similar apotheosis takes place in E. Grey Walter's *The Curve of the Snowflake*. The shrunken utopia takes another route to the same goal: It is much more admissible to think of oneself as a psychologist creating and unobtrusively ruling a commune than to exalt oneself into a king.

In our other paradigms of shrunken utopias the issue is further defused by diffusion. In *Harrad* the leader role is split between a man and his wife, and they remain too shadowy to raise embarassment. In *Lost Horizon* the founder-ruler, Father Perrault, is there in all his authority, but the author seems rather projected onto brilliant young Conway, the master's favorite and chosen successor, eventual renegade and final penitent, playing out the drama of the son coming to terms with the father. In *Old-New-Land*, in a curious reversal, the figure patterned on the author is merely a guest in utopia, but one whose generosity has helped bring it about. All these are devices to make it possible to enjoy fantasies of self-aggrandizement with impunity, for the shrunkenness of the utopia keeps them within the bounds of what is in principle possible and at the same time sufficiently limited in scope not to be unseemly.

VIII

Having weighed all these factors we can no longer be quite contented with our preliminary answer to the question of why Skinner is more so-phisticated than Gonzalo—namely, because we are living in a psychologically more sophisticated age. Historical forces must have been operative to make it so—the same forces, presumably, that were at work demolishing the proud structure of eutopia, to replace it with the forbidding forts of dystopia and the modest dwellings of shrunken utopia. Three influences stand out, each following the other in the span of one generation: The change of mental climate at the beginning of our century; World War I, culminating in the collapse of great empires and in the Russian Revolution; and fascism, cul-minating in the Nazis' bid for world domination and its destruction in World War II.

At some point in history—say around 1905—something happened. A great rift sprang open in seemingly unrelated areas. In Paris, modern art was invented: Suddenly faces had two eyes on one side of the nose, nudes descended staircases in broken lines where curves had pleased the eye, soon pictures ceased to represent anything. In Vienna, Freud discovered that man was not the captain of his soul, that he was motivated by unconscious more than by conscious fears and desires. The quantum theory and the theory of relativity replaced the Newtonian order. Again in Vienna, music broke out of tonality, its frame for centuries now shown up as illusionary or arbitrary. The reversal in the direction of utopias was but one aspect of this revolution.

While all that happened in the proverbial ivory tower and could therefore go long unnoticed, changes of immediate impact were going on. King Coal, dethroned, was being replaced by Emperor Oil. The railroad age yielded to the automobile age, the era of steam to the era of electricity. These, however, were shifts clearly continuing the established line of development. They were plausible, expectable. The sudden reversal of mental climate was not. It has baffled historians. Was it that scientists and artists, somehow endowed with a finer sense for the course of history, anticipated the break in the coarser reality that was to follow years later? Or were the great political, social, and economic breaks to follow really the result of the cultural breaks that preceded them? Either version seems to ascribe much too much influence to the intelligentsia. But the facts are there and ought to be explained.

Let us apply the question to our subject. The nineteenth century surely had its share of savagery. But that was not its outstanding characteristic. Savagery existed in spots, in dark corners as it were. There seemed to be every reason to hope that the light of civilization would penetrate them (slavery disappeared in one country after the other). What has come instead is an age of relapse into barbarism. Would it be outlandish to say that the vivid description of barbarism in dystopias has contributed to this degeneration, that they have—much against their intent!—helped to bring about, by making them thinkable, the very things they warned against? Or is it reasonable to say that dystopias were written because their authors somehow sensed the world was heading back to barbarism, and that without them our descent would have been even more precipitous?

The eutopists, from More to Bellamy and Howells and beyond, had a very sharp eye for all that was wrong in their contemporary world. They were blind to the possibility that something might be more fundamentally wrong. Their outlook was unclouded, their sense of destiny secure. It was their unshaken conviction that reason and the humanitarian ideas were to triumph. There was no room in their philosophy for either Saint Paul's and Calvin's original sin or for Freud's death instinct. American optimism gave resonance to hymns to future earthly happiness, even though American religious tradition did not, and the mood of the rest of the world buoyed them up. Bellamy and Howells were children of their time even more than of their place.

Dystopia got a start as reaction to Bellamy's eutopia. Then the upheaval in the cultural sphere around 1905 began the demolition of eutopia. World War I completed it. Three great powers that had strutted on the global scene collapsed: the empires of the Hohenzollerns, the Hapsburgs, and the Romanoffs. In the case of the Hapsburgs their land itself disappeared, leaving old remnants and new countries. One of these was Czechoslovakia, where Karel Capek, giving to the world a name for a new concept, the robot, developed science fiction into a successor to defunct types of utopia. In Russia the revolution brought a dichotomy: The Soviet Union produced little utopian writing—Marx and Engels had taken a stand against it—but remarkable science fiction in a predominantly eutopian mode. The paradigms of emigré literature are dystopian: Nabokov (who by now can be considered an American as much as a Russian writer) wrote *Bend Sinister*. Zamiatin (representing the "internal emigration") wrote *We*, a work both pioneering in itself and of importance in the history of utopic literature as the model for Orwell. English utopism became decidely dystopian as the British Empire slipped into the phase of unmistakable decline while retaining enough of its primacy in the world to give its literature resonance: Huxley's *Brave New World* and Orwell's *1984* are universally recognized as the paradigms of dystopia, not merely of England, but of the world. They cover between them much of the ground that dystopias can cover.

We in America have not had to face the dissolution of our empire, though we have faced the dissolution of our imperialism. The difference between our development and that of European nations did not relieve us from obeying the command of history, which decreed the end of the comprehensive nineteenth-century eutopia. But the result differed. Here the lamented departed left other heirs. Still, the mood had changed, irreversibly changed.

A Jewish woman, told that the Messiah was coming any day now, is said to have replied: "The Lord in His mercy has shielded us from Pharaoh and Haman, he will save us from the Messiah, too." It is an old story, but it has popped up again, and for a reason.[24] Many an American has felt that we were taken, or just barely escaped being taken, by one or the other of the Messiahs Europe so abundantly produced. We have become wise; and to be "wise" in America does not mean to have wisdom as much as it means to be leery of being "conned," "taken."

The woman in the joke expressed the loss of faith in leaders; not yet in the led. The horrors of the 1930s and 1940s made that last step inevitable. The French Revolution had led German Romantic writers (most explicitly the gentlest among them: Eichendorff, Stifter) to discover the "tigerish side" of man. Nazism forced its rediscovery. If throughout our century men had been ill at ease feeling the ground beneath them wavering, they now faced the abyss in front of their feet.

The significance for any contemplation of mankind's possible future could not have been more profound. It has drawn innumerable comments and some applications to the narrower field of utopism. Brunngraber's classic formulation is but one of them. All that could still be done was to bend with the storm and to embody the direst forebodings in increasingly great dystopias or to duck from the tempest into the shelter of the shrunken utopia.

IX

To contemplate an ideal society is bound to be in itself pleasurable. It would be naive to believe, though, that with eutopias, full-fledged or shrunken, love of mankind is the principal spur. This role must be ascribed to the Gonzalo syndrome. That the masters of utopia would rather rule over happy than over unhappy subjects is true even of dystopias (*1984* is the one great exception). However, happy or unhappy, people are for these planners essentially raw material, the clay from which to form their masterpiece, the new and better, if smaller society. Existing reality often has no other function than to be cleared away, without nostalgia or regret, to make room for utopia. The difference between the old days and now is not the goal's having become less desirable, only less attainable. The scaling down of the constructive imagination is one of the symptoms of the general malaise of our time. Its other manifestations have been more extensively studied—for example, alienation from government, frustration of liberal and progressive hopes, and pragmatism shading into cynicism.

Anxiety has replaced hope as the main determinant of the tone of our expectations for the future of mankind, while the imagined role of the leader compared to that of his followers has rather grown. The result is that contrary to first impressions man and his handiwork are not found to rank high in the scale of utopian values any more. This is how Shakespeare lets his Prospero contemplate the end of civilization as he knows it:

> The cloud capp'd towers, the gorgeous palaces,
> The solemn temples, the great globe itself,
> Yea, all which it inherit, shall dissolve,
> And, like this insubstantial pageant faded,
> Leave not a rack behind.

Compare this to Skinner speaking *in propria persona* about the possible fall of our cloud capp'd towers: "A few skeletons of cities may survive, like the bones of dinosaurs in museums, as the remains of a passing phase in the evolution of a way of life."[25]

Though it may seem morbid to engage in fantasies of the coming end of civilization, and presumably to enjoy them, occasional fantasies going beyond this to foresee the end of mankind or of the world are actually not uncommon. They are well known to child psychology. A. A. Milne, for example (best known for his Winnie the Pooh), reports having entertained such ideas as a boy.[26] They are rooted in anxiety rather than in that triumphant self-assurance they pretend to express. Chukovsky's collection of spontaneous sayings of children contains this item: " 'Mother,' said four-year-old Anka, 'all the people will die, but someone will have to place somewhere the urn with the ashes of the last dead person, let me do it—all right?' "[27]

Such very last rites are not rare in that subgroup of modern utopias that describes the aftermath of World War III or of some other, usually nuclear, holocaust. *On the Beach*—Nevil Shute's book as well as the film made from it—might serve as paradigm. The tapping of the coke bottle in the film is a ghostly reminder of how close the utopia of extinction is to the utopia of replacing mankind by some other living or nonliving species.

There were such scenes in works written before Hiroshima. The historical event that brought annihilation within the realm of concrete possibility is only one factor. We would doubt whether it could have produced corresponding utopias, were it not for the fact that in all the little Ankas of the world they strike a responsive chord.

Other works envisage instead of a final quietus an eternal repetition, the past forever returning, the future reenacting the past. *Penguin Island* is a paradigm, and George Stewart's *Earth Abides* is a modern American example of the tendency in general. It helps in getting our main theme into perspective to review it against this massive backdrop of gloom. The shrunken utopia is the defensive position of eutopia in an age when so much seems to conspire to affirm Shakespeare's melancholy dictum that for centuries must have sounded very unreasonable:

> The evil that men do lives after them.
> The good is oft enterred with their bones.

In one of the best books on utopias, Robert C. Elliott classifies *Walden Two* and Huxley's *Island* as "Anti-Anti-Utopias." They are "our utopias, the two post-modern visions of the good place that speak most cogently against despair."[28] I would classify *Island* as a reversal utopia (in the opposite sense from the usual, though; in the reversal at the end evil triumphs over good), and I think Professor Elliott has made things needlessly difficult for himself by almost completely shunning such helpful terms as "eutopia" and "dystopia," but no matter. His term "anti-anti-utopia" is not merely classificatory. It also conveys forcefully something about the origin and position of the shrunken utopias. They are reactions to dystopia, though the mechanism isn't as simple or transparent as in some cases of works written as reaction to eutopias. Eugen Richter, as I have noted, was provoked by Bellamy, and E. M. Forster made the sequence explicit, saying that he wrote "The Machine Stops" "as a reaction to one of the earlier heavens of H.G. Wells."[29]

Antiutopism is implicit in Berdiaeff's writings, notably in the brief, almost aphoristic statement that became famous as the motto of *Brave New World*. Berdiaeff, however, followed the nineteenth-century usage: His "utopia" means "eutopia." Huxley was not inconsistent when he followed through with the attack by writing a dystopia.

True antiutopism is preformed in the relevant writings of Marx and Engels, who, however, battled essentially against utopic theory and practice, while literary utopias were of little concern to them. Antiutopism was fully developed by Karl R. Popper in his very influential book *The Open Society and Its Enemies*.[30]

Sir Karl argues against the rigidity and totalitarian aspects of utopism. He opposes "utopian engineering" to "piecemeal engineering," of which, in contrast to Marx, he strongly approves. His attack is directed against those utopias—the only ones he considers—that aim at revamping an entire state or society. His arrows are deadly, but they fly over the heads of the shrunken utopias, for their essence is that they have ducked. The shrinking of utopia thus proves its value as a viable adjustment to the perils of operating in a world that is not as hospitable now as it was to their forebears.

X

It would be nice if at the end of this essay we could say that the outline of the shrunken utopia had appeared ragged when we started but that now it stood out in wholesome clarity. Instead, new problems have bubbled up faster than we could solve old ones. The shrunken utopias impress us most by their variety.

At that, we have not even mentioned some specimens at the fringes, such as H. G. Wells's *Island of Dr. Moreau* or Kafka's *In the Penal Colony*, shrunken dystopias—and "dys" may not even be a strong enough prefix: The critic who called Kafka's *Metamorphosis* "surely the most dreadful story ever written" had perhaps never read *In the Penal Colony*. What happens on Wells's and Kafka's arcane islands is so dreadful that the reader's mind shrinks from taking the authors literally. They do not tell us, we must conclude, that such deeds were or could be perpetrated, but they intimate other events: We are not to read what is written, but to translate it into something that is not written. We are led to another fringe phenomenon, the allegory in the guise of utopia.

There is equally striking variety in the intellectual contexts. The enormous expansion of literature in our age (and perhaps, as some would have it, our growing *anomie*) abet the writer's unbridled individualism: Nobody is compelled to write within the frame of an established or traditional ideology. *Walden Two* is perhaps the only one among the modern shrunken utopias that has the clear purpose of demonstrating the putting into practice of a coherent and comprehensive philosophy of man and society.

Motivation for the shrinking varies no less. Only Herzl had the backing of an ancient faith—it was already so deeply entrenched when Saint Paul challenged it that in the process he split Christianity from Judaism—the idea that the Jews have a special destiny and that it is therefore legitimate or even obedient to design a utopia for Jews only. None of the other shrinkers of utopia had that motivation. Their shrinking conforms to the requirements of giving body to Gonzalo's dream under the restraining conditions of modern sophisticated skepticism.

That a historic change in our sensibility thus led to the shrunken utopia is only one of the historical factors impinging on our field. The impact of history also has been more varied than what we have considered so far. Religious communes were closely connected with religious writings, and the impulse to found secular communes came largely from utopian writers, notably in France under the restored monarchy (1815–48). They invariably ended in disappointment, and their failure was blamed on smallness. Revolutionaries and reformers alike derided them for pettiness of spirit. Big was beautiful. The test came in the largest country of them all, Russia, in 1917. Whatever the verdict of history will be,[31] the West became disenchanted. So—back to the initiative of little groups that had through the nineteenth century dotted the American landscape with utopias; and back from theory to practice. *Walden Two* is small, as Shangri-La is, but not remote.

We must not forget either that terms like eutopia and dystopia are unavoidably relative. The beauty or the ugliness of a utopia is in the eyes of the beholder. Donald C. Williams remarks, a propos *Walden Two* (and presumably without the benefit of a survey of readers' responses) that "this new Atlantis must seem to most Americans both comical and repulsive."[32] I have known a young man (he was, perhaps not entirely coincidentally, an engineering student) who thought *Brave New World* was just the sort of place where he would like to live—as an alpha plus, no doubt. People who regret that they weren't born in the Age of Pericles are prone to see themselves promenading in a shady stoa listening to sages; they do not usually yearn for the life of a miner at Mount Laurion. We are back at the Gonzalo syndrome.

Let us remember how Skinner, indignantly rejecting Rogers's criticism, insisted that *1984* and *Walden Two* were completely different: In the former, control was exercised "for vicious selfish purposes." This may be true, but is it relevant? May not the best intention, as the woman in the joke fears, lead to the worst tyranny? Elliott may be right: "Dostoevski's Grand Inquisitor hovers over" all of them.[33] The road to hell may be paved with good utopias.

From these roots antiutopianism, such as Popper's, draws its sustenance.

The shrunken utopia takes some of that wind out of its sails. Shrinking can be seen as retreat or as adjustment.

It likewise answers the argument that can be formulated—in analogy to the popular quip, if you are so smart, why aren't you rich? If utopias are so great, why have they never succeeded? Contrary to nineteenth-century expectations, the shrunken utopia has a greater chance to be realized. Herzl's vision became reality. Communes have been founded on the model of Walden Two.[34] When Huxley quotes Berdiaeff expressing his anxiety that it may be possible to realize utopias, he has in mind the utopia that becomes dystopia, Gonzalo's dream gone sour. The more a utopia is shrunk, the more can we hope that it has built into it some safeguard against this monstrous trick of fate.

As the individual matures, he accommodates his strivings to the limits of the attainable. The shrinking of utopia may be analogous. It offers the hope that the great experiment with consciousness, unique in the solar system and perhaps in the cosmos, and irreplaceably lost if man is changed into robots or replaced by robots, may not be coming to an end; that utopia may still be a beacon, to guide us to harbors more modest than we had dreamed of, yet to places where we can truly live.

NOTES

1. B. F. Skinner, *Walden Two* (1948) (New York: Macmillan, 1962). Professor Burris is the narrator; Skinner's first name (his mother's family name) is Burrhus.

2. Constantinos A. Doxiadis, *Between Dystopia and Utopia* (Hartford, Conn.: Trinity College Press, 1966).

3. Sinclair Lewis, *It Can't Happen Here* (Garden City, N.Y.: Doubleday, Doran, 1935).

4. Jack London, *The Iron Heel* (New York: Macmillan, 1913). See Beauchamp's essay in Part II of this collection.

5. Ira Levin, *This Perfect Day* (New York: Random House, 1970).

6. Nadia Khouri, "Utopia and Epic: Ideological Components in Jack London's *The Iron Heel*," *Science-Fiction Studies* 3 (July 1976), 174–81.

7. Ursula K. Le Guin, *The Dispossessed* (New York: Harper & Row, 1974).

8. Will I be forgiven a little rhetorical exaggeration? Louise Berneri in *Journey Through Utopia* (Boston: Beacon Press, 1951) devotes twelve pages (281–92) to Richter's utopia.

9. Theodor Herzl, *Altneuland* (Leipzig: H. Seemann, 1902). There have been many editions and translations, for example, *Old-New-Land* (New York: Bloch Publishing and Herzl Press, 1960).

10. Irving Howe, "The American Voice: It Begins on a Note of Wonder," *New York Times Book Review*, July 4, 1976, p. 2.

11. B. F. Skinner, "Walden Two Revisited," preface to the 1976 Macmillan edition of *Walden Two*, p. xi.

12. Richard Gerber, *Utopian Fantasy: A Study of English Utopian Fiction Since the End of the 19th Century* (London: Routledge & Kegan Paul, 1955), p. 112.

13. Fritz Wagner, *Zur Apotheose Newtons* (Munich: Verlag der Bayerischen Akademie der Wissenschaften, 1964), p. 48.

14. Carl R. Rogers and B. F. Skinner, "The Issues Concerning the Control of Human Behavior—A Symposium," *Science* 124 (November 30, 1956), 1057–66.

15. Skinner, "Revisited," p. v.

16. Rudolf Brunngraber, *Der Weg durch das Labyrinth* (1935) (Vienna: Paul Zsolnay, 1949), p. 101.

17. Karel Capek, *R.U.R.* (1923) (Garden City, N.Y.: Doubleday, Page, 1925).

18. The Austrian writer Rudolf Hawel depicted a future in which an artificial life form has wrested dominion of the world from man as early as 1910 in his novel *Im Reiche der Homunkuliden*.

19. Arthur C. Clarke, *The Lost Worlds of 2001* (New York: New American Library, 1972), p. 87.

20. Robert H. Rimmer, *The Harrad Experiment* (1966) (New York: Bantam Books, 1972).

21. Anthony Burgess, "One of America's Glories, with 50 Books and 80 Years Behind Him," *New York Times Book Review*, January 2, 1972, p. 1.

22. Leo Szilard, *The Voice of the Dolphin and Other Stories* (New York: Simon & Schuster, 1961).

23. Michel de Montaigne, "Of the Caniballes," in *The Essayes of Montaigne: John Florio's Translation* (New York: Modern Library, n.d.), p. 164.

24. In a characteristically roundabout way: Leon Wieseltier in a review ("Only in America," *New York Review of Books* 23 [July 15, 1976]) of a book by Irving Howe reports that Hayim Greenberg used the story in an essay on, equally characteristically, Trotsky.

25. Skinner, "Revisited," p. ix.

26. A. A. Milne, *Autobiography* (New York: Dutton, 1939), pp. 55 ff. See Robert Plank, "The Milne Phenomenon," in *The Emotional Significance of Imaginary Beings* (Springfield, Ill.: Charles C Thomas, 1968), pp. 51–55.

27. Kornei Chukovsky, *From Two to Five* (Berkeley: University of California Press, 1963), p. 47.

28. Robert C. Elliott, *The Shape of Utopia: Studies in a Literary Genre* (Chicago: University of Chicago Press, 1970), p. 129. "Anti-Anti-Utopia" is the title of Ch. 7 (pp. 129–53) of Elliott's book.

29. E. M. Forster, *Collected Short Stories of E. M. Forster* (London: Sidgwick & Jackson, n.d.), p. vii.

30. Karl R. Popper, *The Open Society and Its Enemies* (Princeton, N.J.: Princeton University Press, 1950); especially Ch. 9 (pp. 154–64), "Aestheticism, Perfectionism, Utopianism."

31. For a recent verdict see Jerome M. Gilison, *The Soviet Image of Utopia* (Baltimore: Johns Hopkins Press, 1975).

32. Donald C. Williams, "The Social Scientist as Philosopher and King," *The Philosophical Review* 58 (1940), 247.

33. Elliott, *The Shape*, p. 129.

34. In the spring of 1979 a "Nova" program on public television explored the relationships between Skinner's ideas and one of these communes.

BIBLIOGRAPHIC AND HISTORICAL SURVEYS

THE CONTRIBUTORS TO PART IV faced the impossible task of surveying approximately seven hundred American utopian titles extending from the colonial writings discussed by Joel Nydahl to the science fiction utopias published in 1975. Such bibliographic and historical digging is often frustrating and always time-consuming. But the historical essays, bibliographic essays, and bibliographies in Part IV are essential complements to the rest of this collection. As with most of the studies of American utopian literature, many of the essays in Parts I through III focus on the late nineteenth century and/or depend heavily upon well-known works. In Part IV five out of the six period surveys concentrate on eras either before or after the late nineteenth century, and in all the essays numerous obscure utopias are discussed along with the familiar titles. The broad historical frame and the wide selection of utopias should not only help readers to place the golden era of American eutopias and the well-known utopias within large contexts, they should also suggest "new" areas worthy of study for their own sake.

The chronological short-title bibliographies that follow each of the essays except the first are not definitive, because new titles are always being discovered. The only bibliography including American works that approaches completeness is Lyman Tower Sargent's annotated bibliography, *British and American Utopias 1516–1975*. (Glenn Negley's impressive international bibliography, *Utopian Literature: A Bibliography*, should also be consulted.) But the 713 titles listed in the five short-title bibliographies represent the most complete checklists of their kind ever published. (This number swells to approximately 750 titles when the feminist, Lost Tribes, capitalist, and religious writings with utopian content, discussed by Quissell, Teitler, and Sargent in Part III and Nydahl in his first essay in Part IV, are added to the lists in Part IV. Sargent's bibliography in Part IV includes some British works.)

The concluding checklist of secondary sources focuses on general studies of American utopian literature. It includes books, articles, bibliographies, and dissertations.

Joel Nydahl's first essay demonstrates that the story of America as utopia began long before the European discovery of the New World. European history and literature influenced American utopianism in many ways; specifically, Nydahl cites ancient utopian writings, the humanism and geographical discoveries of the Renaissance, the naturalism and rationality of the Enlightenment, and economic and scientific developments of the seventeenth and eighteenth centuries. But Nydahl's primary interest, which he claims is just as important as these pre- and post-European discovery influences, is the effect of European religious beliefs, especially as they were expressed in longings for an Earthly Paradise and the Millennium. Surveying a wide variety of European and American sources, including the Bible and Saint Augustine, Columbus, John Winthrop, Jonathan Edwards, Joseph Bellamy (Edward's great-great-grandfather), Samuel Hopkins, the Connecticut Wits, and early American allegorists, Nydahl traces the gradual secularization and Americanization of Paradise and the Millennium. His study is thus a valuable complement to the renewed interest in the evolution of the American concept of mission evident in such articles as Sacvan Bercovitch's "The Typography of America's Mission," which appeared in the Summer 1978 issue of *American Quarterly*. Nydahl's essay is also valuable because it outlines several characteristics that were associated with American utopian literature up through the early twentieth century; for example, a Protestant outlook, interest in technological development and economic prosperity, and the type of American chauvinism that was so evident at the conclusion of Edward Bellamy's first essay in Part I.

Nydahl's second contribution to Part IV is a bibliographic essay that offers the first thorough and detailed study of early American utopian fiction ever published. (See the secondary sources checklist for other studies that discuss early works.) His book-by-book survey is divided into six parts: early eutopias (1798–1824), satiric utopias, antiutopias, dystopias, secular progressive eutopias, and religious progressive eutopias. Continuities from the colonial period are evident—for example, the emphasis upon secular millennialism and an increasing interest in science and technology, especially after 1850. There were, however, several elements in the very late eighteenth-century and early nineteenth-century works that were rarely seen in the colonial utopian writings: discussions of women's status and economic reforms and the delineation of an idealized garden city. These concerns link the utopian works with the spirit of the early-nineteenth-century communal experiments and foreshadow important themes in post–Civil War utopian literature. Nevertheless, the general critical tone of the early-nineteenth-century utopias—which was often related to fears about the extension of Jacksonian democracy, social mobility, and sectionalism—helps to distinguish the utopian fiction published from 1812 to 1855 from both the optimism of transcendentalism and communal experiments and the outburst of eutopias during the late nineteenth century. The early-nineteenth-century emphasis on political as opposed to economic issues also marks their separation from their post–Civil War heirs.

One other significant finding suggested by Nydahl complements H. Bruce Franklin's contention, expressed in *Future Perfect*, that many major nineteenth-century literary figures attempted utopian or science fiction. Nydahl's focus on purely utopian books excludes discussion of partially utopian, travel, and fantasy literature, such as Melville's *Mardi*, *Typee*, and *Omoo* and Poe's *Pym*. Nevertheless, his survey of early American utopists includes Poe, Charles Brockden Brown, James Fenimore Cooper, James Kirke Paulding, and Nathaniel Hawthorne.

In his bibliographic essay covering 1865–87 Charles J. Rooney begins with a chronological survey of the eutopias and concludes with an examination of three dystopias and one antiutopia. Although there weren't many utopian works published during this period, there was one significant development: an emphasis on economic issues and solutions. Religion and politics were still important, but many of the post–Civil War utopists were especially concerned with the corrupting influence of money power upon the press, politicians, lawyers, landlords, middlemen, and laborers in America. The solutions proposed were often strange mixtures of European utopian socialism, Christian brotherhood, and cooperative or profit-sharing schemes, but the economic questions and answers posed by the authors' characters suggest a growing concern about the efficiency and morality of the early-nineteenth-century American concepts of production, distribution, and even individuality. Few of these utopists, even such well-known figures as Edward Everett Hale, attracted wide audiences. But they certainly paved the way for the enthusiastic reception of the late-nineteenth-century cooperative and socialistic utopias.

My historical essay differs from the preceding contributions in Part IV. Joel Nydahl discovered only twenty-four fictional utopias published during the 149-year period beginning in 1715 and ending in 1864. Charles Rooney located fifteen published during the twenty-two years before *Looking Backward* appeared in 1888. My bibliography lists 172 utopian works published in only eleven years. Thus it was impossible to use the detailed book-by-book approach that was appropriate for Nydahl's and Rooney's periods. Instead I had to use a cumulative approach, depending upon analyses of representative works. My survey also differs from Howard P. Segal's and Lyman Tower Sargent's bibliographic essays. Whereas the many utopian works of the late nineteenth century have been examined in books, articles, and dissertations, the 502 utopian and science fiction works listed in Segal's and Sargent's bibliographies (Sargent includes British works) have not received the attention they deserve, with the notable exceptions of a few well-known works such as *Walden Two* and several popular science fiction books.

Therefore, Segal's and Sargent's primary task was to attempt to map out the general trends and characteristics that have rarely been delineated in studies of American utopian literature. Much of this sort of work has been done for the late nineteenth century; hence I was freer to write a more speculative historical essay.

My essay is divided into two parts. The first section is a brief overview of the popularity, impact, and diversity of the utopian works published between 1888 and 1899, and a biographical profile of the utopists. This profile leads into the second part, which is an attempt to understand the nature of late-nineteenth-century literary utopianism by placing it within the context of Victorian "culture" in America. I compare the broad outlooks, specific values, means of transmitting these values, and ultimate goals defined in Daniel Howe's *Victorian America* and in the utopian works. The comparisons reveal strong continuities with colonial and earlier nineteenth-century utopian literature: the Protestant perspective, emphasis on technology, efficiency, order, and reason, an increasing interest in cooperative and socialistic economic systems, and an emphasis on America as the world's savior. But the comparisons also suggest that despite the fact that the utopists, as defined by their backgrounds, should have been—and in many ways were—proper American Victorians, they had serious doubts about modernization without morality, emphasized equality and cooperation over postponement of gratification and competition, and were ambivalent about the future. These doubts, combined with the utopists' blindness to the positive aspects of America's ethnic diversity and their tendency to champion middle-class utopias and American chauvinism, foretold the collapse of Victorian culture and the decline of American eutopian writing in the twentieth century.

Although there was such a decline, especially after the first two decades of the century, Howard P. Segal's statistical and bibliographic survey of a sample of 236 utopian works published during the first half of the century demonstrates that some authors still hoped to reach the American public by offering them a trip to utopia. As in the nineteenth century, the creators of these journeys to utopia were often respected or popular authors, for example, William Dean Howells, Jack London, Vachel Lindsay, Upton Sinclair, Sinclair Lewis, Ayn Rand, Robert Herrick, Granville Hicks, Austin Wright, and B. F. Skinner. And the economic, political, and ethical problems these authors discussed were often very similar to the issues discussed by the nineteenth-century authors, with the important exception of Skinner's emphasis on behavioral psychology. But there were two significant differences. First, there was a relatively healthy crop of dystopias, although England and Russia led America in the popularization of this genre with the publication of H. G. Wells's scientific romances, E. M. Forster's *The Machine Shops*, Zamiatin's *We*, Huxley's *Brave New World*, and George Orwell's *1984*. Second, as Segal's title indicates, the diversity of the utopian literature during this period is quite remarkable. This phenomenon might suggest a bewildered response to the diversity of modern America and the shock of the Depression years and to the startling international events discussed in Robert Plank's essay, "events" such as the Russian Revolution, Hitler and Stalin, and the entry into two world wars. Whatever the causes, it was evident that during the first half of the twentieth century, American utopists found it difficult to agree upon which vision of utopia would inspire Americans during the twentieth century.

It seems as if there has been a bit more consensus since 1950. Lyman Tower Sargent's bibliographic essay, which covers 1950 to 1975, indicates that there is at least an apparent agreement about how utopian speculation should be written—as a branch of science fiction—and what the tone of the works should be: dystopian.

Utopian fiction hasn't been completely swallowed up by science fiction. During each one of the decades surveyed by Sargent important and popular utopian works have been published that should not be classified as science fiction, works such as Ayn Rand's *Atlas Shrugged* (1957), Robert Rimmer's *The Harrad Experiment* (1966), and Ernest Callenbach's *Ecotopia* (1975). But most of the recent eutopias and dystopias have been presented in works of science fiction. This is a significant change; it often alters the impact of the utopian content, for most science fiction writers are much more interested in the entertainment and speculative opportunities of literature than in the didactic uses of fiction. Hence a science fiction writer might tend to keep those imaginative episodes and details, which (according to Bellamy's first essay in Part I) Bellamy deleted so that they would not distract the readers from his religious and economic teachings.

The dystopian tone is clear; imitators of Zamiatin, Huxley, and Orwell pop up throughout Sargent's bibliography. Whether the narrative focuses on the dangers of military power, pollution, and warfare caused by unchecked technological development, overpopulation, or rampant commercialism, the message seems to be that humanity may be incapable of stunting the seeds of destruction sown in modern industrialized nations. What may be even more frightening is that, as David Y. Hughes points out in Part II, we may not want to stop the cataclysmic forces at work.

The general pessimism, the specific disillusionment with elements of earlier American utopias, such as reason, order, and America's role as the Savior, and the shifts away from explicit religious, political, and economic preaching all seem to create a huge gulf between utopian science fiction and pre-1950 utopian literature. And yet not all is doom and gloom. Sargent's bibliography includes a substantial number of eutopias. Furthermore, the dystopias he surveys often have happy endings, and, conversely, the eutopias described are often flawed. This mixing of hellish heavens and heavenish hells might be seen as a continuation of the long tradition of ambivalence in American utopian literature, and indeed in the dominant American culture. The blending of good and bad imaginary worlds can also be read as evidence that contemporary utopists realize that, except for an occasional trip to a purely escapist Shangri-La, modern readers are quite suspicious of any imaginary worlds that pretend to be absolutely good or absolutely bad.

Of course this awareness is nothing "new"; Friedrich Engels articulated it in *Socialism, Utopian and Scientific* back in the nineteenth century. But the awareness in the hands of competent young writers may prove to be a crucial factor in the future of American utopian literature. During the 1970s several talented authors have utilized and amplified the ambiguities and ambivalences of utopian literature to create an interesting type of fiction typified by works such as Ursula K. Le Guin's "ambiguous utopia" *The Dispossessed*, part of which is the Epilogue to this collection. These "critical utopias," as they are sometimes called, may not inspire neo-Nationalist groups and neo-Bellamy Clubs; I have yet to hear of any activist Le Guin Clubs, Thomas Disch Factions, Samuel Delany Parties, or Joanna Russ Revolutionaries. (Whereas there are communes inspired by Skinner, and Rimmer has received many inquiries about applying to Harrad College.) But the critical utopists do suggest ways to breathe new life into stale imitations of nineteenth-century utopias and equally stale imitations of Zamiatin, Huxley, and Orwell. They—along with Skinner, Rimmer, and an increasing number of authors who attempted eutopian works during the closing years of the 1970s—have provided and will, I hope, continue to provide us with those "fresh crops" of utopias that are such important challenges to the way we see ourselves and the past, present, and future of our planet.

JOEL NYDAHL

From Millennium to Utopia Americana

THE HISTORICAL STREAM FROM MILLENNIUM TO UTOPIA

UTOPIA AMERICANA[1] lies at the confluence of two historically important streams flowing westward from the Old World to the New: Paradisiacal Dreams and Millennial Expectations. Where these two allegorically merge in space is where they actually merge in time—when America became associated in men's minds with both the beginning and the end of time.

The first of these streams has a universal source and is by far the oldest. Represented in the Judeo-Christian tradition by the Garden of Eden (and, to a lesser extent, sometimes by the pre-Flood and pre–Tower of Babel periods), a bygone golden age—a past time and place of ease, abundance, simplicity, and innocence—an image that seems to be a part of the mythology of all peoples. It is an attempt to explain, or at least account for, present imperfection in man and society in terms of past perfection.

The second of these streams has its source in a more particularized location and is more recent. While Charles L. Sanford is correct in stating that "everywhere . . . recur the myths of a lost paradise together with an eschatological view of history in which the end of time reactualizes the beginning of time,"[2] yet the vision of the end of time that dominated much of the early intellectual and religious history of America came directly from the Bible, especially from the book of Revelation. More important, while the belief in the eventual coming of the Kingdom of God goes back in Christian history to the promises in the Gospels, the hope that this Kingdom is to be more than "transcendent, otherworldly, and unhistorical" is, as we shall see, relatively modern; the millennial expectations, which play such a large part in developing eutopian visions in America, have their origin in a period "beginning over three centuries ago" when "there sprang up a hope, what might be called a 'Christian optimism' about the future of humanity and human society."[3]

When the modern belief in an improved future for humanity achieved

237

by means of temporal progress does not exist, the strong desire to recapture
a perfect past still does, and it manifests itself in one of two ways: through
striving for felicity in an otherworldly (heavenly) future reached only by
death, or through searching for paradise on earth in a place only an ocean
or a mountain range away. Both are attempts to transcend time by trans-
muting it into either no-time (eternity) or space. The first of these utopian
strivings—which, when it gives birth to literature, produces the *upward
utopia*, "an other worldly conception of utopia," a "life after death" conception like that underlying the "whole Judaic-Christian tradition" from
"Isaiah to Billy Graham"—is represented in pagan terms by the Islands of
the Blest and in Christian terms by Augustine's City of God; the second—which
produces the *outward utopia*, a conception holding that "utopia exists
now—somewhere—but not here" and that a "better world is open to man
if he will physically move from here to there"[4]—is represented by repeated
attempts to locate a temporal paradise somewhere over the horizon, usually
in the West.

That there were mysterious lands in the West had been known viscerally
long before the discovery of the New World. Columbus's voyages, and those
of others, it must be remembered, only confirmed what had already been
sketched on the maps of men's imaginations by primitive musings on the
astronomical and geographic fact that the sun set in the West—in a New
World, in an undefined yet promising place, frightening in its possibilities,
where, since things end, things might also begin. Homer's Elysian Fields,
Plato's Atlantis, Hesiod's Hesperides—these and other imaginary places in
the West had a real locus in the European mind, and legends about them
gave rise to early reports of fantastic voyages to lands of abundance and
plenitude, where climate and topography were combined ideally and men
lived longer and happier lives—as they had before they sinned.

In the Western imagination, all images of paradise or of a golden age are
eventually transmuted to images of Eden; and the European mind, which,
because of the Reformation, was receptive to ideas of freedom, exploration,
and growth, as well as of purification and simplification, was ready in the
sixteenth century to believe that a New Eden (perhaps the old one re-
created or rediscovered) existed and that a new chance for man *on earth*
could be had merely by going from here to there. Outward utopian strivings
were joined to upward ones. It was a matter of men seeing space as a
metaphor for time—as a short cut to the future and to moral and spritual
"progress," which symbolically and paradoxically took them on a journey
into the past. It was the first fusing of the past to the future in terms of a
cartographically real place—a literal New World. Columbus himself linked
the two traditions of a past earthly paradise and a future millennial period;
he "assumed [that] the Second Coming of Christ . . . [would] restore the
earthly paradise to the faithful" after the gospel had been proclaimed

throughout the world.[5] In his *Book of Prophesies* he established the New World as the stage upon which the last act of history would unfold: "God made me the messenger of the new heaven and the new earth, of which He spoke in the Apocalypse by St. John, after having spoken of it by the mouth of Isaiah; and he showed me the spot where to find it."[6]

Columbus's easy assumption that Saint John's Revelation would have temporal consequences had its origin in the millennial expectations of the earliest years of Christianity—expectations that fell into disrepute before actually triumphing. Church fathers prior to Augustine had read Revelation as prophesying an imminent earthly paradise within the boundaries of time, an ideal state representing a radical spiritual and material transformation of man and society.[7] Augustine, however, denied progress; repelled by the evident sensuality of a materialistic eutopia, he argued for a separation of the City of God (represented on earth by the Church) and the City of Man. Those who dwelled in the second, reveling in the things of this world, could never, because of man's inherent corruption, build a heaven-like city on earth; those who dwelled in the first, living *in* the City of Man but not being *of* it, cultivating a Christian and a spiritual rather than a material life, would ultimately prevail and would find the true City of God as a heavenly reward. Augustine's was, in other words, an upward utopia. In order to destroy the power of Revelation as a dangerous blueprint for supposed temporal progress, Augustine allegorized Saint John's work and "transformed the Apocalypse from a revelation of history into a book of consolation for the spiritually besieged members of the City of God."[8]

Augustine argued successfully; the idea of an earthly utopia lay dormant. Not progress but "decay [was] the essential fact"[9] for a thousand years, and "the peoples of Europe were, for the most part, reconciled to their temporal conditions."[10] Of course, there were important exceptions: for example, peasant rebellions and the writings of the twelfth-century millennialist Joachim of Flora, who held that human history was about to enter the third of three historical stages—an Age of the Holy Spirit, an earthly manifestation of God's Kingdom. While Augustine had preached that at best a slight melioration of the human dilemma was possible, Joachim had an "unmistakable progressivist tone";[11] his views suggested that an earthly paradise might be brought about in and by history. Although Joachim's theory was quickly submerged under an avalanche of criticism by Thomas Aquinas and others, it emerged centuries later in a new context and, though sometimes unrecognized and unacknowledged by those who held it, became a dominant influence in utopian—one can almost say "modern"—thought.

Beginning in the sixteenth century, men once again began to read Revelation not in the ahistorical manner of Augustine, but as a prophecy of earthly bliss for man. Although the ascetic side of the Protestant mind stressed a journey of the soul to a heavenly, not an earthly, reward, yet another side of that same mind—a side dominated by the individualism inherent in Protestantism and later in capitalism—had "expectations of greater, more glorious days for the church on earth."[12]

Luther himself, "partaking of the optimistic futurism of New World idealism,"[13] believed that he was living in a period just on the front edge of the Millennium, which he saw as a time preceding the Second Coming, when Satan would be bound and helpless and there would be a utopia of both secular and religious dimensions. The progressivist viewpoint—that history is dynamic instead of static, that the way things were and are is not the way things have to be, that man (with the aid of God, of course) can shape his own world—was alive and well and would continue to prosper in Protestant theology and later in economic thought (especially capitalism) and in scientific theories of progress (both in Bacon's faith in science and in Darwinism).

As the seventeenth century arrived, views of the Millennium, while always essentially Christian, began to take on an even more secular tint and included (if not emphasized) cultural, moral, and material progress. One of those who helped promulgate this further secularization was the seventeenth-century English biblical scholar Joseph Mede, whose envisioned Millennium, "a period of great happiness for mankind on this earth," helped engender other similar ones. "By the end of the century it was believed that the 'prophetic' books of the Bible foretold a steady ascent of mankind, this improvement being accompanied by an amelioration of the environment, natural and cultural."[14] Whereas Augustine had held that the corrupt nature of man precluded any improvement in his nature or situation, "by the end of the seventeenth century the novel idea that history is moving toward a millennial regeneration of mankind became not only respectable but almost canonical." After an initial skepticism, in fact, even Richard Baxter found little difficulty in finally accepting not only temporal progess as being concomitant with spiritual, but also man's role as being central in God's scheme; in the words of Ernest Lee Tuveson, Baxter saw that "as God desire[d] to work with and through human nature to transform the individual soul, so he worke[d] with and through men and their institutions to regenerate the kingdoms of the world."[15]

THE EARLIEST UTOPIAN VISIONS

Tuveson is undoubtedly correct when he argues that Revelation is "perhaps the first expression of the idea of history as progress."[16] It was, indeed, a recognition that the stream of history flows, as it were, uphill, which made a belief in a golden age of the future possible and led to the symbolic turning from Augustine's to Joachim's ideal state. That this philosophic discovery should occur at approximately the same time as the geographic discovery of the New World was, we might be tempted to say, providential; if Satan was to be defeated before the final conflagration, then here, in the fabled West, was a new stage upon which that drama might be enacted.

It is no wonder that millennial expectations were aroused, for there was a long tradition in England—now invoked and amplified—which portrayed the English as God's chief instrument for spreading the gospel.[17] Our Puritan forefathers "considered themselves in fact as advancing to the next stage beyond the Reformation—the actual reign of the spirit of Christ, the amalgamation of the City of the World into the City of God." They were "intent on establishing what might be called the prototype of the millennium."[18] Listen, for example, to Edward Johnson's ringing statement in the 1628 "Proclamation for Volunteers" to colonize New England: "For your full satisfaction, know this [New England] is the place where the Lord will create a new Heaven, and a new Earth in new Churches, and a new Commonwealth together."[19]

America, as many have noted, has grown up with the idea of utopia; our earliest literature is an amalgam both of annals of discovery and exploration and of plans for the City of God to encompass perfectly the society of men. Paradisiacal images abound in "realistic" general descriptions of New World lushness[20] and of such natives as the "most gentle, loving, and faithful" inhabitants of sixteenth-century North Carolina, who were "voide of all guile and treason, and such as live after the maner of the golden age."[21] That most of the early settlers who came for other than purely economic motives envisioned founding societies that would be ideal in their own eyes goes without saying. John Winthrop's "A Modell of Christian Charity" is an example not only of an embryonic constitution but also of a proclamation of the establishment, at least in hope, of a secularized, temporalized version of Augustine's City of God. John Eliot's tracts advertising attempts to convert and civilize the Indians—a step (along with the conversion of the Jews) that nearly all millennialists believed to be a prerequisite for the Second Coming—also can be viewed as partaking of the utopian spirit.

The earliest fictional American utopias in prose, however, all written in the eighteenth century and all portraying religious utopias, would seem to be Joseph Morgan's *The History of the Kingdom of Basaruah* (1715)—perhaps also the first American novel—Daniel Moore's *An Account of Count D'Artois and His Friend's Passage to the Moon* (1785), and the short, anonymous "An Allegorical Description of a Certain Island and Its Inhabitants" (1790).[22] The first and third of these are completely allegorical works, primarily concerned with presenting the drama of salvation in an easily palatable form in much the same way as Michael Wigglesworth's *The Day of Doom* did; they both portray men (exiled from utopia—Eden in *Basaruah*, Heaven in

"An Allegorical Description") as being under the necessity of returning to a previous state of grace with God. Moore's novella, no less concerned with restoring a previous state of rectitude if not grace, renders the possibility of an earthly utopia.

Basaruah is primarily an explication of and an apology for Calvinist theology. Influenced mostly by Bunyan and to some extent by More, *Basaruah*—the name means *flesh-spirit* in Hebrew—is a first-person narrative by one who once visited (that is, was born into) that kingdom (earth) and is now reporting the details of the generally dystopic life he found there.[23]

Although *Basaruah* dwells in detail on many themes—the necessity of rulers being chosen by God, the potential tragedy of having unregenerate or uneducated clergy, the desirability of religious toleration, the evil of cupidity in business dealings—Morgan focuses most often on attacking both Arminianism and Antinomianism: The Covenant of Faith has replaced that of Works as a means to salvation—*but* good works and proper outward deportment still have significance in that they will always be present in the regenerate; and while man cannot use good works to get into Heaven, *once there* his reward will be commensurate with his earthly behavior.

Morgan shows himself to be a millennialist in the tradition of Joachim, for, besides rendering an otherworldly utopia of Heaven, he mentions "happy times"—"a Period of Time called *Ta Chilia Ete*" (p. 155), which lies within the boundaries of time and precedes the Last Judgment. During this temporal period, marked by the conversion and merciful salvation of many more than have been damned in all previous time, Satan and his forces are completely bound and finally destroyed. Mentioned only in passing at the very end of the book, the millennial period is not particularized in any way; thus, while hinting at an inward conception of utopia, *Basaruah* must be considered as rendering primarily an upward conception.

"An Allegorical Description" reveals no such millennial consciousness. Allegorically representing a more humanized dogma than that in *Basaruah*, it is entirely concerned with showing a return route to utopia-lost that is accessible to all; while Morgan—though he strongly believes in the infinite mercy of God—wrestles mightily with the guardian beast of predestination, the anonymous author of this later tract easily bypasses that potential road-block and leads all sincere souls to salvation.

Prisoners on a remote island (earth) "belonging to the extensive dominions of the King of Utopia" (God), all men must "do penance" for disobedience and be corrected. No one, however, is eternally banished unless he proves incorrigible, for God is eager to forgive all. It is not so much what they actually do—even the erroneous teachings of a misguided clergy cannot block their path—but the zeal and faith with which they apply themselves that determines whether they will return to "the peaceful shores of the Utopian continent"—their "native country," which they have left and to which they may easily return. On a more temporal level, if men are diligent, they may also improve their own lot on earth, for it is "in their power to render the place of their exile agreeable or painful, a place of punishment or enjoyment." Thus, even though "An Allegorical Description" is, like *Basaruah*, primarily an upward utopia, its progressiveness is revealed by its holding out the possibility of an improved community here on earth—though this temporal improvement is not presented in millennial terms. The language used would seem to suggest materialistic (with perhaps a hint of actual scientific) progress; *Basaruah*'s millennialism, on the other hand, is strictly concerned with a temporal utopia of the church. In both, however, we can see a turning from Augustine to Joachim, for men can make a better world for themselves on this transitory earth.

The first essentially inward fictional utopian work—a work suggesting that a transformation of man's nature will lead to a transformation of his environment—is Daniel Moore's *An Account of Count D'Artois and His Friend's Passage to the Moon* (1785), which contains what is apparently the earliest example in American literature of a flight to another planet on which is located an imaginary society. Containing such paradisiacal and millennialist images as those of Eden and the New Jerusalem, and upholding the Joachim tradition of a perfectible human society—yet not suggesting the establishment of an identifiable millennial period—*Passage to the Moon* recounts the adventures of two Frenchmen whose out-of-control balloon takes them ultimately to a lunar world populated by Hebrew-speaking human beings who, being perfectly religious, "live in the most perfect harmony" in an idyllic setting "free from all things . . . hurtful . . . and filled with everything that delights them" (p. 25).

Count D'Artois and his friend Vogtill—both of whom have forsaken the "horrid . . . soul-ruining principles of Rome" (p. 8)—are delighted to discover a society that embodies true religious beliefs as they understand them—a society that proves, contrary to the teachings of detested atheists and deists, that a "just, wise, and good" (p. 6) Supreme Being has created and continues to rule the universe, rewarding and punishing men according to their just deserts.

Awed by the technological marvel of the balloon, the Lunarians assume that the travelers represent a superior race and are delighted to learn of another of God's worlds. Moore, however, does not dwell on the ironic and satiric potential of this Gulliver-like situation to the extent that later utopists will; instead, once having established the mistaken Lunarian assumption, he is content to stress his main theme—that men can become like the Lunarians, who possess "minds adorned in every grace, in every virtue" (p. 26).

Whereas the Lunarians, always described in pre-lapsarian terms, have never fallen from grace and thus have never had to abandon their Eden-like abode, man, by means of Christ's sacrifice, has the same potentially virtuous nature as these utopians and can return, by an act of the will, to a state of innocence. He can, so to speak, pull himself up by his moral bootstraps and make a Christian utopia on earth. The Lunarian society represents the best that man is capable of; and the paradisiacal surroundings—beautiful, idyllic, and verdant (though in a carefully controlled and patterned way, in no way suggesting wild or raw nature)—represent the inevitable material extension of a spiritual perfection.

Even though *Passage to the Moon* does not render a technological utopia—indeed, virtue, not science, is responsible for the idyllic state of the Lunarians—and their society contains none of the materialistically progressive attributes associated with so many ideal American societies, it does offer a hint of the promise technology will whisper to other utopists; the balloon and the Count's telescope are matters of wonder and approval to the Lunarians—gifts of God, the "fountain of all knowledge and invention" (p. 30), to enable man to explore the secrets of His creation.

While many American utopian visions that are direct outgrowths of the millennial tradition give at least equal emphasis to the ease, comfort, and plain wonder of a materialistically advanced civilization, *Passage to the Moon*, despite its science-fiction trappings, is primarily a religious utopia. Moore wants to dramatize the literal truthfulness of the Bible and the truth of Protestantism against both Roman Catholicism and the perversions of the Enlightenment, which speak of man's autonomy in a universe neglected by an absentee landlord. Moore, by wishing to return to the religious purity of the early church even while embracing the scientific advances of his own age—by, in other words, rejecting the philosophy but accepting the technology of the Enlightenment—shows that same nostalgic-progressive tension discernible in most early American utopian writings.

EUTOPIAN TRACTS AND SERMONS

As the eighteenth century progressed in America, otherworldly concepts of utopia increasingly gave way to thisworldly ones; a heavenly utopia gave way in emphasis to a prophesied thousand-year period of prosperity for the church on earth. Even though an earthly Millennium is presented in *Basaruah*—tagged on, as it were, as if the idea were an afterthought—the real utopia exists in Heaven and will be completely realized when all of the saints are gathered there after the Day of Judgment; by the end of the century, utopia will have become more secularized and, as we shall see, more localized.

Although the terms *Millennium* and *eutopia* (or the more common, though less precise, *utopia*) can be, and frequently are, used interchangeably, each really governs an area of meaning pretty much its own: The second is a secularization of the first; indeed, as we proceed historically from the time of Augustine, we find ourselves moving from the city limit of Millennium to that of Eutopia—from a largely religious orientation to a largely secular one; from a belief that Eutopia will happen to man to a belief that man, by means of his own will and strength, can make Eutopia happen. Frequently, however, we shall find ourselves in suburbs between belonging to neither or to both.

Jonathan Edwards, in *A History of the Work of Redemption,*[24] launched the first direct New World attack on Augustine's (and Calvin's) position that the Millennium would have no earthly consequences within history; Edwards, in fact, broke with the current New England tradition of premillennialism—the belief that the Second Coming will be *prior* to the Millennium and hence that the reign of Christ will be literal and outside of history.[25]

No doubt influenced by the writings of the English "originator of postmillennialism in its modern form," Daniel Whitby,[26] Edwards—harking back to Columbus's vision and being perfectly consistent with early beliefs linking the New World with God's plan of salvation—sees every reason to expect an earthly, temporal Millennium, during which the church will flourish gloriously under the radiant sun of America (and especially New England): "This new world is probably now discovered, that the new and most glorious state of God's church on earth might commence there; that God might in it begin a new world in a spiritual respect, when he creates the *new heavens* and the *new earth.*"[27]

Arguing against those who foresee dark days ahead for the church, Edwards sees that the golden age is yet to come and, like Joseph Morgan, believes that the spreading of the gospel will help bring it about; man, from this point on, acting as the conscious agent of God, will play an increasingly important part in bringing on the Millennium and founding Utopia Americana.

What will the Millennium and the age leading up to it be like? First will come a further purification of Protestantism; next the fall of the papacy; then the conversion of the Jews and the enlightenment of the heathens; finally, a world "thoroughly settled in the Christian faith and order," in which all schisms and all vice and all resultant "unhappy commotions, tumults, and calamities" will be absent.[28] But this peaceful, worldwide reign of the Christian spirit has another side that is even more secular—indeed, materialistic—although Edwards makes it clear that the material blessings described are the result of spiritual and intellectual strivings:

'Tis probable that the world shall be more like Heaven in the millennium in this respect: that contemplation and spiritual employments, and those things that more directly concern the mind and religion, will be more the saint's ordinary business than now. There will be so many contrivances and inventions to facilitate and expedite their necessary secular business that they shall have better contrivances for assisting one another through the whole earth by more expedite, easy, and safe communication between distant regions than now. . . . And so the country about the poles need no longer be hid to us, but the whole earth may be as one community, one body in Christ.[29]

The importance of Edwards as a utopian thinker paradoxically is contained within, and yet lies beyond, his millennial expectations; he did more than portray a golden age of the church—more even than portray a golden age of secular accomplishments. He linked, as he quite naturally would, religion and intellectual contemplation—gave, in other words, a resolution to the old quarrel between faith and reason: He assumed that, by the grace of God, man had the power to imagine and make manifest improvements in his environment that would, in turn, work to improve his intellectual and spiritual life. This cycle, it can be assumed, would perpetuate itself upward in a spiral of progress. As C. C. Goen puts it:

The importance of the religious background of the idea of progress can never be disparaged; and though direct evidence may be lacking, it is difficult to believe that Edwards' historicizing of the millennium did not furnish a strong impetus to utopianism in America. . . . Though Edwards knew it not, his historical millennium was of a piece with the liberalizing thought which came to full flower in the following century. The encouragement it gave to the efficacy of human effort made it a natural ally to the new doctrine of human ability which already had begun to make inroads on the older Calvinism. . . . Whatever the tragedy of the ultimate secularization of the millennial hope, it becomes an integral part of the optimistic activism which was destined to crown with success the "errand in the wilderness."[30]

Other millennialists followed Edwards's views closely, merely embellishing what the master had already set down. In 1758 Joseph Bellamy (a student and lifelong friend of Edwards and the great-great-grandfather of Edward Bellamy), for example, preached a sermon on the inevitability of the coming Millennium. Playing in deadly seriousness, as so many before him had done, with the prophetic, though cryptic, numbers hinted at in Revelation, he determines that "these glorious days" still lie in the future.[31] Like Edwards and other postmillennialists, Bellamy debunks the idea that "Christ [is] to reign personally on earth" during this period (p. 508); rather, Christ's reign will be a spiritual one, a "grand harvest-time" (p. 510) during which the Jews and all the heathen will be converted. Furthermore (again taking his cue from Edwards), Bellamy sees that both the subsequent days of universal peace and the destruction of "all luxury, intemperance, and extravagance" (p. 511) will enable "useful labour" (p. 510) to convert the earth into a near-paradise capable of sustaining "with food and raiment, a number of inhabitants immensely greater than ever yet dwelt on it at a time" (p. 511).

Bellamy's Millennium, however, is not exactly a carbon copy of Edwards's; as Ernest Lee Tuveson has pointed out, "Bellamy went farther than did his predecessors . . . in making the true Christians associates of God.[32] In the words of Bellamy,

> It therefore becomes all the followers of Christ [to] exert themselves to the utmost, in the use of all proper means, to suppress error and vice of every kind, and promote the cause of truth and righteousness in the world; and so be workers together with God. [p. 514]

Americans, then, are moving closer to the premise that man can make his own world; he may work with God, but—and this was not lost on the American psyche—God works equally as much with man.

Samuel Hopkins's *A Treatise on the Millennium* (1793) is the earliest nonfictional fully developed utopian work written in America. Dedicated to those who will live during the Millennium, it is an attempt to clear up once and for all the confusion surrounding the advent and the events of "that happy era."[33]

Although *Treatise* is ostensibly a religious document, its real importance to us lies in its close delineation of what we would consider the more secular details of the forthcoming Holy Eutopia. Hopkins—and this is true of most utopists-millennialists in the Joachim tradition—is much concerned with debunking any theories of the Millennium that would make of it a time brought about by supernatural means; the details of its coming and content must be entirely reconcilable with reason. Hopkins's first task in Section II ("The Millennial State, Particularly Described") is to defeat by both logic and scriptural evidence the theories that Christ will physically descend and actually reign and that there will be a literal resurrection of the bodies of the saints; instead, the revitalized church will be made up of the spirits of the departed saints living "again in their successors" (p. 51). Although there will be no absolute perfection "on this side of heaven" (p. 55), the "new heavens, and new earth" will exist in a time of universal peace and friendship when "mankind will be united as one family" (p. 59), when there will be a "great increase of light and knowledge" (p. 56), and when all men will feel and think alike respecting religious doctrine (p. 60).

It would be easy for us to collate details concerning material progress—especially those having to do with technological advancement and cultural, social, and economic rearrangements—and conclude that Hopkins was primarily interested in secularizing and temporalizing the Millennium. Such, however, would be at least an exaggeration if not a grave error, for Hopkins is most concerned with the *holiness* of the prophesied Holy Eutopia. It is just that secular benefits will flow naturally from a society made of new men—men transformed by "disinterested benevolence" (p. 59) from beasts into "harmless humble and benevolent" (p. 60) creatures: A "time of eminent holiness, must be a time of proportionably great light and knowledge" (p. 57). Whether material or spiritual progress comes first—and whether one of necessity leads to the other—has been, and still is, a perennial question in American utopian thought. Hopkins, we see, has reversed Edwards's order; better men, his *Treatise* tells us, will make a better world.

Hopkins, like Edwards, makes it clear that life during the Millennium will be easier than ever before. Not only will it be a "time of great enjoyment, happiness and universal joy" (p. 65), but the blessings of God will provide all of the "outward conveniences, and temporal enjoyment[s]" (p. 70) one might expect in an agrarian society when farming is made easier and more efficient. Foreshadowing the mid-nineteenth-century scientific utopist John Adolphus Etzler, he looks forward to a time when there

> . . . will also doubtless, be great improvement and advances made in all those mechanic arts, by which the earth will be subdued and cultivated, and all the necessary and convenient articles of life, such as all utensils, clothing, buildings, &c. will be formed and made, in a better manner, and with much less labour, than they now are. There may be inventions and arts of this kind, which are beyond our present conception. [p. 71]

Because of new inventions "found out by men, to cut rocks and stones into any shape they please," the landscape will be manipulated—"vallies . . . filled, and the mountains and hills . . . made low"—in order to make travel easier. There will be, in short, "a fulness and plenty of all the conveniences of life [more] than ever before, and with much less labour and toil"—only about two or three hours of work a day (p. 72). Lest the reader forget that spiritual values are all-important, however, Hopkins is quick to point out that all of the resultant leisure time will be spent improving the mind and making "progress in knowledge; especially in the knowledge of divinity" (pp. 72–73). And so the cycle is complete. Edwards's and Hopkins's visions are really part and parcel of each other; better men will make a better world, which, in turn, will make better men. Spiritual and material progress (naively, it might seem to us) are not dichotomized.

EUTOPIAN VISIONS MOSTLY IN VERSE

What we find as we look at the work of these men who kept the millennial tradition of Joachim alive in America is a progressive pattern tending toward the temporalization of millennial expectations—a temporalization that, as we shall see, tends later on to make the New Eden less like a garden and more like a city. Ironically, this secularizing tendency was inherent in the very thought of the great revivalist himself, Jonathan Edwards; his acceptance of Newtonian physics and Lockean psychology could hardly have avoided adding a materialistic emphasis to his millennial extrapolations. His relatively vague map of the Holy Eutopia was eagerly seized by his followers who set about to hypothesize a number of topographical details. From Edwards through Bellamy to Hopkins—the millennial vision of America becomes more secularized as the millennialists themselves become more interested in the materialistic details of comfort and convenience. While the initial emphasis may ostensibly be on the glories of God as manifested in a perfected or improved earth, what caught the fancy of many were Edwards's "contrivances and inventions to facilitate and expedite their necessary secular business."

This secularization of American millennial expectations took place on another level as well. Not surprisingly, the Millennium became associated as much with patriotic pride as with God's great plan for the salvation of mankind. The future glory of God's Kingdom on earth gave way in emphasis to the future glory of America; that the Millennium would appear seemed not so important as that it would appear in America.

Utilizing some of the techniques of fiction—the framework of the vision or dream, for example, or a hint of elementary characterization—and dwelling on the extrapolative details of the imagined Millennium, a number of writers (most of them poets and most of these among the Connecticut Wits) set out to sing the praises of their native land; in the process they rendered some of the first substantial images of Utopia Americana. Some of these works, indeed, are entirely devoted to portraying America as Holy Eutopia—Timothy Dwight's "America: or, a Poem on the Settlement of the British Colonies" (*ca.* 1771, *ca.* 1781), David Humphreys's "A Poem on the Future Glory of the United States of America" (1804), and the anonymous short prose work *The Golden Age* (1785); others have different main themes but still devote substantial time to linking America to the advent of the Millennium—Part VII of Timothy Dwight's *Greenfield Hill* (1794) and Book VIII of Joel Barlow's *The Vision of Columbus* (1787).[34]

While all of these works differ somewhat from one another in emphasis, the millennial-utopian content is so remarkably similar that we can easily construct a representative abstract to stand more or less for all: We can see in history that God's great plan for humanity will soon culminate in bringing society to a state of perfection. The New World was revealed to man at a propitious time in order to serve as a theater for the climax of the drama of salvation—the binding of the forces of evil and the subsequent founding of an earthly paradise, a Holy Eutopia filled with temporal blessings. Its founding will inaugurate the Millennium, a period of peace and prosperity that will flower first in America and then spread to the entire world. Through the ultimate triumph of reason over passion, society will be shaped and dominated by scientific, religious, and cultural enlightenment; new technology, for example, will bring fertility and abundance, religious dissension will disappear, and men will use their free time to improve their minds. Of special importance (all authors stressed this) will be the increase in commerce; its spread, aided by a network of canals and highways connecting distant points in America, will bind men together in the sharing of both material goods and progressive ideas. America will be a beacon to the world, and the rest of mankind will eagerly follow its example. Ultimately, nationalistic designs will fade away and there will be one universal nation, one language, and one governing body.

It would be wrong to say that the emphasis in these works was entirely on humanistic and materialistic concerns at the total expense of religious ones; yet the *tendency* is in that direction. For one thing, while all of the authors stress that God is the primary mover, they also agree that man is His special instrument, a central pawn in a great cosmic struggle. With infinite patience, God works unevenly but relentlessly through the imperfections of the beings He has created. Following Hopkins, all of the authors of these early visions of Utopia Americana agree with Joel Barlow "that such a state of peace and happiness as is foretold in scripture and commonly called the millennial period, may be rationally expected to be introduced without a miracle" (p. 242); because they could not emphasize supernatural causes of a perfected earth, they were left with only natural ones—and with the natural, temporal fruits thereof. The secularization of earlier millennial expectations is well on its way to being complete. Although the framework of these utopian visions is still the essentially religious impulses of Joachim, Luther, and Edwards, the canvas is bright with the gaudy paint of a more materialistic age.

American utopian fiction, then, has an ancestry not unlike that of American literature in general—tracts, sermons, and religious allegories. Although the importance of such secular background materials as Plato's *Republic* and other ancient utopian writings, the humanism and the geographic discoveries of the Rennaissance, the naturalism and rationality of the Enlightenment, and the economic and scientific developments of the seventeenth and eighteenth centuries cannot be disputed, such influences can be overemphasized to the near exclusion of equally (perhaps more) important ones. This essay has been an attempt to get at what is peculiarly American about the early Utopia Americana—the fact that its origins are primarily religious rather than secular, although within a few centuries after its founding a distinct temporalization began to take place.[35]

The images to keep in mind are two shifting ones: Augustine's City of God descends from heaven to earth and becomes populated with men *doing* instead of contemplating and praying; and, while still remaining essentially gardenlike, the Eden of Genesis evolves slowly into the New Jerusalem of Revelation. All of this takes place on the shores (and later in the interior to the West) of a land set aside by God for the establishment of the millennial Kingdom foretold in scripture.

In the minds of its creators, early Utopia Americana was a real, not fictional, place; while its particular aspects might have been extrapolative and hypothetical, its ultimate existence was not. American utopian *fiction* begins only when utopists feel free to speculate in ways, and on subjects, more or less divorced from the specifics of Revelation; as we shall see, however, Utopia Americana, having its roots in millennial expectations, never entirely frees itself from the religious spirit of its past—secularized though it becomes.

NOTES

1. I prefer the utopian terminology presented in my introduction to *The Amazonian Republic* (Delmar, N.Y.: Scholars' Facsimiles & Reprints, 1976). I have, however, modified this terminology slightly in my two essays to conform with the terms used in this collection.

2. Charles L. Sanford, *The Quest for Paradise: Europe and the American Imagination* (Urbana: University of Illinois Press, 1961), p. 5.

3. Ernest Lee Tuveson, *Redeemer Nation: The Idea of America's Millennial Role* (Chicago and London: University of Chicago Press, 1968), p. 1.

4. Harold V. Rhodes, *Utopia in American Political Thought* (Tucson: University of Arizona Press, 1967), pp. 16–20.

5. Sanford, *Quest for Paradise*, p. 40.

6. Quoted in Ibid.

7. Tuveson, *Redeemer*, pp. 13–16.

8. Ernest Lee Tuveson, *Millennium and Utopia: A Study in the Background of the Idea of Progress* (Berkeley and Los Angeles: University of California Press, 1949), p. 17.

9. Tuveson, *Millennium*, p. 46.

10. Sanford, *Quest for Paradise*, p. 33.

11. Tuveson, *Millennium*, p. 20.

12. J. A. De Jong, *As the Waters Cover the Sea: Millennial Expectations in the Rise of Anglo-American Missions, 1640–1810* (Kampen, Netherlands: J. H. Kok, 1970), p. 12.

13. Sanford, *Quest for Paradise*, p. 79.

14. Tuveson, *Millennium*, pp. ix, x.

15. Tuveson, *Redeemer*, pp. 17, 38.

16. Ibid., p. 7.

17. De Jong, *As the Waters*, pp. 5–33 (Ch. 1, "Millennial Views and Missions Prior to 1640").

18. Tuveson, *Redeemer*, pp. 97, 98.

19. Quoted in De Jong, *As the Waters*, p. 30.

20. See Chs. 2 and 3 of Leo Marx, *The Machine in the Garden: Technology and the Pastoral Ideal in America* (New York: Oxford University Press, 1967), pp. 34–144, for a full discussion of such early descriptions.

21. Quoted in Howard Mumford Jones, *O Strange New World: American Culture: The Formative Years* (New York: The Viking Press, 1967), p. 19.

22. [Joseph Morgan], *The History of the Kingdom of Basaruah* (Boston: n.p., 1715); [Daniel Moore], *An Account of Count D'Artois and His Friend's Passage to the Moon*, . . . (Litchfield, Conn.: Collier and Copp, [1785]); and "An Allegorical Description of a Certain Island and Its Inhabitants," *The Massachusetts Magazine*, No. 16, 1790. Page references to these, and to all subsequent primary sources, will appear in parentheses within the text.

23. Although the allegorical framework forces us to consider the narrator as speaking from beyond the grave, this aspect is not even alluded to in the work.

24. Jonathan Edwards, *A History of the Work of Redemption. Containing the Outlines of a Body of Divinity, in a Method Entirely New* (New York: Shepar Kollback, 1786). This was originally a series of sermons that Edwards preached in Northampton in 1739; after Edwards's death, John Erskin edited the manuscripts and published them first in Edinburgh in 1774.

25. Winthrop's "Citty upon a Hill" was in no way meant to be an equivalence of an actual millennial state. The secularization of Augustine's City of God was merely meant to create a society on earth pleasing to God, which facilitated men's living Christian lives and functioned as a fortress—or new beachhead—in the soon-to-be-concluded battle with Satan.

26. C. C. Goen, "Jonathan Edwards: A New Departure in Eschatology," *Church History*, 28 (March 1959), 37.

27. Jonathan Edwards, *Works* (New York: Robert Carter & Bros., 1881), II, 314; quoted in Goen, "Jonathan Edwards," p. 29. See also Perry Miller, *Jonathan Edwards* (New York: Meridian Books, 1959), pp. 326–30, for a discussion of Edwards's belief that the thousand years of heaven on earth would begin in America.

28. Edwards, *Works, II*, 493; quoted in Goen, "Jonathan Edwards," p. 33.

29. Harvey G. Townsand, ed., *The Philosophy of Jonathan Edwards from His Private Notebooks* (Eugene: University of Oregon Press, 1955), p. 207; quoted in Goen, "Jonathan Edwards," p. 29.

30. Goen, "Jonathan Edwards," pp. 38–39.

31. Joseph Bellamy, "The Millennium," *The Works of the Rev. Joseph Bellamy, D. D. Late of Bethlem, Connecticut* (New York: Stephen Dodge, 1811), I, 495–516; the quotation is from p. 514.

32. Tuveson, *Redeemer* (note 3 above), p. 59.

33. Samuel Hopkins, *A Treatise on the Millennium. Showing from Scripture Prophecy, That It Is Yet to Come; When It Will Come; In What It Will Consist;*

Events Which Are First to Take Place, Introductory to It (Boston: Isaiah Thomas & Ebenezer T. Andrews, 1793).

34. [Timothy Dwight], *America: or, a Poem on the Settlement of the British Colonies; Addressed to the Friends of Freedom and Their Country* (New Haven, Conn.: Thomas and Samuel Green, [1780; largely written a few years earlier]; David Humphreys, "A Poem on the Future Glory of the United States of America," *The Miscellaneous Works of David Humphreys* (New York: T. & J. Swords, 1804); *The Golden Age; or, Future Glory of North-America Discovered by an Angel to Celadon. In Several Entertaining Visions. Vision I* (n.p., 1785); Timothy Dwight, *Greenfield Hill* (New York: Childs & Swaine, 1794); and Joel Barlow, *The Vision of Columbus* (Hartford, Conn.: Hudson & Goodwin, 1787).

35. Two recent studies concerning the influence of millennialism on American thought deserve to be mentioned here: David E. Smith's "Millenarian Scholarship in America," *American Quarterly*, 12 (Fall 1965), 535–49, and Jean B. Quandt's "Religion and Social Thought: The Secularization of Postmillenialism" *American Quarterly*, 25 (October 1973), 390–409.

JOEL NYDAHL

Early Fictional Futures: Utopia, 1798–1864

THE EARLIEST UTOPIAN VISIONS in and of America were of millennial expectations fulfilled: Columbus saw on the shores of the New World a stage upon which would be acted out Saint John's great prophetic drama; John Winthrop's "Citty on a Hill" was to be a society of godly men waiting for, and working to bring about, the final apocalyptic defeat of the forces of Satan; John Eliot's missionary work with the Indians (in his view the Lost Tribes of Israel, discussed in Stuart Teitler's introduction) was an attempt to fulfill scriptural prophecies leading up to the Second Coming and the establishment of the Kingdom of Heaven on earth; and the earliest speculative writings portraying spiritual and material progress were exclusively by men who saw America's manifest destiny in terms of a cosmic struggle between darkness and light culminating in a secular millennial age spreading from American to foreign shores.

Beginning in the second decade of the nineteenth century, however, American utopists turned from optimistic millennial speculation about America's future to severe criticism of the present situation. Expressing itself predominantly in satiric and antiutopian attacks, this critical attitude seems to have precluded any positive visions of what actually might have been done to improve matters.

EARLY PROGRESSIVE EUTOPIAS

Before this post–War of 1812 disillusion set in, however, two fictional *eutopias* made their appearance—Charles Brockden Brown's *Alcuin* (1798) and James Reynolds's *Equality—A Political Romance* (1802).[1] Even though its appearance was considerably later, another work, David Stirrat's *A Treatise on Political Economy* (1824), should also be included in our discussion here; not only does it focus, like *Equality*, on economic paths to utopia, but it also represents a positive vision of a significantly early date.[2]

Although *Alcuin* represents an important break in American utopian writing with the millennial tradition, its progressive vision, like that of many subsequent works, no doubt owes much, at least indirectly, to the temporal millennial hopes encouraged by the writings of Jonathan Edwards and his followers. It is the complete secularization of utopia (for the first time really distinct from the Millennium). Equipped with a new "assumption that there exists a 'natural order,' the workings of which can be understood by man's reason,"[3] men no longer have to allow utopia to happen to them; rather, they can now make utopia happen.

Differing in focus from most of the utopian visions preceding it, *Alcuin* stresses the use of the social sciences of economics and politics to effect the ideal society; scientific advances—Edwards's "contrivances and inventions,"—are never mentioned. This new focus is both necessary and logical in *Alcuin*, for it is primarily concerned with social issues—specifically, women's rights.

Modeled in form after Plato's dialogues, *Alcuin* hardly has a plot at all. At a series of *soirées* at the home of the widowed Mrs. Carter, Alcuin, an indigent school teacher, engages in a continuing debate with his hostess on the question of the proper place of women in American society. Touching on such subjects as women's rights to vote and hold property and their subjugation within marriage, *Alcuin* is an economic and political novel in that it focuses on power—in the marketplace, at the polls, and in the home.

After debating with Mrs. Carter throughout the entire first half of the book—her main argument against the conservative views of Alcuin being that mere sexual identification is no rational basis upon which to assign or take away rights—Alcuin visits (but only in his imagination) the Paradise of Women, a utopia created entirely in his own mind from the mortar and boards of Mrs. Carter's arguments. In his vision, the ubiquitous utopian guide shows him a society in which all citizens are treated as rational beings with a basic nature unaffected by gender; environment, not sex, determines aptitudes and prejudices. Marriage, however, does not exist; some other (never specified) arrangement takes care of procreation.

Alcuin illustrates an important aspect of the American character that will be stressed time and again in the utopian literature under discussion—the search for the practical. There is a tension between Alcuin's theoretical ideal society and Brown's belief that it can never really exist. In an act that certainly has a symbolic import, Alcuin travels to utopia only on the wings of fancy; Mrs. Carter's scorn for his Paradise plummets him back to earth. What Alcuin does, however, is give respectability to the imagination in the face of cold reason. When it comes time to change the world, Brown implies, we should imagine the best (even the most farfetched) and then let reason cut the image down to size. Rationality is not all: Both the logical arguments of Mrs. Carter and the fantasy utopia of Alcuin are ideally right—but not practically correct, because neither will work in the everyday world where the two of them are trapped.

Utopia for Charles Brockden Brown, then, is an imaginary land (a work of art) created by fancy feeding on reason—or vice versa; it is a land in which social changes can be tested by visualization; it is itself a means of persuasion, as it shows concretely the absurdity of present-day practices. Ready to be brought forth in time from the soil of the here-and-now, it is not a place to be reached by an outward journey to some distant land; rather, it is to be reached by an inward journey into man's mind.

James Reynolds's *Equality—A Political Romance* is the first fully developed fictional portrayal of utopia in America that utilizes from beginning to end the setting of a distant, mysterious land.[4] Located in the allegorical "regions lately discovered by political philosophers" (p. 1), the island of Lithconia reveals to the nameless sailor who sojourns there numerous reforms, practices, and attitudes that will become common fare in later American utopian fiction. *Equality*, in other words, is a prototypical work—the grandfather, perhaps of *Looking Backward*. There is, however, in spite of the reprints published in 1847, 1863, and 1947, no evidence that it was actually read by any subsequent utopist.

As the title indicates, *Equality* portrays a society in which economic and social differences have been leveled or at least minimized—a society in which the citizens (all of whom dress alike and live in identical houses) lead outward lives cut from the same pattern. Because money and trade are prohibited, and the products of both field and factory are equitably distributed by law, there is no strife, poverty, or greed—in short, no unhappiness whatsoever. Human needs are reduced pretty much to the level of economics and—to ask a question implicitly posed by most modern, progressive utopias—if material needs are satisfied, can perfect bliss be far behind?

Equality is primarily a paean to the ability of man to make a better world for himself by controlling his own economic, political, and physical environment. Whereas in the work of the early millennialists God worked through man, in Reynolds's utopia men, having the necessary tools, work more or less alone. According to Lithconian history, "God delegated to man a certain power of directing the principal operations of nature on this globe of the earth"—that is, He furnished "the means of knowledge, whereby [man] may discover the road to happiness" (p. 16). The watch, in other words, now runs without the watchmaker in attendance. Interestingly enough, the only hint of a Fall (Lithconian history teaches that man's nature is not innately corrupt) is an early failure, because of a life of ease and abundance, to inquire sufficiently "into the operations of nature" (p. 17) in both the political and physical sciences. The Lithconians, however, were given a second chance to earn a kind of secular salvation and through eons managed to regenerate themselves by using reason to change man's temporal condition. Men thus finally learned that their happiness depended solely on how they themselves organized their communities; foolish and dangerous institutions such as private property, they discovered, needed to be, and could be, overthrown.

What the Lithconians learn is a fledgling lesson in bureaucracy, which, it would seem, they managed to pass on to their utopian and real-life descendants right down to the twentieth century—that nature's orderly and regular operations can be reduced to systems that, in turn, can control both machines and men. Not only do technological marvels abound, making work enjoyable by eliminating drudgery, but "order and regularity . . . worthy of being recorded for the instruction of our modern politicians" (p. 1) is what first impresses our narrator. The "whole country," he notes, "has the appearance of one vast manufactory, conducted by one mind"—an "immense machine" that is "much more simple [that is, understandable and efficient] than any other form of government in the world" (p. 7).

Equality is especially noteworthy for being the first American utopia to portray in some detail the garden-city. With typical Jeffersonian bias, the Lithconians have abandoned "large towns, as in Europe" with their "concomitant" "evils, natural and moral" (p. 3). In what will become an increasingly typical attempt by American utopists to combine the best of pastoral and urban life, Reynolds has the Lithconians embrace the order and regularity of civilization and progress while still honoring the virtues of agrarianism. They build a city that is not really a city: "The whole island may be compared to a city spread over a large garden: not a spot can be seen but what is in a high state of cultivation" (p. 10).

This nostalgic-progressive tension—this desire for a new beginning as well as a return, a holdover from, and an extension of, early paradisiacal-millennial dreams associated with America[5]—will be evident, even dominant, in much of American utopian fiction throughout the nineteenth century. (See for example, Donald C. Burt's discussion of the utopian landscape.) It is, indeed, a theme seemingly inherent in the American experience itself: nature versus civilization—the natural desire to return to an Edenlike state of simplistic purity versus the cultural drive to "progress" to an "improved" state of grace earned by mastering, and imposing order on, the environment.

In light of Lyman Tower Sargent's assertion in "Capitalist Eutopias" that too frequently it has been erroneously assumed that utopias, as if by definition, uphold a socialist point of view, it should not be surprising that the early American eutopia most obviously designed to make capitalism work is almost completely unknown. The obscurity of David Stirrat's *A Treatise on Political Economy* (1824) is, in fact, ironic, for this thinly fictionalized tract speaks more directly to us today, in terms we still understand, than almost any other utopia.

In simplest terms, Stirrat proposes a kind of Works Progress Administration in order to bolster a sagging economy, assure the undertaking and completion of great public works, and provide adequately for those who cannot provide for themselves.

Recognizing early, as so many did not, that America is entering a new

era when the economic ethic of rugged individualism will often prove irrelevant, Stirrat boldly faces the problem of how to maintain the prosperity
the country has enjoyed from the beginning. Growing continually in area
and population, America, he maintains, can no longer be a nation only of
landowning yeomen. The history of the utopian society of Oceanus, visited
in a dream, makes quite clear Stirrat's commitment to a mixed economy;
at the very founding of the country, all men would have chosen farming as
their profession had not the Governor advised them to divide themselves
into farmers, manufacturers, and laborers—such an arrangement promising
to be "more congenial for improvement and refinement" (p. 136). This
vocational diversification—not unlike that suggested later on by George
Tucker in *A Voyage to the Moon* (1827)—naturally led to a relatively complex
economy, which, while containing a marvelous potential for a rich life for
all, needs to be first understood and then mastered before its inherent
benefits can be spread over the entire population instead of being concentrated in the hands of a few.

The most impressive result of this national industry is the capital of
Although Stirrat's social conscience dictates that it is one's Christian duty
to care for those who cannot care for themselves, it is a kind of self-interested
altruism—"the interest of every individual is the interest of the whole" (p.
58)—that moves him to propose a plan suggestive in many ways of the New
Deal. Aware that "the foundation of the wealth of all nations" (p. 43) is the
increasing value—that is, the buying power—of the surplus labor, Stirrat
recognizes that all men must have employment so that the "surplus produce"
and the "surplus population" can be brought together. His solution to a
stagnant economy is to have the government use the surplus produce to
employ the surplus population in order to prosecute "useful national improvements" (p. 23) and "put in motion national industry" (p. 46).

The most impressive result of this national industry is the capital of
Oceanus with its technological marvels. Set in the middle of a "green verdant
carpet" with lakes, streams, and "shady bowers" (p. 13), yet arranged with
"exact regularity" (p. 17)—an orderly, balanced mixture of domes and spires,
gardens and baths—the city, like its prototype in *Equality*, renders that
nostalgic-progressive tension symbolized by the settings of so many American utopias. Even so, the city is decidedly progressive; the garden images
are basically elements of embroidery on a forward-looking fabric. Machines
(hydraulics and steam engines) build and regulate the city and perform the
mundane labor while men merely supervise.

As if a more efficient model of Reynolds's prototype, the government
itself is the greatest machine. It alone has the power to undertake grand
projects, such as uniting the Atlantic and Pacific, subduing the wilderness,
and building canals and changing the courses of rivers. Most important, as
the first American bureaucratic machine that openly approximates God as
the dispenser of blessings (p. 94), it alone can organize, distribute, con-

trol—in short, regulate. Stirrat already knew what America would only partially learn, much later, that Adam Smith's "invisible hand" does not exist;[6] government intervention is necessary at times to assure that "by regulation . . . all may have a share" (p. 93).

Although Stirrat's project would distribute the wealth of the country more evenly, it is definitely not intended to promote economic or social equality; rather, it aims at promoting what we would call equality of opportunity. Given the new, deviously complex economic forces of the time, it is vain to say "that man [can always] earn a living if he chooses to be industrious" (p. 73). *Treatise* is a capitalistic eutopia whose aim is to use the benefits of capitalism to raise the living standards of all. To say that every man has a right to the surplus produce is not to claim that some men may not rightfully become richer than others. Stirrat fully supports "the honest and industrious speculator" (p. 85) and finds "no fault with the division of property amongst individuals . . . that naturally has taken place in the various societies of man" (p. 148).

SATIRIC UTOPIAS

Few American millennialists or utopists prior to Stirrat seem to have lacked positive, progressive visions; few later utopists until after the half-century mark seem to have possessed them.[7] If we wish to account for this dearth, we may point to an age of disillusionment and confusion—an age in which sectional contention and factionalism in general abounded to the extent that the survival of the Union itself was in doubt. It was also a time of shifting values and shifting power, of speculation and new, unconventional enterprise replacing plain, old-fashioned work, of wealth and status passing slowly but surely from one level of society to another. It was a time when Americans sensed, but did not really understand, that agrarianism was inevitably giving way to industrialism. It was, in short, a time in which many felt that the so-called golden age of the post-Revolutionary years—that very age eagerly looked forward to by the poet utopists such as Joel Barlow and, later, nostalgically recalled by Cooper—had been betrayed. It is perhaps not surprising, then, that most American utopists found fault with the existing state (always the easiest thing to do) rather than build ideal ones. One typical form that their writings took was the *satiric utopia*, a work, such as most of Swift's *Gulliver's Travels*, rendering a negative vision that indirectly presents an improved or ideal society by portraying an imaginary one as an absurd reflection of the author's own.

The tradition of the fantastic voyage—which was, of course, utilized earlier by Daniel Moore, Reynolds, and, to a lesser extent, Morgan—becomes especially popular in the first half of the century; it is as if American utopists have just discovered *Gulliver's Travels*, for every one of the satiric utopias we shall now consider is influenced to some extent, either in form or in content, by that work—Jonas Clopper's *Fragments of the History of Bawlfredonia* (1819), Adam Seaborn's *Symzonia* (1820), George Tucker's *A Voyage to the Moon* (1827), James Fenimore Cooper's *The Monikins* (1835), Timothy Savage's *The Amazonian Republic* (1842), and Elbert Perce's *Gulliver Joi* (1851).[8]

Of these satirical fantastic-voyage utopias, Jonas Clopper's *Bawlfredonia* has by far the least literary merit. Purportedly a portion of a longer chronicle of the early years of a previously unknown country in the East Indies, the work is full of such bombast and superficial allegory (Thomas Paine becomes Tom Anguish and the southern province of the country, Blackmoreland, is infamous for growing and exporting the noxious "stinkum weed") that it soon begins to wear our patience.

As Vernon Louis Parrington, Jr., has pointed out, Clopper's history is concerned with "debunking tradition"[9]—specifically the tradition that the founding fathers of the Republic were all great and honorable men. Clopper, harking back to early millennial expectations, is certain that America has failed in its mission as God's instrument; irreligion and debauchery have replaced the virtues of early Puritan New England.

The slow drifting apart of God and His commonwealth has been due, according to Clopper, to "the impiety of our great men" (p. 24), and his most vicious satirical barbs are reserved for Jefferson, Paine, and the entire membership of the American Philosophical Society, all of whom are portrayed as being not only an irreligious lot but also drunkards and libertines.

Truly a negative vision, more than is the case with most other American satiric utopias, *Bawlfredonia* is more concerned with attacking the follies of the present (and their historical roots) than with indicating how men may create a better future.

By contrast, Adam Seaborn's[10] *Symzonia*, besides taking Swiftian broadsides at American society, renders a positive vision of an ideal state—albeit one in which the citizens are not quite human and whose virtues and institutions, therefore, seem only obliquely applicable to real men and women. *Symzonia* portrays an ideal society, on the underside of the earth's crust, in which the old Puritan virtues and the old Puritan practicality hold sway—although these have been filtered through the Enlightenment until they are little more than Doing Good and Being Useful.

Ruled by a Best Man and a Council of Worthies (comprising three classes, the Good, the Wise, and the Useful), the citizens of Symzonia reflect Seaborn's simplistic notion—one hauntingly and naively present in much of American utopian fiction—that if only men are right-minded, even potentially complicated matters, like government and economics, will somehow work themselves out properly; "purity of life, usefulness in society, and goodness of heart" (p. 125) are everything. At the root of America's problems, Seaborn believes, are the philosophers (representing everything abstract and impractical) "who have the control of the government" and who becloud the simple truth with arcane and dangerous theories. In Symzonia,

> The community is not bewildered by a voluminous and complex system of political economy, consisting of abstract principles, buried in abstract and unintelligible words, and rendered too intricate to be understood by those who have common sense, or too inapplicable to civilized society to be adopted by those who have any sort of sense—invented by the *Wise* men of one country to mislead the politicians of another, and to depress the Good and the Useful. [pp. 160–61]

The Symzonians are nearly perfectly rational and hence, according to the logic of the book, nearly perfectly virtuous beings. More than the Lithconians and less than the Lunarians in George Fowler's *A Flight to the Moon* (1813)—an antiutopia to be discussed later—they represent the utopist tendency to dichotomize flesh and spirit: "The enjoyments of this refined people were intellectual and pure—not the debasing gratifications of animal passions and sensual appetites" (p. 182). Seaborn attributes this perfection to the Symzonians' "conformity to the law of their natures" (p. 176), thus seeming to hold out the hope that we may emulate them.

Upon witnessing the perfection around him, Captain Seaborn, like Gulliver in Houyhnhnmland, is tempted to make invidious comparisons between Symzonian and American societies. We are thus presented with direct attacks on cupidity in business, the accumulation of wealth, inequality of station, and complex political and economic systems.

Symzonia—part pure imaginary voyage, part satire, and part eutopia—is a hybrid work. Our discussion of it could just as easily have fallen under the heading (which I shall come to later) of *progressive eutopias*. Yet the author's obvious interest in casting Seaborn in the mold of Gulliver and his use of the fantastic voyage to show us a mirror image of ourselves seem to beg us to consider this work as a satiric utopia.

George Tucker's *A Voyage to the Moon* is more obviously a satiric utopia, even though it, too, in a relatively brief section, portrays an ideal state, the "Lunar Paradise" of Okalbia. The plot of *Voyage* is a simple one, in no really important way distinguishable from those of many other fantastic voyages. Joseph Atterley, cast up by a shipwreck on the shores of Burma and held prisoner by the Burmese, is befriended by a Brahmin priest. In a spacecraft utilizing the power of a chemical that is repulsed by the earth and attracted to the moon, Atterley and the Brahmin, who has made the journey before, visit the moon. Their subsequent adventures in various Lunarian countries, obviously derivative of Gulliver's, show that institutions and practices on the moon are merely reflections of absurdities on earth; some Lunarians, born without any "intellectual vigour" but "illuminated with the [shared] mental ray of some earthly brains," have a sense of "understanding" that is divided between two beings whose "modes of thinking" necessarily conform (p. 38).

In episodes closer than any of those in other American satirical utopias—with the possible exception of Cooper's *The Monikins*—to matching the verve and cleverness of similar ones in *Gulliver's Travels*, Tucker sticks his rapier to a variety of earthly follies: the ostentatious display of wealth; grotesque "female fashions"; ridiculous and hypocritical religious practices; impractical inventions (applied science gone mad); irrational quarrels over whether agriculture or industry should be the basis for the national economy; and the poles of abstract philosophy not rooted in experience and empiricism carried to extremes.

It is only when Atterley and the Brahmin visit the isolated country of Okalbia that we have a chance to see a positive vision of Utopia Americana. While journeying to the moon, Atterley and the Brahmin discuss the cause of differences among the races. Because the Brahmin, echoing Tucker, believes that it is more "reasonable to impute the changes in national character to the mutable habits and institutions of man, than to nature, which is always the same" (p. 56), it is not surprising that we are presented with a utopia illustrating that rational, humane institutions will produce rational, humane citizens.

Like America, Okalbia, founded during a time of "religious fervour" (p. 185), is separated from the rest of the world (in this case by huge mountains); thus the Okalbians, who carry their isolation so far as to have no foreign intercourse except a tourist trade, are uncontaminated by the absurdities plaguing the other Lunarians.

The economy of Okalbia, unlike the economy of Stirrat's Oceanus, works itself out naturally, with a minimum of government intervention. First of all, population control—"the most important of all sciences" (p. 189)—holds the population at a level the land can ideally support; the control is left to "individual discretion" (p. 190). Second, the Okalbians have made sure that individual initiative in the economic sphere is interfered with as little as possible; one citizen—as in Stirrat's *Treatise*—may rise above another (although there are no privileged *classes*), for their "institutions have only tempered" ambition (p. 192), not done away with it. By means of equal distribution of land, they "tried first to preserve . . . equality; but finding it impracticable," with typically good Okalbian sense, they abandoned it (p. 186). No problems arise, however, from the fact that not everyone owns land; nonlandowners happily cultivate someone else's soil or practice some "liberal or mechanical art" (p. 194).

Like most other American utopists, Tucker attempts to sketch in a more or less complete society. Thus, we find a number of other positive attributes that make Okalbia the "Happy Valley": Newspapers contain only objective reporting; capital punishment has been outlawed; property qualifications for voting do not exist; women are "under few restraints" (p. 201), just to mention a few.

The American garden-city also makes its appearance in *Voyage*. Although cultivated verdure (as in almost all American utopias, there is no wilderness) and settlements are not homogeneously blended, the yearning to retain a sense of the pastoral is very strong. Atterley's first glimpse of Okalbia is of a "whole surface . . . like a garden, interspersed with patches of wood, clumps of trees, and houses standing singly or in groups"; off to the side, on the edge of a lake, is a town, the road to which is lined by "rows of trees" and paralleled by a "rivulet . . . bubbling along one side or the other" (p. 185).

While the satirical thrusts of *Voyage* are many, one of Tucker's main concerns is the absurdity of certain economic theories and practices prevalent in America. The main attack in this direction comes when Atterley visits a farm family where the husband and wife allegorically represent, in a quarrel over whether their daughters will work in the family garden or make their own clothes, the basic arguments in the American debate over the respective virtues of an agrarian versus an industrial economy. The absurdity, we are clearly shown, lies in the belief that either extreme position—rather than a commonsense middle ground—represents the most viable economic base for an America that is, Tucker feels, inevitably progressing from a predominantly rural to a predominantly urban state.[11]

James Fenimore Cooper's *The Monikins*, on the other hand, while allegorically satirizing many economic (as well as social and religious) absurdities, finally focuses on a political question: Who should rule? Although three-quarters of this utopian animal fable is devoted to presenting the protagonist's background and his adventures in Europe and in the kingdom of Leaphigh (England), we feel, at the end of our visits to these Swiftian lands, that the portrayal of life in the republic of Leaplow (Jacksonian America) should, because of its relevancy, command most of our attention. If, after all, the institutions of American republicanism contain such dangerous absurdities, the degeneration is doubly tragic, for America probably represents man's last chance to found a government devoid of the chicanery, dishonesty, ineptitude, and general foolishness of European monarchies and aristocracies.

Son of a self-made multimillionaire who believed that states exist solely for the protection of property, Gulliver-like John Goldencalf develops his own theory that only those who have a "stake in society" are fit to rule. In his attempt to gain an economic interest in all parts of the known world in order to make himself the most fit of all men to rule, he encounters a group of intelligent monkeys (the monikins) who have been enslaved as street performers and returns them to their native land of Leaphigh, a kingdom hidden behind a ring of ice in the region of the South Pole. After being rudely treated by these aristocratic monkeys, Goldencalf and his crew set sail for republican Leaplow, a country founded many years earlier by those fleeing Leaphigh and now representing, supposedly in all respects, everything antithetical to Leaphigh.

Although many faults—political, social, and religious—are found in republican Leaplow, *The Monikins* is not an antirepublican work. Quite the contrary; in the spirit of all relevant satire, we are asked to laugh at Leaplow's republican excesses so that we—Americans living in the Age of Jackson—may make amends. Goldencalf's "social stake" theory of government—whether embodied in English or Whiggish aristocracy—is debunked insofar as it demands a propertied ruling elite; *all* men (or monkeys), merely by being human (or monikinian), have a sufficient stake in society. The narrative interest of *The Monikins*, in fact, focuses on Goldencalf's gradual conversion from commercial aristocracy (as bad as, and similar to, the social aristocracy in Leaphigh/England) to republicanism.

There are, however, dangers inherent in republicanism—party politics, for instance. The perils of politics loom as large here as they do later in Timothy Savage's imaginary voyage to the land of the Amazons. Party politics is depicted as depending for its existence on a selfish disregard of principle. Before Goldencalf departs for home he is forced to contemplate the possible alternative to a Whiggish commercial aristocracy—a Democratic state of "political chaos" (p. 350). Later, the faults of republicanism will bulk even larger to Cooper; while *The Monikins* ends on a happy and generally hopeful note. *The Crater*, as we shall see, can only promise the apocalyptic destruction of republican America.

Timothy Savage's *The Amazonian Republic*, even though devoting much time to attacks on Jacksonian economic institutions and practices—bankruptcy laws, rampant speculation, and the new economic power of the masses—also focuses on the question of who will run the country.[12]

Savage, the probable author and implied narrator, discovers in Peru a remote Amazonian republic that embodies the political as well as the economic and social follies of America. The title of the work focuses our attention on its most important theme—the weaknesses of republicanism. That *women* govern is not the problem in the republic of Amazonia; the problem is that power is in the hands of officials who must prostitute themselves in order to win votes from the masses. Savage's thrust is clear: Universal suffrage—described as an excess of republicanism and "the greatest defect . . . in the [American] political constitution" (p. 157)—is responsible for sending uncultured, quarrelsome individuals to the legislature, where they have little to do but debate too much over matters that are essentially simple, pass superfluous laws to win the votes of their constituents, subvert the Constitution by stretching its meaning when convenient, and, through legislation designed primarily to keep themselves elected, encourage an unhealthy and dangerous dependence of the people on government.

Savage is a worried man voicing the objections of one side in an old quarrel when he speaks of the dangers of "vagabonds and ruffians" holding power over "those who have an interest in the country" (p. 157). This—the foundation of John Goldencalf's "social stake" theory—is the main fear of an American aristocracy of property living in the new age of Jacksonian democracy, an aristocracy that sees its power and position being eroded and feels its foundations being shaken by a social upheaval that it is unable either to understand or to accept.

While the main theme of *The Amazonian Republic* is antiegalitarianism in politics, Savage's antagonism toward the rise of the common man does have an economic basis as well. What Savage fears as much as anything else is *new* money. The love of wealth—a "natural instinct" (p. 170) in republics, where gold and silver are fashioned into a new kind of social ladder—is "one of [America's] chiefest faults" (p. 163), says Savage. Money is worshiped, and men who wish to be admired must devote themselves entirely to acquiring property. Especially upsetting to Savage are the new ways of acquiring wealth, such as by declaring bankruptcy and speculating.

In spite of the author's concern with economic matters, however, *The Amazonian Republic* is a political rather than an economic utopia. The question indirectly addressed throughout this satirical work is not which economic system will lead to Utopia Americana, for, as in the case of many of the pre-Civil War utopias, capitalism is a given; rather, the question addressed is which political system will lead there. The answer is only partially indicated, and even then only in negative terms: Universal suffrage, if left unchecked, will probably lead to Dystopia Americana. What the alternative system might be (or how it could be implemented) is left in the vaguest of terms.

Elbert Perce's *Gulliver Joi* is certainly the least interesting and least important of this group of satiric utopias. While style makes *Bawlfredonia* tedious reading, that work at least renders the honest vitriol of a staunch anti-Jeffersonian, antideist, and dyed-in-the-wool conservative on many important matters both secular and religious. *Gulliver Joi*, on the other hand, in its satirizing of relatively minor aspects of American society, hardly seems to come to grips with major issues or with much of anything that would interest a reader today. After dressing his work in fantastic garb—a Merlin-like old magician-scientist on a small island in the middle of the ocean invents airships of various kinds to transport Gulliver to distant lands—Perce settles down to presenting pretty much the kind of utopia that Mrs. Trollope might have written in one of her more petulant and less inspired moods.

Dealing almost entirely in social criticism, *Gulliver Joi* does not go beyond such things as castigating young women for hurrying into society and becoming old before their time.

Women, in fact—their place and behavior—occupy much of Perce's interest. In Ejario, for example, where Gulliver is largely responsible for returning the legitimate male ruler to the throne of a country disastrously ruled by usurping women, the deposed Amazon-like queen thanks Gulliver for putting her and the other ladies back in their proper places at home with their families.

Among other contemporary aspects of society that Perce attacks are slavery, imperialism, and crime in the streets; but these and other themes are taken up superficially, are dropped suddenly, and furnish no coherent pattern in this rather wild-eyed work.

ANTIUTOPIAS

Although, as we have seen in both *Symzonia* and *A Voyage to the Moon*, a basically satiric utopia can contain within it eutopian sections, we nevertheless refer to satiric utopias as negative visions because they emphasize criticism rather than construction. We must keep in mind, however, that satire, far from precluding the hope of progress, actually suggests the possibility of improvement. Far more likely, on the other hand, to be negative in philosophy as well as in form are the *antiutopias*—works that seek to invalidate others' imaginary, theoretical, or communal eutopias. Often calling into question the validity of any eutopian dream while focusing attention on a particular one, they function as (whether, indeed, they are or not) antimillennial treatises—especially to the extent that they imply a repudiation of Joachim's vision of an improved earthly state.

What we have already called an age of disillusionment and confusion in America produced five of these essentially negative visions—George Fowler's *A Flight to the Moon* (1813), James Kirke Paulding's "The Man Machine" (1826), Ezekiel Sanford's *The Humours of Eutopia* (1828), James Fenimore Cooper's *The Crater* (1847), and Nathaniel Hawthorne's *The Blithedale Romance* (1852).[13]

The earliest antiutopia in America, George Fowler's *A Flight to the Moon*, uses the technique of the dream vision (compounded here because the narrator has a series of visions within the main one) to tell the story of Randalthus, who learns, from discussions with the Lunarians and from glimpses of various lunar paradisiacal states, that within man, as God has constituted him, wisdom and virtue are forever dichotomized. An implied embracing of Augustine's vision of an otherworldly City of God necessarily apart from the corruption of the City of Man, the book is really an attempt to come to terms with the ape-angel, flesh-spirit nature of man, who in theory is capable of so much, in practice of so little.

To the sensitive, philosophical individual like Randalthus it first appears to be a tragedy that man is constituted as he is. Yet the theme of *Flight*—driven home in the didactic final sentence—is that it is our "duty to be satisfied on the world on which we are destined to exist!" (p. 185). Because only God knows why we have been created with aspirations to a perfection that we can never realize, we must learn to live contentedly with the nature of things as they are; to criticize "the laws of divinity" (p. 66) is to criticize God.

In many ways *Flight* can be considered a progressive utopia—that is, a positive vision—for it praises and upholds the practical uses of science. In the discussions between Randalthus (wisdom) and the Lunarians (virtue), it is made quite clear that man's reason, while in the moral world unfortunately ruled by passion, in the physical world can aid in manipulating the environment and plumbing the mysteries of the universe. What man cannot do, however, is create a paradise of innocents. Randalthus finds that such Eden-like states do exist in God's vast creation, but they are populated by ethereal nonhuman beings of pure virtue; men, on the other hand, need to be controlled by a world of laws. Like Hawthorne after him, Fowler discovers that what is admirable and desirable in theory is impossible in fact.

A disbelief in the perfectibility of man, in fact, lies at the heart of all American antiutopias. These works, unlike satiric utopias, portray absurdity not so much in society as it is currently constituted as in the presumably oversimplified plans put forth by various utopists to correct existing conditions. While Fowler is content with attacking the entire concept of utopianism, James Kirke Paulding levels his guns not only in that general direction but also at the specific utopian edifice constructed by the transplanted English industrialist-philosopher Robert Owen with his theories of the perfectibility of man.

Paulding's "The Man Machine" tells the story of Mr. Harmony, the Man Machine himself. Having spent years as an abused child laborer, Mr. Harmony falls under the influence of a philanthropist who, on the basis of his "new view of society," has founded a community dedicated to the dual aim of perfecting man and producing cotton cloth.[14] The "new view" holds that there are no inherited traits or passions in men; that because men's actions are caused by environmental factors, men are not responsible for their actions and should not be punished for what they cannot help; that there are no natural inequalities in men; and that men can be perfected if only certain "counteracting principles" in society can be eliminated. In the course of putting these theories into practice, however, the Man Machine loses all of his property, is thrown into jail for his debts, and is finally reduced to a mindless automaton before leaving for concentric spheres inside the earth to find there the perfectibility of man lacking here!

The two aspects of Owen's "new view" that receive most of the satirical lashes are the placement of man at the tail end of an oversimplified cause-effect relationship, which obliterates all moral responsibilities and, ultimately, denies free will, and the treatment of man as a mere producer in an economic system geared to an efficiency that dehumanizes him.

Even while denying the existence of any innate passions, our hero's master paradoxically conceives of controlling man by discovering "certain fixed and inflexible rules" that *are* inherent in him, "like the laws of motion which govern the spinning jenny" (p.33). By reducing man to a machine entirely governed by external influences, the master can utilize him—now a man machine—in industry for greater production.

Paulding renders the "manufacturing philosopher" Owen (p. 26) as concluding, quite inhumanely in spite of his avowed humanitarianism, that "productive labour [is] the grand and only desideratum of the social compact" (p. 25). Naturally, in a system geared to efficient production—a system in which morals are based on economics—even if total mechanization is not possible, it is still an advantage to have workers who closely approximate machines. It is precisely Owen's apparent willingness to treat men as machines—and thus help transform them into actual machines—that raises Paulding's ire.

Paulding also satirizes the common utopian concepts of perfect equality and communitarianism. Indeed, one of his two main objections to the communal life of withdrawal from society (the other being that isolation unbalances the delicate equilibrium between the human passions that society maintains) is that in communal experiments true equality—usually the foundation of the community itself—is a theoretical position never actually achieved. Men, after all, are imperfect and imperfectible—a fact often overlooked by philosophers more interested in preconceived ideas found only in their own minds than in the concrete experience of men.

"The Man Machine," indeed, has this theme (the ideal clashing with the real) in common with many other American utopias; and here, as in the other works, without exception there is the absolute preference for experience over theory, almost to the point of an eschewal of abstract thought entirely. Seaborn, we recall, noted that in America the so-called Wise only foul up actual and workable political and economic systems with their airy theories; and Fowler, to give only one more example, reiterates time and again the unfortunate but nevertheless very real discrepancy between the way abstract philosophers view human nature and the actual nature itself.

Ezekiel Sanford's *The Humours of Eutopia*, which concerns the early history of a New England community founded by a minority faction in a dispute over religious doctrine, is the first example of an American utopia (Savage's *The Amazonian Republic* and Cooper's *The Crater*—and, in some ways, *The Monikins*—are later ones) that openly questions egalitarianism and democracy as absolute virtues.

Like Tucker and Cooper (in *The Crater*), Sanford establishes that in the past, in some golden age of America, the relatively small size of communities made it possible for a simple kind of government (in this case theocratic) to function effectively. Religious and secular quarrels, however, frequently caused dissenting minorities to withdraw into the wilderness to found other religious good places. But in the case of one particular good place, actually named Eutopia, religious controversies erupt again and the citizens of Eutopia are finally forced to separate church and state. Problems still arise, though, and they are ultimately traceable to the original theocratic, individualistic, and democratic basis of government. Civil government does not work now because the colony has had a regretable tradition of independence, secession, and self-government in religious matters.

Sanford, unlike Cooper, does not attempt to develop a solution to the problem of creating a viable government, though he implies, as does Sylvester Judd later in *Margaret,* that a charismatic hero, such as Captain Homebred, through his example and presence, might be able to unite the community. Rather, this antidemocratic and implicitly authoritarian work renders only what will not work—communism, for example, for "Eutopia dated her increase in strength and numbers" (p. 39) from the time when men stopped working in common and took private land.

In general—and this does not surprise us—what will not work is any visionary scheme not grounded in the reality of human nature and things as they are. Skendo, chief of the nearby hostile Mingo Indians, is Sanford's example of the well-intentioned but naive utopian thinker who has only the crudest of materials—real men and women—to work with in building his imagined ideal society. An example of the typically blind, impractical visionary who has no concept of what must eventuate when dream comes up against reality, Skendo makes two serious errors in trying to improve the life of his people: He assumes that Eutopia can be built in a day and, misreading human nature, puts too much faith in the common man.

Like Cooper, Sanford has little faith in the masses; he has faith only in the enforcement by secular authorities of codified laws imposed from above and (again like Cooper) in the ability of a hero figure to impose order on the chaos resulting from ill-conceived liberal experiments in majority rule.

This authoritarian and aristocratic bias, found in many American utopias written during the Age of Jackson, is nowhere more powerfully expressed than in James Fenimore Cooper's *The Crater.* In essence a political novel, this antiutopia is an elaborate working out of the proper relationship between those whom God has chosen to lead and those whom God has chosen to follow; it is an attempt to render dramatically the strengths and weaknesses of the aristocratic and democratic positions in both society and politics.

The Crater concerns the founding of a potentially utopian state—in many ways representing the golden age which America embodied for the first few decades after the Revolution—on an island providentially thrust up in the

South Seas by a volcanic eruption. Originally discovered by two shipwrecked American sailors (officer Mark Woolston and seaman Bob Betts), this island quickly becomes a New Eden because of the industriousness of the two young men and the proper (hierarchical) social-political relationship immediately established between them. Later, when a carefully selected cross-section of the best of American society has immigrated, the community of Vulcan's Peak prospers because the divinely ordained relationship between the natural leaders and the natural followers is not violated.

Eutopia quickly becomes dystopia, however, after a flood of undesirables (a second minister, a newspaper editor, and a lawyer among them) arrive. The rights of the aristocracy are soon violated, and religious, political, and economic dissensions prevail where once only peace and plenty ruled; the heads and hearts of the people are easily turned away from God's great plan and toward man's selfish desires by various demagogues. All thought and feeling are given to making money and to prideful concern with what "the people" want. Finally, God writes large His (and Cooper's) judgment on this failed New Eden; while Mark and his family are visiting America, another volcanic eruption submerges the islands in the eternal, unchanging sea. (Edgar Allan Poe's short stories "Mellonta Tauta" and "The Colloquy of Monos and Una" contain similar attacks on Jacksonian democracy.)[15]

Cooper laments the passing of a time when, and a place where, God's hierarchical arrangement of the members of society was honored—a golden age when an aristocracy of power, money, and virtue quite naturally imposed its superior views and designs on a properly malleable population. It is the inability or unwillingness of the new masses to see and accept their designated position in God's scale that most disturbs Cooper about American democracy in the middle of the nineteenth century; the political and social chaos that John Goldencalf was warned about in *The Monikins* has come to pass. That Vulcan's Peak represents a third chance for mankind and a second chance for Americans is obvious. *The* Golden Age was, of course, prelapsarian; but after the Fall mankind had a second chance in the New Eden of the New World. Cooper, however, believes that Americans have botched their opportunity badly by failing to recognize that man's inherently sinful nature needs to be controlled. Like George Fowler, Cooper sees that man is a creature of "indulgence" and "wantonness"; God will not allow a state based upon the cultivation of these traits—that is, a pure democracy—to exist, much less thrive. Eutopia on Vulcan's Island, therefore, is doomed.

But all the while he is ostensibly positing an America that might have been, Cooper is, in reality, positing not only an America that never could have been, but also an America that never will be. Cooper's Utopia Americana, we come to see, greatly depends on three conditions that could hardly have been met in the America of 1847: a community-nation limited in size both in land area and population; a prophylactic agent to filter out the undesirable elements from the stream of immigration; and the happy acceptance by the population of a paternalistic and aristocratic government.

Not surprisingly, Cooper would make the future by returning to the past—if he could. But he finally indicates violently his own subconscious recognition of the impossibility of the survival of Eutopia. As the omniscient author, he settles the issue once and for all: "The supreme folly of the hour is to imagine that perfection will come before its stated time" (p. 444). With this glance ahead at the Millennium, Cooper forces the reader to recognize that perfection, as George Fowler has already pointed out, lies in the hands of God, not men—a decidedly antiutopian view in modern times. After flirting with Joachim, Cooper turns back, reluctantly, to Augustine.

No one would have agreed more with Cooper's final judgment than Nathaniel Hawthorne, whose *The Blithedale Romance* is a reluctant rebuttal of the standard modern utopian proposition that earthly perfection is possible because men, if divorced from the corrupting institutions of the past, are really better than they seem to be.

Hawthorne not only debunks the optimism of utopianism in general but also finds grave weaknesses in a specific brand—the communal withdrawal from society. First of all, the come-outers of Blithedale, by being "inevitably estranged from the rest of mankind" (p. 43), have broken the great chain of humanity—one of the most serious acts a Hawthorne character can commit; the narrowness of their concerns (especially Hollingsworth's) makes it easy for them to view the world and its inhabitants as objects upon which to work their designs. Second, in such a community, where virtue is attached to newness, there is "no scruple of oversetting all human institutions" (p. 68) and destroying not only what is rubbish but also what is valuable from the past. Third, such a community is inherently unstable, being made up of "crooked sticks . . . not the easiest to bind into a fagot" (p. 89). Finally, Hawthorne's vision of the world precludes any return to Eden—to a time, before the world became complex, when "the earth [really was] a green garden" (p. 88). As Richard Harter Fogle puts it, "Blithedale is an Arcadia exposed to the criticism of nature, of economics and society, and of human passions."[16] It is, in a word, pathetically innocent and prey to the complexities of experience. Recognizing the pathos in such innocence and no doubt feeling himself that the desire to reach the Millennium on earth by returning to Eden is a very human one, Hawthorne (through the mask of Coverdale) alone of all early American utopists recognized the ambiguity and paradox at the heart of all attempts at reconciling ideal theory with practical reality and praised the impossible dream even while criticizing it:

Yes, after all, let us acknowledge it wiser, if not more sagacious, to follow out one's day-dream to its natural consummation, although, if

the vision have been worth the having, it is certain never to be con-
sumated otherwise than by a failure. And what of that? Its airiest
fragments, impalpable as they may be, will possess a value that lurks
not in the most ponderous realities of any practicable scheme. They
are not the rubbish of the mind. What ever else I may repent of,
therefore, let it be reckoned neither among my sins nor follies that I
once had faith and force enough to form generous hopes of the world's
destiny,—yes!—and to do what in me lay for their accomplishment.
[pp. 31–32]

Coverdale's and Hawthorne's sympathies with a lost cause do not, however, make it any the less lost. The members of the community fail to
reconcile the tragically real differences between theory and practice, between idealism and reality; like most utopists before and since, they fail to
account for human weaknesses and complexities.

That utopia is founded on a misunderstanding of human nature is, of
course, a perennial criticism of that ideal realm. Paulding, as we have seen,
believed that Owen's theories erroneously presupposed man to be machine-
like and perfectible; Sanford criticized those who believed that men could
be perfected overnight; Cooper finally attacked those who held that the
common man was able to know and act in his own best interests and the
interests of the community and to control his base passions. Later on in the
century, others will find the most common panacea offered by utopists for
economic turmoil—socialism—to be contrary to human nature, which is
delimited by social-Darwinian needs for "competition" and "individual initiative." In rejecting all hopes of either returning to Eden or building the
New Jerusalem—though Coverdale is torn between rural and urban retreats—*The Blithedale Romance*, then, fits into a general pattern of antiutopian literature in America, for it criticizes the utopian dreams of others
on the basis of the most elementary kind of pragmatism: Utopia cannot exist
because it presupposes an oversimplification and misunderstanding of human nature. Viewed in such a light, at its best utopia is ridiculous; at its
worst, dangerous.

To the same degree that millennial expectations do not play an equal
part in all American eutopias, neither do refutations of those expectations
play an equal part in all of these utopian works rendering negative visions.
In some of the satiric utopias and antiutopias (*Bawlfredonia* and *Gulliver
Joi*, for example) the millennial vision seems not to be alluded to at all, even
by negation. In others, however (such as "The Man Machine" or *The Blithedale Romance*), where the whole basis of either a secular or a religious
Millennium is questioned if not attacked, we must recognize a strong refutation of the Joachim tradition. In addition, such works as *The Crater* and
The Blithedale Romance not only refute the possibility of man's making a

permanent improvement in his situation but also refute the essentially antihistorical idea that man can reach a better future by traveling physically—across the ocean or over the next hill—into a new, hopeful version of the past that merely awaits him there.

ONE LONE DYSTOPIA

In spite of the preponderance of negative visions in American utopian fiction during the Age of Jackson, only Nathaniel Beverley Tucker's *The Partisan Leader* (1836)[17] is a *dystopia*—a negative vision of a failed society in which certain dangerous elements present in the author's own society have fully manifested themselves. While other early works contain dystopian elements (Seaborn's ideal beings, for example, develop a weapon that has potentially genocidal applications, and one of George Tucker's Lunarians and Paulding's philanthropist-philosopher carry the fascination with mechanical theories and practices to absurd and dangerous extremes), no other utopia has portrayed in such detail, and without satirical relief, the complete and nearly final dissolution of the author's idea of a good society.

Dystopia, more or less a child of the modern world, can only exist when and where men see a negative force strong enough to subvert and completely dominate the minds and bodies of men. In most dystopian fiction that force is technology, quite often in the service of totalitarianism. In *The Partisan Leader* that force is Jacksonian democracy—"a mobocracy . . . dominated by the Yankee merchant at that"[18]—which has established a powerful political tyranny dedicated to supplanting agrarianism with industrialism, destroying state sovereignty, and abolishing the "sacred" institution of Negro slavery.

The Partisan Leader is similar in basic plot formula to Orwell's *1984* in that it deals with an attempt to defeat dystopian elements already in control when the story opens. By 1849[19] a powerful and corrupt federal government in Washington, controlled by "northern cupidity and northern fanaticism" (p. 32), is busy subverting the Constitution. The South, beseiged for years by Northern attempts to abolish slavery and establish hated manufacturing as the basis of the nation's economy—thus denying "the South the full benefit of its natural resources" (p. 49)—has seceded from the Union. Because Virginia is obviously the key to the South's success, President Martin Van Buren, preparing to be elected for his fourth term, and his lackeys station federal troops in the state capital of Richmond in an attempt to control the legislative elections. The survival of the South as a viable nation is assured only when these troops, cleverly deceived into withdrawing from the capital, are so decisively defeated by a makeshift Southern force that Virginia gains its independence.

While its continual warnings against "the progressive usurpations of the

Federal Government" (p. 29) force us to read *The Partisan Leader* as a
political novel primarily concerned with upholding the principle of states
rights, it can also be seen as a profoundly antidemocratic doctrine; it is, in
fact, the most openly pro-aristocratic of all American utopian works. Even
more than Cooper, Tucker feared the great majority into whose hands Jacksonian politics had placed so much power. But whereas in reading Cooper
we sense an inner conflict, a wrestling with the bear of democratic reform,
and a compulsion to come to terms with the realities of new political and
social forces, we sense none of that in reading Tucker. As Carl Bridenbaugh
puts it, "In a period when Websters and Calhouns faced about like weather-
cocks before the changing winds of economic and political doctrine, Tucker
went on talking and writing as if nothing had happened since 1798."[20] His
language, in fact—as when he bemoans the "revolution in public sentiment
which . . . encouraged the unwashed artificer to elbow the duke from his
place of precedence" (p. 96)—reveals an aristocratic revulsion, almost vis-
ceral in nature, toward the masses that goes far beyond Cooper's fears of
political and social leveling.

PROGRESSIVE EUTOPIAS: SECULAR, RELIGIOUS, AND HYBRID

It would not be an exaggeration to say that the main thrust of American
utopian fiction during most of the first half of the nineteenth century was
antiprogressive. But even while such negative visions held sway, a few noteworthy positive ones made their appearance—John Adolphus Etzler's *The
Paradise Within the Reach of All Men* (1833), Mary Griffith's "Three
Hundred Years Hence" (1836), and Sylvester Judd's *Margaret* (1845); these
were followed in the next decade and a half by David A. Moore's *The Age
of Progress* (1856); Alexander Lookup's three works, *The Soldier of the
People*, *Excelsior*, and *The Road Made Plain to Fortune for the Millions* (all
1860); Calvin Blanchard's *The Art of Real Pleasure* (1860); and Thomas Low
Nichols's *Esperanza* (1860).[21]

Of special importance is the fact that these eutopian visions, harking
back to earlier ones near the turn of the century, prefigure what will become
the mainstream of American utopian fiction. Consciously or unconsciously
carrying on the millennialist tradition—both religious and secular—these
inward utopias suggest that "the better life must be carved from out of the
existing human conditions" and that "existing society must be transformed
for man to live the good life."[22] They look forward to the fulfillment on the
shores of the New World of the Biblical promise of an improved spiritual
and material life on earth. Expanding and embellishing the edenic image
of America—until in some instances the paradisiacal garden and the city of
the New Jerusalem become one—and capturing once again the essential

optimism of Brown, Reynolds, and Stirrat, these eutopists generally see science as one of the keys to the gate of Utopia Americana. In most of these works—the exceptions are Judd's and, to some extent, Moore's and Nichols's—Millennium has become Eutopia; the ideal state, even while trailing clouds of paradisiacal and millennial rhetoric behind it, has become almost entirely secular.

The first complete manifestation of the secular, progressive eutopian spirit after the eighteenth-century millennial visions of men like Jonathan Edwards, Samuel Hopkins, and some of the Connecticut Wits, and the eutopian visions of Stirrat and Reynolds in the first quarter of the nineteenth century, is a work of nonfiction[23] by a German immigrant who came to the New World to spread the gospel of science and build the garden-city of the New Jerusalem in the West. Divorced entirely from outright religious concerns, John Adolphus Etzler's *The Paradise Within the Reach of All Men* is a natural extension and development of the religious-become-secular faith in spiritual and material progress of the Joachim tradition.

More than merely a manual on the proposed application of technological speculation, Etzler's work is also a philosophic treatise; not content with gadgets (though there are plenty of those), Etzler sees himself not only as the inventor of mechanical marvels to make life easier, but even more important, as the creator of "a superior and more systematic order" of civilization (I: 62). What at first glance may seem to be only a grandiose version of *Popular Mechanics* turns out to be also a manual for the construction of utopia. Etzler is like a god who wishes to create a New Eden. The organization of the book, in fact, is indicative of this dual concern—invention and creation. The first volume discusses the harnessing of the powers of nature—the wind, the tides and the waves, sunlight, steam, falling water—and the resultant technological advances; the second volume details how such inventions can be economically feasible and how they can best be utilized to establish and run planned communities, suggestive of (and certainly influenced by) both the form and content of Fourier's phalanxes, where "a new state of society" will inevitably develop.

It is instructive to read Etzler after having read Henry Nash Smith's *Virgin Land* and Leo Marx's *The Machine in the Garden*, for he would use the machine to manipulate "Any wilderness, even the most hideous and the most sterile," until it has been "converted into the most fertile and delightful [of] gardens" (I: 67). Etzler, in fact, goes about as far as one can in proposing a radical transformation of nature into art, for he goes on to propose the construction of covered aqueducts and canals, irrigated gardens, and "enchanting sceneries," which will give "the relief of a paradise" in which one can glide on gondolas (I: 69). There would seem to be no more violent wrenching of nature into man's image in American literature. Etzler sees the wilderness—which he seems to equate with the West in general—as existing solely for man's use; it will furnish space for the American destiny to realize itself and also function as a safety valve for the bloody revolutions in Europe.

Etzler's evocation of the paradise of Genesis is different in kind from the evocations of most other utopists, who, as we have seen, hope to reach the future by returning to the past. Etzler hopes to reach the past by plunging headlong into the future. Embodying the progressive spirit at its highest point of intensity, he will not *find* paradise—he will *make* it. An inward utopist, he is convinced that he can "change the world into a most delightful paradise" (I: 60). Prepared as he is "to relinquish entirely all our customary notions of human wants" (I: 62), he will also change men into New Adams; earlier paradisiacal-millennial expectations are brought up to date by the proclamation that we "may henceforth cause a regeneration of mankind to a far superior kind of beings with superior enjoyments, knowledges and powers" (I: 118).

Mary Griffith's "Three Hundred Years Hence" seems to be the earliest work in which a Utopia Americana existing in the more or less distant future is reached by means of a dream. Edgar Hastings falls asleep and dreams—the reader does not learn until the end of the story, however, that it is only a dream—that an avalanche of ice and snow preserves him in slumber until he is discovered by his own descendants in the year 2135. He awakens to a world changed radically from that of the mid-nineteenth century: Women have assumed an equal status with men; science has made possible a neater, safer, more comfortable world; and society has finally adopted many of the sensible minor reforms that Mary Griffith evidently advocated, such as the elimination of dangerous steamboats, the education of orphan girls, the "cleansing" of literature, and the prohibition of dogs and loose livestock. The author makes it clear that this "new era," as prim as a proper lady can make it, is due entirely to the improved status granted to women. Because they are, we are somehow not surprised to learn, higher-minded, more sensitive, and more humanitarian, they have dragged the rest of the country, the men, upward with them.

Stressing some of the same issues as *Alcuin*, "Three Hundred Years Hence" is, to a great extent, an economic novel, for it is of paramount importance that women are economically independent and "equal as to property" (p. 87). The work fits into a common pattern discerned by one student of American utopian fiction who has noted that American utopists have "commonly assume[d] marital unhappiness to be the effect of woman's financial dependence"; in "Three Hundred Years Hence" women have generally been made financially independent of their husbands, either by means of "the same competence" from the state as their husbands or by means of "the prevailing wage" for the duties they perform.[24]

Technology plays a relatively important part in Griffith's ideal society—as it will increasingly in later versions of Utopia Americana. As Hastings is taken on the standard tour by his utopian guide, he notes that "New wonders sprung [*sic*] up at every step—vessels, light as gossamer" (p. 46) and "curious vehicles that [move] by some internal machinery" (p. 33). Most important, as if Griffith is taking a cue from Etzler, the machine has found its way into the garden. Machines help the farmer by mowing, raking, and gathering hay; by threshing, storing, and grinding the grain, and even distributing it to the merchants. Machines also manipulate the landscape by uprooting trees, leveling hills and filling in gullies, and turning streams in their courses. Readers familiar with late-nineteenth-century utopian fiction will recognize here a prototype for many of the utopias discussed in Donald Burt's essay in Part III of this collection.

Two other pre–Civil War utopias that carry on the theme of science and technology as the key to utopia—David A. Moore's *The Age of Progress* and Calvin Blanchard's *The Art of Real Pleasure*—present diametrically opposed views of the place of religion in the ideal American society. Moore contends that Utopia Americana can be built only if science and religion work hand in hand; Blanchard vitriolically attacks all of "that mystical and moral savagery, our Puritan forefathers cursed America with" (p. 108) and proclaims that "the Good Time" can come only if scientific positivism completely replaces religious supernaturalism.

Blanchard's work is both confused and confusing. Almost plotless, it bespeaks the author's inability to explicate clearly his social and political theories, and his attempts to do so only make apparent the unsettled morass of half-digested ideas that passes for his mind. He bases his social theories on Fourierism and his political theories on Comte's positivism—and then treats both kinds of abstract constructs as if they are subject to the physical laws of the Newtonian universe as he dimly understands it!

Perhaps the most striking aspect of *Real Pleasure* is Blanchard's open advocation—an offshoot of his Fourieristic belief that men must be true to their nature—of complete sexual freedom. Because man has a nature that demands, among other pleasures, those of the flesh, he must have unlimited access to sexual intercourse.

Blanchard's importance as an American utopist, however, rests not only on his sexual theories but also on his positivistic vision of utopia—a state made possible by man's dedication to the understanding of the laws of nature and his harnessing of the powers therein in order to abolish the drudgery of work, transform America—especially the West—into something suggestive of Etzler's paradise, and, ultimately, enable him to live a life that actually becomes surfeited with pleasure. Like Etzler and Griffith, Blanchard carries on the tradition of the manipulated landscape and the controlled environment. "Palatial residences" (based on Fourier's phalanxes) spring up in the "semi-deserts" of the West, storms and volcanoes are controlled, and "marshes and deserts are [put] in a state of high cultivation" (p. 18).

Blanchard, who speaks of a world run by "majorityism" as "dreadful" (p. 44), has created one of the most undemocratic of American utopias. Reigning in "the Good Time" is an ostensibly benevolent dictatorship of "scientists and artists, whose business it is to discover the best solutions" to problems such as "who will reproduce or what the people will wear" (p. 50). Blanchard, however, assures us, in positivistic fashion, that his social organization is devoid of any real totalitarian threat: "The masses follow the leaders, as inevitably as the planets revolve around the sun's centre" (p. 61); after all, a "reciprocalness of interests" means that the people "know [that their leaders] cannot betray them" (p. 47). The leaders, in turn, in their omniscient benevolence, not only make it "impossible for the people to do wrong" (pp. 49–50) but also make sure that all citizens of Eutopia experience the utmost happiness and pleasure.

Not every progressive utopian work of the time, however, was as secular as Blanchard's and Etzler's. David A. Moore's *The Age of Progress*, for example, a series of four dreams projecting us 2,000 to 3,000 years into a perfected future, has as one of its themes the belief that "true Science is a ladder which reaches to heaven; and faithfully pursued, it can lead only in that direction" (p. 33). This intimate linking actually makes of science a means of grace. Moore, in fact, always subordinates science's secular applications to its religious and moral ones. While carefully delineating science's relative importance in aiding man's progressive journey from the imperfect but promising nineteenth century to "a glorious harvest of Progress in the Future" (p. 215), he is careful to emphasize that the road to utopia begins at Moral Education; only then, with no shortcuts, does it pass through Good Character, the Study of Books, the Study of the Bible, and, finally, the Study of Nature where the secrets of power lie.

Moore's work, however, does not imply that heaven on earth—in either a religious or a secular sense—can be achieved without spiritual and physical struggles. Although showing the same spirit that enabled Samuel Hopkins and others to proclaim confidently that "knowledge, mental light, and holiness, are inseparably connected,"[25] *Progress* also pays tribute to the image of Armageddon. Harking back to earlier millennialists who saw much darkness before the Dawn, Moore—evidently a reader of current millennial literature—picked up the common feeling of the times that violence and revolution would be requisite to bring about the Millennium. Although an evolutionary process will help, natural development will not suffice to rid the world of its evils.

Keeping in mind both the full title of this work—*The Age of Progress; or, A Panorama of Time. In Four Visions*—and the fact that its "plot" encompasses the final apocalyptic battle in which the forces of Satan are "defeated and driven . . . from the earth" (p. 12), we find it instructive to discover the following passage in an 1853 issue of *Presbyterian Quarterly Review:*

> When the visions of the far distant future pass before the ancient seers like panoramic processions, almost invariably scenes of terror and desolation, falling dynasties and crumbling thrones are precursive of the glorious close. Along the strings of the harp of prophecy swept by the Almighty, there is a wail almost like agony, preceding the Hallelujah of consummation. These views do not accord with the usual tone of uninspired prophecy that peals out perpetually from the press, grounded on the wonderful physical and mechanical triumphs of these last days.[26]

We are witnessing a backward glance in history, not only to the apocalyptic theories of the Jews, which "envisioned a final battle between the armies of God and those of the enemies of the chosen people,"[27] but also to their spiritual heirs, the Puritans, who frequently used the language of war to describe the cosmic struggle between God and Satan. In this way, then, *Progress* is primitive as well as progressive; not supernatural in the way to which Hopkins objected, *Progress* yet portrays the necessity of heaven's intervention in man's affairs. The line between temporality and spirituality is finely drawn—as is the boundary between Millennium and Eutopia.

The Age of Progress illustrates so well the two central themes of this and my previous essay in this volume that it could pass for a classroom illustration written according to formula. First of all, its amalgamation of religious and secular concerns renders the slow and subtle historical merging of Augustine's City of God and City of Man until there exists a new entity, the City of Godly Man—a city in which the Joachim tradition can, and does, thrive. Second, its fusion of paradisiacal and millennial images—its first vision is of a "state analogous to that of our primitive Parents in Eden" (p. 11), its last of "SATAN, with all his Legions, [being] shut up in the prison of HELL, to remain forever" (p. 13)—makes it a logical sequel to Columbus's vision.

If there is one image that links early American utopian literature with what came later, it is that of the garden-city, that paradoxical amalgam of progress and nostalgia which represents the American psyche's timid longing for the future with vestiges of the past still clinging to it. To leap into the future by stepping into the past has long been part of the American Dream, and building the New Jerusalem in the Garden of Eden has seemed a good way to realize this dream. From James Reynolds's "city spread over a large garden" (p. 10), through Etzler's fantastic palaces in man-made Edens in the West, to the myriad garden-cities in late-nineteenth-century utopian works, American utopian literature abounds with "scientific paradise[s] modified by beautiful parks and gardens."[28]

The Age of Progress contains the quintessential image of this complex paradisiacal-millennial urge. As in so many other utopian works, the protagonist is given a bird's-eye view of Utopia Americana, enabling him to see "one continuous, interminable city" with "every area of ground . . . covered with verdure" (p. 20). Not content with placing gardens in the city, however, Moore is compelled to go even farther in revealing that the fruits of the Millennium will be brought forth in an urban context; in the "GARDEN of the NEW EDEN" he places "the earthly TEMPLE of the ALMIGHTY" (pp. 30–31)—a temple whose walls have the "appearance of massive glass" and whose "domes and spires . . . and towers and collonades" nearly touch the clouds (pp. 28–29). This is the Holy City of Augustine come down to earth. No longer, in fact, do the two cities of God and Man exist in parallel; they have merged. The City of Godly Man has sprung up in the New Eden of the New World; the cycle of history has been completed with the advent of the Millennium; the end is like the beginning; Revelation and Genesis have been linked.

Sylvester Judd's long and often tedious novel *Margaret* shows us Utopia Americana through Emerson's transparent eyeball, the key to earthly perfection being transcendental knowledge, especially as it operates through Unitarianism. *Margaret*, differing in emphasis from most other utopias in that it focuses on the individual instead of on the state, proposes that the transformation of society into heaven on earth cannot take place until all men as individuals have accepted the long-buried truth of Christ—that they in themselves have worth and potential as children of God. In the process of accepting this truth, they must reject "the ridiculous enginery of God's wrath and eternal damnation" (p. 424).

The bulk of the work traces the spiritual growth into a state of true Christianity of Margaret, a young New England girl born into poverty and ignorance. The last section of *Margaret* illustrates how the love of Christ and a clear, simple, intuitive knowledge of His teachings, working through the agency of Margaret and her husband, transform the community of Livingston into an ideal Christian society.

Love—physical as well as spiritual—is all. Margaret's husband, who, along with Margaret, represents the kind of hero figure who frequently leads Americans into utopia, teaches her that "the Fall, consist[ed] in this, that men ceased to love" (p. 249) and thus to know how to govern themselves properly. The formalized social, moral, and religious systems—the intellectual residue of the centuries—used by most men as a basis for their communities make it difficult to establish an original relationship with the world. Such a relationship can be established only when men learn to love, when unnatural, man-made laws give way to natural, God-originating love—a transformation symbolized near the end of the book by the erection of a statue "representing *Moses kneeling to Christ* and surrendering the Book of the Hebrew Code" (p. 457). Old law is thus replaced by new love.

As with other utopian works that fall directly in the millennial tradition, *Margaret* portrays America as the place intended by God to give man a fresh start. Although it is clear to Judd that so far New England, having succumbed to the debased and corrupt teachings of Calvin and Wesley, has failed in its mission of establishing the Millennial Age, hope for the future lies in those who, like Margaret, know that men "are ever-living as the Divinity himself" (p. 243). Being new Adams because "our ancestors were very considerably cleansed by the dashing waters of the Atlantic" (p. 266), we have every right to expect the road to the Millennium to begin eventually in New England. As Margaret's husband puts it,

> "I think [New Englanders] might lead the August Procession of the race to Human Perfectibility; that here might be revealed the Coming of the Day of the Lord, wherein the old Heavens of sin and error should be dissolved, and a New Heavens and New Earth should be established, wherein dwelleth righteousness." [p. 268]

Although *Margaret* is a progressive eutopia and "modern" in its view of human potential, science and technology are not of major importance in establishing Utopia Americana. Judd is primarily interested in spiritual, not material, progress. In the tradition of transcendentalism, however, spiritual progress is reflected in material progress in the form of a better life for everyone: "High calculation [science], which is only the symbol of a higher Moral Sense, is even now at work; and they are ripping up the earth for a Canal from Worchester to Providence; and what shall next be done, who knows" (pp. 268–69). It is a natural progression—from Idea to Act—which Emerson and Thoreau would approve, though they might not approve of the specific application. As it turns out, however, Judd does not dwell much on specific applications; we learn only that "Waste lands have been redeemed; sundry improvements in agriculture and mechanical arts adopted, whereby at once is a saving, and a profit" (pp. 443–44) and that the roads are the best in the state. The focus instead is on moral improvements, and in this respect *Margaret* deviates from most other progressive eutopias. The deviation, though, is one of emphasis, not exclusion. In all progressive eutopias written in America (and in this they take their cue from the early millennial tracts and sermons), moral improvement and technological advances leading to material abundance are linked by a cause-effect relationship—though which is the cause and which the effect is not always made clear.

Alexander Lookup's three chaotic, illiterate utopian works—two allegorical closet dramas in the supposed style of Shakespeare, *Excelsior* and *The Soldier of the People*, and a dramatic (though essentially nonfictional) monologue, *The Road Made Plain to Fortune for the Millions*—share with *The Age of Progress* the distinction of being the most millennial of all fictional American utopian visions.

Lookup must be thought of paradoxically as a religious writer with essentially secular concerns: He fully utilizes the millennial and paradisiacal language that evidently was part and parcel of his own intellectual background to translate religious allegory into historical events that focus on "Humanity's prime era" (*Excelsior*, p. 60); and his complaint that all governments "postpone [the Kingdom of God] to another existence" (*Road*, p. 6) shows that his sense of priorities places the earthly present over the heavenly future.

As in *The Age of Progress*, there is no distinct boundary between Eutopia and the Millennium; Utopia Americana, ultimately extending itself throughout the world, is Biblical prophecy coming true in a way in which no one supposed. Most important, apocalyptic events can be triggered by human action; "the enlightened future" is easily attainable once the "Sovereign people" transcend what only seems to be reality and realize that "heaven is perpetually about them" (*Soldier*, pp. 16, 32). The ideal state can then be brought about by mere acclamation. All that is needed is for all men to determine at once not to abide by the old rules and be led astray by the deliberate distractions—"furious wars, intrigues, and elections"—of the "Tyrants and Pharisees." Immediately, Enlightened Law—God's great plan—will descend and ravish "all the earth" (*Road*, pp. 32, 57, 29), "magnetically elevat[ing], raptur[ing] and unit[ing]" all men (*Soldier*, p. 16) according to a "perfectly heavenly pattern" (*Road*, p. 29) intuitively available. This rule of Enlightened Law is the literal meaning of the allegory of the millennial reign of Christ; "Enlightment," says Lookup, " . . . is the New Messiah" (*Soldier*, p. 17), the "Son of Man" coming to rule the earth during the Millennium (*Road*, p. 55). As anxious as was Samuel Hopkins to encourage millennial expectations divorced from supernaturalism, Lookup confidently proclaims that the prophesied reign of Christ on earth will be in spirit, not in flesh; there will be a momentous change in the way men think and feel about themselves and their institutions. Once Enlightened Law has been inaugurated—an act likened to "the White Horse of Revelations" (*Road*, p. 18)—the further prophecies of Saint John will be fulfilled; "the New Jerusalem [will descend] from God out of Heaven," and all "Tyrants and Pharisees" will be brought to justice and removed from power—an "obscurity" allegorically equated to "the lake of fire and brimstone of the Scriptures" (*Road*, pp. 93, 57).

Whereas previous utopists have attacked particular aspects of contemporary society—Savage, for example, the influence of political parties, and

Blanchard the hindrance of religion to progressive thinking—Lookup is the first to attack the entire social-political-economic system. The problem with America is not that any particular interest group has temporarily achieved extraordinary influence, but that *everyone* in power is corrupt and in league to squeeze the blood out of the common man; "Caesars and Saints [are] in collusion" (*Soldier*, p. 20).

Lookup's three utopian works, in fact, are certainly among the earliest documents to put forth the conspiracy theory of American politics. Not only have "tyrants . . . converted the direct resources for Paradise to their own purposes," but they have also deliberately interfered with the functioning of the "natural straightforward Enlightened Law of God" (*Road*, pp. 21, 28) which, if allowed to operate without interference, would obviously spread the blessings of this potential paradise among all men. The symbolic Armageddon in these works is, in fact, the culmination of the battle between the Enlightened Law of God and the "inventions" of the "Pharisaic confederates of the Prince of Darkness" (*Road*, pp. 5–6). This battle—emphatically nonviolent, culminating in victory by an acclamation of the people—will have the result that each man, previously victimized by "tax grinding courts" (*Soldier*, p. 19), will become his own landlord, an event symbolically representing "the angel with the seals, chaining down asperant Lucifer in the Bottomless Pit of his own iniquitous invention" (*Road*, p. 176).

Lookup, like Stirrat, is one of the strongest advocates of capitalism among American utopists and certainly the strongest advocate of rugged individualism. A lack of property, he says, is responsible for all crime; when men have no stake in society, they will attack it. His aim is to see that "the middle class" and the "mechanics and laborers" enjoy the fruits of capitalism (*Road*, p. 16), not just the "cutthroats of trade, business and population" (*Soldier*, p. 83)—to see that capital is circulated among *all* men to stimulate manufacturing. After all, "whatever will realize a countless harvest of cash customers is the desideratum before all else" (*Road*, p. 147).

Certainly the least readable of all American utopias—some passages literally defy all principles of English syntax—these works are, at the same time, among the richest of documents in the tradition of American millennial-utopian literature. Lookup, like so many before him, steps backward to the beginning of time as he steps forward to the end of time; his "Diamond America" (*Excelsior*, p. 84) is a Jeffersonian eutopia of small landowners—a nostalgic return to an economic Eden, a place-time before things got complicated. Not only does the establishment of Enlightened Law cause "the New Jerusalem [to descend] from God out of Heaven," but also "inaugurates a Western Hesperides, or Garden of Eden in every country" (*Road*, pp. 93, 65). Echoing the utopist Connecticut Wits, Lookup predicts that under Enlightened Law America will "[merge] the nations in a glorious republic of the globe" (*Road*, p. 20). Thus Lookup, perhaps unknowingly, reiterates the vision of Columbus and the related sense of manifest destiny that has been part of the Anglo-American intellectual baggage for centuries.

Even though the apparent themes of Thomas Low Nichols's *Esperanza* (1860) are myriad (eugenics and human sexuality, a modified Fourierism, individual rights and freedom—especially of women—in a patterned and controlled society, the economics of selflessness, and Spiritualism), its main focus, too, is on the vision of Columbus.

The novel takes us down a tributary of the Mississippi River to a "Land of Promise in the Far West" (p. 7), where a group of devotees have founded a harmonist community isolated from the world's influence until it can change the world and merge the nations into Nichols's version of a glorious kingdom of heaven on earth. Like Samuel Hopkins, Nichols is concerned with historicizing this kingdom and debunking any suggestions that it will be supernatural in origin and primarily spiritual in essence; he, in fact, repeatedly makes it clear that the coming paradise will be an earthly one brought about through the efforts of men and women, working within a Fourieristic system of harmony and brotherhood, to change the world around them. Although the pattern of this system has descended from heaven (pp. 128–29) and although aid is given by "angel friends, in the land of Spirit life" (p. 311) who "retain [their] sympathetic connection with the human race" (p. 323), Esperanza is constantly held up as the prototype of a world-wide community that will arise in the here-and-now of the future and fulfill the prophecies of Saint John. There is "a whole planet to be transformed" (p. 123). "Earth [is] our home," proclaims one of the members of the community; men have foolishly "grow[n] faithless of [the Millennium's] possibility on earth" and "have either prayed without faith, or looked forward to some mystical and illy [*sic*] conceived millennium" (p. 64). The spirit of Christ, not Christ himself, will reign on earth because of the sacrifices and industry of a select few who have banded together. Nowhere in American utopian fiction are the visions of Augustine and Joachim more directly opposed.

Through all of this, of course, peeps the specter of America's manifest destiny to be the beacon to the world. As strongly as in *Margaret* (though not so regionally chauvinistic), the city-on-a-hill syndrome is clearly evidenced: "It has been our high mission to show mankind the possibility of a harmonic society, free from all the cares, discords, and miseries of civilization" (p. 131).

The clearest of all points, of course, is that because man "has the power of making his own conditions, and therein is the possibility of his destiny" (p. 232), temporal progress is possible. Temporal progress is, in fact, not only possible, but ordained by God, for "the divine energy that resides in humanity, struggling ever upward to light and life, [is the only thing] that has prevented the utter depravation and annihilation of the race" (p. 194).

Finally, it is clear also that progress means setting the Millennium in the New Jerusalem, not in the Garden of Eden; nostalgic dreams may dictate where it all begins—in "this truly Arcadian scene" (p. 117)—but, in spite of the surface agrarian bias, not where it ends. "All art," says our narrator, "seems to me the expression of hope, or aspiration, of an idealization which looks forward into the future of our destiny, rather than back into the past" (p. 236). The complex Fourieristic phalanstery; the bureaucracy inherent in family planning; the emphasis on the cultural and spiritual benefits of opera, ballet, painting, and music; the deliberate cultivation of intellect and taste; and the continual paeans to organizational and social principles that are (paradoxically) both organic and mathematical—a "beautiful and perfect order" like "the controlling forces of the planetary systems" (p. 286)—all these foreshadow a life fully realized only in the complexity of the city.

A SUMMARY

The early years of American utopian fiction—from the appearance of Joseph Morgan's *The History of the Kingdom of Basaruah* in 1715 to what may be a rather arbitrary cutoff point near the end of the Civil War—divides into three periods, which somewhat overlap. During the first, a period of optimism in utopian thought lasting roughly a century, most American utopists, inspired by expectations of a millennial period in the New World and by faith in the saving grace of God, created imaginary ideal societies along essentially religious lines; they portrayed a religious utopia as accessible to all, either an otherworldly one (Heaven) after death for those who truly strove to reach it or a thisworldly one during the millennial reign of Christ on earth.

As the ideas of the Enlightenment struggled successfully for a place alongside the tenets of Calvinism, fictional portrayals of the fulfillment of Saint John's prophecies took on a more temporal nature as some utopists, motivated primarily by confidence in the survival of the Republic, pictured the Millennium not only as a period of prosperity for the church but also as one of ease and material abundance for America. This emphasis on earthly progress was not long in producing what can be called the first "modern," progressive eutopias—that is, works showing man in control of his own destiny. From mere hints at the potential of scientific and technological progress in the essentially religious *An Account of Count D'Artois and His Friend's Passage to the Moon* it was only a few short steps to detailed portrayals, by the Connecticut Wits and others, of an America (and, ultimately, a world) transformed into a progressive paradise in which the spirit of Christ descended not only to change men's hearts, but also to build cross-country canals and tame the West. Near the turn of the century, this developing temporal utopian spirit finally manifested itself in works wholly devoted to proclaiming man as the maker of his own world—*Alcuin* and *Equality*.

Shortly after the conclusion of the War of 1812, a four-decade period of national disillusionment and confusion set in. Sectional strife, factionalism, and a general social unrest generated by expanded suffrage and concomitant shifting economic and social prestige led many Americans to lose what had been, during the early days of the Republic, faith in the future of their country. By 1825 the "heady nationalism of the immediate postwar years had broken down . . . into sectional contention. The idealism of Jefferson had now become a self-interested struggle for wealth; the old dependence upon Europe, a new and aggressive form of isolation."[29] By 1836 a French observer of the American scene could write that the "American system no longer works well" and could fear for the preservation of the Union.[30] Some men who saw the need for an offensive against what they believed to be dangerous social, economic, and political forces in Jacksonian America took to creating imaginary societies that were absurd reflections of the one they saw around them. Many of these works, as we have seen, manifested both a general lack of faith in human potential to perfect, or even drastically improve, the world and a specific lack of faith in the common man—that very creature usurping, in the market place and at the polls, the rights and privileges traditionally held by his betters.

Whereas the main concern of utopists of the late nineteenth century would be the economic reconstruction of American society, the main one of those of the Age of Jackson was political reconstruction. Most American utopists, in attempts to confront the problem most often singled out as the most serious—the political and social leveling inherent in Jacksonian democracy—were content to emphasize the limitations of the masses who threatened to overrun things. There were exceptions, of course, in this general pattern of pessimism; we therefore must speak of these periods as overlapping one another. Stirrat, Griffith, and Judd, for example, during these years saw great potential in man; even such satirists as Adam Seaborn and George Tucker, in the midst of rendering America's and man's follies, briefly depicted the ideal society America might become.

Near the middle of the century a third period began as these few earlier hopeful visions of Jacksonian utopists were reaffirmed in a series of works produced during the decade and a half prior to the end of the Civil War. Science and technology especially seemed to be the keys to utopia—whether entirely divorced from the supernaturalism of religion or merely accepted as a tool given man by God to be used in good faith. The headwaters of the scientific-utopian stream which flowed out fully developed from *Equality*, in which God was reported as having given man reason and the fruits thereof in order for him to reshape his environment, split into two streams somewhere along the way. One led through Etzler's completely secular realm to Blanchard's positivistic utopia; the other, through Griffith's pious society and Judd's transcendentally revitalized community, to Moore's scientific New Jerusalem and Nichols's isolated society watched over by heaven's angelic representatives.

The millennial image of the New Jerusalem, in fact, became, more and more, the utopian image of progress—the technologically and culturally rich city. Though not without some sense of the dangers of industrialization and urbanization and not without a great deal of nostalgic backward-looking at the imagined pastoral simplicity of America's supposed golden age, American utopists from Reynolds and Stirrat to Moore, Blanchard, and Lookup happily embraced the kind of progress necessarily embodied in the city; for most, however, it was a garden-city, looking forward to the many nostalgic-progressive garden-metropolises of later utopias.

In almost all of these early works, there is, as we have seen, the sense—many times explicit, sometimes implicit—of America as the stage upon which God has chosen to act out the final (or the advanced) stages of his great drama. Whether this nation is thought of as fulfilling its duty or as failing to perform up to its potential, the feeling is always present that upon America's shores the fruits of the Millennium will, or at least should, come forth, whether spiritual or material, or (more likely) both. Utopia Americana has a worldwide, even cosmic, role to play and is waiting anxiously in the wings.

NOTES

1. Charles Brockden Brown, *Alcuin: A Dialogue* (New York: T. & J. Swords, 1798). The second dialogue—parts three and four—was published posthumously in William Dunlap's *The Life of Charles Brockden Brown: Together with Selections from the Rarest of His Printed Works, from his Original Letters, and from His Manuscripts Before Unpublished*, 2 vols. (Philadelphia: James P. Parke, 1815), I:71–105; reprint of complete work, with an afterword by Lee R. Edwards (New York: Grossman, 1971); [James Reynolds], *Equality—A Political Romance* (first published in eight installments in *The Temple of Reason*, 1802). Page references to these, and to all subsequent primary sources, will appear in parentheses within the text.

2. [David Stirrat], *A Treatise on Political Economy; . . .* (Baltimore: n.p., 1824).

3. Martin G. Plattel, *Utopian and Critical Thinking* (Pittsburgh: Duquesne University Press, 1972), p. 32.

4. Daniel Moore's *An Account of Count D'Artois and His Friend's Passage to the Moon* (1785), discussed in the preceding essay, "From Millennium to Utopia Americana," neither qualifies as a fully developed utopia nor has as its entire setting the imaginary lunar society.

5. For an incisive discussion of this paradoxical progressive-regressive urge, see

the first three chapters of Charles L. Sanford, *The Quest for Paradise: Europe and the American Moral Imagination* (Urbana: University of Illinois Press, 1961), pp. 1–55.

6. It is possible to view *Treatise* as a direct response to Adam Smith's *An Inquiry into the Nature and Causes of the Wealth of Nations* (1776), especially in light of Stirrat's use of the phrase "the foundation of the wealth of all nations" (p. 43).

7. This shift from the term *millennialist* to *utopist* is a calculated one; it denotes a shift from primarily religious visions to primarily secular ones—a shift in emphasis, in other words, from God to man, from primary causes to secondary ones.

8. Jonas Clopper [Herman Thwackius], *Fragments of the History of Bawlfredonia: Containing an Account of the Discovery and Settlement, of that Great Southern Continent; and of the Formation and Progress of the Bawlfredonian Commonwealth* ([Maryland]: American Booksellers, 1819) Capt. Adam Seaborn (pseud.), *Symzonia; A Voyage of Discovery* (New York: J. Seymour, 1820); George Tucker [Joseph Atterley], *A Voyage to the Moon: With Some Account of the Manners and Customs, Science, and Philosophy, of the People of Morosofia, and Other Lunarians* (New York: Elam Bliss, 1827); [James Fenimore Cooper], *The Monikins*, 2 vols. (Philadelphia: Carey, Lea & Blanchard, 1835); Timothy Savage (pseud.?), *The Amazonian Republic, Recently Discovered in the Interior of Peru* (New York: Samuel Colman, 1842); Elbert Perce, *Gulliver Joi: His Three Voyages; Being an Account of His Marvelous Adventures in Kailoo, Hydrogenia and Ejario* (New York: Charles Scribner, 1851).

9. Vernon L. Parrington, Jr., *American Dreams: A Study of American Utopias* (Providence: Brown University Press, 1947), p. 13.

10. See R. D. Mullen, "The Authorship of *Symzonia*," *Science-Fiction Studies*, 3 (March 1976), 98–99. Mullen undermines the assumption that John Cleves Symmes wrote *Symzonia*.

11. This sense of America *progressing* from a rural-centered to an urban-centered economic and cultural base is the main theme of Tucker's *Progress of the United States in Population and Wealth in Fifty Years as Exhibited by the Decennial Census from 1790–1840* (New York: Press of Hunt's Merchant's Magazine; Boston: Little, Brown, 1843). The "town population," says Tucker, not only determines a country's "capacity for manufactures" but also "marks the progress of intelligence."

12. In this discussion of *The Amazonian Republic* I have borrowed heavily from my introduction to the Scholars' Facsimiles & Reprints edition.

13. George Fowler, *A Flight to the Moon; or, The Vision of Randalthus* (Baltimore: A. Miltenberger, 1813); [James Kirke Paulding], "The Man Machine; or, The Pupil of 'Circumstances' " in *The Merry Tales of the Three Wise Men of Gotham* (New York: G. & C. Carvill, 1826), pp. 21–142; [Ezekiel Sanford], *The Humours of Eutopia: A Tale of Colonial Times. By an Eutopian*, 2 vols. (Philadelphia: Carey, Lea & Carey, 1828); James Fenimore Cooper, *The Crater; or, Vulcan's Peak: A Tale of the Pacific*, 2 vols. in 1 (New York: Burgess, Stringer, 1847); and Nathaniel Hawthorne, *The Blithedale Romance* (Boston: Ticknor, Reed, & Fields, 1852).

14. This obvious reference to Owen's *A New View of Society* (1813) is merely one of many in "The Man Machine." Paulding frequently uses ironic footnotes to point out a "remarkable coincidence" in the similarity of language or idea between the Man Machine's and Owen's remarks.

15. In "Mellonta Tauta," *Godey's Lady's Book*, February, 1849, pp. 133–38, the narrator can hardly believe that the "ancients" of the nineteenth century ignored the "laws of gradation" and actually embraced republicanism. In "The Colloquy of Monos and Una," *Graham's Magazine*, August, 1841, pp. 52–55, a look backward in history reveals nineteenth-century man's mistake is attempting to dominate nature through so-called scientific progress; having become "infected with system," man accepted the most erroneous and prideful notion of all—"universal equality." It is interesting to note, also, that Poe, like Cooper, portrays God-Nature as passing judgment on the corrupt world of man by means of an act of "purification"—although Poe holds out the hope that the world will "clothe itself anew in . . . verdure" and become a new Paradise (p. 205).

16. Richard Harter Fogle, *Hawthorne's Fiction: The Light and the Dark* (Norman: University of Oklahoma Press, 1952), pp. 142–43.

17. Nathaniel Beverly Tucker [Edward William Sidney], *The Partisan Leader: A Tale of the Future*, 2 vols. ([Washington, D.C.]: James Caxton [Duff Green], 1856 [1836]; reprint, with an introduction by Carl Bridenbaugh, New York: Alfred A. Knopf, 1933).

18. Bridenbaugh, "Introduction," ibid., p. xvi.

19. The novel, issued with a fictitious publication date of 1856, is actually set thirteen years in the future—in 1849.

20. Bridenbaugh, "Introduction," p. xxviii.

21. J[ohn] A[dolphus] Etzler, *The Paradise Within the Reach of All Men, Without Labor, by Powers of Nature and Machinery. An Address to All Intelligent Men*, 2 vols. (Pittsburgh: Etzler & Reinhold, 1833); [Mary Griffith], "Three Hundred Years Hence" in *Camperdown; or, News from Our Neighborhood: Being Sketches, by the Author of "Our Neighborhood," &c.* (Philadelphia: Carey, Lea & Blanchard, 1836), pp. 9–92; [Sylvester Judd], *Margaret, A Tale of the Real and the Ideal, Blight and Bloom: Including Sketches of a Place Not Before Described, Called Mons Christi* (Boston: Jordan & Wiley, 1845), David A. Moore, *The Age of Progress; or, A Panorama of Time. In Four Visions* (New York: Sheldon, Blakeman, 1856); [Thomas Low Nichols], *Esperanza; My Journey Thither and What I Found There* (Cincinnati: Valentine Nicholson, 1860); Alexander Lookup (pseud.?), *Excelsior; or, The Heir Apparent. . . .* (New York and London: Kennedy, 1860); idem, *The Soldier of the People; or The World's Deliverer. A Romance* (New York and London: Kennedy, 1860); idem, *The Road Made Plain to Fortune for the Millions: or, The Popular Pioneer to Universal Prosperity* (New York and London: Kennedy, 1860); [Calvin Blanchard], *The Art of Real Pleasure: That New Pleasure, for Which an Imperial Reward Was Offered* (New York: Calvin Blanchard, 1864).

22. Harold V. Rhodes, *Utopia in American Political Thought* (Tuscon: University of Arizona Press, 1967), p. 20.

23. Etzler, *Paradise*. The grounds upon which I have elected to include this nonfictional work in a discussion of utopian fiction are many; its more or less total view of an improved society, for example, and its secular millennial vision are only two. In 1977 Scholars' Facsimiles & Reprints issued a facsimile edition of Etzler's collected works, with an introduction by me. The definitive study of Etzler is an unpublished dissertation by Patrick Ronald Brostowin, "John Adolphus Etzler: Scientific-Utopian During the 1830's and 1840's," New York University, 1969.

24. Margaret Thal-Larsen, "Political and Economic Ideas in American Utopian Fiction, 1868–1914," Ph.D. dissertation, University of California, Berkeley, 1941, p. 215. Financial independence is given partial credit for women's having obtained equal rights in Jane Sophia Appleton's "Sequel to the 'Vision of Bangor in the Twentieth Century,' " in *Voices from the Kenduskea* (Bangor, 1848). Its companion piece, Edward Kent's "A Vision of Bangor, in the Twentieth Century," had reduced women's rights to an absurd, abstract theory unable to stand the test of reality.

25. Samuel Hopkins, *A Treatise on the Millennium. Showing from Scripture Prophecy, That It Is Yet to Come; When It Will Come; In What It Will Consist; Events Which Are first to Take Place, Introductory to It* (Boston: Isaiah Thomas & Ebenezer T. Andrews, 1793).

26. "Laws of Progress," *Presbyterian Quarterly Review*, 2 (December 1853), 433; quoted in Ernest Lee Tuveson, *Redeemer Nation* (Chicago and London: University of Chicago Press, 1968), p. 78.

27. Tuveson, *Redeemer*, p. 2.

28. Charles L. Sanford, *The Quest for Paradise: Europe and the American Moral Imagination* (Urbana: University of Illinois Press, 1961), p. 186. Although Sanford's description is of the Boston of *Looking Backward*, it can apply equally well to many other fictional utopian cities of the time.

29. Charles M. Wiltse, *The New Nation, 1800–1845* (New York: Hill & Wang, 1961), p. 76.

30. Michael Chevalier, *Society, Manners and Politics in the United States: Being a Series of Letters on North America*, ed. T. G. Bradford (Boston: Weeks, Jordan, 1839), p. 394.

SHORT-TITLE BIBLIOGRAPHY

Major Utopian Fiction, 1715–1864	Type of Utopia
1715 Morgan, Joseph. *The History of the Kingdom of Basaruah.*	eutopia
1785 [Moore, Daniel]. *An Account of Count D'Artois and His Friend's Passage to the Moon.*	eutopia
1798 Brown, Charles Brockden. *Alcuin: A Dialogue.*	eutopia
1802 [Reynolds, James]. *Equality—A Political Romance.*	eutopia
1813 Fowler, George. *A Flight to the Moon.*	antiutopia
1819 [Clopper, Jonas]. *Fragments of the History of Bawlfredonia* by Herman Thwackius (pseud.).	satiric utopia
1820 Seaborn, Adam (pseud.). *Symzonia: A Voyage of Discovery.*	satiric utopia
1824 [Stirrat, David]. *A Treatise on Political Economy.*	eutopia
1826 [Paulding, James Kirke]. "The Man Machine," in *The Merry Tales of the Three Wise Men of Gotham.*	antiutopia

1827	[Tucker, George]. *A Voyage to the Moon*, by Joseph Atterley (pseud.).	satiric utopia
1828	[Sanford, Ezekiel]. *The Humours of Eutopia: A Tale of Colonial Times.*	antiutopia
1835	[Cooper, James Fenimore]. *The Monikins.*	satiric utopia
1836	[Griffith, Mary]. "Three Hundred Years Hence," in *Camperdown; or, News from Our Neighborhood.*	eutopia
1836	[Tucker, Nathaniel Beverly]. *The Partisan Leader: A Tale of the Future*, by Edward William Sidney (pseud.).	dystopia
1842	Savage, Timothy (pseud.?). *The Amazonian Republic.*	satiric utopia
1845	[Judd, Sylvester]. *Margaret.*	eutopia
1847	[Cooper, James Fenimore]. *The Crater; or, Vulcan's Peak. A Tale of the Pacific.*	antiutopia
1851	Perce, Elbert. *Gulliver Joi.*	satiric utopia
1852	Hawthorne, Nathaniel. *The Blithedale Romance.*	antiutopia
1856	Moore, David A. *The Age of Progress; or, A Panorama of Time.*	eutopia
1860	Lookup, Alexander (pseud.?). *Excelsior.*	eutopia
1860	———.*The Soldier of the People; or The World's Deliverer. A Romance.*	eutopia
1860	Nichols, Thomas Low. *Esperanza.*	eutopia
1864	[Blanchard, Calvin]. *The Art of Real Pleasure.*	eutopia

CHARLES J. ROONEY

Post–Civil War, Pre–Looking Backward Utopia: 1865–87

THE HANDFUL OF UTOPIAS WRITTEN in America between 1865 and 1888 was small by comparison with the great outpouring in the 1890s and early 1900s. No doubt the assassination of the President, the great devastation of the Civil War, and the traumas of Reconstruction left the nation in shock. No longer, it seemed, could it afford the heady idealism of the 1840s and 1850s. Transcendentalism, the Fourieristic communities and phalanxes, the factory cooperatives modeled upon those of Robert Owen, and even the religious communities—Hopedale, Oneida, the Shakers—all seemed to be of another generation. These experiments, which cut across the entire spectrum of social, political, economic, religious, and educational practices, had failed to prove themselves on a large scale, but their questioning of the fundamental assumptions of social organization were not entirely lost. They supplied a tentativeness to the great experiment called "democracy"—a tentativeness that saw fewer practical challenges after the Civil War but kept itself alive in the more traditional yet imaginative form of utopian literature.

By the 1870s the great optimistic faith in the noble experiment of American democracy survived the rampant corruption and scandals of the Grant Administration, the panic of 1873, the greenback controversy, the tariff question, and the waves of immigrant workers. Closer to the main pulse of the public heartbeat were the spectacular and dramatic: the transcontinental railroad, the electric light, the telephone, the dynamo, the rise-to-riches stories of Carnegie and Rockefeller, the shootouts in Dodge City, the James boys, Buffalo Bill, and discovery of gold in the Klondike. In the intellectual realm the theory of evolution, popularized by the pupils of Herbert Spencer, together with the Enlightenment values of freedom, reason, nature, and progress—fed the public's hopes and were the as yet unquestioned values of the time. For most, the system seemed to work, and the recent European innovations in the very young science of political economy—the various socialisms, communism, the labor theory of value, the rise of the modern state, imperialism—seemed foreign to the commonsense philosophy of McCosh and the economics of Adam Smith taught as gospel in every college in America. Even the warnings of Walt Whitman against incipient greed and materialism in his *Democratic Vistas* were lost in a panegyric of hope for the American dream.

Yet the American dream took different forms—even besides the utopian fiction of the time. In addition to the usual pieces of reform literature advocating everything from free trade to woman's rights, a great number of "Christian" proposals began to appear more and more in the popular press, from such pearly-gates works as Elizabeth Stuart (Phelps) Ward's *The Gates Ajar* (1868) and William Henry Holcombe's *In Both Worlds* (1870) to the more serious religious reform works of Washington Gladden's *The Christian League of Connecticut* (1884) and Jessie H. Jones's *The Kingdom of Heaven* (1871). Virtually all, in one way or another, attempted to prove what the authors of the colonial utopian visions, surveyed by Joel Nydahl in this volume, attempted to demonstrate—that the kingdom of heaven was meant to be on earth; it seemed as if the most quoted phrase in the idealized writing of the time was one section of the Lord's Prayer: "Thy Kingdom come, Thy Will be done, on earth, as it is in heaven." Truly it was the religious impulse, focused for almost a century upon the idea of individual dignity and freedom, that later turned such writers as Henry George in his *Progress and Poverty* (1879) and James Casey in his *A New Moral World* (1885) to write scathing attacks upon the economic system. They advocated a complete change in the basic structure of economic life. Yet these and other works are peripheral to our story, confined, as it is, to mostly book-length utopian, antiutopian, and dystopian works.

Ironically, the post–Civil War era opened with a satiric treatment of earlier idealism in the form of a pseudononymous work entitled *The Philosophers of Foufouville* (1868) in which the author, calling himself Radical Freelance, denounced transcendentalists and the followers of Charles Fourier. The writer made no effort to disguise his bias. After describing a Fourieristic community of absolute equality, common property, passion subordinate to reason, and all sustaining themselves by the labor of their hands, he facetiously portrayed their ideal as being "secure from the raging passions and numberless temptations that beset less fortunate mortals. Separated from the outer world, from its lusts, its hatreds, its avarice, its contentions, we will tranquilly glide down the vale of years in perpetual harmony, peace, and good will."[1] No longer able to contain his patience, the author (by page 200) in the person of a Reverend Mr. Knox, labeled Harmony Hall, the center of their little community, as a "stronghold of Belial." Later, he described Mr. Goodenough, their leader, as "an artful and determined emissary of the Evil One" (p. 229). For some, it seemed no scheme of universal improvement could refuse to take into account the corrupted nature of man.

Yet even putting aside the Calvinistic reservations of the more conservative segments of the American populace, the basic tenets of our national way of life—individual perfection and personal salvation—were questioned more and more, and very particularly by one of the finest products of that system, Edward Everett Hale. While pastor of the South Congregational Church in Boston in 1867, Hale felt the frustration of preaching to the workers whose lives were squelched by impoverished housing and living conditions. The squalor of tenement life, which he observed daily, caused him to take out his prolific pen to describe life in Boston, as it ought not to be, and life in *Sybaris* as it ought to be. After jolting the citizens of Boston with a fundamental question—"What shall they say when they shall be making their answers on the day of Judgement?"—he proposed a new society in which "the highest work of the nation was to train its people."[2] His models were the ancient Greek city-state and Rome but with a modern twist—the state existed to protect the rights of the individual. In fact, the state's primary role was to punish exploiters, especially those who built inadequate housing or failed to answer claims of injury. Large industries, such as the railroads, were run by the government. Debts were not allowed, and each Sybarite retired on a small pension, "enough to save anybody from absolute want" (p. 55).[3] Before death each Sybarite had to give away his property.

Individual conveniences abounded: sheltered seats on street corners, free newspapers, housework done by large, efficient cleaning concerns. Child labor was forbidden, marriage for men before age thirty and women before age twenty-five and, finally, lateness and gossip were severely punished by law. But the motivating force behind these conveniences was the moral principle of mutual help and service. The real center of life in Sybaris was the church parish, where everyone was induced to do his best and to share with the less fortunate. The only Sunday sermon ever heard anywhere was, "God loves you," and the greatest crime was to advance one's private gain at the expense of the community. Hale's *Sybaris* blended the best qualities of traditional morality and modern efficiency. But the work ethic was notably absent; leisure was the ultimate object of all this efficiency. Hale believed that if everybody worked a little, there would be enough for everybody, and certainly the writings of Saint-Simon, Robert Owen, and John Stuart Mill, all of whom are favorably mentioned, corroborated the point.

Edward Everett Hale was unique in proposing, as early as 1867, that the government take a strong hand in social planning, but already he recognized a different time had come. One of his characters in Sybaris, Laura, says to her husband, the city administrator, "I know you hate to be constantly making laws . . . and I know how your father says that the best government is that which governs least; but I think something should be done to give such people as these [in the slums] a better chance" (p. 173). His New

England frugality recoiled at the collossal moral waste of the city, and he reluctantly admitted the Jeffersonian principle of government fell far short of dealing with deprivation in the cities.

A fellow Bostonian, Edward Bassett, proposed, in his utopian *Model Town* (1869), that "individuals, families, and communities may live in comfort, refinement and in a permanent temporal and moral prosperity in their own town . . . rather than be obliged to emigrate to manufacturing towns and cities."[4] Life in the *Model Town*, as in *Sybaris*, was formed as a Christian community centered on cooperative enterprises in which each person contributed according to his industry or skill. Middlemen, that bugaboo of inefficiency, were eliminated by a town cooperative store. The town members shared the profits of the entire enterprise, leaving little need for government, for when people enjoyed their work, "it is clearly demonstrated that man has the ability for self-government" (p. 64). Conversely, "selfishness is the foundation of sin" (p. 94), and so, in the *Model Town*, each worked for himself but still contributed to the whole with his effort, interest, and Christian concern. The right of private property was staunchly upheld by Edward Bassett, whose town motto, "the hand of the diligent maketh rich" (p. 19), belied his faith in the magic of work.

Bassett's model town combined pastoral simplicity with the natural rights philosophy and modern efficiency. It was supposed to be the best of the Old and New worlds. Both Hale and Bassett wondered, as did Robert Owen, whether manufacturing required slums, exploitation, and an unnatural environment. They both believed that the utopian dreams of the late 1860s had to become realities in the near future. The price of conveniences for the few was too high for the many.

In the 1870s the cultural attack against the abuses of the way of life in America began to sharpen and point directly against the profit motive and big business. All three of the book-length utopias reorganized their economies upon the principles of labor as the basis of value. The economics of Ricardo, I. B. Say, and even Marx served as a preface to the utopias of Thomas Wharton Collens, William Trammell, and Lewis Masquerier. In fact, without the utopian form, all three could have served as economics textbooks elucidating what T. W. Collens declared to be his final aim: "To carry to legitimate and ultimate consequences, the fundamental principal admitted by all economists, viz. Labor is the real measure of the exchangeable value of all commodities and services."[5]

Yet the application of this principle took different turns. Collens himself, like Edward Everett Hale, called upon "the law of neighborly love propounded by Our Lord Jesus Christ . . . and by the self-denial His name implies" (pp. iii–iv) to arrive at a new life in his perfected world. The religious impetus for "fairness" in the distribution of goods grafted itself onto the social commentators, mostly European, of the nineteenth century.

William Trammell spoke in terms of syndicalism and the Internationale; and Masquerier, an early disciple of Albert Brisbane, a Fourierist, subtitled his work *The Reconstruction of Society*. As a consequence, the *Dictionary of American Biography* labeled Lewis Masquerier an "anarchic agrarian reformer."[6]

William Trammell proposed to destroy utterly the wage system of labor, substituting "cooperative societies who take under their own control the producing energies of the country."[7] This, he maintained, would put a stop to "those periodic convulsions incident to the capitalist system, and so direct and regulate production that every producer shall get what he produces and no more" (p. 269). All else was subordinate to this principle. The purpose of the Internationale in his ideal society was to make sure that every energy and capacity to work would never be wasted or involuntarily idle. Outside of a harsh and severe criticism of the status quo, Trammell pays little attention to education, the arts, social mores, religion, or the comforts of life. His utopia is a grim affair, with efficiency of production and distribution saving the day.

William Trammell's future society undoubtedly did much to add to the conviction that man's salvation rested in the hands of the economic planners, coming as it did during the throes of the Panic of 1873—a prime example of artificially manipulated money supply, corrupt political practices, speculation, and overextended banking houses. All these practices added support to Trammell's conviction that a new society was in order.

Just two years later, on January 16, 1876, Thomas Wharton Collens, a New Orleans resident who had already authored two books, one on science of "Humanics" and the other a history of charity, dedicated his *Eden of Labor* to the Holy Name of Jesus—whose feast day it was. Essentially, Collens contrasted two societies: one a dystopia named Nodland, where selfishness and unbridled greed prevailed; the other the "Christian Utopia," where the selfish principle is overcome by the principle of charity.

Collens did not, however, believe in any giveaways. Labor, he asserted, is the fundamental principle upon which all distribution of wealth should depend. Most of his utopia is spent applying an elaborate system for calculating the "average labor-time," which becomes the common standard of value. In using "co-operative job work"—that is, various labor cooperatives for different industries and producing units—each person is progressively freed from the slavery of serfdom, wagedom, and piecework to working together for a common wage. The demands of taxes, usury, rent, and profit are circumvented and ultimately eliminated. "Labor" is then the only creator of exchangeable value, the only cost of any commodity (p. 210).

In Collens's *Eden of Labor* two great advances over the present system are accomplished. First, the principle of private profit and individualism passes before what he calls "enlarged minds, who see that there is no severance from society, know that the only avenue to private happiness is through public happiness" (p. 2). Second, man is forced to create through his labor and his dependence on God. As his life is simplified, he will return to the joys of Adam and Eve, whom God provided for through a bountiful nature.

Thomas W. Collens's system is but one of many suggestions in this era for simplifying the economic system. The realization that the machinations of Jay Gould and other stock manipulators could make fortunes for a few and break the economy for so many drove him to consider a better way. In this respect, he was no different from Henry George, who, in his *Progress and Poverty* three years later, offered a system for taxing the unearned increment of rent investment, or capital—in short, tax the manipulators and reward the working man. In that same year, 1879, Lewis Masquerier proposed an advanced society in his utopia entitled *Sociology,* wherein middlemen and profiteers were banned. Masquerier, a Kentuckian whose father was driven from France by the Edict of Nantes, spoke eloquently about religious freedom, the removal of capital punishment, and the banning of priests. His family heritage dictated many of his biases, but fundamentally Masquerier was interested in economic reforms whereby each person was entitled to as much land as he could use. There were no landlords, however. Town assemblies legislated laws administered by a larger "department," which also published the only newspaper. Education was acquired during afternoons at home from free encyclopedias distributed to each family.

The pattern of Masquerier's utopia was to become typical of a great number of utopias later in the century. His deep suspicions of the press, of politics, of large corporations, lawyers, landlords, and middlemen alongside his basic faith in the democratic process, the salutary effect of living close to nature, and the value of hard work all combined to set the basic pattern of the late nineteenth century's utopian concerns.

Few utopists had a tougher view of human nature than John Macnie, a classics scholar and mathematician who emigrated from Scotland in 1867, taught in Connecticut and New York, and eventually joined the faculty of the University of North Dakota in 1885. Even though his book *The Diothas* (1883) closely resembles the traditional utopia in format, he immediately set the reader straight in the preface, denying any connection with "the communistic ideas so attractive to so many." "To become," he claimed, "well fed slaves of an irresistible despotism with its hierarchy of walking delegates seems hardly the loftiest destiny of the human race."[8] The setting of his ideal society in the year A.D. 9600 would give mankind sufficient time to match his technological progress with commensurate moral progress. Fascinated with submission to law, social order, and intelligence, he harbored little hope in the immediate future for what he regarded as an ill-disciplined and depraved human nature.

Yet, his Calvinistic view of mankind had its millennial side, for in A. D. 9600, after much devotion to science and the ruthless elimination of idleness, laziness, and crime ("mercy to the bad is cruelty to the good"), the world emerged as a well-ordered society with a natural aristocracy, a republican form of government, and everyone skillfully laboring toward some definite goal or object. Each of the inhabitants of utopia in *The Diothas* took his turn serving at law at some time during his life—he might even become an unenviable object of that law if caught drinking, propagating smutty literature, or dishonoring the very highly regarded moral stature of women.

Aside from Macnie's Victorian view of women and his love of hard work, it is doubtful that his speculation was popular in his time, as the small reception of his book indicated, but a curious sidelight to this utopia occurred in a biographical sketch appended at the end of the book. Here, Macnie attributed his inspiration to his friend "E . . . ," the subsequent description of which fits Edward Bellamy, whose utopia, published five years later, does bear a close resemblance in some details to Macnie's. Even so, the matter of initial inspiration or plagiarism brings us down a blind alley—the two works do differ greatly on essential points (see Darko Suvin's essay in Part II of this collection).[9] What is interesting is the tremendous public reception Bellamy received as opposed to Macnie.

But before Bellamy was to write his famous *Looking Backward*, three other utopias were written, two in 1884 and one in 1885. A year after Macnie's book appeared in New York, Alfred Denton Cridge's ideal society, described in *Utopia, or, The History of an Extinct Planet*, appeared in pamphlet form in Oakland, California. Apparently this perennial reformer, who wrote tracts advocating proportional representation and democracy (in Portland and San Francisco in the 1890s) chose the utopian format to advocate the idea of equality and democracy in a communal society. Cridge's *Utopia* resembled the older political utopias rather than his contemporary's economic reform proposals. The government did not play a large part in this agrarian, Jeffersonian society; however, a good portion of his tract is spent extolling the virtues of democracy, which inaugurated an "era of grand improvement in every way. Disease disappeared as education advanced. Science, art, literature, and mechanics were in the midst of the people."[10] Utopia was achieved when the people learned to rule themselves.

Alfred Cridge's unbridled faith in human nature, in stark contrast to John Macnie, ran parallel to a more common faith in the late nineteenth century: the transformation of man's environment. This social scientist's dream received its best expression in Laurence Gronlund's *Coöperative Commonwealth*. Gronlund, who came to America from Denmark in 1867, became a lawyer, lecturer, and propagandist for the cause of socialism. He had no quarrel with human nature. He did not think men needed reform but chose rather "to reform their *surroundings*, the *constitution of society*, the *mould* in which their lives, thoughts, and feelings are cast."[11] "Sin," he claimed, "comes from poverty and ignorance"; consequently, "man saves his soul best by helping his neighbor" (p. 247). His ideal socialist society allowed each worker to be paid the true value of his labor, but "everyone who pockets gains without rendering an equivalent to society, takes what does not belong to him" (p. 230). Actually, the representative government owned the means of production, although the workers did have the right to private property, a condition that few American utopists were willing to change.

The *Coöperative Commonwealth*, besides being one of the earliest socialist tracts in utopian form in America, attempted to bridge the individualism of John Stuart Mill and the later German socialist writers for whom Gronlund had high praise. He projected a community no longer pastoral or cityless, but a worker's paradise where the profits of labor were shared and individual degradation disappeared. As a matter of fact, Gronlund added his own twist to this socialist paradise: The individual was subordinate to the "will of the universe . . . that Supreme Will which is Providence for Humanity, though not for the individual . . . it enters into vital relations with the individual only through Humanity as the mediator, it commands the interdependence of mankind" (p. 246). Perhaps his heavy reading in the German socialist utopians had led Gronlund to the Hegelian principle that the total is more than the sum of the parts and that society is more than the sum of individuals, acquiring, then, a personality and destiny of its own. In any case, his "religion of humanity" was not spelled out in any detail but simply mentioned as the binding force of his unique paradise. (In 1891 he described this religion at length in *Our Destiny*, a series of essays first published in *The Nationalist*.)

Despite the title of Alonzo Van Deusen's work, *Rational Communism* (1885), he was no socialist. His guiding principle was the notion that the Herbert Spencer school of philosophy was, in his words, "akin to barbarism"[12] and that the human race could only improve itself through *united effort*, a remarkable change for someone who admitted being "well schooled in the habits of industry and frugality, and the importance of securing for himself a competence" (pp. 14–15) on his New England farm. The radical change came after visiting and taking up permanent residence in New York City—the setting for his idealized great metropolis of the future.

The inhabitants of this futuristic city were divided into communal tracts with communal homes and communal representation in the government. Production and distribution were supervised by the government through a warehouse system—for Van Deusen's frugality could not bear the endless shops and myriad wares of the old New York. The waste of effort in time and labor Van Deusen deemed colossal—but not as much as the waste caused by ignorance. "Long in advance of the time of which I speak," he wrote, "the conviction had become universal that the power and privilege to acquire and utilize knowledge were the most precious boon that had been bestowed upon man" (p. 237). Understandably, scientific advancements abounded in his utopia; education was compulsory. The only penalty ever imposed upon a human being was expulsion from the community.

Van Deusen believed that the most complete individual liberty and the highest possibilities attainable by the human race could come only through united effort, and so, he asserted, "I can conceive of no plan which appears to me so feasible as the banding together in communities" (pp. 50–51). Essentially, Van Deusen's dream combined the Enlightenment principles of specific rational inquiry and the natural efficiency of common effort. He did not anticipate any of the usual problems attendant upon human weaknesses or variability, he simply asked that all work together, and if they didn't care to share in the enormous benefits, they could leave the community. Unlike Gronlund's, his limited community did not embrace universal mankind.

Toward the later part of the 1880s, the utopian writer concentrated more and more on the problem of the distribution of goods. Like Alonzo Van Deusen and Laurence Gronlund, Henry F. Allen projected a community, this time on Venus, where everyone contributed to the support of the entire group in return for a share of the profits. This profit-sharing plan centered on a highly efficient system of distribution, a system that attempted to satisfy every need. The central government determined what would be produced and how—a problem simplified by the fact that no one was allowed to accumulate possessions worth more than $10,000.

By this time the solution of efficient government distribution systems began to sound hackneyed among the utopian writers—though it was still heretical to the public at large. Yet this solution, bordering on socialistic or communistic principles, offered a unique attack upon the evils of human nature, public greed, and unbounded "license for trespass and tyranny," which, according to Henry Allen, prevailed under the laissez-faire philosophy of the Republican party in the 1880s.[13] Allen truly believed that a noncompetitive system would transform the minds and souls of the general populace, which he regarded as essentially good. "All life is but an expression of truths or forces that are inherent in nature and are not our creations" (p. 71). Thus our minds are receptacles of higher intelligences, which flow into us as we prepare ourselves by "soul discipline" (p. 7). This worship of nature in the Emersonian sense (Allen was also a Swedenborgian) brought a "clearer power of elucidation of the essence of life" (p. 105). The motto of this perfect society was conformity to nature—mankind was not condemned always to endure vice; and as for individualism, each person would assert himself "without the assistance of artful pretense" (p. 18).

Yet, despite the use of intuitive thought transmission and other "gadgets" for advancement in moral and social understanding, the prime purpose of

Allen's *The Key of Industrial Co-operative Government* (1886) was to demonstrate that "the least expenditure in enterprises will insure the largest pecuniary profit"—and that governmental co-ops were superior to "selfish competitive enterprise." (p. 7).

A perennial reformer, Allen did not give up on his ideal society. After lecturing in Chicago for the Young Men's Mutual Improvement Association and again in Saint Louis on the "Need for Reform," he wrote another utopia in 1891 called *The Strange Voyage*, with essentially the same ideas except to deal more harshly with laziness and idleness. His plan, though novel in some respects, was an economic alternative to the free enterprise system—and in that respect he joined his fellow utopians of the 1880s.

Allen's solution seemed optimistic compared with another variety of utopian literature in the 1880s. Generally speaking, the doomsday approach to future speculations had not been greatly developed as a literary form. Yet the dystopian form of utopian writing was well represented in Pierton Dooner's *Last Days of the Republic* (1880), D. R. Loche's [Petroleum V. Nasby's] *A Paper City* (1878) and Joaquin Miller's *The Destruction of Gotham* (1886). All these writers concentrated on the excesses of social and economic injustice—Loche satirizing the speculative fever in the money markets, Dooner depicting an armageddon of revenge by mistreated Asiatics, and Miller projecting the destruction of a future debauched, sinful New York City. Miller's story comes closest to later satirical future states, such as Huxley's *Brave New World*. In it, after he describes the future New York City, where the rich condemn cab drivers and prostitutes to long years in jail for stealing and selling to survive, he blandly compares the degenerate state to a Darwinian world in which "the animal—all the wild animal—is aroused in man."[14] He goes on to state how he could be persuaded to believe momentarily that man descended from the ape and "doubt the ability of God to create man directly and at once after his own Image" (p. 24). Indeed, to Joaquin Miller the whole scene closely resembled a true "death of the soul" (p. 5).

The depth of anguish these writers felt did not match the satirical tone of one other variant utopian form during this era: Mark Twain's satire of America's contradictory love of intelligence and espousal of democracy. Yet Twain's moralism guided him as he revealed some utopian elements in his "Curious Republic of Gondour." Here, for instance, the educated had more respect and voting power than the merely rich; schools were free, the spoils system was abolished, and public employees were judged according to their talents and behavior. In addition, women could become heads of government. The final barb of this very short essay is a typical Twain barb—he claims to be happy to leave Gondour because of the citizens' incessant proud commentary about their land. He was delighted to return home where he found so little of this attitude.

One other type of literary utopia appeared during this period—the antiutopia. It was a direct response to the socialistic utopias that criticized the American faith in individualism. Anna Bowman Dodd, a literary woman who specialized in travelogues of English and French cathedrals, took time out in 1887 to mock these socialistic visions in *The Republic of the Future, or, Socialism, a Reality.*[15]

The traveler in this futuristic land journeyed through pneumatic tubes to hotels run completely by machinery; no humans were seen. The houses, examples of mass-produced, tasteless architecture, were constructed from identical sets of plans, and shops were run by government clerks who took no interest in what they sold. Dodd's description of the typical street scene characterized the entire society: The "inhabitants have the look of people who have come to the end of things and who have failed to find it amusing. The entire population appear to be eternally in the streets, wandering up and down with their hands in their pockets on the lookout for something that never happens" (p. 23). Indeed, in her thinly disguised bias, the traveler to this wearisome land complained that in a place where the government is founded on the principle of equality "there must of necessity be a lack of initiative, a feebleness in aggressive attack, and a want of determination in the pursuance of a given policy" (p. 71). The final blow descended upon this now disgruntled visitor when she discovered that religion was banned. Maybe, she surmised at the end of the story, a sense of humor and human variety may once again prevail in this otherwise dreary scene, but as for now it presented a hopeless debacle.

Anna Bowman Dodd, though hankering for the earlier values of variety, individualism, freedom, and competition as the best stimuli for human growth, posed a fundamental question to her predecessors: How could a highly organized, efficiently run, scientifically advanced society help the individual person live a better life? The utopian authors addressed themselves, in all sincerity, to this very question by asserting that individuals would be better off in their ideal societies; nevertheless, when examined closely, they spoke in very different terms.

The way the utopian authors answered Anna Bowman Dodd's question tells us much about the growing dilemma in the utopian literature of post–Civil War America. Edward Everett Hale was the first and last utopist during this period to cite the Benthamite principle that "each individual is protected in his enjoyment . . . so long as his choice injures no other man" (*Sybaris*, p. 39). Understanding the naiveté of this principle, his followers in the 1870s, William Trammell and Lewis Masquerier, did not even speak in terms of the individual—to Trammell, the Internationale assumed higher responsibility and to Masquerier, the individual became an economic integer. His only right was to procure the product of his labor—all else was subordinate to this. Alfred Cridge, who spoke so rhapsodically of democracy, abolished cities and the ownership of land in his garden of Eden. The most mistrusting of all was John Macnie whose individual freedom in *The Diothas* went as far as obeying the law or feeling its severe response.

By 1884, Alonzo Van Deusen gave lip service to the principle of "extending the widest individual liberty compatible with public order" (*Rational Communism*, pp. 86–87), but he began to lose patience with the "impossibility of attaining, in the aggregate, to a state of existence that may be properly regarded in any degree exalted . . . under the hitherto dominant basic society principles and customs derived from selfish, incoherent, haphazard, unharmonious individual effort" (pp. 49–50). Two years later, Henry F. Allen exasperatingly declared "life has nobler purposes than the ceaseless struggle to amass property for individual ownership" (*Key*, p. 48). Laurence Gronlund's religion of mankind gave the individual significance "only through Humanity as the mediator . . . and our common duty is to obey" (*Coöperative Commonwealth*, p. 246).

Thus, the crisis of post–Civil War utopian literature was the crisis of the time—the insufficiency of the philosophy of individualism. Like their predecessors of half a century before, Owen, Saint-Simon, Fourier, Mill, Ricardo, Malthus, and Marx, the utopian authors advocated a radical change in the social order by questioning the fundamental assumptions of laissez-faire capitalism. But there was a characteristically American difference in the form of their presentation. The antislavery issue gained more momentum from a novel, *Uncle Tom's Cabin*, than from all the abolitionist tracts. Similarly, the ponderous preachings of the political economists went largely unnoticed until the utopian novel popularized their teachings after 1888. The several well-known pre–Civil War utopian works and the trend toward a paradoxical social or communal individualism in the few utopian novels published during the 1870s and early 1880s helped to pave the way for the immense popularity of Bellamy's *Looking Backward* and the surge of utopian literature after its publication.

NOTES

1. Radical Freelance Esq. (pseud.), *The Philosophers of Foufouville* (New York: G. W. Carleton, 1868) p. 10. Page references to the works cited appear parenthetically in text.

2. Edward Everett Hale, *Sybaris and Other Homes* (Boston: Fields, Osgood, 1869), p. 11. The Sybaris story first appeared as "My Visit to Sybaris," *Atlantic Monthly*, 20 (July 1867), 63–81.

3. See also Hale's later work, *How They Lived in Hampton* (Boston: J. Stillman Smith, 1888).

4. Edward B. Bassett, *The Model Town* (Cambridge, Mass.: Houghton Mifflin, 1869), p. iii.

5. Thomas Wharton Collens, *The Eden of Labor or, The Christian Utopia* (Philadelphia: Henry Carey Baird, 1876), pp. iii–iv.

6. *Concise Dictionary of American Biography*, 1969 ed., s.v. Masquerier, Lewis, p. 651.

7. William D. Trammell, *Ca Ira* (New York: United States Publishing, 1874), p. 269.

8. John Macnie, *The Diothas, or, A Far Look Ahead*, by Ismar Thiusen, (pseud.) (New York: G. P. Putnam & Sons, 1883), p. iv.

9. See especially Suvin's footnote 13. See also Glenn Negley and J. Max Patrick, *The Quest for Utopia* (New York: Henry Schuman, 1952), pp. 50–51.

10. Alfred Denton Cridge, *Utopia, or, The History of an Extinct Planet* (Oakland, Calif.: Winchester & Pew, 1884), p. 15.

11. Laurence Gronlund, *The Coöperative Commonwealth* (London: n.p., 1886), p. 243.

12. Alonzo Van Deusen, *Rational Communism: The Present and the Future Republic of North America* (New York: Social Science, 1885), p. 51.

13. Henry F. Allen, *The Key of Industrial Co-operative Government*, by Pruning Knife (pseud.) (Saint Louis: author, 1886), p. 43.

14. Joaquin Miller, *The Destruction of Gotham* (New York: Funk & Wagnalls, 1886), p. 23.

15. Anna Bowman Dodd, *The Republic of the Future, or Socialism, A Reality* (New York: Cassell, 1887).

SHORT-TITLE BIBLIOGRAPHY

MAJOR UTOPIAN FICTION 1865–87   TYPE OF UTOPIA

1867	Hale, Edward Everett. "My Visit to Sybaris." *Atlantic Monthly*, 20 (July 1867), pp. 63–81.	eutopia
1868	Freelance, Radical, Esq. (pseud.). *The Philosophers of Foufouville*.	antiutopia
1869	Bassett, Edward Barnard. *The Model Town*.	eutopia
1874	Trammell, William Dugas. *Ca Ira*.	eutopia
1875	[Clemens, Samuel L.]. "The Curious Republic of Gondour," by Mark Twain (pseud.). *Atlantic Monthly*, 36 (October 1875), pp. 461–63.	satirical utopia
1876	Collens, Thomas Wharton. *The Eden of Labor*.	eutopia
1877	Masquerier, Lewis. *Sociology*.	eutopia
1880	Dooner, Pierton W. *Last Days of the Republic*.	dystopia
1883	Macnie, John. *The Diothas*.	eutopia
1884	Cridge, Alfred Denton. *Utopia*.	eutopia
1884	Gronlund, Laurence. *The Coöperative Commonwealth*.	nonfiction eutopia
1885	Van Deusen, Alonzo. *Rational Communism*.	eutopia
1886	Allen, Henry Francis. *The Key of Industrial Co-operative Government*.	eutopia
1886	Miller, Joaquin. *The Destruction of Gotham*.	dystopia
1887	Dodd, Anna Bowman. *The Republic of the Future*.	antiutopia

KENNETH M. ROEMER

Utopia and Victorian Culture: 1888–99

I

THE GOLDEN ERA OF nineteenth-century American utopian—especially eu-topian—writing calls for an approach different from those used by the other contributors to the historical-bibliographic survey section of this collection. The sheer bulk of the utopian literature published between 1888 and the turn of the century eliminates the possibility of the detailed, book-by-book examinations suitable for Joel Nydahl and Charles Rooney in their surveys of literary utopias before *Looking Backward*. Of course, Howard P. Segal and Lyman Tower Sargent were confronted with hundreds of eutopian and dystopian works published during the twentieth century. But their tasks were also different from mine. As Sargent observes in a recent overview of "utopian fiction in English before Wells," "the twentieth century utopia is least studied of all."[1] Therefore, historical surveys covering the post-1900 years must describe broad trends and basic characteristics. Much of this type of spadework has already been done for the late-nineteenth-century utopias (though there is always more digging to be done). Several pioneering articles and dissertations on this period were completed during the 1930s and 1940s; in *American Dreams* (1947; reprint 1964), the published version of one of the dissertations, Vernon Louis Parrington, Jr., focused on 1888 to 1900. These early studies have recently been supported, criticized, revised, and extended in several articles and dissertations, and in my book *The Obsolete Necessity: America in Utopian Writings, 1888–1900* (1976).

Thus the amount of material to be covered and the fact that much of the spadework has been done have shaped the nature and scope of this essay: The survey must be broad rather than microscopic; nevertheless, I am freer than the authors of the other historical essays to attempt an interpretive rather than a descriptive analysis. (Anyone desiring a more detailed descriptive survey should consult the recent dissertations and publications listed in the "Secondary Sources" list in this collection.)

305

The present essay is divided into two sections. The first provides a descriptive overview of important characteristics of this period of American utopian literature. Emphasis is placed upon the popularity, numbers, impact, and diversity of the utopias and upon the authors' backgrounds—the perspectives that shaped their eutopias and dystopias.[2] The second section is less descriptive, more interpretive. Utilizing the December 1975 special issue of *American Quarterly*, "Victorian Culture in America," and other recent scholarship on late-nineteenth-century America,[3] I attempt to place the utopian literature within the context of American cultures by comparing and contrasting the basic characteristics, values, and goals of Victorian culture in America and the American utopian culture imagined by the utopists. This approach should help us to understand why so many people wrote utopias and why they were so popular. It should also help to clarify some of the fuzziest spots in the study of the most studied era of American utopian literature: How liberal or conservative, forward- or backward-looking, typical or untypical, American or un-American were these once popular visions of a new and better America?

II

As Joel Nydahl's essays demonstrate, ever since the beginnings of American fiction our authors have experimented with utopia. But in spite of this continuity, it is clear that the period beginning in 1888 and extending up through the early years of the twentieth century stands out as an especially noteworthy era for eutopias. The most specific impetus for utopists during those years was, of course, Edward Bellamy's *Looking Backward, 2000–1887*, published in 1888. The tremendous popularity and influence of this book make the late nineteenth century a fertile time for literary utopianism. *Looking Backward* was one of the biggest bestsellers of the nineteenth century. It was a slow starter: In an interview with the Johannesburg (South Africa) *Star*, Mark Twain remarked that the "first edition . . . was about as scrofulous-looking and mangy a volume as I have set eyes on."[4] But after several less "scrofulous" and less expensive editions were printed, sales soared. Within the first year 60,000 copies were sold. After another year, the figure rose to 213,988; sometimes more than a thousand copies were bought on a single day. By March 1890 *The Nationalist*, a magazine inspired by Bellamy's utopia, advertised that 310,000 copies were in print; *The Nationalist* itself boasted about its 69,000 circulation as early as December 1889. The entire June 1890 issue of *Overland Monthly* was devoted to responses to Bellamy, and Robert L. Shurter estimated that at least eleven magazines besides *The Nationalist* and *The New Nation* (edited by Bellamy) were reactions to *Looking Backward*.[5] Another impressive though seldom noted indication of this utopia's popularity is Hamilton W. Mabie's 1893 survey of "all the important libraries in the United States." In only five years *Looking Backward* had surpassed such works as *The Swiss Family Robinson*, *A Tale of Two Cities*, *Pilgrim's Progress*, and *Aesop's Fables* in library circulation. During the twentieth century *Looking Backward* has been translated into numerous languages, and sales have risen into the millions. It is no wonder that as late as 1935 the philosopher John Dewey, the historian Charles Beard, and Edward Weeks, the editor of the *Atlantic*, felt that of the books published since 1885 only Marx's *Das Kapital* had done more to shape the thought and action of the modern world.[6]

But *Looking Backward* was not the only popular late-nineteenth-century utopian work. Ignatius Donnelly's primarily dystopian *Caesar's Column* (1890) sold quite well; Frank Luther Mott lists Twain's eutopian-dystopian *A Connecticut Yankee in King Arthur's Court* (1889) as a "better seller"; and by 1975 Alice Payne Hackett and James Henry Burke estimated that the partially utopian *In His Steps* (1897), written by the Reverend Charles M. Sheldon, had reached the 8-million sales mark.[7] Furthermore, the numbers of eutopian, antiutopian, dystopian, and partially utopian works published from 1888 to 1899 add to the evidence of the interest in utopia. One critic has proclaimed this publishing phenomenon "the largest single body of utopian writings in history."[8] (The bibliography appended to this essay lists 172 titles for the period 1888–99.) Considering this outburst of literary utopianism and the popularity and influence of such books as *Looking Backward*, it may not be too much of an exaggeration to say that for about a decade utopian literature "was perhaps the most widely read type of literature in America."[9]

Besides the popularity and influence of this utopian literature, another characteristic that distinguishes the late-nineteenth-century utopias from their American and non-American predecessors is an explicit, literal brand of utopianism. Many of these utopists hoped that their books would do more than encourage readers to experience utopia and to see the present and the future in new ways. They wanted to implement their utopias, to transform the imaginary into an accomplished fact. The many Nationalist Clubs (estimates range from 160 to 500) inspired by *Looking Backward* attest to the emphasis on applied utopianism, as do F. U. Adams's Majority Rule Clubs, Charles Caryl's New Era Union, King Camp Gillette's incorporation of his World Corporation, and Bradford Peck's Cooperative Association of America.[10] If other utopists didn't start their own reform organizations, they advocated the use of existing parties—Donnelly's *The Golden Bottle* (1892) is a fictionalized Populist platform, for example—or made it clear, with subtitles such as *A Very Possible Story* and *Utopia Made Practical* and explicit prefaces and afterwords with headings like "Why Not an Eden," that their imaginary utopias housed realistic blueprints for the future. (See

Bellamy's essay in Part I of this collection.) In other words, late-nineteenth-century American utopists were approaching a concept of utopia satirized as early as 1905 in H.G. Wells's *A Modern Utopia*: "There is a common notion that the reading of a Utopia should end with a swelling of the heart and clear resolves, with lists of names, formation of committees, and even the commencement of subscriptions."[11]

The literalism combined with the popularity and influence of the late-nineteenth-century utopias make this literature a tempting index to late-nineteenth-century American cultures: The explicitness makes the works "easier to handle" than complex novels such as *Moby-Dick* or ambiguous utopias such as *The Dispossessed*, and the popularity and influence suggest a wide appeal extending far beyond literary interest.

But before we leap to any conclusions relating Victorian America to America as utopia, we must be careful not to oversimplify our index. *Looking Backward* fits everyone's definition of a utopia, and it was popular, influential, and designed for practical application. But this paradigm of late-nineteenth-century utopian literature is not always representative of late-nineteenth-century literary utopias. Many of the utopian works were not popular; even William Dean Howells's Altrurian Romances did not approach the best-seller category. Other books that were best-sellers—*In His Steps*, for instance—did not provide detailed descriptions of utopia (although the Reverend Maxwell's reformed Kansas town is a foreshadowing, even a microcosm, of utopia). Bellamy, Sheldon, and to some degree Howells were earnest and practical, but D. Herbert Heywood was lighthearted and satiric. His *The Twentieth Century* (1889) mocks the whole quest for utopia with incoherent lists of inventions, irrelevant illustrations, and absurd "Ballads of the Rockies"—supposedly the music of the future. Finally, there are fascinating eutopian dystopias and vice versa, most notably Will N. Harben's *The Land of the Changing Sun* (1894), *A Connecticut Yankee*, and *Caesar's Column*. In other words, any attempts to relate this body of literature to Victorianism must, when appropriate, take into account the diversity that lies outside the vision of Julian West and his creator.

The creators also pose a problem. It would be a sham to pretend that these utopias were Victorian or modern, American or un-American, without knowing the authors' backgrounds. Unfortunately, such biographical information is hard to come by. A few well-known individuals did write utopias: Twain, Howells, Bellamy, Donnelly, Gillette, and Sheldon have already been mentioned. There were also Harold Frederic, Joaquin Miller, the economist Laurence Gronlund, "the Kansas fire eater" Mary Elizabeth Lease, and the millionaire John Jacob Astor. But most of the authors were unknowns who sometimes courted obscurity with pseudonyms such as Anon Moore, Myself and Another, Two Women of the West, Untrammeled Free-thinker, Luke A. Hedd, and Omen Nemo. One approach to the problem of sketching a profile of the utopists has been simply to assume that they were "average" Americans; another is to concede that "information is too incomplete to make any sweeping generalities."[12] Although the second conclusion is much closer to the truth, a careful examination of nineteenth- and twentieth-century biographical sources, comparisons with 1890 census reports, and a random sample of a hundred late-nineteenth-century authors taken from a list of 26,000 writers reveal some definite trends that should help to determine how representative the utopian authors were.[13]

In two respects the utopists were representative Americans. Except for Southern writers, their geographical distribution was a much closer approximation of the population distribution in 1890 than was the distribution of the "typical" author as defined by the random sample.[14] The other representative characteristic was the migration from the country to the city. Of the sixty-five authors for whom relevant information is available, fifty-two (80 percent) moved from rural or small-town environments to large urban centers such as New York, Boston, or Chicago. The locations of the authors when they wrote their utopias are available for at least thirty-five more utopists; twenty-nine (83 percent) lived in large cities. Even though the evidence is incomplete, the move to the cities is obvious.

The geographical distribution and flight from the country support Jay Martin's contention that "in some senses, the utopian novel became for a brief period the true National Novel."[15] An occupational survey also reveals that the utopists were more vocationally representative than the authors in the random sample. For instance, their occupations were more diversified than the occupations in the random sample, which were more heavily weighted toward traditional professions: random sample—clergy, 18 percent; lawyers, 13 percent; physicians, 15 percent; teachers, 13 percent; utopists—clergy, about 13 percent; lawyers, about 5 percent; physicians, about 4 percent; teachers, about 4 percent. In contrast to the random sample, the utopian authors included many who either modified traditional professions to become social-gospel ministers or reform lawyers, or they chose "newer" professions: about 15 percent were businessmen, inventors, engineers, or scientists; about 14 percent described themselves as political reformers; and at least 25 percent, the largest occupational concentration, were journalists (random sample: about 7, 5, and 5 percent respectively). The ranks of the utopists, moreover, included some occupational black sheep as well as examples of the economic extremes of progress and poverty.[16]

But despite the trend away from traditional professions and the occupational and economic diversity, and hints that as many as one-half of the authors experienced financial difficulties during their lives, available information suggests that a clear majority of the utopists were middle- and upper-middle-class professionals. Educational and family data support this profile. During the academic year 1891–92, less than 1 percent of the population were attending college, and estimates indicate that only 28 percent of the business elite and 29 percent of the national leaders had college degrees. In contrast, about 72 percent of the utopists went to college.[17] Because college degrees usually meant "good" homes, it is not surprising to discover that most of the utopists were the scions of respected families. For instance, John Bachelder's ancestors founded his home town in New York; Ralph Albertson's kin were among the first Dutch settlers in New York; Mary Agnes Tinckner's ancestors came over on the *Mayflower*; and Will N. Harben could claim kinship with Daniel Boone.

The religions, nationalities, races, sexes, and ages of the utopists also suggest how unrepresentative they were of the diversity of the late-nine-teenth-century American population. With few exceptions, they were Prot-estant, American-born, Caucasian, male, and middle-aged (about fifty years old in 1894). Even some of the exceptions were not so exceptional. Donnelly, for instance, was born a Catholic, but he was not devout and drifted toward spiritualism in later life. The only truly notable exceptions were two suc-cessful Jewish immigrants, Rabbi Solomon Schindler and Rabbi Henry Per-eira Mendes; one respected black minister, Dr. Sutton E. Griggs; and a handful of women (see Barbara Quissell's essay in Part III of this collection.)

Thus, in spite of the popularity, influence, and diversity of late-nine-teenth-century utopian literature and the geographical distribution, the migration to the cities, and the occupational diversity that characterize the utopists, it would be foolish to assume that these utopias are foolproof in-dices to late-nineteenth-century American culture, even if one could define one "culture" during this pluralistic era. But the limitations of the utopists' backgrounds may make their utopias remarkable indices to the dominant "culture" in America during the late nineteenth-century—the Victorian cul-ture.

III

"Victorian" and "culture" are two words that have acquired as many negative connotations as "utopia," especially when they are put together and debunked by the likes of an H. L. Mencken. Recently, however, there have been attempts to avoid the extremes of praise and censure associated with British and American Victorianism. To quote Daniel Walker Howe:

> The present is an auspicious moment for Victorian studies. The Vic-
> torians themselves were so caught up in the excitement of their era
> [Queen Victoria reigned from 1837 to 1901] and its dramatic changes
> that they usually glorified it in their scholarship, interpreting previous
> eras as incomplete stages en route to their own. The result we call

"Whig history." Then came a period in the twentieth century when intellectuals were struggling against the restraints of Victorian convention, and consequently debunking was in fashion. Now, it would seem, the time is ripe for a kind of understanding that can go beyond an immediate need to celebrate or derogate, that can take a fresh look at the characteristics and dynamics of American Victorian culture.[18]

One example of a recent "fresh look" is the "Victorian Culture in America" issue of *American Quarterly* (December 1975), which Howe edited and published in book form as *Victorian America* (1976). In at least three ways this collection is a very useful and provocative framework for discussing late-nineteenth-century American utopian literature.

First of all, Howe's definition of "culture"—the one I used in the introduction to this collection—provides a useful context for analyzing the functions of late-nineteenth-century American utopias: "Culture" is defined as "an evolving system of beliefs, attitudes, and techniques, transmitted from generation to generation, and finding expression in innumerable activities people learn: religion, politics, child-rearing customs, the arts and professions, *inter alia*." He continues by supporting Clifford Geertz's emphasis on function: Culture is a "distinctive heritage of ideas and values, providing people with nonmaterial resources to cope with life and a world view to make sense out of it."[19] Late-nineteenth-century American utopists hoped to provide their readers with such "ideas and values." Furthermore, in their eutopias they demonstrated how these ideas and values could be learned and expressed "in innumerable activities." (For a detailed interpretation of the various activities, see Chapters 5–8 of *The Obsolete Necessity*.) Finally, as I shall stress later, these authors believed that utopian fiction was a powerful means of transmitting "from generation to generation" the ideals, values, beliefs, attitudes, and techniques that would enable Americans to understand and "cope with life."

Howe's population frame of reference is as applicable to the study of the utopias as his definition of culture. He stresses that "even during the height of American Victorianism," not all Americans were Victorians. American Indian cultures, immigrants (especially recent arrivals from Southeastern Europe and Asia), Mexican Americans, blacks, alienated intellectuals, and many native working-class Americans did not fit the Victorian mold. The most active supporters of American Victorianism were typically of British-American or German-American origins, were Caucasians and Protestants, and had middle- or upper-middle class backgrounds—often urban middle-class backgrounds. But support for Victorianism came from a wider base than the urban middle classes. It came from upwardly mobile workers who realized that "Victorian cultural values and techniques could bring tangible rewards" and from rural and small-town Americans who absorbed Victorianism via "the network of railways, print, and telegraphy."[20] As the foregoing biographical sketch of the utopists suggests, Howe's Victorian profile fits the utopists quite well, making them full-fledged Victorians who should have "learned" Victorian culture long before they wrote their utopias. The only glaring difference is the scarcity of women utopists. In part this is explained by the prejudices against "serious" female writers, and in part it is countered by the utopists' desire to reach the large Victorian female reading audience.[21]

The third, and possibly most important, frame of reference provided by Howe and the other contributors to "Victorian Culture in America" is their general delineation of the *broad perspectives, specific values* (and the means of *transmitting* these values), and *ultimate goals* that characterized Victorian culture in America. This profile can be used to determine just how Victorian these Victorian utopists were. The similarities between the Victorian and utopian views will thus help to establish to what degree the utopists' visions were rooted in the dominant culture of their era. The differences may be even more interesting, however. They will illuminate some of the nagging contradictions and doubts within the Victorian ranks that led to the decline of Victorian culture in America during the closing years of the nineteenth century.

Howe's introduction and several of the other essays, most notably Richard D. Brown's "Modernization: A Victorian Climax," stress the importance of three *broad perspectives* that were central to American Victorianism. First, this "was a time when people were particularly self-conscious about their culture. . . . The new awareness of culture is understandable in an era of rapid change, when everything from art forms to criminal law was being rethought, and habits of long standing came under critical examination."[22] According to D. H. Meyer, this self-consciousness was often expressed as a "peculiar mixture of doubt and confidence" about America.[23] Closely related to the self-consciousness was "an intense preoccupation with national identity," especially after the United States had "vindicated its national unity" with a bloody Civil War. Of course, the rapid industrialization and urbanization that pushed us toward self-sufficiency and our first international war at the end of the Victorian period augmented this tendency toward nationalism. The rapid industrial and urban growth also supported a third crucial attitude—"central to the Victorian era in the Western world was modernization." Modernization is most frequently associated with the knowledge and techniques that facilitate economic and urban growth; but, as Howe points out, modernization also suggests a broad, "multivariant approach . . . stressing causal interconnections among economic resources, social structure, and cultural values, as well as knowledge of specific skills."[24]

Self-consciousness, nationalism, and modernization were all central concerns for the late-nineteenth-century utopists, concerns that exposed fundamental contradictions and stresses. Because "self-consciousness" is rather difficult to define when it is not clear as to what the self is being conscious about, it seems wisest to begin with the other two perspectives, proceed through the analysis of values and goals, and then examine how the Victorians and utopists were self-conscious about the combination of perspectives, values, and goals.

If only the most idealistic rhetoric of the utopian authors were examined, their utopias would seem broadly humane, not nationalistic. Again and again there is a general call for cooperation and brotherhood for all humanity. But when the utopists get down to details, this universal appeal usually translates into Americanized brotherhood. Thus, Bellamy's revisions of *Looking Backward* are both typical and revealing: When he transformed his utopia from a vague social fantasy into a detailed blueprint, he moved from an "Ideal World" to an ideal America. (See Bellamy's first essay in Part I of this collection.)

Only a few works—most notably *Looking Forward: A Dream of the United States of the Americas in 1999*, written by Arthur Bird, a former consul to Haiti—were dominated by an international outlook; and even these focused on Americanization, not interrelation. Only fourteen authors predicted powerful world courts; a couple emphasized trade relationships; and eleven envisioned large-scale international ventures—Americanizing ventures. Of more significance than these rare glances beyond our shores was the general tendency to define utopia as the future of America. All but eight of the authors in my sample located their improved societies in America. This generality even applies to utopists who set their utopias on distant planets, within the earth's center, or on imaginary islands, for these no-places were obvious analogies for a potential someplace, an idealized America. To quote William Dean Howells's Mr. Homos, "America prophesies another Alturia."[25]

How did these utopists resolve their general hopes for humanity with their scant attention to international relations and their Victorian America-First attitude? John Winthrop and a long tradition of patriotic rhetoric offered one answer. Once America was utopia, it would become "a beacon to guide [humanity's] Steps," "a guiding star," "a pattern for all the world to follow," for "all eyes [would be] centered on it," to borrow phrases used frequently by the utopists. Winthrop would have understood this rhetoric; it was simply an echo of his City-upon-a-Hill motif. But this traditional patriotic appeal certainly didn't silence the contradictions between humanism and nationalism; it was also a backward-looking setup for disillusionment and misguided international policies in the twentieth century.

The utopists' version of the Victorian enthusiasm for modernization also exposes weaknesses in the Victorian outlook. As Howard P. Segal has emphasized in two recent studies,[26] the utopists seem quite modern in their

attitudes about technological advances, economic efficiency, and urbanization. To be sure, there were some important dissenters. Howells's Altrurians
tear up some of their railroad tracks; the dangers of total automation are
dramatized in Walter D. Reynolds's *Mr. Jonnemacher's Machine* (1898);
Harben warns about the intrinsic threats of technology in *The Land of the
Changing Sun*; and of course there is Twain's frightening ambivalence about
his Yankee's inventions in *A Connecticut Yankee*. But even Howells's Altrurians ride streamlined railroads to glorious urban centers. Moreover, no
late-nineteenth-century American utopists championed William Morris's
rejection of modernization in *News from Nowhere*.[27] Instead most of their
utopias dazzle visitors with magnificent aluminum, electric railroads, planes,
cars, spaceships, mechanized factories and farms, plastics, computers, solar
and wind power, and Polaroid cameras. Visitors are also impressed by the
modern cities: Chauncey Thomas envisioned gigantic city pyramids not
unlike Paolo Soleri's arcologies; Charles Caryl included full-page and foldout
city plans; in *The Human Drift* (1894) King Camp Gillette even used city
plans, building designs, and apartment blueprints—all modeled on the latest
construction designs in New York and Chicago. As for economic efficiency,
Bellamy imagined an ingenious warehouse–pneumatic tube system that
eliminated middlemen and reduced transportation and delivery costs. Bradford Peck (listed in Segal's bibliography under eutopias for 1900) emphasized
the merits of his efficient department store cooperatives by attacking nineteenth-century economies in an encyclopedic table entitled "Conservative
Table Representing the Estimated Wasted Energy in Every Department
of Life at the Close of the Nineteenth Century." Most other utopists weren't
as ingenious as Bellamy or as comprehensive as Peck. But whether they
supported capitalistic or socialistic systems, they emphasized the importance
of efficient technology, the elimination of obsolete personnel (especially
middlemen and lawyers), and the widespread use of experts—frequently
economic, industrial, and agricultural brain trusts governed important national departments.

All this enthusiasm for technological advances, urban development, and
economic efficiency seems to fit the Victorian desire for modernization. The
quest for modernization in the utopias was, however, predicated upon an
important assumption. The utopists wanted a "just" modernization, one
founded upon equality and cooperation. Otherwise, as John F. Kasson has
recently observed, modernization, especially technological advance, "might
serve as an instrument not of liberty but of repression, not order but chaos,
not creation but destruction."[28] For example, Bellamy likened the combination of advanced technology and efficient monopolies to "the body of the
spider [that] swells as he sucks the juices of his victims." Bert J. Wellman
agreed: This powerful combination reduced honest workers to "the slaves
and hirelings of the owners of [machines]."[29] In *Caesar's Column* Donnelly

foresees the ultimate results of the league of technology, grand cities, efficient economies, and immoral leaders. In his Orwellian future the workers slave beneath the surface of a modern city; they slave, suffer, smolder, hate. Finally they unleash their fury and destroy their glittering prison. Their testament to the future is a gigantic pile of bloody corpses.

Donnelly's dystopian catastrophe was an expression of the utopists' worst fears about modernization. But even the more typical moderate doubts suggest that the utopists were more aware than their fellow Victorians that modernization was not simply a matter of engineering and growth. Ethics and morals had to adapt to the new knowledge and techniques; or, again to borrow Howe's words, modernization involved "stressing causal interconnections among economic resources, social structure, and cultural values." Without these interconnections, eutopia could quickly become dystopia.

The Victorian emphasis on nationalism and modernization, especially modernization, was closely related to a cluster of *specific values* that were usually expressed in terms of desirable character attributes. These were the values that were supposed to help Victorians to "cope with life." They were sometimes "new" values, sometimes "old"; some were specific, others general. The ones most frequently stressed by Victorian spokesmen and women on a spectrum ranging roughly from specific to general are: cleanliness, punctuality, repression of sexual urges, postponement of gratification, specialization, efficiency, hard work, devotion to duty, competitiveness, seriousness, self-improvement, a future orientation, rationality, orderliness, valuing a sense of unity and stability, and a "Christian" outlook. Of course, Victorians weren't all that. Both the debunkers of the 1920s and scholars have shown that Victorian values and Victorian behavior could diverge widely. But these specific values represented what Victorian Americans were supposed to strive toward and be rewarded for; hence they were important normative prescriptions.

And the utopists knew it. They knew that there had to be some sense of continuity between their eutopias and what was familiar to their readers. Otherwise their imaginary futures might be just as confusing to the readers as the rapid changes of the late nineteenth century. One obvious source of continuity was the cluster of Victorian values listed above. Utopia would bring drastic changes, but many of these changes would preserve or even enhance familiar values. Thus there is no dirt in the streets of utopia and the trains are always on time. Albert Waldo Howard permits his young utopians to "love naturally" before marriage and enjoy polygamy after the wedding.[30] But most of the utopian authors, including Bellamy, implied that the sex act was to be experienced after marriage and mainly for procreation. For instance, in *Equality* (1897), Bellamy's second book-length utopian work, Dr. Leete argues that economically secure couples control their "impulses of crude animalism" better than poor people do. His proof: Without the aid of birth control devices, the secure citizens of the year 2000 have few children, which means that they can lavish attention on each child.[31] Hence, as in many of the sex manuals of the day, sex was chastized and idealized simultaneously. "Crude animalisms" were repressed, but pure love, untainted by economic motives, made perfect matches and occasionally inspired them to produce an ideal cherub. Accordingly, Henry Olerich's ideal Martian proclaims that "the person who has the sexual function so adjusted that he exercises it only for the special purpose of sexual reproduction, is the most complete person sexually."[32]

Victorian values that suggested broader patterns of behavior than cleanliness, punctuality, and sexual repression were also stressed by the utopists. As their attitudes about modernization indicate, they championed specialization and efficiency. Hard work, devotion to duty, and competitiveness are reflected in a variety of ways ranging from Bellamy's young utopians striving for public awards to glimpses of school children competing in athletics and academics and later for positions in an Industrial Army in Rabbi Schindler's *Young West* (1894). Seriousness is most often exemplified in the narrators, heroes, and guides. Whether we consider Bellamy's West and Leete, F. U. Adams's John Smith, Chauncey Thomas's John Costor, James M. Galloway's John Harvey, Archibald McCowan's Abraham Lincoln Homeborn, Joaquin Miller's beautiful Jewess, Miriam, or Sutton E. Griggs's two black heroes, Bernard and Belton, one common trait stands out: They are all earnest, serious-minded people, devoted to their causes. The emphasis on self-improvement and a future orientation are self-evident in most of the utopias. Utopia was where Americans could develop all their capacities during their abundant leisure hours, and the futuristic settings of the majority of the works give a sense of concreteness to the utopists' future orientation. (Twain's *A Connecticut Yankee*, Franklin H. North's *The Awakening of Noahville* [1898], some of the Lost Race tales, and the antiutopias and dystopias do, of course, reject, criticize, or question this orientation.) Rationality, another important Victorian value, was most clearly expressed in the utopists' belief that to convince readers, to get them to experience utopia, they had to (1) expose the evils of the present, that is, disclose the "facts," and then (2) present a commonsense blueprint for a much better future. This rational approach was combined with religious, patriotic, and emotional appeals, but the utopists believed that the exposé-blueprint logic was the key to change without irrational revolutions. The city plans of utopia—rectangles, squares, and especially circles—underline the utopists' love of orderliness, and so does the architecture. We see it in Gillette's rows of identical apartment complexes that make up his beehive city of "Metropolis," in the "harmonies" of Charles Caryl's concentric circles and in the revulsion against the "ragged spasmodic, violently contrasting and utterly incongruous monster" of the nineteenth century, the city.[33]

Finally, these were Christian utopias. With the exception of the few works written by Jewish authors and the ones by a handful of critics of all religions,[34] the concept of a Christian Heaven on earth permeated late-nineteenth-century utopian literature. The utopists relied upon the millennial image of the "chosen people" to define the role of America in history; they sometimes associated the transition to eutopia with the Resurrection; some of the most popular utopists—Bellamy and Sheldon, for example—used the conversion experience as an analogy for how individuals would change during the transition; heroes were often compared to Jesus; and economic systems were frequently presented as applications of Christ's teachings. Add to these characteristics the many religious titles and subtitles and the fact that the two most popular utopists, Sheldon and Bellamy, were, respectively, a Protestant minister and a scion of a long line of Protestant ministers; then the utopian literature seems to be a wholehearted endorsement of the Victorian celebration of a Christian world view combined with a resounding endorsement of the Victorian values.

Not quite; not quite on several counts. The cluster of values identified by the contributors to "Victorian Culture in America" does encompass many of the utopists' values, with one very significant omission: equality. In Charles Rooney's unpublished content analysis of 101 late-nineteenth- and early-twentieth-century utopian works, he shows that the most important value for the utopists was equality, particularly equality of opportunity.[35] This does not mean that all the utopists supported Bellamy's scheme for absolute economic equality. Very few did. But the political, economic, and social systems advocated by the utopists suggest that the elimination of economic and social inequality was a prime goal: Approximately 20 percent of the authors advocated socialism, usually labeled with an Americanized name such as Nationalism; over 50 percent envisioned national cooperatives regulated by government departments; a little over 10 percent described capitalistic eutopias that included equalizing reforms such as inheritance taxes and income limits; and less than 10 percent advocated totalitarianism.

The utopists' desire for equality clashed with several Victorian values, and in the inevitable tradeoffs equality almost always got the nod. For example, most of the utopists assumed that certain forms of gratification postponement fostered "character." But with the exceptions of J. W. Roberts, David Hilton Wheeler, and a few other critics of Bellamy, the utopists believed that too much gratification postponement destroyed character. Their primary illustrations of this tragedy were the victims of urban and rural inequalities. Continual postponement of adequate education, economic opportunity, and social respect ended in stunted self-development, apathy, or bitterness. The value conflict between postponement and equality also raised questions about the application of Christianity. The utopists championed the ethics of the life of Christ, but they could not tolerate certain Victorian forms of Christianity that preached postponement as the answer to poverty. Sheldon's hero confesses that bars often comfort the poor better than churches because many ministers could offer them only endurance and the promise of heavenly rewards as an answer to poverty. And then there were the "Acres-of-Diamonds" preachers who justified, even glorified inequality. In *Caesar's Column* Gabriel is so shocked by one of these sermons that he protests. The congregation responds by pelting him with ornate Bibles and throwing him out of the church.

Equality also met head-on with competition. Certain types of constructive competition that fostered academic excellence, physical fitness, and public service were lauded by the utopists. But the "cutthroat" competition of free enterprise was banned from most of the utopias. In part the utopists' complaints against competition reflected their desire for efficiency, stability, rationality, and order: Wide-open competition seemed so redundant, so wasteful, so chaotic. As Bellamy's famous coach parable implies, even the wealthy might be toppled from their high perches by an unforeseen lump in the road. Some sort of planned, centralized economy seemed much more sensible. But the utopists' attacks went beyond reason. To them the present system of economic competition was immoral and unjust: How could a hundred-yard dash be fair if most of the runners had to start on the zero yard line and a few were permitted to start at the ninety? (Bellamy and other utopists used distribution of wealth statistics to emphasize this point.) But most of the utopists went beyond criticisms of nineteenth-century competition. Even if equality of opportunity existed, they preferred cooperation (another value left out of the Victorian list) over competition. In part this attitude reflected the utopists' attitude toward personality formation: Competition, argued the Christian mystic Thomas Lake Harris, encouraged the "outlet and satisfaction of egotistic lusts," which in turn led to "the savagisms, the barbarisms of all the past."[36] Cooperation, on the other hand, encouraged kindness and love and an awareness of the complex interrelationships among all humans, while still fostering self-development. To quote Laurence Gronlund, "I must make myself valuable, for if myself is paltry, so is every other self, so are all selves put together."[37] The utopists' Christian outlook also inclined them toward a cooperative society rather than one governed by a competitive survival of the fittest. As Sheldon's question "*What Would Jesus Do?*" suggests, Christ would have prefered to help the weak instead of eliminating them from the species.

The value conflicts of equality and cooperation versus postponement of gratification and competition are striking examples of where the Victorian utopists and the "typical" Victorians parted company. Less obvious perhaps, but just as significant, were the utopists' ambivalences about at least two other Victorian values, hard work and a future orientation. Hard work was a prime virtue during the late nineteenth century; even "prominent New York reformers" reacted to their state's Half-Holiday Act (1887) with predictions that the workers would spend their free half Saturdays "dancing, carousing, . . . rioting, shooting, and murder[ing]."[38] So it is not surprising that in an anti-Bellamy series of essays entitled *Our Industrial Utopia and Its Unhappy Citizens* (1895) David H. Wheeler, a Methodist minister, argued for "more rather than less" work in his utopia,[39] or that the utopists rarely described lazy utopians. And yet the authors' sympathy for factory hands forced to work twelve to fourteen hours a day and their enthusiasm for advanced technology and efficient economic systems meant that most of the citizens of their utopias would spend at least half of their lives in "leisure." The typical work day was eight hours or less—often four hours—and retirement ages were as early as thirty-five in Gillette's Metropolis and forty-five in Bellamy's Boston. Most of the utopists tried to circumvent the apparent contradiction between the hard-work ethic and this life of leisure by showing the narrator (and readers) all the wonderful libraries, theaters, concert halls, schools, and gymnasiums of eutopia, that is, people didn't just lie around during their time off, they worked hard at their leisure. This resolution may seem a bit strained, but it does indicate that the utopists knew that they had to consider the importance of increased leisure in the future; otherwise lives formerly wasted by senseless toil would be wasted in senseless boredom. Furthermore, at least two authors realized that in the future it might be necessary to have a new concept of work. In the Altrurian Romances Howells respected the value of the agricultural and industrial work that contributed to the society's welfare. But for the Altrurians the primary motivation for doing work was "the pleasure of doing a thing beautifully."[40] Whether the task was done during "work" or "leisure" was of secondary importance. In *Looking Backward* retirement comes at forty-five. Then people are free to "fully devote [themselves] to the higher exercise of their [facilities], the intellectual and spiritual enjoyments which *alone* mean life"[41] (italics mine). Like Howells, Bellamy does not denigrate work done for society. But, again like Howells, he depicts a very personalized concept of work, one that coincides perfectly with the Victorian emphasis on self-improvement.

Bellamy, Howells, and their colleagues were less successful with their ambivalence toward a future orientation. In their explicit statements about historical process, they were all eyes to the future, assuming the present could be changed so that the future could be utopia. They spoke of the "idea of progress in a right line," a glorious escape from the meaningless cycles of civilized peaks and barbaric troughs in the Old World.[42] But this quest for infinite progress in the future had a rather low ceiling. In part this was a literary limit; in a work of fiction it is very difficult to dramatize infinite change; readers need bits of the familiar to hold on to. But time was more than a literary problem for the utopists. It confronted them with a clash between their future orientation and their desires for order, unity, and stability. The typical response was a sincere advocacy of drastic changes in many aspects of American culture in order to achieve a changeless and thus understandable existence in the future. By the year 2000, Dr. Leete can proclaim that his America embodied "fundamental principles [that] settle *for all time* the strifes and misunderstandings which in your day [West's nineteenth century] called for legislation"[43] (italics mine). Similarly in William Simpson's Martian utopia we find a "stationary state" economy, and in Chauncey Thomas's forty-ninth century we find "the Government of Settled Forms . . . fixed inflexibly in the minds and consciousnesses of the people."[44] Evidently these utopian authors believed that if they incorporated too much futuristic Progress into their utopias, they and their readers might feel that these imaginary futures were more confusing than the present, more change heaped upon change, future shock upon future shock.

Despite the disagreements and questions about certain specific Victorian values, both the Victorian exponents and the utopists agreed that a key element in an ideal America was the *transmission of the proper values* throughout America and from generation to generation. Here we can see how deeply rooted the utopists were in Victorian culture.

Advocates of Victorian values were preoccupied with a didactic communication system. The ticket to this system was the English language, and the primary means of communication was the printed word. (Hence many Americans, including Indians, blacks, the Spanish-speaking, and some immigrants, were automatically excluded from the network.) Newspapers, magazines, tracts, and books "became important vehicles for communication."[45] Books were especially important. To quote David D. Hall, "the publishing revolution of the 1830's and '40's, by lowering the price of books, had brought them within the reach of an enormous audience." The "Victorians' hope" was that everyone would read "serious" literature that encouraged self-improvement. Therefore much emphasis was placed on the importance of didactic books as a means of transmitting proper values.[46] Howe agrees:

> It was a great age of prescriptive writing of all kinds: child-rearing manuals, books on household management, etiquette books, even joke books to tell people how to be funny. It was also an age when poetry and fiction legitimated themselves by the morals they taught.[47]

There was only one hitch: The "type of book which people actually bought in huge quantities was fiction," and much of it was trash, according to the Victorians.[48] The utopists thought they had an answer to this question:

popular utopian fiction. *Looking Backward* was serious, prescriptive, and immensely popular; its values were even translated into action for thousands of active supporters of Bellamy and Nationalist Clubs. With this striking example (along with *Uncle Tom's Cabin*) to inspire them, it was natural for authors of utopian fiction to hope that their books could change the world. At least twenty-two plots included the writing of a book that transformed America, or a modest hint by the utopist that his book would do the trick. This faith in book power is captured by the economist-reformer, Laurence Gronlund, in a partially utopian series of essays entitled "Our Destiny: The Influence of Nationalism on Morals and Religion" (1890–91): "When I reflect that what remains to be said may prove [to be] the spark that . . . may turn [readers] into the Leaders of men . . . , I almost tremble from the excitement that masters me."[49]

Of course, other literary and popular sources could be cited that illuminate the utopists' attitude toward writing—past utopian literature, the sentimental reform novel, and the "oral conventions of the pulpit, the lecture platform, and the stage."[50] But to understand late-nineteenth-century American utopian authors fully, one must be especially aware of the Victorian attitude toward the tremendous power of didactic, prescriptive fiction. As Friedrich Engels had already pointed out in *Socialism, Utopian and Scientific*, this utopian faith in book power was naive: a "rational" exposé of the present followed by a "rational" blueprint for a relatively static utopia—which in the case of the late-nineteenth-century American utopists was often a projection of middle- or upper-middle-class values—was not a likely means of rousing the masses or understanding the past and present. But the utopian authors' Victorian belief in book power, coupled with the popularity of *Looking Backward* and the early achievements of the Nationalist Clubs, helped to blind the utopists to certain social and historical realities that seem painfully clear to Engels.

The foregoing examinations of the Victorians' broad perspectives, specific values, and one means of transmitting these values have included the delineation of important Victorian *goals*: a dominant and modernized America—an America where the behavior and thought of Americans are shining examples of the Victorian values that were born in England, developed and perfected in America, and destined to sweep the world. There was, however, at least one other crucial Victorian goal:

> The intended product of Victorian didacticism was a person who would no longer need reminding of his duties, who would have internalized a powerful sense of obligation and could then safely be left to his own volitions. Such a person has been described by David Riesman as "inner-directed," possessed of a moral gyroscope that would function

even amidst the unfamiliar surroundings in which Victorians so often
found themselves. A society composed of such persons, the Victorians
hoped, could get along with a minimum of government.[51]

The utopian authors accepted this ultimate goal wholeheartedly. In
Henry Olerich's Martian utopia there are "no parties, no politicians, . . . no
kings, queens, and presidents; no political congress, parliaments and leg-
islatures." Why? because, as in Chauncey Thomas's eutopia, all the proper
values are "fixed inflexibly in the minds and consciences of the people."
There is "no government," argues James Cowan's Martian, because "no
one . . . needs governing."[52]

But there was a rub. How do you implant a moral gyroscope? The
Victorians and the utopists agreed that the right type of didactic literature
in school and in the home would help. The utopists also believed in the
Victorian "cult of domesticity. The home was conceived of as an orderly and
secure place where children were indoctrinated with the proper values
before being sent forth to make their way in a rapidly-changing world."[53]
Within this shelter motherhood was enshrined. Several utopists celebrated
motherhood with rhetoric that would have pleased any devout Victorian:
Richard C. Michaelis, one of Bellamy's critics, proclaimed that "nearly all
our good qualities can be traced back to the influence and unfathomable
love and patience of the mother."[54]

Nevertheless, approximately 90 percent of the utopian authors, including
Bellamy and Howells, could not accept the conventional Victorian view that
didactic literature and the "great socioanatomical institution" of the nineteenth century, the mother's knee,[55] would ensure inner-directed Americans. In part this was because of the new roles they prescribed for women
in utopia. With the exception of a few authors who eliminated the mother's
role or greatly reduced it by sending the children off to live-in preschools,
the utopists felt that motherhood was important. With the efficient economies and technology of utopia, mothers would have ample time for loving
and indoctrinating their children. But the utopists also argued that it was
wrong to restrict a woman's role to motherhood. They believed that women
should have the opportunity to pursue careers (Edith Leete was a farmhand
in *Equality*); after all, should not women also participate in the Victorian
drive to self-improvement?

Most of the utopian authors also believed that transforming average
Americans into the inner-directed citizens of utopia called for more than
books and home life. Other important catalysts were experiences akin to
religious conversions, the inspiration of heroic figures, a considerable dash
of "Anglo-Saxon" genes, and a conscious manipulation of the environment
designed to reinforce the correct character attributes.[56] Except for the last
method—the utopists' version of Reform Darwinism, a precursor to Skin-

ner's positive reinforcement—the individual elements of this conglomerate theory of personality development would have been familiar to most Victorians. The differences are that the utopists expanded the woman's role and placed special emphasis on a multilevel approach to implanting the moral gyroscope. Both changes indicate that the utopists sensed that at the end of the nineteenth century it would take more than the printed word and mother's knee to allow Americans to "cope with life" and "function even amidst unfamiliar surroundings." Look at what happens to that Victorian of Victorians, Julian West. Soon after awakening to the twenty-first century he crumbles: "In my mind, all had broken loose, habits of feeling, associations of thought, ideas of persons and things, all had dissolved and lost coherence and were seething together in an apparently irretrievable chaos. There were no rallying points, nothing was left stable."[57]

IV

Comparing and contrasting American Victorianism and Victorian utopianism means leaving a lot unsaid about both. Furthermore, Howe's "Victorian Culture in America" and *Victorian America* may not be the "definitive," and certainly are not the "last," words on this topic. Nevertheless, a comparative approach does permit a survey of most of the major perspectives, values, and goals of late-nineteenth-century American utopists, and Howe's collections do provide meaningful historical and cultural contexts within which the relationships between the utopists and their era can be examined.

These relationships indicate that neither the American Victorians nor the American Victorian utopists represented the diversity of American cultures during the late nineteenth century. Their views were limited by their racial, religious, economic, and social backgrounds and by their nationalism, which might not have been too appealing to immigrants and minorities from "alien" cultures. It could also be argued that the utopists were not very typical Victorians. They fitted the Victorian profile in many ways—especially in their backgrounds and in their faith in book power, which helps to explain why their books appealed to so many Victorian readers. But there are too many deviations from the mold: the questions about modernization without justice and order, the value conflicts that place postponement of gratification and competition second to equality and cooperation, the ambivalence about the work ethic and a future orientation, and the "new" attitudes about woman's role and personality formation. These blemishes on the Victorian profile call for more than plastic surgery. They may represent a different American face.

Similar problems crop up when we try to pigeonhole the utopists into

liberal or conservative and forward- or backward-looking slots. The honest
historian will inevitably end up revising Gilbert and Sullivan's lyrics from
Iolanthe to read: Every Conservative is born a little bit Liberal / Every
Liberal is born a little bit Conservative. Such equivocating is not necessarily
weak-kneed ambiguity. It simply suggests that terms such as *liberal* or
conservative and *forward-* or *backward-looking* are almost irrelevant when
applied to the study of utopian literature published from 1888 to 1899. If
not irrelevant, at least they get in the way.

A better way to approach this particular American phenomenon is to say
that the utopists were disciples of Victorian culture in America, but they
were preaching Victorianism strained to the breaking point by the changes
occurring in late-nineteenth-century America. Which brings us back to
Howe's comment about the self-conscious Victorians who, in Meyer's words,
expressed a "peculiar mixture of doubt and confidence." Reading these
eutopian and dystopian works is like holding a distorting lens over the
American Victorian profile. Certain elements of Victorianism—faith in
American technological knowhow and its moral reserves, faith in book
power, Christianity, rationality, earnestness, order, and the promise of
America—were enlarged by the utopists' optimism about America. Other
characteristics were blurred or hidden by the utopists' fears about the inequalities and chaos of late-nineteenth-century America.

This Victorian exercise in euphoric future shock is certainly a risky index
to the diversity of American cultures toward the close of the nineteenth
century and a distorted index to conventional Victorianism in America. But
the utopian literature is just as certainly a provocative index to the decline
of Victorian culture in America: the decline of Victorianism and the exciting
but troubled birth of twentieth-century America.

NOTES

1. Lyman Tower Sargent, "Themes in Utopian Fiction in English Before Wells,"
Science-Fiction Studies, 3 (November 1976), 279.

2. Part of this section first appeared in a slightly different version in Kenneth
M. Roemer, *The Obsolete Necessity: America in Utopian Writings, 1888–1900* (Kent,
Ohio: Kent State University Press, 1976).

3. See footnote 78 in Daniel Walker Howe, "American Victorianism as a Culture," *American Quarterly*, 27 (December 1975), 532.

4. "A Chat with Mark Twain . . . ," *Star*, May 18, 1896, p. 4.

5. Robert L. Shurter, "The Utopian Novel in America, 1865–1900," Ph.D. dissertation, Case Western Reserve University, 1936, pp. 160–61.

6. "The Most Popular Novels in America," *Forum*, 16 (December 1893), 508–10,
and Robert L. Shurter, "Introduction" to *Looking Backward, 2000–1887* (New York:
Modern Library, 1951), p. xv.

7. Alice Payne Hackett and James Henry Burke, *80 Years of Best Sellers, 1895–1975* (New York and London: R. R. Bowker, 1977), p. 11.

8. A. James Stupple, "Utopian Humanism in America, 1888–1900," Ph.D. dissertation, Northwestern University, 1971, p. 2.

9. Robert L. Shurter, "The Utopian Novel in America, 1888–1900," *South Atlantic Quarterly,* 34 (April 1935), 143.

10. For an interesting analysis of Peck's efforts see Francine C. Cary, "*The World a Department Store:* Bradford Peck and the Utopian Endeavor," *American Quarterly,* 29 (Fall 1977), 370–84.

11. As quoted in Richard Gerber, *Utopian Fantasy,* 2d ed. (New York: McGraw-Hill, 1973), pp. 8–9.

12. J. F. Normano, "Social Utopias in American Literature," *International Review for Social History,* 3 (1938), 290, and Allyn B. Forbes, "The Literary Quest for Utopia, 1880–1900," *Social Forces,* 6 (December 1927), 188.

13. The random sample was drawn from W. Stewart Wallace, ed., *A Dictionary of North American Authors Deceased Before 1950* (Toronto: Ryerson Press, 1951). The biographical data include utopists who published in 1900.

14. See Roemer, *Obsolete Necessity,* p. 10.

15. Jay Martin, *Harvests of Change: American Literature, 1865–1914* (Englewood Cliffs, N.J.: Prentice-Hall, 1967), p. 225.

16. See Roemer, *Obsolete Necessity,* p. 10.

17. *Statistical Abstracts of the United States* (Washington, D.C.: Bureau of Labor Statistics, 1892), p. 266; William Miller, "American Historians and the Business Elite," *Journal of Economic History,* 9 (November 1948), 207; and Seymour Martin Lipset and Reinhard Bendix, *Social Mobility in Industrial Society* (Berkeley: University of California Press, 1967), p. 126. Relevant information was available for only sixty-two authors in my sample. But even if none of the others went to college, the utopists would compare favorably with the other groups.

18. Howe, "American Victorianism" (note 3 above), p. 532. Besides Howe's collection, another indication of the new interest in American Victorian studies is the primary source collection *Victorian Culture in America 1865–1914,* edited by Wayne Morgan and published by F. E. Peacock in 1973; the primary focus is on the "arts."

19. Howe, "American Victorianism," p. 509.

20. Ibid., p. 515.

21. See Virgil L. Lokke, "The American Utopian Anti-Novel," in Ray B. Browne et al., eds. *Frontiers of American Culture* (West Lafayette, Ind.: Purdue University Studies, 1968), pp. 123–53, esp. p. 142.

22. Howe, "American Victorianism," p. 510.

23. D. H. Meyer, "American Intellectuals and the Victorian Crisis of Faith," in "Victorian Culture in America," full issue of *American Quarterly,* 27 (December 1975), 578.

24. Howe, "American Victorianism," pp. 511, 512.

25. William Dean Howells, *A Traveler from Altruria. A Romance* (New York: Harper & Brothers, 1894), p. 281.

26. Howard P. Segal, "*Young West:* The Psyche of Technological Utopianism," *Extrapolation,* 19 (December 1977), 50–58, and idem, "American Visions of Tech-

nological Utopia, 1883–1933," *Markham Review*, 7 (Summer 1978), 65–76.

27. See T. M. Parssinen, "Bellamy, Morris, and the Image of the Industrial City in Victorian Social Criticism," *Midwest Quarterly*, 14 (Spring 1973), 257–66.

28. John F. Kasson, "Technology and Utopia," in *Civilizing the Machine: Technology and Republican Values in America, 1776–1900* (New York: Penguin, 1977), p. 191. See also Christine McHugh, "Abundance and Asceticism: Looking Backward to the Future," *Alternative Futures*, 1 (Fall 1978), 47–58.

29. Edward Bellamy, *Equality* (New York: Appleton, 1897), p. 314, and Bert Wellman, *The Legal Revolution of 1902* (Chicago: Charles H. Kerr, 1898), p. 323.

30. Albert Waldo Howard, *The Milltillionaire* (Boston: The author, 1895).

31. Bellamy, *Equality*, pp. 269–70, 410.

32. Henry Olerich, *A Cityless and Countryless World: An Outline of Practical Co-operative Individualism* (Holstein, Iowa: Gilmore & Olerich, 1893), pp. 65–66.

33. William Dean Howells, *Letters of an Altrurian Traveller*, in *The Altrurian Romances*, eds. Clara Kirk and Rudolph Kirk (Bloomington: Indiana University Press, 1968), p. 202, and [John Brisbane Walker], "A Brief History of Altruria," *Cosmopolitan*, November 1895, p. 88.

34. See the short-title bibliography for 1888–99 for works by Mendes (1899), Schindler (1894), Chavannes (1892, 1895), Dail (1890), Schwahn (1892), Michels (1899), and Giles (1894, 1896).

35. Charles Rooney, "Utopian Literature as a Reflection of Social Forces in America, 1865–1917," Ph.D. dissertation, George Washington University, 1968, Ch. 5, pp. 194 ff.

36. Thomas Lake Harris, *The New Republic* (Santa Rosa, Calif.: Fountaingrove Press, 1891), pp. 49, 59.

37. Laurence Gronlund, "Our Destiny," *The Nationalist*, July 1890, p. 305.

38. David J. Pivar, *Purity Crusade: Sexual Morality and Social Control, 1868–1900* (Westport, Conn.: Greenwood Press, 1973), p. 233.

39. David A. Wheeler, *Our Industrial Utopia and Its Unhappy Citizens* (Chicago: A. C. McClurg, 1895), p. 292.

40. See Howells, *Traveler from Altruria* (note 25 above), pp. 262, 278–80, 283–84.

41. Edward Bellamy, *Looking Backward, 2000–1887* (Cambridge, Mass.: Belknap Press of Harvard University Press, 1967), pp. 221–22. See also David Bleich, "Eros and Bellamy," *American Quarterly*, 16 (Fall 1964), 445–59.

42. Bellamy, *Looking Backward*, p. 281.

43. Ibid., p. 230.

44. [William Simpson], *The Man from Mars* (San Francisco: Bacon, 1891), p. 134, and Chauncey Thomas, *The Crystal Button* (Boston: Houghton, Mifflin, 1891), 254–55.

45. Howe, "American Victorianism" (note 3 above), p. 521.

46. David D. Hall, "The Victorian Connection," in "Victorian Culture in America," p. 571.

47. Howe, "American Victorianism," p. 527.

48. Hall, "Victorian Connection," p. 571.

49. Laurence Gronlund, "Our Destiny," *The Nationalist*, September 1891, p. 141.

50. See Roemer, *Obsolete Necessity* (note 2 above), pp. 6–7; and Lokke, "Utopian Anti-Novel" (note 21 above), p. 141.

51. Howe, "American Victorianism," p. 528.

52. Olerich, *Cityless and Countryless World* (note 32 above), pp. 245–46; Thomas, *Crystal Button*, pp. 254–55; and James Cowan, *Daybreak: A Romance of an Old World* (New York: George H. Richmond, 1896), p. 56.

53. Howe, "American Victorianism," p. 529.

54. Richard C. Michaelis, *Looking Further Forward . . .* (Chicago and New York: Rand-McNally, 1890), pp. 78–80.

55. William E. Bridges, "Warm Hearth, Cold World: Social Perspectives on the Household Poets," *American Quarterly*, 21 (Winter 1969), 769.

56. See Roemer, *Obsolete Necessity*, Ch. 4.

57. Bellamy, *Looking Backward* (note 41 above), pp. 141–43.

SHORT-TITLE BIBLIOGRAPHY

The following bibliography is divided into six sections to suggest the diversity of the utopian literature published from 1888 to 1899. As mentioned in my introduction to this collection, it is difficult to find "pure" American eutopias and dystopias, so I had to categorize each work according to its main emphasis. Thus, Bachelder (1890) is listed with the eutopias, even though it contains anti-Bellamy material; and Twain (1889), Donnelly (1890), and Reynolds (1898) are placed with the dystopias, even though they sometimes express eutopian sentiments. For the definitions of antiutopias, satiric utopias, and partial utopias, see my introduction. I have included a brief list of nonfictional works. Most of them are only partially utopian, and many, many others could have been listed. But at least the list indicates some of the types of expository responses to the utopian fiction. For other titles of partially utopian fiction and nonfiction and for annotations to the following entries, see the bibliographies in *The Obsolete Necessity* and in Sargent's *British and American Utopias 1516–1975.*

As further evidence of the diversity and popularity of the utopian literature during this period, I have appended a supplemental list. These additional titles are selected from lists of works sent to me by Stuart Teitler and Lyman Tower Sargent. Except for works by Janet Von Swartwout (1895) and Charles Wooldridge (1898), I have included only titles that I could verify in *The National Union Catalogue; Pre-1956 Imprints.*

EUTOPIAS

1888 Bellamy, Edward. *Looking Backward, 2000–1887.*

1888 Hale, Edward Everett. *How They Lived in Hampton.*

1889 Bellamy, Charles Joseph. *An Experiment in Marriage.*

1889 [Lane, Mary E.]. *Mizora: A Prophecy.* (Serialized in the *Cincinnati Commercial,* 1880–1881.)

1890 [Bachelder, John]. *A.D. 2050. Electrical Development at Atlantis.*
1890 Cole, Cyrus. *The Auroraphone.*
1890 Fuller, Alvarado M. *A.D. 2000.*
1890 Leggett, Mortimer Dormer. *A Dream of a Modest Prophet.*
1890 Salisbury, Henry Barnard. *The Birth of Freedom, A Socialist Novel.* (A later edition was entitled *Miss Worden's Hero.*)
1890 Stone, Mrs. C. H. *One of "Berrian's" Novels.*
1890 [Worley, Frederick U.]. *Three Thousand Dollars A Year,* by Benefice (pseud.).
1891 [Allen, Henry Francis]. *A Strange Voyage. A Revision of the Key of Industrial Co-operative Government.*
1891 Fiske, Amos Kidder. *Beyond the Bourn.*
1891 Geissler, Ludwig A. *Looking Beyond.*
1891 [Simpson, William]. *The Man from Mars,* by Thomas Blot (pseud.).
1891 Thomas, Chauncey. *The Crystal Button.*
1892 Chavannes, Albert. *The Future Commonwealth, or, What Samuel Balcom Saw in Socioland.*
1892 [Crocker, Samuel]. *That Island,* by Theodore Oceanic Islet (pseud.).
1892 Donnelly, Ignatius. *The Golden Bottle, or, The Story of Ephram Benezet of Kansas.*
1892 Everett, Henry L. *The People's Program: The Twentieth Century Is Theirs.*
1892 Harben, William Nathanial. "In the Year Ten Thousand." *Arena,* November 1892, pp. 743–49.
1892 [McCowan, Archibald]. *Philip Meyer's Scheme. A Story of Trades Unionism,* by Luke A. Hedd (pseud.).
1892 [Moore, M. Louise]. *Al-Modad; or, Life Scenes Beyond the Polar Circumflex.*
1892 Tibbles, Thomas Henry, and Mrs. Elia (Wilkinson) Peattie. *The American Peasant, a Timely Allegory.*
1892 Tinckner, Mary Agnes. *San Salvador.*
1893 *The Beginning, a Romance of Chicago as It Might Be.*
1893 Howells, William Dean. *Letters of an Altrurian Traveller.* (Serialized in *The Cosmopolitan,* November 1893-September 1894; parts later incorporated into *Impressions and Experiences,* 1896, and *Through the Eye of the Needle,* 1907.)
1893 [Jones, Alice Ilgenfritz, and Ella Merchant]. *Unveiling a Parallel.*
1893 Miller, Joaquin. *The Building of the City Beautiful.*
1893 Olerich, Henry. *A Cityless and Countryless World: An Outline of Practical Co-operative Individualism.*
1893 Swift, Morrison Isaac. *A League of Justice, or, Is It Right to Rob the Robbers?*
1894 Astor, John Jacob. *A Journey in Other Worlds.*
1894 Brooks, Byron Alden. *Earth Revisited.*
1894 Giles, Fayette Stratton. *Shadows Before; or, A Century Onward.*
1894 Howells, William Dean. *A Traveler from Altruria. A Romance.* (Serialized in *The Cosmopolitan,* November 1892–October 1893.)
1894 Rosewater, Frank. *'96; A Romance of Utopia.* (A later edition was entitled *Utopia: A Romance of Today.*)
1894 Schindler, Solomon. *Young West.*

1894   Welcome, S. Byron. *From Earth's Centre, a Polar Gateway Message.*
1895   Bishop, William Henry. *The Garden of Eden, U.S.A. A Very Possible Story.*
1895   Chavannes, Albert. *In Brighter Climes, or Life in Socioland. A Realistic Novel.*
1895   Holford, Castello N. *Aristopia. A Romance-History of the New World.*
1895   [Howard, Albert Waldo]. *The Milltillionaire,* by M. Auburré Hovorrè (pseud.).
1895   Phelps, Corwin. *An Ideal Republic; or, Way Out of the Fog.* (©1895; American Politics, No. 10, February 1896.)
1895   Smith, Titus Keipler. *Altruria.*
1895   [Walker, John Brisben]. *A Brief History of Altruria,* by Sir Robert Harton (pseud.). (Serialized in *The Cosmopolitan,* November 1895–March 1896.)
1896   Cowan, James. *Daybreak; A Romance of an Old World.*
1896   [Emmens, Stephen Henry]. *The Sixteenth Amendment.*
1896   [McCoy, Dr. John]. *A Prophetic Romance, Mars to Earth.*
1896   *Man or Dollar, Which? A Novel.*
1896   Stump, D. L. *From World to World. A Novel.*
1897   Adams, Frederick Upham. *President John Smith.* (Originally published in serial form in the *Chicago Times.*)
1897   Bellamy, Edward. *Equality.*
1897   [Caryl, Charles W.]. *New Era.*
1897   [Galloway, James M.]. *John Harvey: A Tale of the Twentieth Century,* by Anon Moore (pseud.).
1897   Windsor, William. *Loma; A Citizen of Venus.*
1898   Athey, Henry, and A. Herbert Bowers. *With Gyves of Gold.*
1898   [Clarke, F. H.]. *The Co-opolitan; a Story of the Co-operative Commonwealth of Idaho,* by Zebina Forbush (pseud.).
1898   Craig, Alexander. *Ionia; Land of Wise Men and Fair Women.*
1898   [Rehm, Warren]. *The Practical City. A Future City Romance, or, A Study in Environment,* by Omen Nemo (pseud.).
1898   Sullivan, James William. "A Modern Co-operative Colony," in *So the World Goes.*
1898   [Wellman, Bert J.]. *The Legal Revolution of 1902.* (Occasionally attributed to William Stanley Child.)
1899   Bird, Arthur. *Looking Forward: A Dream of the United States of the Americas in 1999.*
1899   Bond, Daniel. *Uncle Sam in Business.*
1899   Mendes, Henry Pereira. *Looking Ahead. Twentieth Century Happenings.*
1899   Merrill, Albert Adams. *The Great Awakening; The Story of the Twenty-Second Century.*

DYSTOPIAS

1888   [De Mille, James]. *A Strange Manuscript Found in a Copper Cylinder.* (De Mille was born in Canada.)
1889   [Clemens, Samuel L.]. *A Connecticut Yankee in King Arthur's Court,* by Mark Twain (pseud.).
1889   Mitchell, John Ames. *The Last American.*

1890   [Donnelly, Ignatius]. *Caesar's Column: A Story of the Twentieth Century*, by Edmund Boisgilbert (pseud.).
1893   Niswonger, Charles Elliot. *The Isle of Femine*.
1894   Harben, William Nathanial. *The Land of the Changing Sun*.
1898   [Reynolds, Walter Doty]. *Mr. Jonnemacher's Machine. The Port to which we Drifted*.
1898   *The Rise and Fall of the United States. A Thin Leaf from History, A.D. 2060*.

ANTIUTOPIAS
1890   Michaelis, Richard C. *Looking Further Forward*.
1890   Satterlee, W. W. *Looking Backward and What I Saw*.
1890   Vinton, Arthur Dudley. *Looking Further Backward*.
1891   McGlasson, Eva Wilder (Brodhead). *Diana's Livery*.
1893   Roberts, J. W. *Looking Within*.
1894   Chamberlain, Henry Richardson. *6,000 Tons of Gold*.
1894   Pomeroy, William C. *The Lords of Misrule. A Tale of Gods and Men*.
1896   Lockwood, Ingersoll. *–1900—or, The Last President*.
1897   Orpen, Mrs. Adel (Elizabeth Richards). *Perfection City*.

SATIRIC UTOPIAS
1889   Heywood, D. Herbert. *The Twentieth Century. A Prophecy of the Coming Age*.
1890   Holmes, Oliver Wendell. "Over the Teacups, III." *Atlantic Monthly*, February 1890, pp. 232–43.
1894   Browne, Walter. *"2894"; or, The Fossil Man. (A Mid-Winter Night's Dream.)*
1895   Haedicke, Paul. *The Equalities of Para-Para*.
1898   North, Franklin H. *The Awakening of Noahville*.

PARTIAL UTOPIAS
1889   Bunce, Oliver Bell. *The Story of Happinolande and Other Legends*.
1889   [Petersilea, Carlyle]. *The Discovered Country*, by Ernst von Himmel (pseud.).
1889   Stockton, Frank Richard. *The Great War Syndicate*.
1889   [Woods, Katharine Pearson]. *Metzerott, Shoemaker*.
1890   Dail, Charles Curtis. *Willmoth the Wanderer; or The Man from Saturn*.
1890   Pittock, Mrs. M. A. (Weeks). *The God of Civilization*.
1890   [Porter, Linn Boyd]. *Speaking of Ellen*, by Albert Ross (pseud.).
1891   Bartlett, Mrs. Alice Elinor (Bowen). *A New Aristocracy*, by Birch Arnold (pseud.).
1891   Fitch, Thomas, and Anna M. Fitch. *Better Days, or A Millionaire of To-morrow*.
1891   Houston, Benjamin F. *The Rice Mills of Port Mystery*.
1891   McDougall, Walter Hugh. *The Hidden City*.
1891   Ramsey, Milton Worth. *Six Thousand Years Hence*.
1891   [Walker, Samuel]. *The Reign of Selfishness. A Story of Concentrated Wealth*. (Published later as *Dry Bread*.)
1892   [Austen, Edward J.]. *The Lost Island*. (Published also with Louise Vescelius Sheldon in *The Cosmopolitan*, January 1893, pp. 365–84.)

1892 Bradshaw, William R. *The Goddess of Atvatabar.*
1892 Daniel, Charles S. *Ai. A Social Vision.*
1892 Doughty, Francis Worcester. *Mirrikh; or, A Woman from Mars; A Tale of Occult Adventure.*
1892 Granville, Austyn. *The Fallen Race.*
1892 Grimshaw, Robert. *Fifty Years Hence: or What May Be in 1943.*
1892 Schwahn, John George. *The Tableau; or, Heaven as a Republic.*
1892 Stockwell, Lucius A. *The Earthquake. A Story of To-day.*
1894 Pope, Gustavus W. *Journey to Mars. The Wonderful World.*
1895 Davenport, Benjamin Rush. *"Uncle Sam's" Cabins. A Story of American Life Looking Forward a Century.*
1895 [Fitzpatrick, Earnest Hugh]. *The Marshal Duke of Denver; or, The Labor Revolution of 1920,* by Hugo Barnaby (pseud.).
1895 Lloyd, John Uri. *Etidorhpa or the End of Earth.*
1895 Mitchell, Willis. *The Inhabitants of Mars.*
1896 Burnham, Elcy. *Modern Fairyland.*
1896 Chambers, James Julius. *"In Sargasso." Missing.*
1897 Colburn, Frona Eunice Wait. *Yermah the Dorado.*
1897 Morris, Henry O. *Waiting for the Signal.*
1897 Sheldon, Charles Monroe. *In His Steps. "What Would Jesus Do?"* (First serialized in *The Advance* in 1896.)
1898 Bellamy, Edward. *The Blindman's World and Other Stories.*
1898 Davenport, Benjamin Rush. *Anglo-Saxons, Onward!*
1898 Farnell, George. *Rev. Josiah Hilton, the Apostle of the New Age.*
1898 Frederic, Harold. *Gloria Mundi.*
1898 Waterloo, Stanley. *Armageddon; A Tale of Love, War, and Invention.*
1899 Beale, Charles Willing. *The Secret of the Earth.*
1899 Franklin, Abraham Benjamin. *The Light of Reason.*
1899 Griggs, Sutton E. *Imperium in Imperio; A Study of the Negro Race Problem.*
1899 [Michels, Nicholas]. *The Godhood of Man,* by Nicolai Mikalowitch (pseud.).

SOME NONFICTION WITH UTOPIAN CONTENT
1889 Griffin, Crawford S. *Nationalism.*
1890 Gilpin, William. *The Cosmopolitan Railway Compacting and Fusing Together All the World's Continents.*
1890 Gronlund, Laurence. *Our Destiny. The Influence of Nationalism on Morals and Religion.* (First appeared in *The Nationalist,* March–September 1890.)
1890 Longley, Alcander. *What Is Communism? A Narrative of the Relief Community.*
1891 Harris, Thomas Lake. *The New Republic.*
1893 Russell, Addison Peale. *Sub-Coelum: A Sky-Built Human World.*
1893 Von Swartwout, Dr. William H. *Olumbia; or Utopia Made Practical.*
1894 Flower, Benjamin Orange. *The New Time.*
1894 Gillette, King Camp. *The Human Drift.*
1895 Call, Henry Laurens. *The Coming Revolution.*
1895 Lease, Mary Elizabeth (Clyens). *The Problem of Civilization Solved.*
1895 Wheeler, David Hilton. *Our Industrial Utopia and Its Unhappy Citizens.*
1896 Giles, Fayette Stratton. *The Industrial Army.*

1897   Flower, Benjamin Orange. *Equality and Brotherhood.*
1897   Harris, George. *Inequality and Progress.*
1898   Albertson, Ralph. *The Social Incarnation; Studies in the Faith of Practice.*
1898   Sanders, George A. *Reality; or Law and Order vs. Anarchy and Socialism.*
1899   Fishbough, William. *The End of Ages.*

SUPPLEMENTARY LIST OF UTOPIAN WORKS: A SAMPLE OF TITLES RECENTLY "DISCOVERED" BY TEITLER AND SARGENT

1888   Batchelor, John M. *A Strange People.*
1888   Leonhart, Rudolph. *The Treasure of Montezuma.*
1889   Clark, Francis Edward. *The Mossback Correspondence, . . . with a Short Account of His Visit to Utopia.*
1890   McMartin, Donald. *A Leap into the Future; or, How Things Will Be; A Romance of the Year 2000.*
1890   [Miller, George Noyes]. *The Strike of a Sex.*
1891   Fitzporter, John L. *My Vacation; or, The Millennium.*
1891   Leland, Samuel Phelps. *Peculiar People.*
1891   Norton, Seymour Francis. *Ten Men of Money Island.* (Originally published in the Chicago *Sentinel* in 1879 and 1885.)
1892   Beard, Daniel Carter. *Moonblight, and Six Feet of Romance.*
1892   Braine, Robert D. *Messages from Mars.*
1892   Cowdon, James Seldon. *Pantocracy; or, The Reign of Justice.*
1893   Leonhart, Rudolph. *Either, or.*
1895   Aikin, Charles. *Forty Years with the Damned; or, Life Inside the Earth.*
1895   Marshall, Luther. *Thomas Boobig.*
1895   Miller, George Noyes. *After the Sex Struck.*
1895   Von Swartwout, Janet. *Heads; or, The City of the Gods; A Narrative of Olumbia in the Wilderness.*
1896   [Burg, Swan]. *The Light of Eden; or, A Historical Narrative of the Barbarian Age.*
1897   Bellsmith, Henry Wentworth. *Henry Cadavere: A Study of Life and Work.*
1897   [Flood, John Heber]. *The Great Seven—The Greater Nine; A Story for the People,* by Jno. H. Flood, Jr. (pseud.).
1897   Little, William. *A Visit to Topos, and How the Science of Heredity Is Practiced There.*
1898   Dail, Charles Curtis. *The Stone Giant. A Story of the Mammoth Cave.*
1898   Hix, J. Emile (pseud.). *. . . Can a Man Live Forever?*
1898   Odell, Samuel W. *The Last War; . . . A Story of the Twenty-sixth Century.*
1898   Wooldridge, Charles William. *The Kingdom of Heaven Is at Hand.*
1899   [Adolph, Anna]. *Arqtiq; A Study of the Marvels at the North Pole.*
1899   Brady, Adhemar. *The Mathematics of Labor.*
1899   Dake, Charles Romyn. *A Strange Discovery.*

HOWARD P. SEGAL

Utopia Diversified: 1900–1949

I

EVEN THOUGH THERE was a decline in utopian literature during the first half of the twentieth century, the genre certainly did not disappear. I am aware of 236 utopian works published between 1900 and 1949. Of these, 121, or about half, have been available for this study.[1] Although the availability of all 236 works would naturally allow for a fuller analysis, the basic contention about utopian writings during this period probably would not be altered. For the outstanding characteristic of these 121 works is their diversity, both of general orientation toward the future and of the specific kind of future envisioned. There is no one prevalent attitude toward utopia per se and no one prevalent vision of utopia. Nor is there any one apparent historical event or trend during this half century that might account for these diversities.

To be sure, such diversities characterize the utopian writings of most other periods of American history, as the other surveys in Part IV of this collection make clear. Utopias are by their very nature as often individualistic as imitative. Furthermore, the relative length of the period examined here, the comparatively large number of utopian works published, and the considerable number of major historical events—wars, revolutions, depressions, migrations—that occurred ought to make such diversities expected rather than unexpected. Still, the diversification of utopia does not preclude a search for other, perhaps "middle-range" generalizations.

II

There was a definite decline in the number of utopian works—eutopias, partial utopias, and dystopias alike—published during these years in comparison with the preceding eleven, the years after the appearance of Edward Bellamy's *Looking Backward* (1888). For that book's extraordinary popularity prompted an unprecedented and in fact unsurpassed flood of visionary writings. Whereas Roemer's list supplemented by the findings of Teitler and Sargent totals 172 titles for 1888 to 1899, I find 93 for 1900–1911, with a further marked decline in the decades after 1910, when 88 such works appeared: 36 for 1910–20, 39 for 1920–30, 46 for 1930–40, and 27 for 1940–49.

Comparisons with the pre-1888 and post-1950 periods are also revealing. Joel Nydahl finds only 24 eutopias, satiric utopias, and dystopias for the entire period 1715–1864, and Charles J. Rooney only 15 for that of 1865–87. In contrast, Lyman T. Sargent's bibliography in this collection totals 266 American and British works for the period 1950–75. Yet Sargent's works are mostly in the form of science fiction, the principal form utopianism took after 1950—a form which, he readily admits, differs significantly from "genuine" utopianism in intention, in style, and in content. Sargent's figures therefore reflect no necessary resurgence of utopianism after 1950.

As in the other periods there is, to repeat, a diversity of general orientations toward the future. Of the 121 works in the present sample, 80 are authentic eutopias, with full-fledged descriptions of supposedly perfect societies to be brought about by various means. Fourteen others are partial utopias, whether "mere" reform tracts seeking only modest changes within existing society or "exotic" science fiction tales seeking escape from (though also eventual return to) that same society or "realistic" accounts seeking its substantial improvement but not—given imperfect human nature—its outright perfection. A final 27 are dystopias, whether satiric utopias mocking the pretensions of would-be perfectionists or antiutopias lamenting the fatal flaws of seemingly successful perfectionists.

Also, as in the rest of the history of American utopian literature, there is a diversity of specific visions of the future. Apart from details, this diversity is most apparent in terms of principal theme: that is, at once the principal mechanism for realizing utopia and the principal objective of its realization (other than personal fulfillment and societal advance, the objectives of presumably all eutopias). Of the 80 eutopias in the sample, 16 have as their principal theme "pure" socialism; 23, semisocialist or nonsocialist profit sharing and cooperation; 5, revived Bellamy Nationalism; 7, a combination of private enterprise and public welfare; 3, "pure" capitalism; 13, a combination of religious altruism and agrarian simplicity; 7, benevolent dictatorship; 2, monetary changes; 2, greater equality for blacks; 2, greater equality for women; and 1, syndicalism.

These thematic divisions are not, however, completely rigid. Certain components of several principal themes also appear in other of these 80 works, but as subsidiary themes rather than as parts of the principal one. When their numbers are added to those just cited the thematic divisions are partially erased. The most important such components are government-sponsored public welfare programs and institutions, found in 60 of the 80 works (whether as part of the principal theme or as a separate subsidiary one); cooperation, found in 50; civic and economic equality, whether as absolute economic equality or as equality of opportunity, found in 47; scientific and technological advance, found in 45; religion, usually Christian and invariably altruistic, found in 31; honest, effective, nonpartisan government, whether democratic, representative, or elitist, found in 31; businesslike efficiency, found in 27; and private enterprise, found in 20.

In addition to these component themes, others appear in fewer than 20 of these 80 works, again either as parts of the principal theme or as separate subsidiary themes. These more minor component themes include individualism; the eradication of war, crime, and poverty; the simplification of legal codes and the elimination of lawyers; the application of the single tax; educational, occupational, and political advancement strictly by merit; the improvement of the species through eugenics; and the erection of model cities and model landscapes.

It is notable that these same principal and component themes also characterize both the 14 partial utopias and the 27 dystopias. Their function in the case of the former is similar to their function in that of the eutopias: as both the means and the end(s) of utopia or at least of a society better than the existing one. Thus David Lubin's *Let There Be Light* (1900) is a "mere" reform tract advocating semisocialist cooperation, quasi-religious altruism, and scientific advance, albeit within existing society; Mark Wicks's *To Mars Via the Moon* (1911) is a science fiction tale describing a technologically advanced, thoroughly egalitarian, and fully cooperative society implicitly resembling heaven; and Granville Hicks's *The First to Awaken* (1940) is a "realistic" account nevertheless seeking a substantial measure of socialism, cooperation, and scientific and technological advance. In contrast, the function of these themes in the case of dystopias is as both the means and the end(s) of fatally flawed would-be utopias or of antiutopias. Thus the objects of criticism in such dystopias as Caroline Mason's *A Woman of Yesterday* (1900), William Wright's *The Great Bread Trust* (1900), David Parry's *The Scarlet Empire* (1906), Henry Sedgwick's "The Coup D'Etat of 1961" (1908), and Victor Rousseau Emanuel's *The Messiah of the Cylinder* (1917) are, as a whole, cooperation, altruism, religion, capitalism, socialism, political corruption, and scientific and technological advance.

As this overlapping of themes among the utopias suggests, the fundamental ideological and structural differences between, for example, a semisocialist cooperative utopia and a Bellamy Nationalist one, or between a semicapitalist utopia and a strictly capitalist one, are comparatively modest. Such similarities bind others of the 80 eutopias. Thus practically all the socialist, semisocialist, semicapitalist, Nationalist, and agrarian utopias seek some measure of cooperation, equality, efficiency, and honest government.

Most of them also seek some measure of scientific and technological advance and of religious or quasi-religious altruism.

Further thematic connections may be drawn, and not only within the present sample but also between it and Roemer's sample of late-nineteenth-century utopian works. For as with many of the 80 eutopias, so with many of his several seemingly antithetical themes regularly appear: individualism and cooperation; scientific and technological change and social order; private enterprise and public welfare; hard work and leisure; and religious or quasi-religious altruism and businesslike efficiency. And as with Roemer's works, so with these, the antitheses are indeed only seeming, for to the utopists of both periods not conflict but rather a definite complementarity exists within each pair. As both groups of utopists attempt to prove, under their respective schemes citizens would find individual fulfillment by working with one another, would create a new social order through scientific and technological change, would pursue private enterprise in a public welfare state, would enjoy leisure after working hard, and would be altruistic after being efficient.

Thematic connections may be drawn among as well as within these pairs and simultaneously again to Roemer's sample. For many of these utopists, like many of their immediate predecessors, view material progress as less an end in itself than a means to social and moral progress. To both groups material improvements, though not unimportant in their own right, are more important in providing the basis for a harmonious social order in which in turn moral virtues like cooperation, altruism, equality, and efficiency may be fully realized.

Chronological as well as thematic connections may be drawn to many of Roemer's works. For, as the table opposite demonstrates, a majority of the 80 works and, for that matter, a majority of the 121 in the sample, appeared between 1900 and 1920—the years closest to Roemer's period. This concentration holds true, moreover, for almost every thematic division and for partial utopias and dystopias as much as for eutopias. That there should be at least some thematic overlap with Roemer's works is, consequently, hardly surprising.

Notwithstanding this chronological concentration in the early twentieth century, works expressing most of these principal themes span the bulk of this half-century. Thus those works "about" socialism run from Henry Drayton's *In Oudemon* (1900) to Robert Frank's *Social Integration* (1935); those "about" semisocialist or nonsocialist profit sharing and cooperation, from Milan Edson's *Solaris Farm* (1900) to Emanuel Posnack's *The 21st Century Looks Back* (1946); those "about" revived Bellamy Nationalism, from Paul Devinne's *The Day of Prosperity* (1902) to A. T. Churchill's *The New Industrial Dawn* (1939); those "about" combined private enterprise and public welfare, from George S. Morison's *The New Epoch* (1903) to Prestonia Martin's *Prohibiting Poverty* (1932); those "about" capitalism, from Edward

NUMBER OF UTOPIAN WORKS PER DECADE, BY THEME

Utopian Themes	1900–10	1911–20	1921–30	1931–40	1941–49
Bellamy Nationalism	2			3	
Socialism	11	2	2	1	
Semisocialistic or non-socialistic profit sharing and cooperation	11	3	5	2	2
Private enterprise and public welfare	4	1	1	1	
Capitalism	1	1		1	
Religious altruism and agrarian simplicity	8	1	1	1	1
Benevolent dictatorship	2	3	1		1
Black equality	1	1			
Female equality		1	1		
Monetary reform			2		
Partial utopias	9	3		2	
Dystopias	13	6		4	4

Caswell's *Toil and Self* (1900) to Ayn Rand's *Anthem* (1938); those "about" benevolent dictatorship, from Simon Newcomb's *His Wisdom, The Defender* (1900) to B. F. Skinner's *Walden Two* (1948); and those "about" religious altruism and agrarian simplicity, from Frank Baum's partial utopia *The Wonderful Wizard of Oz* (1900) to Austin Wright's *Islandia* (1942). The time span for works expressing the leading component themes, whether as parts of the principal themes or as subsidiary themes, is even broader but need not be detailed here. It is notable that the time span for both the partial utopias and the dystopias is similarly broad: from Albert Hoskin's *The City Problem* (1900) to Granville Hicks's *The First to Awaken* (1940) in the one case and from Charles Bayne's *The Fall of Utopia* (1900) to George Stewart's *Earth Abides* (1949) in the other.

III

No one work shapes the utopian writings of this period or even part of this period in the way *Looking Backward* shaped the last decade of the nineteenth century, but then no other single work does that for any other period in the history of American utopian literature. Still, among the several works of these years one may retrospectively call "important,"[2] the diversity of both general orientation toward the future and the specific kind of future envisioned is striking. In chronological order, these works include Simon

Newcomb's *His Wisdom, The Defender* (1900), which advocates the achievement of permanent and universal peace via the selective use of advanced
weapons and the consequent establishment of a benevolent dictatorship;
William Dean Howells's *Through the Eye of the Needle* (1907), a sequel to
his *A Traveler from Altruria* (1894), which emphasizes cooperation, altruism, agrarianism, and village life; Jack London's *The Iron Heel* (1907), a
utopian dystopia, to borrow Beauchamp's term, which opposes capitalist
plutocracy—and despite its pessimism, points toward a socialist eutopia;
King C. Gillette's *World Corporation* (1910), an extension of *The Human
Drift* (1894), which predicts a giant joint stock company that will eventually
control all the material resources of the United States and the consequent
creation of a society based upon material equality and efficiency; Edward
House's *Philip Dru* (1912), which advocates a benevolent American dictatorship to effect various political, constitutional, economic, and social
changes; Ralph Adams Cram's *Walled Towns* (1919), which calls for the
restoration of medieval Catholicism, small communities, guilds, crafts, and
order in opposition to the bigness, materialism, and impersonalization of
the modern world; Vachel Lindsay's partial utopia *The Golden Book of
Springfield* (1920), which contrasts the material progress in Springfield,
Illinois, between 1918 and 2018 with the moral, political, and intellectual
stagnation within that same period; Harold Loeb's *Life in a Technocracy*
(1933), which delineates the platform of the Technocracy movement as the
economic basis for a society stressing social and cultural as well as material
progress; Sinclair Lewis's dystopia *It Can't Happen Here* (1935), which
opposes a native American fascist regime and advocates—and like *The Iron
Heel* does not rule out—some form of democratic socialism; Ayn Rand's
Anthem (1938), which criticizes collectivism and socialism and advocates
individualism and capitalism; Granville Hicks's partial utopia *The First to
Awaken* (1940), which argues for socialism, cooperation, and scientific and
technological advance but like *The Golden Book of Springfield* is skeptical
about the prospects for human perfectibility; Austin Wright's *Islandia* (1942),
which advocates agrarianism, simplicity, and close personal relations in retreat from Western materialism, selfishness, and complexity; and the primary subject of Robert Plank's essay, B. F. Skinner's *Walden Two* (1948),
which depicts a benevolent dictatorship in a commune based upon behavioral engineering, psychological conditioning, and, specifically, positive reinforcement.

IV

In the absence of a historical explanation of their overall diversity, one
can still make specific correlations between certain of these 121 works and

certain historical events of the period under discussion. For example, Morrison Swift's *The Monarch Billionaire* (1903) advocated syndicalism over trade unionism and socialism just when such ideological conflicts plagued "real" world radicals; E. A. Johnson's *Light Ahead for the Negroes* (1904) and Lillian Jones's *Five Generations Hence* (1916) both argued for greater freedom and equality for blacks just when their fortunes had reached the lowest point since the Civil War; Charlotte Perkins Gilman's three utopias—*Moving the Mountain* (1911), *Herland* (1915), and *With Her in Ourland* (1916)—emphasized female equality with men just when the women's suffrage crusade reached its peak; Edward House's *Philip Dru* (1912) seemed a virtual blueprint for the incoming President Woodrow Wilson; Thomas Dixon's *The Fall of a Nation* (1916) advocated both American isolationism and a strong national defense on the eve of the Russian Revolution and the entry of the United States into Europe's "Great War"; William H. Harvey's *Paul's School of Statesmanship* (1924) offered paper currency in reaction to the depression, especially in agriculture, of the post–World War I years; Harold Loeb's *Life in a Technocracy* (1933) was an explicit blueprint for the then fledgling Technocracy movement; Sinclair Lewis's *It Can't Happen Here* (1935) opposed the real prospect of nascent fascism; and Erwin Lessner's *Phantom Victory* (1944) opposed a potential Fourth Reich arising from the ruins of the still potent Third.

One can also make somewhat broader correlations between certain groups of these 121 works and certain historical trends of the period. For instance, those works advocating or opposing socialism, concentrated as they are in the first two decades of the twentieth century, were obvious reactions to the rise and fall of socialism in America during those same years. Similar correlations apply to those works advocating or opposing large-scale corporate capitalism in its rise during those same years and to those advocating or opposing a revived Bellamy Nationalism following its decline after 1900.

Finally, one can make still broader correlations between most of the eutopias of the early twentieth century and the "Progressive Ethos" of the same period as described in an important essay by Clyde Griffen.[3] Insofar as these works differ from those discussed by Roemer, it is largely as a reflection of this new ethos. Although Griffen himself links this ethos to the intellectual, cultural, and social currents of both the pre-1900 and the post-1920 eras, he emphasizes the blend of such currents that made the two decades unique: an equal balance of religion and science. As indicated, a similar balance characterizes many of these eutopias.

To be more precise, these Progressives and utopists both sought a perfect or perfectible society in which such religious or quasi-religious values as brotherhood, cooperation, equality, justice, and altruism could mesh easily with such scientific or quasi-scientific values as efficiency, planning, management, and professionalization. The society both groups envisioned, moreover, would be a scientifically and technologically advanced and thoroughly meritocratic and democratic one. It would be founded upon the assumption that "man can [scientifically] direct social change to rational purposes"[4] but also to ethical purposes, there again being no conflict between the two. For to utopists as to Progressives it appeared possible "to accommodate the methods and values of an emerging urban, bureaucratic, and relativistic society without seeming to abandon those of an older America of smaller communities and simpler, more secure faith."[5] And to both groups ultimate success seemed assured.

Success, however, came to neither group. At least some of these objectives have, of course, been partially fulfilled in the United States—the "real" world—since 1920. Yet the particular orientation toward both religion and science was, as Griffen admits, lost after that date. Just as these religious or quasi-religious values had, as he shows, been emphasized to the near exclusion of the scientific ones before 1900, so the reverse took place after 1920.[6] The "Progressive Ethos" consequently does not describe, much less account for, the utopian works published beyond that year.

The diversification of American utopias from 1900 to 1949 is not necessarily problematic, save perhaps to the overly zealous scholarly synthesizer. For what John Veiby wrote in *The Utopian Way* (1917) about such diversity still bears repeating:

The main trouble with utopians heretofore seems to have been that they sought to make their utopias *one*. For my utopia may not be your utopia, and ours not that of a third, etc.; for this must be the first question in regard to any and all utopias proposed: What is there in it for me? By making them many and *different* we shall avoid that stumbling block.[7]

NOTES

1. The remaining 115 works have, for various reasons, been unavailable for use for this essay.

2. The importance of these works in retrospect has no bearing, of course, upon their reception by critics, much less upon their popularity, at the time of their publication.

3. Clyde Griffen, "The Progressive Ethos," Stanley Coben and Lorman Ratner, eds., *The Development of an American Culture* (Englewood Cliffs, N.J.: Prentice-Hall, 1970), pp. 120–49. Griffen's conception of Progressivism will not accord with that of certain other historians, so multifaceted and therefore so controversial is the phenomenon. His conception is nevertheless the most balanced and persuasive I know.

4. Ibid., p. 138.

5. Ibid., p. 124.

6. On these changes before and after 1900–1920 see the essays here by Charles J. Rooney and Kenneth M. Roemer, as well as Howard P. Segal, "Technological Utopianism and American Culture, 1830–1940," Ph.D. dissertation, Princeton University, 1975, Chs. 1, 4.

7. John Veiby, *The Utopian Way* (South Bend, Ind.: n.p., 1917), p. 9.

SHORT-TITLE BIBLIOGRAPHY

The following bibliography is divided into four sections: eutopias, dystopias, partial utopias, and supplementary utopias. The first three categories have already been defined. The fourth consists, quite simply, of the remaining 115 known utopias of whatever kind that were not available for use for this essay. I'd like to express my gratitude to Lyman Tower Sargent, who called my attention to many of the titles listed in this bibliography.

EUTOPIAS

1900 [Caswell, Edward A.]. *Toil and Self.*
1900 Drayton, Henry S. *In Oudemon.*
1900 Edson, Milan C. *Solaris Farm.*
1900 [Grigsby, Alcanoan O.]. *Nequa; or, The Problem of the Ages*, by Jack Adams (pseud.).
1900 Newcomb, Simon. *His Wisdom, The Defender.*
1900 Peck, Bradford. *The World a Department Store: A Story of Life Under a Cooperative System.*
1900 Persinger, Clark E. *Letters from New America; or, An Attempt at Practical Socialism.*
1901 Frisbie, Henry S. *Prophet of the Kingdom.*
1901 McGrady, Thomas. *Beyond the Black Ocean.*
1901 Paine, Albert Bigelow. *The Great White Way.*
1901 Taylor, William A. *Intermere.*
1902 Cooley, Winnifred H. "A Dream of the Twenty-first Century." *Arena*, 28 (November 1902), 511–16.
1902 Devinne, Paul. *The Day of Prosperity: A Vision of the Century to Come.*
1902 Wooldridge, Charles William. *Perfecting the Earth.*
1903 Dague, Robert A. *Henry Ashton.*
1903 Morison, George S. *The New Epoch as Developed by the Manufacture of Power.*
1903 Noto, Cosimo. *The Ideal City.*
1903 Swift, Morrison I. *The Monarch Billionaire.*
1904 Davis, Nathan. *Beulah; Or A Parable of Social Regeneration.*
1904 Johnson, E. A. *Light Ahead for the Negroes.*
1905 Armour, John P. *Edenindia: A Tale of Adventure.*
1905 Fry, Lena Jane. *Other Worlds.*
1905 Peterson, Ephraim. *An Ideal City for an Ideal People.*
1905 Rogers, Bessie S. *As It May Be, A Story of the Future.*

1906 Hillman, H. W. *Looking Forward.*
1907 Howells, William Dean. *Through the Eye of the Needle.*
1907 Hutchinson, Alfred L. *The Limit of Wealth.*
1907 Lull, D. *Celestia.*
1907 Sinclair, Upton. *The Industrial Republic.*
1907 [Spaulding, Wayland]. *When Theodore Is King.*
1908 Hatfield, Richard. *Geyserland, 9262 B.C.: Empiricisms in Social Reform.*
1908 London, Jack. "Goliah." *The Red Magazine* (London), 2 (December 1908), 115–29.
1908 Rice, Harry E. *Eve and the Evangelist: A Romance of A.D. 2108.*
1908 Rosewater, Frank. *The Making of a Millennium.*
1908 Steere, C. A. *When Things Were Doing.*
1909 Brant, John Ira. *The New Regime, A.D. 2202.*
1909 [Kirwan, Thomas]. *Reciprocity in the Thirtieth Century*, by William Wonder (pseud.).
1909 Peterson, Ephraim. *Redemption.*
1909 [Phelps, George Hamilton]. *The New Columbia; or, The re-United States,* by Patrick Quinn Tangent (pseud.).
1910 Chambless, Edgar. *Roadtown.*
1910 Gillette, King Camp. *World Corporation.*
1911 Gilman, Charlotte Perkins. *Moving the Mountain.* (See also Gilman's *Herland,* 1915, and *With Her in Ourland,* 1916; all three works were serialized in *The Forerunner.*)
1911 [Horner, Jacob W.]. *Military Socialism*, by Walter H. Sensney (pseud.).
1912 Brinsmade, Herman Hine. *Utopia Achieved.*
1912 [House, Edward M.]. *Philip Dru, Administrator.*
1913 Hayes, Jeff W. *Portland, Oregon, A.D. 1999.*
1914 Henry, Walter O. *Equitania; or, The Land of Equity.*
1915 England, George A. *The Air Trust.*
1915 Olerich, Henry. *Modern Paradise.*
1916 Chapman, Richard Marvin. *A Vision of the Future.*
1916 Hughes, Thomas J. *State Socialism After the War.*
1916 Jones, Lillian B. *Five Generations Hence.*
1917 Veiby, John. *The Utopian Way.*
1919 Cram, Ralph Adams. *Walled Towns.*
1921 Bruce, Stewart E. *The World in 1931.*
1921 Fowler, Horace D. *The Industrial Public.*
1922 Kayser, Martha. *The Aerial Flight to the Realm of Peace.*
1923 Clough, Fred M. *The Golden Age; or The Depth of Time.*
1923 Olerich, Henry. *The Story of the World a Thousand Years Hence.*
1923 Pauer, Louis. *Eurekanian Paternalism.*
1924 Bottomley, Samuel. *A Message from "Mars."* (Bottomley published sequels to this book in 1925 and 1926.)
1924 Gillette, King Camp. *The People's Corporation.*
1924 Harvey, William H. *Paul's School of Statesmanship.*
1927 Maxim, Hudson. "The City of the Future." In Clifton Johnson, *The Rise of an American Inventor,* pp. 280–88.

1929 Fuller, Frederick T. *Beyond the Selvas: A Vision of a Republic.*
1930 Harris, Frank. *Pantopia.*
1931 Wilkins, Hilliard. *Altrurian Farms.*
1932 Martin, Prestonia M. *Prohibiting Poverty.*
1932 Palmer, Frederick. *So a Leader Came.*
1933 Loeb, Harold. *Life in a Technocracy: What It Might Be Like.*
1934 Sumner, Park. *Tomorrow Comes.*
1935 Frank, Robert. *Social Integration.*
1935 Parker, Joseph W. *Doctor Crosby's Strange Experience; or, A New World by 1944.*
1936 Sinclair, Upton. *Co-op.*
1938 Rand, Ayn. *Anthem.*
1939 Churchill, A. T. *The New Industrial Dawn.*
1942 Wright, Austin T. *Islandia.*
1944 Ardrey, Robert. *Worlds Beginning.*
1946 Posnack, Emanuel R. *The 21st Century Looks Back.*
1948 Skinner, B. F. *Walden Two.*

DYSTOPIAS
1900 Bayne, Charles J. *The Fall of Utopia.*
1900 Mason, Caroline A. *A Woman of Yesterday.*
1900 Rogers, Lebbeus H. *The Kite Trust: A Romance of Wealth.*
1900 Wilson, John Grosvenor. *The Monarch of Millions.*
1900 Wright, William H. *The Great Bread Trust.*
1903 Cook, William W. *A Round Trip to the Year 2000.*
1903 Snyder, John. *The Wind Trust.*
1906 Burroughs, Joseph B. *Titan, Son of Saturn: The Coming World Emperor.*
1906 Parry, David M. *The Scarlet Empire.*
1907 London, Jack. *The Iron Heel.*
1908 Sedgwick, Henry D. "The Coup D'Etat of 1961," in *The New American Type and Other Essays.*
1909 Dixon, Thomas. *Comrades.*
1910 Gratacap, Louis P. *The Mayor of New York.*
1911 *Our Sister Republic: A Single Tax Story.*
1911 Schuette, H. George. *Athonia; or, The Original Four Hundred.*
1915 Stauffer, Mack. *Humanity and the Mysterious Knight.*
1917 [Emanuel, Victor Rousseau]. *The Messiah of the Cylinder*, by Victor Rousseau (pseud.).
1919 Pallen, Conde B. *Crucible Island.*
1920 Hastings, Milo. *City of Endless Night.*
1933 Herrick, Robert. *Sometime.*
1935 Lewis, Sinclair. *It Can't Happen Here.*
1937 Serly, Ludovicus Textoris. *Stop! . . . Distracted People!*
1937 Wilson, Henry L. *Of Lunar Kingdoms.*
1944 Lessner, Erwin C. *Phantom Victory: The Fourth Reich, 1945–1960.*
1947 Heard, Henry Fitzgerald. *The Doppelgangers.*
1949 McCarthy, Mary. *The Oasis.*

1949   Stewart, George. *Earth Abides.*

Partial Utopias

1900   Baum, Lyman Frank. *The Wonderful Wizard of Oz.*
1900   Hoskin, Albert. *The City Problem.*
1900   Lubin, David. *Let There Be Light; The Story of a Workingmen's Club.*
1900   Myers, Cortland. *Would Christ Belong to a Labor Union?*
1903   Gratacap, Louis P. *Certainty of a Future Life in Mars.*
1905   Harris, William C. *Life in a Thousand Worlds.*
1909   Alexander, James B. *The Lunarian Professor.*
1909   Rock, James. *Thro' Space.*
1910   Dowding, Henry W. *The Man from Mars.*
1911   Wicks, Mark. *To Mars via the Moon.*
1916   Dixon, Thomas. *The Fall of a Nation.*
1920   Lindsay, Vachel. *The Golden Book of Springfield.*
1934   Reitmeister, Louis A. *If Tomorrow Comes.*
1940   Hicks, Granville. *The First to Awaken.*

Supplementary Utopias

1900   Evans, Chris. *Eurasia.*
1900   Williams, Frank P. *Hallie Marshall.*
1901   Borders, Joe H. *The Queen of Appalachia.*
1901   Gilman, Bradley. *Back to the Soil.*
1901   Henley, Carra D. *A Man from Mars.*
1902   Perry, James R. "The Constitution of Carnegia." *North American Review,* 175 (August 1902), 243–53.
1903   Bunker, Ira S. *A Thousand Years Hence.*
1903   Sinclair, Upton. *Prince Hagen.*
1904   Lloyd, John W. *The Dwellers in Vale Sunrise.*
1904   Ross, Olin J. *The Sky Blue.*
1905   Marks, William D. *An Equal Opportunity.*
1906   Casparian, Gregory. *An Anglo-American Alliance.*
1907   Firmin, Albert B. "The Altrurian Era." *Altruria,* 1 (September 1907), 9–17.
1907   Harding, Ellison. *The Demetrian.*
1908   Emerson, Willis G. *The Smoky God.*
1908   Martin, Nettie Parrish. *A Pilgrim's Progress in Other Worlds.*
1908   Maxim, Hudson. "Man's Machine-made Millennium." *Cosmopolitan,* 45 (November 1908), 569–76.
1908   *The Reverend John Smith Died.*
1908   Stevens, Isaac N. *The Liberators.*
1908   Stevens, John. *The Realm of Light.*
1909   Blanchard, Henry P. *After the Cataclysm.*
1909   Clarke, Francis H. *Morgan Rockefeller's Will.*
1909   Pressey, Edward P. *The Vision of New Clairvaux.*
1909   Rhodes, H. Henry. *Where Men Have Walked.*
1909   Wright, Allen Kendrick. *To the Poles by Airship.*

1912 Hile, William H. *The Ostrich for the Defense.*
1912 Lewis, Dewitt F. *A Trip to the North Pole.*
1912 Newman, H. E. *The Prophet.*
1914 Neff, M. A. *Paradise Found.*
1915 Tracy, Roger S. *The White Man's Burden.*
1917 Reynaert, John H. *The Eldorado of Socialism.*
1918 Morrill, Fred B. *Beyond the Horizon.*
1919 Bruere, Martha B. *Mildred Carver, U.S.A.*
1919 Carnevali, Emanuel. "Utopia of the Men Who Come Back from the War" (poem). *Touchstone*, 5 (July 1919), 308.
1919 Fairfield, Frederick P. *Story of the City of Works.*
1919 Guthrie, Kenneth S. *A Romance of Two Centuries.*
1919 Koepsel, Louis H. *A Prophecy: The Human Community.*
1919 Marshall, James. *1960 (A Retrospect).*
1920 Rosewater, Frank. *Doomed.*
1921 Hall, Austin. *The Blind Spot.*
1921 Roche, Arthur S. *The Day of Faith.*
1922 Scrymsour, Ella. *The Perfect World.*
1922 Wright, Allen Kendrick. *Dalleszona and the Seventh Treasure.*
1922 X (pseud.). *1943.*
1923 Ball, Frank P. *My Wondrous Dream.*
1923 Griesser, Wilhelm. *The Welcome Island: Story and Laws.*
1923 Pauer, Louis. *The Day of Judgment.*
1923 [Thompson, Harriet Alfarata (Chapman)]. *Idealia.*
1923 Tilden, Freeman. *Mr. Podd.*
1923 Veiby, John. *Utopian Essays.*
1924 Pettersen, Rena O. *Venus.*
1924 Triplett, Henry Franklin. *Negrolana.*
1925 Dell, Berenice V. *The Silent Voice.*
1925 Fox, Richard A. *The People on Other Planets.*
1925 Rosewater, Frank. *Easy Millions.*
1925 Williams, Arthur. *Looking Forward.*
1925 Willoughby, Frank. *Through the Needle's Eye.*
1925 Winship, Glen B. *Volonor.*
1927 Barker, Arthur W. *The Light from Sealonia.*
1927 Mette, John Allen. *The Ideal State.*
1929 Clock, Herbert. *The Light in the Sky.*
1929 Salisbury, William. *The Square Heads.*
1930 Baxter, Garrett. *Bamboa.*
1930 Bradford, Columbus. *Terrania.*
1930 Schinagel, Geza. *Possibilities.*
1930 Vassos, John, and Ruth Vassos. *Ultimo.*
1931 Dalton, Charles Test. *The Richest Man on Earth.*
1931 Schuette, H. George. *The Grand Mysterious Secret Marriage Temple.*
1932 Baxter, Garrett. *Rosma.*
1932 Blanchard, Charles E. *A New Day Dawns.*
1932 Lawrence, James C. *The Year of Regeneration.*

1932 McCutchen, Duval. *America Made Young.*

1932 O'Sheel, Shaemas. *It Could Never Happen.*

1933 Rizk, C. M. *The Paradise City.*

1934 Bradley, Charles M. *Me-Phi Bo-Sheth (If The Gods So Decide).*

1934 Cooke, David E. *The History of Lewistonia.*

1934 Yerex, Cuthbert. *Christopher Brand.*

1935 Goldsmith, John Francis. *President Randolph.*

1935 Gotthelf, Ezra G. *The Island of Not-Me.*

1935 Meyer, John J. *Thirteen Seconds That Rocked the World.*

1935 [Wybraniec, Peter Frank]. *Speratia*, by Raphael W. Leonhart (pseud.).

1936 Allen, Henry W. *Prosperity in the Year 2000 A.D.*

1936 Lyonds, Edgar A. *The Chosen Race.*

1936 Nelson, Albert D. *America Betrayed.*

1936 Nicolaides, Nicholas. *At the Dawn of the Millennium.*

1936 Samuels, Philip F. *Bensalem and New Jerusalem.*

1936 Wolf, Howard. *Greener Pastures.*

1937 Pritcher, Jacob L. *A Love Starved World.*

1937 Smith, David E. *Every Man a Millionaire.*

1938 Morris, Martha M. *No Borderland.*

1939 Sullivan, Philip A. *Man Finds the Way.*

1940 Denturk, Henry C. *Vision of a State of Rightness on Spiritual Foundation.*

1940 Gieske, Herman E. *Utopia, Inc.*

1940 Gilbert, John W. *The Marsian.*

1940 Glenn, George A. *When Loneliness Comes.*

1940 Smart, Charles A. *Rosscommon.*

1941 Twiford, William Richard. *Sown in the Darkness, A.D. 2000.*

1941 Walton, Nathan. *Utopia Right Around the Corner.*

1941 Wilson, Philip W. *Newtopia.*

1942 Davenport, Basil. *An Introduction to Islandia.*

1942 Hall, Harold Curtis. *The Great Conflict.*

1943 Dardenelle, Louise. *World Without Raiment.*

1943 Zahn, Oswald Francis. *Let's Triumvirate.*

1943 Zori, Henri. *America's Sin Offering.*

1944 Gallego, Serapio G. *John Smith, Emperor.*

1945 McElhiney, Gaile C. *Into the Dawn.*

1945 Rogers, Frederick R. *Prelude to Peace.*

1946 Gross, Werter L. *The Golden Recovery.*

1946 Joseph, Marie G. H. *Balance the Universe.*

1947 Matthews, Carleton. *Flight to Utopia.*

1948 Liston, Edward. *The Bowl of Light.*

1949 Short, Gertrude. *A Visitor from Venus.*

1949 Stanley, Alfred M. *Tomorrow's Yesterday.*

1949 Sutton, Paralee S. *White City.*

1949 Walsh, Chad. *Early Christians of the 21st Century.* (Listed in Library of Congress as 1950.)

LYMAN TOWER SARGENT

Eutopias and Dystopias in Science Fiction: 1950–75

AFTER 1950, utopian fiction became almost entirely a part of science fiction. Science fiction, being popular literature, presents a volume and style of publication different from the norm of the utopian tradition. First, the utopia is often background to an adventure story rather than the reverse, which is the usual form in literary utopias. Second, science fiction has been as badly served by scholarship as has utopianism, and thus the scholar must face bibliographical and definitional problems anew and with many more books. Third, most science fiction is primarily designed to entertain, not educate or convince. Fourth, a major vehicle for science fiction is the short story which, from the utopian perspective, is limiting.

Here I have undertaken to survey a high percentage of the science fiction published in book form in the past twenty-five years. From that I have analyzed all (that I have so far been able to obtain) of those works presenting a picture of the future that includes a fairly detailed description of a functioning society in a variety of aspects and takes a stance regarding that society. There are two qualifications in that sentence that must be made very explicit: (1) fairly detailed descriptions of a functioning society in a variety of aspects, and (2) a society pictured as good or bad.[1] Anyone familiar with the amount of science fiction published and the very serious problems of keeping track of it all will know that I have fallen short of my goal. But I think that a perusal of the bibliography will demonstrate that I have some basis for generalization.[2] Although the essays in *America as Utopia* concentrate on American utopian literature, I have included a fair number of works by English authors for two reasons. First, science fiction is primarily an

An earlier version of this paper was presented at the 1974 Annual Meeting of the American Political Science Association, Palmer House, Chicago, Illinois, August 29–September 2, 1974. Copyright, 1974, The American Political Science Association. Research for this paper was supported by grants from the Office of Research Administration, University of Missouri–St. Louis.

Anglo-American phenomenon, and to limit one's consideration to the American literature alone would greatly falsify the picture. (Of course, science fiction is not exclusively an Anglo-American phenomenon, as, for example, Darko Suvin's essays about and bibliographies of Russian science fiction demonstrate.) Second, for about half the period under consideration the best-known and best writers of science fiction were English; to ignore them would be foolhardy to say the least.

NEGATIVE FUTURES: DYSTOPIAS

The first generalization, and one that strikes one immediately, is that science fiction writers are very pessimistic, though most of their dystopias have happy endings. As Arthur C. Clarke has written, "Marlan was bored, with the ultimate boredom that only utopia can supply."[3] And Thomas M. Disch seems to agree: "Paradise has a considerable flaw, however, from the narrative point of view. It is anti-dramatic. Perfection doesn't make a good yarn."[4] Of course, as H. G. Wells said many years ago and Ursula K. Le Guin has more recently demonstrated in *The Dispossessed* (1974), utopia no longer means static perfection.[5] But we must take Clarke and Disch seriously for two reasons. First, they're writing the stuff. Second, because we are looking for generalizations, we should not ignore the fact that eutopias rarely intrude upon the imagination of these writers, for whatever reason, and this message is being given to their readers. Later I shall develop a third reason why, for these writers, utopia is almost always rotten at the core.

Most of the negative futures follow the classic outlines of the great dystopias, Zamiatin's *We* (English translation, 1924), Huxley's *Brave New World* (1932), and Orwell's *1984* (1949). There is a dictatorship, power has corrupted, man is coerced and generally accepts his coercion, except, of course, for the lone rebel. The best recent dystopia in the classic mold is probably L. P. Hartley's *Facial Justice* (1960). Most of these works simply present one form of authoritarianism or another. (See the short-title bibliography appended to this essay for works by Anderson, 1953; Asimov, 1970; Aycock, 1954; Ballard, 1961; Upchurch, 1968; Bradbury, 1951, 1953; Bryant, 1973; Bulmer, *The Patient Dark*, 1969; Charbonneau, 1963, 1965; Compton, 1966, 1974; Dick, *The World Jones Made*, 1956, 1964, 1974; Disch, 1968; Groves, 1968; Harrison, 1962; Hartridge, 1970; Heinlein, 1953; Hughes, 1975; Jones, 1962; Klass, 1955; Kornbluth and Pohl, 1960; Le Guin, 1973; Leiber, "Coming Attraction," 1950, and 1959, 1968; McCutchan, 1968; Mackenzie, 1959; Mead, 1957; Mitchell, 1970; Moore, 1957; Pohl and Williamson, 1968; Reed, 1969; Ryder, 1969; Sheldon, 1973; Silverberg, *A Time of Changes*, 1971; Spencer, 1975; Spinrad, *Agent of Chaos*, 1967; Trains,

1974; Tucker, 1968, 1969, 1970; Wylie, 1971; Youd, 1955, 1970; and Zelazny, 1967). It is important to note that no single type, Communist, capitalist, fascist, or scientific, seems to predominate, with two very important exceptions, the military and the machine.

Indeed, science fiction is profoundly antimilitary, which is somewhat striking in view of the fact that a significant number of science fiction writers have military backgrounds. In fact, Heinlein is the only author I know of who consistently speaks favorably of the military. In all other cases, when the military is the topic, the tone is negative. It is clear that many science fiction authors are profoundly concerned about the role of the military in contemporary society (Brunner, 1971; Bunch, 1971; Burgess, *Wanting Seed*, 1962; Casewit, 1960; Chandler, 1968; Dick, 1959; Disch, 1966; Ellison, 1971; Geston, 1967; Harrison, 1965; Roshwald, 1962; Saberhagen, 1969; and Spinrad, *The Men in the Jungle*, 1967, among others). They see a world or worlds constantly at war, and the military as rulers who want to socialize the population to accept and live by military values, particularly the value of obedience. Man obeys much too readily for these writers; he is much too willing to stop thinking and follow orders. There is, of course, almost always some rebel who jars men into thinking and acting on their own again, but he arises only rarely and in extreme conditions, if at all. Most men are simply content to be ciphers, to be used and destroyed by the military machine. They fight and die for nationalism, the earth, the leader, mankind, without ever questioning the rightness of the war. Again and again First Contact (for the neophyte First Contact refers to the first meeting of man and alien) is marred or destroyed by some man in uniform who figuratively or literally shoots first and asks questions later. As Heinlein recently put it (but as praise), "thus far we have encountered not one race as mean, as nasty, as deadly as our own."[6] To understand this trend, one has only to remember the arrival of the benign aliens in Clarke's *Childhood's End* (1953) and the attempt to shoot down the ships. We have trigger-happy, power-hungry men, largely in the military, and a docile, easily led population that emulates the lemmings by regularly destroying itself. There are also, of course, a number of works that focus on the bomb and the fallout shelter fad (Pohl and Kornbluth, "Critical Mass," 1961; Roshwald, 1959).

Even more striking, in fact startling, is the attitude toward technology and scientific advances. Even though technology may bring about utopia (for example, Pohl, 1969), it is unlikely to, and if it does we won't like it. Given a chance man will make the wrong use of the opportunities he has.

There are a number of ways in which this distrust of man's ability to live with his technological advances is expressed. First, it may be that such advances will give corrupt men significant advantages. For example, Gunn's *The Immortals* (1962), Herbert's *The Eyes of Heisenberg* (1966), Niven's *A Gift From Earth* (1968), and Weatherhead's *Transplant* (1969) focus on the ways in which medical advances, such as transplants, could be used to keep the powerful in power by greatly extending their normal life span. Second, a few people might be able to use their access to information systems to gain political power, or sentient or nearly sentient "thinking" machines could simply take over from man (for example, Anderson, 1955; Asimov, 1975; Bourne, 1967; Caiden, 1968; Cooper, 1969; Dagmar, 1963; Davidson, 1975; Effinger, 1973; Elder, 1970; Fairman, 1968; Girad, 1974; Green, 1968; Gunn, 1961; High, 1966; D. F. Jones, 1966; G. Jones, 1968; Leiber, 1961; Long, 1964; Pohl, "Rafferty's Reasons," 1955; Sheckley, 1962; Sladek, 1967; Thompson, 1968; Tubb, 1954; and Vonnegut, 1952). And this theme leads directly to a third one, one that is also expressed in many of the works listed above, that while technology may produce a seemingly perfect society, machine perfection is not good for men (C. Anderson, 1970; P. Anderson, 1967; Biggle, 1967; Brunner, 1967; Cooper, 1958; Dickson, 1973; Frayn, 1968; Hough, 1967; Lafferty, 1968; Leiber, 1959; Levin, 1970; and Van Vogt, 1968). Again, of course, a rebel usually reasserts man's superiority to machine.

Closely connected to the man-machine problem is a strong tendency to see mankind degenerating mentally and physically, often as a direct result of too much dependence on machines. (See, in addition to those mentioned above, Aldiss, 1965; Asimov, 1957; Biggle, 1961; Brown, 1955; Klass, 1950; Kornbluth, 1951; Levene, 1968; Lorraine, 1953; Pohl, 1954 and "What to Do Till the Analyst Comes," 1955; Rocklynne, 1973; and Yorke, 1953.) Along this same line there are a few in which teenagers or children have come to control society, or part of it, largely because adults were too weak (Bova, 1973; Gotschalk, 1975; Jonas, 1970; Nolan, 1967; Pohl and Kornbluth, "A Gentle Dying," 1961; and Rocklynne, 1972).

The message is clear: Men are weak. They are all too willing to accept rule, perhaps particularly technological rule, because we are so used to thinking our lives are improved by technological advances that we miss the point where improvement changes to control. This message is particularly striking coming from science fiction, a genre whose beginnings and early development dealt almost exclusively with the advantages of technological advances. A later generation of science fiction writers has become more and more disillusioned.

Along these same lines, there are the catastrophe novels. These fall into two categories: the pollution stories, which extrapolate our current way of life into its inevitable future (Blish, 1969; Brunner, 1972; Cooper, 1970; Elwood and Kidd, 1973; Peck, 1972; and Vonnegut, 1972), and the catastrophe stories, in which the bomb and/or innumerable other events (science fiction is amazingly inventive about the ways we shall destroy ourselves) destroy civilization as we know it and force us back into some type of barbarian state, a state, interestingly, that is often pictured as somehow desirable (see Section II in the short-title bibliography).

The antipollution literature can be devastating. Among the most effective science fiction works is Brunner's *The Sheep Look Up* (1972); it made me feel dirty every time I read part of it. Here is one small illustration: " 'Is there somewhere I could wash up?' he added, displaying his palms to prove he meant *wash*. They were almost slimy with the airborne nastiness that had eluded the precipitator on his car. It wasn't designed to cope with California.'"[7] And this is on page 9, before it gets bad. James Blish also does an excellent job:

Twenty years ago, he liked to remember, Morningside Heights had consisted mostly of some (by modern standards) rather mild slums, completely surrounding the great university which had been their landlord. Today, like all other high ground in the city, the Heights was a vast skyscraper complex in which worked only the most powerful of the Earth. Lesser breeds had to paddle for it in the scummy, brackish canals of Times Square, Wall Street, Rockefeller Center, and other unimportant places, fending off lumps of offal and each other as best they could.[8]

These works are obviously intended as warnings, though Brunner's work implies that it is already too late.

The other catastrophe literature is in one sense more depressing because it tends to present ways of destroying the world that man could not have done anything to avoid. We are insignificant beings controlled by the totally impersonal forces of nature. But of course if we do try to control these forces, we will probably bring about the catastrophe. For example, the disaster in Silverberg's *Nightwings* (1969) was brought about by attempts to control the weather.

On the other hand, as in all these works, the catastrophe and barbarianism novels have a few men (rarely women, but women are becoming more frequent) who show extremely high survival tendencies. Being resourceful, intelligent, and able to deal with totally unheard-of conditions, they lead the rest into some sort of safety or manage to begin to improve the barbarian civilization against all the prejudices of the times. Youd's *A Wrinkle in the Skin* (1965) and Anderson's *Vault of the Ages* (1952) are good examples of the two courses of action. The position is definitely elitist. Men are on the whole incompetent, but there are a few who are significantly better physically, intellectually, and morally. Do the writers believe this, or is science fiction still largely formula literature? I don't know; but I do know that this is what is written in most science fiction, although there are, of course, exceptions.

Authoritarianism, militarism, control by technology, catastrophe, barbarianism, and degeneration are the principal themes of science fiction writers picturing negative futures or dystopias, but there are a number of other themes, some closely related to these, some more or less unrelated. Among the related ones, there are futures of violence (Ballard, 1975; Brunner, 1969; Burgess, *Clockwork Orange*, 1962; Cooper, 1970; Disch, 1972; Heinlein, 1971; Karlins and Andrews, 1974; Morland, 1974; Rankine, 1968; and Sheckley, 1959, 1960, 1966), and racism (Brunner, 1969; Dick, 1967; Heinlein, 1964; Lupoff, 1972; and Silverberg, 1970).

But the favorite theme used to describe what man is doing to himself is overpopulation. Brunner's *Stand on Zanzibar* (1968) is, of course, the masterpiece among the many works that use this theme, but its construction makes it difficult to quote. Fortunately there are many others that can be used. For instance, this appears in Robert Bloch's *This Crowded Earth* (1958):

> There were so many people, so many faces. After awhile it got so they all seemed to look alike. Yes, and breathed alike when you were squeezed up against them, and you were always being squeezed up against them, wherever you went. And you could smell them, and hear them wheeze and cough, and you went falling down with them into a bottomless pit where your head began to throb and throb and it was hard to move away from all that heat and pressure. It was hard enough just to keep from screaming—[9]

Other authors vary this theme only slightly. In most cases, the picture presented follows the lines of the above quotation, though there are exceptions, such as Robert Silverberg's *The World Inside* (1971):

> "Good morning," the screen says heartily. "The external temperature, if anybody's interested, is 28°. Today's population figure at Urbmon 116 is 881,115 which is + 102 since yesterday and + 14,187 since the first of the year. God bless, but we're slowing down! Across the way at Urbmon 117 they've added 131 since yesterday, including quads for Mrs. Hula Jabotinsky. She's eighteen and has had seven previous. A servant of god, isn't she."[10]

Ultimately the picture of a healthy, happy, well-adjusted world that is primarily oriented to population growth breaks down, again showing us a perfect society that is rotten at the core. Later I shall contrast this with the society described by James Blish and Norman L. Knight in *A Torrent of Faces* (1967), where they argue that the earth can support a huge population. The usual picture, however, is of a dystopia produced by overpopulation (Aldiss, 1968; Anderson, 1957; Asimov, 1954; Ballard, 1960, "Billenium," 1961; Bass, 1971; Bloch, 1958; Brunner, 1968, 1975; Burgess, *Wanting Seed*, 1962; Charbonneau, 1958; del Rey, 1962; Disch, 1972; Dozois, 1972; Ehrlich, 1971; Harrison, 1962; Hill, 1972; Hoffman, 1972; Klass, 1956; Mc-Allister, 1971; Maclean, 1971; Malzberg, 1973; Peck, 1972; Sheckley, "The People Trap," 1968, "Street of Dreams, Feet of Clay," 1968; and Silverberg, 1967, *To Open the Sky*, 1970, and *The World Inside*, 1971). One work shows a horrible society produced by a drop in the birthrate (Jones, 1967).

Yet another popular theme is the society that has become even more commercialized than contemporary American society, a society in which advertisers or, alternatively, a few capitalists control the population. For example, in one such society each house has two rooms; one contains a reciprocal (every viewer can be viewed) television that cannot be turned off twenty-four hours a day. It covers all four walls (Aldiss, 1957). In others all art has been replaced with commercials (Biggle, 1957), or one is required to consume vast quantities to keep the economy going (Pohl, 1954). (Others with similar themes are Biggle, 1961; Dick, *The Man Who Japed*, 1956; McCann, 1958; Pohl and Kornbluth, 1953, 1954; Pohl, "Tunnel Under the World," 1954; Sheckley, 1954; and Silverberg, 1958.)

A few other points are mentioned by one or more writers. Women ruling men is presented as a dystopia by six writers (Bloch, 1968; Cooper, 1968; Kettle, 1969; Klass, 1951; Maine, 1973; and Wilson, 1955).[11] In contrast Russ (1975) presents the disappearance of men as a utopia. Several other types of dystopias include a commune system dystopia (Maclean, 1971), an overly moral society (Brunner, 1973), a future slave society (Disch, 1963), a state of sensory overload (Skal, 1972), and three drug-addict societies (Bulmer, *The Ulcer Culture*, 1969; Lombino, 1956; and Tubb, 1972).

Obviously most of the works mentioned are not limited to only one theme; I have only mentioned the dominant theme or themes. Clearly science fiction writers are pessimistic, even if we keep in mind the optimism of the rebel and the belief that a dystopia is more entertaining than a eutopia. They also are despairing about the ability of most men to cope with the world, though they seem to believe that there are a few rebels, an elite, who can provide leadership, which, of course, provides a neat paradox. In most cases, it is clear that the people must be led, but they usually got into the problem in the first place by being too easily led. No solution to this difficulty is provided. Perhaps the positive futures, often written by the same people, will provide an answer.

POSITIVE FUTURES: EUTOPIAS

If the writers of the dystopias could be called optimistic pessimists, the writers of the eutopias, usually the same people, can be called pessimistic optimists, for there is almost always a flaw in the good society they present. In fact, it was sometimes hard to determine which category best described a particular work. This is certainly true, of course, with Heinlein's *Stranger in a Strange Land* (1961), which is known for its utopian elements even though they are revealed only in a small, isolated community in an essentially dystopian society. Similar observations can be made about Clarke's works. In *Against the Fall of Night* (1953; see also the revised version, *The City and the Stars*, 1956), he presents two fundamentally flawed utopias, and in *Childhood's End* (1953) utopia only comes as an alien importation at the end of the human race. Moreover, this utopia kills human creativity—"The end of strife and conflict had also meant the virtual end of creative art."[12] Ursula K. Le Guin makes the same point in a different context: "The only thing that makes life possible is permanent, intolerable uncertainty: not knowing what comes next."[13] Her own utopian work, *The Dispossessed* (1974), is subtitled *An Ambiguous Utopia* because the good society has begun to lose its way and may not be able to find its way back to openness. Chapter 11 of *The Dispossessed*, which is the Epilogue to this collection, offers a glimpse of this ambiguity. (Other fundamentally flawed good societies are Adlard, 1975; Disch, 1968; Mitchison, 1975; and Sheckley, 1955. Remember also all those perfect-society dystopias mentioned earlier.)

Three other works, all short stories, present good societies with a single flaw (Disch, 1966; Ellison, 1959; and Le Guin, 1973). In two of them the flaw is the suffering of a single child. The point is, of course, is utopia worth the suffering of a single child?

These writers provide a fundamental challenge to our whole conception of utopia.[14] In the best of these stories, Le Guin's "The Ones Who Walk Away from Omelas (Variations on a Theme by William James)" (1973), after presenting a most delightful sketch of a livable eutopia, she adds:

> . . . they all understand that this happiness, the beauty of this city, the tenderness of their friendships, the health of their children, the wisdom of their scholars, the skill of their makers, even the abundance of their harvest and the kindly weathers of their skies, depend wholly on this child's abominable misery.[15]

The title refers to those who assert that utopia cannot justify such suffering. Even if we could achieve utopia, what costs are we willing to have others pay?

Leaving this issue aside for the moment, what would utopia look like if we found it? First, and not at all surprisingly, it would be much more free sexually (Adlard, 1975; Aldiss, 1961; Appel, 1959; Disch, 1968; Heinlein, 1961, 1973; Pohl, 1969; Russ, 1972; Smith, 1962; and Upchurch, 1969, among others). Also, it would be likely to be small-town, even rural (Appel, 1959; Keilty, 1971; Oliver, 1954; Priest, 1970; Russ, 1970; Sheckley, 1954; Smith, 1962; and Waldo, 1960). Some of these utopias show man giving up all technology and returning to a life of toil on the land; others show him using technology but leaving the cities for a healthier life. Of course, a number of works stress utopia brought about through technology (Adlard, 1975; Leach, 1962; Moorcock, 1972; Pohl, 1969; Russ, 1972; and Walter, 1956). But it is still noteworthy that science fiction writers are hesitant about the value of technology in their utopias. And here it is clear that it is not man's use of technology that is at issue but the value of technology itself.[16] Interestingly enough, all utopias that use technology extensively tend to have equality of power as the basis of the society.

Equality, however, is an area of controversy in these new utopias. On the one hand there are the anarchist utopias (Lafferty, 1966; Le Guin, 1974; Russell, 1951; and Upchurch, 1969) that stress equality. On the other hand, Heinlein takes a strong stand against any form of equality, particularly equality of political power: "Killing an anarchist or a pacifist should not be defined as 'murder' in a legalistic sense."[17] While not taking as strong a position, Anderson (1955, 1963, 1973) rejects equality in utopia for similar reasons. Macgregor (1953) also establishes his utopia on an inegalitarian basis—intelligence. (See Lafferty, 1966, for a different treatment of intelligence and education.)

Other utopias are based on leisure (Appel, 1959; Pohl, 1969), telepathy (Russ, 1970; Upchurch, 1969), or the climate (Aldiss, 1957). Leiber (1953) presents a delightful example of a society rejecting commercialism, at least for a while. Russ (1975) presents a healthy, well-developed eutopia without men. It should be noted that some of these themes had also appeared among the dystopias.

An interesting example of a utopia produced on much the same basis as a number of dystopias is James Blish and Norman L. Knight (1967), who show a world coping with the tremendous world population of one trillion in the year 2794. They do this through a corporate state and argue that a quasi-democratic fascism is more likely to exist and work than a democratic socialism. Their society is horrifying, and one might want to reject the utopian label that they insist upon. But it does sustain the population, which could hardly be said of all those dystopias of overpopulation.

Even though most science fiction writers seem still to believe that utopia equals static perfection, virtually none of the utopias discussed fit that model. In all of them men tend to fall away from their professed beliefs into dependency. Man is probably not capable of establishing a perfect society, but he certainly can do better than he has—this is the optimistic message of these science fiction utopists. But, as was noted before, even if he does, there's a good chance he'll louse it up.

It would be possible to go into great detail on any number of these works, but I am convinced that what I have attempted to do here is more important now—to sketch in the main themes and patterns in science fiction.

It may be argued that I have taken some of the material too seriously, even after my own warning, and I admit to being hesitant about some of my comments on Pohl and Klass, the two best satirists in the group. But although satire is always a difficult mode to analyze, comments on the themes the satirist portrays and the mood he projects are not likely to be led too far astray.

Science fiction is first and foremost designed to entertain. Most science fiction does express the current hopes and fears of an intelligent, imaginative, and creative individual. Thus it should not be discounted as suggestion or warning. But rarely is science fiction intended to be taken seriously as extrapolation or scenario. It deserves to be taken seriously as such just as rarely. The accurate prediction of certain inventions by a variety of authors and the short-term projection of some social trends by some authors have led us to expect too much from science fiction. The fact that eutopias and dystopias appear in science fiction and are, at times, used to explore complex societies, the possible ramifications of social change, and present alternative futures that can be worked for or avoided must be set against the fact that most science fiction does not, and is not intended to, do any of these things. It can be sophisticated social analysis, as Le Guin has often shown. It can be excellent satire, as Pohl and Klass have often shown. It can be many things, as can any literary form, and science fiction is used to explore ideas more than any other genre, but we must not demand that it be something it isn't. Eutopias and dystopias are useful means of testing ideas. Positive and negative futures are important ways of communicating concerns. But science fiction is not a study of the future, so we should not expect it to be.

NOTES

1. In addition to these two categories, I have also included catastrophe–barbarianism novels. See Lyman Tower Sargent, "Utopia and Dystopia in Contemporary Science Fiction," *The Futurist*, 6 (June 1972), 93–98, for an earlier consideration of some of this material from a different perspective.

2. The works included can be faulted on two grounds. First, given the importance of the short story to the genre, there are not enough included. In defense let me simply say that the attempt to use fairly detailed descriptions of society precludes most short stories. See Lyman Tower Sargent, "Utopia: The Problem of Definition," *Extrapolation*, 16 (May 1975), 137–48 for further comment. Second, I have probably been too strict in excluding works, particularly in the list of negative futures.

3. Arthur C. Clarke, "The Awakening (1951)," *Prelude to Mars* (New York: Harcourt Brace Jovanovich, 1965), p. 264.

4. Thomas M. Disch, "White Fang Goes Dingo," *White Fang Goes Dingo and Other Funny S.F. Stories* (London: Arrow, 1971), p. 160. First published in 1966 as *102 H-Bombs*.

5. See H. G. Wells, *A Modern Utopia* (Lincoln: University of Nebraska Press,

1967; originally published 1905), and Ursula K. Le Guin, *The Dispossessed: An Ambiguous Utopia* (New York: Harper & Row, 1974).

6. Robert A. Heinlein, *Time Enough for Love: The Lives of Lazarus Long* (New York: Berkeley, 1973), p. xi.

7. John Brunner, *The Sheep Look Up* (New York: Harper & Row, 1972), p. 9.

8. James Blish, "We All Die Naked," in *Three for Tomorrow* (New York: Meredith Press, 1969), p. 140.

9. Robert Bloch, *This Crowded Earth* (New York: Belmont, 1958), p. 10.

10. Robert Silverberg, *The World Inside* (Garden City, N.Y.: Doubleday, 1971), p. 2.

11. For further consideration of this topic, see Barbara Quissell's essay in Part III of this collection. See also Lyman Tower Sargent, "Women in Utopia," *Comparative Literature Studies*, 10 (December 1973), 302–16; Beverly Friend, "Virgin Territory: Women and Sex in Science Fiction," *Extrapolation*, 14 (December 1972), 49–58; and Joanna Russ, "The Image of Women in Science Fiction," in Susan Koppelman Cornillon, ed., *Images of Women in Fiction* (Bowling Green, Ohio: Bowling Green University Press, 1972), pp. 79–94.

12. Arthur C. Clarke, *Childhood's End* (New York: Ballantine Books, 1953), p. 75.

13. Ursula K. Le Guin, *The Left Hand of Darkness* (New York: Walker, 1969), p. 52.

14. For another such challenge, see Lyman Tower Sargent, "A Note on the Other Side of Human Nature in the Utopian Novel," *Political Theory*, 3 (February 1975), 88–97.

15. Ursula K. Le Guin, "The Ones Who Walk Away from Omelas (Variations on a Theme by William James)," in Robert Silverberg, ed., *New Dimensions* (Garden City, N.Y.: Nelson Doubleday, 1973), 3, 6.

16. Here it would be useful for the reader to compare my comments with Mulford Q. Sibley's *Technology and Utopian Thought* (Minneapolis: Burgess, 1971).

17. Heinlein, *Time Enough for Love* (note 6 above); p. 346.

SHORT-TITLE BIBLIOGRAPHY

Included in the bibliography are all the American and British works used in this study arranged in chronological order in three groups: negative futures, novels of catastrophe or barbarianism, and positive futures. I have included works that present both negative and positive futures in the positive list, for there are relatively few positive works. Given the bibliographic problems of science fiction, it is certain that some of the short stories were published earlier, as I have used the date of the collection they appear in when the original date of publication is not available. Also, although many of the novels were originally published in part or in whole in magazines before being published in book form, I have used the copyright date. Even with these reservations, the lists do give a generally accurate picture of the publication record of that science fiction that has portrayed positive or neg-

ative future societies. There are many different editions of these books. The
edition listed is the one I used. Unlike the other bibliographies following
the historical and bibliographic surveys in Part IV, this listing includes the
publisher and place of publication. This added information indicates in most
cases which works are American and which are English.

Because the focus of my survey was eutopias and dystopias in science
fiction, several popular titles are not included in the bibliography, for instance, Ayn Rand's *Atlas Shrugged* (1957), Ernest Callenbach's *Ecotopia*
(1975) and Robert Rimmer's *The Harrad Experiment* (1966). (For discussions
of Rand's and Rimmer's utopias, see Sargent's and Plank's essays in Part III
of this collection and Rimmer's own essay in Part I—Ed.)

NEGATIVE FUTURES: DYSTOPIAS
1950   Asimov, Isaac. *Pebble in the Sky*. New York: Bantam, 1957.
1950   Capon, Paul. *The Other Side of the Sun*. London: William Heinemann.
1950   Leiber, Fritz. "Coming Attraction," in *The Best of Fritz Leiber* (Garden City,
       N.Y.: Nelson Doubleday, 1974), pp. 104–14.
1950   [Klass, Philip]. "Null-P," by William Tenn (pseud.), in *The Wooden Star*
       (New York: Ballantine, 1968), pp. 57–71.
1951   Bradbury, Ray. "The Pedestrian," in *Twice Twenty-two* (Garden City, N.Y.:
       Doubleday, 1966), pp. 16–20.
1951   [Klass, Philip]. "Venus Is a Man's World," by William Tenn (pseud.), in *The
       Square Root of Man* (New York: Ballantine, 1968), pp. 145–69.
1951   Kornbluth, C. M. "The Marching Morons," in Ben Bova, ed., *The Science
       Fiction Hall of Fame*, 2 Vols. in 3 (Garden City, N.Y.: Doubleday, 1973),
       Vol. 2A, pp. 204–32.
1952   Frankau, Pamela. *The Offshore Light*. London: William Heinemann. U.S.
       ed. published under pseud. Eliot Naylor.
1952   Vonnegut, Kurt, Jr. *Player Piano*. New York: Dell. Also entitled *Utopia 14*.
1953   Anderson, Poul. "Sam Hall," in Robert Hoskins, ed., *The Liberated Future*
       (Greenwich, Conn.: Fawcett, 1974), pp. 13–51.
1953   Bradbury, Ray. *Fahrenhit 451*. New York: Ballantine.
1953   Heinlein, Robert A. *Revolt in 2100*. New York: New American Library.
1953   Lorraine, Paul. *Dark Boundaries*. London: Curtis Warren.
1953   Pohl, Frederik, and C. M. Kornbluth. *The Space Merchants*. New York:
       Ballantine.
1953   Yorke, Preston. *Space-Time Task Force*. London: Hector Kelly.
1954   Asimov, Isaac. *The Caves of Steel*. London: Panther, 1958.
1954   [Aycock, Roger Dee]. *An Earth Gone Mad*, by Roger Dee (pseud.). New
       York: Ace.
1954   Mead, Shepherd. *The Big Ball of Wax*. New York: Simon & Schuster.
1954   Pohl, Frederik. "The Midas Plague," in Ben Bova, ed., *The Science Fiction
       Hall of Fame*, 2 Vols. in 3 (Garden City, N.Y.: Doubleday, 1973), Vol. 2B,
       pp. 259–312.
1954   Pohl, Frederik, and C. M. Kornbluth. *Search the Sky*. Harmondsworth,
       England: Penguin.

1954   Pohl, Frederik. "Tunnel Under the World," in *Alternating Currents* (New York: Ballantine, 1956), pp. 112–43.

1954   Sheckley, Robert. "Cost of Living," in *Untouched by Human Hands* (New York: Ballantine, 1954), pp. 12–23.

1954   [Tubb, E. C.]. *Enterprise 2115*, by Charles Grey (pseud.). London: Merit Books.

1955   Anderson, Poul. *No World of Their Own*. New York: Ace.

1955   Brown, Alec. *Angelo's Moon*. London: Bodley Head.

1955   [Klass, Philip]. "The Servant Problem," by William Tenn (pseud.), in *The Human Angle* (New York: Ballantine, 1956), pp. 44–75.

1955   Knight, Damon. *Hell's Pavement*. New York: Lion. Also entitled *Analogue Men*.

1955   McCann, Edson. *Preferred Risk*. New York: Simon & Schuster.

1955   Pohl, Frederik, and C. M. Kornbluth. *Gladiator-at-Law*. New York: Ballantine.

1955   Pohl, Frederik. "Rafferty's Reasons," in *Alternating Currents* (New York: Ballantine, 1956), pp. 83–96.

1955   Pohl, Frederik. "What to Do till the Analyst Comes," in *Alternating Currents* (New York: Ballantine, 1956), pp. 143–54.

1955   Wilson, Richard. *The Girls from Planet 5*. New York: Ballantine.

1955   [Youd, C. S.]. *The Year of the Comet*, by John Christopher (pseud.). London: Michael Joseph.

1956   Dick, Philip K. *The Man Who Japed*. New York: Ace.

1956   Dick, Philip K. *The World Jones Made*. London: Panther, 1968

1956   [Klass, Philip]. "A Man of Family," by William Tenn (pseud.), in *The Human Angle* (New York: Ballantine, 1956), pp. 137–52.

1956   [Lombino, S. A.]. *Tomorrow's World*, by Hunt Collins (pseud.). New York: Avalon. Also entitled *Tomorrow and Tomorrow*.

1957   Aldiss, Brian W. "Panel Game," in *Space, Time and Nathaniel* (London: New English Library, 1971).

1957   Anderson, Poul. "License," in *Seven Conquests* (New York:Collier Books, 1969), pp. 140–166.

1957   Asimov, Isaac. "Profession," in *Nine Tomorrows* (Greenwich, Conn.: Fawcett, 1959), pp. 11–68.

1957   Biggle, Lloyd, Jr. "The Tunesmith," in *The Metallic Muse* (Garden City, N.Y.: Doubleday, 1972), pp 4–48.

1957   Mead, Harold. *Mary's Country*. London: Michael Joseph.

1957   Moore, C. E. *Doomsday Morning*. Garden City, N.Y.: Doubleday.

1958   Bloch, Robert. *This Crowded Earth*. New York: Belmont Books.

1958   Charbonneau, Louis. *No Place on Earth*. Garden City, N.Y.: Doubleday.

1958   Cooper, Edmund. *The Uncertain Midnight*. London: Hutchinson. Also entitled *Deadly Image*.

1958   Silverberg, Robert. *Invaders from Earth*. New York: Avon.

1959   Dick, Philip K. *Time Out of Joint*. Philadelphia: J. B. Lippincott.

1959   Leiber, Fritz. "The Haunted Future," in Gardner Dozois, ed., *A Day in the Life* (New York: Harper & Row, 1973), pp. 154–99.

1959   Mackenzie, Compton.*The Lunatic Republic*. London: Chatto & Windus, 1959.

1959 Roshwald, Mordecai. *Level 7*. New York: McGraw-Hill.

1959 Sheckley, Robert. *Immortality Inc*. New York: Bantam. Also entitled *Immortality Delivered*.

1960 Aldiss, Brian W. *The Interpreter* [c. 1960]. London: New English Library, 1972.

1960 Ballard, J. G. "Build-up," in *Chronopolis and Other Stories* (New York: Putnam's, 1971), pp. 175–93.

1960 Casewit, Curtis W. *The Peacemakers*. New York: Macfadden-Bartell.

1960 Hartley, L. P. *Facial Justice*. London: Hamish Hamilton.

1960 Kornbluth, C. M., and Frederik Pohl. *Wolfbane*. London: Victor Gollancz.

1960 Sheckley, Robert. *The Status Civilization*. New York: Dell. .

1961 Ballard, J. G. "Billenium," in *Chronopolis and Other Stories* (New York: Putnam's, 1971), pp. 137–51.

1961 Ballard, J. G. "Chronopolis," in *Chronopolis and Other Stories* (New York: Putnam's, 1971), pp. 152–74.

1961 Biggle, Lloyd, Jr. "Well of the Deep Wish," in *The Metallic Muse* (Garden City, N.Y.: Doubleday, 1972), pp. 138–57.

1961 Gunn, James. *The Joy Makers*. London: Victor Gollancz, 1963.

1961 Leiber, Fritz. *The Silver Eggheads*. New York: Ballantine.

1961 Pohl, Frederik, and C. M. Kornbluth. "Critical Mass," in *The Wonder Effect* (New York: Ballantine, 1962), pp. 11–46.

1961 Pohl, Frederik, and C. M. Kornbluth. "A Gentle Dying," in *The Wonder Effect* (New York: Ballantine, 1962), pp. 47–54.

1962 Burgess, Anthony. *Clockwork Orange*. New York: W. W. Norton.

1962 Burgess, Anthony. *The Wanting Seed*. New York: Ballantine.

1962 del Rey, Lester. *The Eleventh Commandment*, rev. ed. New York: Ballantine, 1970.

1962 Gunn, James. *The Immortals*. New York: Bantam, 1962.

1962 Harrison, Harry. *Planet of the Damned*. New York: Bantam.

1962 Jones, Raymond. *The Cybernetic Brains*. New York: Avalon.

1962 Roshwald, Mordecai. *A Small Armageddon*. London: Heinemann.

1962 Sheckley, Robert. *Journey Beyond Tomorrow*. New York: Dell.

1963 Charbonneau, Louis. *The Sentinal Stars*. New York: Bantam.

1963 Dagmar, Peter. *Sands of Time*. London: Brown, Watson.

1963 Disch, Thomas M. "Thesis on Social Forms and Social Controls in the U.S.A.," in *Fun with Your New Head* (Garden City, N.Y.: Doubleday, 1968), pp. 177–92.

1963 Pohl, Frederik, and Jack Williamson. *The Reefs of Space*. New York: Ballantine.

1964 Dick, Philip K. *The Penultimate Truth*. New York: Leisure Books.

1964 Heinlein, Robert A. *Farnham's Freehold*. New York: Putnam's, 1964.

1964 Long, Frank Belknap. *It Was the Day of the Robot*. London: Dennis Dobson.

1965 Aldiss, Brian W. "Man on Bridge," in *Who Can Replace a Man?* (New York: New American Library, 1965), pp. 82–98. English edition entitled *Best Science Fiction Stories of Brian W. Aldiss*.

1965 Charbonneau, Louis. *Psychedelic—40*. New York: Bantam. Also entitled *The Specials*.

1965 Harrison, Harry. *Bill, the Galactic Hero*. Harmondsworth, England: Penguin, 1969.
1965 Pohl, Frederik. *A Plague of Pythons*. New York: Ballantine.
1966 Compton, D. G. *Farewell, Earth's Bliss*. London: Tandem.
1966 Disch, Thomas M. "102 H-Bombs," in *White Fang Goes Dingo and Other Funny S.F. Stories* (London: Arrow Books, 1971), pp. 7–33. First edition published as *102 H-Bombs*.
1966 Herbert, Frank. *The Eyes of Heisenberg*. London: Sphere, 1968.
1966 High, Philip E. *The Mad Metropolis*. New York: Ace. Also entitled *Double Illusion*.
1966 Jones, Dennis Feltham. *Colossus*. London: Rupert Hart-Davis.
1966 Sheckley, Robert. *The Tenth Victim*. London: Mayflower.
1967 Anderson, Poul. "Eutopia," in Harlan Ellison, ed., *Dangerous Visions* (Garden City, N.Y.: Doubleday, 1967), pp. 274–91.
1967 Biggle, Lloyd, Jr. "And Madly Teach," in Edward L. Ferman, ed., *The Best from Fantasy and Science Fiction: Sixteenth Series* (Garden City, N.Y.: Doubleday, 1967) pp. 25–58.
1967 Bourne, John. *Computer Takes All*. London: Cassell.
1967 Brunner, John. *Quicksand*. Garden City, N.Y.: Doubleday.
1967 Dick, Philip K. *Counter Clock World*. New York: Berkeley.
1967 Geston, Mark S. *Lords of the Starship*. London: Sphere, 1972.
1967 [Hough, Stanley Bennett]. *The Paw of God*, by Rex Gordon (pseud.). London: Tandem.
1967 Jones, D. F. *Implosion*. New York: Putnam's.
1967 Nolan, William F. and George Clayton Johnson. *Logan's Run*. New York: Dial.
1967 Silverberg, Robert. *The Time-Hoppers*. Garden City, N.Y.: Doubleday.
1967 Sladek, John T. "The Happy Breed," in Harlan Ellison, ed., *Dangerous Visions* (Garden City, N.Y.: Doubleday, 1967), pp. 414–31.
1967 Spinrad, Norman. *Agent of Chaos*. London: New English Library.
1967 Spinrad, Norman. *The Men in the Jungle*. New York: Avon.
1967 Zelazny, Roger. *Lord of Light*. London: Panther.
1968 Aldiss, Brian W. "Total Environment," in Donald A. Wollheim and Terry Carr, eds., *World's Best Science Fiction 1969* (New York: Ace, 1969), pp. 287–331.
1968 Bloch, Robert. *Ladies' Day*. New York: Belmont Books.
1968 Brunner, John. *Stand on Zanzibar*. Garden City, N.Y.: Doubleday.
1968 Caidin, Martin. *The God Machine*. New York: E. P. Dutton.
1968 Chandler, A. Bertram. *False Fatherland*. 1969 ed. as *Spartan Planet*. New York: Dell.
1968 Cooper, Edmund. *Five to Twelve*. New York: Putnam's.
1968 Disch, Thomas M. *Camp Concentration*. London: Rupert Hart-Davis.
1968 Fairman, Paul W. *I, The Machine*. New York: Lancer.
1968 Frayn, Richard. *A Very Private Life*. Harmondsworth, U.K.: Penguin.
1968 Green, Robert. *The Great Leap Backward*. London: Robert Hale.
1968 Groves, John Williams. *Shellbreak*. London: Robert Hale.
1968 Jones, Gonner. *The Dome*. London: Faber & Faber.

1968   Lafferty, R. A. *Past Master*. London: Rapp & Whiting.
1968   Leiber, Fritz. *A Spector Is Haunting Texas*. New York: Walker.
1968   Levene, Malcolm. *Carder's Paradise*. London: Rupert Hart-Davis.
1968   McCutchan, Philip. *The Day of the Coastwatch*. London: Harrap.
1968   Niven, Larry. *A Gift from Earth*. New York: Ballantine.
1968   [Rankine, John]. *Ring of Violence*, by Douglas R. Mason (pseud.). London: Robert Hale.
1968   Sheckley, Robert. "The People Trap," in *The People Trap* (London: Pan, 1972), pp. 7–27.
1968   Sheckley, Robert. "Street of Dreams, Feet of Clay," in Robert Hoskins, ed., *The Liberated Future* (Greenwich, Conn.: Fawcett, 1974), pp. 139–58.
1968   [Thompson, Anthony A.]. *Catharsis Central*, by Antony Alban (pseud.). London: Dennis Dobson.
1968   [Tucker, Allan James]. *The Alias Man*, by David Craig (pseud.). London: Jonathan Cape.
1968   [Upchurch, Boyd]. *The Last Starship from Earth*, by John Boyd (pseud.). New York: Weybright & Talley.
1969   Blish, James. "We All Die Naked," in *Three for Tomorrow* (New York: Meredith Press, 1969), pp. 139–80.
1969   Brunner, John. *The Jagged Orbit*. New York: Ace.
1969   Bulmer, Kenneth. *The Patient Dark*. London: Robert Hale.
1969   Bulmer, Kenneth. *The Ulcer Culture*. London: Macdonald.
1969   Cooper, Hughes. *Sexmax*. London: New English Library, 1970.
1969   Kettle, Pamela. *The Day of the Women*. London: Leslie Frewin.
1969   Reed, Kit. *Armed Camps*. London: Faber & Faber.
1969   Ryder, James. *Kark*. London: Robert Hale.
1969   Saberhagen, Fred. *Brother Berserker*. London: Macdonald.
1969   [Tucker, Allan James]. *Message Ends*, by David Craig (pseud.). London: Jonathan Cape.
1969   Weatherhead, John. *Transplant*. London: Harrap.
1970   Anderson, Colin. *Magellan*. London: Sphere.
1970   Asimov, Isaac. "2430 A.D.," in *Buy Jupiter and Other Stories* (Garden City, N.Y.: Doubleday, 1975), pp. 159–66.
1970   Cooper, Edmund. *Son of Kronk*, 1972 ed. as *Kronk*. London: Cornet Books.
1970   Elder, Michael. *Paradise Is Not Enough*. London: Robert Hale.
1970   Hartridge, Jon. *Earthjacket*. London: Macdonald.
1970   Heinlein, Robert A. *I Will Fear No Evil*. New York: Putnam's.
1970   Hoyle, Fred, and Geoffrey Hoyle. *Seven Steps to the Sun*. Greenwich, Conn.: Fawcett.
1970   Jonas, Gerald. "The Shaker Revival," in Donald A. Wollheim and Terry Carr, eds., *World's Best Science Fiction 1971* (New York: Ace, 1971), pp. 263–92.
1970   Levin, Ira. *This Perfect Day*. New York: Random House.
1970   Mitchell, Adrian. *The Bodyguard*. London: Jonathan Cape.
1970   Reynolds, Mack. "Utopian," in Harry Harrison, ed., *The Year 2000* (Garden City, N.Y.: Doubleday, 1970), pp. 91–110.
1970   Silverberg, Robert. "Black Is Beautiful," in Harry Harrison, ed., *The Year 2000* (Garden City, N.Y.: Doubleday, 1970), pp. 175–93.

1970 Silverberg, Robert. *To Open the Sky*. London: Sphere.
1970 [Tucker, Allan James]. *Contact Lost*, by David Craig (pseud.). London: Jonathan Cape.
1970 [Youd, C. S.]. *The Guardians*, by John Christopher (pseud.). London: Hamish Hamilton.
1971 Bass, T. J. *Half Past Human*. New York: Ballantine.
1971 Brunner, John. *The Wrong End of Time*. Garden City, N.Y.: Doubleday.
1971 Bunch, David R. *Moderan*. New York: Avon.
1971 Ehrlich, Max. *The Edict*. Garden City, N.Y.: Doubleday.
1971 Ellison, Harlan. "Silent in Gehenna," in Ben Bova, ed., *The Many Worlds of Science Fiction* (New York: E. P. Dutton, 1971), pp. 196–217.
1971 McAllister, Bruce. "Benji's Pencil," in Edward L. Ferman, ed., *The Best from Fantasy and Science Fiction: Nineteenth Series* (Garden City, N.Y.: Doubleday, 1971), pp. 273–83.
1971 Maclean, Katherine. "The Missing Man," in Lloyd Biggle, Jr., ed., *Nebula Award Stories Seven* (New York: Harper & Row, 1973), pp. 167–210.
1971 Silverberg, Robert. *A Time of Changes*. Garden City, N.Y.: Doubleday.
1971 Silverberg, Robert. *The World Inside*. Garden City, N.Y.: Doubleday.
1971 Wylie, Philip. *Los Angeles: A.D. 2017*. New York: Popular Library.
1972 Brunner, John. *The Sheep Look Up*. New York: Harper & Row.
1972 Disch, Thomas M. *334*. London: MacGibbon & Kee.
1972 Dozois, Gardner R. "Machines of Loving Grace," in Damon Knight, ed., *Orbit II* (New York: Putnam's, 1972), pp. 147–52.
1972 Hill, Richard. "Moth Race," in Harlan Ellison, ed., *Again, Dangerous Visions* (Garden City, N.Y.: Doubleday, 1972), pp. 539–48.
1972 Hoffman, Lee. "Soundless Evening," in Harlan Ellison, ed., *Again, Dangerous Visions* (Garden City, N.Y.: Doubleday, 1972), pp. 422–26.
1972 Lupoff, Richard A. "With the Bentfin Boomer Boys on Little Old New Alabama," in Harlan Ellison, ed., *Again, Dangerous Visions* (Garden City, N.Y.: Doubleday, 1972), pp. 676–765.
1972 [Maine, Charles Eric]. *Alph*, by David McIlwain (pseud.). Garden City, N.Y.: Nelson Doubleday.
1972 Peck, R. E. "Gantlet," in Damon Knight, ed., *Orbit 10* (New York: Putnam's, 1972), pp. 152–68.
1972 Rocklynne, Ross. "Ching Witch!" in Harlan Ellison, ed., *Again, Dangerous Visions* (Garden City, N.Y.: Doubleday, 1972), pp. 10–26.
1972 Skal, Dave. "They Cope," in Damon Knight, ed., *Orbit II* (New York: Putnam's, 1972), pp. 153–57.
1972 Tubb, E. C. *Century of the Manikin*. New York: DAW Books.
1972 Van Vogt, A. E. "Future Perfect," in Jerry Pournelle, ed., *20/20 Vision* (New York: Avon, 1974), pp. 151–74.
1972 Vonnegut, Kurt, Jr. "The Big Space Fuck," in Harlan Ellison, ed., *Again, Dangerous Visions* (Garden City, N.Y.: Doubleday, 1972), pp. 267–72.
1973 Bova, Ben. "Blood of Tyrants," in *Forward in Time* (New York: Walker, 1973), pp. 17–34.
1973 Brunner, John. *The Stone That Never Came Down*. Garden City, N.Y.: Doubleday.

1973   Bryant, Edward. "The Legend of Cougar Lou Landis," in Terry Carr, ed., *Universe 3* (New York: Random House, 1973), pp. 135–50.

1973   Dickson, Gordon R. *The R-Master*. Philadelphia: J. B. Lippincott.

1973   Effinger, Geo. Alec. "The Ghost Writer," in Terry Carr, ed., *Universe 3* (New York: Random House, 1973), pp. 61–73.

1973   Elwood, Roger, and Virginia Kidd, eds., *Saving Worlds*. Garden City, N.Y.: Doubleday.

1973   Malzberg, Barry N. "Conversations at Lothar's," in Robert Hoskins, ed., *The Liberated Future* (Greenwich, Conn.: Fawcett, 1974), pp. 229–34.

1973   Rocklynne, Ross. "Randy-Tandy Man," in Terry Carr, ed., *Universe 3* (New York: Random House, 1973), pp. 101–12.

1973   [Sheldon, Alice]. "The Girl Who Was Plugged In," by James Tiptree (pseud.), in Robert Silverberg, ed., *New Dimensions 3* (Garden City, N.Y.: Nelson Doubleday, 1973), pp. 60–97.

1974   Compton, D. G. *The Unsleeping Eye*. New York: DAW Books. Also entitled *The Continuous Katherine Mortenhoe*.

1974   Dick, Philip K. *Flow My Tears, the Policeman Said*. Garden City, N.Y.: Doubleday.

1974   Girad, Dian. "Eat, Drink, and Be Merry," in Jerry Pournelle, ed., *20/20 Vision* (New York: Avon, 1974), pp. 121–26.

1974   Karlins, Marvin, and Lewis M. Andrews. *Gomorrah*. Garden City, N.Y.: Doubleday.

1974   Morland, Dick. *Albion! Albion!* London: Faber & Faber.

1974   Trains, Robert. *Android Armageddon*. New York: Pinnacle.

1974   [Upchurch, Boyd]. *The Doomsday Gene*, by John Boyd (pseud.). New York: Weybright & Talley.

1975   Asimov, Isaac. "The Life and Times of Multivac," *The New York Times Magazine*, January 5, 1975, pp. 12, 51, 56, 58, 70.

1975   Ballard, J. G. *High-Rise*. London: Jonathan Cape.

1975   Davidson, Michael. *The Karma Machine*. New York: Popular Library.

1975   Gotschalk, Felix C. *Growing Up in Tier 3000*. New York: Ace.

1975   [Hughes, Zack]. *The Stork Factor*, by Hugh Zachary (pseud.). New York: Berkeley.

1975   Le Guin, Ursula K. "The New Atlantis," in Robert Silverberg, ed., *The New Atlantis* (New York: Hawthorn Books, 1975), pp. 59–85.

1975   Spencer, John. *The Electronic Lullaby Meat Market*. London: Quartet.

CATASTROPHE AND BARBARIANISM: A SELECTED LIST

1951   [Cove, Joseph Walter]. *Late Final*, by Lewis Gibbs (pseud.). London: J. M. Dent.

1951   Tucker, Wilson. *City in the Sea*. New York: Rinehart.

1952   Anderson, Poul. *Vault of the Ages*. New York: Avon, 1969.

1954   Budrys, Algis. *False Night*. New York: Lion.

1954   Crowcroft, Peter. *Fallen Sky*. London: Peter Nevill.

1955   Brackett, Leigh. *The Long Tomorrow*. Garden City, N.Y.: Doubleday.

1956   Stark, Raymond. *Crossroads to Nowhere*. London: Ward, Lock.

1956   [Youd, C. S.]. *No Blade of Grass*, by John Christopher (pseud.). New York: Avon.

1958   [Klass, Philip]. "Eastward Ho," by William Tenn (pseud.) in *The Wooden Star* (New York: Ballantine, 1968), pp. 73–93.
1961   Galouye, Daniel F. *Dark Universe*. New York: Bantam.
1964   Aldiss, Brian W. *Greybeard*. London: Panther, 1972.
1964   Ballard, J. G. *The Burning World*. 1968 ed. as *The Drought*. Harmondsworth, U.K.: Penguin.
1965   Disch, Thomas M. *The Genocides*. London: Panther.
1965   [Youd, C. S.]. *A Wrinkle in the Skin*, by John Christopher (pseud.). London: Hodder & Stoughton.
1966   Cooper, Edmund. *All Fools' Day*. London: Hodder & Stoughton.
1966   [Rankine, John]. *From Carthage Then I Came*, by Douglas R. Mason (pseud.). London: Hale. Also entitled *Eight Against Utopia*.
1967   Cowper, Richard. *Phoenix*. New York: Ballantine.
1968   Farmer, Philip José. *Flesh*. New York: New American Library.
1968   Harrison, Harry. *Deathworld 3*. New York: Dell.
1968   Kapp, Colin. "The Cloudbuilders," in Donald A. Wollheim and Terry Carr, eds., *World's Best Science Fiction 1969* (New York: Ace, 1969), pp. 144–85.
1968   [Youd, C. S.] *Pendulum*, by John Christopher (pseud.). New York: Simon & Schuster.
1969   Lightner, A. M. *The Day of the Drones*. New York: Bantam.
1969   Silverberg, Robert. *Nightwings*. New York: Avon.
1970   Platt, Christopher. *The City Dwellers*. London: Sphere.
1970   Tucker, Wilson. *The Year of the Quiet Sun*. New York: Ace.
1973   Coney, Michael. *The Hero of Downways*. New York: DAW.
1973   Stableford, Brian M. *Rhapsody in Black*. New York: DAW.
1975   Delany, Samuel R. *Dahlgren*. New York: Bantam.

POSITIVE FUTURES: EUTOPIAS

1951   Russell, Eric Frank. ". . . And Then There Were None," in Ben Bova, ed., *The Science Fiction Hall of Fame*, 2 Vols. in 3 (Garden City, N.Y.: Doubleday, 1973), Vol. 2A, pp. 275–341.
1953   Clarke, Arthur C. *Against the Fall of Night*. New York: Pyramid.
1953   Clarke, Arthur C. *Childhood's End*. New York: Ballantine.
1953   Leiber, Fritz. "The Big Holiday," in *The Best of Fritz Leiber* (Garden City, N.Y.: Nelson Doubleday, 1974), pp. 165–72.
1953   [Macgregor, James M.]. *World Out of Mind*, by J. T. M'Intosh (pseud.). Garden City, N.Y.: Doubleday.
1954   Oliver, Chad. "Rite of Passage," *Astounding Science Fiction*, 53 (April 1954), 49–86.
1954   Sheckley, Robert. "Skulking Permit," in *Citizen in Space* (New York: Ballantine, 1955), pp. 154–80.
1955   Anderson, Poul. "Inside Straight," in *Seven Conquests* (New York: Collier, 1969), pp. 93–116.
1955   Sheckley, Robert. "A Ticket to Trainai," in *Citizen in Space* (New York: Ballantine, 1955), pp. 108–47.
1956   Clarke, Arthur C. *The City and the Stars*. New York: Harcourt, Brace & World.

1956   Walter, William Grey. *The Curve of the Snowflake*. New York: W. W. Norton. Also entitled *Further Outlook*.

1957   Aldiss, Brian W. "The Shubshub Race," in *Space, Time and Nathaniel* (London: New English Library, 1971), pp. 63–79.

1959   Appel, Benjamin. *The Funhouse*. New York: Ballantine. Also entitled *The Death Master*.

1959   Ellison, Harlan. "Eyes of Dust," in *Alone Against Tomorrow* (New York: Macmillan, 1971), pp. 171–79.

1960   [Waldo, Edward Hamilton]. *Venus Plus X*, by Theodor Sturgeon (pseud.). New York: Pyramid.

1961   Aldiss, Brian W. *The Primal Urge*. London: Sphere, 1967.

1961   Heinlein, Robert A. *Stranger in a Strange Land*. New York: Putnam's.

[1962] Leach, Decima. *The Garthians*. Ilfracombe, U.K.: Arthur H. Stockwell.

1962   Smith, Evelyn E. *The Perfect Planet*. New York: Lancer.

1963   Anderson, Poul. "No Truce with Kings," in *Time and Stars* (London: Panther, 1966), pp. 9–66.

1966   Disch, Thomas M. "Utopia? Never!" in *White Fang Goes Dingo and Other Funny S.F. Stories* (London: Arrow, 1971), pp. 67–69. Also entitled *102 H-Bombs*.

1966   Lafferty, R. A. "The Primary Education of the Camiroi," in Judith Merrill, ed., *SF 12* (New York: Dell, 1968), pp. 161–74.

1967   Blish, James, and Norman L. Knight. *A Torrent of Faces*. Garden City, N.Y.: Doubleday.

1968   Disch, Thomas M. "The City of Penetrating Light," in *Fun With Your New Head* (Garden City, N.Y.: Doubleday, 1968), pp. 165–68.

1969   Pohl, Frederik. *The Age of the Pussyfoot*. New York: Ballantine.

1970   Priest, Christopher. *Indoctrinaire*. London: New American Library.

1970   Russ, Joanna. *And Chaos Died*. New York: Ace.

1971   Keilty, James. "The People of Prashad," in Thomas A. Disch, ed., *The New Improved Sun* (New York: Harper & Row, 1975), pp. 49–80.

1972   Moorcock, Michael. *An Alien Heat*. London: MacGibbon & Kee.

1972   Russ, Joanna. "Nobody's Home," in Pamela Sargent, ed., *Women of Wonder: Science Fiction Stories by and About Women* (New York: Vintage, 1974), pp. 235–56.

1972   Russ, Joanna. "When It Changed," in Harlan Ellison, ed., *Again, Dangerous Visions* (Garden City, N.Y.: Doubleday, 1972), pp. 252–60.

1973   Anderson, Poul. *The People of the Wind*. New York: New American Library.

1973   Heinlein, Robert A. *Time Enough for Love*. New York: Berkley.

1973   Le Guin, Ursula K. "The Ones Who Walk Away from Omelas," in Robert Silverberg, ed., *New Dimensions 3* (Garden City, N.Y.: Nelson Doubleday, 1972), pp. 1–8.

1974   Le Guin, Ursula K. *The Dispossessed*. New York: Harper & Row.

1974   Moorcock, Michael. *The Hollow Lands*. New York: Harper & Row.

1975   Adlard, Mark. *Multiface*. London: Sidgwick & Jackson.

1975   Mitchison, Naomi. *Solution Three*. New York: Warner Books.

1975   Russ, Joanna. *The Female Man*. New York: Bantam.

KENNETH M. ROEMER

A Selected Checklist of Secondary Sources

THE FOLLOWING CHECKLIST represents a very thin slice of the mass of utopian studies. My cutting edge was guided by two criteria: (1) I chose studies that focused on American utopian literature as opposed to American utopian thought or American utopian communities. Therefore I did not include general studies, such as Charles L. Sanford's *The Quest for Paradise* (1961) or provocative essays, such as Rush Welter's "The Idea of Progress in America," *Journal of the History of Ideas*, 16 (June 1955), 401–15, and Robert F. Sayer's "American Myths of Utopia," *College English*, 31 (March 1970), 613–23, or Harold V. Rhodes's less stimulating *Utopia in American Political Thought* (1967). Nor did I list Robert Fogarty's survey of communalism, *American Utopianism* (1972), or diversified collections such as Ivan Doig's *Utopian America* (1976). (2) I selected general studies of American utopian literature (thematic or period approaches) as opposed to essays about one or a few utopists. Therefore I have not mentioned studies of major figures, such as Cooper, Hawthorne, Bellamy, Howells, and Skinner, or "minor" utopian authors, who have been the subjects of several good recent articles (for example, see the essay by Francine C. Cary in the Fall 1977 issue of *American Quarterly* and one by Howard P. Segal in the December 1977 *Extrapolation*). Nor have I included the relevant "utopian" chapters in Vernon Louis Parrington's *Main Currents of American Thought*, Vol. III (1930), in A. N. Kaul's *The American Vision* (1963), in Michael Fellman's *The Unbounded Frame* (1973), in Elisabeth Hansot's *Perfection and Progress* (1974), in David Ketterer's *New Worlds for Old* (1974), and in Allan M. Axelrad's *History and Utopia* (1978), because their authors focused only on Cooper, Hawthorne, Bellamy, Howells, Twain, or other individual authors. I have, however, included Joel Nydahl's "Introduction" to Timothy Savage's *Amazonian Republic*, though I omitted my "Introduction" to Gillette's *Human Drift*: Nydahl's essay includes a survey of early American utopian fiction, whereas mine focuses exclusively on Gillette.

My two guidelines may seem arbitrary and restrictive, but they are also appropriate and practical. This collection emphasizes the study of American utopian literature, so it is appropriate that the checklist reflects that emphasis. Furthermore, general bibliographies, especially lists of works on utopian thought and literature, are available elsewhere. For example, see the brief listing of general American studies in *The Obsolete Necessity*, pp. 181–83; the checklists of recent studies in *Utopus Discovered*, which, beginning in 1978, has become the "News Center" section of the Fall and Spring *Alternative Futures*; some of the titles listed in the "Works Influential in Utopian Thought" section of Glenn Negley's *Utopian Literature: A Bibliography*; Gorman Beauchamp's more inclusive secondary bibliography "Themes and Uses of Fictional Utopian Studies" in *Science-Fiction Studies*, 4 (March 1977), 55–63; and Lyman Tower Sargent's comprehensive bibliography of secondary sources in *British and American Utopias 1516–1975: An Annotated Bibliography*. There are also many extensive bibliographies of major utopists, and both major and minor American utopists are covered in such standard reference tools as Lewis Leary's *Articles on American Literature* and the annual, *American Literary Scholarship*. The decision to omit studies of individual authors was also a practical necessity; their inclusion would require a book-length volume instead of a brief checklist.

Considering the selective nature of this checklist, it may seem strange to reserve so much space for unpublished dissertations. But anyone acquainted with the study of American utopian literature knows that much of the important bibliographic and critical work in this field first appeared in dissertations. And, as the increasing number of recent dissertations suggests, this trend will probably continue into the near future. In spite of my emphasis on unpublished works, I have not included masters theses (see Patsy C. Howard's *Theses in American Literature*) or dissertations that were never completed, such as H. H. Eddy's "The Utopian Element in American Literature" (Stanford University) and Barry Love's "Technology in American Utopian Literature" (University of Pennsylvania).

One final note on the following checklist: I could have listed many bibliographies of primary works; for example, practically all the dissertations listed include useful primary sources bibliographies. I chose instead to mention only nine published bibliographies, which I thought were particularly useful (see "Chapters, Articles, and Bibliographies"). Of these the most wide-ranging is Glenn Negley's new international bibliography, *Utopian Literature: A Bibliography* (1977). But for students of American utopian literature the most valuable bibliography is Lyman Tower Sargent's *British and American Utopias 1516–1975: An Annotated Bibliography* (1978). It includes the most comprehensive listing of American utopias ever compiled.

I would like to thank Gorman Beauchamp, Arthur O. Lewis, Joel Nydahl, Lyman Tower Sargent, and Howard Segal for their advice about the entries in this checklist.

BOOKS

Parrington, Vernon Louis, Jr. *American Dreams: A Study of American Utopias* (Providence: Brown University Press, 1947; 2nd ed.: New York: Russell & Russell, 1964).

Roemer, Kenneth M. *The Obsolete Necessity: America in Utopian Writings, 1888–1900* (Kent, Ohio: Kent State University Press, 1976).

DISSERTATIONS

Aiken, John. "Utopianism and the Emergence of the Colonial Legal Profession, New York, 1664–1710: A Test Case." University of Rochester, 1966.

Berger, Harold L. "Anti-Utopian Science Fiction of the Mid-Twentieth Century." University of Tennessee, 1970.

Bleich, David. "Utopia: The Psychology of a Cultural Fantasy." New York University, 1968

Burt, Donald C. "Utopia and the Agrarian Tradition in America, 1865–1900." University of New Mexico, 1973.

Cary, Francine Curro. "Shaping the Future in the Golden Age: A Study of Utopian Thought, 1888–1900." University of Wisconsin, 1975.

Curzon, Gordon Anthony. "Paradise Sought: A Study of the Religious Motivation in Representative British and American Literary Utopias, 1850–1950." University of California, Riverside, 1969.

Leitenberg, Barbara. "The New Utopians." Indiana University, 1975.

Nydahl, Joel. "Utopia Americana: Early American Utopian Fiction, 1790–1864." University of Michigan, 1974.

Panage, John H. "Representative Late Nineteenth Century Utopias." University of Minnesota, 1939.

Parrington, Vernon Louis, Jr. "The Utopian Novel in America." Brown University, 1942.

Pfaelzer, Jean. "Utopian Fiction in America, 1880–1900: The Impact of Political Theory on Literary Forms." University College, University of London, 1975.

Pratter, Frederick Earl. "The Uses of Utopia: An Analysis of American Speculative Fiction 1880–1960." University of Iowa, 1973.

Quissell, Barbara C. "The Sentimental and Utopian Novels of Nineteenth Century America: Romance and Social Issues." University of Utah, 1973.

Ransom, Ellene. "Utopus Discovers America or Critical Realism in American Utopian Fiction, 1798–1900." Vanderbilt University, 1946. Reprint, Folcroft, Pa.: Folcroft Press, 1970.

Roemer, Kenneth Morrison. "America as Utopia, 1888–1900: New Visions, Old Dreams." University of Pennsylvania, 1971.

Rooney, Charles J., Jr. "Utopian Literaure as a Reflection of Social Forces in America, 1865–1917." George Washington University, 1968.

Samuelson, David Norman. "Studies in the Contemporary American and British Science Fiction Novel." University of Southern California, 1969.

Schectman, Aaron Henry. "The Uses of Utopia in Selected American Educational Proposals." Rutgers University, 1971.

Segal, Howard P. "Technological Utopianism and American Culture, 1830–1940." Princeton University, 1975.

Shurter, Robert L. "The Utopian Novel in America, 1865–1900." Case Western Reserve University, 1936. Reprint, New York: AMS Press, 1973.

Solberg, Victor. "A Source Book of English and American Utopias." Ohio State University, 1932.

Stupple, A. James. "Utopian Humanism in America, 1888–1900." Northwestern University, 1971.

Sweetland, James H. "American Utopian Fiction, 1798–1926." University of Notre Dame, 1976.

Thal-Larsen, Margaret. "Political and Economic Ideas in American Utopian Fiction, 1868–1914." University of California, Berkeley, 1941.

Thomas, George Boyd. "Blueprint for Tomorrow: American Novels of Future Change." Harvard University, 1970.

CHAPTERS, ARTICLES, AND BIBLIOGRAPHIES

Bailey, J. O. "To the Islands of the Blest: Scientific Fiction," in *Pilgrims Through Space and Time: Trends and Patterns in Scientific and Utopian Fiction* (New York: Argus Books, 1947), pp. 51–78.

Blotner, Joseph Leo. "The Novel of the Future," in *The Modern American Political Novel, 1900–1960* (Austin: University of Texas Press, 1966), pp. 139–63.

Boggs, W. Arthur. "Looking Backward at the Utopian Novel, 1888–1900," *Bulletin of the New York Public Library*, 64 (June 1960), 329–36.

Clareson, Thomas D. "Major Trends in American Science Fiction: 1880–1915," *Extrapolation*, 1 (December 1959), 2–4. Followed by an "Annotated Checklist," pp. 5–20.

Dupont, V. "Bellamy: ⟨⟨Looking Backward⟩⟩" and "Littérature Utopique des Etats-Unis," in *L'Utopie et le Roman Utopique dans la Littérature Anglaise* (Cahors: A. Coueslant, 1941; Paris: Librairie M. Didier, 1941), pp. 753–822. Originally a dissertation for the University of Lyon.

Erisman, Fred. " 'Where We Plan to Go': The Southwest in Utopian Fiction," *Southwestern American Literature*, 1 (September 1971), 137–43.

Flory, Claude R. "The Answer as the Novelists Give It: Signposts to Utopia" and "The Utopian Novel a Peculiar Continuation of Romanticism," in *Economic Criticism in American Fiction, 1792–1900* (Philadelphia: University of Pennsylvania Press, 1936), pp. 129–96, 227–41. Originally a dissertation for the University of Pennsylvania.

Forbes, Allyn B. "The Literary Quest for Utopia, 1880–1900," *Social Forces*, 6 (December 1927), 179–89.

Franklin, Howard Bruce. "Introduction" [and several headnotes] in *Future Perfect: American Science Fiction of the Nineteenth Century* (New York: Oxford University Press, 1966; 2nd ed., 1978), pp. ix–xiii.

Hillegas, Mark R. "Dystopian Science Fiction: New Index to the Human Situation," *New Mexico Quarterly*, 31 (Autumn 1961), 238–49.

Kasson, John F. "Technology and Utopia," in *Civilizing the Machine: Technology and Republican Values in America, 1776–1900* (New York: Grossman, 1976; reprint, New York: Penguin, 1977), pp. 181–234.

Lewis, Arthur O., Jr. "The Anti-Utopian Novel: Preliminary Notes and Checklist," *Extrapolation*, 2 (May 1961), 27–32.

————. "The Utopian Dream," in Stanley Weintraub and Philip Young, eds., *Directions in Literary Criticism* (University Park: Pennsylvania State University Press, 1973), pp. 192–200.

————. "Utopian Literature." New York: Arno Press, 1971. Twelve-page booklet.

————. *Utopian Writings in the Pattee Library: A Selected List, with Random Annotations.* University Park: The Pennsylvania State University Libraries, forthcoming.

Lokke, Virgil L. "The American Utopian Anti-Novel," in Ray B. Browne, et al., eds., *Frontiers of American Culture* (Lafayette, Ind.: Purdue University Studies, 1968), pp. 123–53.

Martin, Jay. "Paradises (To Be) Regained," in *Harvests of Change: American Literature, 1865–1914* (Englewood Cliffs, N.J.: Prentice-Hall, 1967), pp. 202–39.

Negley, Glenn. "Modern Utopias, 1850–1950," in Glenn Negley and J. Max Patrick, eds., *The Quest for Utopia; An Anthology of Imaginary Societies* (New York: Henry Schuman, 1952), pp. 12–19.

————. *Utopian Literature: A Bibliography with a Supplementary Listing of Works Influential in Utopian Thought.* (Lawrence: The Regents Press of Kansas, 1977).

Normano, J. F. "Social Utopias in American Literature," *International Review for Social History*, 3 (1938), 286–300.

Nydahl, Joel. "Introduction" to Timothy Savage, *The Amazonian Republic* (Delmar, N.Y.: Scholars' Facsimiles & Reprints, 1976), pp. v–xv.

Pfaelzer, Jean. "American Utopian Fiction 1888–1896: The Political Origins of Form," *Minnesota Review*, n.s. 6 (Spring 1976), 114–17.

Roemer, Kenneth M. "American Utopian Literature (1888–1900): An Annotated Bibliography," *American Literary Realism*, 4 (Summer 1971), 227–54.

————. "Eyewitness to Utopia: Illustrations in Utopian Literature," *Prospects*, 4 (New York: Burt Franklin, 1979), 355–64.

————. "The Heavenly City of the Late 19th-Century Utopians," *Journal of the American Studies Association*, 4 (1973), 5–17.

————. "Sex Roles, Utopia and Change: The Family in Late Nineteenth-Century Utopian Literature," *American Studies*, 13 (Fall 1972), 33–49.

————. "Utopia and Methodology: Uses of Fiction in American Studies," *Social Science Journal*, 12 (January 1975), 21–28.

————. "Utopia Made Practical," *American Literary Realism*, 7 (Summer 1974), 273–76.

Rose, Lisle A. "A Bibliographic Survey of Economic and Political Writings, 1865–1900," *American Literature*, 15 (January 1944), 381–410. Unpublished supplements: I (April 28, 1944) and II (October 1, 1944) Houghton, Mich.; III (October 5, 1949) and IV (1949–1951) Urbana, Ill.

Sargent, Lyman Tower. *British and American Utopias 1516–1975: An Annotated Bibliography.* Boston: G. K. Hall, 1979.

————. "English and American Utopias: Similarities and Differences," *Journal of General Education*, 28 (Spring 1976), 16–22.

————. "Utopia and Dystopia in Contemporary Science Fiction," *The Futurist*, 6 (June 1972), 93–98.

Segal, Howard P. "American Visions of Technological Utopia, 1883–1933," *Markham Review*, 7 (Summer 1978), 65–76.

Shurter, Robert L. "The Utopian Novel in America, 1888–1900," *South Atlantic Quarterly*, 34 (April 1935), 137–44.

Taylor, Walter. "Bibliography," in *The Economic Novel in America* (Chapel Hill: University of North Carolina Press, 1949), pp. 341–64; also pp. 106, 206.

Addendum: *Utopian Thought in the Western World* by Frank E. Manuel and Fritzie P. Manuel (Cambridge, Mass.: Belknap Press of Harvard University Press, 1979) appeared while *America as Utopia* was in press. Although the Manuels concentrate on non-American utopian thought, their book is essential reading for anyone seeking to understand the Christian and Enlightenment roots of American utopian fiction, as well as the influences of socialism, Victorianism, Darwinism, and Freudianism on American utopian literature.

EPILOGUE

URSULA K. LE GUIN's *The Dispossessed: An Ambiguous Utopia* (1974) is an ambitious fictional re-examination of the nature of utopian literature. Indeed, Le Guin and the other authors of "critical" utopias mentioned in the introduction to Part IV may do for modern utopian science fiction what Melville did for the sea adventure tale. Le Guin and Melville mastered and transcended their genres—transcended in the sense that they used the conventions of sea stories and utopian and science fiction to re-evaluate the philosophical assumptions of these literatures and to broaden their scopes. This process of re-examination and expansion is obvious in *Moby-Dick*. Similarly in *The Dispossessed* Le Guin utilizes many of the conventions of classical, nineteenth-century, and modern utopian literature and science fiction to present an exciting and complex re-evaluation of the utopian hero and the quest for utopia. The result eludes such traditional classifications as utopian, dystopian, or antiutopian. The "ambiguous utopia"—that paradoxical phenomenon mentioned in Robert Plank's essay—comes closest to the mark. In *The Dispossessed* there are moments of technological, bureaucratic, and ecological despair as dark as any Orwellian or Huxleian nightmare mentioned in Lyman Tower Sargent's survey of modern dystopias. But these counterpoint and merge with equally intense moments of optimism about the ability of humanity to endure and prevail, to borrow Faulkner's words, and a refreshing honesty about our inability to predict doomsday and eutopia with accuracy. In other words, Le Guin points toward a new type of utopian fiction that escapes the one-dimensional simplicity and absolutism of much eutopian and dystopian literature but still maintains the intensity and integrity of a Bellamy, Skinner, Rimmer, or Rand.

How does she do this? A brief headnote and an extract cannot answer that question. But at least they can hint. In *The Dispossessed* Le Guin juxtaposes two settings often found in nineteenth- and twentieth-century eutopian and dystopian works: an isolated utopian settlement (the barren moon colony of Anarres founded by the followers of Odo, an anarchist) and a powerful capitalistic nation (Urras, a country on the mother planet). The dramatic link between the two is a brilliant, courageous, and troubled physicist, Shevek, whose awareness of both the moral superiority and the inhumane limitations of his homeland, Anarres, inspired an unprecedented event: his voyage to Urras. There he is dazzled by natural wonders, luxury, diversity, and freedom of thought. But gradually he discovers the oppressive sexual, racial, and economic inequalities of this Paradise. He even helps to lead a short-lived revolution. Shevek's dual vision of both worlds is complemented by the structure of the novel—the chapters alternate between Shevek's prevoyage experience on Anarres and his Urras experience—and hints about several other potential dystopias and eutopias, including a totalitarian, ruined world (Terra), a Soviet state (Thu), and an ancient civilization, the Hainish, who have experienced practically all forms of ideal and not-so-ideal commonwealths. The overall result is a richly textured quest: an honest and ever shifting series of Paradises Lost and Paradises-to-Be-Regained unified by an intense awareness of bestial and angelic human urges. (For a very frank and personal critique of the novel, see the monograph-length essay "To Read *The Dispossessed*" in *The Jewel-hinged Jaw* [1977], by Samuel R. Delany, the author of *Dahlgren* [1975] and *Triton* [1976]. Delany measures the novel's strengths and weaknesses against his concepts of language and science fiction and against relevant personal experiences.)

The following extract is taken from Chapter 11. Shevek is on Urras. He has just climaxed his visit from Anarres by inspiring a mass demonstration against the government. He is almost killed for his efforts. Luckily he escapes, after spending the night with a dying man in a cellar, and finds asylum in the embassy of the Terrans, a people from another world. During his confrontation with the Ambassador, he and she become more aware of many of the eutopian and dystopian possibilities of their sector of the universe, and their dialogue effectively summarizes and evaluates many of the alternative futures created by early and modern American utopian authors.

URSULA K. LE GUIN

Extract from "An Ambiguous Utopia"

AFTER TWO DAYS' SLEEP and two days' meals, dressed again in his grey Ioti suit, which they had cleaned and pressed for him, he was shown into the Ambassador's private salon on the third floor of the tower.

The Ambassador neither bowed to him nor shook his hand, but joined her hands palm to palm before her breast and smiled. "I'm glad you feel better, Dr. Shevek. No, I should say simply Shevek, should I? Please sit down. I'm sorry that I have to speak to you in Iotic, a foreign language to both of us. I don't know your language. I am told that it's a most interesting one, the only rationally invented language that has become the tongue of a great people."

He felt big, heavy, hairy, beside this suave alien. He sat down in one of the deep, soft chairs. Keng also sat down, but grimaced as she did so. "I have a bad back," she said, "from sitting in these comfortable chairs!" And Shevek realized then that she was not a woman of thirty or less, as he had thought, but was sixty or more; her smooth skin and childish physique had deceived him. "At home," she went on, "we mostly sit on cushions on the floor. But if I did that here I would have to look up even more at everyone. You Cetians are all so tall! . . . We have a little problem. That is, we really do not, but the government of A-Io does. Your people on Anarres, the ones who maintain radio communication with Urras, you know, have been asking very urgently to speak with you. And the Ioti Government is embarrassed." She smiled, a smile of pure amusement. "They don't know what to say."

She was calm. She was calm as a waterworn stone which, contemplated, calms. Shevek sat back in his chair and took a very considerable time to answer.

"Does the Ioti Government know that I'm here?"

"Well, not officially. We have said nothing, they have not asked. But we have several Ioti clerks and secretaries working here in the Embassy. So, of course, they know."

"Is it a danger to you—my being here?"

"Oh no. Our embassy is to the Council of World Governments, not to the nation of A-Io. You had a perfect right to come here, which the rest of the Council would force A-Io to admit. And as I told you, this castle is Terran soil." She smiled again; her smooth face folded into many little creases, and unfolded. "A delightful fantasy of diplomats! This castle eleven light-years from my Earth, this room in a tower in Rodarred, in A-Io, on the planet Urras of the sun Tau Ceti, is Terran soil."

"Then you can tell them I am here."

"Good. It will simplify matters. I wanted your consent."

"There was no . . . message for me, from Anarres?"

"I don't know. I didn't ask. I didn't think of it from your point of view. If you are worried about something, we might broadcast to Anarres. We know the wave length your people there have been using, of course, but we haven't used it because we were not invited to. It seemed best not to press. But we can easily arrange a conversation for you."

"You have a transmitter?"

"We would relay through our ship—The Hainish ship that stays in orbit around Urras. Hain and Terra work together, you know. The Hainish Ambassador knows you're with us; he is the only person who has been officially informed. So the radio is at your service."

He thanked her, with the simplicity of one who does not look behind the offer for the offer's motive. She studied him for a moment, her eyes shrewd, direct, and quiet. "I heard your speech," she said.

He looked at her as from a distance. "Speech?"

"When you spoke at the great demonstration in Capitol Square. A week ago today. We always listen to the clandestine radio, the Socialist Workers' and the Libertarians' broadcasts. Of course, they were reporting the demonstration. I heard you speak. I was very moved. Then there was a noise, a strange noise, and one could hear the crowd beginning to shout. They did not explain. There was screaming. Then it died off the air suddenly. It was terrible, terrible to listen to. And you were there. How did you escape from that? How did you get out of the city? Old Town is still cordoned off; there are three regiments of the army in Nio; they round up strikers and suspects by the dozen and hundred every day. How did you get here?"

He smiled faintly. "In a taxi."

"Through all the checkpoints? And in that bloodstained coat? And everyone knows what you look like."

"I was under the back seat. The taxi was commandeered, is that the word? It was a risk some people took for me." He looked down at his hands, clasped on his lap. He sat perfectly quietly and spoke quietly, but there was an inner tension, a strain, visible in his eyes and in the lines around his mouth. He thought a while, and went on in the same detached way, "It was luck, at first. When I came out of hiding, I was lucky not to be arrested at once. But I got into Old Town. After that it was not just luck. They thought for me where I might go, they planned how to get me there, they took the risks." He said a word in his own language, then translated it: "Solidarity. . . ."

"It is very strange," said the Ambassador from Terra. "I know almost nothing about your world, Shevek. I know only what the Urrasti tell us, since your people won't let us come there. I know, of course, that the planet is arid and bleak, and how the colony was founded, that it is an experiment in nonauthoritarian communism, that it has survived for a hundred and seventy years. I have read a little of Odo's writings—not very much. I thought that it was all rather unimportant to matters on Urras now, rather remote, an interesting experiment. But I was wrong, wasn't I? It is important. Perhaps Anarres is the key to Urras. . . . The revolutionists in Nio, they come from that same tradition. They weren't just striking for better wages or protesting the draft. They are not only socialists, they are anarchists; they were striking against power. You see, the size of the demonstration, the intensity of popular feeling, and the government's panic reaction, all seemed very hard to understand. Why so much commotion? The government here is not despotic. The rich are very rich indeed, but the poor are not so very poor. They are neither enslaved nor starving. Why aren't they satisfied with bread and speeches? Why are they supersensitive? . . . Now I begin to see why. But what is still inexplicable is that the government of A-Io, knowing this libertarian tradition was still alive, and knowing the discontent in the industrial cities, still brought you here. Like bringing the match to the powder mill!"

"I was not to be near the powder mill. I was to be kept from the populace, to live among scholars and the rich. Not to see the poor. Not to see anything ugly. I was to be wrapped up in cotton in a box in a wrapping in a carton in a plastic film, like everything here. There I was to be happy and do my work, the work I could not do on Anarres. And when it was done I was to give it to them, so they could threaten you with it."

"Threaten us? Terra, you mean, and Hain, and the other interspatial powers? Threaten us with what?"

"With the annihilation of space."

She was silent a while. "Is that what you do?" she said in her mild, amused voice.

"No. It is not what I do! In the first place, I am not an inventor, an engineer. I am a theorist. What they want from me is a theory. A theory of the General Field in temporal physics. Do you know what that is?"

"Shevek, your Cetian physics, your Noble Science, is completely beyond my grasp. I am not trained in mathematics, in physics, in philosophy, and it seems to consist of all of those, and cosmology, and more besides. But I know what you mean when you say the Theory of Simultaneity, in the way I know what is meant by the Theory of Relativity; that is, I know that relativity theory led to certain great practical results; and so I gather that your temporal physics may make new technologies possible."

He nodded. "What they want," he said, "is the instantaneous transferral of matter across space. Transilience. Space travel, you see, without traversal of space or lapse of time. They may arrive at it yet; not from my equations, I think. But they can make the ansible, with my equations, if they want it. Men cannot leap the great gaps, but ideas can."

"What is an ansible, Shevek?"

"An idea." He smiled without much humor. "It will be a device that will permit communication without any time interval between two points in space. The device will not transmit messages, of course; simultaneity is indentity. But to our perceptions, that simultaneity will function as a transmission, a sending. So we will be able to use it to talk between worlds, without the long waiting for the message to go and the reply to return that electromagnetic impulses require. It is really a very simple matter. Like a kind of telephone."

Keng laughed. "The simplicity of physicists! So I could pick up the—ansible?—and talk with my son in Delhi? And with my granddaughter, who was five when I left, and who lived eleven years while I was traveling from Terra to Urras in a nearly light-speed ship. And I could find out what's happening at home *now*, not eleven years ago. And decisions could be made, and agreements reached, and information shared. I could talk to diplomats on Chiffewar, you could talk to physicists on Hain, it wouldn't take ideas a generation to get from world to world. . . . Do you know, Shevek, I think your very simple matter might change the lives of all the billions of people in the nine Known Worlds?"

He nodded.

"It would make a league of worlds possible. A federation. We have been held apart by the years, the decades between leaving and arriving, between question and response. It's as if you had invented human speech! We can talk—at last we can talk together."

"And what will you say?"

His bitterness startled Keng. She looked at him and said nothing.

He leaned forward in his chair and rubbed his forehead painfully. "Look," he said, "I must explain to you why I have come to you, and why I came to this world also. I came for the idea. For the sake of the idea. To learn, to teach, to share in the idea. On Anarres, you see, we have cut ourselves off. We don't talk with other people, the rest of humanity. I could not finish my work there. And if I had been able to finish it, they did not want it, they saw no use in it. So I came here. Here is what I need—the talk, the sharing, an experiment in the Light Laboratory that proves something it wasn't meant to prove, a book of Relativity Theory from an alien world, the stimulus I need. And so I finished the work, at last. It is not written out yet, but I have the equations and the reasoning, it is done. But the ideas in my head aren't the only ones important to me. My society is also an idea. I was made by it. An idea of freedom, of change, of human solidarity, an important idea. And though I was very stupid I saw at last that by pursuing the one, the physics, I am betraying the other. I am letting the propertarians *buy the truth* from me."

"What else could you do, Shevek?"

"Is there no alternative to selling? Is there not such a thing as the gift?"

"Yes—"

"Do you not understand that I want to give this to you—and to Hain and the other worlds—and to the countries of Urras? But to you all! So that one of you cannot use it, as A-Io wants to do, to get power over the others, to get richer or to win more wars. So that you cannot use the truth for your private profit, but only for the common good."

"In the end, the truth usually insists upon serving only the common good," Keng said.

"In the end, yes, but I am not willing to wait for the end. I have one lifetime, and I will not spend it for greed and profiteering and lies. I will not serve *any* master."

Keng's calmness was a much more forced, willed affair than it had been at the beginning of their talk. The strength of Shevek's personality, unchecked by any self-consciousness or consideration of self-defense, was formidable. She was shaken by him, and looked at him with compassion and a certain awe.

"What is it like," she said, "what can it be like, the society that made you? I heard you speak of Anarres, in the Square, and I wept listening to you, but I didn't really believe you. Men always speak so of their homes, of the absent land. . . . But you are *not* like other men. There is a difference in you."

"The difference of the idea," he said. "It was for that idea that I came here, too. For Anarres. Since my people refuse to look outward, I thought I might make others look at us. I thought it would be better not to hold apart behind a wall, but to be a society among the others, a world among the others, giving and taking. But there I was wrong—I was absolutely wrong."

"Why so? Surely—"

"Because there is nothing, nothing on Urras that we Anarresti need! We left with empty hands, a hundred and seventy years ago, and we were right. We took nothing. Because there is nothing here but States and their weapons, the rich and their lies, and the poor and their misery. There is no way to act rightly, with a clear heart, on Urras. There is nothing you can do that profit does not enter into, and fear of loss, and the wish for power. You cannot say good morning without knowing which of you is 'superior' to the other, or trying to prove it. You cannot act like a brother to other people, you must manipulate them, or command them, or obey them, or trick them. You cannot touch another person, yet they will not leave you alone. There is no freedom. It is a box—Urras is a box, a package, with all the beautiful wrapping of blue sky and meadows and forests and great cities. And you open the box, and what is inside it? A black cellar full of dust, and a dead man. A man whose hand was shot off because he held it out to others. I have been in Hell at last. Desar was right; it is Urras; Hell is Urras."

For all his passion he spoke simply, with a kind of humility, and again the Ambassador from Terra watched him with a guarded yet sympathetic wonder, as if she had no idea how to take that simplicity.

"We are both aliens here, Shevek," she said at last. "I from much farther away in space and time. Yet I begin to think that I am much less alien to Urras than you are. . . . Let me tell you how this world seems to me. To me, and to all my fellow Terrans who have seen the planet, Urras is the kindliest, most various, most beautiful of all the inhabited worlds. It is the world that comes as close as any could to Paradise."

She looked at him calmly and keenly; he said nothing.

"I know it's full of evils, full of human injustice, greed, folly, waste. But it is also full of good, of beauty, vitality, achievement. It is what a world should be! It is *alive*, tremendously alive—alive, despite all its evils, with hope. Is that not true?"

He nodded.

"Now, you man from a world I cannot even imagine, you who see my Paradise as Hell, will you ask what *my* world must be like?"

He was silent, watching her, his light eyes steady.

"My world, my Earth, is a ruin. A planet spoiled by the human species. We multiplied and gobbled and fought until there was nothing left, and then we died. We controlled neither appetite nor violence; we did not adapt. We destroyed ourselves. But we destroyed the world first. There are no forests left on my Earth. The air is grey, the sky is grey, it is always hot. It is habitable, it is still habitable, but not as this world is. This is a living world, a harmony. Mine is a discord. You Odonians chose a desert; we Terrans made a desert. . . . We survive there, as you do. People are tough! There are nearly a half billion of us now. Once there were nine billion. You can see the old cities still everywhere. The bones and bricks go to dust, but the little pieces of plastic never do—they never adapt either. We failed as a species, as a social species. We are here now, dealing as equals with other human societies on other worlds, only because of the charity of the Hainish.

They came; they brought us help. They built ships and gave them to us, so we could leave our ruined world. They treat us gently, charitably, as the strong man treats the sick one. They are a very strange people, the Hainish; older than any of us; infinitely generous. They are altruists. They are moved by a guilt we don't even understand, despite all our crimes. They are moved in all they do, I think, by the past, their endless past. Well, we had saved what could be saved, and made a kind of life in the ruins, on Terra, in the only way it could be done: by total centralization. Total control over the use of every acre of land, every scrap of metal, every ounce of fuel. Total rationing, birth control, euthanasia, universal conscription into the labor force. The absolute regimentation of each life toward the goal of racial survival. We had achieved that much, when the Hainish came. They brought us . . . a little more hope. Not very much. We have outlived it. . . . We can only look at this splendid world, this vital society, this Urras, this Paradise, from the outside. We are capable only of admiring it, and maybe envying it a little. Not very much."

"Then Anarres, as you heard me speak of it—what would Anarres mean to you, Keng?"

"Nothing. Nothing, Shevek. We forfeited our chance for Anarres centuries ago, before it ever came into being."

Shevek got up and went over to the window, one of the long horizontal window slits of the tower. There was a niche in the wall below it, into which an archer would step up to look down and aim at assailants at the gate; if one did not take that step up one could see nothing from it but the sun-washed, slightly misty sky. Shevek stood below the window gazing out, the light filling his eyes.

"You don't understand what time is," he said. "You say the past is gone, the future is not real, there is no change, no hope. You think Anarres is a future that cannot be reached, as your past cannot be changed. So there is nothing but the present, this Urras, the rich, real, stable present, the moment now. And you think that is something which can be possessed! You envy it a little. You think it's something you would like to have. But it is not real, you know. It is not stable, not solid—nothing is. Things change, change. You cannot have anything. . . . And least of all can you have the present, unless you accept with it the past and the future. Not only the past but also the future, not only the future but also the past! Because they are real: only their reality makes the present real. You will not achieve or even understand Urras unless you accept the reality, the enduring reality, of Anarres. You are right, we are the key. But when you said that, you did not really believe it. You don't believe in Anarres. You don't believe in me, though I stand with you, in this room, in this moment. . . . My people were right, and I was wrong, in this: We cannot come to you. You will not let us. You do not believe in change, in chance, in evolution. You would destroy us rather than admit our reality, rather than admit that there is hope! We cannot come to you. We can only wait for you to come to us."

Keng sat with a startled and thoughtful, and perhaps slightly dazed, expression.

"I don't understand—I don't understand," she said at last. "You are like somebody from our own past, the old idealists, the visionaries of freedom; and yet I don't understand you, as if you were trying to tell me of future things; and yet, as you say, you are here, now! . . ." She had not lost her shrewdness. She said after a little while, "Then why is it that you came to me, Shevek?"

"Oh, to give you the idea. My theory, you know. To save it from becoming a property of the Ioti, an investment or a weapon. If you are willing, the simplest thing to do would be to broadcast the equations, to give them to physicists all over this world, and to the Hainish and the other worlds, as soon as possible. Would you be willing to do that?"

"More than willing."

"It will come to only a few pages. The proofs and some of the implications would take longer, but that can come later, and other people can work on them if I cannot."

"But what will you do then? Do you mean to go back to Nio? The city is quiet now, apparently; the insurrection seems to be defeated, at least for the time being; but I'm afraid the Ioti government regards you as an insurrectionary. There is Thu, of course—"

"No. I don't want to stay here. I am no altruist! If you would help me in this too, I might go home. Perhaps the Ioti would be willing to send me home, even. It would be consistent, I think: to make me disappear, to deny my existence. Of course, they might find it easier to do by killing me or putting me in jail for life. I don't want to die yet, and I don't want to die here in Hell at all. Where does your soul go, when you die in Hell?" He laughed; he had regained all his gentleness of manner. "But if you could send me home, I think they would be relieved. Dead anarchists make martyrs, you know, and keep living for centuries. But absent ones can be forgotten."

"I thought I knew what 'realism' was," Keng said. She smiled, but it was not an easy smile.

"How can you, if you don't know what hope is?"

"Don't judge us too hardly, Shevek."

"I don't judge you at all. I only ask your help, for which I have nothing to give in return."

"Nothing? You call your theory nothing?"

"Weigh it in the balance with the freedom of one single human spirit," he said, turning to her, "and which will weigh heavier? Can you tell? I cannot."

Notes on the Contributors

GORMAN BEAUCHAMP, Associate Professor of Humanities, College of Engineering, University of Michigan, chaired the first MLA Seminar on Utopian/Dystopian Literature in 1974 and the Second Conference on Utopian Studies in 1977. He is Associate Editor of *Alternative Futures: The Journal of Utopian Studies* and has written a number of articles on utopian literature and thought.

EDWARD BELLAMY (1850-98) was the son of a Massachusetts Baptist minister. Bellamy wrote the bestselling utopian work *Looking Backward*. He also wrote several psychological romances, the novel *Equality*, and a collection of short stories entitled *The Blindman's World* and edited *The New Nation*, the activist voice of the Nationalist Party.

DONALD C. BURT received his degrees from Mankato State University (B.S. and M.A.) and the University of New Mexico (Ph.D.). His doctoral dissertation was entitled "Utopia and the Agrarian Tradition in America, 1865–1900." He has been an Instructor at Mankato State University and an assistant professor at Washburn University, and his essays have appeared in *Mankato Studies in English* and *Inscape*.

THOMAS M. DISCH's latest novel, *On Wings of Son G*, was published early in 1978. In 1978 Dragon Press published Samuel Delany's *The American Shore*, an intensive analysis of "Angouleme," a part of Disch's book *334*. His own criticism appears in *New Statesman* and the *Times Literary Supplement*; and his fiction and poetry, in *F & SF*, *Poetry*, *Partisan Review*, *Harper's*, and many other journals.

DAVID Y. HUGHES teaches in the College of Engineering of the University of Michigan in the Humanities Department. He has written numerous essays on H. G. Wells's science fiction and utopias and edited (with Robert M. Philmus) *H. G. Wells: Early Writings in Science and Science Fiction*.

URSULA K. LE GUIN's *The Dispossessed* won the 1975 Nebula and Hugo awards. She also won the Nebula and Hugo awards for her earlier novel *The Left Hand of Darkness*, and a National Book Award for *The Farthest Shore*. Her short story "The Day Before the Revolution" won the 1975 Nebula Award for best short story. Her stories have appeared in many magazines, including *Fantastic*, *Amazing*, *Playboy*, and *Redbook*. She graduated from Radcliffe College and earned a master's degree at Columbia University.

ARTHUR O. LEWIS is Professor of English and Associate Dean of the College of Liberal Arts at The Pennsylvania State University. He received his B.A.

and M.A. at Harvard and his Ph.D. at Penn State—all in English. His books include *Of Men and Machines* and *American Utopias: Selected Short Fiction*. He is editor of the forty-one–volume series *Utopian Literature*, published by Arno Press, and he compiled the *Directory of Utopian Scholars*. He has been President of the Science Fiction Research Association and chaired the Third Conference on Utopian Studies in 1978.

JOEL NYDAHL earned his Ph.D. in American Studies from the University of Michigan. He has taught at Northern Michigan University, the University of Maryland (Far East and European divisions), the Federal University of Brazil, and the University of Michigan. Besides teaching, he is also active in the wine business.

JEAN PFAELZER received her Ph.D. from University College, University of London. Her doctoral dissertation was entitled "Utopian Fiction in America 1880–1900: The Impact of Political Theory on Literary Forms." She has taught in the Department of Literature of Revelle College at the University of California, San Diego. Her articles have been published in several journals, including *Women's Studies* and the *Minnesota Review*.

ROBERT PLANK, originally a lawyer in Austria (his doctorate is in law, from the University of Vienna), came to the United States in 1938, studied social work, and for nearly thirty years was a psychiatric social worker. He is now an Adjunct Associate Professor at Case Western Reserve University, where he teaches the psychology of literature. The author of *The Emotional Significance of Imaginary Beings*, he has contributed sections to books on Tolkien, C. S. Lewis, Heinlein, and Arthur C. Clarke, as well as numerous articles to scholarly journals.

FREDERICK PRATTER wrote his doctoral dissertation on speculative fiction while in the American Civilization Program at the University of Iowa. He has been a steelworker, a fruit picker, a roofer, a stereo salesperson, and a survey researcher. He is currently working as a programmer-analyst for the Health Sciences Computing Facility at the Harvard School of Public Health and pursuing his utopian interests in his spare time.

BARBARA C. QUISSELL received her B.S. from Augustana College, her M.A. from New Mexico State University, and her Ph.D. from the University of Utah. Her doctoral dissertation was entitled "The Sentimental and Utopian Novels of Nineteenth Century America: Romance and Social Issues." She has written for *Western American Literature*, and she has taught at New Mexico State University, the University of Utah, and Idaho State University.

ROBERT RIMMER received his B.A. from Bates College and his M.B.A. from Harvard. Until 1977 he was the Chairman of the Board of the Relief Printing Corporation. He is the author of the bestselling novel *The Harrad Experiment*, as well as several other novels, including *Proposition 31*, *The Harrad Letters*, *The Premar Experiment*, and *Love Me Tomorrow*.

KENNETH M. ROEMER received his B.A. in English from Harvard and his M.A. and Ph.D. in American Civilization from the University of Pennsylvania. He teaches at the University of Texas at Arlington, where he developed a course entitled "Build Your Own Utopia." He is the author of *The Obsolete Necessity: America in Utopian Writings, 1888–1900*; the Introduction to a facsimile edition of Gillette's *The Human Drift*; and essays on utopian literature and American Indian fiction and poetry. From 1972 to 1978 he was the Managing Editor of *American Literary Realism*.

CHARLES J. ROONEY received his Ph.D. from Georgetown University. His doctoral dissertation was entitled "Utopian Literature as a Reflection of Social Forces in America, 1865–1917." He has been active as a teacher and as an administrator at Felician College in New Jersey.

LYMAN TOWER SARGENT received his Ph.D. from the University of Minnesota. He is Professor of Political Science at the University of Missouri–St. Louis, and he has been a Visiting Professor at the University of Exeter. He is the author of *British and American Utopian Literature: An Annotated Bibliography; Contemporary Political Ideologies; New Left Thought; Techniques of Political Analysis* (with Thomas Zant); and many articles on utopianism.

HOWARD P. SEGAL is an Assistant Professor of Humanities and History at the University of Michigan. He received his Ph.D. in history from Princeton University and has been a Taft Post doctoral Fellow at the University of Cincinnati and a Killam Postdoctoral Fellow at Dalhousie University. His doctoral and postdoctoral research and publication have centered on "technological utopianism" in America.

B. F. SKINNER received his B.A. from Hamilton College and his M.A. and Ph.D. from Harvard. He has taught at Indiana University and Harvard and was granted a Guggenheim Fellowship in 1944. He has received many awards and honorary degrees for his work in behavioral psychology. His book publications include *Behavior of Organisms, Walden Two, The Technology of Teaching, Beyond Freedom and Dignity, About Behaviorism*, and *Particulars of My Life*, among others.

DARKO SUVIN is a Professor of English and Comparative Literature at McGill University and editor and publisher of *Science-Fiction Studies*. He received his B.A., M.Sc., and Ph.D. from Zagreb University (Yugoslavia) and engaged in additional study at Bristol University, the Sorbonne, and Yale University. His specialties are modern drama, utopian and science fiction, and theory of literature. His major publications in English include *Russian Science Fiction 1956–1974, H.G. Wells and Modern Science Fiction, Metamorphoses of Science Fiction, Science-Fiction Studies 1973–1975*, and *Science-Fiction Studies 1976–1977* (the last two coedited with R. D. Mullen). Approximately three hundred of his articles have appeared in various European and North American periodicals.

STUART TEITLER is owner of Kaleidoscope Books of Berkeley, California. He has knowledgeably examined and summarized more speculative fiction than any other dealer or collector living. Having issued many informative catalogues and introductions, he is responsible for much research by other scholars, a considerable amount of it unacknowledged.

Author Index

Short-Title Index

This index includes listings of pages where the title does not appear but the author's name is used to represent a work.

Subject Index

Cross-references to people's names refer to the Author Index, which precedes.